CHILD CARE DESIGN GUIDE

CHILD CARE DESIGN GUIDE

ANITA RUI OLDS

McGraw-Hill
New York San Francisco Washington, D. C. Auckland Bogotá
Caracas Lisbon London Madrid Mexico City Milan
Montreal New Delhi San Juan Singapore
Sydney Tokyo Toronto

Library of Congress Cataloging-in-Publication Data
Olds, Anita Rui.
Child care design guide / Anita Rui Olds.
p. cm.
Includes bibliographical references and index.
isbn 0-07-047449-4
1. Day care centers—Design and construction. I. Title: Childcare design guide. II. Title.

NA6768.O43 2000
727′.083—dc21 00-058381

McGraw-Hill
A Division of The ***McGraw-Hill*** *Companies*

6 7 8 9 0 QWC 0 9 8 7 6

ISBN 0-07-047449-4

The sponsoring editor for this book was Wendy Lochner, editing supervisor was Sally Glover, and the production supervisor was Pamela Pelton. The designer was Gary Head and the illustrator was Fernando Marti. It was set in Berkeley by Detta Penna of Penna Design and Production.

Printed and bound by Quebecor World Bogotá

This book is printed on recycled, acid-free paper containing a minimum of 50% recycled, de-inked fiber.

McGraw-Hill books are available at special quantity discounts to use as premiums and sales promotions, or for use in corporate training programs. For more information, please write to the Director of Special Sales, McGraw-Hill, Two Penn Plaza, New York, NY 10121-2298.

This book is dedicated to my daughter,
Loren Arienne Olds, whose joyous, loving,
and luminous spirit has been the source of my healing.
And to Lulu Torbet, whose unwavering friendship,
devotion, and extraordinary editorial gifts have
brought it to completion.

CONTENTS

FOREWORD

THROUGHOUT HER LIFE, MY MOTHER, ANITA RUI OLDS, embodied the wisdom of healer, artist, and activist. Her life's work merged the healer's sensitivity and sacrifice, the artist's vision and insight, and the activist's determination to effect change. As a healer, she carried within her heart the pain of the breakdown of our collective family and community values and the impact of this dissolution on our childrearing and education practices. Out of this deep concern and compassion for the children of our communities came her lifelong devotion to seeing that children be given what they must in order to thrive and to realize their potential. As an artist, she heightened our sensitivity to the impact of our environments and inspired us to envision how we might transform and improve them. Deeply aware of children's joyful spirits and their profound connection to the natural world, she sought to bring beauty and opportunities for creative play into even the most marginal of institutions. As an activist, she challenged the status quo, and pushed for the "impossible," insisting that our day care centers honor the critical developmental needs of growing children. The daughter of a revolutionary, she inherited a will for change and a hunger for justice. As the statistics of institutional child care grew more and more grim, and substandard practices more entrenched, she continued to voice the needs of those who could not yet speak and led a fight for the sanctity of their lives.

Anita Rui Olds and Loren Arienne Olds, 1976

Throughout my life I experienced my mother as a woman consumed by her mission. I also experienced a mother whose capacity and desire to love was truly stunning. The fire of her love has forever permeated the fabric of my being. As I stayed by her in her final days, I heard stories—from friends, colleagues, students, neighbors—of the profound and myriad ways in which her love and vision affected their lives. Watching the slides shown at her memorial service, I glimpsed environments that have transformed the lives of countless children and caregivers. From these rich experiences I know more deeply not only the woman who was my mother, but also the "Great Mother" that this extraordinary woman was, in her work, her love, her life, and her death.

I am humbled by the forces that compelled my mother to complete this summation of her life's work before she died, and grateful that we are now able to offer it as her final gift. Anita believed the completion of this book marked a new beginning: the close of one phase of her life and the doorway to the next. As she worked tirelessly on the book's writing and production, she spoke longingly, and with great anticipation, of the freedom she would find on the other side. How deeply mysterious that the hour of her greatest anticipation should meet the hour of her death. It is this mystery that we as the living now hold. It is to this mystery that she has gone. My wish is that her life continues to inspire and propel us toward the realization of our own unique visions. May we never forget the laughter, the curiosity and the wonder of the child—within and without. This is what she most deeply would have wanted.

LOREN ARIENNE OLDS
Forest Knolls, California

ACKNOWLEDGMENTS

THIS BOOK IS THE CUMULATIVE PRODUCT NOT ONLY of many years of work and study, but of the cumulative support, collaboration, assistance and counsel of many colleagues and friends.

At McGraw Hill, I would like to thank my editor, Wendy Lochner, and especially Editing Supervisor Sally Glover and her staff for their careful attention and patience.

Judith Cope and Beverly DeWitt, my editorial sidekicks throughout this project, made invaluable contributions to the editing, revising, and restructuring of the many drafts of the book.

The design and production of this complex project are the result of the skills and dedication of production manager Detta Penna, in collaboration with designer Gary Head and illustrator Fernando Marti. Detta's hands-on attention to seeing this project through to the end is deeply appreciated.

Murray Silverstein, Barbara Winslow, Max Jacobson and Helen Degenhardt at JSW/D Architects in Berkeley, with whom I worked on several projects in this last decade, helped in myriad ways throughout the process. I am especially grateful to Murray and to Barbara for their careful reading and critique of large sections of the book. Consummate colorist Carla Mathis offered steadfast support, and made huge contributions to the chapter on color.

During the nine years that I taught the Child Care Institute at Tufts/Harvard, Angela Foss was the dedicated and supportive coordinator, and champion, of the program. I am very appreciative of her efforts and of many others affiliated with the program. I would like to give credit to Tufts University, the Office of Professional and Continuing Education, the Conference Bureau, and the Department of Child Development. At Harvard, I want to thank the Graduate School of Design, Office of External Relations, Professional Development.

I hope I have not omitted anyone from the long list of people, who, in their capacity as friend or colleague, or both, served as support, sounding board, and/or reader of various sections or chapters of the book. This list includes Toni Jackson, Megan Freeman, Horst Hencke, Ed Howe, Bruce Brook, Bruce Kennett, Carol Venolia, Margaret (Heidi) Lobenstine, Jay Hollman, Steven Rosen, Tiffany Field, Wendy Goldberg, Jennifer Kagiwada, Arlene Uss, Bruce and Shona Davison, Jeanne Comeau, Cindy Beacham, Linda Ruth, Peg Sprague, Linda de Hart, Cate Riley, Joan Drescher, Martha Casselman, and Beth Wallace.

Finally, there is no way to fully express my love and gratitude to my daughter Loren Olds and my dear friend Lulu Torbet, to whom this book is dedicated, for their unstinting efforts in bringing this book to completion.

To all of you, for all you did, my profound appreciation and thanks.

INTRODUCTION: HOW TO READ THE CHILD CARE DESIGN GUIDE

Concern for the welfare of children and the environments in which they grow, learn, and heal, has been my passion for almost thirty years. During this time I have designed or consulted on the design of spaces for children ranging from pediatric hospitals, therapeutic centers, and playgrounds, to children's museums, elementary and secondary school classrooms and, above all, child care centers.

In an attempt to understand and to help others create settings in which children can thrive, I have written articles and books, given speeches, seminars, and countless workshops—including the *Child Care Design Institute,* a weeklong training session sponsored by Tufts University and Harvard University's Graduate School of Design, which I present annually for architects, designers, and child care professionals from around the world.

Yet I have many reservations about raising children in child care centers. These include concerns about the ability of group care to meet the astonishing receptivity to life, and potential for growth and learning, of the preschool child; the effects of institutionalization on children during their crucial formative years; and doubts about the lack of personal attention and affection which may result when children are separated from home and family. I am particularly uneasy about center-based care for infants and toddlers. Personally, I believe the United States should follow in the footsteps of other industrialized nations which support parents to stay at home with their babies for at least the first 6–9 months of life. And I am concerned about the quality of the child care environment itself: the staff, the curriculum, and the physical plant in which children spend these crucial days, weeks, months, and years of their young lives.

My personal reservations notwithstanding, the fact that most children will spend so much time in a child care center is a reality of modern life. It is estimated that sixty million square feet of new child care space will be needed annually for the foreseeable future. So the question becomes: If it is unavoidable that today's children will be raised in child care centers, what role can design play in making this experience a positive and supportive one? Every program grapples with the issue of facility design but, due to a conspicuous lack of information, many centers learn after the fact, rather than before, what might have made the building work better. My personal goal—and the reason I have written *The Child Care Design Guide*—is to do whatever I can to see that young children are raised in nurturing, spirited settings that honor their precious young souls.

The Child Care Design Guide takes a two-pronged approach to the issue of providing well-designed spaces for children: It offers design information and guidelines, and it offers philosophical and psychological commentary, based upon my training as a developmental psychologist, on what constitutes good design and a good program.

Information

The Child Care Design Guide provides detailed information about every aspect of the planning and design of child care centers, for all of the parties involved—architects, interior designers, developers, and child care professionals. Much of this information has never before been gathered in one place. Intended as a reference, it is organized so that the reader can quickly find information on each specific aspect of center design as it arises. The book is amply cross-referenced, but, for the reader's convenience, core information is repeated in some instances.

Addressing several different professions simultaneously has seemed important to me, even at the risk of presenting material which will be simplistic to some and overly technical to others. Given our current state of knowledge, I do not believe we can create good centers without the collaboration of child care and design professionals. I have tried, however, to avoid including information which delves too deeply into the expertise of either profession, such as the different types of curricula and daily schedules, or the code requirements of different types of construction. In this attempt at balance, I hope I have not omitted detail that either profession believes should have been provided—or overly simplified concepts.

The information presented here represents a culling from diverse sources of the most pertinent material gathered during my thirty years in this field. Taken in one dose, it may seem dauntingly dense and detailed. But I know from experience that all of these issues and considerations do arise, and do need to be grappled with, in the course of planning and designing a center.

Organization of the Book

The book is organized into four parts. *Part One: The Child's Environment* looks at the current state of child care in the United States, and offers an overall philosophical concept—the spirit of place—as the framework for all center design.

Part Two: The Design Process takes you through the series of issues centers typically encounter when starting a design project: formation of a design team, establishing a program, evaluating a site and possible existing building, choosing between new construction and renovation, doing preliminary layouts for the center on a specific site, and honoring the key ingredients of children's group room design. It is recommended that those unfamiliar with the design process read these chapters in the sequence in which they are presented. Later on, you can refer back to specific ones. Rather than being organized according to topics, factors such as plumbing, heating, and storage may appear in several different locations, because the book follows the design progression typical of many projects. Extensive cross-referencing should help you find what you need when you need it.

Part Three: Ingredients of Good Design addresses specific aspects of design in greater detail—sound, light, color, finishes, furnishings, building systems, and windows, doors, and security. Some of these relate to the building's structure, others to its interior. Many represent the fine points and details which distinguish a mere building shell from a place of true habitation and delight for its occupants. You will want to refer to these chapters at different point in the design process.

Part Four: The Functional Spaces addresses design elements unique to different parts of the building and site, such as the children's group rooms; areas for staff, parents, and the community; and outdoor play. In the last chapter I describe two recently completed centers whose design is based on the residential core model, which I am proposing as one possible new prototype for child care center design. One of these centers—the Copper House—an on-site child care center for Husky Injection Molding Systems, Inc. in Bolton, Ontario, is referred to frequently because it embodies many of the principles and practices presented in this Guide. Both centers were designed by JSW/D Architects, of Berkeley, California, in consultation with Anita Olds and Associates. The last chapter also concludes with a philosophical inquiry into the relationship between the design of facilities for children and the evolution and transformation of human society.

Throughout the text you will find displays entitled **Questions** and **Guidelines** highlighted by a different typeface. **Questions** are intended to pose design options and possibilities and encourage you to think about what is most appropriate for your unique circumstance. **Guidelines** summarize key points in the text and elaborate upon design solutions that will ensure a better facility; they should be read by everyone. The text also contains a number of boxes highlighting key **Facilities** and **Supports** that need to be present in different areas of the children's group rooms.

The book is also heavily illustrated with sketches, floorplans, and photographs depicting the concepts presented, and showing various ways in which they have been executed. Most of the photographs are of my own work. While many fine centers exist, I was not seeking in this Guide to document the state of the art, but rather to explain and illustrate concepts which I have developed, or which have proven important to me, over the years.

Notes at the end of each chapter expand on material in the text or make reference to sources. I have been sparing with these, so as not to make the material overly academic. Appendixes provide additional material where it seemed merited.

Awareness and Intention

It has been my experience that the more those involved in planning a child care center understand about the developmental needs of young children, and about the design process itself, the better the outcome. When a planning team is aware of the impact of the environment on children, they work harder to ensure that their design decisions benefit the child. To that end, information which philosophically and psychologically supports the design enterprise is included throughout *The Child Care Design Guide.*

The true client in the building of a child care center is the child, and the mission of the design team—from architect to center administrator to caregiver—is to provide the optimum environment for that child. There are, of course, many constraints and restrictions—budgetary, logistical, regulatory, political—that intrude between the ideal and the real. But the more that we can be aware of what we want and what works, the more informed and detailed a vision we have for our children, the more energy and good intentions we can bring to keeping that dream alive, and to make what we envision a reality.

You may be tempted to skip over the theoretical or philosophical material in your need to get to the nuts-and-bolts information that appears more important. It may not seem necessary (in fact it may feel burdensome or guilt-inducing!) to read about the importance of sound or natural light or color to childrens' growth or well-being. When you are struggling to figure out how to accommodate too many children, doing too many things, with too few dollars, considering the impact of green building materials may seem like one too many concerns to think about. But when this issue is part of your knowledge and awareness, you automatically factor it into your design deliberations, and you are more likely to produce an outcome that is beneficial to the child, in many cases without additional cost.

The material presented in this book promotes an optimum scenario by encouraging you to strive for the highest quality possible. Obviously, this has to be tempered with realism and practicality. No center should feel badly if it cannot meet all the recommendations suggested here. Rather, by attempting to meet some, you will contribute to raising standards nationwide. Some recommendations are unquestionably costly; some might be difficult to implement, given a particular location or set of circumstances. But many design decisions—and many suggestions presented in this book—are not a matter of money. They are the result of concern, time, and planning on the part of the team. In other words, they are matters of intention and awareness.

In the debate about better and more affordable child care, the design of center facilities has been a neglected variable. We seem to assume that if personnel and policy issues are resolved, the necessary facilities will miraculously materialize. Instead, facility design needs to be right up there—along with subsidies, staff salaries, staff/child ratios, and group sizes—as one of the key issues related to quality. If I have erred on the side of idealism, it is only in the interests of bringing national awareness to this critical aspect of children's lives.

You are an advocate for our children and our future. I hope *The Child Care Design Guide* helps you in your mission.

Anita Rui Olds
Woodacre, California 1999

PART ONE

THE CHILD'S ENVIRONMENT

CHAPTER ONE

RAISING AMERICA'S CHILDREN

Isn't it strange that Princes and Kings
And clowns that caper in sawdust rings
And common folks like you and me
are builders of Eternity?

To each is given a bag of tools,
A shapeless mass and a book of rules
And each must make ere life is flown
A stumbling block or a stepping stone.

— ANONYMOUS

As a reader of this book, you are most likely involved or soon to be involved in the design, construction, or renovation of a child care facility. The above verse suggests that you, like all of us, are a "builder of eternity." But your role has special significance, because you will shape the lives of countless youngsters and future generations. Whether you are trained in design, or are a lay person with little knowledge of where to begin, it is essential to understand the far-reaching impact of using a bag of tools, a shapeless mass of mortar and bricks, and a book of construction rules, to build a place of caring for children.

The Dilemma of Child Care

Today, children as young as three weeks of age are placed in child care centers for the major part of the day, sometimes overnight, and sometimes when they are ill. Although group care of children has existed in this country and abroad for more than 100 years, rarely has it extended to children younger than two. Nor was it considered the norm to place children below kindergarten age, who were neither orphans nor in foster care, in the custody of strangers on an extended full-day basis. But the technological revolution, which made it necessary for parents to leave home in order to work; women's liberation; the necessity for dual-incomes; increasing mobility; a rising divorce rate; and an increasing number of adolescent and single parents have created a burgeoning need for care of children under school age.

Unlike other industrialized nations, the United States does not have policies of publicly-funded child care programs, paid leaves and job protection for employed parents.[1] The United States stands alone among major industrialized nations in not ensuring income protection for parental leave. Many new mothers must return to work earlier than they desire or is desirable for the child, often sacrificing the quality they would like for a center slot that is simply available, safe, and affordable. Lack of subsidies often result in inadequate compensation and poor working conditions for staff, poor quality of care for children, and lack of affordability for parents.

Number of Children in Care and Types of Care

The statistics are staggering. *Today's child in center-based care—whether 3 weeks or 3 years of age—spends an average of 10 hours a day, 5 days a week, 50 weeks a year essentially within the four walls of one room.* Before reaching the age of 5, a child may have spent as many as 12,500 hours in a child care center—the amount of time that most adults have spent in elementary and high school combined.

By the end of 1995, approximately 1 out of every 3 of the nation's nearly 20 million children under 5 was enrolled in a center on a full-day or part-day basis. Although Figure 1.1 indicates that 48% remained in the care of relatives, and 22% in the care of nonrelatives, center-based care is on the rise. As new federal legislation deprives mothers of welfare support and requires that they enter the workforce, more and more children are being enrolled in centers at younger ages. Indeed, infant/toddler and school-age care are the fastest growing forms of child care.

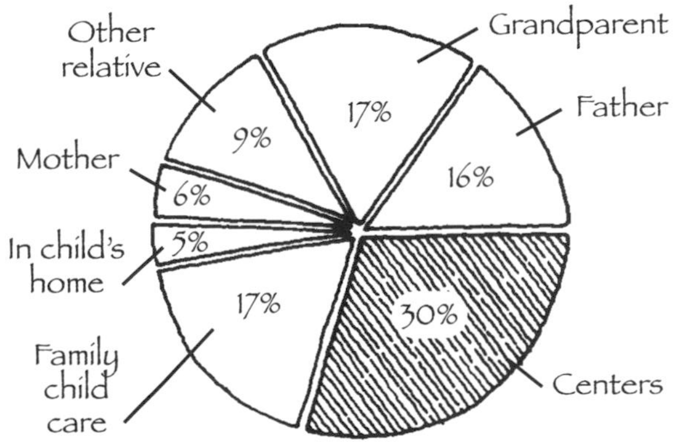

Figure 1.1
United States child care arrangements for children under 5 as of 1996.

Infant Care: A Major Concern

Fifty percent of all mothers with babies younger than a year work away from home, and that number is steadily rising. Nearly half of these infants are enrolled in center-based care. Infants and toddlers are the fastest-growing population requiring care, and they are the ones who have historically been kept close to home and shielded from group settings because of their profound need for consistency, warm physical contact, and nurturance. Many experts would argue that breast feeding is nature's way of ensuring both that infants stay close to their mothers for at least the first six to nine months, and that they not share their mothers with a same-aged peer except in the case of twins or triplets. A one-to-one ratio may be crucial to development in the first year.

In center-based care, by comparison, even the best ratio of one adult to three babies is abysmally low. Three infants cannot receive the same amount of attention and physical affection any child would receive one-on-one. Yet today it is usual for groups of 6–10 infants and 8–18 toddlers, with two caregivers per group, to be exposed, in two shifts per day, to as many as four "trained caregivers," who have an average annual turnover rate of 40%. This means that infants may expect to change caregivers twice per day, and twice per year, hardly the stability and consistency that is required. We do not yet know the developmental impact of these practices.

Recent Research—The Importance of the First Three Years

What we do know—from new scientific evidence—is that warm and loving attachments between infants and adults, and positive age-appropriate stimulation from birth onward, critically affect brain and neurological development. The first three years of life are particularly important because of the pace at which children are growing and learning. In no other period do such profound changes occur so rapidly: A newborn grows from a completely dependent human being into one who walks, talks, plays, and explores in less than three years. The downside of the brain's plasticity is its acute vulnerability to trauma, especially in the early years when its organizing framework is being established.

Research confirms that babies raised by caring, attentive adults in safe, predictable environments, are

better learners than those raised with less attention in less secure settings. New research techniques, including sophisticated brain scans, have also enabled scientists to study the developing brain in greater detail than ever before. The findings reveal that the effects of the environment on the developing brain are more profound and wide-ranging than previously recognized. It has been established that during the prenatal period and the first year of life, the brain develops more rapidly and extensively than earlier research demonstrated. The vulnerability of the brain to early environmental influence is now seen as profound and long-lasting. Early stress on brain function negatively affects the number of brain cells, and both the number and the circuitry by which these cells are connected.

Thus, the risks are more clear than ever: If infants and toddlers are cared for in unpredictable and inconsistent fashion, their stress and fear levels elevate. An adverse environment can compromise a young child's brain function and overall development, placing him or her at greater risk of developing cognitive, emotional, and physical difficulties.

Number of Centers and Their Size

In 1967, when the first child care census was completed, the typical center served 49 children. Rising costs for facilities and staff now dictate that centers serve more children in order to survive. By 1990, the average center size had increased to 62 children, by 1996 to 72. Most new centers are in the 100–125 child range. Caregiving is among the fastest growing occupations in the United States. In fact, the lack of child care workers qualified to staff the burgeoning number of centers is creating a minicrisis in the field.

As of 1997, there were approximately 101,000 child care centers accommodating around 10 million infant through school-age children. Using even the most conservative estimate of a 6% increase per year, by the year 2001 there will be approximately 124,000 centers serving about 12 million children. Estimating facility needs, based either on the absolute minimum space requirement of 35 square feet per child, or on an average overall building size of 100 square feet per child, indicates that an additional 21–60 million square feet of space are needed annually.

Care Quality

It is not surprising, given these numbers and the snowballing rate of growth, that quality suffers. A landmark 1995 study[2] came to the disturbing conclusion that only 24% of the facilities studied were "good," 66% were "mediocre," and 10% were of "poor" quality at or below minimum standards. Children in the large middle range were physically safe but received scant or inconsistent emotional support and little intellectual stimulation. This remained true across all levels of maternal education, child gender, and ethnicity. Of the centers for infants and toddlers, 40% provided inadequate care (52% were mediocre, and only 8% were good), for reasons including unresponsive caregivers, safety hazards, and poor equipment. Centers for infants and toddlers especially were sufficiently poor in quality as to interfere with children's emotional and intellectual development.

In this study, centers with better quality also had higher staff/child ratios, staff education, and staff wages; administrators with greater prior experience; specialized staff training; and more stringent licensing standards. Very little in the study concerned the physical environment per se. However, two of the items on which most centers scored the lowest related to the amount of homelike comfort and privacy provided for children: The average center provided an environment that "lacks in creature comforts" with very little "space to be alone" and few "furnishings for relaxation." Although most centers provided furnishings for routine care, the average environment is described as hard and institutional: Rooms might have a rug on the floor, but not a cozy area to snuggle up in.

Food was nutritionally adequate, but the mealtime atmosphere did not tend to encourage the development of social or self-help skills. Similarly, encouraging children's creativity through art and dramatic play activities was not a strength in the average center, nor was the display of children's work. The average center also fell short in providing good space to meet adults' personal needs, such as separate restrooms, a comfortable staff lounge, or safe and adequate storage for teachers' belongings. As will become clear in the following pages, most of these factors are aspects not of program design but of facility design, which can be improved!

The study also found that market forces—including strong price competition and lack of consumer demand for quality—constrain the cost of child care and thereby depress the quality of care provided. In most communities, the child care market is highly competitive, forcing all centers to hold fees to a similar level. Public funding typically comes with mandates to set subsidies at or below the market rate, offering little incentive to centers to provide quality services and, in reality, precluding them from doing so. Ironically, the study found good-quality services cost only about 10% more than those of mediocre quality, assuming the 10% is spent on items related to quality enhancement.

Perhaps the most startling finding was that parents are not very effective evaluators of quality. Ninety percent of parents tended to rate the quality of centers where their children were enrolled as "very good," while trained observers rated the care in most of these same programs as poor to mediocre. It would appear that parents do not know what they should be looking for and substantially overestimate the quality of the services their children are receiving. Perhaps they tend to disregard problems as a form of self-protection when they feel uncomfortable or guilty about leaving a child in group care. The result is that parents are not getting the best value for their child care dollar and not demanding real quality in the services they purchase.

The only exceptions to these dismal statistics were

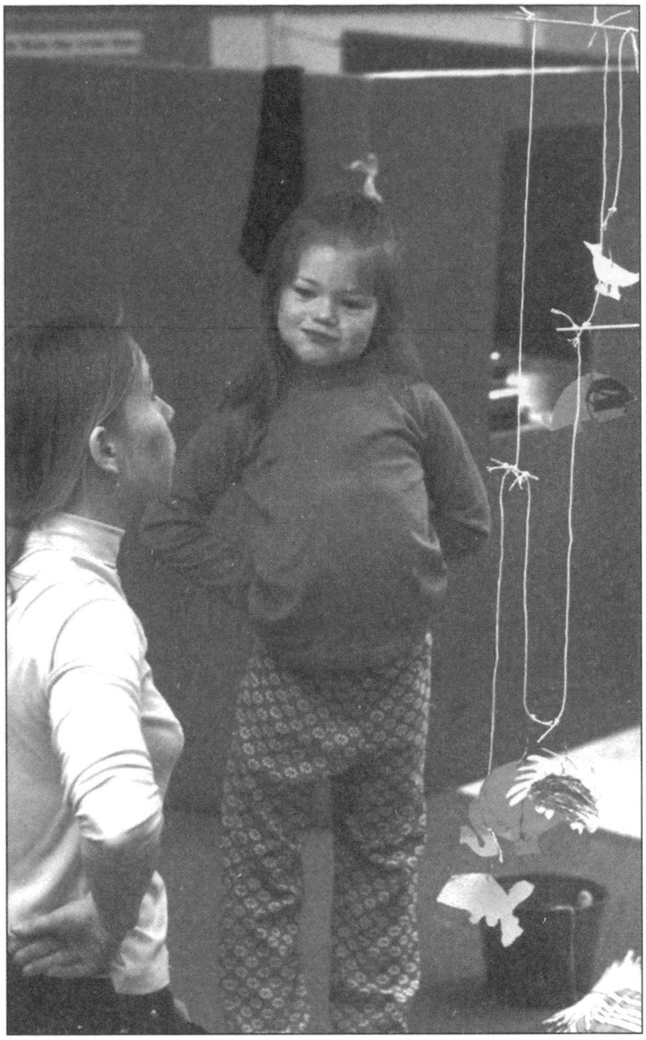

accredited centers[3] (a small fraction of America's total child care programs), which were able to provide better quality and to charge higher fees. The study concluded that where there is an indicator of quality that parents can identify, they are willing and (in this case at least) able to pay for it.

Quality and Costs

The fact is that child care is expensive. Most experts now agree that without support and subsidies either from the federal government or private enterprise, it is difficult if not impossible to make care affordable, or to provide the quality of facility and staffing that children require. Similar to the heavily subsidized, largely universal child care throughout Europe (from age two or three to compulsory school age), the Carnegie Corporation, in its 1994 report on the needs of children under three,[4] strongly recommended that this nation:

- Improve parental leave benefits
- Ensure quality child care for infants and toddlers
- Provide parents with affordable quality child care options
- Develop networks of family-centered child care programs for infants and toddlers

In 1996, the Carnegie Corporation's report on Learning in the Primary Grades,[5] proposed that universal preschools (ages three to five) be established to help assure success in school for young children. As of this writing, about 30 states have established mandates to provide universal pre-K programs. We are headed in the right direction, but discrepancies between what is required and the money available to do it still remain.

While these studies provide evidence of the growing need for reassessment of our priorities, practices, and monetary allocations, none of them really addresses the quality of a center's physical environment. This book is intended to fill that gap by highlighting the role that facility design plays in creating a good program. As the number of centers continues to rise, we can no longer simply "make do" with whatever space is available. Instead, we must consciously create facilities that ensure children's safety and developmental well-being, staff comfort and ease of caregiving, and parental involvement in center activities. This text outlines the extensive physical supports needed to create well-functioning programs. Although no single center is likely to meet all of these goals, each can strive to incorporate some, thereby helping to improve the standards and quality of facilities nationwide.

The Child Care Center: A Building Type In Search of a Model

The care of large numbers of children for long hours, in confined space, is unprecedented. And the effects of such practices are truly unknown. Who among us, reading this, is a product of child care? Who can attest to its impact or guide our design and decision making? We are on virgin terrain, flying by the seat of our pants, without answers. We do not really know the ideal setting in which to raise children outside their homes. Nor what scale, forms, textures, space, and colors will most support the astonishing receptivity of the growing child.

Child care centers are a new building type in search of a model. Most of the over 100,000 centers in existence in the United States today were created in found space under extremely tight budgets and time frames requiring them to have been done "yesterday." Church basements, supermarkets, and assorted "leftover" spaces have been pressed into service as centers. Now that it is desirable to keep children near their parents' place of work, offices, banks, hospitals, government buildings, and corporate headquarters also qualify as potential child care sites. Even structures built as stand-alone child care facilities have not had a tested model on which to base their designs. Most were built in haste, and many were designed more to meet the owner's bottom line than the needs of children and staff. The examples that do exist have "grown like topsy"—hybrids of the nursery school, the elementary school, the corporate office, conventional wisdom, and whatever available resources would allow. Few of these centers operate on the premise that the real client is the child and the family rather than the owner or funder. Few have asked what is the best environment for children and staff, as opposed to what is necessary for adult productivity, for breaking even, or making a profit.

Many architects, child care professionals, and human resources personnel confronted with the task of providing a space for child care assume that there are "accepted" ways to do it and exemplary facilities to emulate. This is, unfortunately, a false assumption. Often, the elementary school is seen as the model, but elementary schools are not appropriate for babies who cannot talk, toddlers just learning to walk, or preschoolers who need to move in order to learn. Without a body of knowledge from which to draw, teams designing new centers have practically had to invent strategies for each new situation.

Research Related to Child Care Center Design

Because child care in the United States has been viewed as a domestic responsibility rather than a basic component of a community's infrastructure, there has been limited concern for the impact of institutional settings on children's development. The relationship between facility design and children's needs is relatively unexplored, and research regarding the impact of facility design on program quality and children's development is limited. Not only is it difficult to delineate which aspects of the environment are most relevant to development, but the effect of the environment is mediated by the policies governing its use. Physical parameters cannot be separated from behavioral ones—teaching styles, educational philosophies, socioeconomic status, etc. Yet research shows that the physical environment does influence children's development. So the logical starting point for designing child care centers is an understanding of how children develop and what they need.

What Children Need: The Foundation of Center Design

Experts agree that the first three to five years of life lay the foundation of each individual's personality, belief systems, and ways of seeing and being in the world. Children's good health and development are predicated first and foremost on affectionate interaction with at least one adult or a few familiar people from whom they can receive intensive, personalized, and predictable care on a consistent basis. While this is primarily an issue of staffing and curriculum, the design of a center can either promote or discourage contact between child and caregiver. It can create a pleasant work environment that eases the task of caregiving and makes caregivers want to stay on, or it can add to staff burdens, burnout, and turnover. *Facilitating predictable, consistent, and intimate care for each child needs to be an overarching concern in all design decision making.*

Childrens' Four Basic Environmental Needs

In addition to the need for consistent and personalized care, children have four basic environmental needs, (which adults share), for movement, comfort, competence, and control. Keeping these four needs foremost in mind during every aspect of center design, and especially in developing the interiors, will go a long way towards assuring an optimal outcome.

An Environment That Encourages Movement

A key design requirement is to allow children the greatest possible variety of large muscle movement both indoors and out. The entire ambience should offer an invitation to move within safe and tolerable limits.[6] Motion permits children to locate themselves freely in space, create their own boundaries, access diverse territories, and explore their abilities. Moreover, movement

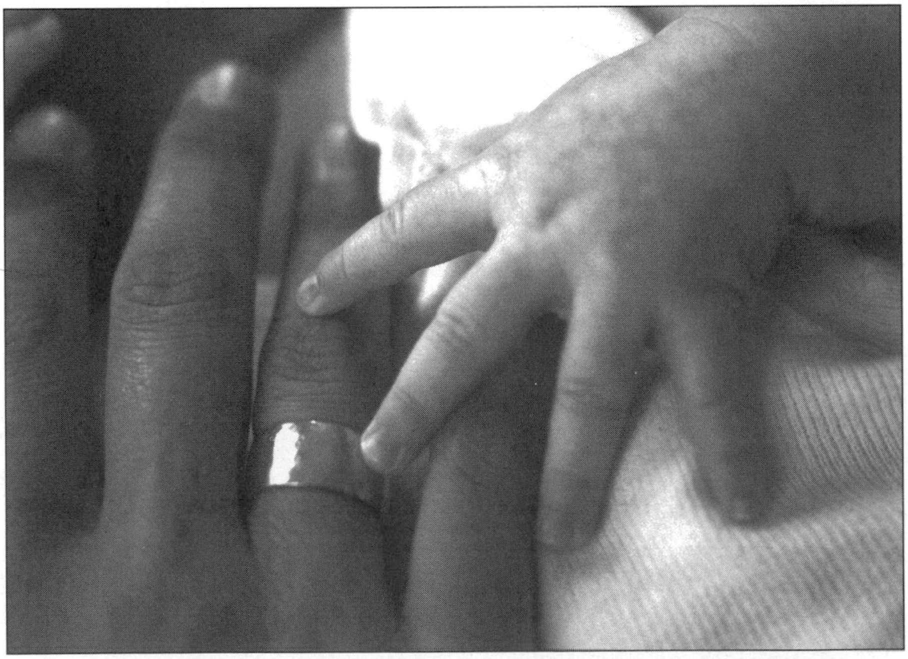

An environment that encourages movement.

is considered to be the bedrock of all intellectual development.

Adults can easily become aggravated by many little bodies each moving to a separate drummer. In an attempt to constrain movement indoors, caregivers sometimes eliminate gross motor equipment, restrict the territory available for action, or require children to sit in chairs, cribs, or playpens.

If restricted too much, children become frustrated and their attempts to learn are diverted into inappropriate expression—they fidget in their seats or incessantly try to gain access to prohibited materials. When these behaviors become repetitive or lead children consistently to disobey established rules, teachers may begin to locate the causes for the misbehavior *within the child,* and to suspect deficiencies such as poor motivation, attention deficits, and hyperactivity. But often it is merely limited opportunities for movement that create many so-called behavioral and learning difficulties. Group rooms designed with appropriate indoor supports for large muscle activity (such as climbers, lofts, movement areas, and equipment with movable parts) and opportunities to run, climb, swing, slide, and crawl outdoors, can resolve the tension between children's needs to move and caregivers' needs to organize the movement.

An Environment That Supports Comfort

When children feel comfortable in their physical surroundings, they will venture to explore materials or events around them. Consider places which make you feel comfortable. Most likely, these settings involve moderate and varied levels of stimulation for all the senses.

Our sense organs are designed to detect *changes in stimulation* rather than to monitor a steady state or constant input. They therefore require movement and change, even though the built environment tends to be static and unchangeable. While dramatic fluctuations in stimulation level can be frightening and disorienting, patterns of movement that are moderately diverse help to maintain optimal levels of responsiveness and make us feel "comfortable."

The bell-shaped diagram in Figure 1.2 shows how behavior is optimum at *moderate levels of stimulation*—the "comfort zone"—rather than when there is too much or too little stimulation. The relationship between performance and stimulation is actually nonlinear: Although performance tends to increase with

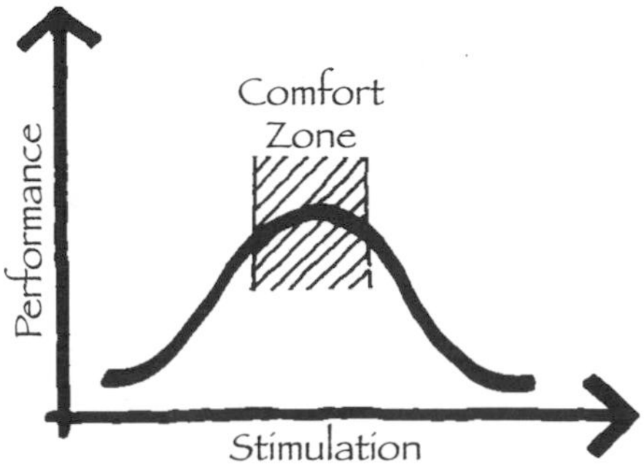

Figure 1.2
Moderate degrees of stimulation create feelings of comfort and optimize performance.

An environment that supports comfort.

increasing stimulation, at some point, too much stimulation leads to a decrease in performance. In fact, because behavior at the two ends of the spectrum looks identical, it is often difficult for a teacher to know whether a child's disinterest is due to boredom or overarousal.

Comfortable settings provide neither too much sameness nor too much contrast, but what Fiske and Maddi[7] call "difference-within-sameness." Nature best exemplifies this difference-within-sameness concept, providing us with some of our most comforting experiences—wafting breezes, babbling brooks, sunlight dancing on leaves. The sense of calm we experience in a beautiful natural setting is perhaps due to nature's capacity to establish rhythmic patterns of change akin to our own physiological rhythms. Children also appreciate, and need to have, extensive experiences outdoors.

By contrast, the over- or underarousing levels of sensory stimulation present in many child care centers—long, echoing corridors; cold tile floors; groups of identical tables and chairs; glaring fluorescent lights; artwork hung indiscriminately; bright, chaotic colors and patterns everywhere—exacerbate feelings of "disease."

The many ways in which design can provide difference-within-sameness are discussed throughout this book. Among the most important are variation in architectural elements such as scale, floor height, ceiling height, and lighting, variety in the texture of finish materials, and the presence of soft elements such as carpets, couches, and pillows. Each group room also presents opportunities to create separate "places" for engaging in different activities: areas that are warm and cozy; hard and sterile; dark or light; noisy or quiet. Varied spaces prevent boredom and discomfort by enabling children to seek out stimulation that suits their moods and levels of arousal at different times of the day. "Variety is the spice of life" is a good adage to keep in mind when designing for comfort.

An Environment That Fosters Competence

Children need to feel successful in negotiating the world around them. Yet, their immaturity and small size constantly force them to confront intimidating and frustrating experiences: light switches too high to reach, faucets too tight to turn, clay too hard to pound. A supportive environment helps children fulfill their own needs, execute tasks easily, manage their own tools and materials, and control their own movements from place to place.

Listed below are three design factors that enhance children's ability to work competently:

1. **A variety of things to do.** To assure that children will find things at which they can succeed and through which they can reveal themselves.
2. **A variety of places in which to do them.** To reduce the overall scale of the room and group, and help children perceive the possibilities and limits of each activity.
3. **Well-organized and accessible things and places.** To invite child use, help focus attention, clarify ideas, and support possibilities for execution.

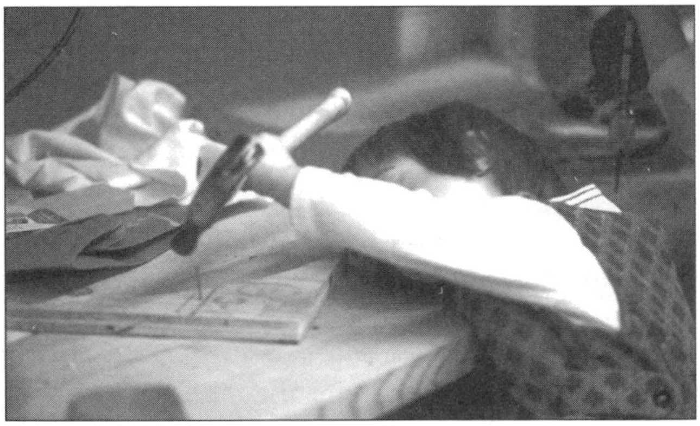

An environment that fosters competence.

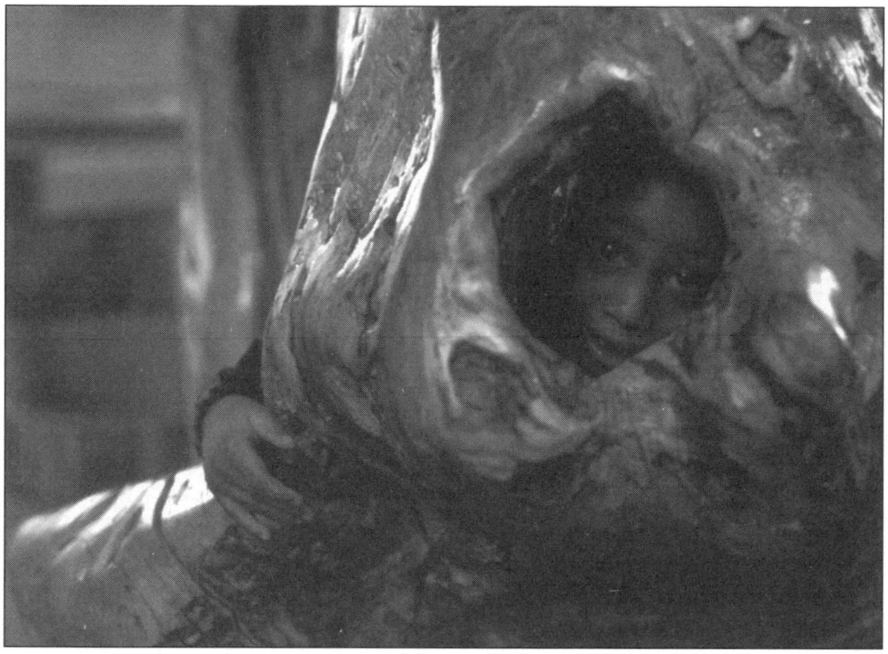

Privacy is part of a sense of control.

An Environment That Encourages a Sense of Control

It is also important that children have the ability to exercise control over their immediate personal environment by being able to have some privacy, to make predictions, and to appropriately orient their bodies in space.

Privacy. Because adults must have full view and ready access to children in child care settings, a child's opportunity for privacy is often neglected. However, like adults, children suffer when possibilities for retreat are not available. Window seats, platforms, cubbyholes, fiberboard barrels with cutouts, and small enclosures provide ideal spots to get away from it all. Certain design tactics can also assist in maintaining a balance between access to the child and the child's need for privacy.

Predictability. Institutional settings are inherently unpredictable: one is never sure what will happen next, who will arrive, and for what purpose. Unpredictability increases children's lack of ease and control.

A well-designed center is "decipherable" by a child. For example, upon entering a room, the first thing a child wants to know is: "How did I get in here? How do I get out? What other spaces is this space connected to?" Boxlike rooms with few connections, or womblike enclosures that create too much environmental protection, are as distracting and unsettling as too much physical stimulation or visual input; children feel cut off from things around them, not knowing what might occur to interfere with their activity. Doors and windows that are informative and distinctive give reassuring answers to these questions.

Spaces designed to support predictability often involve a vista or an elevated position so that occupants can scan all areas of the room and anticipate future events. This is one reason why lofts and changes in level can be valuable. A building whose scale is small, and designed as a cluster of spaces, is more interpretable than one consisting of many rooms off long corridors. Predictability also can be increased by using interior windows or walls of glass, by keeping boundaries low and partially transparent, by well-modulated lighting and sound, and bold graphics.

Orientation. Solidity at one's back is another essential of environmental control. Adults instinctively place their own chairs and desks against a wall or in a protected corner, but they often leave children vulnerable in the more exposed areas such as on the floor in the middle of the room. For children to experience a sense of safety and control, they need to sit so their backs are against the walls in the room's most protected places.

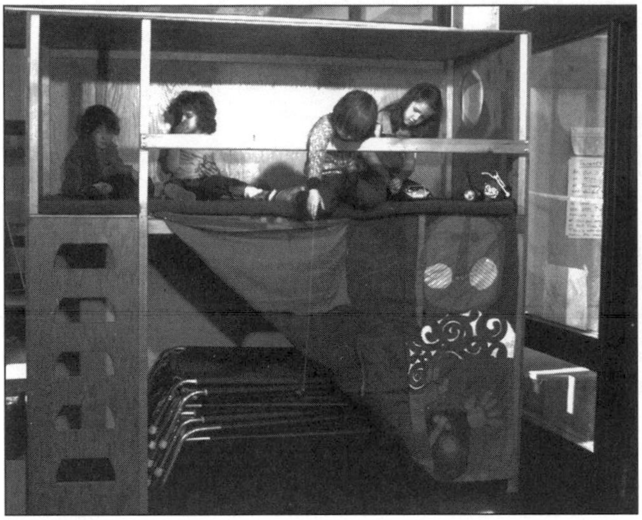

Predictability enhances children's sense of control. From this perch children can survey the entire room and look through peep holes and the window beyond to glimpse visitors before they enter.

Balancing the Four Needs

The design of any child care setting needs both to provide for and to balance these needs for movement, comfort, competence, and control. Whenever one factor is limited, the others have to be increased. For example, if children are required to sit still—as in a group meeting—they will need to be provided interesting things to attend to, a comfortable place to sit, and a vista or view that gives them considerable control over the room. If a child is disabled and experiences many limitations at once, such as ineptitude, decreased movement, and decreased control, then the comfort dimension must be given more attention than normal.

From Theory to Reality

As our children in their most formative years are raised in institutional contexts, the child care center rather than the home is becoming the child rearing "habitat" for this country's future generations. Quality child care center design emerges as a crucial social need to which architects, interior designers, developers, corporations, child care specialists and educators must respond. This book, while providing guidelines for design, also strives to prompt a deeper inquiry into the profound question: How do we really want to be raising our children?

Action Follows Thought

A fundamental law of psychology states that "action follows thought." We may act and then think about what we have done, but we cannot act without first having some mental construct—a thought, belief, felt sense—that precedes the act. Conversely, whatever is created through action reflects the nature and quality of the thought that preceded it. To change the action, we must first change the thought or belief.

Raising children in concrete boxes without much sensory variation or relationship to nature suggests that we believe sterility will not hurt them and that nature is not very important. Cutting corners because of budgetary limitations suggests we believe money is scarce, the sole resource, and the only way to get the job done.

A major problem with child care center design lies in our limited visions and imaginations. Instead of striving for ideals, we tend to allow circumstances, budgets, and timelines to dictate what becomes manifest. Too often, minimum licensing standards—below which children's welfare is jeopardized—become the accepted goal, not the bedrock lower limit to be avoided. Just as minimum daily requirements of vitamins are not sufficient to create good health or a long life, licensing requirements do not ensure developmentally appropriate centers, only minimally adequate ones. If we set our sights on the lowest common denominator—rather than on the loftiest and most far-reaching possibilities—we will do only what is required, and challenge ourselves to do little more.

There is a simple key to designing buildings that enable children to move expansively through space, play lavishly with water and paint, hear harmonious sounds, smell marvelous odors, and touch fabulous textures. The key is to design buildings that establish beliefs in opportunity and possibility. *The key is to understand what nourishes our children and use this awareness to inform every step of the design process.* When we operate on the assumption that "where there is a will, there is a way," we dramatically increase the chances that what children really deserve will materialize before our eyes.

In the end, our attitudes and beliefs are the legacy we leave to our children. Our thoughts, as reflected in our designs, in turn shape children's beliefs about themselves and life. Buildings that constrain or offer limited choice result in beliefs that life is finite, controlling, inaccessible. But committed and compassionate design can instead offer freedom, caring, comfort, competence, and control.

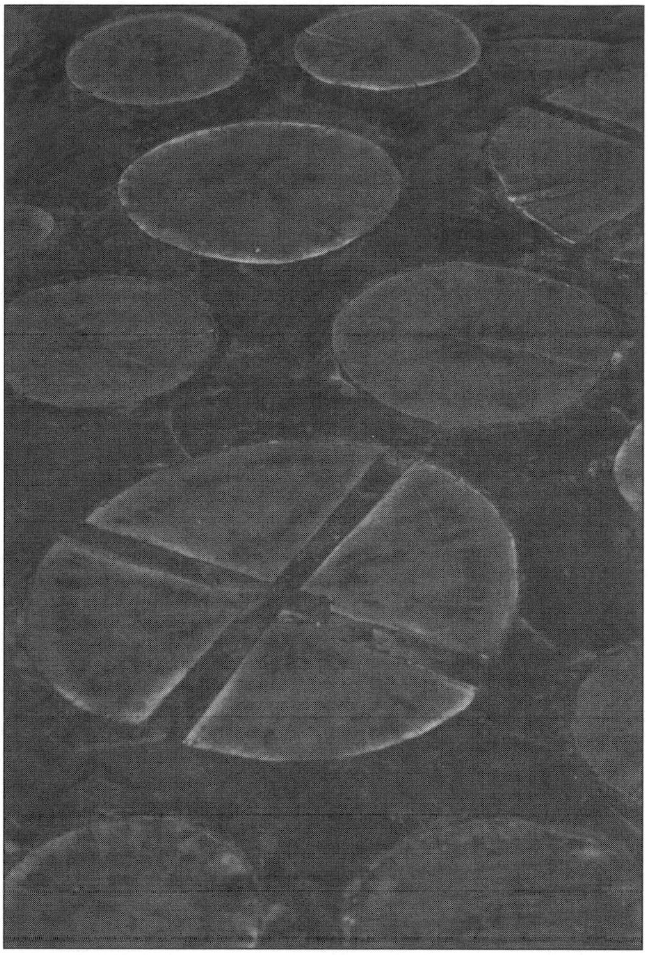

Minimums versus Miracles

Children are *miracles*. Believing that every child is a miracle can transform the way we design for children's care. When we invite a miracle into our lives we prepare ourselves and the environment around us. We may set out flowers or special offerings. We may cleanse ourselves, the space, or our thoughts of everything but the love inside us. We make it our job to create, with reverence and gratitude, a space that is worthy of a miracle!

Action follows thought. We can choose to change. We can choose to design spaces for miracles, not minimums.

The Task for Designers

A great deal is at stake in the design of environments for children. The task begins with acknowledging that creating a child care center is like no other design enterprise. Society's future is in our hands. We are not just providing an office, hotel, library, bank, or factory to which adults go voluntarily for a limited number of hours. Children in child care do not go by informed choice. Often, they are removed from contact with the places and people on whom their security and trust most depend. In part, they will build their sense of expectation, understanding, and love of life on the space, colors, materials, and furnishings that *those of us who design their spaces intentionally provide.*

Designing spirited, wholesome places for children is what this book is about. In the author's experience, this means doing more. It means questioning every choice and decision, not only in terms of client satisfaction, schedules, and the budget, but also in terms of the welfare of the real client—the child. It means finding ways to do the job better with the limited resources at hand. It means saying "no" more often to compromises that diminish children's spirits and saying "yes" more often to feasibility studies and alternative ways of solving problems. It means holding to the highest standards while being clever in manipulating the real constraints. In sum, it means commitment, energy, and time but, most of all, vision.

Every project provides the opportunity to improve the concept of child care center design and the lives of the children who are shaped by it. If we are bold, we will allow our design vision to exceed what we currently believe to be possible. For ultimately, we are being asked not only to avoid known and unforeseen stumbling blocks, but also to care enough to commit to creating solid, supportive, enticing, and beautiful stepping stones.

Notes

[1]Carnegie Corporation of New York, *Starting Points: Meeting the Needs of Our Youngest Children* (Carnegie Task Force on Meeting the Needs of Young Children, August, 1994). Page 7 cites the following statistics for Germany, France, Sweden, Finland, Austria. Germany: New parent receives modest financial sup-

port while at home for up to 1.5 years or can work part-time at previous workplace. France: modest compensation at home for up to 3 years, or work and have subsidized child care. Sweden: full pay at home for 1.5 years or work part-time for longer and receive full pay. Finland: full pay for 1 year, and a lesser amount for 2 more years, job waiting until mother returns; or she can use subsidized child care. Austria: stay at home for 2 years or work part-time until child is 3, while receiving financial support equivalent to the wage of an unskilled worker.

[2]Cost, Quality, and Child Outcomes Study Research Team, *Cost, Quality, and Child Outcomes in Child Care Centers* (Denver: University of Colorado at Denver, 1995).

[3]Accreditation is provided primarily by the National Association for the Education of Young Children (NAEYC) via a process of self-study, correction, and evaluation, in which centers voluntarily engage for as long as required. Once received, accreditation lasts 3 years. At the end of 1995, NAEYC had 4,300 accredited programs and 8,000 in the self-study phase, but these 12,300 programs constitute a small fraction of America's early childhood programs.

[4]Carnegie Corporation of New York, *Needs of Our Youngest Children.*

[5]Carnegie Corporation of New York, *The Task Force on Learning in the Primary Grades,* September 15, 1996.

[6]M. Montessori, *The Montessori Method* (New York: Schocken Books, 1964). Montessori considered the first design requirement to be that of helping children control "the instrument," by which she meant children's own bodies.

[7]D. W. Fiske and S. R. Maddi, *Functions of Varied Experience* (Homewood, IL: Dorsey, 1961).

CHAPTER TWO

THE SPIRIT OF PLACE

If only our own faces
would allow the invisible carver's hand
to bring the deep grain of love to the surface.

If only we knew
as the carver knew how the flaws
in the wood led his searching chisel to the very core,
we would smile too,

And not need faces immobilized
by fear and the weight of things undone.

–DAVID WHYTE, *The Faces At Braga (excerpted)*

Our goal as designers is to create places of freedom and delight where the enchantments and mysteries of childhood can be given full expression. A spirited design satisfies children's souls. It does not simply "equip" a center to serve children's needs.

The "spirit" of a place—as of a person—is an intangible "something" that we intuit to be its characteristic energetic quality. While some people can be "mean-spirited" and some places dark and foreboding, the spirit of place as used here denotes a setting whose integrity helps people feel more fully alive and without fear. Such a place mixes peace and excitement, happiness and pain, fragility and strength, roughness and perfection. It possesses a wholeness that makes the heart sing, the soul rejoice, the body feel safe and at rest. It is the spirit of a place that makes it memorable, that expands our sense of possibility, and puts us in touch with what is most loving, creative, and human about ourselves.

. . . a spirited place enlivens the soul.

Children delight in soaking up the richness of the world through their senses. Everything around them—the sparkling, the foaming, the gooey, the sticky, the slippery, the tall, the tiny, the flat, the shiny, the smooth, the rough, the heavy, the delicate, the loud, the whispered—is "food" for their developing bodies, minds, and souls. A building weak in spirit adversely affects children's development; it lacks the sensory nourishment and sense of wholeness on which they thrive.

The spirit of a place is hard to quantify or prescribe.[1] It is not the same for any two places, nor will all the elements of which it is comprised necessarily be present all the time. Indeed, part of its mystery stems from the fact that a unique set of ingredients converges in a unique spot, in a unique way, at a particular time, to produce a unique result. Difficult as it is to describe, when we experience it, we know it is there. Understanding the qualities that contribute to the spirit of a place can improve the chances of its appearance in the environments we design.

Children delight in soaking up the world's richness.

Prelude to Design: Recalling Our Own Spirited Places

Spirited child care places honor children's spirits—their inimitable curiosity and unrestrained receptivity to the moment—and also the adults who provide their care. Unfortunately, adult emotional responses to places are often "civilized" and repressed. Our skilled designer-minds have limited access to the wonder and abandon we once knew. The guided visualization presented in Box 2.1 is intended to help you tap into the child's point of view. In a relaxed state, you are asked to remember yourself as a child, and to move progressively through recalling three different childhood settings:

1. A favorite, special place
2. A disliked or uncomfortable place
3. A special place that belonged to a favorite adult

This visualization exercise is an important first step in the overall design enterprise. You are encouraged to take the time to work through it before continuing with the text.

Qualities of Favorite Places

Over the years, thousands of adults have participated in this visualization—architects, designers, teachers, parents, therapists, psychologists, administrators. Regardless of the project's mission, or the age, sex, or socioeconomic background of the participants, the results are strikingly similar. Most favorite places involve the *outdoors*. A predominant number involve large *trees* with particular features (gnarls; long, bent branches. . .)—trees in which children spent long, lazy hours alone, with a secret overview of scenes below. Many involve play in or beside water—streams, rivers, lakes, oceans. Some involve favorite rocks, grassy hillsides, golden sunshine, open fields, flower gardens, hammocks, swings, animals. The most unusual favorite place was that of a New Zealand woman who loved to "ride her tricycle under the cows in the family barn!" Some favorite places involve hideaways, huts, small outbuildings, a place under the stairs or bulkhead. Some are personal bedrooms, attics, stair landings. . . .

Despite the uniqueness of these favorite places, all generally share these characteristics:

BOX 2.1

Being A Child: A Visualization

If possible, have someone else read these next paragraphs to you while you sit with your eyes closed. Ask them to pause between each sentence, inviting reverie. Have them slow down to dream time. If you've no companion, read these paragraphs into a tape recorder. Or simply read them first to yourself. Then, sitting back with your eyes closed, take time to envision what they address. Allow yourself to access inner information.

Note: Should you find that you cannot access memories from your own childhood, consider the experiences from the standpoint of a child you know and love.

Sit back comfortably, close your eyes, and take a few deep cleansing breaths. Forget the day's concerns. Sit peacefully for two or three minutes, just focusing on your breathing, until you feel calm and relaxed.

Imagine yourself now as your young child self. Whatever age comes to mind is perfect. See your little feet and hands; feel the smallness and lightness of your body. Perhaps you had a name or nickname. Notice what you are wearing, how your hair is cut, what shoes and socks you have on. Did you tie or buckle them yourself this morning, or did you need help? Allow yourself to fully enjoy being this little person, with all your specialness, uniqueness, and peculiarities.

After you have taken some time to get reacquainted, ask your little feet to walk you to **your most favorite place**, where you most loved to play and to go when you were that young person. Take yourself there now. Notice everything you can about this place: its size, its shape, the quality of light that is there, any special textures or odors, any sounds that have significance for you, any features you treasure. Allow the memories to flood in. Put yourself back there, in your favorite place. Take time to play there. See yourself doing, making, creating the things you loved to do. Enjoy it fully. Notice, all the while, as much as you can about what makes it special.

After you have fully enjoyed playing in this favorite place, prepare yourself to leave it. Thank it for all the wonderful times and memories it has given you. Know that you can always return to it, whenever you like, in your imagination. Wave goodbye and have your little feet move you on.

Now, as you walk, ask your feet to take you to **a place you really did not like** as a child. It may have been a scary place or just somewhere that made you feel bad or sad. Unlike your favorite place, it was not somewhere that you would choose to go or to spend a long time. Once you get there, notice its size and shape. Notice the quality of light, the unique textures, odors, colors, sounds, objects that seem to contribute to its unappealing nature. Pluck up your courage and allow yourself to spend a little time there once again, experiencing its unique qualities and some of your own feelings associated with it. As you do so, see if you can notice the particulars of place that contribute to your feelings. After you have been there for a while, prepare yourself to leave. Say "thank you" to this place as well, for the knowledge it has provided you of things you prefer not to create in your life. Wave goodbye, and walk on.

Now, for a third time, ask your little feet to take you to a special and likeable place. But this time, it is **a place that belongs to a favorite adult** who matters a great deal to you. This is an adult who is very important in your life, and you rejoice in being able to go to a place that belongs to them. Take yourself there now. Notice who this person is and where they are. What are they doing? What do you do together that is so special? What qualities of light and color, texture and odor, sound and space, does their world possess? Are there objects or events of significance? Take time to enjoy reconnecting and being with this wonderful adult, in his or her special place. Have a nice long visit. When it is time to go, give them a big hug and thank them for contributing so much to your life. Tell them they will always be a part of you, held tenderly in your heart. Wave goodbye, knowing you can return to them in your imagination.

Now look at your little child self and thank him or her for being true to you all these years. Invite them to come around more often as you design spirited places for children. Tell them you really need their help. Give them a big hug of gratitude and appreciation, and wave goodbye.

Bring your awareness back to your feet on the floor and your body on the seat. Wiggle your fingers and toes. When you feel ready open your eyes. Then take a large piece of paper and some crayons or markers, and draw the three settings you just envisioned. These simple sketches will be your invaluable guides forever. Never forget them and never lose touch with them.

- A relationship to nature
- Sensorial richness
- A sense of territoriality and ownership
- Privacy and control of intrusion
- An emphasis on being, not doing
- A sense that one has free, timeless play without rules and schedules
- A sense that one is trusted by adults

The participants remember feeling in *control* of themselves as children. They made the *choice* of what to do, were able to become lost in their activities, as well as to be *daring* and *risk-taking* in their explorations.

Qualities of Disliked Places

The shared characteristics of disliked places tend to be the opposite of those of favorite ones:

- Indoors (often), dark and unfamiliar
- Uncomfortable and unpredictable
- Lacking in privacy, freedom, trust, exploration, or ability to move about

Generally speaking, these memories involve *extreme levels of sensory stimulation*. Everything seems too hot or too cold, too big or too small, too bright or too dark. Instead of caressing the senses, these places blast them. The extremes tend to induce boredom/deprivation or hyperarousal. The memory is one of *powerlessness*.

Qualities of a Favorite Adult's Place

Often the favorite adult in a child's life is a grandparent or relative; sometimes it is Mom or Dad. What is unique about these people is their unconditional love for and deep personal interest in the child, and their desire to spend one-on-one time sharing something of value to themselves. It might be cooking, woodworking, building a boat, having a tea party with adult china, fishing, gardening, hiking, or telling stories together.

The favorite adult tends to treat the child as an equal. There is no routine, few rules, much sharing and appreciation. The child is trusted to handle fragile and prized possessions, dangerous tools, or things that adults often consider off-limits. Time is taken to just be together, or the child is given freedom to be with the adult as he or she engages in routine activities. The adult world of work is fascinating and informative. In being privileged to share it, the child feels special and unique.

In summary, the characteristics of the favorite adult's place are:

A loving adult makes a child feel unique and special.

- Equality
- Freedom from rules and routines
- Trust
- Connectedness
- A feeling of specialness

Creating the Spirit of Home: Building Centers on a Residential Model

It is not surprising that the qualities of favorite places are similar to the qualities archetypally associated with "home": protection, belonging, intimacy, familiarity, stability, predictability, comfort, lack of inhibition, choice, autonomy, rest, self-expression, privacy, territoriality, individuality, and memories and symbols of personal and family history. But what makes a building a "home," and how it differs from a child care center, is neither easy to determine nor to agree on.

Nonetheless, most of us would probably agree that the home and the child care center are very different building types. In being places of care outside the home, which serve groups larger than the average family, child care centers are usually seen as more similar to schools, nursing homes, and small institutions, than to houses and residences. Yet institutional settings for care such as birthing rooms, assisted living for the elderly, and hospitals are increasingly incorporating more "residential" elements into their designs, at the request of users who wish these places to be more homelike and less institutional. In the case of child care centers, creating a homelike setting is not only desirable but essential.

For millennia, young children have been sheltered and protected within the "sacred" realm of the home until mature enough to handle the "profane" world outside. This period of protection has been considered important for the formation of a personal identity and sense of self, both of which are forged in relationship to family members, and the unique architectural features and artifacts associated with a dwelling. Indeed, in western society, home is often viewed as a mirror of the self.[2] Historically, the bedrock developmental stages of basic trust, autonomy, and initiative[3] are established in the home before a child is considered ready to enter school.

In these earliest years, children most need the opportunity to be, to create as the inspiration moves them, to impose their own structure on things, in a predictable and secure place, under the watchful eye of a few constant and loving adults. They need, in other words, to feel "at home."

Growing up in a child care center is not the same as growing up in a home. Research indicates that

Children need the opportunity to simply be.

At home, children have access to everyday activities.

children's play in homes is more intimate, self-expressive, and complex than it is in centers.[4] Even the smallest home has quiet places, territories children can claim as their own, and few time constraints. Children typically have access to rooms linked to everyday activities (kitchens, bathrooms, living, and dining rooms) for personal use and play.

With more privacy and (usually) freedom from interruption, children are able to incorporate a diversity of available objects and props into their play. And adult help in procuring the props seems to enhance the expression of self-identity. Activities which start with a clear focus often slowly turn into something else.

Group care settings, on the other hand, appear to dictate a more regimented and structured program, with less room for individual choices by children.[5] The space and the artifacts within them belong to someone else. All aspects of life—including the physical environment, the activities, and the time frame in which they occur—are structured by an outside power.

Homes as places for relationship tend to support conversation and opportunities for children to eavesdrop on adults. In the home, researchers report hearing long discussions between adults and children, revolving around everyday activities and concrete acts. Children greet the mail carrier and various service people and accompany adults in their tasks and errands. By contrast, centers emerge as places primarily for learning cognitive and group social skills, where conversations are brief and focused on naming and categorizing. The logic for behavior is often unclear or abstract: Children might be taught about "community helpers," for example, but rarely encounter them.

While houses typically have contiguous room layouts supporting spontaneous activity, centers have corridors that symbolize conformity and orderly movement from one place to another. Privacies associated with home such as dressing, undressing, bathroom use, and grooming, usually occur in full view of others in centers. Moreover, children are expected to share their feelings and materials with 8 to 18 others and may even be reprimanded for failing to demonstrate a group spirit of cooperation. A child who tries to get out of view, to go outside the designated space, or uses daydreaming as a form of retreat, may be suspected of having a behavior problem, or be called inattentive and disinterested. Constant surveillance, enforced sociability, and lack of privacy are counter to the experience of being "at home."

Thus, it is important to acknowledge that once the context of growing up is transferred from the informality of the home to the structured requirements of a child care center, *the entire experience of being a child changes*. This may not be all bad, and it may require us to re-examine the nature of childhood in modern society, but we must not pretend it is the same. In truth, we do not yet know the emotional consequences of this type of care. However, if the child care center is now to replace the home as the context for the development of trust, autonomy, inititive, and sense of self, we need to ensure that the child care environment tampers with such formative processes as little as possible. Why design the center like an institution when it can as easily be more like a home and stand a better chance of providing the essential ingredients for children's growth?

A place filled with spirit helps relax institutional tendencies toward programmed management and control. Centers designed more like homes than schools, more like an informal natural area than a playground, come closer to providing the archetypal childhood experience. Such settings can provide both the emotional freedom "to be" and the mental opportunity "to learn" that characterize home and center.

To ensure that the child care centers we design today become the "favorite places" in the adult memories of the children who attend them, a residential model, and the incorporation of residential elements in center design, is at the heart of this book. Examples of this model—featured in Chapter 21, "A Model for the Future"—can be found throughout the book.

Designing Spirited Places: The True Purpose of Architecture

Architecture plays a key role in creating the experiences we want for our children. The etymology of the word itself, reveals a relationship between the spirit of a place and the true purpose of the architectural profession:

Root	Meaning	Representation	Symbol
ARCHI	ideal	heaven	○
TECT	to make	man	△
URE	material	earth	□

Architecture is the act of using material to make the ideal become manifest. It is the place where mind and matter combine to produce built forms reflecting the values and ideals of the institution, the designers, the builders, and the society as a whole. It is a process used by humanity to bring heaven to earth, spirit into matter. Conscientious architects can contribute to healing the earth; it is part of their charter.

Different architectural shapes convey different meanings. Rounded or curved forms, typical of religious and spiritual structures, represent the "ideal." Triangular forms represent technology. Square forms represent the earth. In a wholesome child care center, all three forms are represented, especially curved ones that enable the spirit to soar.

While the question of which shapes and materials to use is significant, the matter of greatest import pertains to the *ideals*. **What** is it we wish to manifest? What is the "heaven" we wish to bring to children's earth? What is it we most want them to understand (to "stand" under them)? In terms of what architect Louis Kahn calls a building's "existence will," what does a place for children **want** to be? Can the building offer them tranquillity in a troubled world? Can it assist them in the realization of selfhood? Most importantly, can it make them, in all their uniqueness and diversity, feel loved?

As was stressed in Chapter 1, *action follows thought*. Our beliefs and thoughts about the ideals we wish to manifest ultimately determine the quality, and the depth of spirit, of the places we create for children. It is on these ideals that we need to focus, first and foremost.

Developing a Child's Perspective: Broad-based Perception

Children under five perceive the world differently from adults. We might call the child's innate mode of perception holistic, broad, and simultaneous, whereas the adult's is focused, narrow, and goal-oriented. Children approach experiences with their senses and bodies wide open, exquisitely receptive to *all* the qualitative aspects of the environment. They live continuously in the here and now, feasting upon the nuances of color, light, sound, odor, touch, texture, volume, movement, form, and rhythm around them. Their play is often a response to subtle variations in the places and sensations that surround them, many of which leave deep and long-lasting impressions.

> Children use the environment to improve themselves; adults use themselves to improve the environment. Children work for the sake of process; adults work to achieve an end result.[6]

Research documents that children remember places and sensations far more than they remember people.[7] Often, they are deeply affected by details of which adults are unaware. Rooms, toys, and play structures tell children what they can do. But it is the sensorial qualities of a facility that most affect children's emotions and convey messages about their safety, self-worth, and freedom to be expressive.

So every design detail matters; none is neutral. Children instinctively sense when a setting's wholeness, integrity, and underlying unity are weak. This knowledge might be called "the intelligence of the heart," as opposed to that of the brain. While much emphasis is placed on the visual aspects of architecture, it is really the **feeling** of buildings and our sense of well-being or dis-ease when we are in them that are at the roots of the architectural experience. Feeling relates to broad-based perception, which we need to practice and consciously bring to the design of any space for children.

A good way to practice broad-based perception is to *spend time with children*, seeing the world through their eyes. It is also helpful to meditate, to retreat into nature, and to perform physical activities that require such complete attention that they keep us from becoming absorbed in thought. The critical factor in all these options is to slow down our pace, open our senses, and deepen our awareness of the subtle properties of the physical world around us. We might then ask ourselves:

- How many different types of wind can I hear and feel in this place?
- How many colors appear to my naked eye in a leaf?
- Can I smell if this place is arid, damp, acrid, or sweet?
- What is different about sitting on earth, a rock, a brick ledge, concrete?
- Can I experience the wonder in common objects, such as a pen and a piece of paper?

. . . a lively dialogue between building and light.

Qualities of Spirited Places

With the visualizations of our own childhood experiences of spirit of place as a starting point, and an understanding of how children's and adult's perceptions differ, we can now examine more closely some common qualities of spirited places.[8]

Natural Light

Light changing with the time of day and the seasons alters the appearance of places. The various and subtle cues of daylight—its changing brilliance, warmth, colors, intensity and direction as it illuminates and casts in shadow—are processed continually by broad-based perception. This helps us balance our biological clocks, as well as orient ourselves in time and space. For a place to be fully "understood" there needs to be a lively and informative dialog between a building and the light, weather, and seasons around it. Organic architects often shape windows specifically to reveal the different qualities of light coming from the north, south, east, and west sides of a room.

Difference-within-Sameness

As discussed in Chapter 1, the nervous system is more attuned to noticing *changes* in the environment than to monitoring steady states. Uniformity and lack of change are unnatural and require a great deal of energy to maintain. Settings that provide both varied forms of stimulation and subtle changes in that stimulation, similar to what is found in the natural world, are the most nourishing. The task for designers is to suffuse the static, built world with "difference-within-sameness" at all levels of experience.

Safety

Children have great concerns about their personal safety, but their strategies for dealing with danger are limited. When we subject them to group experiences in confined spaces for long hours, children are forced to learn to watch out for and guard against the movements of others long before they are ready. Living in a state of continual concern about personal safety can wear down the body's immune system, capacity to relax, and overall health. A spirited place, however, reduces the number of alarm signals by providing varied spaces, options for privacy and small groupings, ownership of territory, nooks and crannies—all of which help the body relax so it can interact creatively with its surroundings.

Beauty

Spirited places are beautiful, and beauty is powerfully regenerative. The physical wholeness of a beautiful place transmits psychic wholeness and tranquillity, helping us feel connected yet free, closer to personal sources of vitality and well-being. Currently, so long as child care centers are safe and clean, aesthetic considerations beyond the basics are thought to be "luxuries." However, it is open to question whether today's children can afford not to be given more aesthetically pleasing play and learning spaces.

The two ends of the design continuum shown in Figure 2.1 often characterize center design. One end is budget-driven, with no funds for much beyond space and code requirements, resulting in a container lacking spirit or beauty. The other end is driven by arbitrary aesthetics. Based on adult (architect, interior designer, or both) preconceived notions of a childlike environment, these centers often involve a frenzy of colors, fractured forms, and stylized "houses" that may be both difficult and expensive to build. They may look good in design publications but are rarely beautiful or comforting to a child. The balance point between these two extremes can create an environment where aesthetics enhance function but do not dominate or overwhelm it.[9]

Sometimes a small gesture, such as a transition from straight to curved forms, can change everything. Curves are shaped like the human body and the way it moves through space. Curves and angles wider than 90 degrees invite us to nest and inhabit a space, whereas sharp angles seem cold and rejecting. Although we need straight lines for order, concentration, and doing, we need curves for protection, sociability, and being. Archetypally, curves represent the feminine, straight lines the masculine. Flat ceilings can turn rectangular rooms into lifeless boxes. But placing a life-giving curve at the ceiling/wall junction can be transformative, provided that the transition between the two is gradual and integrated.

Designing for aesthetic richness involves giving similar attention to all of a building's or room's elements. From the child's perspective, everything is an interactive surface with the potential to be sculpted, painted, draped, or molded artististically. Craft, from the hands and hearts of designers, tradespeople, artisans, and caregivers, can counterbalance mass-production. It can transform raw materials into substances of spirit and beauty. Then a space is "alive," and its qualities beckon the senses to play and to respond.

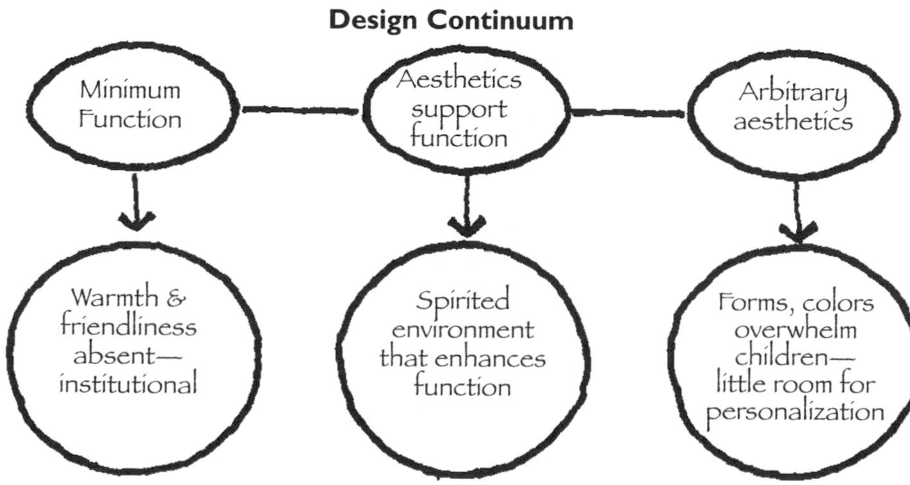

Figure 2.1
To be more than minimally functional, a child care center needs a moderate budget but not arbitrary aesthetics.

A rectangular room with a flat plaster ceiling is transformed by the addition of some curvature where its ceiling and wall juncture meet.

Integration with Nature and the Site

Most cultures have a tradition of geomancy (the art of placement) to determine the most propitious and healthful location of buildings in relationship to the natural landscape, or of furniture in relationship to the building's orientation and design. The Romans believed buildings needed to honor the *genius loci* of a place—the guardian or spirit guide that gave the place its unique spirit or generative energy. The Chinese science of *feng shui*, gaining increasing credence in our culture, is based on the concept of creating a harmonious flow of the life force "chi" in people, objects, rooms, buildings, and the natural landscape.

Other civilizations, acknowledging that our sustenance and well-being depend upon the natural energies of earth, air, fire, and water, and the cycles of the seasons, sun, moon, and stars, built their structures in relationship to these visible and invisible forces. For example, teepees, kivas and yurts, and the Pantheon were designed, respectively, to keep humans in touch with the sky, the earth, and the movement of light from above. As a result, human beings, their settlements, and the landscapes they inhabited tended to be deeply and spiritually bound to one another.

By honoring, improving upon, and being integrated with the site on which they are placed, spirited buildings always have a similar inextricable connection with the natural world . Rather than being designed according to a preconceived "plan," they are built to relate to the unique features of a particular location, often using

The touch points between materials and planes in a building are places particularly amenable and sensitive to beautification.

. . . *the experience of the unseen forces that transform and nourish.*

materials indigenous to the area. Instead of competing for attention, the buildings merge with the site, so much so that plants and structures may grow up, around, and even inside one another. Nature is disturbed as little as possible.

Substantial research[10] verifies that places with spirit also involve such elements as: winding paths; a sense of mystery; vistas; refuges; legibility (enough openness to see where one is going); imageability (richly detailed, well-defined areas filled with landmarks, nodes, and paths); lovable objects; niches; and many ways in which people can actively and passively interact. The more diverse and ubiquitous these qualities, even when subtle, the better we feel in a place.

Current standardized design and construction processes make it extremely challenging to give contemporary buildings and sites the quality of spirit inherent in many older structures. Spirited places require contrast, diversity, and imperfection, not uniformity and flawlessness. Our work is cut out for us.

Personal and Place Identity

A building marks a location in space. Together, the building and its surroundings create a "place" with a particular identity. However, the true spirit of places resides not only in their physical parameters, but also in the symbolic meanings that grow up around them as a result of the history, participation, and belonging of the people who use them. This is why uninhabited

. . . *a deep connection with the natural world.*

deteriorated ruins still have power to move us. Repeated experiences in a place, over time, give both the inhabitants and the place a unique spirit which is part of both their identities.

Children come to know every inch of the territory where they play: exactly how it feels to walk a particular path, to stand under a particular cluster of trees, to experience rain, snow, fog, ice, heat, and cold in this one location. They also mold these elements according to their own fancy by appropriating territories and giving them a personal mark. Experiences growing up in a predictable environment filled with "character" create personal identities, emotional security, and place identities that are inextricably bound together. Such memories are indelible, as our own vivid images of childhood places substantiate.

The symbolic meanings associated with built forms also are learned during the early years: Floors symbolize support and emotional security, walls represent both separation and enclosure, windows expansion and letting in life, and roofs nurturing shelter. Concepts such as ownership, exclusion, access, and control become part of a child's identity as they are learned in relationship to particular spaces.

Every space and object both teaches properties of the physical world and is incorporated into a child's thoughts and feelings. The stair tread that creaks, the warped cabinet door, the crescent-shaped doorknob, the latched gate, the sunken living room, the A-frame roof—which gather layer upon layer of information as they are shaped by the builder, worn by the weather, used by inhabitants, and subjected to the passage of time—then become part of the identities of the children who experience them. The unique history of specific built worlds and the children are one. Child care centers rich in place identity and the freedom to create, help to build rich personal identities connected to place.

Contrast

What makes a building beautiful and spirited has been the subject of extensive inquiry.[11] Especially relevant is *The Good House* by Jacobson, Silverstein, and Winslow,[12] which postulates that good building design depends upon the presence of contrast in everything we experience—specifically, the six contrasts of *In/Out, Up/Down, Light/Dark, Exposed/Tempered, Something/ Nothing,* and *Order/Mystery*. To truly know one dimension we must also experience its polar opposite. Contrast is the starting point for making places interesting.

A design may starkly juxtapose a pair of bipolar contrasts: for example, an interior room *(in)* can be separated from a yard *(out)* by a solid building wall. Alternatively, the contrasts may be mediated by some form of *link* (itself an architectural or design element): for example, a porch that allows you to experience the inside room and the outside yard simultaneously. In serving as the transition between opposing contrasts, links actually enliven rather than reduce contrast. They tend to be the places where the building can be most responsive to the changing needs of its occupants.

The spirit of a structure is deepened when *linked contrasts* occur at *every level of scale*, i.e., the site plan, the building plan, the rooms, the areas within rooms, and the room's architectural elements (windows, doors, floor patterns, wall trim). Thus designers are urged to recognize where more contrast is needed between any two elements, provide a link between the contrasting parts, and extend this treatment to larger and smaller scales.

Contrast tends either to be notably absent in child care center design, especially where budgets are low—or, in centers with arbitrary aesthetics, vividly present with few links. Because the use of linked contrasts at many levels of scale can be transformative, brief descriptions of the six contrasts and their links are provided in Box 2.2. You are urged to consult *The Good House* for fuller explanations, as well as extensive illustrations and analyses of buildings that express these principles.

Spirited Design

The spirit of place is inherent in sites of natural beauty. But in the architectural world it is reflected in the intentions of the designer, the builder, and their clients. Creating spirited places depends upon our ability to let go of ego and—as the opening verse of this chapter suggests—let go of our tendency to be "immobilized by fear and the weight of things undone." It depends upon welcoming the flaws and difficulties in the design process as doorways to our own creativity. When we allow our own hands, like those of the "invisible carver," to bring the deep grain of our abiding love for children to the surface, we create beautiful places to house and liberate their spirits.

BOX 2.2

Six Dimensions of Contrast

In/Out

The IN/OUT dimension refers to the degree of enclosure or exposure created by built elements, and also to the relationship of inside and outside. A space expresses more IN to the degree that it is concave, closer to us, has well-defined corners and edges, increased mass or opacity of its walls, and accessibility only through layers. The size, shape, and distribution of windows and doors also affect the sense of enclosure. The feeling of OUT is increased by transparency, by the degree to which an element is larger, further away, or beyond the walls of a room or building.

Some LINKS between IN and OUT include porches, balconies, decks, courtyards, front and rear yards, fences, arcades, deep roof overhangs, deep door and window reveals, and the extension of a building's walls into the surrounding landscape.

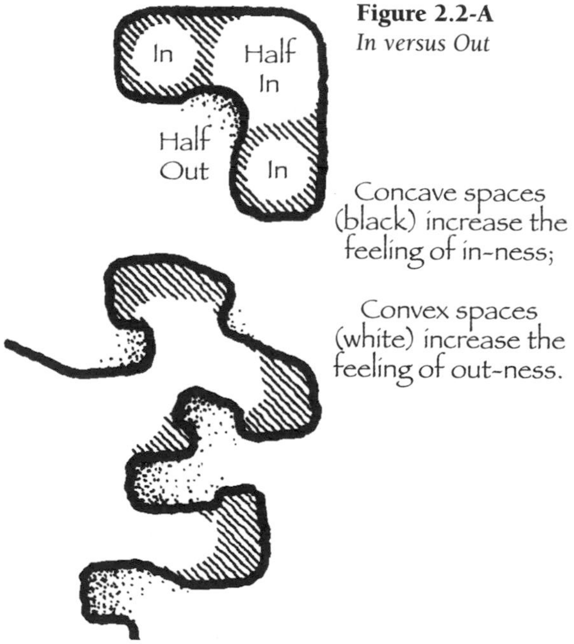

Figure 2.2-A
In versus Out

Children love nooks and crannies, hideaways, and spaces more in scale with the size of their own bodies, thus making them feel in control, protected, and safe. Spaces with more IN provide privacy and intimate groupings that shield individuals from the larger group. On the other hand, children's expressive natures also call for a great deal of OUT, where they can move freely and expansively through space. Children will also endlessly cross and manipulate the boundary between IN and OUT, preferring to play on a porch or sidewalk near the house to playing inside or on the street. Since the feeling of IN comes from being able to observe OUT from a safe place, the growth potential of being OUT is easier if there is a clear escape to a protected IN associated with it. Thus, LINKS between IN and OUT are essential in child care centers.

Up/Down

The UP/DOWN dimension concerns high and low, how buildings rise, and their relationship to earth and sky. UP/DOWN mirrors the verticality of our own bodies. Ways of increasing the contrast between UP and DOWN include varying ceiling and floor heights; the presence of baseboards, wainscoting, fireplace mantels, furniture, and pictures at different levels; long and short views provided by stairlandings, balconies and catwalks; and increasing the steepness, lightness, breeziness, and apparent sense of danger.

The LINKS between UP and DOWN can be expressed by making the distinction between the two very apparent and sharp: for example, cellar versus attic; by varying their temporal connection (giving circulation spaces ceilings of one height, and adjacent rooms ceilings of anoth-

(continued)

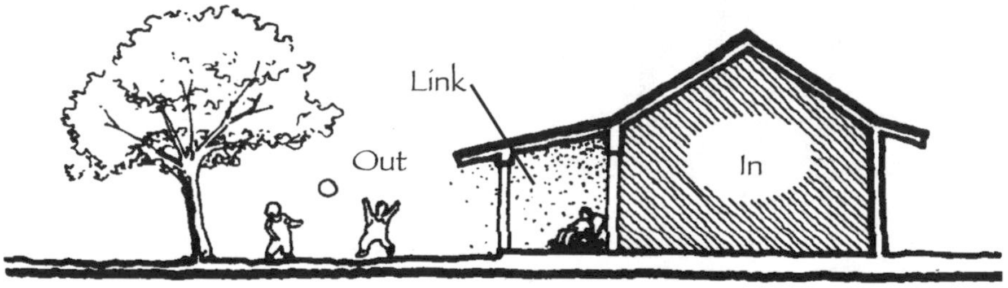

Figure 2.2-B
In versus Out

BOX 2.2

Six Dimensions of Contrast *(continued)*

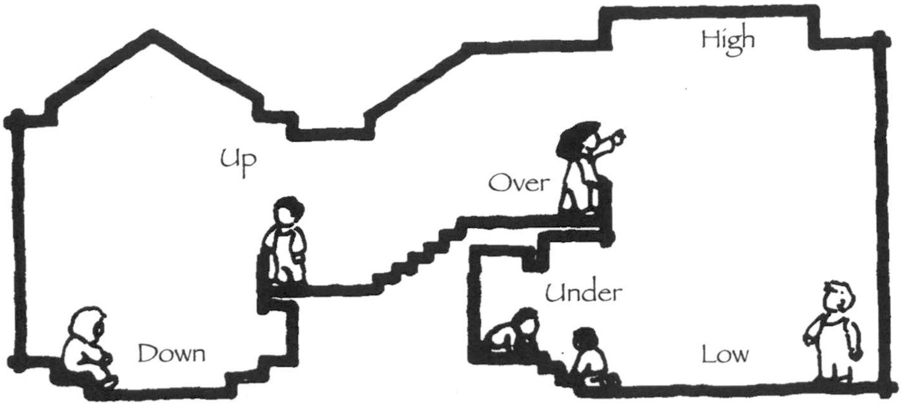

Figure 2.2-C
Up versus Down

Light versus Dark

er height); by using a transitional link that is different in height from either the high or the low, or is continuous—such as a ramp. The design of a building's footings and base (especially if wide) express its link to the ground, just as its posts, beams, joists, braces, walls, and columns express how its vertical load is carried.

Children are both fascinated and intimidated by height. Feeling small relative to the world around them, opportunities to be up high "above it all," give them a sense of power and of privacy. They also enjoy being "down under" tables, stairs, lofts, and being able to hide. Platforms, risers, and lofts are important ways to create spatial variety and offer children possibilities to develop competence in negotiating UP/DOWN variations.

Light/Dark

Much has already been said about the importance of light to the human spirit. But LIGHT is experienced only in relationship to DARK and to the ways in which it is reflected or absorbed by objects and colors in the physical world. Thus, dark spaces are balanced by the contrast of light from large windows and skylights; light spaces welcome the relief of moving shadows and dappled light effects. Rather than even light levels throughout, pools of light to focus activity, and darker areas of retreat, are important.

Anything introduced at the boundary between light and dark can serve as a LINK: windows broken into small panes, awnings, trellises, filmy curtains, extended eaves,

Figure 2.2-E
Exposed versus Tempered

deep window reveals, skylights, and interior lighting providing secondary light sources.

Because children are fascinated by shadow play and by the way different materials process light,[13] designers can make concerted efforts to use natural light as a nurturing "being" in children's lives. A small grove of leafy trees outside, which casts reflections indoors and creates dappled light to play under, leaves impressions lasting a lifetime.

Exposed/Tempered

The contrasts of EXPOSED and TEMPERED concern the primary physical qualities of wet and dry, hot and cold, and windblown versus still. LINKS created between these dimensions can be deeply satisfying to the soul: the protected feeling of retreating during a rainstorm under a roof with deep eaves; the comfort of a campfire on a chilly night; warming one's hands at a wood stove after making snowballs; showering outdoors on a hot day. Porches, outdoor rooms, window seats, enclosed courtyards, garden walls, sheltering trees, and interior pools and fountains are all powerful linking strategies.

Children gravitate to south-facing seats inside or outside, and cozy fireplace inglenooks. Partly enclosed courtyards, trees that provide protection from the elements, and unique places that counterbalance the experience of extremes leave lasting memories in their minds.

Something/Nothing

The contrast of SOMETHING versus NOTHING concerns the presence of mass, form, and decoration, and their absence. SOMETHING is expressed by the solidity of a building's walls, the use of dense materials such as stone and thick timbers, and the presence a deep window reveals. A palpable feeling of protection is created by a building whose base is heavier and thicker at the bottom than at the top. NOTHING is reflected by the absence of decoration and by light, transparent, flexible materials. SOMETHING, such as a rock, in a large open field (NOTHING), can become a point of reference and orientation.

The LINKS between SOMETHING and NOTHING, which connect areas with lots of contents to those relatively free of contents, contribute to tranquillity, balance, and reassurance. Buildings which have a "common area at the heart," some internal place of focus and arrival, or a place of rest such as a window seat or small alcove, provide an intense SOMETHING of focused energy so that what is around it appears to be NOTHING. Roof parapets, decorated rafter ends, and the thickened edge or lip of doors and windows, can differentiate SOMETHING and NOTHING.

Children need opportunities to do SOMETHING and to be NOTHING. Centers often lack enough space for any to be empty. However, a wall of stored toys (SOMETHING) adjoined by an empty platform (NOTHING)

(continued)

BOX 2.2

Six Dimensions of Contrast *(continued)*

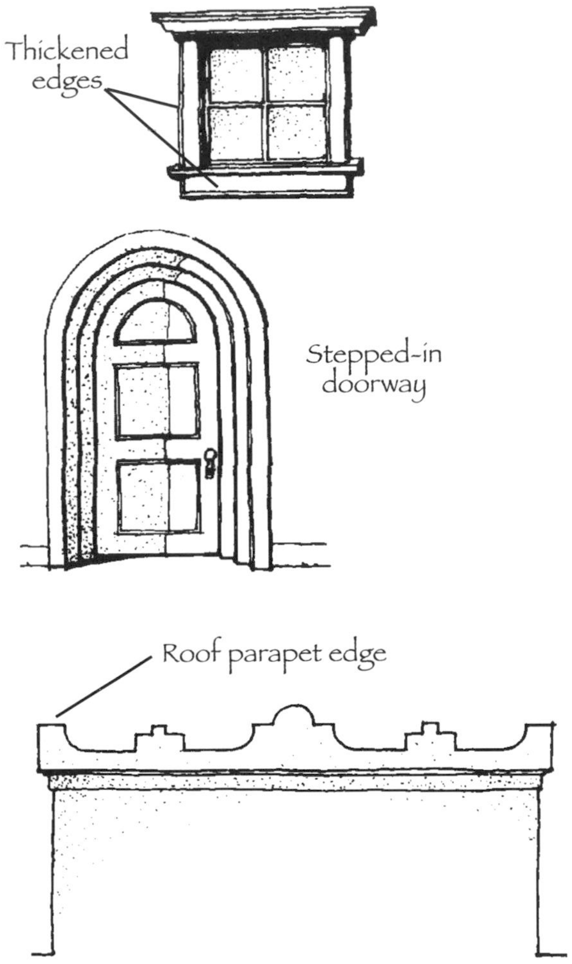

Figure 2.2-F
Something versus Nothing

creates a sense of opportunity and is more conducive to creativity than the same space filled only with toys (SOMETHING) or an empty platform with no toys nearby (NOTHING only).The boxlike uniformity of spaces, and the prefabricated nature of many of the building elements used in child care center design today, deprive children of the experience of this dimension perhaps most of all.

Order/Mystery

The presence of ORDER is apparent in predictable street and building layouts, machine-made products, and the invariant sequence and size of windows on a standard high-rise building, whereas MYSTERY is reflected in that which is handmade, partially hidden, and not entirely predictable. Creating ambiguity between spaces with clearly defined functions, such as designing a kitchen to be both a functional and a social space, can introduce MYSTERY and assist people in relating more informally to one another.

To LINK ORDER and MYSTERY, both machine-made and handmade materials can be present; interior windows and half walls can partially separate and join dis-

Notes

[1]Indeed, Christopher Alexander has called this "the quality without a name." C. Alexander, *The Timeless Way of Building* (New York: Oxford University Press, 1979).

[2]Clare Cooper Marcus, *House As a Mirror of Self: Exploring the Deeper Meaning of Home* (Berkeley, CA: Conari Press, 1995).

[3]E. Erikson, *Childhood and Society,* 2d ed. (New York: W.W. Norton & Co. Inc., 1963).

[4]E. Prescott, "The Environment as Organizer of Intent in Child-Care Settings," in C. Weinstein and T. G. David, *Spaces for Children: The Built Environment and Child Development* (New York: Plenum Press, 1987), 82–86.

[5]Maxine Wolfe and Leanne G. Rivlin, "The Institutions in Children's Lives," in *Spaces for Children*, 103.

[6]Paula Polk Lillard, *Montessori—A Modern Approach* (New York: Schocken Books, 1972), 38.

[7]E. Prescott and T. G. David, *Concept Paper on the Effects of the Physical Environment on Day Care* (Pasadena, CA: Pacific Oaks College, 1976). Concept paper prepared for the U.S. Department of Health, Education and Welfare, Office of Child Development.

[8]Christopher Alexander has identified 15 "Properties" or "Ordering Principles" as the basis of wholeness and beauty in great art, the natural world, and the built world:

Figure 2.2-G
Order versus Mystery

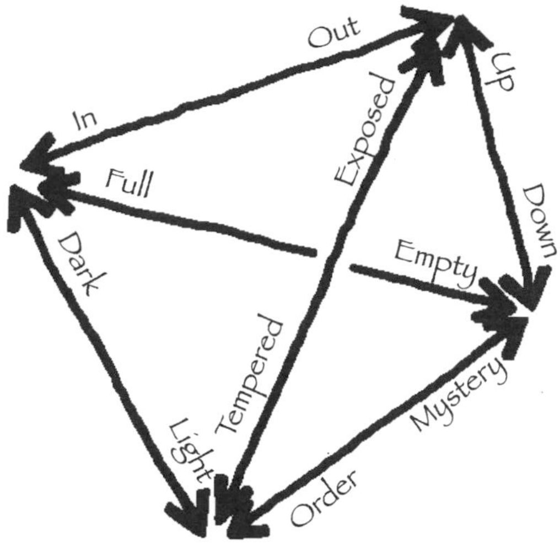

Figure 2.2-H
The six interrelated dimensions of contrast. The poles of each dimension are associated with each other.

tinct functional areas such as rooms and hallways; permanent niches can contain changing displays of flowers and artwork; wall-to-wall carpets can be offset with area rugs and changing furniture arrangements.

Children frequently gravitate to ambiguous spaces linking specific functions because such spaces help explain the relationship of things and implicitly allow the child a freedom of expression otherwise molded by expectation in more ordered realms. Children need order for security and mystery to satisfy their sense of wonder.

Linking the Six Contrasts

When these six dimensions of contrast are made to cooperate with and reinforce each other, a center's design is deeply enriched. The simultaneous presence of several contrasts creates more impact: For example, giving an alcove a lower ceiling, a reduced floor area its own spot of light and its own color makes it very special. Intuitively, certain dimensions are naturally linked: UP with LIGHT; DOWN with DARK; DOWN with MYSTERY and EMPTINESS; IN with DARK and FULL (SOMETHING); OUT with LIGHT and EMPTY. These relationships are expressed by the accompanying diamond.

1. Levels of Scale
2. Centers
3. Boundaries
4. Alternating Repetition
5. Positive Shape
6. Good Shape
7. Local Symmetries
8. Deep Interlock and Ambiguity
9. Contrast
10. Graded Variation
11. Roughness
12. Echoes
13. The Void
14. Inner Calm
15. Not Separateness

Readers are referred to his exhaustive three-volume work-in-progress, *The Nature of Order: An Essay on the Art of Building and the Nature of the Universe*, 1986, because space does not permit discussion here.

[9]Adapted from Bruce Brook, The Child Care Design Institute, Harvard University, June, 1996.

[10]Stephen Kaplan and Rachel Kaplan, *Cognition and Environment: Functioning in an Uncertain World* (New York: Praeger Publishers, 1982); Kevin Lynch, *The Image of the City* (Cambridge: The M.I.T. Press, 1977); Tony Hiss, *The Experience of Place: A New Way of Looking at and Dealing with Our Radically Changing Cities and Countryside* (New York: Vintage Books, 1990).

[11]In particular, Christopher Alexander, *The Timeless Way of Building*; Alexander, et al., *A Pattern Language* (New York: Oxford University Press, 1977); Christopher Day, *Places of the Soul* (San Francisco: Harper, 1994); and Anthony Lawlor, *The Temple in the House* (New York: Tarcher/Putnam, 1994). The

principles in these richly illustrated works deserve intensive study and are articulated throughout this book.

[12]Jacobson, Silverstein, and Winslow, *The Good House* (The Taunton Press (1990).

[13]The preschools in Reggio Emilia, Italy are considered by some to be the finest programs for early education in the world today. One notable aspect of their approach is a focus on the properties of light, through extensive use of light tables, shadow screens, projected images, and beams of light from many sources.

PART TWO

THE DESIGN PROCESS

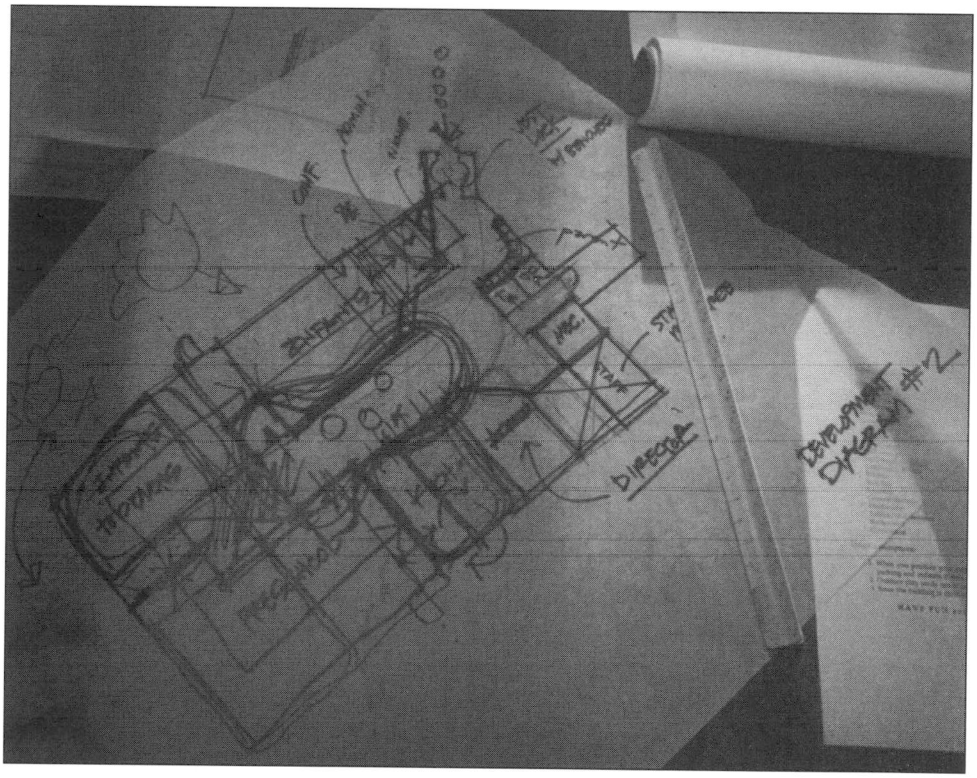

C H A P T E R   T H R E E

THE DESIGN TEAM AND PROCESS

Creative design is a contact sport.

—David Lash

When completed, a center's program and design will ideally reflect the interaction of three sets of forces:

- The needs of children and families
- Guidelines for architectural and interior design
- The needs of child care providers

Effective child care center design involves a diverse team: design and child care professionals, management, contractors, and building and licensing professionals. It is up to the design team to keep the real clients—the child, the child care staff, and the family—in mind throughout the design process. This and the following two chapters outline the process of assembling the design team, addressing preliminary design considerations, finding a site, and designing or renovating the building.

Teamwork: The Essence of a Successful Design

Centers most responsive to children and staff usually result from the genuine collaboration of a congenial team of players. Because collaboration requires dialogue and consensus among people with varied agendas and expertise, it can be difficult, cumbersome, and time-consuming. But failure to institute a process with a diversified, representative approach has been the single greatest factor in creating facilities that do not support the needs of children, even where projects are well funded. A good team always includes both child care and design professionals, as well as management, building professionals, and representatives of regulatory agencies (Figure 3.1).

The collaboration of a congenial team of players is key to an integrated design process.

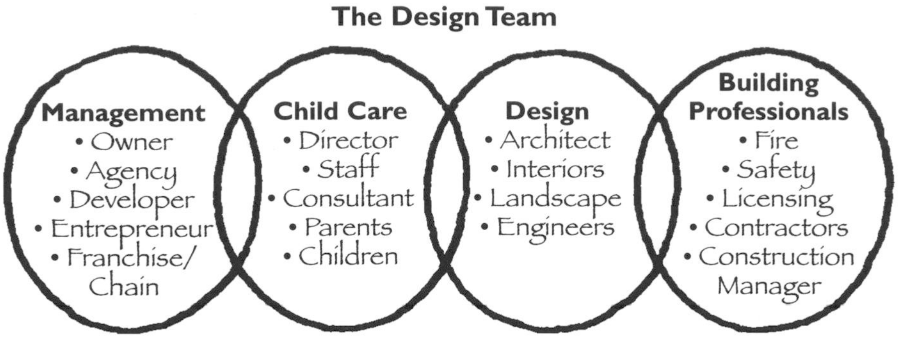

Figure 3.1
An effective design team includes representatives from the child care and design professions, management, contractors, and regulatory agencies.

The impetus for forming a team can come from the client, the architect, management, or an individual. New centers may have to work harder than existing ones to find individuals who—in addition to being committed and willing to lend their time and expertise—have the personal qualities of flexibility, patience, and ability to meld personal priorities with team concerns that are needed to negotiate the intricacies of the design process. Commitment on everyone's part must be first and foremost to the experiences and welfare of the *true client*—the child.

The success of any child care center project depends upon the *ongoing involvement of people familiar with the day-to-day realities of child care*: the director and staff. Sadly, child care staff—the building's primary users—typically carry the least power in terms of design decisions. Architects generally seek staff input initially but often fail to check out the consequences of design solutions with them later on. The all-too-frequent post-occupancy complaint—"we told them not to. . . but they didn't listen," is the result of a design process that did not insist on several cycles of input/critique to the designer and sufficient cross-checking of design with functional consequences. Because subtle factors can carry profound operational weight, meeting the stated requirements of a program does not guarantee fulfillment of its actual intent: Only feedback, dialog, and collaboration can.

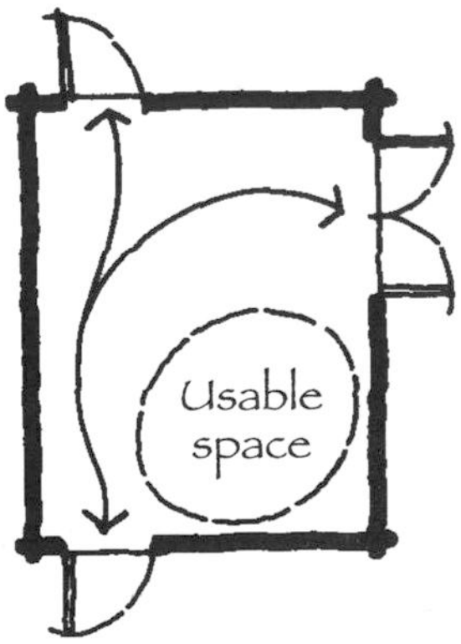

Figure 3.2
A room with too many doors loses valuable corners and floor space.

> ***Example:*** An architect met the programmed square footage requirements for primary play space in a preschool room. But,when the staff moved in with furniture and equipment, they discovered that the movement generated through the room by its three doors reduced the effective play space available. Only a single protected corner remained for quiet activities (Figure 3.2).

The collaborative design process recommended here takes time and therefore can be more expensive with respect to architect's fees than a less interactive approach. Contracts need to address the iterations, models, and extra design time that will be involved. However, the process usually results in fewer mistakes being made and the saving of untold dollars in the long run. The result is a more economical, efficient, and well-designed building.

For the design process to be participatory, meeting schedules and substitute-care arrangements that make it possible for all team members to be present must be established, and decision-making procedures must acknowledge the importance of each individual's expertise. Consensus rather than majority vote is the ideal form of decision making, provided there is a facilitator to move the group along. Knotty design issues require respect for a dissident voice sensitive to aspects that are not working, or important features others have overlooked. A good team strives to "massage" a plan, considering alternatives and trade-offs, until all basic requirements are met. Deliberately preparing alternative designs at the outset assists nondesigners to better understand their options. Satisfactory solutions are never a question of someone winning or losing, but arise out of all team members listening to and understanding the needs of the *situation*.

Decision making by consensus is not design by consensus. Architects and interiors specialists still pro-

Mock-ups make collaboration between architect and center staff possible.

vide the forms and aesthetic they are trained to create. However, decisions that involve functions, budgets, material performance, and a host of other parameters tied to form and aesthetics are improved when people knowledgeable in these areas contribute their experience and expertise to the entire design enterprise. Having team members provide the following types of information early on saves dollars in the long run:

- ask architects and/or contractors to provide cost estimates for alternative designs, systems, and materials.
- Ask interior designers to provide furniture and facility layouts.
- Ask architects to provide study models and mock-ups of areas where it is essential that staff evaluate the 3-dimensional qualities of a space.
- Ask landscapers to provide a sense of the views outside each window and the way the building will relate to the site.
- Ask licensers and inspectors to specify their criteria in writing and review/rule on preliminary designs.
- Ask staff to role-play how they will use each space.

A collaborative, interactive process encourages people to think about how they are currently doing things and how they would really like to be doing them in the future.

A Word About Team Leadership

Successful projects generally involve a pioneering leader with the will and power to bring the project to fruition. The choice of chairperson is critical. While consensus lies at the heart of successful design collaboration, a need remains for sensitive and effective leadership from someone with authority to assist in the resolution of constantly changing tensions, to coordinate communication, and to see that decisions are implemented. If things do not turn out as expected, it is rarely the fault of one person but more often the failure of the organization to identify such an individual to manage the project.

Timing: Avoiding the Express Train

A good process allows enough time for the design to unfold so communication corners are not cut or decisions made without adequate evaluation. *Too many projects are on an express train, racing to their destination.* There is a real contradiction between trying to design a "spirited" facility—intended to last 20 or more years—and a time frame that demands the building be done "yesterday." The schedule (and the budget) need to build in time for stops, refueling, and getting off to stretch one's legs, as well as for deliberation, feedback, and consensus resolution. Successful designs are those that do not stall but allow time to find the optimal *compromise* for a situation.

Time, Costs, and Quality

Three things of concern to owners in managing a design/construction project are time, costs, and quality. An old adage cautions that it is possible to have your wishes in any two, but not all three, of these categories:[1]

- A short schedule and low costs make it difficult to attain high quality.
- A short schedule and high quality make it difficult to keep costs down.
- Low costs and high quality make it difficult to work on a short schedule.

This guide encourages teams and owners to strive for a reasonable project schedule and a moderate-sized budget that will make a good-quality center possible.

Because costs are not consistent across projects, it is impossible to provide general estimates in this guide. However, the recommendations made here for a team process; strong internal leadership; and for *on-going* cost-estimating, construction management, construction administration, and review by inspectors and regulators, are all intended to contribute to cost containment. Where all aspects of the budget (building, interior, site) are generated and reviewed simultaneously as the design evolves, imbalances, shortfalls, and difficult last-minute trade-offs are less apt to occur. This cannot be overemphasized.

GUIDELINES:
COLLABORATION AND DECISION MAKING

- Institute a diversified, representative design approach.
- Make rules about decision making at the outset. Success is predicated on the *equal* participation and power of design *and* child care professionals.
- A responsive process establishes meeting schedules, substitute-care arrangements, supports, and decision-making procedures that acknowledge the importance of every participant.
- Integrate structural, mechanical, acoustic, electrical, interior, landscape, budgetary, and construction decisions early on. Discontinuities will be reflected in increased costs and a lack of building integrity which, in turn, affect children's well-being.
- Choose a leader for the design process from within the facility's administration who can assist in the resolution of constantly changing tensions before, during, and after completion of the project.
- Allow enough time for the process and the design to unfold. This will probably require a larger architectural fee at the outset, but fewer changes and add-on costs for the construction budget.

The Mission Statement: The Team's First Task

A mission statement is an overarching concept expressing the team's ideals for the building and how it will serve the needs of children, families, and staff. The mission statement acts as one of two informing documents (the program is the other) for all decision making. A sample mission statement, written for the Copper House, appears in Box 3.1.

Writing a mission statement, or approving any existing statement written by an agency, is the design team's first task. (The "childhood places" visualization exercise in Chapter 2 and the visioning techniques described at the end of this chapter can help with this effort.) Mission statements written with clarity and consensus help shift the basis of decision making away from individual control to the intentions of the whole. *At major junctures, always examine the ramifications of specific decisions against the original mission statement to be certain the project is still on course.* When the going gets rough, a review of the original purpose often brings focus and compromise by renewing a committee's efforts to stand by its original intent. The team leader can be helpful in reminding the team of this need.

> ***Example:*** After many months of pavement pounding for new space to replace an existing center, the design team found two moderately desirable office complexes with differing attributes. The team spent much time weighing the pros and cons of each site, but even a majority decision seemed difficult to attain. Finally, a team member pointed out that the choice was difficult because neither space had the qualities the team had initially envisioned as appropriate for children. Reminded of the goals set forth in their mission statement, everyone willingly abandoned both sites in search of a more suitable ambience.

The Design Team: Members and Their Roles

An effective design team usually involves 6–12 people: management, child care professionals, designers,

BOX 3.1

The Copper House Mission Statement

The mission of the Copper House is to assist and share in the joys and burdens of parenthood by providing an environment that offers the necessary resources for the full emotional, spiritual, intellectual, and physical development of children in their first five years of life, while nourishing and supporting their families and the staff to the highest degree possible.

Essential Ingredients of the Center are:

1. **Expansion of Children's Potential** by honoring the unique capacities of each individual.
2. **Creating Community** by fostering links between parents, children, and siblings; different families; the home and the workplace; senior citizens and the young.
3. **Caring for Caregivers** by providing a nurturing and supportive environment for staff.
4. **Environmentally Sustainable Design** by minimizing the building's impact on the earth for present and future generations, and giving children direct experience with ecologically sound, sustainable, appropriate technologies.
5. **A Residentially Scaled Building** whose intimacy, form, materials, and environs enable children and adults to feel as safe and comfortable as they would in their own homes.
6. **Health-Giving Resources** of sunlight; pure, uncontaminated air, water, food; nontoxic materials; natural and man-made beauty.
7. **Access to Nature** by providing immediate, personal, ongoing contact with nature's cycles and a diversity of plants and animals.
8. **Aesthetic Integration** of the forms, proportions, spaces, textures, and volumes in the environment to nourish children's exquisite aesthetic sensibilities.
9. **Natural Materials and Craft** to complement mass-produced and standardized fittings, giving evidence of response to the uniqueness of circumstance, organic growth and repair, artistry, and construction by the human hand.
10. **Light, Sounds, and Colors** that uplift the spirit by being balanced, melodious, and harmonious.

building professionals, regulatory personnel, funding and sponsoring agencies. Players in one category can sometimes substitute for those in another, depending upon circumstance.

Management Personnel

The support of corporations, real estate developers, public and private agencies, franchises and chains, and private entrepreneurs in helping to meet the growing demand for child care is invaluable. However, when the ownership of a center—and the motivational incentive—originates with business rather than with child care professionals, the potential pitfall is a developmentally inappropriate center. Endorsing a team approach, and noting the following recommendations, helps management maximize appropriate solutions to difficult issues:

- At least one individual who *intimately knows children, day care, and center design* needs to be appointed to the team to represent the child, the staff, and the family as part of all decision making. This professional may come from inside or outside management, provided he or she is not compromised in making recommendations.
- Architects generally do not know enough about child care to adequately weigh its complex performance criteria against architectural and budgetary demands. For a facility to provide children with what they require, child care professionals must have some role in design decisions and architects must be allowed to speak and work with the end user.
- If the project is for an existing facility, officially include staff in the decision-making process. Not doing so fosters resentment and reduces willingness

to stay on the job in the face of other factors known to contribute to high staff turnover. Negative staff attitudes always affect children adversely.

- When a child care consultant is hired as the prime informant to the architect, do not reduce or eliminate the consultant's involvement when the budget gets tight and everyone is worried about sufficient funds to build or renovate. "The bottom line is that those centers that did not...utilize child care expertise throughout the process, including construction, suffered in terms of time, cost, and overall quality and efficiency of the completed facility."[2] In addition, when management has assured child care staff that the consultant will represent their interests, and the consultant is eliminated, staff confidence in the enterprise is severely undermined.
- In summary, the team should contain as least one representative who is both knowledgeable about and committed to quality child care—and who has the authority to act on the child's behalf.

Child Care Personnel

Some or all of these child care personnel belong on the design team:

- Center director
- Caregivers/staff
- Child care consultant
- Parents
- Children (where possible)

It is important that the facility be designed with the ongoing involvement of a center director and someone representing each of the major age groups the center will serve. Social workers, psychologists, special-needs teachers, nurses, dietitians, and other special interest groups can be consulted as needed.

The Role of the Center Director

Good directors represent the needs of children, families, and staff and help evaluate operating costs, program policies, licensing requirements, and a facility's design. When the center is created before staff are hired, at the very least have the future director on board or have a director from a comparable local program participate on the design team. If a child care consultant (see the discussion that follows) substitutes for a center director to be hired later, have some overlap between these individuals to assure continuity of practice and intent.

The Role of Caregivers and Staff

The role of caregivers and staff members is to inform the designers of their unique user needs and to give feedback about the evolving design. Although centers are not created for particular individuals, the team needs to include a director and teachers from each of the major age groups the center will serve—people who have personally experienced the day-in-day-out realities of child care. Given continued evidence that their expertise matters, their involvement on the design team usually results in a better facility and in staff's greater commitment to and satisfaction with the facility.

Although rarely trained in design issues, child care professionals can practice and learn to communicate about them, especially when given alternative approaches to consider. Experience suggests that staff need to become more outspoken about their desire to be part of the team and more willing to bear responsibility for decisions that will significantly affect their work lives. No team member should be ashamed to acknowledge his or her design inexperience and to insist upon receiving the help required to make a design solution clear. For their part, most designers lack experience with child care and need assistance of a comparable nature.

GUIDELINES: TAPPING THE EXPERTISE OF THE CHILD CARE STAFF

- Encourage staff to "dream" and to extend their realm of experience. Most child care staff have learned to "make do" with limited resources. They are more used to adapting to difficult circumstances than imagining perfect solutions or workable possibilities.
- Encourage staff to articulate patterns, routines, or features critical to center operation. Staff often need to learn to communicate what may seem obvious to them.
- Ask architects to provide staff with assistance in learning how to read floor plans and evaluate scaled drawings. Child care professionals may be embarrassed to reveal their lack of competency in these areas and need encouragement to express their misunderstanding. Provide study models, so staff can assess a given design's effect upon their activities.

The Role Of The Child Care Consultant

A professional child care consultant (CCC) may substitute for a director if one has not been hired, or complement the skills of a director who is unfamiliar with the design process. The CCC both represents the child and acts as a translator between the child care and architectural domains. Early involvement and continuity of an experienced CCC during design, construction, and initial operation can contribute significantly to center quality. Select someone who can provide the project with a set of detailed written program criteria, not just the licensing regulations, and evidence of how they impacted the design of other centers. The CCC may be a hired consultant from a local resource and referral agency, a college or university, a child care design firm, or an agency specializing in center start-up and organization. Since architects sometimes are reluctant to avail themselves of this type of expertise, it is up to the administrator of the project and/or the team to find an architect and consultant who are eager to collaborate, and to structure the process and budget so this expert can be present for the project's duration.

Representing the Child. The foremost job of the CCC—who typically has a background in early childhood development and curriculum, center design, and day care programming and administration—is to ensure that the physical, emotional, and intellectual needs of children and families are met despite conflicting priorities. A CCC's skills complement those of the staff and the architect by assisting both to better understand how design impacts the needs of children and the program.

Translating Child Development for the Architects. The fit between a building's design and its functionality requires constant evaluation throughout the design process and especially as the interior of each room is addressed. Since the staff's availability as a group is limited, a CCC can expedite the design process by anticipating some of the staff's concerns for the designers, and by checking with staff about matters that lend themselves to multiple design solutions. A good CCC helps architects understand the intricate requirements that make a center developmentally appropriate and functional.

Translating Architecture for the Staff. A CCC with environmental planning skills and knowledge of child development can:

- Help the staff read floor plans or translate plans into three-dimensional reality, to better interpret the consequences of design alternatives.
- Convey the consequences of a design to both staff and architect, especially when tight budgets and time frames unwittingly cause communication to be cut short.

> ***EXAMPLE:*** The infant teacher at one center requested a diapering station placed so she could see the entire room. The architect responded by locating the station near the room's center. This location reduced the flexibility and future organizational possibilities of the room as a whole. The CCC noticed this drawback and was able to communicate it to the staff. She then worked with them and the architects to find a new diapering location that permitted staff observation but kept room arrangement options open.

The Role of Parents

Successful child care centers involve families and support their needs. Parents' points of view about what can help them feel welcome, communicate with staff, and feel secure about their children's welfare is invaluable. Their early participation builds community at the outset, enables a center to better supplement resources lacking at home, and ensures a design that is responsive to the needs of families.

The Role of Children

Children "tell" us what they need by their behavior in different contexts. Where design parameters are in doubt, observe how children behave in relation to the issue.

> ***EXAMPLE:*** A team wanted to decide between a 27-inch-high sand table versus an indoor sandbox in which children sit. Observation revealed that more sand is dispersed by children getting out of a sand box than is spilled from a table. The table was therefore the better indoor choice.

In addition to being observed, children over three can be questioned about their preferences, while those over six certainly can participate in generating design alternatives.

Design Personnel

Include some or all of the following design personnel on the design team:

A child working on top of a counter "tells" us the surface is too high.

- Architect
- Interior designer
- Landscape architect
- Engineers (mechanical, electrical, acoustical, etc.)

The Role of the Architect

Architects are responsible for designing or renovating buildings to express the client's goals and program, providing drawings for obtaining all necessary permits and approvals, and monitoring the construction involved. They are trained to see the possibilities inherent in space and to provide design alternatives others may not think of—especially in the face of limited space and dollars—while balancing form, function, structural integrity, codes, and regulations. Some architectural firms also handle the design and selection of interior finishes and fittings; others work with a consulting interior designer.

The Role of the Interior Designer

An interior designer specializes in space planning, furniture layout, the selection of appropriate colors, interior finishes and fittings, and the aesthetic integration of all these elements.

The Role of Additional Engineers and Design Personnel

Typically, the architect will contract with **mechanical**, **electrical**, **plumbing**, and **structural engineers** to assist in the design, permitting, and approval of these aspects of the building. Depending on the project, other professionals may also be involved, such as a **soils engineer** to assess the structural integrity of the building site; a **civil engineer** to assess its relationship to existing public utilities and to plan required grading and drainage; an **environmental engineer** to assess soil toxicity; and a **landscape architect** or **designer** to configure and improve the site around the center, including variations in terrain, path design, plant selection and layout, and play yard design; an **acoustical engineer** to enhance the acoustic performance of the building; a **lighting consultant** or **engineer** to recommend lighting fixtures for the center.

Building Professionals

Include some or all of the following building professionals on the design team, at least on a consulting basis:

- Fire inspector
- Building/safety inspector

- Licensing inspector
- Construction manager or general contractor

The Role of Fire, Building, and Licensing Inspectors

Early input from and consistent consultation with fire, building, and licensing inspectors helps avoid the uncertainties of code application and interpretation that can lead to extensive conflicts, loss of time and money, and compromised center quality. Even so, the design team and budget need to be prepared to deal with last-minute code enforcement issues sometimes requiring building changes.

Where states and local agencies do not have a sufficiently broad range of tested codes and regulations to meet the varied circumstances that arise in child care, and inspectors, as well as architects, are inexperienced in code interpretation and application, many geographical, regional, and even center-by-center variances exist. Regulations can be too lenient, too strict, or inconsistently enforced. Conflicts even exist between the codes of various agencies—fire versus building security, for example. It is important that all regulatory agencies understand how a building's design affects *children* so that the program's requirements—rather than the regulations— become the *raison d'être* of a decision. (See Chapter 4.)

Architects unfamiliar with local codes and regulatory personnel can hire someone to expedite the permitting and approval process. There is more room for negotiation between designers and building inspectors than is commonly believed. However, this depends upon establishing relationships *early*, receiving all requirements and approvals *in writing*, and making every effort to have the original inspectors be the same as those who make the final inspection.

The Role of the Contractor and the Contractual Process

By hiring a construction manager (CM) or general contractor (GC) as a member of the design team in the early planning stage, choices of materials and aesthetic options can be more directly related to cost. This person can contribute to the center's goals and have an investment in the team's decisions and outcome.

Typically, contractors are asked to bid on a project once all the drawings are completed. Then the contractor with the lowest or a reasonably low bid is chosen. Subsequently, that contractor is held to completing the building at the bid price regardless of changes that arise, most of which he or she is expected to have predicted in advance. Thus there is a dichotomy between a building that should grow as a living process and a contractual arrangement demanding a fixed budget. Although contractors frequently have valuable suggestions for design changes, their lack of familiarity with child care can also lead to highly inappropriate choices when they attempt to make substitutions based on a fixed bid.

Negotiated bids, rather than fixed competitive ones, allow the contractor and the team to arrive jointly at a set of documents and a price. The contractor will subsequently be held to this bid, but there are fewer surprises, and a different level of understanding is established. A time and materials bid allows for changes during construction but requires a contract defining that process.

Contractual processes that makes changes possible in a timely and cost-effective fashion, subject to review for child-appropriateness, are predictors of project success. At the deepest level, the issue is to breathe enthusiasm into the process because the

GUIDELINES: THE CONTRACTUAL PROCESS

- **Hire a construction manager or general contractor as early as the planning stage.** *Involve the CM or GC in facility cost estimation throughout the process.* A negotiated bid (rather than a fixed, competitive bid) that is based on a CM's or a GC's early involvement is likely to more closely reflect later on-the-job performance and true costs.
- **Establish a generous contingency budget, with line items for design changes.** A construction phase governed by flexible contractual terms—where all parties are protected if things get costly and where all benefit if a surplus is realized—enables greater customization of the facility.
- Particularly in public bid projects, consider a process called "partnering" wherein the owner, the design team, and the contractor, in effect, pledge to work together from the outset.
- Where a CM or GC cannot be part of the team, an architect skilled in cost estimating or a consultant cost estimator are indispensible.
- Be prepared to do some value engineering (explained below) if the project comes in over bid.

contractor and subs understand the building requirements and become creative contributors to it, not simply workers with an eye on the dollar. Labor without meaning and care imbues a building with a negative energy that can palpably affect its users. All workers want to be nourished by and appreciated for their work. What greater reward than to be part of a process which encourages people's finest contribution to the welfare of children?

Choosing Design Personnel

The following suggestions are intended to assist design teams in the selection of an architect and/or interior designer—a decision that can be definitive in a project's success or lack of it. (Also see Appendix I for a list of questions to ask prospective architectural firms.)

The Architect

Child care center design is a new field that welcomes architects who appreciate the vulnerabilities of childhood and wish to create settings commensurate with the importance of these early years. Many firms now seek these contracts in order to compete in a growth arena and become known as child care center design experts. This is all to the good.

However, child care center design is not like other design projects. Both the design team and architects need to be aware of at least one potential area of conflict. A practiced way for architectural firms to give expression to their artistic inspiration and to make their work "visible" is to create an eye-catching building that delights the public and looks appealing in photographs and architectural magazines. Unfortunately, unusual design or appearance does not necessarily create a facility that supports children and staff. In fact, experience indicates that where novel design is given higher priority than function, the building rarely works. Children suffer, and the reputation of any innovation is limited.

Child care management is often nervous about choosing an architect, and rightly so. The relationship with this individual will be long-lived and leave an indelible stamp on the center. Management will want to choose someone with whom it has interpersonal rapport, who is modest about child care center design, whose design philosophy resonates with the center's mission, and whose fees are compatible with the budget. For new construction, architects may charge a standard percentage of the building's construction costs, or a fixed fee based on an identified project scope. However, additional fees may be involved for a consensus process and for development of the interior. Small firms are often in a better position to provide the attention to detail that child care centers require.

In the selection process, consider both the professional and personal characteristics of the firm's project architect—the individual who will be assigned to your project—as well as the firm's principal(s). Make certain the project architect will be available for the life of your project. Where this has not been the case, much time and money have been lost.[3]

Previous Experience

Although experience in designing for children is helpful, it is less critical than an architect's ability to honor client needs, to work within a group process, and to handle residential scale. Examine closely the firm's experience with residential design to be certain they are not too commercially or institutionally inclined. If the firm has designed facilities for children, be certain to visit at least one site and talk with the users about its strengths and weaknesses. Evaluate what works and what does not work. Ask questions. The team's best information will come from noting its own feelings during site visits.

The architect will need to be familiar with the type of child care facility being planned and/or with the problems of any existing facility. Management can require the architect (and the interior designer) to spend several days in an existing center going through the children's routines: eating breakfast at 7 A.M., playing with blocks, sitting in the reading corner, taking a nap, playing outside. Such experiences give designers a personal perspective likely to result in a more responsive and functional design.

Willingness to Embrace a Team Approach

Architects honor their ultimate responsibility to the design team and the center's mission by being able to communicate effectively with varied participants; remain flexible as a plan evolves rather than adhering to a fixed design; provide design alternatives, especially at the beginning; and think about the building from the inside out. The single most important factor in evaluating a firm is its experience with a team approach. Listed below are some questions the design team might ask.

QUESTIONS:

- How much give and take between client and architect does the firm encourage, expect, and build into the budget?
- How does the firm feel about working with a team of diverse players?
- Is the firm willing to generate alternative design solutions?
- Is the firm willing to produce simple study models and mock-ups or computer-generated perspective sketches throughout the project to help team members visualize and contribute to the design development of actual spaces?
- Is the firm willing to participate in creating the program for the center?

Conventional architectural contracts and budgets do not allow for intense teamwork, multiple design changes, frequent modeling, and interpretation of plans. It may not be possible to select an architect by price alone and receive these valuable extra services. Teamwork requires and merits additional funding.

Concern About Interiors

It is important to know, from the outset, if the firm views interiors as integral to the project. Do they have their own interiors department, or do they work with an outside firm? Can they show you examples of either approach?

A major source of poor functioning in child care settings arises when various aspects of the design are treated separately or move on different time frames. For example, the architectural form—square footage and shape of rooms—may be established before the furniture layout, finishes, and lighting are considered. Only later are the real consequences of how the spaces do or do not support user behavior uncovered. Square footage alone, in isolation from layout and adjacencies (spaces or functions that need to be physically close to one another), cannot reveal how furnishings will fit in a space, how much space is lost to transit, or what leeway there is for expansion of activities. Unless the interior and exterior are designed simultaneously and there is a constant cycling back and forth between the interiors and the building as the design is being generated, the space may not support everything it is intended to accommodate. Study models and computer aided design (CAD) can be used to facilitate this approach.

The layout of a child care group space is perhaps more complex than any other type of room layout. To create a facility that works well for children and staff, the building must be designed from the inside out, as well as from the outside in, and many options must be evaluated. Some architects endorse this approach, others do not. If an architect claims to be able to handle both the interior and the building design with similar high quality and commitment to function, make sure to see evidence of this.

Aesthetic Sensibilities

In the ideal world, an architect chosen to design a child care center would meet the following aesthetic criteria:

- Ability to *listen* to the needs of the client and the site and then design in *collaboration with both.*
- Appreciation for the "spirit" of place and evidence of having built at least one structure that is imbued with such spirit. Such a building not only supports certain activities, but also has the capacity to make people feel good.
- Appreciation for *craft* and willingness to find ways, within the budget, to minimize the use of mass-produced materials and standardized fittings, and to respond to the uniqueness of circumstance.
- Ability to work magic with natural light entering through windows and to relate/integrate—through shadows, dappled effects, highlighting, etc.—natural light with artificial light sources.
- Ability to integrate the indoor/outdoor relationship so that nature is always present in the interiors and access to the outdoors is effortless.
- Willingness to play with sketches, models, rough images, role playing, and computer-aided perspective views of the interior and exterior to get a "best fit" between visions, functional requirements, and practical limitations.
- Appreciation for ways in which a building can be integrated with a site. Alternatively, where the site has few natural features, an ability to add landscaping and topography to create a unique sense of "place."

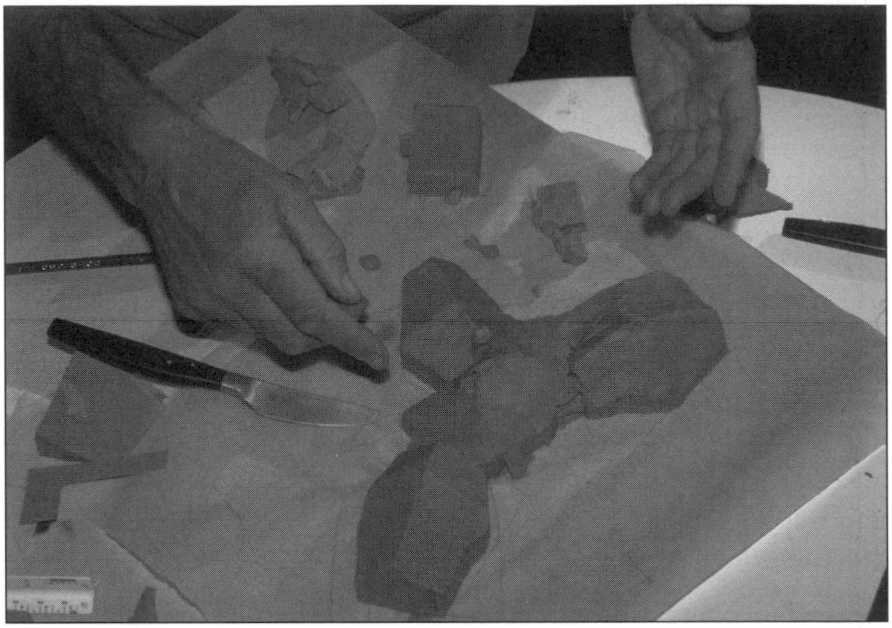

Simple clay models help team members evaluate a building's design.

- Recognition of how spatial variety—curves versus straight lines and flat planes—contributes to a child's experience.
- Ability to create spaces/places that convey peace and tranquillity.
- Willingness to be involved with the interior designer throughout the process, viewing the final project as a whole rather than as an architectural form to be decorated. Appreciation for the impact of color.

Technical Skills

Some technical skills of a good architect include:

- Ability to assist with programming. While the center management typically writes the program, the architectural firm can be helpful in setting its parameters and guiding its creation.
- Ability to state and meet time schedules and bring the project to completion within the time frame established by the team.
- Ability to do accurate cost-estimating, and/or to work with cost estimators and contractors doing estimates, at every stage of the project; evidence of having brought previous projects in on budget.
- Ability to produce quality documents and drawings whose accuracy is substantiated by previous contractors.
- Experience in providing ongoing construction administration leading to successful completion of previous projects.
- Experience working with local codes and permitting processes.
- Knowledge of, or willingness to address, new environmental technologies and systems involving alternative energy sources, the use of nontoxic materials, and Americans with Disabilities Act (ADA) standards for handicapped accessibility.

GUIDELINES: CHOOSING AN ARCHITECT

- Above all, look for an architect who is flexible, client-responsive, and open to a group process and to new ideas.
- Avoid architects who are primarily concerned with making a name for themselves through emphasis on the look and design of the facade.
- Identify and evaluate both the aesthetic sensibilities and the technical skills you wish the architect to have.
- Choose an architect who recognizes the significance of interiors and of working from the inside out, and who provides or works closely with interior designers.
- Visit sites—residences and any previous child care centers—designed by the prospective architect. Honor your own feelings as well as information from users about what works and what doesn't.

The Interior Designer

Usually, interior designers are concerned with spatial relationships, furniture layouts, specification of finishes, and aesthetic integration on the inside, while architects address the building's form, mechanical and electrical systems, corridors, exits, and overall public-use parameters. However, as indicated above, the complex nature of child care center interiors calls for both aspects to be designed simultaneously. In renovation jobs, the skills of the interior designer can become paramount to those of the architect. Many architectural firms have an interiors department that provides specifications for carpets, paints, furniture, moldings, lighting, etc. Other firms choose to work in collaboration with a designer who specializes in these matters. Good communication between the two is essential.

Since the interior finishes and furnishings are the materials with which children and staff interact most, it is important to touch, feel, smell, and absorb the atmosphere of the interior designer's style and previous work by being in the spaces, observing your own reactions as well as the responses of those who use it regularly. Slides and photographs can be useful but often distort colors, finishes, and scale. Site visits are a critical means of assessing an interior designer's approach. Talk with people and ask questions.

Because interiors are not a standard part of an architectural contract, the following two practices are strongly advised:

- Generate a budget for interior finishes, furnishings, and custom-designed equipment at the same time as the construction/renovation budget is created. In the absence of an "interiors" budget, it is common to find the money for the project increasingly going towards building and construction costs while the interiors are left to future years when more funds can be raised. This spells disaster for the program and the children.
- Ensure that the architect and/or interior designer collaborate with the child care professionals in making decisions about key interior elements such as wall, floor, and ceiling finishes; window coverings; lighting; sinks; toilets; cabinets; office furniture; and built-ins. Otherwise, interior features may not work for the program.

The layout of each room—including the location of freestanding furniture, and the custom-design of elements such as lofts and risers—often falls into "a no-man's land" where architect, interior designer, and staff each assume that the other has responsibility for its implementation. Room layout is not the exclusive purview of any one of these players. Rather, all three need to be involved, or the necessary design considerations and budgetary appropriations will not be made. (See Chapters 7 and 15.)

GUIDELINES: CHOOSING AN INTERIOR DESIGNER

Many of the points listed for choosing an architect also apply to the choice of an interior designer. In addition, look for:

- Sensitivity to the maintenance and durability of finishes and fabrics, as well as to appearance.
- Awareness of health-related issues connected with products, finishes, adhesives, and surfactants.
- Color sensibility and awareness of children's color experience.
- A design style and ability to use products that are residential rather than corporate or institutional.
- Willingness to spend time in a child care center understanding routines, space, and materials usage.
- Willingness to provide *large* samples (1–4 feet square rather than 2x2 inches) for floor and wall materials, colors, fabrics, window treatment, etc., so the team can better evaluate their real impact in a room. (See Chapters 12–14.)

The Design Process: Eight Stages

Listed below are the typical stages of the design process, for both renovation and new construction:

1. Programming
2. Schematic design
3. Design development
4. Construction drawings
5. Contract/bid documents
6. Awarding the bid
7. Construction administration
8. Occupancy and postoccupancy evaluation

The design team's greatest involvement is during the first three stages: programming, schematics, and design development. However, contracts need to

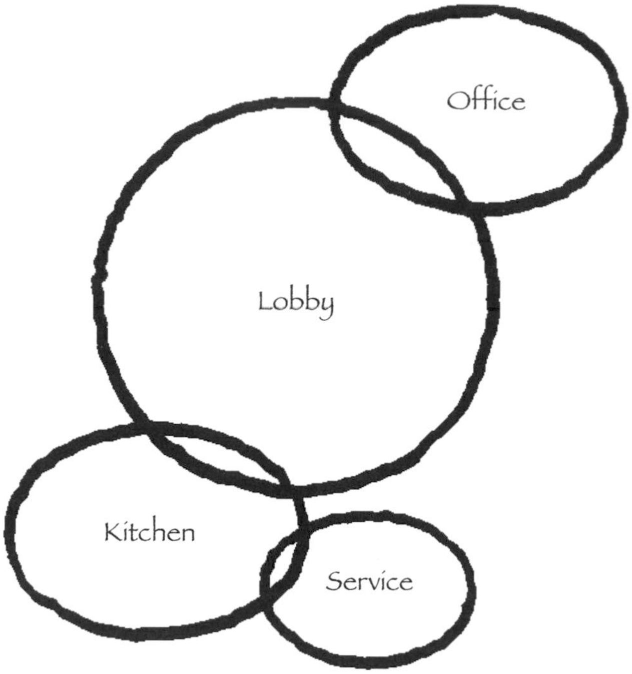

Figure 3.3
Bubble diagrams visually express desired adjacencies—for example, the kitchen remote from the office but near the service entrance. Bubble size indicates relative scale.

specify that a formal letter indicating team approval is required for the completion of each of the eight stages.

Programming

The program is a detailed statement of the spaces, their uses, dimensions, and functional relationships that a building needs to provide. Simply put, it is the definition of the design problem, identifying all the center's desired qualities and functions. The program is the single most critical baseline for generating and evaluating designs (along with the mission statement). It is well worth the time and effort involved (sometimes as long as one year for those unfamiliar with the issues!) to write a comprehensive one. Poor programming can result in loss of time and money changing designs and details during design development. Architects need to be involved in creating the program, but only child care professionals can provide its content.

A good program specifies the ages and numbers of children per group, grouping patterns, ratios, square footage requirements (see Chapters 4, 5, 19, and 21) and how each space should *feel*—its "spirit of place" (see Chapter 2). It identifies design patterns and images, visual connections, sun orientations, the primary activities in and supports needed for each space, code issues, budget goals, and adjacencies. Lists, charts, and bubble diagrams (Figure 3.3) are used to concretely and visually express relationships. Desired orientations and adjacencies might include, for example, infant rooms facing south and the director's office adjacent to the entry lobby. Figure 3.4 (on the next page) presents a sample page from a program document showing one program's identified needs for an infant sleeping area and a young toddler room.[4]

Timelines for the project are often generated along with the program, or even before programming is initiated. For suggestions on how to generate a good program, see "Enhancing the Skills of the Design Team" at the end of this chapter.

Schematic Design

Schematics are when the architect translates the program into some preliminary design form—both on paper and sometimes through the use of study models. For *renovation*, this means allocating the requisite spaces and facilities, locating the plumbing, making certain each space has the desired square footage, and that exits, windows, corridors, etc., correspond to code. For *new construction*, this usually involves orienting the building on the site, beginning a preliminary layout of interior spaces and square footage, and giving the building an exterior form or footprint, as well as all of the above. (See Chapters 6 and 7 for more information on schematics.) *It is important to generate*

Room # and Name	Quantity Needed	Room Census	General Function	Floor Area Required	Preferred Shape	Adjacent to	Close to	Special Equipment	Special Characteristics	Comments
124 INFANT SLEEPING	one	7 infants	Sleeping area for 7 infants	16.5 SF per child	As required based on module of crib	Infant room but not between Infant room and YT room	Sleeping porch Diaper changing area	7 cribs Dutch door Artificial lighting rheostat Some daylight Ventilation, fresh air Closed room Rocking chair	Visual separation needed: glazed opening in wall Space for rocking chair for caregiver and child having difficulty sleeping	
125 YT ROOM	One	9 young toddlers	Cubby area	50 SF	Long and narrow	At entrance to YT room	Porch, outdoor play area	See Infant room	See Infant room	See Infant room for general comments
		2–3 caregivers	Storage area staff belongings and supplies	2' x 10'= 20 SF		Near entrance to room		See Infant room	See Infant room	
			Kitchen/Eating	120 SF		Along one side of room opposite changing area		Sink (adult) 3/4 size refrig. Microwave tall enough for bottles Low tables	Kitchenette w/counter and cabinets Designated but not fixed eating area	Kitchenette should be in alcove
			Diaper area	50 SF	Alcove	Opposite side of room from eating		See Infant room	See Infant Room	
			Activity space	310 SF (34.5 per child)	As required	Infant room; visual penetration through playful windows to Infant room		Moderate level changes Climbing equip. Places to climb on top of or inside Work tables Water/sand trough	Entire space sculpted for activities Messy zone is only fixed area—defined by materials	Minimize fixed objects

Figure 3.4
Program Document Sample Page

Lea Cromwell

and evaluate several different translations of the program during the schematic stage.

Simple study models, including the site if possible, are especially useful at this stage so the team understands what is being proposed, can explore the ramifications of each scheme generated, and check them against the mission statement and program.

QUESTIONS: SCHEMATICS PHASE

- Does the design provide the environmental atmosphere and quality of relationships the team desires for children, staff, and parents?
- Are *all* the functions identified in the program accounted for in the design? If not, why not? What can be done to include them?
- What compromises in the program are required by the design? Are these acceptable to all? Can they be minimized? How does the two-dimensional design convert to three-dimensional form?
- Does the location of plumbing support program activities and staff caretaking activities (Chapters 4 and 19)? Does it allow for clearly defined messy, active, and quiet zones within each room (Chapter 7)?
- What is the relationship of indoors to outdoors? What is the quality of natural light in each room? Do entrances and exits support ease of coming and going and security? Is outdoor play accessible and nearby?

The schematics phase usually ends with a complete design proposal including floor plans; a model and/or perspective sketches; a preliminary cost estimate; and sometimes preliminary electrical, mechanical, and materials specifications.

Design Development

At the design development stage, the team's consensual scheme (solution) is refined. Dimensions, locations, and materials for the building and its interior are finalized and coordinated with structural, mechanical, lighting, and other specifications. Here the team gives close attention to the size and height of rooms, ceilings, doors, windows, toilets, sinks, fixtures, and built-in furnishings; the location of tile and carpet, lighting fixtures, and storage; and the selection of interior finishes and built-ins. It is important for child care professionals to know how to read and evaluate the scaled drawings generated for design development.[5] Chapters 15–18 and 20 are intended to assist with design development of the children's group rooms and outdoor play spaces. As the project moves toward the next stage, Construction Drawings, the design transitions into more technical information. The team needs to be comfortable with how this transition occurs.

Construction Drawings

Construction drawings (CDs) are the building and renovation plans which the architect prepares for the contractors, electricians, plumbers, etc., to communicate the design solution to these parties. Although these plans may be too technical for most team members, it is important that the architect appraise the team of primary systems (e.g., radiant versus convection heat) and critical building details (e.g., location of outlets and switches).

Contract/Bid Documents and Value Engineering

The construction drawings, along with specifications (written descriptions of the processes and materials required in the contract), constitute the contract documents and eventually become part of the formal bid documents disseminated among prospective contractors seeking to be awarded the project. As mentioned earlier, there is good reason to bring the CM or GC (and even the subcontractors) on board earlier, in the programming and planning stages and to handle the bid process differently. In either case, because the documents at this stage are final ones both for the building and for the budget, owner/team review and approval are essential.

Because projects often come in over bid even when there has been ongoing cost estimation, it is wise to be prepared to "value engineer" the project. If funds are short, cost savings need to be found. While contingencies are intended to assist with these circumstances, using up all the contingency funds means they will not be available for surprises and opportunities found during construction. Instead, look for cuts in material selection (ceramic tile rather than colored concrete flooring); phased development where funds can be raised to do some things later (such as climbers and lofts); and use of good standard rather than custom elements (Anderson windows rather than custom windows). Finding more off-the-shelf items helps to bring some costs down.

Awarding the Bid and Construction Administration

Once the owner, in agreement with the architect, awards the bid to a contractor and related firms of choice, construction begins. While the facility is being built, the architect and various other parties have specific roles to play.

The Role of the Architect

The architect (in addition to others below) periodically monitors the construction to ensure it corresponds to the contract documents and the program. Hidden conditions—especially for renovations, but also for new construction—sometimes dictate revisions in the CDs, as do changes in the availability and cost of materials. Because even the most precise plans can undergo some change during the construction phase, it is vital that there be ongoing communication among the architect, the contractor, and the design team.

The Role of the Owner's Representative

Sometimes the center management (developer, corporation, agency), will appoint its own construction administrator from within its facilities department or hire an outside construction manager, called an "owner's rep," to act as its on-site liaison between the architects, the contractors, and, ideally, the child care center director and staff. The owner's rep is on-site to represent the owner's interests (largely financial), translate the concerns of all interested parties, and resolve issues related to the impact of the construction on the site and related facilities. Absence of an individual acting in this capacity can sometimes create real weakness in the process. Where present, it is essential that this person understands the child care center's mission so that difficulties are resolved in ways that take the center's concerns about quality to heart. To avoid conflicting directives to the contractor, very clear lines of communication are needed between the owner, the architect, and the contractor(s).

The Role of the Center Director or Child Care Consultant

During construction administration there needs to be someone representing the child care center itself who will communicate with the architect, the owner's rep, contractors, etc., to ensure that all decisions favorably affect children, staff, and the program. Because many features in question affect function, safety, and maintenance, the need for participation and vigilance by a center director or other child care professional cannot be overemphasized! This is both an exciting and grueling part of the process, since many details will only be caught by the keen eye of an experienced child care professional reviewing every aspect of what is happening on site. Initially, site visits are recommended weekly, eventually daily. Continuing on-site review, and immediate communication of and response to discrepancies, are the only ways to avoid expensive rebuilds or inadequate substitutions.

Design Changes During Construction

Changes to the design of a child care center are often correlated with architect, team, and contractor inexperience with facilities for children. The scale of elements, myriad details, unforeseen circumstances related to the site or to mixed-use projects, reinterpretation of codes, and the difficulties child care professionals have translating plans and models into three dimensional reality, can all generate a need for changes throughout the project, especially during construction. This is why design cannot be rushed in the earlier stages and why time must be taken to anticipate and understand the "built reality."

Plans approved and signed by municipal departments and agencies are no guarantee against change orders imposed by inspectors. In addition, if allowed in the construction documents, contractors frequently make substitutions and alterations based upon site conditions, material availability and cost, and previous experience, many of which may be inappropriate. These should be submitted for review to the design team, and not installed without approval.

> ***Example:*** Adult-sized toilets and sinks are installed by contractors in children's bathrooms approximately 25% of the time, despite specs to the contrary.[6]

Although changes are common, the recommendations discussed so far are intended to keep them to a minimum. Budgets with line items built in for design change contingencies can assist contractors and the team in making changes that are both timely and cost-effective.

Occupancy and Post-Occupancy Evaluation

When construction is completed, the architect and center management tour the building and generate a "deficiency" or "punch" list of things that need to be corrected. Once these changes are made, the architect, owner, and building inspectors sign off on the building, giving the owner the right to occupy and the contractor approval to demobilize and remove his temporary facilities from the site. This completes the occupancy evaluations.

The architect may or may not continue to stay on the project once the center is in operation. About six months after occupancy, a Post-Occupancy Evaluation (POE) is typically conducted, ideally by the architect and the interior designer. A firm that has a POE as part of a its standard practice indicates a willingness to learn from experience. A center also can require a POE as part of the initial contract.

Where the architect is not involved, the center can undertake an internal POE—a room-by-room review in which the staff and director identify what does and does not work well and assess the impact of the design on the program. Questionnaires, followed by interviews and group sharing, are most useful. Primary issues are:

- How well is the building working?
- Are the spaces being used the way they were intended? If not, why not?
- What opportunities are being missed?
- What changes are required?

The time and energy required to adapt to a new facility, plus the desire to "get on with it," frequently make environmental evaluation and change a low priority. In addition, staff may be so delighted to have something better than their former quarters that they hesitate to complain about anything. Yet every new space brings with it new ways of functioning that ultimately affect everyone: One person needs space in the corridor, another lacks storage space for certain items. Such inevitable issues require joint resolution and collaboration.

If the center conducts the POE on its own, it is helpful to provide the architect and interior designer with feedback to better inform their firms' future projects.

Evaluation: An Ongoing Process

With rapid changes taking place in child care, the design process continues well beyond the completion of most projects. In addition to the six months post-occupancy evaluation, semiannual or annual in-house reviews are desirable—some of which might be shared nationwide.

All parties need to be prepared to handle the inevitable changes that arise as a child care program matures. Refinement, modification, and extensions of the facility will be needed as priorities and circumstances shift, requiring efficient and collaborative mechanisms for implementing change. Including design issues as part of staff meetings and in-house reviews acknowledges the environment as a vital aspect of the program, requiring total staff participation.

Enhancing the Skills of the Design Team

A lively, educated, and informed design team produces a lively and functional center. The following skill-building techniques—to be applied particularly at the beginning of the project—demystify the design process and help the design team generate alternative design solutions collaboratively. They also heighten participation by giving the team and community a sense of being involved in an invigorating creative process. Some or all of these techniques can be applied before or during the programming and schematics phases of the project.

Design Log Books and Image Boards

Design log books and image boards are ways to elicit and display those qualities of place and design which team members hope to have in their center. The images can be original sketches, photographs, magazine clippings, even three-dimensional objects expressing any and all design details and qualities that make people's hearts sing. Keep the book or board in a central location so team members can easily add to and enjoy the collective contributions.

BOX 3.2

Our Ideal Center: A Visioning Session

Hold this visioning session in a comfortable, informal setting. Consider inviting the entire center staff (if one exists), the architects, board members, and interested community leaders. Create groups of six to eight with representatives from each of the different constituencies. Give everyone some reading to do in advance, and encourage them to bring photographs and images of favorite environments. Have someone conduct the "childhood places" visualization in Chapter 2 (see Box 2.1) to get people in touch with their own childhoods and the world of children. Show slides, movies, videos of children playing, or center activities to stimulate discussion, images, and dreams. Consider transforming lunchtime into a children's birthday party, complete with party hats, bubbles, balloons, and food choices ranging from peanut butter and jelly to standard adult fare, topped off with birthday cake and ice cream.

Tap into everyone's ideas of what their new building should be like by having them envision each aspect of the child's experience at the center over the course of one day: the approach from bus or car, what is seen as you get closer, the front door, who greets you, the place where you put your coat, how you say good-bye to Mom or Dad, your room, the special places in it, where you eat, where you take a nap, what you do when you go outdoors, etc. Place particular emphasis on envisioning the "quality" or "spirit" of the spaces, as well as details of design. Then give everyone paper, crayons, and markers to draw and write down their dreams.

Have the members of each group share, explain, and clarify their images, while a group scribe records the information on big pads. Towards the end, ask each group to star their 10 most important concerns. Then have the groups summarize their experiences for one another. Compile the material in a book of images and comments to guide the design process thereafter.

Ideal Centers and One-Word Images

At a team meeting or visioning session, ask team members to write a paragraph or page describing their ideal center. Share and discuss these descriptions. Then compile a list of their critical elements to guide the center's program. Similarly, ask members to call out one-word descriptions for aspects of their ideal center—its scale, interior feeling, building exterior. When renovating an existing center, have team members list their likes and dislikes.

Visioning Sessions

Visioning sessions—during which team members and other interested individuals use visualization and guided imagery techniques to imagine their desired goals—are a powerful way to involve all relevant parties at the beginning of the design process. These might be led by a hired consultant, by the architect/designers, or by other members of the team. A full day or weekend away from daily responsibilities is ideal for getting everyone to relax, communicate, and get in touch with their dreams. The purpose of the sessions is to bring forth people's latent ideas and images of the center's qualitative features—its scale, mood, and feel—and for people to begin sharing these with one another. The two techniques described previously can be part of the exercises for this day. Box 3.2 provides suggestions for such a session.

Site Visits

Team walk-abouts on the proposed site or sites are essential for site selection, and for resolving many site-related design issues such as orientation of the building and front door, preservation of trees and outcroppings, etc.

Visits to other facilities (ideally when occupied) can be helpful at different phases of the planning process, especially when new resources are being added—a new infant or toddler room, or when alternative ways of providing care are being considered—climbers in each group space versus a large motor room. By observation and discussion with staff and users of another facility, the design team can benefit from the successes and problems experienced by others. If possible, take a camera along. Structure and record observations around previously identified areas of concern so findings can be referred to in later planning sessions. While it may not be feasible for everyone to visit the same sites, the sites most similar to the proposed center should be seen by all team members, giving everyone a common reference point.

It is useful for the team to keep an ongoing record of the dimensions and floor plans of different infant, toddler, preschool, staff, etc., spaces visited. This record is invaluable in helping team members compare design alternatives or evaluate space allocations for their new center.

Design Charrettes

A design charrette is a short, intense period of time (two to five days) when a design team focuses on and defines critical project requirements. It is similar to a visioning session, and can incorporate some of its exercises, but usually lasts longer and aims to address specific design parameters. Architects may begin a design process with a charrette to maximize their access to the team and accomplish a great deal in a limited amount of time. Ideally, the charrette takes place close to the proposed site. The product is a written and visual depiction of the design program or of schematic designs.

Three-Dimensional Study Models

Inexpensive, three-dimensional models of cardboard, clay, sticks, and computer-aided designs improve a design team's perceptions of the proposed building, so they can more effectively participate in design decisions, especially those involving three-dimensionality such as roof and ceiling heights. Using a model scope and placing scaled figures down "in" the model to role-play or rehearse various behavioral sequences (entering the building, bidding parents good-bye, diapering, getting outdoors) can reveal strengths and weaknesses in the design not apparent by simply viewing the model from above.

Full-Scale Chalk and Masking Tape Models

Because most people have difficulty interpreting the dimensions of spaces they cannot see, teams often begin by comparing their plans to other known spaces, including the team meeting room itself. Chalk, masking tape, and CAD can also help ensure that team members appreciate the actual size of a building's spaces and features.

Three-dimensional scaled models and figures make designs become real.

Cardboard boxes create a full-scale mock-up of an interactive play system for infants.

Simply chalk or tape a feature onto an existing room's walls and floors to indicate the perimeter of rooms, windows, doors, cabinets, furniture, platforms, and lofts. Children and adults can then sit, stand, and move around these demarcated areas until their proposed or preferred size becomes clear. The taped area can be supplemented with actual furnishings placed inside it, or with blocks and cardboard masses used to represent the three-dimensional qualities of critical elements.

Full-Scale Mock-Ups

Sometimes it is worth the expense of creating a full-sized mock-up of an area, or furnishings and equipment, either in an empty space or within an already functioning room.

EXAMPLES: The staff of one recently remodeled center placed full-sized diapering counters, cutouts for toilets, and wooden storage units in an area that was to be taken from their two adjoining rooms to create a bathroom for toddlers. Moving about in this mock-up convinced them of the minimum and maximum amount of space the bathroom would require.

In another instance, a new building shrunk the size of existing preschool rooms in favor of an additional multipurpose play area. To be certain they could still function effectively in smaller space, the staff carefully measured the dimensions of the new rooms within their existing classrooms and operated within the reduced parameters for a week.

Behavior Mapping

"Behavior mapping" consists of recording where certain activities occur over a number of days.[7] This creates a composite picture of activity, a technique especially useful prior to renovation of an existing area. It is often helpful to have someone other than the customary users of the space do the mapping, so the staff's behavior can be part of the information gathered, and also to gain an objective outsider's perspective. Such information may reveal sources of difficulty as well as stimulate discussion of how spaces might function better. Team members then can be given model building materials and scale figures to design a new, more effective space.

Role Playing

Role-playing sessions can help to:

- Indicate whether a new design will allow users to perform all essential tasks effectively.
- Reveal ways that a new design may change habitual communication and use patterns.
- Prepare staff for different patterns of behavior that are bound to emerge as a result of the new design, when role playing is used at the end of the design process.

When using role-play, it is best to mock-up the space in ways that acknowledge its critical features and its true size, as well as its relationship to important contiguous areas or activities. The users of the spaces then "enact" their routines, revealing what does and does not work in the new configuration.

When there is no clear idea how a space should be designed to support a certain behavior sequence, it is helpful to enact the routine in the presence of observers, at least to inform the architect/designers of the particular tasks involved.

Notes

[1]Adapted from Bruce Brook, The Child Care Design Institute, Harvard University, 1996.

[2]Gretchen Lee Anderson, *Removing Barriers to Childcare Facilities Development* (California State University, Northridge, CA, 1993), 7.

[3]Ibid.

[4]Brook Design Associates, Concord, NH, 1996; Program for the Acton Infant/Toddler Center, Acton, MA.

[5]Floor plans can be scaled in various sizes. Psychologically, non-designers often find that half-inch plans tend to make spaces feel larger, whereas l/8-inch plans and below make spaces feel smaller than they actually are. Especially in the design of the group rooms, one-quarter inch plans seem to provide the best balance between how space is perceived on paper and how it is experienced three-dimensionally,

[6]Gretchen Lee Anderson, *Removing Barriers to Childcare Facilities Development.*

[7]W. H. Ittleson, L. G. Rivlin, and H. M. Proshansky, "The Use of Behavioral Maps in Environmental Psychology," in *Environmental Psychology: Man and His Physical Setting* (New York: Holt, Rinehart, and Winston, Inc., 1970) 658–668.

CHAPTER FOUR

STARTING OUT: PROGRAM AND SITE CONSIDERATIONS

A vision without a task is but a dream,
a task without a vision is drudgery,
a vision and a task is the hope of the world.

—from a church in Sussex, England, c. 1730

This chapter identifies basic program and initial siting factors the design team will want to consider as it starts out: program size and age groups served, building square footage, site area, group room sizes, plumbing and storage needs, and preliminary site and location options. However, before addressing any of these issues, we must first look at the premise underlying all child care center design.

The Premise Underlying Center Design: Organizing Children By Age

The driving force behind the layout of U.S. child care centers is a basic licensing requirement that says children must be organized into self-contained "classrooms" or "groups" based upon age. Age-based groups then have specific size limitations, staff/child ratios, and minimum room square footage requirements. (To avoid the connotation that centers are schools, this guide refers to these spaces as children's group rooms, not as classrooms.)

While age-appropriate care has much validity in honoring the needs of children at different points in their development, the regulations are silent on many matters, including two critical ones:

- How much contact can or should there be between children of different ages?
- What kinds and amounts of space are needed in a center above and beyond the minimum square footage required per child?

By placing little value on contact between children of different ages, the licensing regulations treat centers more like elementary schools than the preschool years spent with differently aged siblings in a family. In emphasizing the importance of self-contained groups, they say nothing about community, or about where a center's children, parents, and staff can or should spend time together. They also say nothing about the various types of space needed in addition to space for children's play.

Thus, design teams must address not simply the regulations, but also the *limitations* in the licensing requirements, and the fact that they specify *minimum*, not optimum, conditions for group care. *Centers which do not provide space and facilities beyond the licensing and building code minimums are far more institutional than necessary and cannot provide developmentally or functionally adequate child care.*

Defining Groups by Age

Generally, a child is assigned to one of four categories, depending upon age: infant, toddler, preschool, school-age. Exactly what ages fall into these categories varies across states and programs. The greatest discrepancies exist at the infant and toddler levels. In other words, states can consider a child over 12 months, or over 18 months, or over 2 years to be a toddler, thereby classifying children under these ages as infants. There seems to be general, but not universal, agreement that preschoolers are between 3 and 5 years of age (sometimes between 2½ and 5), and that school-age children are 5 years old, up to 8, 10, or 12 years.

For purposes of this guide, groups are defined as:

- Infants — birth to 18 months
- Toddlers — 18–36 months
- Preschoolers — 3–5 years
- School-age — 5–10 years

This breakdown is used because it corresponds to major developmental milestones; minimizes the number of times children need to change groups in the first 5 years; and allows for some cross-age experiences while still meeting the licensing requirements of most states. It is also the breakdown endorsed by many of the states considered to have higher licensing standards for developmental appropriateness.

Some programs are so concerned about age-appropriate care that they have children change groups every 6–12 months. This is NOT recommended! Children also need, in equal or greater doses, predictable care from one or two consistent caregivers throughout their preschool years (see Chapter 1). Indeed, primary care, where children stay with the same teacher for the first 3 years, is developmentally the most sound but difficult to achieve within many current licensing parameters.

Same-Age versus Multiage Clusters

Where a center serves all three or four age levels, and there are several rooms of children at each level, a decision is needed concerning the relationship of these rooms to one another, or their adjacency within the building. Many programs segregate the age groups by locating infants in one part of the building, toddlers in another, preschoolers in a third. Organizing the building according to age has the advantage of making it easy for groups at similar levels to share materials and play yards, and for staff to share experiences and concerns. However, it reinforces age segregation and can mean that preschoolers never have contact with infants except on special occasions.

Instead, a center can use the cluster concept in its design (Figure 4.1). That approach makes it possible for a child care center to both honor the age group distinctions required by law *and* maximize contact between groups at different ages. The solution is to create clusters of multiage groups, instead of clusters of single-age groups (Figure 4.2). In other words, rather than locate three infant rooms side by side at one end of the building, and three preschool rooms at the other, an infant, a toddler, and a preschool room can be clustered near one another. This physical proximity makes it eas-

Figure 4.1
This building design clusters 2, 3, or 4 rooms together. Each cluster has its own small vestibule/common area.

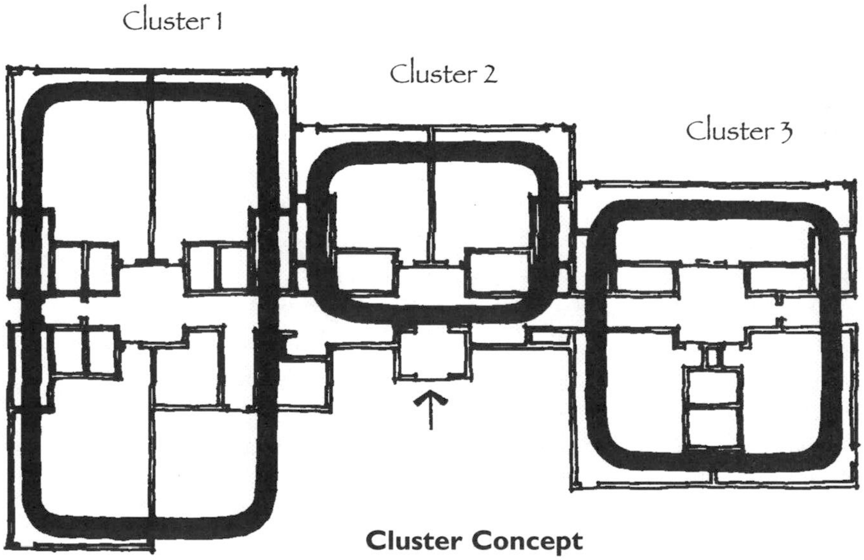

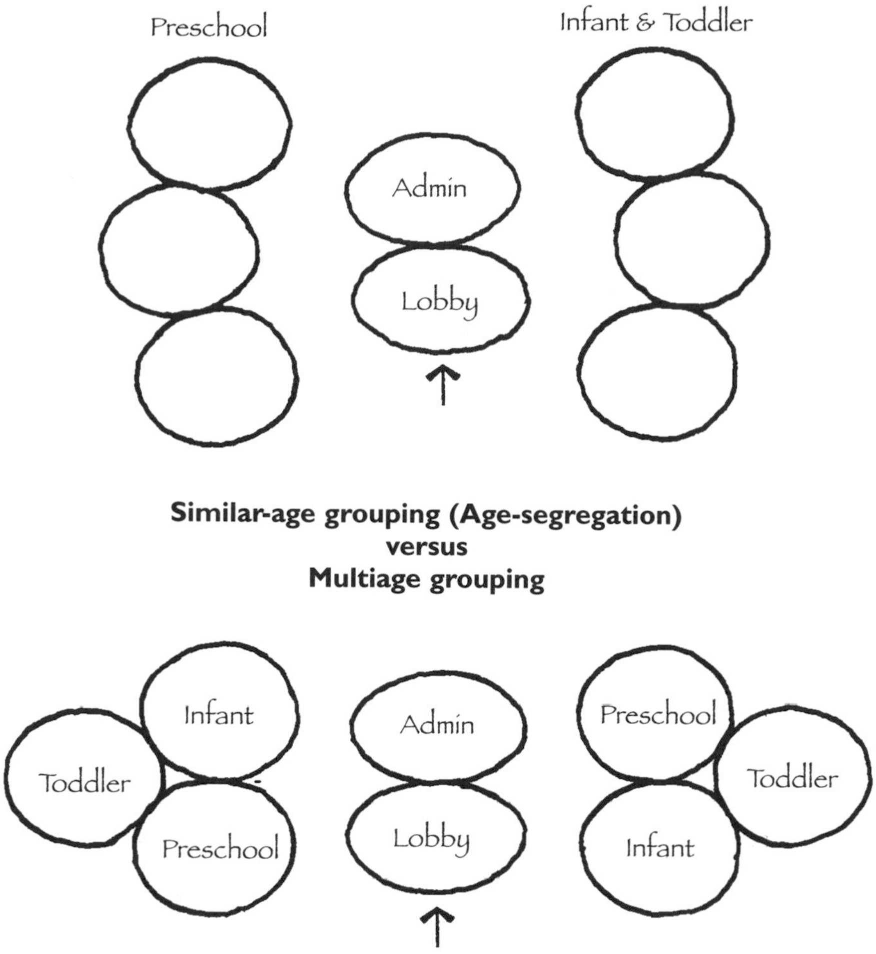

Figure 4.2
Buildings can be organized in at least two ways: by placing the group rooms of similar ages, or the group rooms of different ages, near one another.

ier for children in the different age groups to have contact, provided staff place value on making it happen.

The design team needs to determine what priority it places on cross-age contact and how this can be reflected in building layout and design. Early childhood educators have recently begun to examine the benefits of developmental continuity[1] as provided either by a layout that clusters groups of different aged children near one another, or by greater mixed-age grouping within the rooms themselves. Younger children learn a great deal from passive observation as well as direct interaction with older children. An older child assisting a younger one gets to feel important, express nurturance, and practice skills he or she may have recently learned. (It is said that we learn best what we teach another.) As children spend increasing amounts of time in child care centers, they interact less with siblings. They are missing what can be the rich fabric of family life, woven in part by the spontaneous responses, viewpoints, and shared experiences of different-age children. For these social, psychological, and developmental benefits, design teams are encouraged to consider the concept of multiage clusters.

Creating Community: A Common Area at the Heart

In most centers, space above and beyond the children's group rooms, the offices, a kitchen, and sometimes a staff lounge (also perhaps a "multipurpose" room), is rare and considered a luxury. Staff areas are often treated as luxuries as well. Shared space—created for the purpose of bringing children, families, and staff together—is virtually nonexistent.

However, centers do not only provide care for children. And, even in caring for children, they cannot do their job unless the needs of families and staff are also addressed. In order for people to meet, interact

Figure 4.3
Every center needs a "common area at the heart" to link all the spaces together and provide a welcoming gathering place for everyone

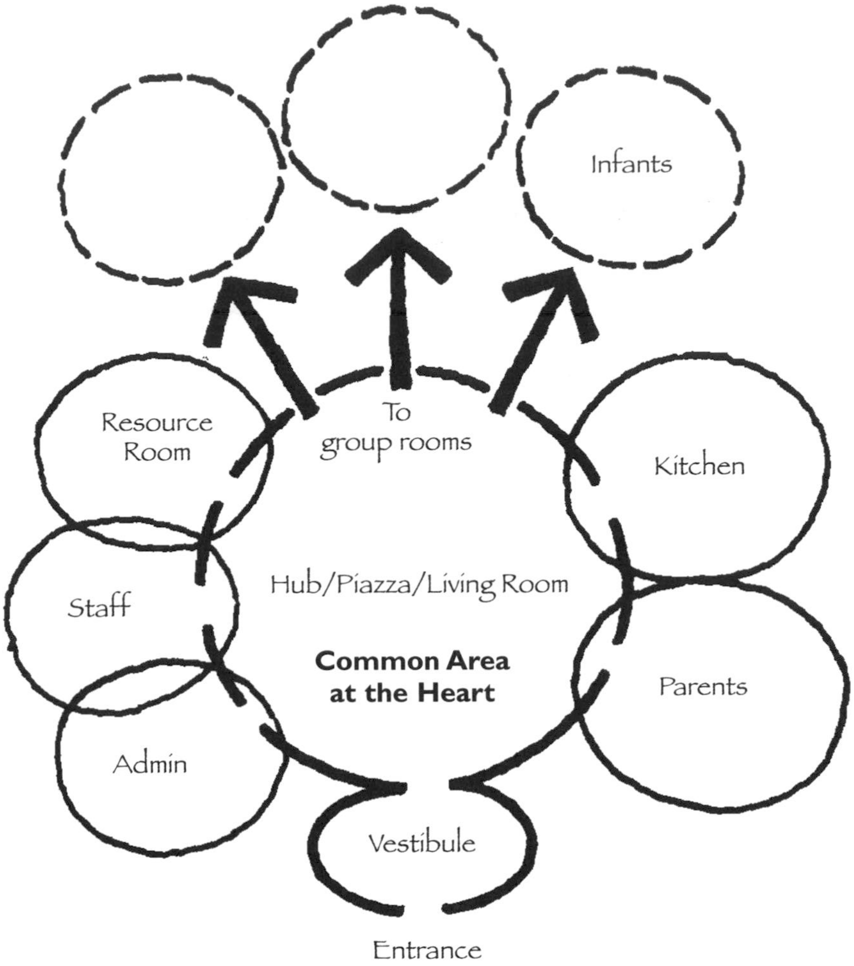

informally, and have shared experiences, there must be places other than corridors in which to do so.

A supportive, quality program has at least one area where people spontaneously rub shoulders as they go about their daily tasks, because major circulation paths lie tangent to, or lead in and out of, this space. Alexander et al call this "a common area at the heart."[2] Kitchens in homes, and hearths in ski lodges, are common areas at the heart with great power to bring people together in those building types. In child care centers, the common area might be a generous entrance room—almost like a living room—complete with fireplace and a children's play area; an administrative area with contiguous spaces for parents, staff, or reception; an assembly/gross motor room; a kitchen/dining area; a sitting or living room. A space that involves food and drink, invites people to linger, and which has interesting views to a part of the center or the outdoors, can serve as a common area at the heart. However, it must be designed as a "place"—not simply as a vending machine area.

A well-designed center makes certain to provide a meaningful common area at its heart (Figure 4.3). Thus the design team needs to establish which activities constitute the core of the center's social fabric and design its prime common area with this function in mind. In large centers especially, a common area at the heart is essential in assisting everyone to feel part of the whole.

In large buildings with separate modules or in a campus plan, it is desirable to have secondary "areas at the heart," forming the common spaces for subsections of the center. Although these secondary areas will be used most frequently, a main common space that everyone has access to on a daily basis is important as well.

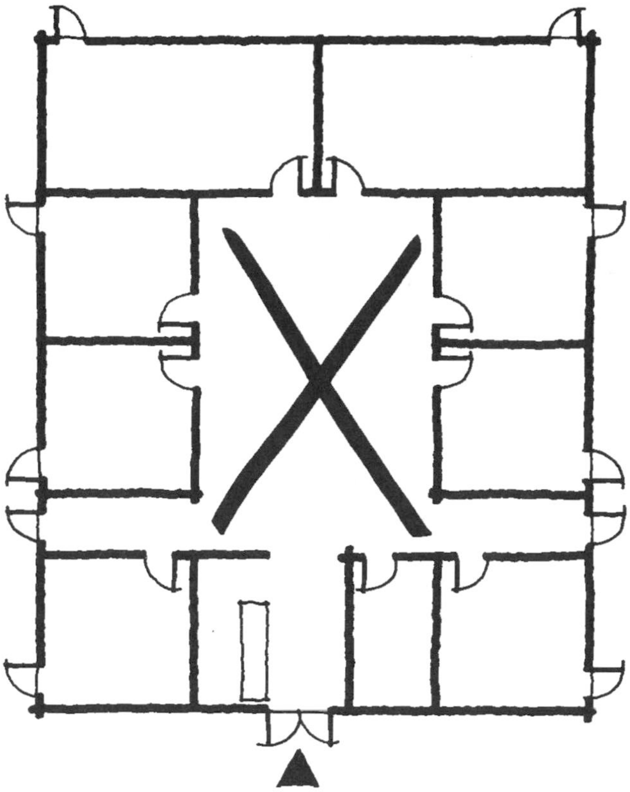

Figure 4.4
Making the multipurpose/gross motor room serve as the center's common area at the heart, and surrounding it with group rooms, usually does NOT work. Transit across the central space interferes with children's play, and sound from the play interferes with the children's rooms. There is no place to sit quietly to have a conversation, eat, or look at interesting views.

Multipurpose/Gross-Motor Rooms

Some centers create "multipurpose" rooms intended as additional space for communal activities and for children's indoor gross motor play. These two functions rarely mix well. Either it is a place for play or it is a place for gathering. And if it is a place for gathering, then the location of the room and its furnishings ultimately determine how successful it will be as a common area at the heart. Having an indoor space for gross motor play, especially in harsh climates, is excellent. But this room works best when it is self-contained, soundproofed, and used for no other function on a day-to-day basis.

Placing a multipurpose room in the middle of a building, and locating group rooms off of it (Figure 4.4), usually does not work well for two reasons. First, the space becomes a massive transit zone used primarily as a way of getting people to and from the children's spaces. Unless the doors are properly positioned, and the furniture is large and protected from peripheral activity, no one will want to sit in it for long. Second, if the multipurpose space is an indoor gymnasium for gross motor play, the area usually works even less well. Noise from the play will infiltrate the surrounding rooms, and transit through the area will constrain children's ability to move about or use equipment freely. This arrangement is not recommended.

Clusters with Something in the Middle

The issues of multiage group contact and shared space actually dovetail because clusters of rooms located adjacent to one another (whether the clusters are same-age or multiage), can be linked by a shared central or common area through which people need to come and go. A vestibule or exterior courtyard might be one such type of shared space, at least hinting at a relationship between the adjoining rooms.

However, if real interaction among the rooms in a cluster is desired, then the shared space needs to support activities of value to all the groups. In other words, the shared space itself has to become "a common area at the heart." Each design team can decide what activities would best function as the common area at the heart at this level of scale: Perhaps it is a living room, a kitchen, a play space, a greenhouse filled with plants and animals, a garden courtyard for temperate climates? For example, the Copper House has a living room entrance lobby for the entire building, and a smaller living room/dining area/servery in the middle of each house. Every children's room also has a group meeting space, which is *its* common area at the heart as well (see Chapter 21).

The Residential Core Model

In an attempt to supply the ingredients missing from licensing regulations, to make centers less institutional in character, and to find a solution for a common area at the heart of a mixed-age-group cluster, the author developed the residential core model illustrated in Figure 4.5. This model places an infant room, a toddler room, and a preschool room around a common living, kitchen, and dining area. The idea is to simultaneously introduce residential features into the center and create a shared space that will be of value to

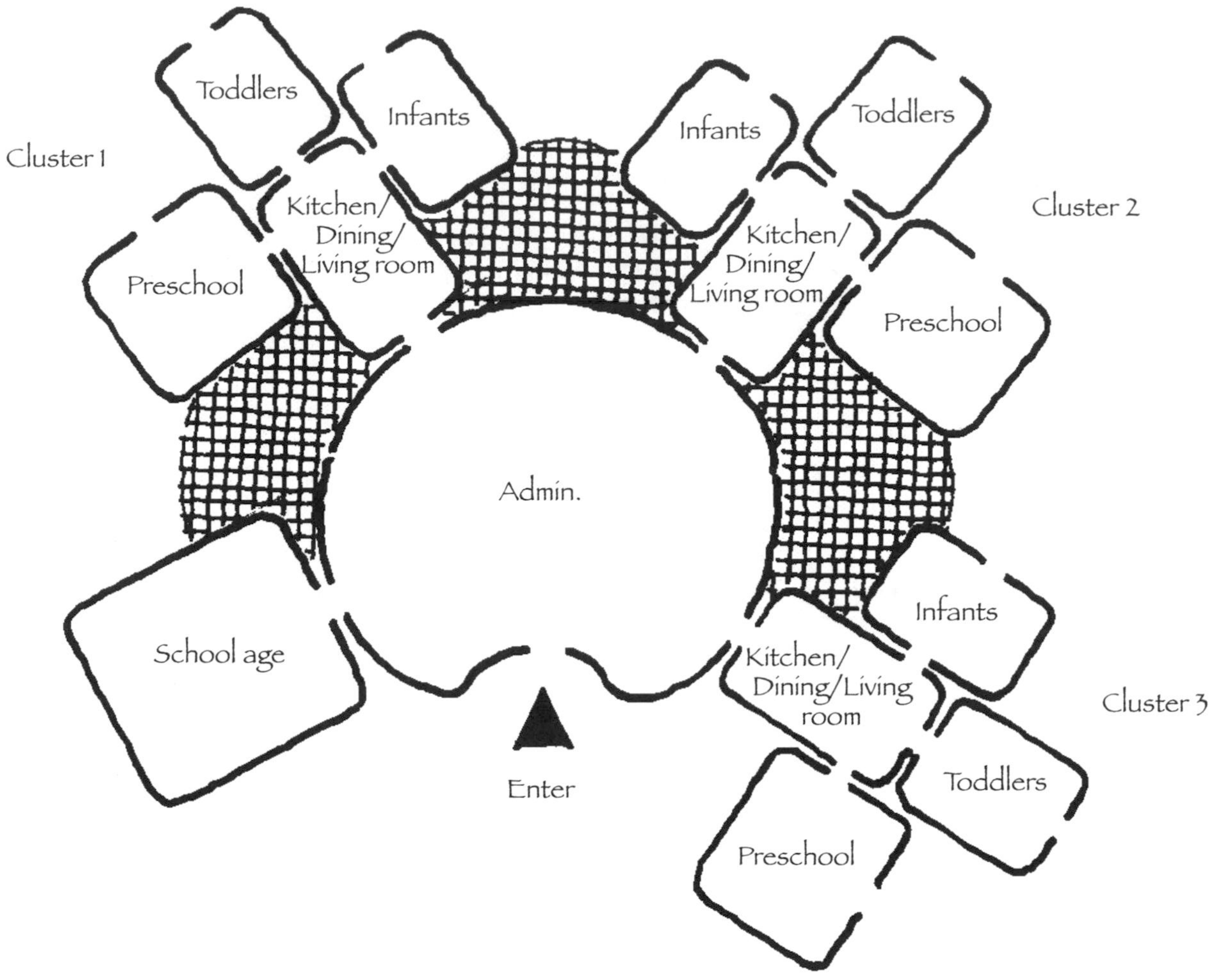

Figure 4.5
In the residential core model, three multiage clusters are organized around an administrative and school-age area under one roof. Each cluster consists of an infant, a toddler, and a preschool room surrounding a living room, dining area, and kitchen —its residential core.

children and adults alike because it provides something that the group rooms do not.

A residential core could also consist of a living room and kitchen with children eating in their group rooms, or it could be just a living room with food preparation and eating occurring elsewhere. The residential core could also exist in the middle of a cluster of same-age group rooms and—in single story buildings (so skylights can bring light into the core) on sites with sufficient space—it is possible to cluster as many as five or six rooms around it (see the plan in Figure 6.24).

The developmental and social advantages of a residential core supporting a multiage group cluster are many. If children from one family are all enrolled in the same cluster, parents have only one drop-off point, and siblings can see each other throughout the day. Children can stay within the same cluster for the entire five years, thereby having a home-base within the larger center domain. The core enables all the teachers and children in a given cluster to get to know one another, reducing the trauma of transition as children move from one group to the next. Indeed, transitions can be very gradual, even almost imperceptible, taking place over a period of weeks or months. The new teacher and child will know one another beforehand, and the old teacher and child can still make contact and remain friends. Chapter 21 presents the residential core model in greater detail, along with descriptions of the two centers that have been built so far, based on its design.

Center Size

The size of any new center depends upon:

- The demand for child care in a given community
- The funds available for design/construction/renovation
- The size center a prospective site/building can accommodate.

In addition to these three factors, a center's "size" is related to its program: the number of children actually served, their ages, the staff/child ratios, the size of groups as a function of children's ages, and the size of rooms as a function of group size and age. Hopefully, the order in which these issues are discussed below will assist the team in understanding their complex interrelationship.

Number of Children Served

Centers range in size from 12 children to several hundred. Many owners feel they cannot break even financially unless a center serves at least 100 children. Some centers have double and triple this number. Franchises, seeking to make a profit, assume they require larger numbers to realize savings from bulk supplies and a centralized administration. However, national experts on center financing have found that larger is not necessarily cheaper and certainly not better.

The Relationship Between Size and Quality

Both the scale of a building and the number of bodies within it affect children profoundly. A number of nationally recognized studies have found that center size is a reliable predictor of center quality, provided the number of children in a single building is no greater than 60–75.[3,4]

Centers with 60 or more children tend to emphasize routines and rules, and to offer less individualized attention and instruction, as well as less time for pleasure, wonder, and delight. Where small centers tend to mix ages and enable older children to enrich the play of younger ones, larger centers are likely to age-segregate. Sadly, research indicates that children in large centers may be less interested and involved in their surroundings, which can be poorly organized and lacking in a variety of things to do.

In general, small centers have the advantages of a less institutional atmosphere; more flexibility and spontaneity in the program; more individualized attention to children, families, and staff; unified goals and philosophy; greater quality control and supervision of staff; and greater parent involvement.[5]

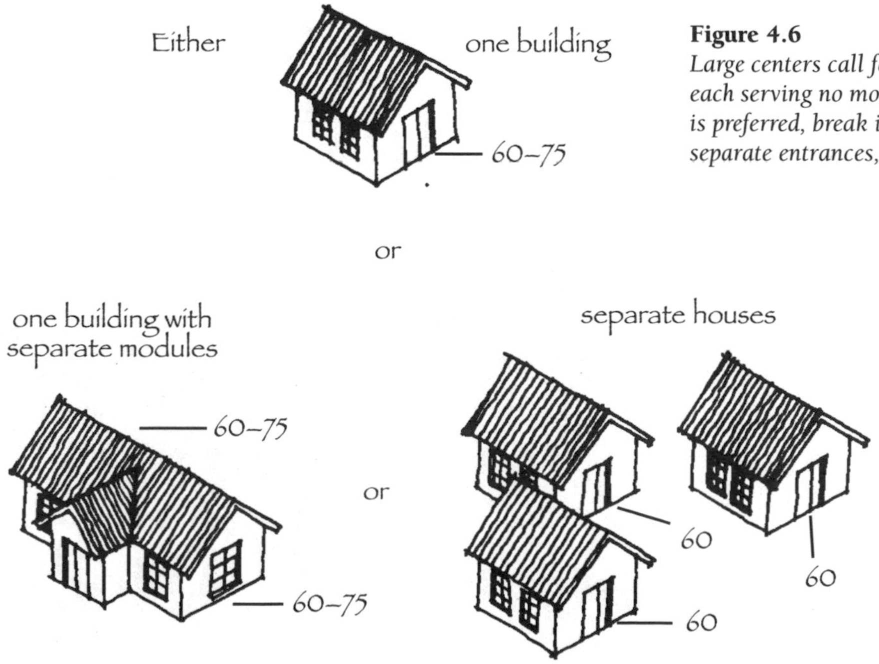

Figure 4.6
Large centers call for a campus plan of separate buildings, each serving no more than 60–75 children. If a single building is preferred, break it down into separate modules, with separate entrances, for 60–75 children each.

These effects of center size on the quality of care children receive cannot be taken lightly! Since children can be easily overwhelmed by the size of a facility and the number of people in it, it is desirable not to place them in programs larger than 60–75 children.

One Building with Modules or a Campus Plan?

This does not mean, however, that a center cannot accommodate more than 75 children. Rather, the issue is one of physical organization and design. If a single building is designed or chosen to accommodate more than 75, it is important to cluster its services into separate modules—with separate entrances—each serving 75 or less. (It is ideal if the modules accommodate only 35–40 children each, rather than 60–75.) To mitigate the impact of overall size, the exterior of the building should not appear monolithic, but instead be broken down to differentiate the group areas inside. (For an example of a modular approach, see the floor plan for the Copper House in Chapter 21.)

An alternative approach for centers with more than 75 children is a campus arrangement of separate but linked buildings, none of which holds more than 60–75 children (Figure 4.6). In such an arrangement, each building is semiautonomous, and day-to-day decisions are made by the staff within it. A building may house only one age group (age-segregation), or be

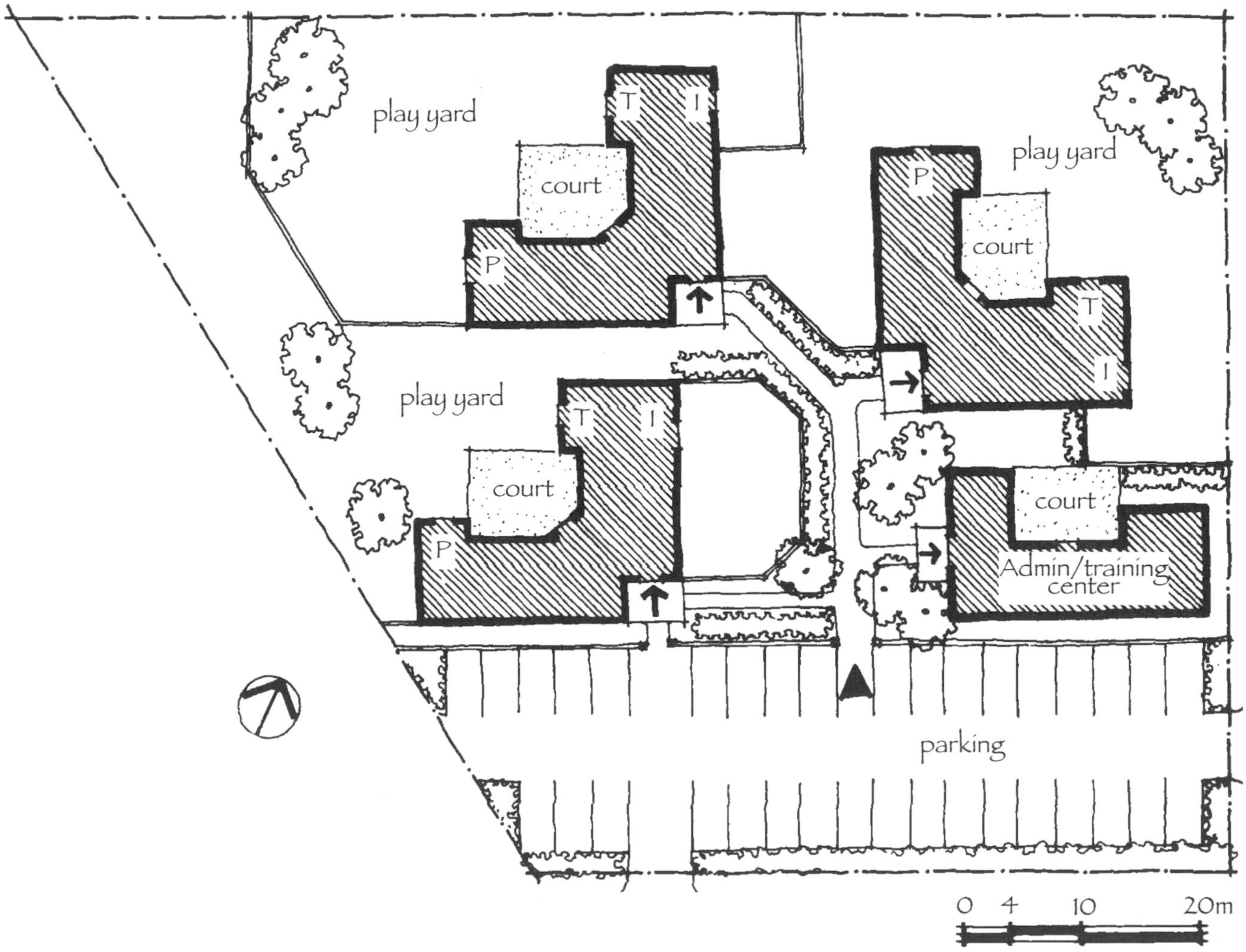

Figure 4.7
This site accommodates four buildings, three houses of 40 children each, plus a central administrative/training facility, in a campus approach to center design.

vertically organized with different ages. One of the buildings can accommodate administrative and staff supports that all the buildings share. The critical feature is that no single child relates to more than 75 others—ideally, to as few as 35 other children—at one time. Figure 4.7 shows the floor plan for a campus-type center design in New Zealand. (For guidelines for building and site considerations for modular and campus designs, see Chapter 5.)

Assessing Building Size

The number of children a center serves determines, in part, the square footage requirements for the building and site. Centers are licensed based upon a *minimum* number of square feet per child that they are required to provide—a figure that varies from state to state. As indicated in the discussion concerning the overriding premise of center design, this figure is confusing because it fails to account for all the space actually needed to operate a child care program. Square footage is the single most important design-related factor affecting the quality of the program, the welfare of children and staff, and the budget. It is therefore crucial that design teams understand the issues involved.

Primary Space in the Group Rooms

Primary space in the group rooms—the space needed for children's developmental activities and play—is the first consideration. Licensing in most states requires a minimum of 35 square feet of activity space per child in each group room. Primary activity space does NOT include bathrooms, cribs, diapering areas, kitchenettes, cubbies, kitchens, offices, staff areas, storage, or any parts of rooms with built-in furniture or equipment, all of which are considered secondary space. It also does not include corridors, stairways, mechanical and electrical supports, or walls, all of which are considered tertiary space. (Primary space may include a multipurpose/large motor activity space; shared art rooms, libraries, etc., if these are used frequently by children to supplement offerings in their group rooms. Exactly how this is calculated is discussed later.)

First, it must be understood that 35 square feet of play space is a *minimum* below which children's welfare is endangered and a program will not be licensed. This minimum, of unknown origins—perhaps adopted from fire ordinances in public buildings—bears little relevance to the actual spatial requirements of child care.

Second, this legal minimum of 35 square feet per child refers *only to activity space*—to that territory available to children for play. It does *not* include space for all the necessary functions that take place in secondary space or in tertiary space (Figure 4.8 on the next page). A design team that assumes it can simply multiply the anticipated number of children by 35 in order to determine the requisite size of a center is in grave error!

As discussed in Chapter 2, young children relate to the world through their bodies and their senses. They require large amounts of space in which to learn by moving and doing. Thirty-five sq ft/child is a 5'-x-7' space—a little over twice the dimensions of the average playpen—hardly the "free-range" toddlers need for gaining assurance on their feet, or that rambunctious five-year-olds need to let off steam and develop physical coordination.[6]

Analysis of the effect of density on children's social behavior reveals that densities of one child per 40–45 sq ft optimize positive social interaction.[7] High densities (more than one child/30 sq ft) produce aggression and less relevant involvement, while low densities (less than one child/50–55 sq ft) can cause low social interaction. As indicated in Table 4.1, this guide endorses 42 sq ft/child (rather than 35 sq ft) as the minimally adequate amount of primary play space required to conduct a "workable" (but not a "better" or "recommended") program.

Secondary Space

Other essential functions must be accommodated in addition to primary activity space. These are referred to as *secondary* and *tertiary* space requirements. There are two types of secondary space—space required in the children's group rooms and space required by adults or the center as a whole. (Chapter 19 addresses adult secondary space needs in detail.)

Secondary Space in the Group Rooms

Secondary space in the group rooms refers to space that is not primary activity space but that is nevertheless essential to support care-giving aspects of the program: bathrooms, diapering areas, kitchenettes,

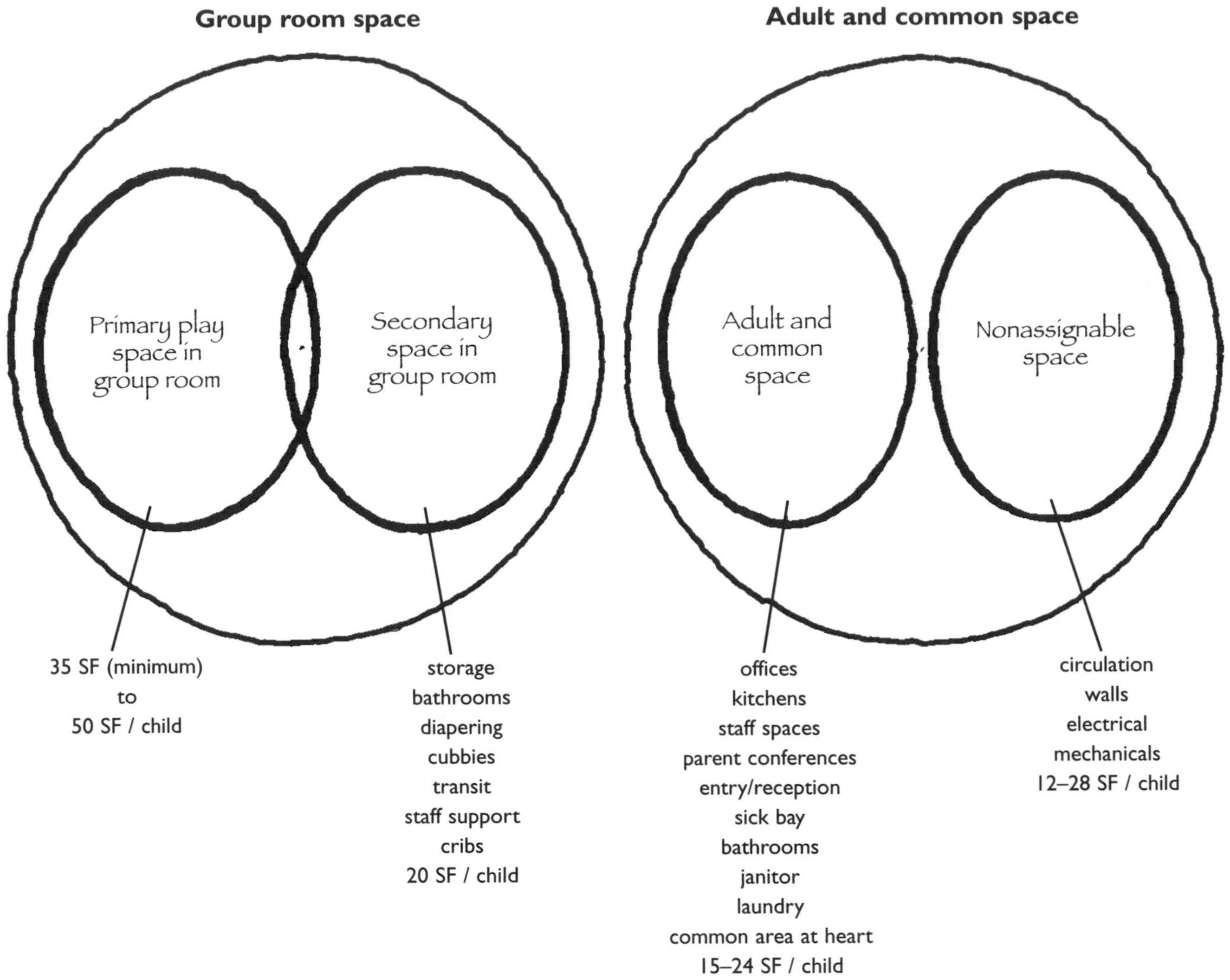

Figure 4.8
Aside from the minimum 35 square feet per child of unencumbered play space cited in licensing regulations, many other functions require square footage in a center.

storage, cubbies, laundry, and built-in furniture. In the case of infants, an additional 30 sq ft/child must be added for each crib and the 2–3-foot clearance required between adjacent cribs.

While the facilities included in secondary activity space in the group rooms are often measured solely by the amount of square footage they occupy, it is important to recognize that, in addition, *circulation space* (often as much as 3 feet deep) is required around diapering stations, toilets, cubbies, kitchenettes, etc. Depending upon room layout, the recommended allocations for secondary space may need to increase in order to prevent circulation around these facilities from infringing on children's primary activity space. Additionally, observation space of 5–12 sq ft/child may be desired in laboratory schools and other training programs.[8]

Secondary Space for Adults and the Common Areas

Adult/common secondary space is the space outside the group rooms that is needed for administrative offices; staff lounge, work, resource and training areas; parent areas; conference rooms; entry/reception; sick child bay; ADA staff/visitor bathrooms; utility and janitor's rooms; the main kitchen and recycling area; resource and other storage; and communal areas, gathering places, and a common area at the heart.

Tertiary Space for the Building

Tertiary space refers to areas that do not directly affect children or adults but are essential for the architecture and the building's structure: entries, corridors, stairways, mechanical and electrical equipment, and wall thicknesses. Tertiary space is generally calculated as a percentage (25–30%) of the sum of both primary and secondary space (also called net or assignable square footage). However, corridors with niches and meeting places, and other amenities that bring real life to a building, may require calculating tertiary space at 35 or 40%. How much tertiary space is actually required ultimately depends upon the degree of sprawl or compactness in the building's design, and upon climate. Buildings in warmer climates often can use exterior space for circulation, whereas buildings in cold climates may require airlocks, thicker wall mass, and ability to circulate through the building solely indoors. Generally, wall thicknesses and mechanical/electrical equipment use 5–10% of the assignable space, while circulation uses 20–25%.

Combined Space Needs

Table 4.1 indicates the amount of secondary group room, adult/common, and tertiary space required for a given amount of primary space at four levels of quality. (The figures in parentheses indicate the percentage of primary and secondary space at which the tertiary space was calculated.)

A rich, developmentally appropriate program is difficult to achieve with less than 100 sq ft/child of indoor space *overall*, and less than 42 sq ft/child of primary activity space in each group room. However, the author's experience over the past 10 years indicates that even these figures are minimums. A quality program providing 8 to 10 hours of care daily really requires 115–125 square feet per child overall. Lesser amounts work only when offset by plentiful outdoor space in a climate that permits extensive outdoor play most of the year. The Italian Reggio Emilia centers, reputed to be the finest early childhood programs in the world, generally provide about 125 square feet per child.

These square footage estimates are intended as guidelines only. The importance of carefully assessing the particular needs of your center cannot be overemphasized. Especially in centers with intended enrollments under 50–55 children, it will not usually work merely to "plug in" the square footage formulas suggested here. In these situations, community, common, and staff spaces will often come up short; a higher percentage of the total space will need to be allotted for them. It is important that the design team evaluate carefully everything they hope to offer in the way of community programs, after-school activities, and parent/family functions in assessing their actual square footage needs. When it comes to center populations, small is beautiful, but accommodating a full range of activities will cost more.

Table 4. 1 ***Determining Building Size***

Space Standard (Quality)	Primary Activity Space in Each Group Room	Secondary Activity Space in Each Group Room*,**	Adult & Common Space (Outside the Group Rooms)	Tertiary (Nonassignable) Space	Total Building Square Footage
Minimum (Insufficient)	35 sq ft/ch	20 sq ft/ch	15 sq ft/ch	17.5 sq ft/ch (25%)	88 sq ft/ch
Workable	42 sq ft/ch	20 sq ft/ch	18 sq ft/ch	20 sq ft/ch (25%)	100 sq ft/ch
Better	46 sq ft/ch	20 sq ft/ch	22 sq ft/ch	26 sq ft/ch (30%)	115 sq ft/ch
Recommended	50 sq ft/ch	22 sq ft/ch	24 sq ft/ch	29 sq ft/ch (30%)	125 sq ft/ch

* In infant rooms, an additional 30 sq ft/child is needed for each crib and the 2–3-foot clearance required between adjacent cribs.

** Because toddlers need both diapering and toileting, an additional 3 sq ft/child are desirable.

Assessing Site Size

Site size is based on four factors: the size of the building, the amount of outdoor play space needed to meet licensing requirements, the amount of pathways, parking and vehicular space needed for the center, plus some amount of free green space calculated at approximately 30% of the above (Figure 4.9).

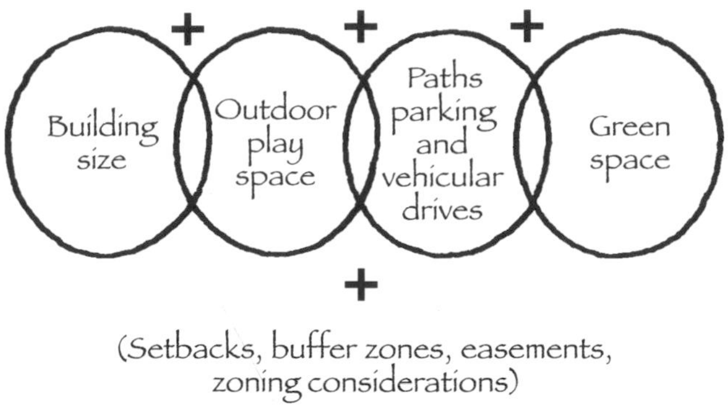

Figure 4.9 *Site size*

Outdoor Play Space

The accepted *minimum* requirement is 75 sq ft/child of outdoor space for all the children enrolled in a center. However, national experts recommend between 100 and 200 sq ft/child. National Association for the Education of Young Children (NAEYC) accreditation guidelines recommend 75 sq ft/child of outdoor space, with the caveat that where space is limited and must be shared by groups, the calculation can be based simply on the maximum number of children who will be *outside at any one time* (usually a group of 18–20 preschoolers). While this limitation may be necessary in certain urban settings, it is best that a design team not begin by assuming scheduling of play yard use. Outdoor play is ideally 50% of the program. Since child care is a year-round affair, and all children benefit from being outside as much as possible, it is important to provide sufficient outdoor space for a center's full enrollment at one time.

Parking and Vehicular Space

The space allocated for vehicular drives, service drives, drop-off, and short- and long-term parking varies enormously and can easily range from 55–100 sq ft/child. It depends upon the site size and location, access to public transportation, the number of staff, number of families and services frequenting the center at peak times, provisions for on-street parking, zoning ordinances, etc. One car occupies approximately 150–200 sq ft. With drives, and entry and access roads added on, this figure can increase, on average, to 300–400 sq ft per car. Usually, 1 short-term parking space per every 10 children is desirable. Long-term parking is required for all staff in attendance at one time (or at peak crossover times), either on-site or nearby, as allowed by local ordinances, unless staff arrive by public transportation or walking. Approximately 1 long-term parking space per every 20 children is desirable.

Table 4.2 indicates the gross square footage requirements for a site—including outdoor play space, vehicular space, building space, and green space—at four levels of quality. Calculations do not include any additional space required as a result of set backs, easements, zoning ordinances, or buffer zones.

Estimating Building and Site Square Footage

When the design team first starts looking for space or considering center size, it is sometimes useful to have a ballpark figure for the amount of square footage required. This figure will later be refined according to the level of quality selected for the center in Tables 4.1 and 4.2. To make a first pass at *estimating* the approximate amount of space required, follow the rules of thumb in Table 4.3 on the next page.

Table 4.2 *Determining Site Size*

Space Standard (Quality)	Outdoor Play Space	Parking	Building Size	Green Space (30–35% of total)	Total Site Size
Minimum	75 sq ft/ch	25 sq ft/c	88 sq ft/ch	56 sq ft/ch (30%)	244 sq ft/ch
Workable	100 sq ft/ch	50 sq ft/ch	100 sq ft/ch	75 sq ft/ch (30%)	325 sq ft/ch
Better	150 sq ft/ch	75 sq ft/ch	115 sq ft/ch	119 sq ft/ch (35%)	459 sq ft/ch
Recommended	200 sq ft/ch	100 sq ft/ch	125 sq ft/ch	149 sq ft/ch (35%)	574 sq ft/ch

Table 4.3 *Estimating Building and Site Size*

- *For indoor space, estimate a* minimum *of 100 square feet per child* overall. This figure includes:

primary play space:	approximately 42 sq ft/child
secondary spaces:	approximately 38 sq ft/child
tertiary space:	approximately 20 sq ft/child

- *For outdoor space, estimate a minimum of 100 square feet per child overall.*
- *For space for vehicle movement, parking, and green space estimate 100–200 sq ft/child* if some needs are met by the urban street network.
- Thus the total size of the site adds up to between 300 and 400 square feet per child, not including setbacks, buffer zones, easements, and local zoning ordinances for the number of car spaces required. As per the levels of quality in Table 4.2, the recommended figure is closer to *400 square feet per child.*

Table 4.4 *Comparisons of Four Sets of National Standards*[10]

	Age	Maximum Group Size	Maximum Adult/Child Ratio
APHA/AAP	1–12 mos	6	1:3
	12–24 mos	6	1:3
	25–30 mos	8	1:3
	31–35 mos	10	1:5
	3 yrs	14	1:7
	4–5 yrs	16	1:8
FIDCR	0–2 yrs	6	1:3
	2–3 yrs	12	1:4
	3–6 yrs	16	1:8
NAEYC	0–2 yrs	6–8	1:3 – 1:4
	2–3 yrs	8–10	1:4 – 1:5
	3 yrs	14–18	1:7 – 1:9
	4–5 yrs	16–18	1:8 – 1:9
NCCIP	0–8 mos	6	1:3
	8–18 mos	9	1:3
	18–36 mos	12	1:4

APHA/AAP: American Public Health Association/American Academy of Pediatrics

FIDCR: Federal Interagency Day Care Requirements

NAEYC: National Association for the Education of Young Children

NCCIP: National Center for Clinical Infant Programs

Assessing Group Room Sizes

The following discussion provides information to assist teams in determining the size of the children's group rooms.

Age Determines Staff/Child Ratios and Group Sizes

Most states have regulations concerning staff/child ratios, (i.e., the number of staff required per number of children in a group), and the group size allowed at each age level. Some states have regulations for ratios but not for group size. Generally speaking, the staff/child ratios and group sizes permissible by law are maximums above which children's welfare is jeopardized, and not standards reflecting a high quality of care. Research indicates that staff/child ratios are the most significant determinant of center quality, and that group size is the next most significant factor.[9] (The effect of square footage on center quality was not prioritized in relation to these factors.)

Ratios affect group size in the following way. Because staff are costly, programs often want to have as many children per adult as the law allows—for example, five infants per one adult in some states. Although permissible, this ratio does not necessarily provide infants with optimum care. Indeed, most evidence suggests that even three babies per one adult is stressful. Precisely because licensing requirements do not reflect developmentally sound procedures, a number of prominent child-advocacy organizations have established their own standards for ratios and group sizes. These have been adapted, for purposes of comparison, in Table 4.4.

Consistent with these standards, this guide assumes the following group sizes and ratios:

infants, 0–18 months	6–7/group	2 caregivers	1:3–1:3.5
toddlers, 18–36 months	8–10/group	2 caregivers	1:4–1:5
preschoolers, 3–5 years	14–16/group	2 caregivers	1:7–1:8
school-age, 5–10 years	16–20/group	2 caregivers	1:8–1:10

Group Size, Ratios, and Quality

The design team needs to consider the staff/child ratios and group sizes that will provide optimum care as seriously as they consider the center enrollment that will balance the budget. Weighing these two factors can be challenging.

Table 4.5 *Estimating Room Size By Age Group*

Primary + Secondary Activity Space			
Age Group	**# of Children**	**Recommended (50 sq ft/ch)**	**Workable (42 sq ft/ch)**
Infants	6–8	x 102* = 612–816 sq ft	x 92* = 552–736 sq ft
Toddlers	8–10	x 75** = 600–750 sq ft	x 65** = 520–650 sq ft
Preschooler	14–16	x 72 = 1,008–1,152 sq ft	x 62 = 868–992 sq ft
School-age	16–20	x 72 = 1,152–1440 sq ft	x 62 = 992–1,240 sq ft

* Includes 30 sq ft/child for each crib and 2–3 foot clearance required between cribs.

** Includes 3 sq ft/child for two toilets and sinks in addition to a diapering area.

When grappling with child care's complex program and budgetary issues, it is easy to lose sight of the fact that group numbers and staff/child ratios represent real, active children and adults. Adding one or two more children may make sense in terms of the budget, but it does not always make sense in terms of the reality of staff and children's lives. Most mothers find caring for a single infant exhausting, and "pity" anyone with twins or triplets. Being around eight babies, with primary responsibility for four, is no small feat! Similarly, although it is "legal" in some states for centers with small rooms to place one staff member alone with four infants or five toddlers, this does not mean it is manageable. (Indeed, this practice is strongly discouraged. At least two adults should be present in a room at all times, so that children are not left unattended if one adult needs to leave or assist a single child.)

Also, adding more children to a group always needs to be done in accordance with the allowed ratios, if the budget is to balance. For example, suppose the ratio is 1:3 for an allowable group size of 12. Thus, groups of 3, 6, 9, or 12 children correlate with the ratio. However, if groups of 7 or 10 children are preferred, an additional staff person is required for the 7th or 10th child. The additional caregiver's salary usually can only be compensated by three children, not by one child alone, thereby adding enormous additional cost.

Table 4.5 shows one way to *estimate* room sizes for each age group, at two levels of quality.

It is essential to note that Table 4.5 is really only good for *estimating* purposes because the smaller the group size, the higher the square footage per child needed to provide space for all necessary facilities (which remain constant despite a lower number of children). Since groups of infants are smaller than groups of preschoolers, some states acknowledge this limitation by requiring 50 sq ft/child of primary activity space for babies. The larger the group, the lower the square footage per child that can be tolerated overall. The fact is that even at the "recommended" level in Table 4.5, the infant and toddler rooms tend to be small, while the preschool and school-age rooms are a bit generous at full capacity. Infant and toddler rooms tend to operate best at around 850–900 sq ft each, preschool and school-age rooms at about 1100 sq ft each, for the group sizes indicated or even for groups slightly larger. It would be preferable to take 100 square feet total (i.e., not per child) off of the latter two rooms if they will have more than 14 children, and add an additional 100 sq ft to each infant and toddler room. How much square footage each room requires also depends, ultimately, on the compactness of room layout that is possible.

Faulty Space Trade-offs

Inappropriate manipulation of building square footage negatively impacts the program in the following four common ways.

Inclusion of Multipurpose Rooms in Primary Space Calculations

Some states do not stipulate that the minimum primary play space must be in the group room only. Instead, it is possible to multiply the minimum—say 35 sq ft/child—times the number of children in the center to get an overall building requirement. Then any space in the center that is used by children exclusively for play—such as a multipurpose, gross motor, shared art, or computer room—can count as part of the minimum requirement. This strategy may yield 35 sq ft/child overall, but it results in inadequately sized and congested rooms where children spend most of their time. Developmentally, this practice is acceptable only when the secondary spaces are contiguous with a group's primary space, are *continuously* available to children for play, and never subject to scheduled use.

Inclusion of Corridors in Group Room Secondary Space Calculations

Another dysfunctional way of cutting building square footage is to have corridors, transit pathways, or other nonassignable functions actually occur within the group rooms. While the measurable space within a room may provide 35 sq ft/child of primary play space, the secondary space and actual usable space in the room is diminished because portions of the room function as passageways for people to get from one part of the building to another. Design teams evaluating the potential of a site, or a set of architectural plans, are cautioned to be wary of such strategies. The loss of space and the confusion introduced by transit within a group room are detrimental to children's welfare and the tranquil, secure functioning of their home base.

Changing a Center's Density at the Last Minute: A Cautionary Note

Sometimes adequate square footage is allotted initially, but late in the planning process the budget begins to get unmanageable. Then there may be pressure to increase the number of children while keeping the square footage constant, or to cut the total square footage of the project without reducing the census. When this decision is made after the building's plans are quite developed, rearrangements of space or the shrinking of adequately sized rooms forces all kinds of programmatically poor compromises. Shrinking the program to fit the available dollars is a balanced decision; shrinking the primary or secondary square footage in group rooms to fit the available dollars is untenable. (See Chapter 3 for ways to avoid getting into this fix.)

Failure to Provide Enough Space for Cribs

A small-sized crib measures approximately 27″ x 40″, a full-sized crib approximately 27″x 52″. To prevent infection, most licensing regulations require that cribs do not touch each other on any of their sides—unless the touching ends have Plexiglas panels in them—and to be separated on all adjacent sides by 2–3 feet. Thus the average crib takes up about 30 sq ft of space. When either crib size or crib clearance space is not honored in square footage allocations for infant rooms, the rooms become overrun with cribs and have barely any free floor space for babies to crawl about.

Costs and Design Alternatives

One possible way to better utilize a facility with limited square footage is to take advantage of overhead space in its group rooms. Suggestions for ways to use vertical space may be found in Chapters 15–18.

Other options include: reducing corridors, using external circulation, creating greater efficiency in the layout of staff areas and laundries, using common areas as support spaces during non-child-care hours, etc. Alternatively, reduce all three types of space—primary, secondary, tertiary—by an equivalent percentage, or go down one quality level in Table 4.1 (assuming you are not already at the lowest quality level). Then try to do the best job with the interiors that you can. The advantage of using Table 4.1 is that it ensures that all types of space receive some representation, at all levels of quality.

Center Size, Costs, and Ages Served

Center size also needs to be determined in relation to construction/renovation costs, start-up costs, and operating costs. The larger a center's census, the larger the site and/or building required, the greater the cost to build or renovate, and the greater the cost to operate and maintain the facility in the long run.

However, cost is not related just to sheer numbers of children, but also to their ages. Staff salaries constitute about 80–85% of a child care center's budget. Because infant care is so labor intensive (one caregiver per every three to four babies) and requires a high per-capita investment in square footage and equipment, it incurs the highest operating (as well as building) costs. In many communities, this cost is barely offset by parental fees. Costs to operate toddler programs are slightly lower. As a result, revenues may not begin to exceed basic operating expenses until children are three to five years of age, and staff/child ratios approach one to eight.

Thus projected costs to serve children at different age levels, and expected revenues at each age level, need to be factored into a determination of center size and composition. Sometimes adding a small infant/toddler program to a larger preschool population helps address a community's growing demand for quality infant/toddler care, while keeping the budget balanced. It may also be a built-in way to help a center grow.

Key Secondary Space Requirements: Plumbing and Storage

Plumbing

Plumbing is one of the largest fixed renovation or building costs for a child care center, (second only to heating, ventilation, and air-conditioning systems—HVAC). Because it is unlikely to change over time, its placement—critical to the functioning of each room—is described in some detail in Chapter 7. Table 4.6 outlines plumbing requirements by age group. Follow local building code and licensing requirements as well.

Table 4.6 *Average Plumbing Requirements by Age Group*

Infants	1 toilet per group (for adult use and feces disposal)
	2 adult sinks (diapering, food preparation)
	1 tub or deep sink for infant bathing (optional, or one of above)
	1 child handwashing sink (optional)
	1 plumbed water play trough (optional)
Toddlers	2 toilets (preferably child-size) per 10–14 children (some still in diapers)
	2 adult sinks (diapering, food preparation)
	1–2 child handwashing sinks per 10–14 toddlers
	1 tub or deep sink for child bathing (optional)
	1 plumbed water play trough (optional)
Preschoolers	2 toilets per 10–20 children
	1 adult sink
	1–2 child handwashing sinks per 10–20 preschoolers
	1 plumbed water play trough (optional)
School-age	2 toilets per 10–20 children (1 each for males and females)
	1 adult sink
	1–2 child handwashing sinks per 10–20 children
	1 plumbed water play trough (optional)
Adults	1 toilet per 10 adults
	1 fully-accessible toilet per building or floor (can be one of above)*
	1 handwashing sink per 10 adults
	2–3 kitchen sinks
PLUS	water fountains in each room and public spaces

*Check ADA and local regulations

Toilets and Hand Sinks

Most states require 1 toilet and 1 handwashing sink in a ratio of 1:10 for toddlers and preschool children, and 1:15 for school-age children. However, because young children have poor bowel and bladder control, it is preferable to have two toilets per group when the group size approaches 10, especially for children between two and three years of age. Where a toddler group consists of approximately 50% children in diapers and 50% in the process of toilet training, over the course of the year, all children in the group are likely to advance to toilet use. If the number of children in the ratio is exceeded by one, an additional fixture is required.

It is standard practice to combine toileting areas for boys and girls under five years of age. However, most states require separation of male and female toilets for school-age children.

Heights and Sizes. Toilet heights for children under five are best at 11 inches; handsink heights for infants are 16 inches, for toddlers 18 inches, and for preschoolers 22 inches. Depending upon the age range of school-age children anticipated, their sink and toilet heights can either be the same as those for preschoolers, or for adults. Toilets are usually 1 foot wide and 2 feet long. At least 2 feet of space is needed in front of each toilet for an adult to assist a child. Therefore allow approximately 3′ x 4′ of space per toilet. Use Table 4.7 to *estimate* the space needed for bathrooms. Actual square footage required will depend entirely upon layout.

Table 4.7 *Approximate Sizes for Bathrooms*

Diapering Only	6′ x 5′ minimum
Diaper + 1 sink + 1 toilet	9′ x 7′
Diaper + 2 sinks + 2 toilets	8′ x 12′
2 sinks + 2 toilets	8′ x 7′
Adult ADA[11] sink + toilet	7.5′ x 7.5′

For Infants. Toilets in infant areas are for adult rather than child use. An adult toilet within the infant room is desirable to reduce staff absence. The toilet required for disposing of feces from cloth diapers (if these are used), can be the adult toilet, in which case it is best located near the diapering area. Some teams may want to put a child-height toilet in each infant room so it has the possibility of being converted to a toddler room in the future. A child-height handwashing sink 16 inches high is an optional addition for independence training if an infant group includes children over 12 months. This sink can be located close to art or eating to encourage children to use it before or after these activities.

For Toddlers. Since toddlers toilet train between the ages of 24 and 36 months, toddler rooms need to have one or more toilets as part of the group room. These are best if child-scaled but can be outfitted with supports for children if child-size is not an option. The area need not be a fully enclosed room; indeed, toddlers are often more content to "sit" on the toilet if they can observe and do not feel cut off from ongoing activities. Allow for staff visibility in and child visibility outwards at all times.

For Preschoolers and School-age Children. To promote supervision and safety, locate toilets and hand washing sinks in or near the entrance to the group room and/or near the entrance to the playground.

For Adults. Adult bathrooms are best placed near the staff lounge or administrative area and near the central entrance core for parents and visitors.

Chapter 7 provides essential information on the positioning of bathrooms and activity sinks in the group rooms. See Chapter 19 for allocating toilets in adult spaces.

Activity Sinks

Both adults and children need activity sinks in the group rooms that are separate from handwashing sinks related to toilets.

In infant and toddler rooms there must be two adult-height sinks—one for diapering and one for food preparation and other uses—to avoid contamination. In preschool and school-age rooms one adult sink is needed. Because water play is a primary sensory experience for children of all ages, possibilities for its occurrence need to be maximized, ideally, by providing a built-in water play table in each group room. (See Chapters 16–18 for details and heights.)

Since the location of adult and child activity sinks is the most critical design issue in laying out a group room, it is covered extensively in Chapter 7. The impact of sink placement on the functionality of group rooms cannot be overemphasized. *It is always worth the added expense to extend or reroute the plumbing to desired locations, rather than to design group spaces around a limited or inappropriately located plumbing system.*

Storage

The first design requirement expressed by every child care teacher is for more storage space. There never seems to be enough! Adequate, well-organized, and accessible storage is a vital adjunct to a good curriculum and frees teachers to be facilitators of learning. It is essential that the design team factor storage space square footage requirements into center design at the outset.

The Storage Needs Inventory

An important task for the center's staff during preliminary design is to make an exhaustive inventory of all their storage needs. The inventory should address not only the type of item to be stored but also the preferred type of storage for the item, the quantity of each type of storage unit needed, and the approximate dimensions of the cabinets, shelves, closets, etc., desired.

Centers make use of a broad range of storage type options: small and walk-in closets (sometimes with much open floor space for large items); open and closed shelving; bins, hooks, and drawers; freestanding and built-in cabinets; outdoor sheds. When designing a new center that does not yet have a staff, the team will need to estimate storage needs by enlisting the cooperation of an ongoing program of a size similar to the proposed program. Table 4.8 categorizes many of the common items centers must store and suggests storage types to accommodate them. The text that follows offers some general pointers for making storage decisions.

Square Footage Requirements

A shocking fact is that 10% of a center's square footage—both 10% of the floor area in each group room and 10% of the building's square footage—needs to be allocated for storage of materials and equipment in such a way that they are not accessible to children. Smaller rooms usually require proportionately more storage space than 10%. Non-child-accessible storage options include closets, shelving (4′ or above), above- and below-counter cabinets, and freestanding storage units.

Point-of-Use Placement

Place storage as close as possible to the point of use. This means that many materials need to be stored in the group rooms themselves. Each group room should have a storage closet of at least 40–60 square feet (make this part of the room's secondary space allocation). Art supplies will need shelf space, usually both in closets and in cabinets in the teacher's prep area in each group room. Storage for sleeping mats or cots (Chapters 16 and 17) is in addition to this requirement. Determine whether mats/cots will be stored within structures (i.e., inside climbers) or whether to allocate a storage closet/cabinet specifically for them. For each stack of 10–15 cots, add an additional 8 square feet of closet space. Also provide space for staff personal belongings (8–10 square feet of closet space for coats and other personal effects) in each group room.

Bulk consumables (tissues, toilet paper, hand towels, etc.), bulk art supplies, and curriculum materials that will be shared centerwide (books, toys, audiovisual and electronic equipment) need to be accessible to all pertinent staff. These might best be kept in closets fitted with shelving or in cabinets in or near central support facilities, such as staff lounges, teacher preparation areas, resource and conference rooms, or common spaces used by clusters (Chapter 19).

Oversized Equipment

Do not forget about storage for the buggies and carriages used to transport infants and toddlers. When deciding where to place storage for these items, remember that children who are not yet walking will need to be carried to the buggies and that corridors, doors, and rooms will need to be large enough to accommodate these vehicles. The average buggy-for-six is 30″ wide x 7′ long x 39″ high (including handle). (See Chapter 16). Some possible storage solutions for these items include special closets near group rooms, under staircases, or in an outdoor shed or lean-to. Also provide some storage for car seats that one parent may leave for the other parent to pick up.

Seasonal Storage

Allot space for storing supplies that are used only once or a few times a year (holiday decorations, etc.), extra furniture, and extra equipment. Some possibilities are a basement or attic, a shed, a large walk-in closet.

Food Supplies

Bulk food supply storage may be placed in or adjacent to the kitchen. Storage for bulk snack foods (juice and crackers, for example) might best be placed close to the group rooms.

Administrative Storage Needs

Provide for the center's administrative storage needs as well. Student files need to be kept for up to five years. Secretaries, bookkeepers, specialists, and directors will need storage for bulk supplies used in center operation (stationery, brochures, fax/computer/copy paper, etc.), as well as for personal items.

Outdoor Storage

Don't neglect outdoor storage needs (Chapter 20). Provide play yard sheds for storing tricycles, bicycles, and wagons and a multitude of loose parts. Plan to store large and small items in separate locations to reduce the possibility of accidents resulting from large equipment hampering access to smaller items (Chapter 20). Also plan for sheds, lean-tos, or closets accessible from the outside of the building for storing tools and equipment needed for garden and yard maintenance.

More details on storage considerations appear in Chapters 14 (cabinet sizes and materials), 15–18 (group-room storage needs), 19 (staff and maintenance needs), and 20 (outdoor storage).

Table 4.8 *Common Storage Needs of Most Centers*

Type of Item	Examples	Storage Requirements	Preferred Type of Storage
Curriculum materials used on a part-time or rotating basis in group rooms	Manipulations, puzzles, books, games	Immediately accessible but out of children's reach	High (above 4′) shelves; closets; cabinets
Consumables used in group rooms	Paint, paper, clay, paste; juice and crackers	One week's supply	Closets; cabinets; shelves
Mats/cots		Immediately accessible in group rooms for naps	*Inside other structures or multiple-use storage units*: climbers, lofts, cabinets, closets. *Solo storage*: own closet or cabinet
Children's belongings	Coats, boots, blankets, etc.	Immediately accessible in group room	Cubbies (see Chapter 15)
Indoor large-muscle equipment	Balls, rocky boats, mats	Accessible to both group rooms and the gross motor room	Closets; cabinets
Bulk supplies for center	Paint, paper, scrounged material, beautiful junk	Easily accessible to all adults who need them	Closets; cabinets
Shared curriculum materials; audiovisual and electronic equipment	Books, toys, projectors, TVs and VCRs, computers, stereos, cameras, tape recorders	Accessible to entire center or to subgroups or clusters	Closets; cabinets
Buggies, carriages		Accessible without carrying children long distances	In a special closet near group rooms; under stair cases; in an outdoor shed or lean-to
Seasonal Supplies	Decorations (Christmas tree stands, lights; menorahs; props for holidays and festivals	Access by staff needed only occasionally	Basement; attic; large closet; shed
Extra furniture and equipment	Tables, chairs, dramatic play props, computers	Access by staff needed only occasionally	Basement; attic; large closet; shed
Kitchen supplies	Bulk food; paper and other necessities	Easily accessible to cook	Pantry
Outdoor equipment for children	*Large*: tricycles, bicycles, wagons, minitrampolines *Small*: balls, ropes, pails and shovels, large hollow blocks and boards, children's gardening tools	Easy access by staff, and sometimes by children, without having to transport equipment long distances	Outdoor shed
Equipment/tools for outdoor maintenance	Mowers, leaf blowers, snowblowers, wheelbarrows, rakes, shovels, hand tools	Accessible to maintenance staff from outside of building	Shed or lean-to; closet that opens to building exterior

BOX 4.1

Environmental Considerations in Site Selection

Avoid sites that are exposed to, adjacent to, or contain:

- Industrial dust emissions or fumes; exhaust from furnaces, incinerators, food-processing or waste-handling operations; or any potentially toxic source
- Concentrated automotive fumes
- Wind-carried pollutants
- Toxic substances such as asbestos, lead paint, radioactivity, radon
- Disruptively high noise levels from traffic, airports, or manufacturing facilities
- Major long-term construction projects
- Electromagnetic radiation from high voltage transformers, etc.
- Toxic vegetation
- Open pools, cesspools, wells, exposed ledges and cliffs

Be certain that:

- The soil has sufficient bearing capacity (engineering evaluation)
- There is no floodplain "up stream" surface water run off
- There is sufficient top soil for landscaping
- The water comes from a safe source. Be aware of what chemicals are added to it and how readily filters remove undesirable pollutants
- No concealed hazards lie beneath the soil from previous use—old gasoline storage, fertilizer dumps, etc.—that might migrate to the surface

Preliminary Site Considerations

In addition to all that has been discussed concerning center composition; site, building, group, and room sizes; and plumbing and storage, there are factors related to the site that the design team will want to keep in mind as it starts out. For example:

- Zoning requirements (for setbacks, buffer zones, pedestrian, and vehicular access)
- Climatic influences of sun and wind paths
- Natural features (slopes, trees, rocks, wet areas)
- Off-site impacts (access points, sources of noise, pollution, shade, views, and utility locations)
- Proximities (positive and negative)
- Site size and potential for expansion

Some of these factors, as well as others, are discussed in greater detail below.

Health and Safety

For an extensive treatment of health and safety issues that this guide cannot possibly cover, readers are referred to the excellent *Caring for Our Children: Health and Safety Guidelines*, published jointly by the American Public Health Association and the American Academy of Pediatrics.[12]

Potential sites need first to be evaluated in terms of their impact on children's health. Obviously, child care centers should be located away from flagrant dangers such as heavily used arterial streets, railroads, waste treatment plants, and hazardous machinery. But increasing evidence indicates that our health is affected by many "unseen" forces—the quality of the air, water, earth, and electromagnetic fields in the surrounding environment. No longer can the purity of these elements be taken for granted. Growing children are far more susceptible to the deleterious effects of pollutants than are adults. (See Chapter 8.)

Environmental Considerations

Fundamental issues of environmental health and safety need to be evaluated at the very beginning of the site-selection process. Unless mitigation is possible, failure to meet any of the guidelines in Box 4.1 should probably disqualify a site, before consideration of other issues.

Another aspect of health, not normally considered, reverses these concerns by asking how the child care center impacts the environment. The center has an ecological responsibility to the community at large. Analyses should project operation, maintenance, and replacement costs over a 25-year period so that materials and energy systems selected are less costly in the long run and more conservative of resources. Plan so that the center's electricity, plumbing, heating/cooling, and waste disposal systems do not pollute the air, use excessive power, or damage fragile ecosystems. (See Chapter 8.)

Safety Concerns

Order and cleanliness are essential for health and safety and communicate messages of professionalism and responsibility to prospective users. Where possible, determine that buildings, sidewalks, and streets near a center are clean and well maintained. Dead-end industrial parks or areas strewn with refuse make a site inappropriate and difficult to protect from crime and vandalism. Positive proximities would include schools, libraries, interesting workplaces, museums, parks, artists' studios, small shops, gardens and nurseries, streams, ponds, woods, as well as hospitals, fire stations, and other emergency resources. These provide varied learning opportunities, abundant contact with nature, and a sense of safety and security.

Ascertain that access to and from the building can be controllable by staff or other observers. Crime and vandalism tend to be reduced in spaces that have natural surveillance—i.e., occupation during the day and evening by those who normally observe activities in the area. See Box 4.2 for general safety and health guidelines.

Ground-Floor Location at Grade

Unless a building code exception is obtained, most states require all infant and toddler spaces, and usually preschool spaces as well, to be located at ground level—i.e., on the first floor (or under very special circumstances a basement area) which exits directly outdoors. This ensures the fastest evacuation possible in case of fire or other emergencies. Some states even require direct egress to the outdoors from all infant and toddler sleep rooms. Carefully check local codes and ordinances in the preliminary planning stage to ensure that any building under consideration meets all building-level requirements, or can be affordably modified for compliance.

BOX 4.2

Overall Health and Safety Concerns in Site Selection

- Clean and well-maintained environs
- Controllable access and easy surveillance
- Clearly defined territory and jurisdiction
- Positive, safe proximities
- Access to nearby hospitals, fire stations, and emergency resources
- Requisite number of fire exits from each group room (if a renovation)
- Access to all major public utilities—gas, electricity, water, sewers, garbage disposal, etc.

Proximities

Zoning, local ordinances, and community acceptance affect where centers can be located. Areas zoned as industrial may violate health and safety considerations. Residential neighborhoods are often fearful of the amount of traffic, parking requirements, and overall noise a center may generate. Areas zoned commercial may be more receptive but quite expensive.

There are several considerations as to desirable proximities:

Near Home

Most parents prefer centers close to home. Parents are often reluctant to take their children to unfamiliar locations, which also heighten a child's anxiety and sense of separation from the family. Being able to walk to the center provides children with direct experience about their neighborhood. The walk between home and center can be an integral part of children's child care experience and their concrete learning about their world. It is also something pleasurable for parent and child to share. Children who arrive at a center by bus or car have a less detailed understanding of the center's relationship to their home and of neighborhood features en route. These children require a certain amount of "down time" to turn off the intensity of the highway and to switch to a more tranquil pace.

At the Workplace

The location of centers is shifting to the workplace as businesses are increasingly providing child care for their employees. At these centers, Mom or Dad can drop in to feed an infant, exchange hugs, have lunch, or simply share a few moments with their children throughout the day. The trip to and from work extends the limited hours parents and children have together. Worksite-related centers are less effective if they are not within walking distance of the parent's work station and if management does not support break periods for parents to see their children.

For Socioeconomic Integration

A center can be located between neighborhoods that are typically segregated from one another. Children thus benefit from playmates of different socioeconomic, ethnic, and racial backgrounds.

Near Civic Resources

A center can be located near valuable community resources—nature areas, museums, artisans—that may expand the center's learning opportunities.

In an Ideal Setting

It is also possible for the team to focus its search on a setting that matches its ideals for children. Perhaps this is a rural area replete with woods, streams, and natural features. When all parties understand the developmental value of a site, they are often willing to make necessary accommodations in order for children to be there.

Natural Features

The natural features and varied topography of a site are as critical to its selection as square footage and other locational criteria. Children thrive on rich experiences outdoors and are entitled to spend as much time outside as they do inside. Trees, gardens, animals, water, and views provide many physically and emotionally healing benefits, in addition to enhancing a child's knowledge of the natural world. Indeed, if we are to save this planet, exposing children to the wonders of nature at a very young age is essential. (See Chapters 2 and 20.)

Vegetation on a site affects its sun/shade balance and wind patterns, just as plants help purify the air and provide acoustic barriers to noise from roadways and other sources. The quality of the land around a center, and the building's connection to the outdoors, cannot be overemphasized as a criterion of site selection. Yet even in urban settings, where natural features are limited, it is always possible to improve existing conditions and the indoor/outdoor relationship between the building and its land. Chapter 5 suggests ways to do this.

Space for Outdoor Play

Outdoor play is richest when there is no distinction between the site's natural features and the "playground" where children climb, run, slide, and swing. The original playscape, after all, consisted of fields and woods, routes and shops, just beyond home. Still, for purposes of licensing and safety, especially in urban areas, it is necessary to build an enclosed play yard of vegetation and man-made equipment.

Ideally, each group room will connect to an outdoor play yard, at grade, which includes a 10–15-foot deep covered porch next to the building (Figure 4.10; see also Chapter 5). If a potential site in an urban area has insufficient space for immediately accessible play yards, serious consideration needs to be given to locating the center elsewhere. Sites that require a long walk to the play yard result in children getting outside less often. Although nearby parks may be a necessary substitute, transporting groups of young children outdoors, particularly infants and toddlers, is exhausting and potentially hazardous.

Relationship with the Community

In determining a center's location and estimating its size, consider both the ways in which the community can benefit the center, and vice versa.

How the Community Can Benefit the Center

No center is an island unto itself. Young children need nurturance but they also need exposure to the rich fabric of the adult world.

Neighborhood Resources. Growing up involves becoming familiar with adult life and with the wealth of activities that take place in communities. The poten-

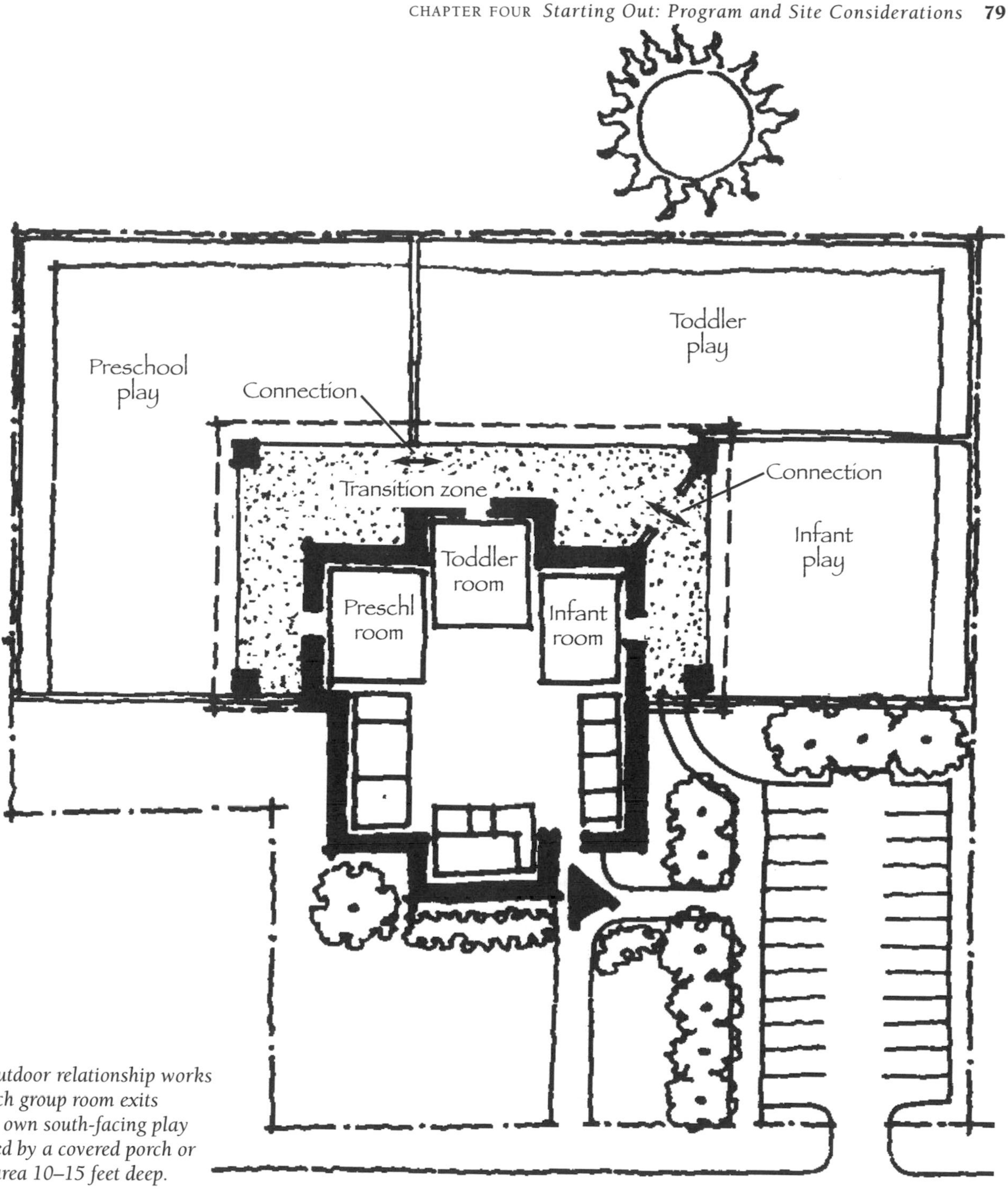

Figure 4.10
The indoor/outdoor relationship works best when each group room exits directly to its own south-facing play yard, mediated by a covered porch or transitional area 10–15 feet deep.

tial for children to learn from community resources such as museums, libraries, and workplaces is enormous. Furthermore, neighborhood resources that are reasonably accessible to groups of small children and involve visible human activities—the grocer, the baker, the shoemaker, the printer—actually add a sense of life and activity to the environs.

Child Care Network. Consider ways in which a child care center can both benefit from and contribute to other child care facilities in a given area. Such coordination can be:

- A valuable means of sharing information and educational materials

- A link for in-service training
- A way to access other resource personnel such as social workers, nurses, and psychologists

Civic Benefactors. Corporations, office complexes, government agencies, and large organizations are sometimes willing to free up a portion of their own real estate for on-site child care. Locating a center within these larger facilities can be beneficial in reducing both the initial capital investment and ongoing costs. Such "encapsulation" of a center presents a major design challenge, yet it is increasingly the reality for many urban programs. See Chapter 5, Centers Located within a Larger Building, for guidelines concerning such potential sites.

How the Center Can Benefit the Community

The word community has as its roots the words "common" and "unity." Communities exist for the common good, to bring together and unify individuals and parts. Child care can make positive social and educational contributions to an area, giving agencies, individuals, nuclear families, and single parents more cohesion and connection to human and material resources. When choosing a place to locate a center, a question for the design team is: How can the presence of our center enrich the quality of community life in this place?

The ways in which a center can benefit a community are limited only by the imagination and a site with sufficient square footage to support such ideas. Never underestimate the ability of a child care center, when conceived as a community facility that gathers diverse resources under one or related roofs, to effect enormous change in the quality of people's lives!

For example, some centers are now providing dinner meals that parents can purchase at the end of the day, dry cleaning services, a swimming pool, coffee and pastries in the morning for parents on the run, and meeting room space for use during nonoperational hours. Such centrality saves travel time and energy, serves as a link in the neighborhood, and encourages the participation of all—especially fathers. Additional services might include:

- A small health care service—perhaps an infirmary
- Senior citizen day care activities and meal services
- Social service and mental health offices
- community center activities including crafts, library, meeting rooms
- Community service programs such as continuing education, literacy classes, and vocational training
- A teacher resource center, including a library, workshop space, and observation facilities for local teachers, family day care providers, educational organizations, parents
- A parent resource center of books, toys, resource materials, workshop space, and personnel addressing parenting issues
- A mini children's museum or petting zoo for community visits after hours
- Spaces for birthday parties on the weekends
- Spaces for activities such as photography, gymnastics, nature study, theater, and physical education that are partly used by the center and partly available for after-school activities on an income-producing basis

Some centers place child care and day care for seniors side-by-side, so seniors and children can easily interact with one another. Such sharing of facilities is not only beneficial to both ends of the generational spectrum, but also often results in a savings in capital investment and ongoing maintenance. The convenience of having different resources in a single place is a boon to busy, road-weary parents, those with disabilities, and the elderly, and brings vitality to a geographical area. Ascertain, however, that the affiliated programs are compatible (in terms of size, noise, safety, etc.) with the needs of young children.

New Construction versus Renovation

The decision to erect a new building versus renovating an existing facility will depend upon a number of interrelated factors unique to the individual circumstance. The availability of a building suitable for renovation is one of them. The availability of land, its cost, and the cost of new construction are others.

Because child care has historically had an affinity for adapted places, it may be assumed that renovation is easy and a way to keep costs down. However, child care centers are an extremely complex building type. Renovation can be costly, sometimes in ways that are not readily apparent, and may not cost less than new construction. Older buildings often need to be upgraded for users with disabilities, fire exits, appropriate means of egress by children, adequate distribution of plumbing, good circulation patterns, the right size spaces and desirable adjacencies, visual and physical access to the outdoors, new fire codes and sprinkler systems, lighting, aesthetics, and outdoor play space—in ways that may be difficult and costly. If there are other occupants in the building, noise, density, and incompatible activities can add further soundproofing and circulation redesign costs.

Where renovation is an option, it is best to meet early on with local building inspectors to discuss what changes would be required to bring the building and site up to code. The list may include items such as those in Box 4.3.

For existing sites, the allocations in Tables 4.1, 4.2 and 4.3 can be used to determine how space might be apportioned to accommodate the intended groups. A site which appears acceptable from other standpoints may turn out to have rooms that cannot be adjusted for the planned groupings. If the program has to be modified in too many ways to make a good fit, probably other sites should be considered.

BOX 4.3

Typical Conversions Required to Bring a Facility up to Code

- Removal of lead paint, asbestos, noxious substances, etc., from the building and surrounding soil
- Installation of sprinkler systems
- Installation of a commercial kitchen
- Installation of extensive plumbing required for child care
- Installation of soundproofing to improve acoustical quality
- Installation of windows to bring natural light into group rooms
- Installations for users with disabilities
- The addition of parking, paving, and walkways

From the Child's Perspective

For child care centers, as for residential and commercial real estate, "location is everything." Whether the choice is to renovate space in an existing structure or to erect a new building, location will affect the center's appeal, the quality of the child's environment, and the availability of outdoor and community resources.

A center's location indelibly imprints images, memories, and feelings of place in each child's mind and body—impressions that will affect his or her development profoundly. Before a team sets out to consider sites, it may want to get in touch, once more, with the child's perspective.

Similar to the "childhood places" visualization exercise in Chapter 2 (Box 2.1), allow yourself to connect with your young child self again and envison yourself attending the most wonderful children's setting imaginable. *What would it be like?* Ask yourself these questions:

- How would you travel to it from your home?
- What would you experience approaching the building?
- How might the front door appear?
- What colors, sounds, and textures would you like to encounter outside and then inside?
- What would you find there that was special for you?
- Where would you eat, sleep, go to the bathroom, sing, dance, and play?
- What would you most want to do outside?

Do not set your mind to figuring out how these spaces might feel, or to looking only at what is "possible." Just sit quietly, with your eyes closed, asking your young heart what it most desires . . . and watch as the images appear.

In the scramble to find available, affordable space, design teams often forget that these mental images are as real and important as the criteria they will be considering in the weeks to come. Not to be written off as "impossible ideals," such images are sequences of experience which, in their own way, tell the team what matters to children. Remember: Action follows thought. To the degree that the team values its images and gives them weight in its search, it will find space that comes closer to having the qualities that matter most. The team may even decide to change its assumptions about where to look in the first place. Chapter 5 examines in greater detail some of the considerations discussed here. It is recommended that the team read it before making final site decisions.

Notes

[1]L. Katz, D. Evangelou, and J. A. Hartman, *The Case for Mixed-Age Grouping in Early Education* (Washington, D.C.: NAEYC), 1990.

R. Theilheimer, "Something for Everyone: Benefits of Mixed-Age Grouping for Children, Parents, and Teachers," *Young Children* (July 1993): 82–87.

[2]C. Alexander et al., *A Pattern Language* (New York: Oxford University Press, 1977), 618–621.

[3]E. Prescott and T. G. David, *Concept Paper on the Effects of the Physical Environment on Day Care.* (Pasadena, CA: Pacific Oaks College, 1976). Concept paper prepared for the US Department of Health, Education and Welfare, Office of Child Development.

[4]R. Ruopp et al., *Children at the Center: Final Report of the National Day Care Study*. (Cambridge, MA: Abt Associates, 1979).

[5]Karen Stephens, "Small is Beautiful—Advantages of a Small Center," *Exchange* (January 1995): 15–19.

[6]Jay Hollmann (personal communication) offers the following comparison of 35 square feet/child to the average child's room at home, which is about 120–140 square feet. Assuming a bed, dresser, and desk take up 30–40 square feet, the remaining floor space—for play that is usually not "active"—is 90–100 square feet.

[7]Prescott and David, *Effects of the Physical Environment on Day Care.*

[8]Gary T. Moore, "Determining Overall Space Needs in Campus Child Care Centers," *Campus Child Care News*, (January 1996).

[9]"Cost, Quality and Outcomes Study Research Team," *Cost, Quality, and Child Outcomes in Child Care Centers,* (University of Colorado at Denver, Denver, CO, 1995).

[10]Adapted from Louis Torelli, "Comparison of Four Sets of Standards of Group Size, Adult:Child Ratio, and Staff Qualifications,": Spaces for Children, Berkeley, CA.

[11]ADA refers to requirements of the "Americans With Disabilities Act," a federal civil rights law.

[12]Available for approximately $50 from: American Public Health Association, Publication Sales, Department 5037, Washington, D.C. 20061-5037, Tel: 202/789-5636, ISBN 0-87553-205-5, 450 pages.

CHAPTER FIVE

ELEMENTS OF BUILDING AND SITE DESIGN

. . . the public building is not an abstract symbol, but partakes in daily life, which it relates to what is timeless and common.

—Christian Norberg-Shulz

Because a building cannot really be separated from the land or community around it, the "building-in-its-neighborhood" constitutes the potential child care place. This chapter looks at design qualities that are desirable for a new building and its environs, as well as at ways to assess and/or improve the potential of an existing building and site. *It assumes that any prospective site first addresses the square footage issues and the health and safety mandates listed in Chapter 4 and is in alignment with the qualities of spirit of place discussed in Chapter 2.* Chapter 6 then looks at ways to lay out a center once the site and/or building have been chosen.

The issues related to building and site design explored here are:

- The child care setting's image
- Visibility and access
- Parking
- Approach and entry
- Interior circulation
- Relationship between indoors and outdoors
- Centers located within a larger building
- Campus plans

A brief discussion of each issue is followed by some key questions for the design team to answer, and then by guidelines that develop pertinent aspects more fully. References made to "the building" concern both the plans for buildings being designed from scratch and existing buildings being evaluated for renovation.

The Child Care Setting's Image

Some buildings and settings have high imagability, readily evoking a mental picture. Others are fairly nondescript. Generally, the more memorable the image, the richer the spirit of place. Rather than the building *per se* proclaiming its existence, ideally it is the entire child care setting—landscaping, play yards, fences, signage, setbacks and structure—that creates a memorable impression and nourishes the senses.

The goal is to create a setting that says "This is a place for children." Design teams usually claim this message is important, but it frequently becomes a low priority in the face of other demands such as finding available space. Wall murals and gigantic stuffed animals added later are superficial touches that do not make up for what a building and site fail to communicate. In considering a prospective location, a new design, or an existing structure, the question that needs to be asked is: Do this building and site create a safe and nurturing setting that beckons children inside and assures parents that the center is offering quality care?

Whether a building and its site convey messages of child-appropriateness and security depends upon:

- The compatibility of building and landscape
- The scale of the building, the site, and the windows
- The building materials
- The shape and height of the roof
- The building's edges

. . . a setting that beckons children inside.

Compatibility of Building and Landscape

A greater sense of place and invitation exist where the child care building is compatible with the natural terrain and the architecture of the surrounding neighborhood. Ideally, the building will be positioned to take maximum advantage of existing site resources and amenities and to create favorable microclimates for outdoor play. In rural areas, buildings need to honor, not offend, the surrounding terrain; a wild site definitely calls for an unobtrusive structure.

Modern urban buildings rarely relate to anything around them; as a result, their spirit of place can be quite weak. The absence of visible sky and long-range views, the use of rigid horizontal and vertical planes, and the coldness of steel and glass, account in part for the tension and entrapment people can feel in urban areas. Where little can be done to transform the exterior of a nondescript urban site, the building's interior will need to be especially harmonious and welcoming.

IMAGE GUIDELINES: COMPATIBILITY AND SCALE

What image and spirit of place does the design team wish the center to convey? What are the messages, images, and impressions conveyed by any building and land under consideration? Is the building's design compatible with the natural terrain and the architecture of the surrounding community? What is communicated by the building's size? What shapes and forms predominate (hard and rigid versus undulating and soft)? How much sky is visible? What are the nearby views and vistas?

Compatibility with Neighborhood and Site

- Evaluate the positive and negative features of neighborhoods within a half-mile or some reasonable radius around the site. Pay particular attention to the quality of air and sound, the presence of pleasing and foul odors, the views, the average moisture and humidity. Assess whether these features would contribute a positive, memorable sense of place to the center.
- Strive to design or select a building whose form and relationship to the site enhance the existing spirit of place.

Scale

Scale refers to size—height, width, and volume—of the overall site, of the building(s), and of the building's parts (windows, doors, columns, roof, stairs) relative to some standard of human measurement. Adult-scale is different from child-scale. A building's scale is part of its "personality" and an aspect of expressing its appropriateness for children.

At least two levels of scale are familiar to most of us: institutional and residential. Centers in high-rise buildings usually feel more institutional than those in houses. In the absence of precise guidelines, where possible it is best to err on the side of "small is beautiful," to honor the fact that children's small size limits

A center at residential scale.

Consider locating the building on the site's least desirable parts, in order to leave its most beautiful areas intact for pathways, play yards, and experiences in nature.

- In siting and constructing or renovating a building, adapt construction methods and machinery to keep most healthy trees intact.
- Shape the volume of the building and the volume of space around it at the same time. Wherever possible, physically and visually extend the building's design into the outdoor space in a way that enhances the land's natural features.
- Include design features that will assure parents the center is safe and offers quality care.

Building Scale

- A residential scale, as reflected in the size and height of the building; the size and length of the approach paths; the size and height of the roof, front door, and windows; the amount of uninterrupted wall surface; and the presence of porches, overhangs, etc., makes a center clearly recognizable as a facility for children. At the same time, the setting needs to convey an image of professionalism and competence.

their ability to interpret large spaces, interact with large numbers of strangers, or understand complex areas and large building elements.

The Building's Materials

Keeping the building within human scale extends also to its exterior and interior materials. Materials which can be applied by hand—brick, stone, clapboards, stucco, adobe, small panes of glass—express a human scale that is not present where cranes and machines are required to position steel girders or slabs of concrete.

Human scale refers to the size of elements relative to various aspects of the human body: body height, eye-level height, walking distance, length and width of the human hand (graspability), and length of the human arm (reachability). The weight of an object as compared to our own weight or strength is also a factor of scale.

Tree-trunk columns that can be walked around and pebbles that can be held, reduce a building's scale at its entry. (The Copper House)

Artistic details applied by hand express a human scale.

. . . materials that invite a child's touch.

Most of us intuitively "measure" our surroundings in relation to these anthropometric dimensions.

For a young child, dimensional differences as small as one-half to one inch can make a dramatic difference! As a result, adult scale often appears large to a child—one reason why places from our childhood are remembered as being so much bigger than they appear years later. Since materials at or below eye level catch our attention first, especially children's attention, a building's scale can be reduced both outside and in by applying architectural and artistic details and embellishments at eye level—a lower roof line or windows; friezes, recesses, etchings, reliefs, and sculptural effects—to suggest that human hands have shaped the structure and are welcome in it.

The Roof

A building's roof line affects its image and can be a dramatic architectural feature. Low, visible, sloping roofs, with dormers and chimneys, play a primal role in our lives and in providing feelings of shelter and security —qualities highly appropriate for a child care center. The invisible roofs on tall urban buildings fail to convey their ability to shelter. A building's perceived size is also affected by the proportion of roof to wall.

Soft Edges

The image and perceived scale of a building is also affected by the way in which its edges relate to the ground. Unlike urban skyscrapers that rise straight up out of the ground with dead space around them, friendly buildings often have soft edges. Those nestled

Varied roof lines reduce the scale and increase the friendliness of large buildings. (The Copper House)

IMAGE GUIDELINES: BUILDING MATERIALS

What are the messages/impressions conveyed by the materials used in this existing building? Alternatively, what messages does the design team wish to convey with materials chosen for a new building?

- Aim to use materials on the building's exterior and interior that are human-scale, ideally even child-scale. Materials that can be laid by hand (wood, glass, masonry), grasped, reached, walked around, and embraced are preferable to materials applied in expansive sheets.
- Where appropriate, use warm materials—wood, brick, stucco, adobe, and rammed earth (rather than metal and concrete)—on the building exterior. Natural materials—which give children roots and connections to the source of substances in their world—are preferable to synthetic ones.
- Use soft, warm materials on the interior. Wall surfaces of glazed brick or concrete block, while cheap and easy to maintain, have a decidedly institutional image and poor acoustic qualities (see Chapter 13, Finishes).
- Varying textures can help alter the flatness and apparent scale of some materials.
- Use easy-to-clean, nonabrasive materials that invite a child's touch. Avoid toxic, flammable, sharp-edged, or otherwise hazardous materials.

IMAGE GUIDELINES: THE ROOF

What spirit of place is conveyed by the existing building's roof, or what image does the design team wish the roof of a new building to convey?

- Where possible, design the building's roof to feel sheltering and protective. Make some edges almost touchable, especially at the entry.
- A sense of intimacy can be lent to large buildings by lowering the roof edges at least over the entry to the building, or the center's entrance.
- Flat roofs can become roof gardens with places to sit and to play. For such uses, be certain the roof has proper strength and drainage, is sheltered from sun and wind, and protected with fencing or walls to keep children safe. Secure any fire exits off a roof from unsupervised use by children.
- In geographical locations where flat or differently shaped roofs are typical (adobe dwellings in the Southwest), the local style is apt to feel the most homelike.
- Roof lines that indicate a hierarchy of functional spaces make a building feel more interpretable and usually more friendly.

Buildings with soft edges feel more approachable and more "rooted" in the ground where they are placed.

into hillsides, or sheltered by berms, appear intimate and integrated with their surroundings. The earth comes up to the building's edge, hiding it a bit and making it impossible to know where the building ends and the earth begins. Such a structure feels "rooted" in the ground around it.

A building's perceived size can also be softened and reduced by placing benches, trellises, trees, bushes, and earth berms of varied shapes and heights next to it to balance its dimensions, or by creating places where people can contact and use the building's exterior (see Relationship Between Indoors and Outdoors: Courtyards and Sitting Gardens).

Buildings are diminished and magnified according to the nearby foliage and the season—appearing smaller when surrounded by fully-leafed trees and appearing larger and bare in fall and winter when leafless trees expose more of their "skin." Whether the trees on a site are deciduous or evergreen will affect how the building appears at different times of the year.

IMAGE GUIDELINES: SOFTENING THE BUILDING'S EDGES

How do we plan to treat the "edges" of the building, existing or to be designed? Could they benefit from some "softening"?

- Construct paths, terraces, and steps at the edge of the building, making the boundary between earth and structure ambiguous. Ascending to enter is more "monumental," descending to enter is more "intimate."
- A building whose base is wider than its top feels more "rooted" in the earth. Shaping the building's edge with earth mounds, ground plants, climbing plants, benches, and places where people can sit and gather will also help to soften it.
- Well-thought-out indentations or extrusions of a building's perimeter (i.e., not just "bumps") make its exterior more interesting, less monolithic, and provide places for people to stop, sit, and enjoy a view. They will also provide light on two sides of some rooms (see Chapter 10, Light).
- Use some forms with softness and curvature, not only sharp angles, hard edges, and flat planes.

Visibility and Access

High visibility makes a center's existence known, assists first-time and infrequent visitors, and facilitates protection of the buildings and grounds. This is especially true in urban areas. Sight lines from parking areas, access roads, and footpaths need to be oriented so that the center's main entrance is always clearly in view.

Various techniques, illustrated in Figure 5.1, for shaping the building's entry can make it more visible. Concave entrances are always more receptive and inviting than convex ones.

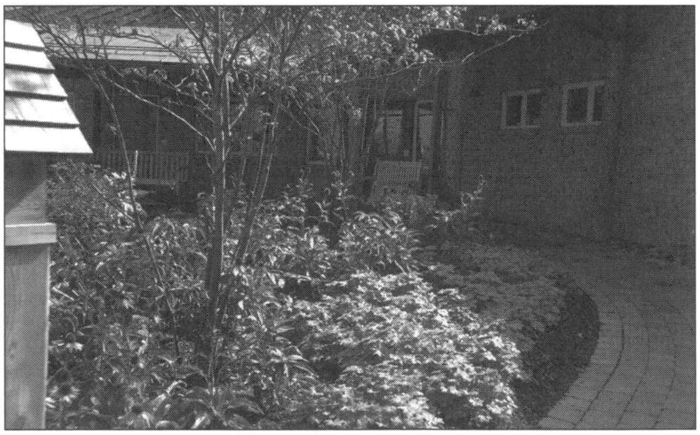

Soft, curved forms mute demarcations between earth and structure. (The Copper House)

GUIDELINES FOR VISIBILITY AND ACCESS:

How appropriate is any prospective site for the degree of visibility we require or desire for the center? What accommodations may be needed to provide screening and privacy? What are the pros and cons of accessibility to this site? Can both pedestrians and vehicles be accommodated safely?

Visibility

- Where appropriate, site the center so that it is visible to, but not adversely affected by, passing traffic and pedestrians.
- Increase a center's visibility by locating it near recognized landmarks—statues, the town hall, well-known routes and stores—provided these enhance the sense of place.
- Emphasize the entry by a change in building form, such as an extrusion or indentation set prominently at a 45-degree angle to the line of approach. Or introduce a curving wall.
- Signs placed at right angles to the building (and near the curb if the building is set back), often help motorists and pedestrians locate the center.
- Plan to provide notice boards, signs, and interesting features outside the center that encourage pedestrians to stop and find out more about its activities.
- Temper visibility with protection (low fences, setbacks, driveways, recessed windows), so the center does not draw unwanted attention or invite inappropriate visitors.

Access

- Centers located near, but not directly on, major traffic arteries, and bus stops within one-half to one block of the main entrance are easily accessed.
- Strive to design approach routes from parking areas or bus stops that do not require parents and children to cross major traffic arteries or, ideally, any streets within one block of the center.
- Negotiate bus stops and routes with local transit authorities if these can be made more convenient and integral to the approach sequence.
- On the center's site, separate pedestrians from vehicles, so no one on foot has to cross turnarounds or driveways used for curbside drop-offs in order to reach the front door. (Figure 5.2 on the next page).
- Ensure that the center's main entrance is always in view from a reasonable distance along footpaths from the parking area or adjacent streets.
- Provide the shortest route possible, that is safe and pleasant, from parking and bus stops. Walking parents will be carrying a great deal of paraphernalia and children.
- A sheltered walkway leading directly from parking to the building may be appropriate in some climates.

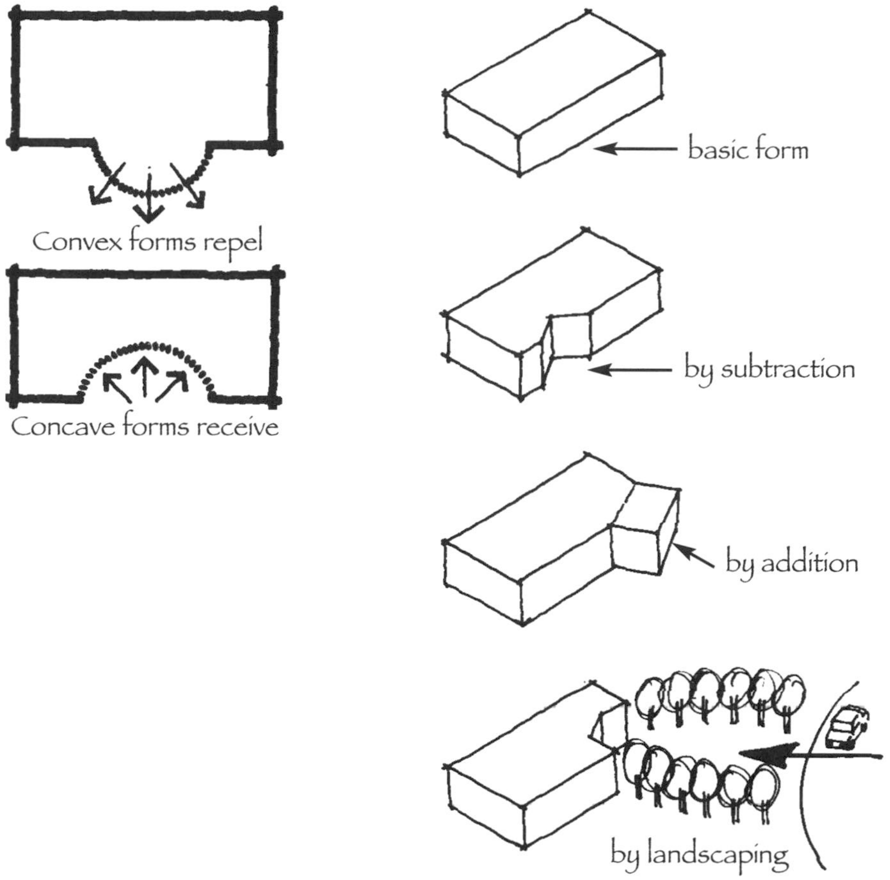

Figure 5.1
Design the building's main entrance to be visible, welcoming, and memorable.

Centers are easiest to access when they are within walking distance of public transportation and major traffic arteries. But nearby highways and traffic must not make the site unsafe or noisy (see Chapter 9, Sound). Also try not to allow parking areas, access roads, and pavement to dominate the site. Footpaths must separate pedestrians from vehicles, provide the shortest, most protected route possible—especially in inclement weather—and keep the center's entry always in view.

Parking

Child care centers need parking for parents and visitors, staff, and service and delivery personnel. The location of the facility—urban, suburban, or rural—and the availability of public transportation, affect the type and amount of parking needed and/or possible. (See Chapter 4 for square footage recommendations.)

The appearance of the parking area, and the experience of getting from the car to the building, affect people's impressions of the center and its image as being a place for children and families. Large, shopping-mall-type parking areas create a cold, impersonal feeling, suggesting that cars are more important than people or the natural terrain. Instead, try to preserve as many natural features on the site as possible and use landscaping to accent natural contours, break up space, reduce the scale of the parking lot, and de-emphasize the presence of automobiles (see Figure 5.2). Parking areas under and around trees, shrubs, and earth mounds covered with plants provide shade, reduce heat buildup in cars, and create natural barriers that direct visitors toward their destination. Underground parking—so that unpaved land can be preserved—although more formal and expensive to build than surface parking, is sometimes a desirable alternative to surrounding a building with asphalt.

In addition to aesthetics, parking facilities also need to have driveways and pathways that are clearly marked, well-surfaced or paved, and lit at night to make them accessible and safe during all kinds of weather. Parents usually carry a lot of materials—food, clothing, carriages, and one or more children—that they need to get into the building easily.

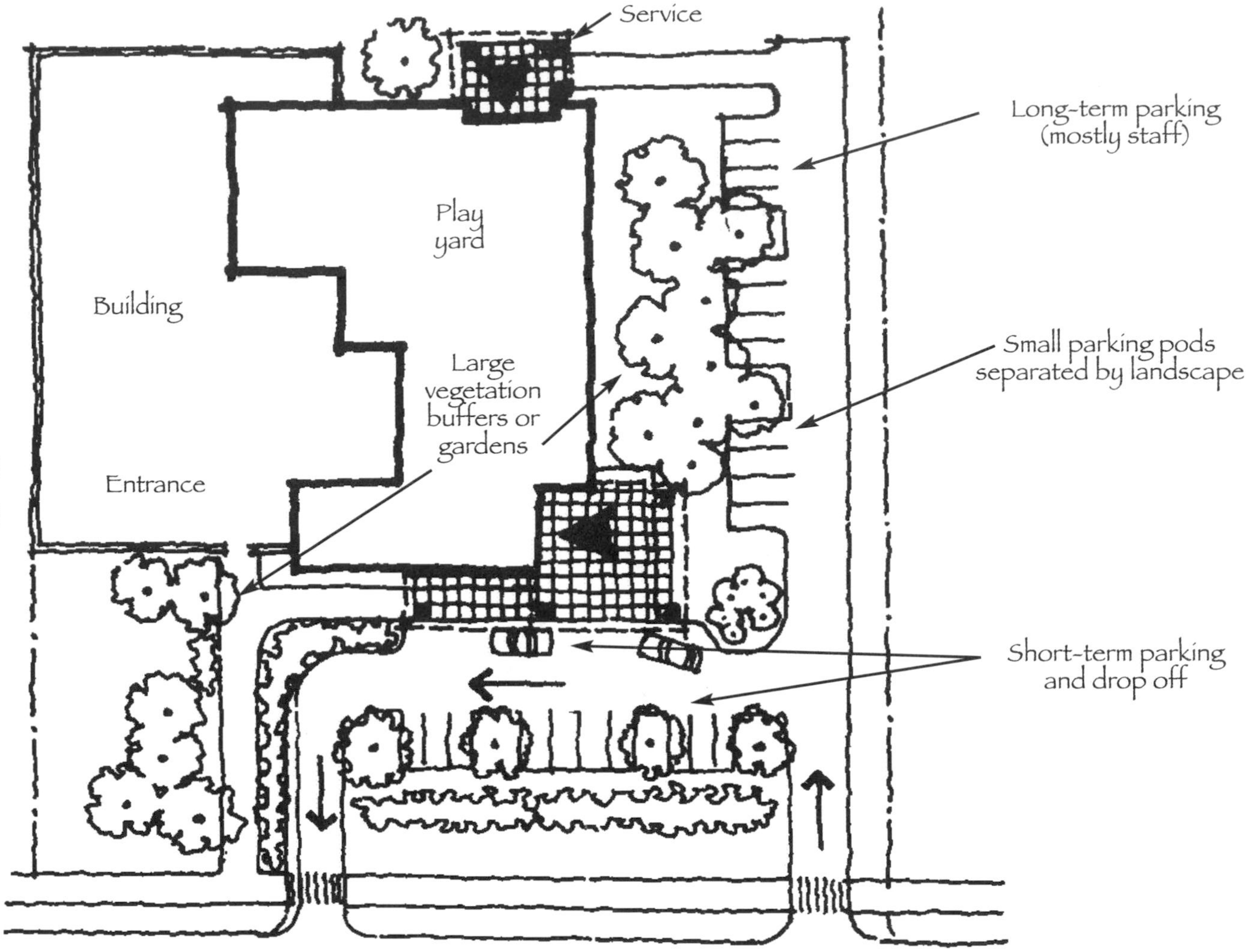

Figure 5.2
Ensure safe pedestrian access to the building along sheltered walkways. Distinguish long-term from short-term parking. Use landscaping to break up large parking areas and visually shield cars.

Providing both long-term and short-term parking options encourages parents to linger at drop-off and pickup times so they can observe what is going on, talk with staff and other parents, or play with children. However, to prevent bottlenecks outside, vehicle circulation needs to be well organized. Some parking for staff close to the building is also desirable, for times when they bring many things to work.

Service/delivery areas must be physically separated from children's outdoor play areas, pedestrian walkways and, ideally, from visitor parking. They are best located close to the center's kitchen for easy drop-off of supplies, and will require controlled access to the interior (lock, buzzer/voice system).

Approach And Entry

A child's acceptance of a new environment is deeply influenced by the aesthetic quality of its approach paths and entry. Impressions are formed by sensorial experiences all along the way and especially by the ease of finding the front door. A pleasant approach enhances everyone's anticipation of what they will find inside the building and ensures that the center's entrance is visible from a reasonable distance away so that people can orient their movements in relation to it and not have to change direction unexpectedly.

GUIDELINES FOR PARKING

What messages are conveyed by any new parking areas and paths being designed, or by existing parking areas and pathways to the building?

General

- Four types of clearly designated parking are required: (1) short-term parking for parents, (2) long-term parking for parents/visitors, (3) long-term parking for staff, and (4) parking for service or emergency vehicles.
- Locate most parking as close to the building's main entrance as possible, with the entrance clearly in view.
- Where residential scale permits, provide small, shielded lots of five to seven cars surrounded by garden walls, hedges, slopes, trees, and fences. Ideally, cars can be blocked from view without compromising access and safety.
- Consider spacing parking lots, used for different purposes, 100 feet apart, and making them almost invisible from beyond the site.
- Locate parking and service areas away from pedestrians and play areas for safety, so children are not tempted to see parking areas as play spaces.
- Install high-quality lighting for both the parking area and approach paths.
- Single-lane drives require a 12-foot width, two-way double lanes a 20-foot width.

Parent/Visitor Parking

- Site parking for parents and visitors near the building and afford a view of the entrance.
- Provide long-term parking for about 1 out of 20 parents.
- Provide drop-off and short-term parking for an average of 1 out of every 10 parents—as close to the entrance as possible—so parents can spend 10–15 minutes in the building at the start and end of each day. Keep this separate from any tenant parking and from interfering with cars going to the long-term parking area.
- Circular turnarounds (for one-way traffic moving in a counterclockwise direction so passengers are closest to the curb), and long or large covered entryways (porte cocheres), tend to increase the formality of a building. For some work sites or large centers they may be vital; for small buildings they may be inappropriate or unnecessary.

Staff Parking

- Parking for the center's director needs to be near the building to expedite emergency access.
- If necessary, staff parking can be somewhat remote from the building. Both on- and off-street parking are possibilities, depending on local regulations. Be sure to have a one-to-one parking/staff ratio for the number of staff present at any one time or during the largest shift/crossover period. Also provide some parking near the building for staff carrying equipment and materials.

Service/Delivery Parking

- Situate service/delivery parking close to the appropriate service entrance. Make use of physical barriers—ideally the same natural screening techniques described for other parking areas—to separate any outdoor children's areas and pedestrian walkways from service drives, dumpsters, and maintenance-related equipment. The service drive can also be depressed to give children a clue that the area is "off limits."
- Ensure that access to the building's interior from the service entry is under administrative control.

Approach Paths

When designing circulation paths to get people from the street or parking area to the building, strive to make them *memorable* and to have them provide an *experience of transition*. Circulation paths that are long and nondescript—like many highways—make the journey monotonous and foster the impression that one is not welcome. On the other hand, paths like back country road—rich with pleasurable sights and impressions—make the journey memorable and as important as the goal. Passing under a honeysuckle-bedecked trellis and sitting momentarily on a swing can transform an ordinary trip to the center into something special. Children instinctively take time "to smell the flowers" if given an opportunity to do so.

Sensitively designed pathways are the design team's first real opportunity to say, "This is a place for children." Welcoming messages can be communicated through landscaping: for example, paths with gentle curves and changes in view that widen or narrow, pass under overhanging trees, are darker or more sunlit, have flowers and bushes nearby, and provide places to stop or vary the pace. Passing through a gate, archway, or trellis is especially powerful in marking a point of transition between the outer world and the center's territory and giving definition to the area truly under the center's jurisdiction. As "gateways to experience,"

Paths that serve as thresholds to experience make the journey memorable.

opening a gate to pass beyond it into a new place has considerable subliminal impact on our impressions of that place.

Elements such as these create *transition zones* or *thresholds* that foster a shift in our inner state along the way. The path itself need not be long. Indeed, it is possible to pass under a trellis, over a bridge (with or without water), and down a curved walkway in just a few feet. In fact, the shorter the route, the more it requires variations in plant material, arches, and gates to create a sense of entry transition.

In designing a kindergarten for children who would be driven to school during rush-hour traffic, Welsh architect Christopher Day purposefully placed parking a short distance from the building. Children then walk through a little wooded glen, over a stream, round a bend, and through a latched gate before entering the enclosed sunlit brick courtyard leading to the school's front door. Each feature, he felt, helped to calm and center children for the more focused activities inside the building.

Alexander et al. powerfully describe the transition sequence that they feel should occur as one approaches a building's entry:

> Buildings . . . with a graceful transition between the street and the inside are more tranquil than those which open directly off the street...Therefore, make a transition space [that exists as an actual physical place] between the street and the front door. Bring the path which connects street and entrance through this transition space, and mark it with a change of light, a change of sound, a change of direction, a change of surface, a change of level, perhaps by gateways which make a change of enclosure, and above all with a change in view...It is the physical changes—above all, the change of view—which create the psychological transition in your mind.[1]

An entry courtyard contained between an exterior door/gate and a second door that opens into the interior of the building is ideal (Figure 5.3). If this is not possible, at least consider curving the entry path, giving it a change in texture, adding a trellis or gate posts, and planting flowers and bushes alongside it.

APPROACH AND ENTRY GUIDELINES: TRANSITIONS AND PATHS

How can we make the experience of approaching the center a memorable and pleasurable journey, however brief? What primary messages does the approach convey, and how might they be improved to be more child-friendly?

- Does the entry sequence have, or can it be designed to provide various "thresholds" along the way: changes in light, sound, direction, surfacing, gates, a transition space, and especially changes in view?
- Strive to create a tranquil, reassuring entry transition sequence that says: "This is a place for children." Consider including sculpture, decorated rocks, swings in trees, gliding swings on the path, sweet-smelling flowers and bushes, fountains, bridges, banners, footprints, as well as repeated lights, ornamental, or interactive devices. (See Figure 5.4 on

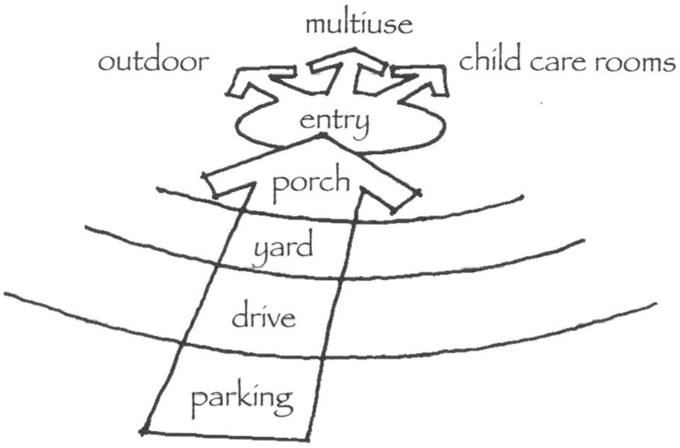

Figure 5.3
A memorable entry transition sequence includes: a trellis and gate; a short, curved approach path varying in width; seats; vegetation; children at play; a porch for lingering; and a welcoming front door.

the next page, and also page 96 for a plan illustrating how one center transformed its exterior approaches.)

- Even if paths undulate, ensure that the building's entrance is visible from both the parking lot and major walkways.
- Seeing children playing in a small yard at the front of the building adjacent to the approach paths helps those arriving feel more at ease.
- Employ a gate, archway, or arcade as a transition marker at the point where people enter the center's domain.
- The shorter the approach paths, the more they need to undulate and vary, to help people slow down and experience a greater sense of transition. If the path is long, provide intermittent seating and rest points, some of which offer protection from sun, wind, and rain.
- Vary the width of the pathways, providing occasional bulges that serve as intimate transitional goals or rest points: a tiny garden or grassy knoll, a bench to enjoy a view of nature.
- Where possible, route the path through natural features—a stream, wooded glen, field, or garden.
- Keep all walkways barrier-free for persons who are in wheelchairs, on crutches, or who have perceptual or mental disabilities.
- Make certain paths are well-lit at night, only pass through safe areas, and are shielded from dangerous activities, equipment, or environmental factors.
- Surface paths with materials that drain well and that prevent mud and erosion. Softer materials—brick, flagstone, wood chips, earth (if weather and drainage permit), and stamped, colored concrete—are warmer and more inviting than asphalt.

(continued)

Figure 5.4
Approach paths to this center were transformed by adding brick paving to replace asphalt; hand-carved benches; wood plank fencing; new shrubs and bamboo plants along the building's long side; an outdoor cafe; a small amphitheater and "performance area;" a shallow fountain; and an interactive musical wall, all leading to a wooden porch with glass roof and inlaid mosaic tile columns.

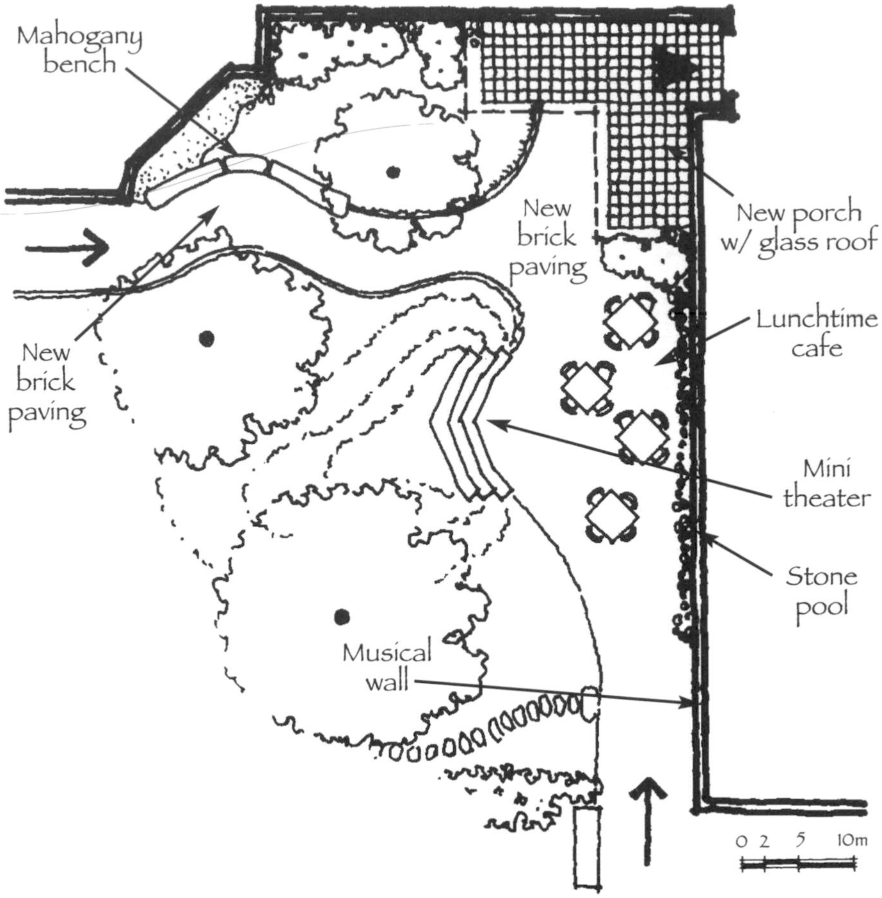

- Off the main circulation path, irregular paths of brick or flagstone, with grass and moss growing up around them, add an element of invitation.
- Use only nonpoisonous plants (children sometimes try to eat leaves or flowers), that are native to the area (ecologically appropriate), and not imposing or scary to small children.
- Ideally, make the entire approach visible from the inside so monitoring the entry is easy.
- Ensure that all paths meet ADA requirements for accessibility.

The Main Entrance: A Third Threshold

The approach paths from parking and streets provide one experience of transition to the building. A second significant transition zone occurs at the entry courtyard or, if there is no courtyard, then simply on the path immediately in front of the entry. The third transition occurs at the center's front door, where the

An irregular path off the beaten track lends intrigue.

threshold to the building itself should create a "feeling of arrival" helping people prepare inwardly to move inside from outdoors. Such a passage is rarely available in modern urban buildings that are entered abruptly from the street, without the benefit of extended roofs, porches, or vestibules that straddle the space between indoors and out, giving people places to pause and prepare for the experience of entering the building.

The location of a center's main entrance controls the building's entire design, including its overall layout and all movement to and from it. Even when the center is to be housed in an existing structure, take time to consider the appropriateness of the location where people will enter. The main entrance should be the only means of public access and egress from the building (although children and staff may enter or exit elsewhere), and lead directly to a staffed administration/ reception area where it can be easily monitored.

For new construction (sometimes even for renovated buildings), the location of the main entrance is best determined by walking the site, observing site lines and views, and imagining the entry at various locations. If a few members of the design team take time to explore the options, the best location usually becomes "obvious" to everyone. This method encourages people to use broad-based perception (see Chapter 2) to absorb information about diverse aspects of the site and the building simultaneously.

The main-entrance door can speak of home or institution, of enticement or intimidation, affecting the degree of clarity or mystery people experience when reaching their destination. Doors with character—distinctive windows, materials, colors, shape—that people can unlatch and pull open easily to step into the new space contribute to memorable entry-transition experiences. Windows in or beside the door, at two heights, will give children, as well as adults, a glimpse inside (Figure 5.5). For more on door design, see Chapter 10.

In many climates, an airlock may be necessary behind the front door. Optimally, this space will be designed as a vestibule—an aesthetically pleasing light-filled room, uncluttered by equipment, inspired perhaps by plants, seating, and appealing graphics. Then it serves as a place where people coming in out of the weather can get their bearings, perhaps sit for a while when waiting to be picked up, or meet others.

Figure 5.5
Front doors with sidebars of glass enable children as well as adults to preview the interior.

APPROACH AND ENTRY GUIDELINES: MAIN ENTRANCE

Will the center's main entrance be clearly visible as soon as the building comes into view? What design tactics and lighting are needed and desired to create a transition zone and mark the threshold around the center's entry? Will the door and entrance convey messages of welcome, security, and child-appropriateness?

Porches

- Strive to create a roof overhang, porch, or deck compatible with the building's design, which is itself a threshold and place to pause, protected from the elements, in front of the building's main door.
- A covered porch, with the homey feel of front porches earlier in the century, might have seating for two to three persons, a table and bench, rocking chairs, wide shelves for sitting and placing articles, a hanging- or glider-swing, sculpture, and potted plants. Include windows into the vestibule for children to glimpse the inside, and for staff to see who is entering at all times.
- Avoid large expanses of glass, which are reflective and disorienting and apt to make those inside feel on display.
- In following ADA requirements for accessibility at the entry and front door, avoid long ramps by eliminating steps or notable changes in elevation at the entry.

Vestibule

- A light-filled vestibule beyond the porch and front door gives people a place to pause once inside the building. (See the floor plan for the Copper House in Chapter 21.) It also serves as an air lock to control drafts of cold or hot air

A nondescript, hidden entry (top) was made distinctive and sheltering (bottom) by the addition of a glass-roofed wooden porch, with inlaid mosaic tile columns

which can be uncomfortable for receptionists and those without coats inside.

- Design the entry vestibule to provide clear sight-lines and direct access to a staffed administrative/reception area.
- Use washable flooring and built-in matting to absorb water, mud, and street dust in the vestibule or area closest to the door.

The Front Door

- Locate the front door in a favorable microclimate, not in the path of prevailing winds or overheated areas of the site.
- Choose a front door that is human-scaled and homelike, with distinctive aesthetic appeal (see Chapter 11).
- Enhance the experience of opening the door through the choice of a knob or lever that has a unique "feel," making the user aware of his motions, while meeting ADA requirements.
- Provide windows in the door or along side it, at adult and child height, so those entering can see into the interior.
- Entrances accessible to the public need to function as controlled filters between indoors and outside by being secure from unwanted interference and carefully monitored. A door bell, buzzer system, electronic card or pad system, or auto opener for those with disabilities will be required (see Chapter 11).

A small, but nonetheless welcoming lobby/reception space.

The Lobby and Reception Area

When we enter a building, our impressions of a place continue to build. Once through the front door, children are likely to have some or all of these questions on their minds:

What kind of a place is this? Is it safe?

Who will take care of me here?

Where am I supposed to go, and who will I play with?

Where can I . . . take off my snow suit and boots, get a drink of water, go to the bathroom?

Even if the site itself has many of the transition features discussed above, the center's lobby/reception area is the place, above all others, where the statement "This is a place for children" needs to be made. In a caring center, the lobby is neither bland nor formal but intimate in scale, like a living room, and filled with things to capture a child's interest: an aviary, a live tree, a rare creature in a terrarium, books and toys, something magical, perhaps other children at play. In some instances, the lobby may be the building's common area at the heart—located more or less near the building's center. The lobby need not be large but it must convey warmth and welcome.

A welcoming lobby always has a friendly face immediately visible and accessible to those entering, not a large "mega" counter. Each center needs to work out how to best fulfill this function: Will a full-time receptionist, secretary, bookkeeper, director, or other staff person be the one to welcome people and monitor the front door?

The lobby/reception area also serves as the point of security, orientation, and transition to other parts of the building. With concerns for children's safety on the rise, many centers are adding computerized check-in facilities and T.V. screens with videotaped views of children's rooms, in the lobby/reception area. These measures serve adult needs for efficiency and control but are not welcoming, nor are they reassuring to children. Strive, instead, to have the lobby/reception space create a friendly "living room" atmosphere in the main greeting area. Locate check-in and surveillance systems, as well as other supports, nearby or in alcoves.

APPROACH AND ENTRY GUIDELINES: LOBBY AND RECEPTION AREA

What qualities of place do we want the lobby/reception area to convey?

- The lobby and reception area needs to be a special place for children and families. Residential furnishings, textures, and decorations, along with things for children and adults to do are the best ways to communicate this message: seating, toys, interactives, plants, fish, and birds—all of which reflect the "aliveness" of the center itself. Objects behind glass, or large, immovable stuffed animals, are less convincing.

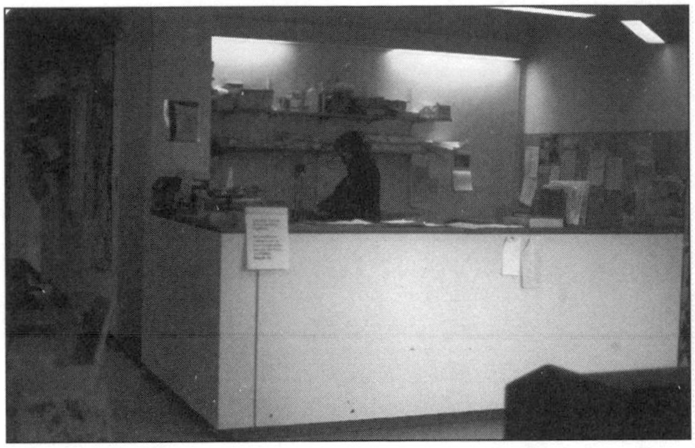

A tall, enclosed, and cluttered reception area (left) transformed with a low, free-form, inlaid mosaic tile desk, improved lighting, and better organization (right) into an artistic child's delight.

- Arrange seating in conversational groupings (L- or U-shaped) to encourage people to pause and linger. Comfortable seating and items of interest to adults in the lobby will create an informal meeting place for conversation and staff breaks and a pleasant place for visitors to wait to see the director, etc.
- Add magical elements to the lobby to make the center memorable in children's eyes.
- Ensure that a friendly face is always present to greet anyone entering the front door. Design teams can work out the most affordable way for each center to fulfill this essential function.
- If a reception "station" is required, try to use a low surface, rather than a formal desk or "mega" counter that feels institutional and forms a barrier between those entering and the person behind it. Children want to see the face of a seated receptionist. Placing the surface at an angle allows it to be approached from more than one side and also allows the person behind it to come forward to personally greet and assist visitors. The photos show how one center transformed its reception area.
- Use pools of light (see Chapter 10) to create a warm atmosphere and to highlight different zones (seating, play, reception) within the lobby/reception area. The reception area may need to be brighter than most.
- An area off to the side, but not in the lobby/reception space, can offer amenities such as telephones; water fountains; rest rooms; notice/bulletin boards; coffee and snacks; storage for coats, wheelchairs, carriages; and security systems.
- Visually and acoustically shield supplies, fax and copy machines, and other supports for the receptionist in nearby alcoves (see page 183).
- Include sufficient space for the passage of wheelchairs, carriages, carts, or other transport devices.
- In large centers where group rooms are some distance from the entry, consider providing carts or wagons adjacent to the reception area to assist parents in transporting children and personal effects through the building.

Interior Circulation

Circulation is a key organizer or armature of a building's design. Determining how people will move through the interior of a center is part of evaluating the appropriateness of its plan (whether the building is new or existing). Corridors and hallways are the most common forms of circulation, but also are the least informative and the most institutional. Movement through a building, like movement outdoors, is most satisfying when the journey gains value through memorable experiences along the way.

Way-finding: Architectural Cues versus Signage

Well-designed circulation realms enable people to orient themselves to the facility as a whole, regardless of their specific location. Having to ask directions is a clue that one is an outsider and that pathways and key areas are not organically arranged. Architectural cues such as landmarks, nodes, views, small niches, places to pause, and changes in the shape and size of pathways and lighting provide the best orientation; these can be supplemented by graphics, unique furniture, and activities. The use of signs to direct movement indicates that the building exceeds residential scale and that the architecture itself is insufficiently informative.

Length and Width of Circulation Realms

Interior circulation routes influence how occupants identify with the overall program and how individual program segments relate to one another. A center designed with the isolationist architecture of a hospital or corporate headquarters —with numerous doors off endless corridors—will have difficulty promoting cooperation among children's groups and staff, regardless of programmatic efforts to do so.

Wherever possible, corridors per se should be avoided, or made to feel more like hallways in homes or even like real rooms, with space for activity and interaction (Figure 5.6). A great deal of important communication and "business" occurs in circulation spaces—momentary conversations and passing remarks—especially when facilitated by gathering spaces that vary the pathway's width and shorten its length. The recommendations below, which should be examined in light of local building codes, can all assist in making transit zones appear wider, more pleasant, and informative. Chapter 6 also provides details on interior circulation.

Pleasant halls and corridors encourage communication and interaction during transit.

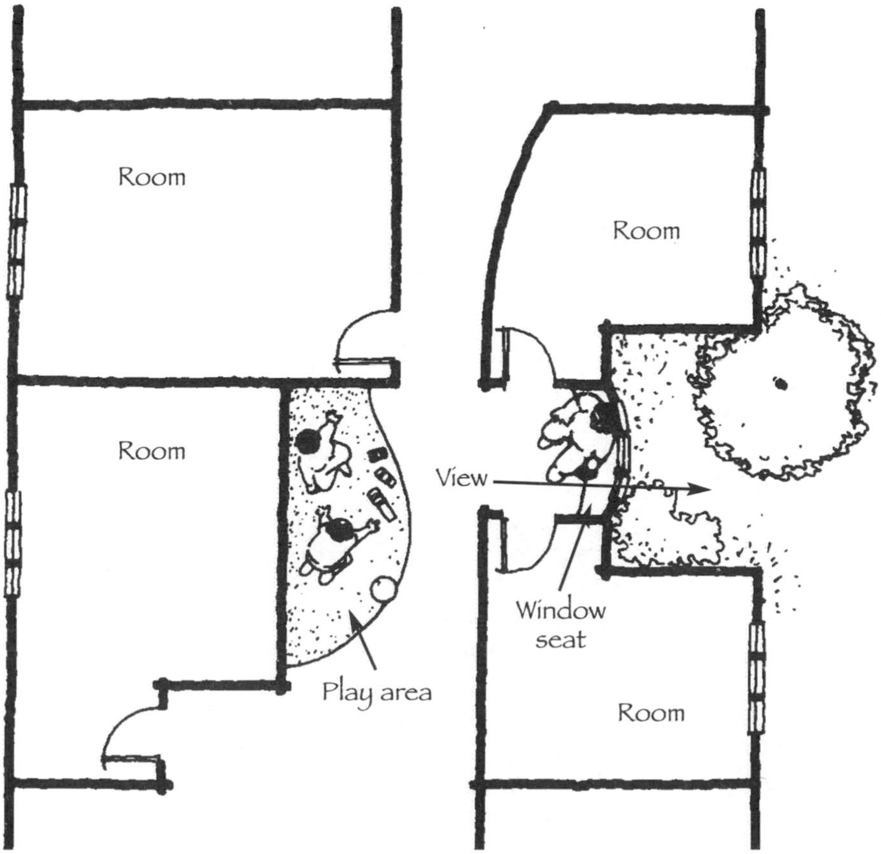

Figure 5.6
Corridors of varying widths, and angled entries, become interesting "rooms" for socializing, playing, and viewing the outdoors.

"Popping" adjacent rooms in or out varies the shape of corridors and rooms.

Lighting perpendicular to its length, carpet, wood-shuttered closet doors, and artwork transform a dark, narrow corridor into a pleasant place to be.

GUIDELINES FOR INTERIOR CIRCULATION

Is the building's design dominated by long, monotonous corridors with isolated rooms? If so, can the corridors be improved by varying their length and width?

- Because corridors are linked to public safety, local building codes must be honored. Explore with inspectors ways to provide amenities that do not jeopardize safety. Twelve-foot widths are sometimes required if furniture is to be part of a corridor.
- Plan to vary the width of corridors and to create areas for social contact (as well as to assist in orientation), especially in new construction. Making corridors generous in size and shape may require additional floor area but is well worth the price. Furniture, plants, play structures, or art objects in these areas can give them distinctiveness and beauty.
- Placing the doors to rooms at an angle, and giving them special lighting, creates entry alcoves that help widen a corridor and give the doors distinction. (See p. 127.)
- To vary the width of circulation realms in renovated buildings, consider "popping" the adjacent rooms in or out at strategic points along the route. This may also vary the rectilinear nature of the rooms themselves, introducing variety and semiprivate "niches."
- Install seating, carpeting, bookshelves, lighting, attractive furnishings, and art, and where possible views to the outdoors, to transform long, narrow, dimly lit corridors into gathering places for people.
- Interior windows or walls of glass that meet code requirements, and do not violate privacy, can break up and increase the feeling of spaciousness in hallways.
- Emphasize architectural and artistic cues rather than signs as keys to way-finding through the building.
- Angled corners rather than those at 90-degrees facilitate the flow of people, strollers, and carts.
- Lighting, banners, and signage (if necessary) placed perpendicular to a corridor's length can help to shorten even institutional-length corridors.

Signs hung perpendicular to a corridor's length, as shown here at Boston's Quincy Market, help shorten it and make destinations more visible.

Relationship Between Indoors and Outdoors

A critical feature in renovating or designing a child care facility is to enhance the relationship between inside and outside. This involves creating access from the center to outdoor play space so the outdoors can be 50% of the program, ideally year-round (as in Scandinavia), but especially during the good-weather months.

Sun/Shade, Wind, Water, and Plants

The first step in integrating indoors and outdoors is to evaluate the unique conditions of sun, wind, and drainage on the site and work with these natural elements, along with plant material and landscaping, to suitably shape the outdoor space. This involves identifying and/or creating possible microclimates on the site (Figure 5.7 on the next page). The guidelines that follow offer some key factors to keep in mind. For more information on light, see Chapter 10.

GUIDELINES FOR NATURAL ELEMENTS AND MICROCLIMATES

Where does the sun rise and set in relation to this site? What types of microclimates does the site offer or can we create?

- With new construction, in the northern hemisphere, orient the long axis of the building east-west so the most important rooms face south toward the sunlight. If play yards must be placed on the north side, step the building down on the northeast and northwest sides to minimize the amount of shade created by the building. Alternatively, place the play area beyond the shadow's deepest range.
- Locate outdoor play areas to capture sun most of the year and cool summer breezes, yet protect them sufficiently from winter winds and shade that they will be usable in any season.
- Locate trees, shrubs, earth forms, and building overhangs to give protection from the wind and rain. Windbreaks placed perpendicular to prevailing winds are most effective and can also help in keeping snow off walkways.
- Consider ways that patterns of sunlight can be used to create different moods. Partial or dappled shade is desirable provided it does not dominate the site.
- In northern climates, plant only deciduous trees on the building's south side to maximize sunlight in winter and make shade available in warmer weather. Plant evergreens on the north side to hold in the heat in winter.
- In southern climates, provide shade that makes it possible for children to be outside most of the day.
- Use plants and landscaping that make the progression of the seasons apparent—seasonal flowers, deciduous plants and trees, edible landscaping.

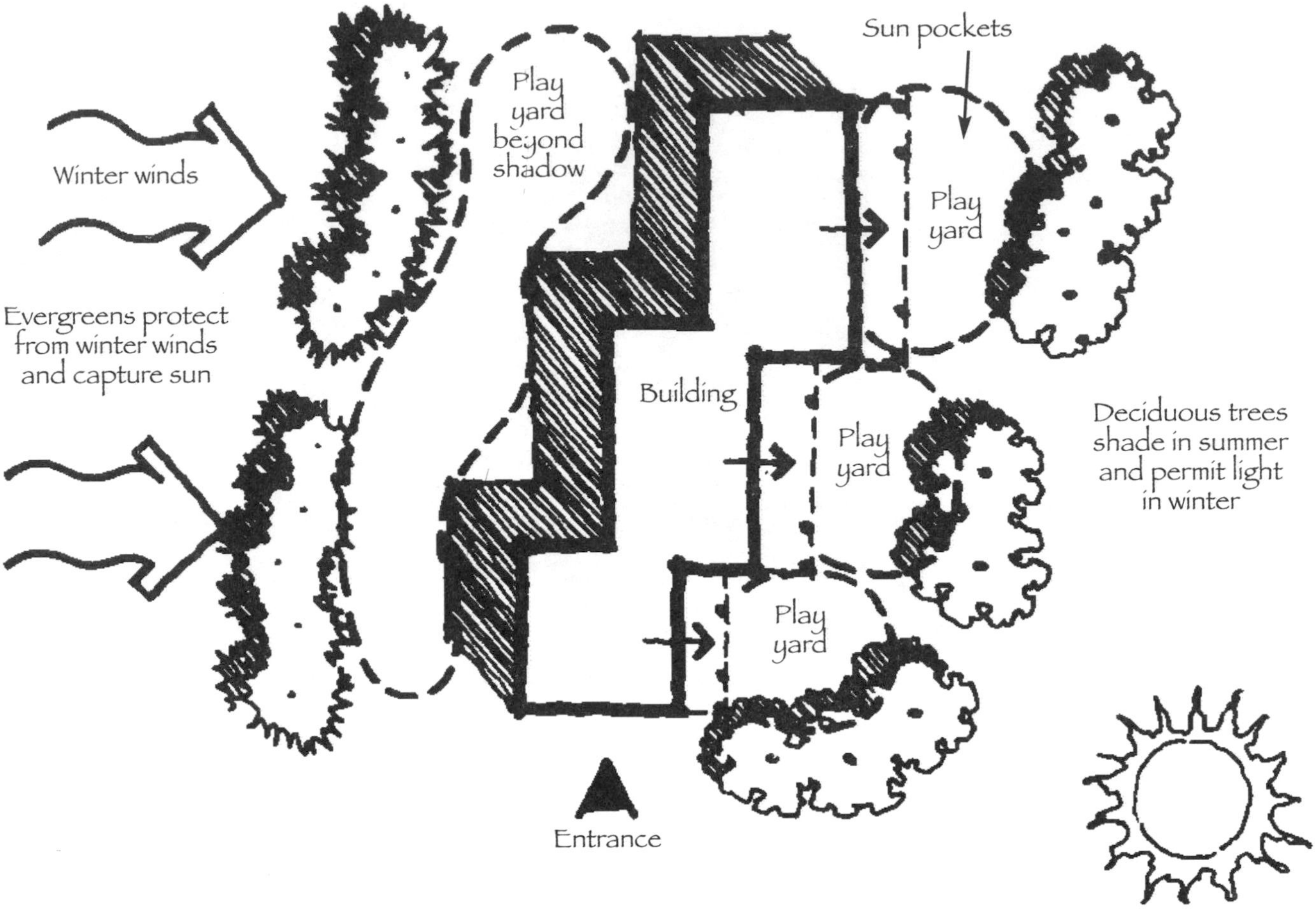

Figure 5.7
Favorable microclimates for outdoor areas include: play yards beyond shadows cast by the building or preferably south-facing; evergreens to protect from winter winds and absorb sound; deciduous trees to shade sunny areas in summer and permit sunlight in winter; earth berms, concrete walls, and trees to buffer traffic and noise.

- Most plants (trees, grass, shrubs), and vines on walls and trellises, can provide considerable cooling and also serve as acoustical buffers.
- Surfaces such as asphalt and concrete, which get hot easily, require shielding from direct midday sun during hot weather. The same is true of sand surfaces.
- All outdoor areas require good drainage to be usable year-round.
- Orient play equipment so children do not have to look directly into the sun.
- Enclose outdoor play spaces by using the building, berms, trees, hedges, fences, etc., as defining elements. These can serve as windbreaks on the side that faces prevailing winds.

Windows and Natural Light

The presence of natural light is more critical to a room's spirit of place than any other element of design. Windows with natural light are essential in every room that children occupy. Natural light connects the indoors and outdoors. (For a full treatment of natural light and windows, in designing a new or evaluating and improving upon an existing building, see Chapters 10 and 11.)

In urban settings, where access to natural light may be limited, consider moderately expensive approaches such as balconies, atria, window wells, lowered win-

Making the most of a transitional outdoor space.

dow sills, windows that can be opened, greenhouses, and clerestories, plus window boxes filled with evergreens in winter and geraniums in spring, to bring the outside in.

Moving Between Indoors and Outdoors

Children take great pleasure in eating lunch on a porch or in the yard, running spontaneously outside to experience a sudden shower or snowfall, or taking materials outside to play. For 50% of the program to occur outside, the building must link the indoors and the outdoors, ideally by giving each group room direct access to a play yard.

But the indoor/outdoor link is made even more powerful and useful when a south-facing porch, or at least a covered hard-surfaced outdoor transitional area, is located immediately outside between each group room and the play yard. It is here that messy activities can easily "spill" over to the outdoors, encouraging experimentation and relieving interior congestion. Lack of immediate access and appropriate outdoor surfaces invariably diminishes use of the outdoors. Because young children want to be able to see staff while they are at play, as much as they need to be seen and supervised by adults, views from the building, as well as access, should be unobstructed.

GUIDELINES FOR INDOOR/OUTDOOR MOVEMENT

Does the building provide a strong relationship between inside and outside? Can children move outdoors easily?

- Strive to create direct access from each group room to outdoor play yards. These same doors sometimes can serve as daily points of entry for parents and children. Otherwise, provide direct pathways from all major indoor child-activity areas to the outdoors.
- Locate a covered, hard-surfaced transitional area (wood, brick, concrete, asphalt) outside each group room, to be used for art, woodworking, science, water and sand play.
- A maximally effective transitional space is no less than 6 feet deep—ideally around 15 feet deep—and equally wide. It is partially covered or naturally shaded to provide some protection from the sun and bad weather. Overhangs of glass or clear plastic allow maximum penetration of natural light into adjacent children's rooms.
- Locate surfaces that dry most quickly closest to the building and entry. Slower-drying grass, earth, and sand should be further away.
- Inside/outside foot traffic can be facilitated through appropriate use of ramps rather than steps. Make all doors child-operable and accessible to those with disabilities.
- Consider installing cozy nooks—places from which to watch the world—both inside and outdoors.
- Awnings and canvas roofs provide flexibility in controlling the amount of heat or glare to the interior—as well as lovely sounds when the rain falls upon them. In some climates they can serve as the cover over the transitional area.

Recessing a portion of a porch into the building enhances the indoor/outdoor relationship.

Fabric "walls" of nylon, with clear plastic inserts, can shield and enclose a covered outdoor transitional space.

Porches, Decks, and Terraces

In addition to a paved outside area, decks, porches, patios, and terraces are relatively inexpensive ways to add space and provide locations for activities outdoors.

GUIDELINES FOR PORCHES, DECKS, AND TERRACES

- Use porches, extended eaves, trellises, covered decks (especially for babies) as outside extensions of group room space.
- Make porches, decks and terraces a minimum of 6 feet deep, ideally 10–15 feet deep.
- Recessing a portion of each porch or terrace space into the building, and giving it partial enclosure, further enhances the relationship between the indoors and outside.

Courtyards and Sitting Gardens

Where space and budget permit, courtyards and semi-enclosed sitting gardens can be delightful ways to provide an outdoor place for pausing, reflecting, and taking advantage of a site's natural features. These might be used primarily by adults—staff and parents—but also by children on supervised "outings." The addition of shrubs, hedges, stone walls, low wooden fences, residential materials, and flowering plants makes such areas feel intimate and welcoming.

To bring a courtyard alive, several specific features can be incorporated (see guidelines below). Sitting gardens also have their own, less stringent, requirements.[2]

GUIDELINES FOR COURTYARDS AND SITTING GARDENS

Courtyards

- Design the courtyard with a view out into some larger open space.
- Place the courtyard so that it has two or three entrances from the building, each connected by a path that requires people to pass through the courtyard (Figure 5.8).
- Provide overhead protection for a portion of the courtyard with a roofed area over at least one of the doors.
- Courtyards work well at the entry to buildings, outside staff areas, and as play yards for sets of group rooms organized around them.

Sitting Gardens

- Locate gardens and sitting areas for maximum exposure to sunlight, or, at least outside any band of shade between the building and the sun.
- Sitting gardens near the building work best if they are "half hidden," i.e., partly hidden from the street and partly exposed, so they are neither too public nor too private to feel comfortable.
- Create a hierarchy of outdoor space so that people look out from their seated location into a larger space (Figure 5.9). This makes a garden feel more intimate and interesting.
- Provide something to support the backs of those sitting (benches, rocks, trees, etc.), and have low seat heights for children.
- Consider having some plants in the garden be "edible landscape" and/or create places where children can grow flowers, fruits, and vegetables.
- Sitting gardens can be created as part of children's play yards, as a feature at the building's entry, along approach paths, and as nooks and recesses to soften a building's edge.

Centers Located within a Larger Building

When a child care center is housed within a larger structure, such as a high-rise office building, creating a positive and appropriate approach to the center is a design challenge. Large multistoried buildings present an overwhelming profusion of people and corridors even to adults!

A center in a larger structure needs to declare itself as "a place for children," just as a freestanding center

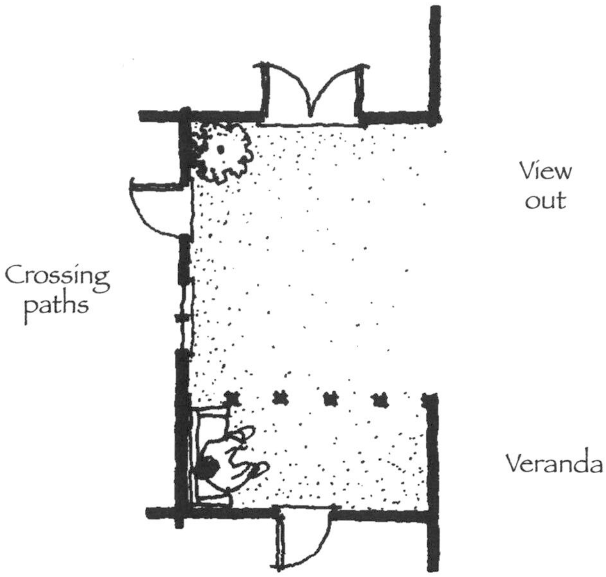

Figure 5.8
"Living" courtyards have two or three entrances from the building, encouraging people to cross them, and a roofed area over at least one of the doors.

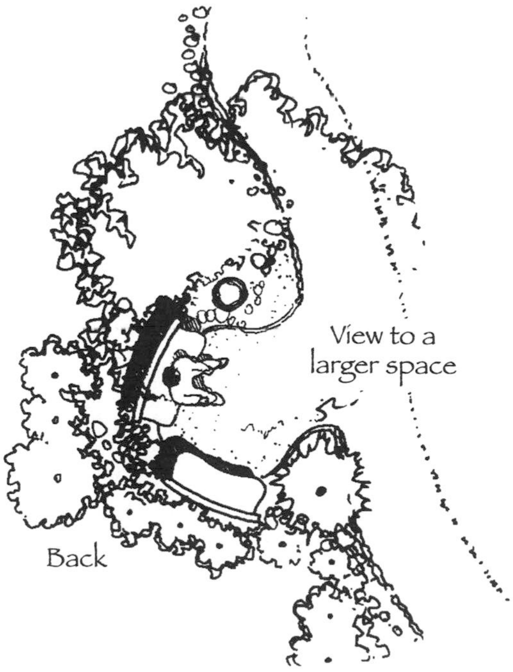

Figure 5.9
Intimate sitting gardens have seats with back protection, and a view outward into a larger space.

Wings of the building, a porch, and fencing (not shown) partially enclose a sitting garden at this center's entry. (The Copper House)

does. However, usually the larger agency and the center treat the exterior of the building and its public spaces as "untouchable," assuming the center begins at its own front door—often deep within the recesses of the larger structure. Because of the psychological and emotional importance of the transition from street to building, and from building to child care entry, strive to give the center its own unique identity somewhere at the building's exterior (Figure 5.10) and throughout the interior entry sequence. Important guidelines for evaluating a location's potential for housing a center, in addition to the issues already discussed, are listed below.

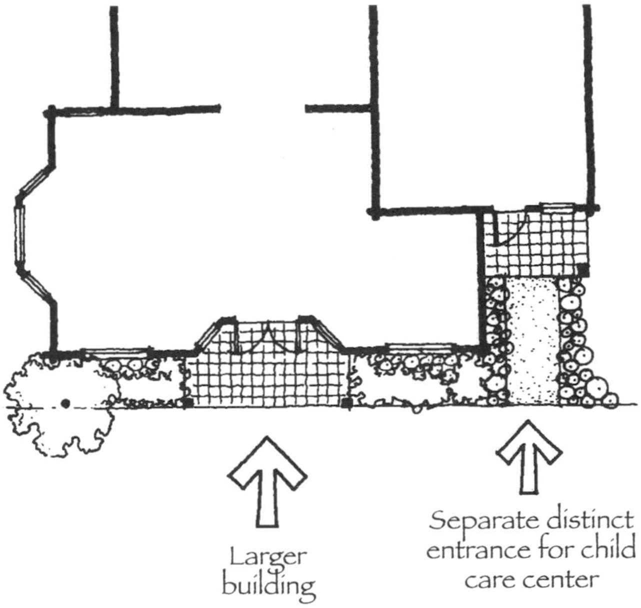

Figure 5.10
Centers housed in multiuse buildings need their own distinctive entrance at the building's exterior.

GUIDELINES FOR CENTERS IN LARGER BUILDINGS

- Determine whether child care is compatible with the activity levels, personnel, and functions that occur in the larger structure.
- House centers, preferably, in buildings less than four stories.
- Locate care for infants and toddlers, and ideally for preschoolers, on the first floor. Regulations in most states require this.
- Strive to provide the child care center with its own approach paths, driveway, and identifiable entrance visible from the street. Techniques that can assist in this task are:
  1. Placing a domestically scaled entrance with low roof lines at an angle to the building.
  2. Adding landscaped walkways, a profusion of natural features, signage, banners, or visible outdoor play yards.

  Use existing parking, drop-offs, paths, and sidewalk areas only where appropriate.
- Create any interior access to the center's entry along the shortest route possible that does not require circuitous paths through the larger building. Where this is not possi-

ble (government buildings, for example), aesthetically compatible, child-appropriate clues—logos, wall-mounted interactives or art, photographs, "footprints" on the floor—can be devised to guide families and staff to their destination.

- Ensure that there is sufficient outdoor play space with natural features.
- Determine whether it will be possible to establish acceptable access between indoor and outdoor activity spaces.
- Assess whether the center and its outdoor play areas can be separated physically from the rest of the building (for purposes of safety and control).

Modules or a Campus Plan?

As explained in the discussion of center size in Chapter 4, whenever a center serves more than 60–75 children, its program and administration are best organized into semi-autonomous buildings of preferably around 35–40 and no more than 60–75 children. This can be accomplished using one of these two approaches:

- A single structure containing separate modules, each with a distinct entrance
- A campus plan of separate but linked buildings

The second option—the campus plan—is the preferable of the two in climates where it is possible to move easily among buildings outdoors.

GUIDELINES FOR MODULES/CAMPUS PLANS

If the center is to accommodate more than 60 children, how do we intend to cluster the children into smaller groups of 35–40 ?

- When a single structure is divided into several parts (modules), provide separate, clearly marked doors to the individual modules. Varied roof lines, and differentiation of the building's facade, can also help to indicate the internal subdivisions (see page 87, earlier).
- When several structures are involved (campus plan), help people identify the main entrance by giving the buildings different roof heights to signal the hierarchy of functional spaces on the interior. Thus the main building would have the higher roof—the lower and more prominent slope at its entry—with the roofs of the other buildings descending around it (Figure 5.11).
- In a campus plan, landscape the residual land between buildings with pleasant sitting gardens and protected walkways to aesthetically and functionally tie the separate pieces of the center together and encourage people from different areas to linger. Arcades, trellised walks, bridges, shared gardens, hedges, fences, and other landscaping techniques can be used to link the parts to one another.
- Use soft edges between the buildings and the surrounding earth to create attractive places where people will want to gather.
- Take advantage of enclosures formed by indentations in the buildings' perimeters to encourage people to meet and interact.
- Make use of interior and exterior connections between the buildings. For example, all of the buildings might front on a common play yard or courtyard, in addition to having their own play areas, or their entrances might pass through a common main entry and administrative core.

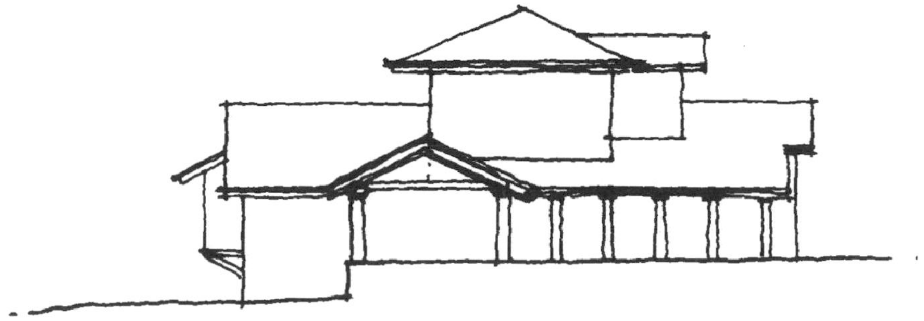

Figure 5.11
Give buildings of a campus plan a hierarchy of roof heights corresponding to the hierarchy of social spaces beneath them.

The Final Assessment

Having assessed the impact of location (Chapter 4), image, natural features, visibility and access, parking, approach and entry, interior circulation, and the relationship between indoors and outdoors, it is again time to step back and ask: ***Does this location, land, and building provide the spirit of place in which we want to raise our children?***

If the location, land, and building don't live up to the ideals the team has outlined, what changes are necessary to make them do so? What things cannot be changed? Are those constraints "tolerable" or does their negative impact on children suggest looking for another site? Where changes are possible, what are the monetary costs of making them versus the human costs of not making them?

Notes

[1]C. Alexander et al., *A Pattern Language* (New York: Oxford University Press, 1977), 549, 552.

[2]C. Alexander et al., *A Pattern Language,* 562–564 , 559–560.

CHAPTER SIX

LAYING OUT THE CENTER

The movement between rooms is
as important as the rooms themselves;
and its arrangement
has as much effect on
social interactions in the rooms
as the interiors of the rooms.

—CHRISTOPHER ALEXANDER

The next step for the design team is to begin schematic design—the process of roughly blocking out the building's interior spaces to fulfill the needs of the program. Parameters and questions to consider in overall center layout are discussed in this chapter.

Detailed considerations for the design of group rooms are then found in Chapters 7 and 15–18, while Chapter 19 discusses the accommodation of staff, parent, and community needs in depth.

However, a good building design does not result from working in this order. The process ideally resembles a spiral, one where you work at several levels of scale simultaneously. You may first want to create a rough outline of the building on the site. But then it is necessary to move forward to Chapters 7 and 15–18 and attempt to give specificity to the shape and contents of the group rooms. (Alternatively, you could begin by doing a schematic design for each of the group rooms and then address the building as a whole.)

After working on the rooms, you will need to return to and modify the overall building design, after which you will want to return and clarify details within the rooms, etc.

Because situations vary so widely, you are asked to be creative in following the basic directives of these chapters, which are offered as guidelines, not prescriptions.

The Schematic Design Process

Creating a good building layout is as much art as science. Laying out a building involves juggling all the guidelines presented in this guide, while simultaneously attempting to satisfy the stated and implied requirements of the program, the advantages and drawbacks of the site, and code, licensing, and other stipulations. This is no small challenge! Fortunately, it is what architects and designers are trained to do.

However, the process demands flexibility, openness, and a willingness to explore options. Layout schemes generated will attempt to optimize all or most of the design parameters specified in the program. Each scheme then needs to be evaluated in terms of its workability overall and at all levels of the building's operation. Usually, some compromises have to be struck between optimum and possible. It is in reaching these compromises that every team member's expertise counts, to ensure that relationships and factors essential to the success and functionality of the building and its components are not ignored or lost.

Alternative Site Utilization Concepts

Most schematic design begins with site analysis. Part of the process of laying out the center involves arriving at two or three alternative site utilization concepts showing various ways in which the building, while

BOX 6.1

Key Site Elements

- Sun and wind paths
- Attractive natural features (rocks, trees, water)
- Locations receiving maximum light (for infants/toddlers)
- Changes in topography and elevation
- Required setbacks, buffer zones, easements, and abutments
- Desirable and undesirable views
- Alternative vehicular and pedestrian entrances and paths
- Possibilities for parking
- Possibile locations for play yards
- Possible locations for the front door.

BOX 6.2

Possible Interior Center Spaces

Entry/Reception
Administrative Area:
  Director's Office
  Secretary's Office
  Bookkeeper's Office
  Social Service Office
  Storage for Files and Records
  First Aid Emergency Records & Supplies
Infant room(s)
Toddler room(s)
Preschool room(s)
Kindergarten room(s)
School-age room(s)
Water play room
Assembly/Multi-purpose Area(s) /Gross Motor Area
Storage of Indoor Equipment
Storage of Outdoor Equipment
Mechanical/Electrical Systems
Circulation paths
*Atelier
*Kitchen or Food Prep Area(s)
*Staff Area:
  Staff Lounge
  Staff Resource Area
  Staff Storage for Personal Belongings
  Staff Individual Work-stations and Files
  Staff Conference Area
Bathroom(s) for Staff and Adults
Toilets/sinks for children
*Parent Area
*Parent/Staff Conference Area
*Central Resource Area (A/V, curriculum prep, library)
*Laundry
*Observation (if required)
*Sick Bay
*Custodian's Space
*Community Based Activities
Separate Service Entrance
Adaptations for those with disabilities

** Discussed in Chapter 19*

meeting the requirements of the center's program, can be positioned on the site. Begin by placing a large site plan on a board and indicating on it the items listed in Box 6.1.

Identification of Desired Interior Spaces

Next, the desired interior spaces need to be identified. These may include, but are not limited to, the categories in Box 6.2. Reviewing this list of possible spaces offers the team a good opportunity to examine its implicit assumptions, to reflect upon the limitations of current models, and to explore alternatives that can breathe life and beauty into its program. A team may want to add to the list in Box 6.2 to suit its needs, or to revise its program to include more of these possibilities.

Spatial Organization

Once you have selected/modified your center's list of desired spaces, you are ready to begin laying out the center. This will probably involve working at two or three levels of scale simultaneously: laying out the building for ideal building/program relationships (adjacencies), using estimated room sizes to see how the building fits on the site, and laying out the rooms so their interior components have the right adjacencies (the subject of Chapter 7). As stated earlier, schematic design involves developing a loose form of adjacencies and relationships that is adjusted and refined as the interior spaces become more fully developed. After reading this chapter, you are encouraged to jump ahead to Chapters 7 and 14–19 to create schematics for

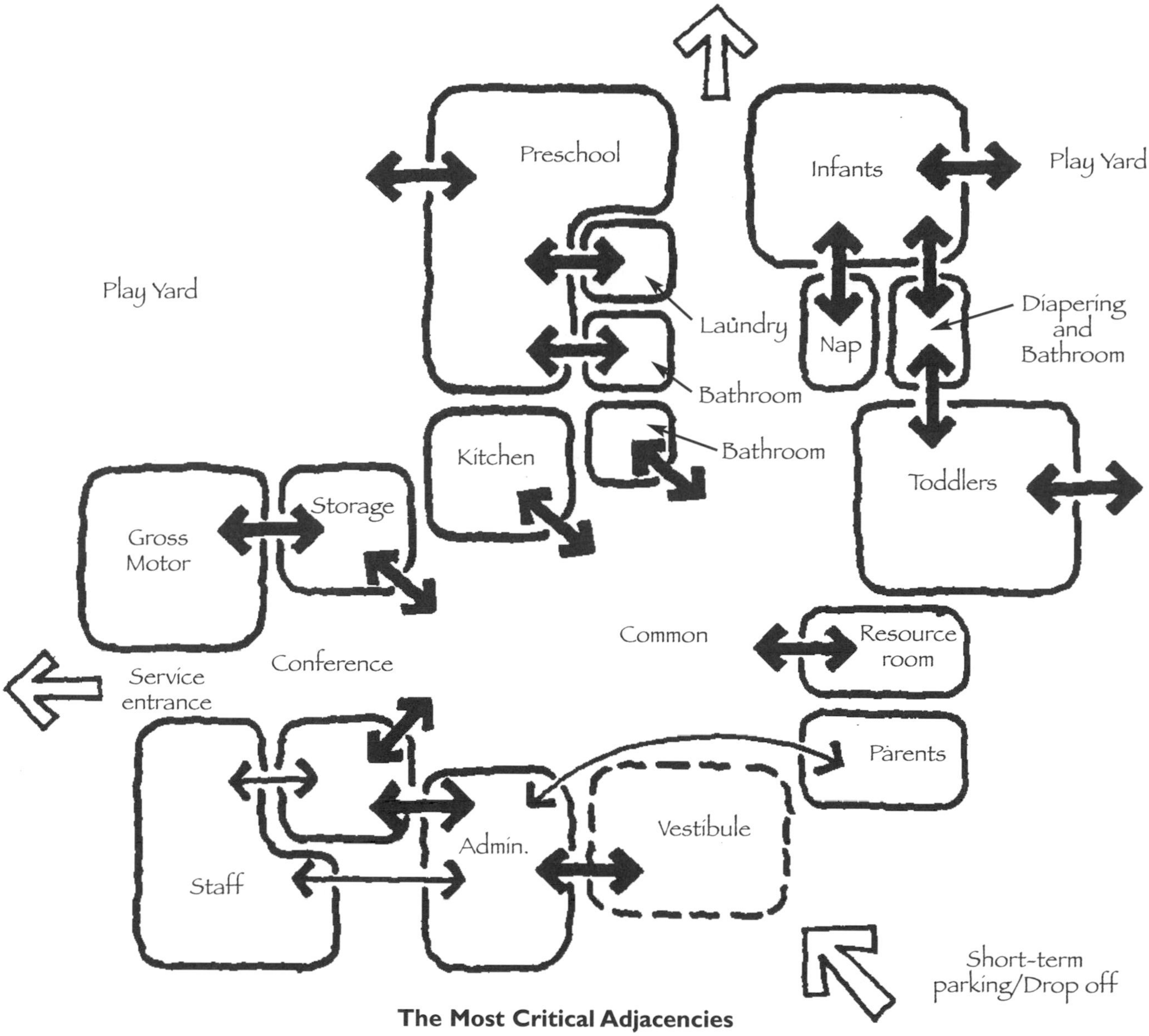

Figure 6.1
Some critical physical adjacencies of a center's plan.

the interior spaces, especially the group rooms, and then work your way back to the overall building plan again.

Identifying Adjacencies

It is helpful to take the list of all the spaces you want to include in your program and organize it into desired physical adjacencies (i.e., clusters of related activities which you want to have in physical proximity). Desired adjacencies can be indicated as bubble diagrams—simple sketches in which circles stand for key elements and show by their positioning the relationships among the elements. Larger circles might represent larger spaces, and so forth. The overriding aim is to identify the relationship of every space to every other space, as specified by the program. This step is critical.

The most important adjacencies concern how the team wishes the group rooms to relate to one another (as discussed in Chapter 4 under Same-age versus Multi-age Clusters, and The Residential Core Model). In addition, clusters of group rooms and the center as a whole will need to have at least one common area at

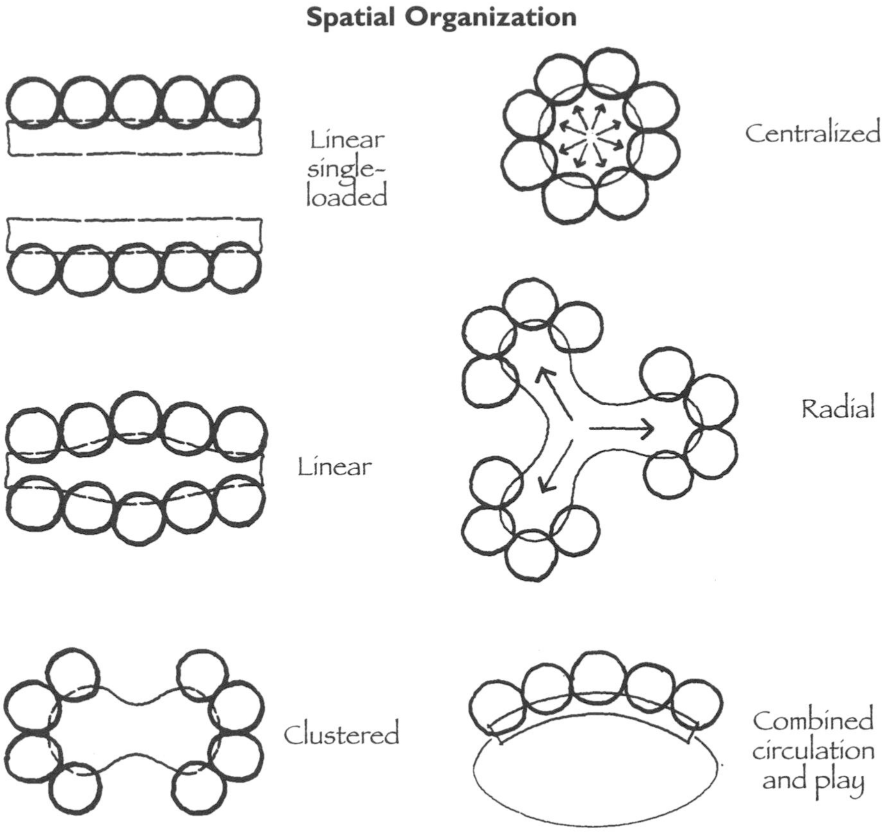

Figure 6.2
Six possible spatial organization plans for a center, using circulation as the organizer.

the heart. These relationships should be explored first and identified with a star so they are the last to change if building constraints require adjustments later on. Then use bubble diagrams to show all the other desired physical adjacencies for your building. Figure 6.1 illustrates some critical physical adjacencies using both bubble diagrams and arrows.

Estimating Room Sizes

At some point, it may be helpful to give your bubble diagrams reality by coordinating them with actual or approximate square footage estimates for each of the spaces in your program. A strategy some teams have found useful is to cut out shapes that have been scaled to represent the approximate sizes of either individual rooms or bubble-diagram groupings. (A reasonable scale might be ⅛ inch represents 1 foot.) Then the team can move these shapes around to create a preliminary set of space relationships for the building, and for the building on its site.

For the purposes of preliminary layout, you might want to estimate the sizes of the children's group rooms at 750 sq ft for infant rooms, 850 sq ft for toddler rooms, and 1,000 sq ft for preschool and school-age rooms, assuming group sizes reasonably similar to those outlined in the text following Table 4.4. Eventually, the team will need to calculate room sizes precisely, according to the guidelines provided in Table 4.1, but estimates are fine when making a first pass at center layout.

Building-Organization Types

Once the team has generated a set of bubble diagrams representing the desired adjacencies and relationships within the center, then it is time to try to lay these out to fit onto the site and create a building footprint. This is where the team needs to draw upon the architect's expertise and ability to visualize space.

There are many ways in which a building can be organized spatially. Six common organizational plans—all based on circulation—are illustrated in Figure 6.2. These include single-loaded, double-loaded,[1] centralized, radial, clustered, and exterior circulation plans. Any given center is likely to embody a variant of one, or a combination of several, of these patterns of circulation. The choice depends largely upon the site, the

QUESTIONS: ADJACENCIES AND SPATIAL ORGANIZATION

1. How does the team wish to organize the relationship of the children's group rooms: same-age, multiage, other?
2. Where might the building benefit from one or more common areas at the heart?
3. What rooms and functions need to be physically near one another? Which require separation?
4. How might the building be organized to meet items 1–3 above and fit on the site: single- or double-loaded corridor; cluster; centralized; radial; exterior circulation; some combination of these?

overiding aims of the program, and the degree of building compactness demanded by the budget and site. Some of the illustrative center layouts provided at the end of this chapter represent these types.

Key Layout Considerations

The following are key factors to address in laying out an entire center, whether it is to be a new building or a renovation. The discussion of each factor is followed by questions the team will want to answer about that consideration. The starred items deserve the highest priority—they are areas about which the team should strive to avoid compromise if at all possible. Of course, each team will want to specify its own priorities.

*Assignment of Prime Spaces

Primary Building Circulation:
The Main Entrance and Exit

Secondary Building Circulation

*Common Areas at the Heart

Access and Separation Requirements

Movement from Public to Private Zones

Flexibility

*Group Room Shapes and Impediments

Mechanical and Service Areas

*Storage

*Plumbing

Heating and Cooling

*Assignment of Prime Spaces

Prime spaces are those that potentially have the best features the building and/or the site can offer: light (which in the northern hemisphere generally means they face south), access to fresh air and good air circulation patterns, and pleasant views from indoors to outside. Young children are especially vulnerable to the effects of light deprivation. They need exposure to full-spectrum light for normal functioning of their nervous systems, as well as for psychological well-being. It is important that the layout maximize the amount of natural light, the number of operable windows, and access to the outdoors in all child-occupied spaces. Ideally, all children's spaces will:

- Face south, southeast, or southwest for maximum exposure to sunlight (in the northern hemisphere)
- Have direct access to the outdoors and to a covered outdoor play space
- Have child-eye-level views to outside activity

Where access to natural light and fresh air is limited, *give the youngest children (infants and toddlers) priority access to sunlight.*

Example: A center located on the top floor of a state office building was configured as a long narrow rectangle. The only windows at child height were along one short end of the rectangle, closest to the entry. These windows looked onto a rooftop play area and provided the best natural light. The spaces behind the entry, on the center's long axis, received natural light only from windows that were 5 feet or more above the floor. For structural reasons, lower windows could not be "punched out" of the walls. A decision had to be made about where to locate infant/toddlers versus preschoolers, and who should have the choice window location. The architects felt the babies should be located at the rear of the center, which was more tranquil and remote from the entry, and was dark for sleeping. Of greater concern to the staff than tranquillity, however, was children's exposure to natural light and views. While 3–5 year olds can walk outdoors unassisted and climb lofts to access windows 5 feet high, infants and toddlers cannot. Ultimately, infants and toddlers were placed closest to the windows, at the front of the building, to offset their immobility and immaturity that put them at greater risk for lack of access to light, air, and outdoor life.

Figure 6.3 shows how to use bubble diagrams and arrows to express the relationship of a building's spaces to solar exposure, views, and access to the outdoors. See Chapter 5 for more on the relationship between indoors and outdoors, and Chapters 10 and 11 for a complete discussion of light, lighting, and windows. In those atypical cases where direct sun is a problem, plan to provide the necessary modulation and control. Keep in mind that each of the group rooms will need to be at grade (unless a building variance is obtained), and to have its own emergency exit, preferably to the outdoors.

QUESTIONS: PRIME SPACES

1. Where is the best natural light on the site? Can children—especially infants and toddlers—and play yards be placed closest to it?
2. What functions, that do not involve children, or that involve sleeping only, can be placed where natural light is poor or limited?
3. How can the building's layout take advantage of the site's best views?
4. Are there at-grade code or site restrictions limiting where infant and toddler groups and sleep areas can be located?

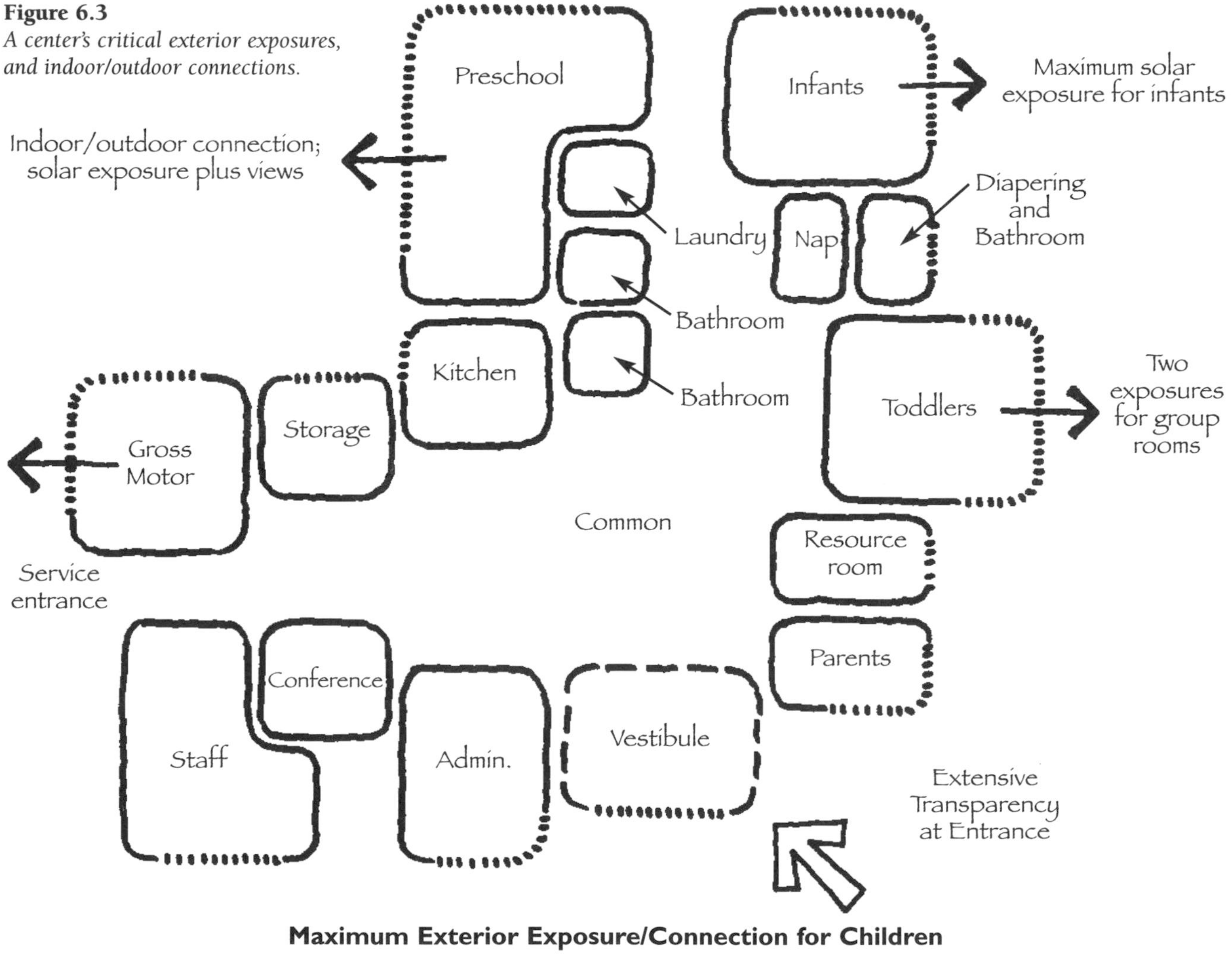

Figure 6.3
A center's critical exterior exposures, and indoor/outdoor connections.

Primary Building Circulation

The location of a center's main entrance determines the building's form and the relationship of the building to the site, as discussed in Chapter 5. Once the front door is positioned, for purposes of safety and control, establish one primary circulation route through the building from the main entrance to the main emergency exit. Sketch out a main circulation route that runs alongside of but not through activity areas, and never through the group rooms themselves. Strive to keep corridors and distances short. (See Chapter 5.) Have the main circulation path lie tangent to, or lead to, at least one common area at the heart of the center where people can meet casually. Figure 6.4 illustrates one way of orienting the building's prime spaces along its primary circulation path. Other primary-circulation arrangements are indicated schematically by the circulation paths creating the different building organization types in Figure 6.2.

In climates with extreme weather conditions, airlocks and vestibules may be desired around doors, as well as "drip and store" places for wet shoes, boots, and umbrellas. Convenient storage for strollers, car seats, and baby packs may also be required nearby. It is also necessary to arrange the building's spaces so the common area at the heart receives some natural light. Without some connection to the exterior, the area will be dark, dead, and unused.

QUESTIONS: MAIN ENTRANCE AND EXIT/CIRCULATION

1. What are some possible locations for the front door? Which one is best? Why?
2. What local codes and site limitations will affect the location of the main entrance and the emergency egress?
3. How can the building be laid out to create a primary circulation route from the main entrance to the center's prime spaces or subgroups?
4. What doors and windows are needed to meet all safety, fire, and functional requirements?
5. Will vestibules and air locks be needed around any doors?
6. How can the common area at the heart be connected to the outdoors and to natural light?

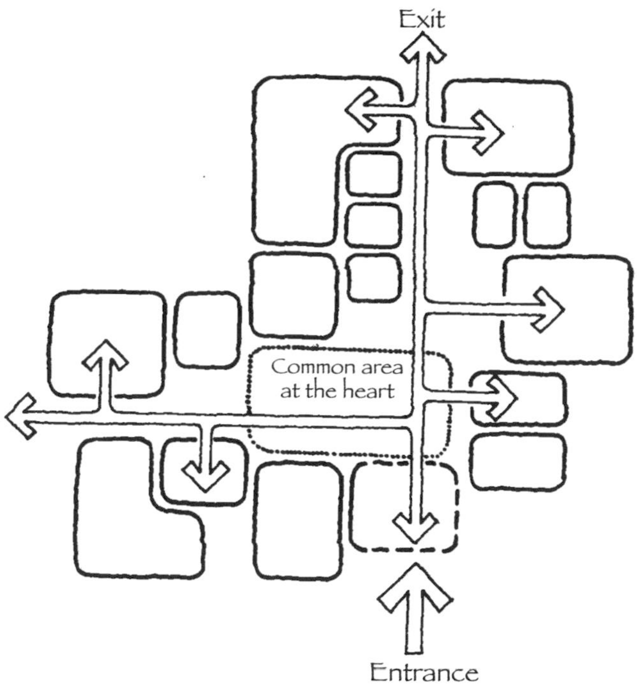

Figure 6.4
For safety and control, design the building with one main entrance and exit and a primary path linking the most important spaces, including a common area at the heart

Secondary Building Circulation

Depending upon the site and the layout of the building, secondary circulation routes may be needed in addition to the primary one. Secondary routes organize circulation for subcomponents of a building and need to connect to the primary route at at least one point. Indeed, these are desirable for giving the building character and breaking down its scale. Secondary routes are most gracious when they are neither too rigid nor too loose and, ideally, when they provide views of center activities en route.

*Common Areas at the Heart

The design team needs to establish which activity(ies) constitute the core of the center's social fabric and position its primary common area at the heart (see Chapter 4) with this function(s) in mind. To work successfully, any common area needs to be placed so that it:

- Is in or near the center of the building, so it is equally accessible to all.

- Has one or more of these essential components—eating, sitting, views of and/or access to the outdoors or to another major attraction.
- Has primary circulation paths tangent to it (Figure 6.5).[2]

As the building footprint takes shape, the team will want to identify its subcomponents and groupings and consider ways in which they can also be given secondary common areas at the heart.

Protected Zones

Common areas at the heart, and central gathering places, work well only when they provide a protected place for people to sit outside of the flow of traffic. Many well-intentioned designs create sufficient space for gathering but fail to provide this essential protected zone. As a result, the space often ends up simply being a large transit area. Figure 6.7 shows what is required. Where multiple doors will be needed off a central gathering space, try to position them to maximize the amount of uninterrupted wall area, so a "cul de sac" can be created for seating and activity.

"Create a single common area for every social group. Locate it at the center of gravity of all the spaces the group occupies, and in such a way that the paths that go in and out of the building lie tangent to it."

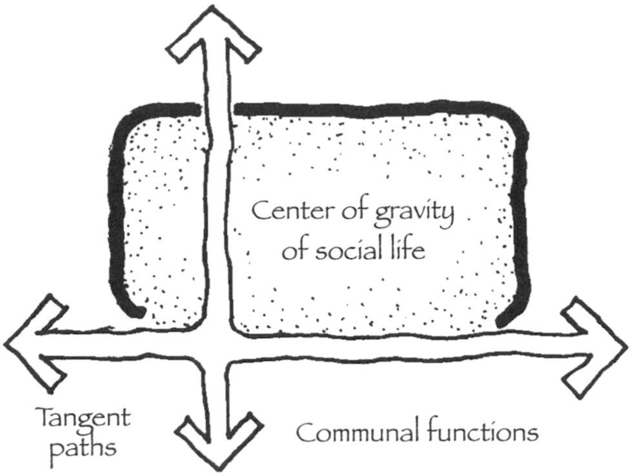

Figure 6.5
A common area at the heart lies near the building's center with major circulation paths leading up to and lying tangent to it.

QUESTIONS: BUILDING CIRCULATION AND COMMON AREA AT THE HEART

1. How can the primary pathway(s) be arranged to link the largest number of center facilities?
2. What secondary and subsidiary pathways and linkages are desirable?
3. What activities/facilities does the team wish to place at the heart of the center and its subcomponents to express its aliveness and interconnection?

Interior Access and Separation Requirements

In addition to the physical adjacencies of the center's spaces and group rooms (see Figure 6.1), and the relationship of rooms to the outdoors (see Figure 6.3), the team will want to consider other forms of adjacency. These can more accurately be called questions of access and separation—visual, acoustic, and olfactory—between the children's rooms and between all the spaces in the building. For example, interior windows can make it possible for children of different ages to have visual access to one another, for adults to provide better supervision, and for children to connect with parents as they come and go. However, some areas of the building, such as the staff lounge, may require complete interior visual privacy. Licensing in most states has visibility regulations for a number of center areas, which need to be followed precisely.

In some parts of the building, it may be desirable to hear children's laughter from one space to another, while elsewhere acoustic access may be undesirable due to differences in the activity levels and sleep cycles of different ages. It is also nice for children to enjoy pleasing aromas from the kitchen, and even to see the cook at work, or to smell flowers and earth outside. On the other hand, toilet and diapering areas may need enclosure or special ventilation and exhaust systems to prevent their odors from spreading. The design team will want to identify all accessibility and separation requirements for its program. Figures 6.7 and 6.8, on the next pages, use bubble diagrams to express some key visual and acoustic-connections and separations between a center's interior spaces.

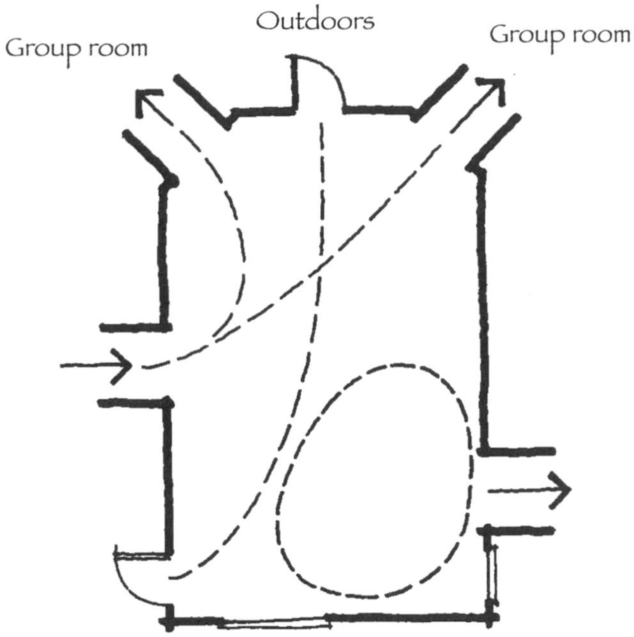

Figure 6.6
To make this large connecting room work as a common area at the heart, the passageway at the lower right needs to be relocated so there is a protected corner for sitting and for activities.

QUESTIONS: ACCESS AND SEPARATION

1. What rooms/functions in the program need to be near one another, visible to one another, within earshot of one another?
2. Which rooms/functions require or can tolerate visual, physical, and/or acoustic separation?
3. What potential odors/aromas in the building need to be shielded or heightened?

Movement from Public to Private Zones

Some of a center's spaces are more public, others more private. Try to lay out the center so that circulation from the entrance leads progressively to activities requiring more privacy and seclusion. For example, the group rooms are usually more private than the entry/administrative area, and the staff lounge is more private than the children's rooms. Especially in large

Figure 6.7
Critical visual connections for integrating center activities.

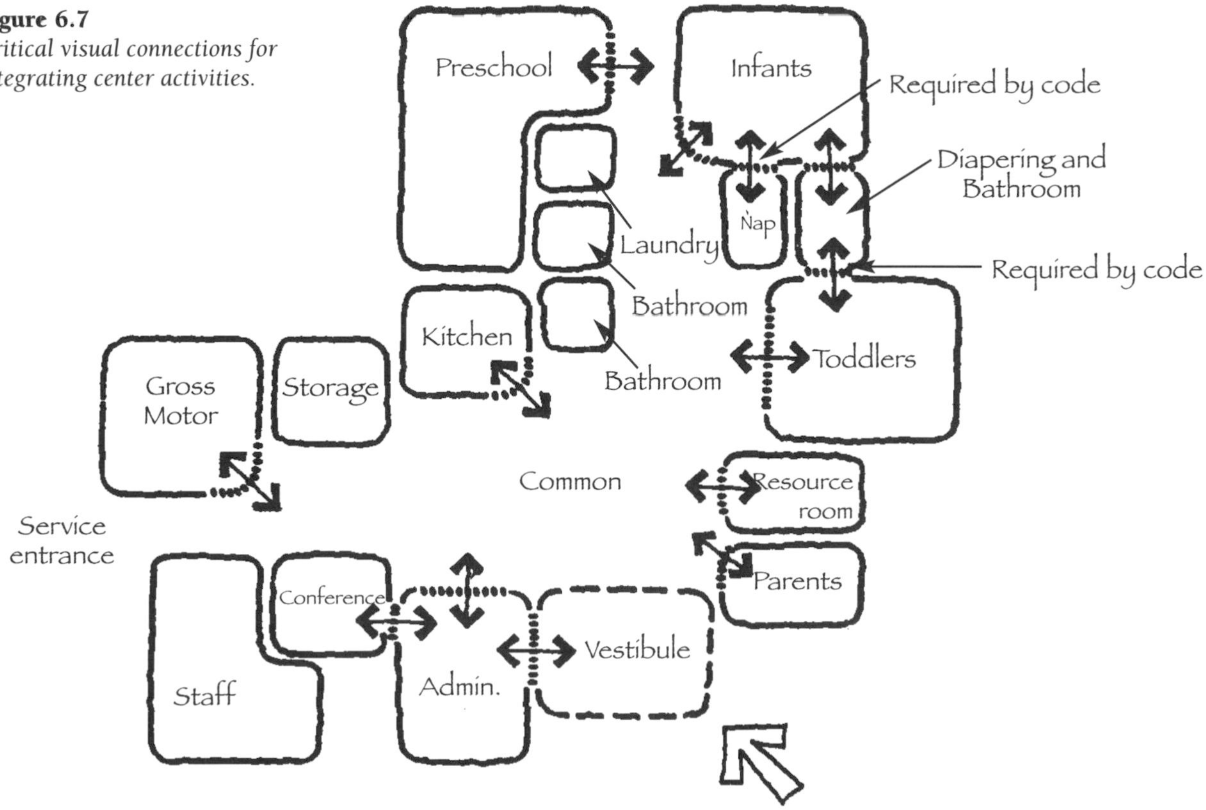

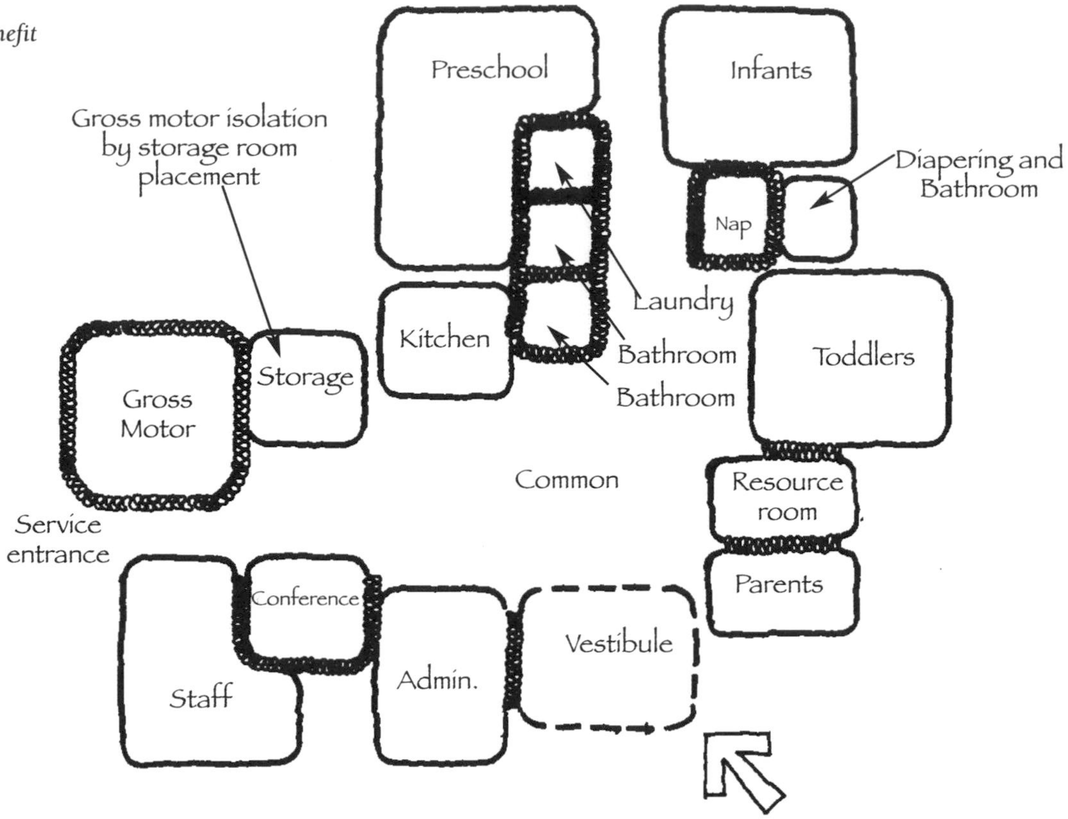

Figure 6.8
Areas of the center that benefit from acoustic separation.

QUESTIONS: PUBLIC TO PRIVATE

1. Which spaces and functions, requiring access to, or tolerance of, high levels of activity, belong near the entrance?
2. Which spaces and functions call for seclusion?

---

centers, progression from more public to private areas can create a series of circulation realms that distinguish different parts of the overall layout. Figure 6.9 illustrates the parallels between this public-to-private continuum as it exists in homes and in centers.

Flexibility

The team may want a layout that can respond easily to a changing census of infants, toddlers, preschoolers, and school-age children over time. If anticipated fluctuations in census merit the additional expense involved, group rooms can be sized to accommodate the larger and developmentally more advanced of two adjacent age groups: i.e., infant rooms can be made the same size as toddler rooms and equipped with one or two toilets and wash basins, so they might accommodate toddlers in the future.

> ***Example:*** An infant and toddler center was concerned that its census might vary over time and could not decide which rooms should be designated for which ages. The team recognized that toddler groups are larger and require toilets as well as diapering facilities, demanding more square footage and plumbing than infant spaces. These factors increase costs, an undesirable outcome. But lack of flexibility was also undesirable. Eventually the team decided to design all the rooms to accommodate the toddler level, concluding that the extra costs would be offset by the potential for improved utilization of the space under changing censuses.

Because preschoolers have larger group sizes and therefore larger room requirements than toddlers, placing toddlers in preschool rooms can leave too much

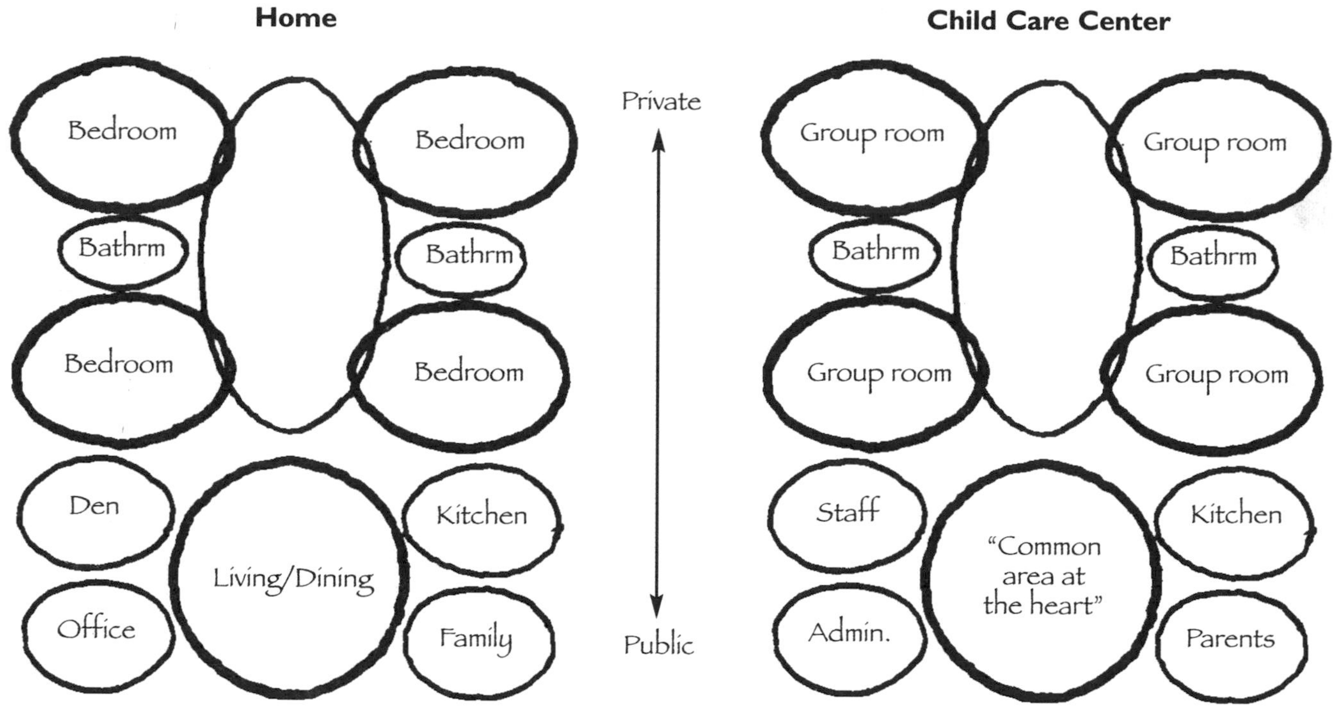

Figure 6.9
Home as a template for child care center: Centers have a public-to-private gradient that is not unlike that of homes.

QUESTIONS: FLEXIBILITY

1. How much age fluctuation in census—and therefore, need for flexibility in room use—is anticipated?
2. How might flexibility increase construction costs, and is it affordable?
3. Where should this flexibility occur: infant/toddler, preschool/school-age, other?

---

spare space. However, a group of school-age children can easily occupy a preschool room, provided the toilets are segregated by sex. If future flexibility/convertibility is desired, plan for two room sizes—one for infants/toddlers and one for preschoolers/school-age children—as a way to build in flexibility and still maintain reasonable space use.

*Group Room Shapes and Impediments

To work well, group rooms need to have balanced proportions—being neither too narrow and long, nor too wide and short. It is difficult to express these relationships precisely. In general, rooms need to be at least 20–25 feet wide so that they can accommodate activities on both sides, plus a 3–5-foot circulation path in the middle. Large square rooms present problems because designers tend to build storage, sinks and counters off the walls, and caregivers tend to place furniture against the walls, leaving dead space in the middle of the room. Triangular rooms can create similarly awkward room arrangements. To vary room shape, consider adding wide bays and alcoves, 4 to 10 feet deep (see the Copper House infant and preschool room plans in Chapters 16 and 17).

Variety in room shape is desirable for providing nooks and crannies, and for a natural separation of noisy/quiet and messy/clean zones (explained in Chapter 7). Regardless of the layout, visual connections specified by licensing must be maintained throughout all the spaces (check local regulations). Certain room shapes and fixed features (structural columns, heating chases, or wall partitions) can obstruct staff visibility and ease of movement. Where impediments exist, or will be needed, careful analysis

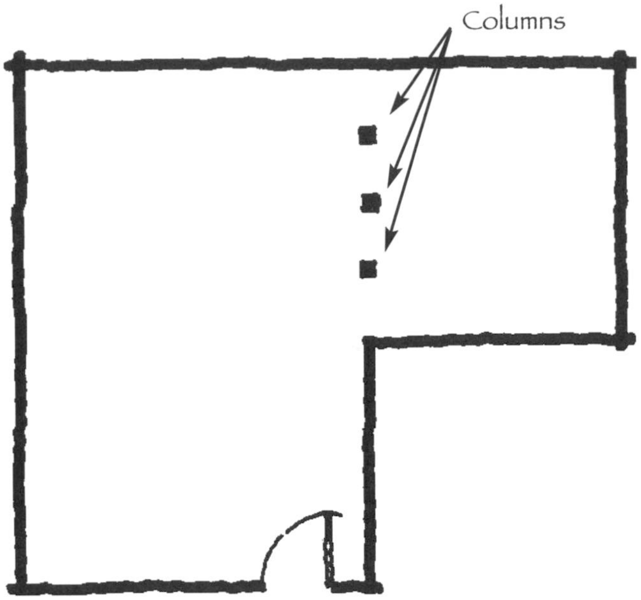

Figure 6.10
Rooms with a deep L-shape, and with impediments such as columns, if they block visibility and/or hamper mobility, are undesirable. The functionality of this room is severely hampered by walls punctuated with too many built-ins and doors.

is called for to ensure that the age level and program assigned to that space can tolerate them. For example, infants and toddlers can accidentally crawl, fall against, or walk into structural columns, or the columns may make it difficult for staff to reach a child quickly. If the columns are in a preschool room, however, they might be used as part of a climber or loft and therefore be less obtrusive.

In general, L-shaped rooms are difficult to monitor when the lower leg of the L is very deep (more than 5–7 feet), especially with infants and toddlers. Any columns in L-shaped rooms add further physical and visual impediments (see Figure 6.10).

Placing too many built-ins—cabinets, sinks, toilets, closets—along a room's major walls on both sides creates another type of impediment to functionality. Most of the furniture will need to be freestanding in the middle of the room, making it impossible to create cozy corners or secure places (see Figure 6.10).

QUESTIONS: ROOM SHAPES AND IMPEDIMENTS

1. What varieties of room shape exist or are proposed? Do they meet code requirements for visual connections?
2. Which age groups and functions can benefit most from which shapes?
3. Are there impediments to visibility and supervision (structural columns, heating chases)? If these cannot be changed, which age groups and functions can tolerate their presence? Which cannot?
4. How can the room's built-ins be positioned to maximize the amount of free wall space in each room?

Service and Mechanical Areas

As illustrated in Figure 6.11, try to locate the kitchen, recycle and garbage collection, janitorial, soiled diaper facilities, and a dumpster close to the service entrance. Place noisy mechanical and service equipment (heating and cooling, laundry facilities) as far as possible from primary group areas. Separate and/or buffer noisy spaces with acoustic shielding or with storage areas (Figures 6.8 and 6.12). Also see the section titled "Custodian" in Chapter 19 for more considerations.

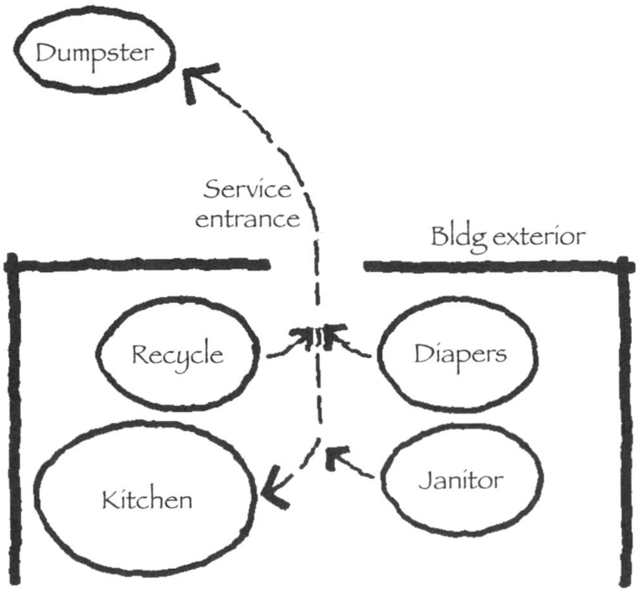

Figure 6.11
Consider locating kitchens, recycling centers, custodial areas, diaper disposal, and a dumpster within proximity of the service entrance. Remember that service vehicles can be noisy and disruptive—maintain acoustic separation.

QUESTIONS: SERVICE AND MECHANICAL AREAS

1. What factors such as noise, mechanical equipment, stairs, elevators, etc., will be present in the facility?
2. Do these require or preclude putting certain functions in certain places?
3. Has sufficient space been allotted for mechanical equipment, ducts, air circulation, etc.?
4. What functions are best located near the service entrance?

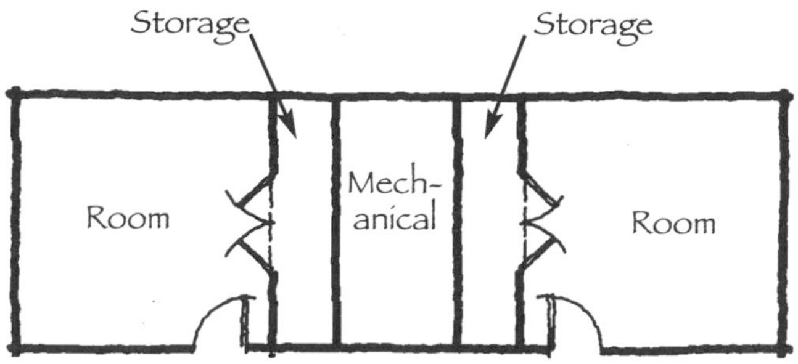

Figure 6.12
Separate noisy facilities and mechanical rooms from adult and children's areas by using storage spaces as acoustic buffers.

*Storage

As explained in Chapter 4, it is essential that the team determine early on how much and which types of storage are to be accommodated inside children's, staff, resource, office, and other rooms. Storage needs outside group and other rooms—for example, large walk-in closets, basements, and sheds—also must be identified. (Refer to Table 4.8 for guidance on common storage needs shared by most centers. Chapters 16–18 identify the types of storage that will be needed inside group rooms for specific age groups, and Chapter 20 discusses outdoor storage needs.) It is essential that the team provide for all identified storage needs on the center's plan. The more specific the team can be about these matters in the layout stage, the more likely that the program's unique requirements will be met and that the curriculum will run smoothly for years to come.

QUESTIONS: STORAGE

1. Have you identified your full range of storage requirements?
2. Can you estimate how much and what types of storage are needed for each group room, each cluster, the central administrative core, outdoors, elsewhere?
3. How should this storage be designed: open shelving, closed shelving, stand-up cabinets, small closets, walk-in closets, open bins, sheds, etc.?
4. Does your building layout honor all your storage requirements?

*Plumbing

Chapter 4 provides guidelines for the types and numbers of sinks and toilets needed for children of various ages and for adults. At this stage it is important to keep in mind that all the sinks and toilets listed in Table 4.6 need to be integrated with the building's main plumbing core and its tributaries, as do water-play facilities if they are included in the program. Also, the plumbing requirements of staff caretaking activities (cooking, laundry, general cleanup) need to be considered (Chapter 19).

Because the impact of plumbing-fixture placement is so profound, it is always worth the expense to extend or reroute plumbing to desired locations, rather than to design group spaces around a limited or inappropriately located plumbing system. During schematic design is the time to ensure that all plumbing concerns are raised and thoroughly addressed.

QUESTIONS: PLUMBING

1. What type of foundation is planned for the building: basement, slab-on-grade, other?
2. How might this impact ability to meet the building's extensive plumbing requirements?
3. For renovation projects: where is the central plumbing core, how far does it extend, and what costs are involved to plumb spaces at some distance from it?
4. Can wet functions be grouped to keep plumbing runs efficient?

Heating and Cooling

The choice of a center's heating and cooling systems is related to its geographic location and climate and is beyond the scope of this guide. However, when considering heating and cooling systems for the building, investigate the use of in-floor radiant heat, at least for the children's group rooms, whenever possible. In extremely cold climates, radiant floor heat may need to be supplemented by another system to better heat the upper regions of the rooms as well. (See Chapter 8.) Keep in mind that the type of system chosen will affect the building's tertiary space requirements, may infringe upon primary and secondary space in the group rooms, and may involve safety concerns.

QUESTIONS: HEATING AND COOLING

1. What are the building's heating and cooling requirements?
2. What systems are being considered to meet these needs, and how visually or spatially obtrusive might they be?
3. Is it physically possible to install in-floor radiant heat, at least in all the children's group rooms? Will the budget allow it?
4. Are all systems under consideration safe for young children to be around?

Renovation Projects

Centers located in renovated buildings often have their own unique layout considerations.

Rooms with Immovable Walls

As indicated in Chapter 4, if the compromises required to accommodate the program within an existing building are too great, the building under consideration may not work. Rooms without load-bearing walls can be more or less adjusted to meet size requirements, but rooms with immovable walls may result in spaces that are larger or smaller than those required for a given group size. The question then is deciding which age groups to place in which rooms. In general, strive to make maximal use of existing rooms by giving the larger-sized groups the larger rooms. Recognize, however, that in some cases infants and toddlers may actually need any additional square footage or "overage" more than preschoolers do.

> ***Example:*** In configuring a gutted space to be renovated, various constraints required that some rooms be disproportionately larger than others. While every child was provided with 42 sq ft of primary activity space, and each room had its requisite secondary space, it seemed to some team members that preschoolers ought to have the larger rooms because they were the larger-sized group, as well as being physically larger and more active than infants. However, the team ultimately chose to give infants rather than preschoolers the larger room, and more space per capita, on the grounds that infants need more space at floor level for equipment and to crawl about, while preschoolers can more readily use lofts and platforms (which add to a room's cubic footage), get to a multipurpose room where they can move about, and get outdoors on their own.

In existing spaces with different ceiling heights, generally the rooms with the lower ceilings are better adapted for infant/toddler areas, provided the rooms also have good light and sufficient square footage. Preschoolers can take advantage of lofts placed in rooms with higher ceilings.

QUESTIONS: FOR RENOVATIONS

1. Which walls can be moved to modify room sizes?
2. What are the ceiling heights? How might these affect the overall scale of the various rooms and placement of different age groups?
3. In terms of available square footage, and space use, which age groups are best placed where?

Making Use of Multiple Small Rooms

A series of small rooms—300–400 sq ft each—may suggest use by a small group with a limited number of caregivers: for example, four infants with one staff (instead of eight infants with two staff), per room. This strategy is undesirable in two respects:

- *It is unsafe to have only one staff person responsible for any group of children.* Should that adult need to give full attention to any one child, or need to leave the room for any reason, the rest of the group will be unattended.

- *It is difficult, if not impossible, to fit the full range of developmentally appropriate activities for any age level in a very small room.* Where space is tight, some desirable activity—such as gross motor play—usually gets left out, thereby shortchanging children's developmental needs.

Where multiple small rooms exist, first explore the option of removing walls to create larger spaces, thereby enabling normal groupings and staff/child ratios. If this is not possible, plan to install a door and operable windows between small adjacent rooms so staff can continually monitor children and communicate with one another (Figure 6.13). Then design small adjacent rooms so a group of children will move across them to access different functions—one room for dramatic and gross motor play, the other for art, quiet activities, and structured materials. This arrangement gives children access to a full range of activities. To avoid scheduled access and arbitrary room shifts when using a series of small rooms, staff needs to be deployed to rooms, rather than to groups, so children can flow freely from one room to another. Using a series of small rooms works best with preschool and school-age children who are mobile, able to separate into smaller groups, and to follow instructions, than it does for infants and toddlers who can easily wander and need to be under the watchful eye of caregivers at all times.

Making Use of One Large Room

Where there is one room large enough to accommodate several groups—1,550–2,000 sq ft—the team may need to decide whether these groups should be at the same or different age levels—i.e., two groups of toddlers, or one group of toddlers and one of infants. When considering placing different ages in one large space, take into account how the physical barriers that will be needed to separate the groups will affect the room's acoustics. Since infants sleep longer than toddlers, and toddlers sleep longer than preschoolers, the younger group may require quiet at times when the older group is active and noisy. Unless appropriate acoustic barriers can be installed, a cross-age combination may be unwise.

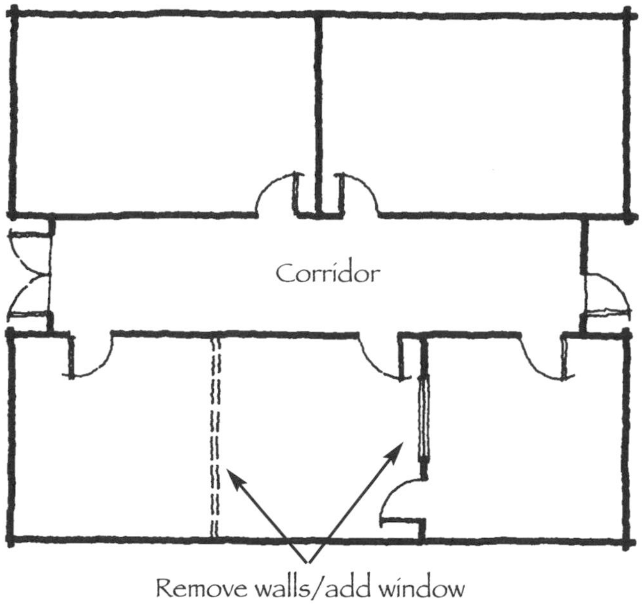

Figure 6.13
In renovations, consider removing walls between small adjacent rooms, or at least adding a window and door.

Putting groups of the same age level together usually works well. In such instances, it may be desirable to choose at least one activity that might be shared—a climber and large-muscle area, a dramatic play complex, or a library/resource area, etc.—to provide a sense of connectedness between the groups. The divider between the groups need not be a full-height stud-and-sheetrock wall. It could, instead, be a functional, movable screen or a half-height barrier that accommodates built-in platforms, levels, hideaways, gross motor and dramatic play spaces that might otherwise not be available.

Making Use of Rooms with Gross Size Differences

Sometimes an existing building has contiguous rooms of grossly different sizes. If walls cannot be moved, a real question arises as to how to use these rooms.

> **EXAMPLE:** A center space for 30 children (two groups of 3–5 year olds) consisted of one very large room, and one small room—remote from the entry—which had the better windows and natural light. It did not seem right to relegate one group of

10 or 15 preschoolers to this smaller room exclusively, because they would then have fewer activity areas, and the other group would have less access to natural light. Therefore the team had to decide what function(s) should be located in the small room to take advantage of its unique qualities. Should it be the art area because of its windows and natural light? Should it be the gross motor room because its location would allow containment of noise and activity? Should it be a quiet space for books, manipulatives, and group meeting?

After much deliberation, it became clear that the most important consideration in terms of the children's welfare was their need for a place of retreat and calm because of the large number of them in the center. Thus the room ultimately became the center's quiet area, as well as the nap space for those children who slept the longest.

A functional dividing wall.

The Necessity for Trade-Offs

In a perfect world, it would be possible for the design team to meet all of the layout objectives discussed in this chapter equally. But in the real world it is impossible to rank priorities across all settings. It is usually necessary to juggle all the variables and then make trade-offs based upon a setting's particular features and the values a design team wishes to emphasize. The team will need continually to refer back to its program and mission statement to determine which considerations remain unchangeable and which can be amended. The good intentions of many programs are lost at this point of choice-making, especially when the architecture is driving the design in ways that affect aspects of the program that have not been clearly articulated or prioritized. It is critical that teams are very attentive at this stage to trade-offs affecting the welfare of children and staff that should not be compromised.

Testing the Layout

As various layouts are explored, the floor plan for the center slowly evolves. However, a building organization that looks neat and tidy on paper may not be experienced as apparent or logical to someone standing in or using the space. Floor plans show the whole, whereas users experience the parts and details, constructing the whole over time, after being present in each of the spaces. Children, in particular, focus mainly on the parts rather than the whole. Architects, who visualize floor plans and layouts in their mind's eye, sometimes fail to realize that people rarely experience the overall space the way it is drawn. Thus it is important that the center's layout (blueprint) be tested against the footprints of people using the space.

The average adult's line of visual focus while in motion extends about 5–15 feet; objects and spaces beyond that distance tend to be somewhat blurred. A child's focus is likely less. Therefore it is important not to rely on such factors as color, lighting, carpet, or tile patterns to provide coherency to a complicated or overextended building layout. Surface treatment can only support—not carry—the plan. The definition needs to come from the architecture, the circulation paths, and the overall scale of the building.

Since it may be impossible to physically test the layout in the real space, role-playing and imagination are invaluable. One method of testing, using models and model-sized figures, is described in Box 6.3 and illustrated in the photo at the top of page 126.

Eight Center Layouts

Eight building floorplans illustrating different center layouts are shown in Figures 6.14–6.21 on pages

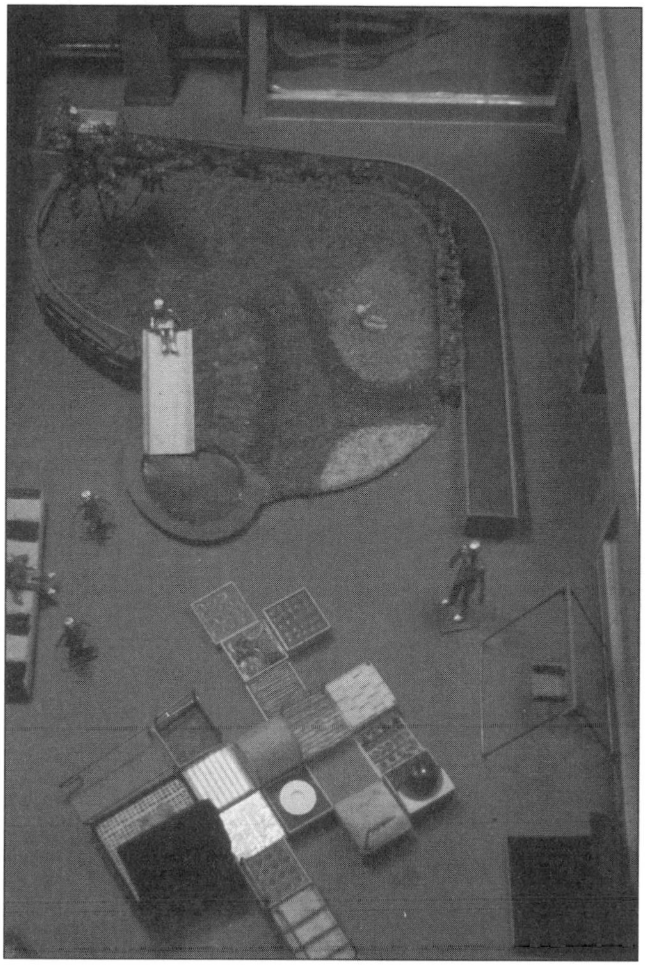

Model-sized figures moved around in scaled models, can help to test an area's layouts.

126–135. (Also see the Copper House plan in Chapter 21.) A brief description highlighting key advantages and drawbacks accompanies each plan. All these plans were developed in response to existing conditions. They therefore meet some, but not all, of the key layout considerations discussed in this Chapter. The purpose in presenting them is not for them to be copied—indeed each is uniquely suited to its individual site—but rather so that they may serve as illustrations of reasonably successful solutions to a variety of site and circumstantial conditions. Careful study of those which most closely resemble your own program requirements and site characteristics will, hopefully, yield insight into ways to resolve some of the issues you are likely to confront. The floorplans at the ends of Chapters 16–18 illustrate numerous different layouts for the children's group rooms.

BOX 6.3

Testing the Layout: A Visualization

Place a small model figure in the center model or on the plan and imagine it to be yourself standing in that area. Alternatively, use a model scope, close-up photographs, and slides of the model as tools for the team to envision and evaluate movement through the building. Notice what you can see within 5 to 20 feet and how far your visibility extends. Experience what it is like moving on foot through the center. Which spaces are obviously connected by visual and physical links? Which are disconnected from one another? Does your experience on foot coincide with the assumptions about spatial connections, circulation zones, and public-to-private gradients that are called for in the program? If not, what needs to be corrected? Let your observations be your guide.

Ascribing Qualities to Spaces

Once the team has arrived at several alternate schematic building layouts, the next step is to develop the interior details of the rooms, especially those for children. At this stage it is helpful once again to explore the "spirit of place" qualities team members want each of the center's rooms to have. Therefore, take time to visualize each space and describe the essence of how you want children and staff to feel in it: tranquil, sociable, adventuresome, etc. Kitchens, for example, can be characterized as "efficient;" "homey" or "institutional;" "compact" or "sprawling." Identifying each individual room's qualities in advance will greatly assist in locating its key supports, and later in the selection of its furniture, finishing materials, and details.

Notes

[1]*Load* refers to the layout of spaces along a circulation path or corridor. A single-loaded corridor has rooms on only one of its sides, a double-loaded corridor has rooms on both sides.

[2]C. Alexander et al., *A Pattern Language* (New York: Oxford University Press, 1977), 621.

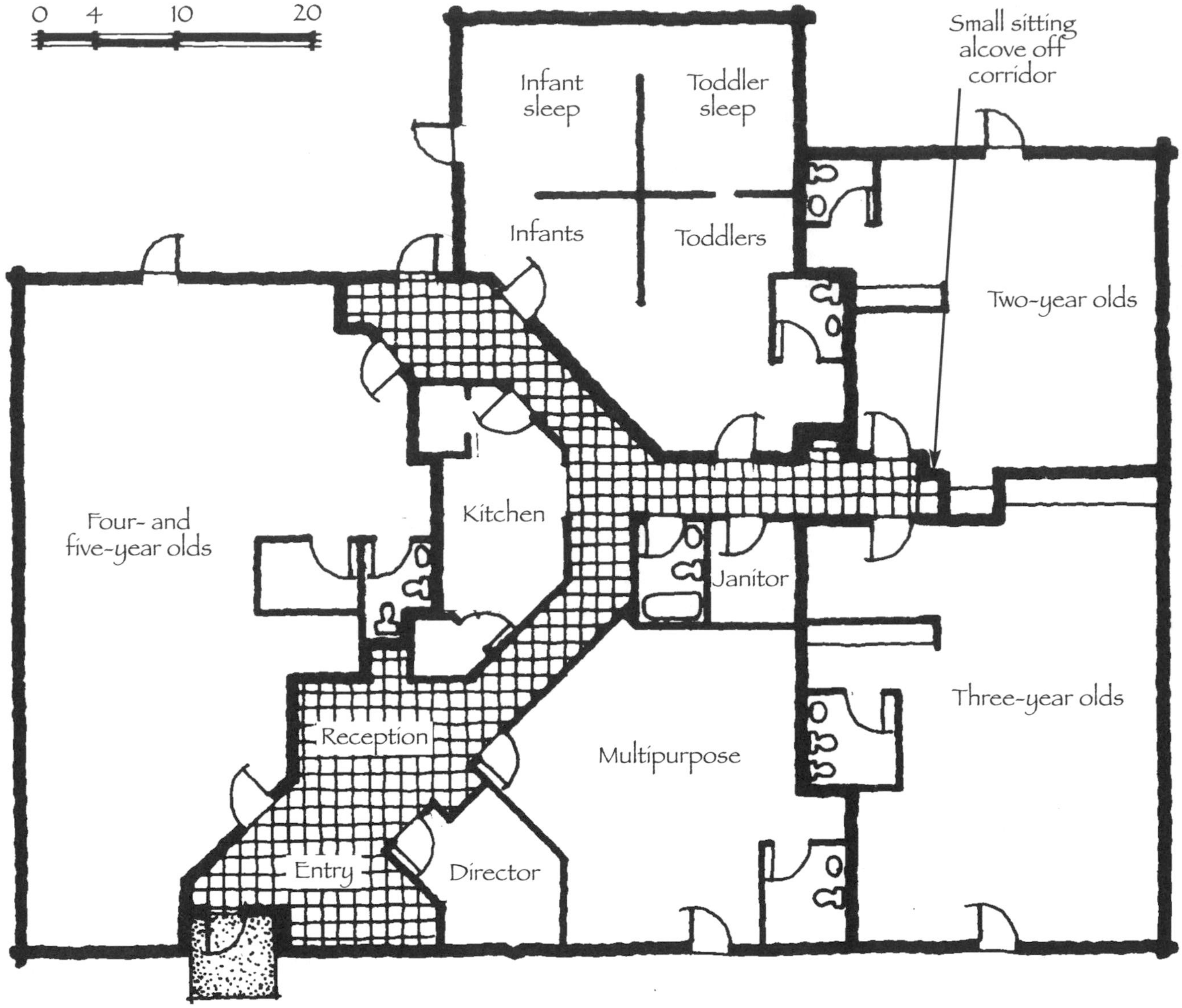

Figure 6.14
A radial circulation plan was used to forge this five-room center out of a small former supermarket and an adjacent house.

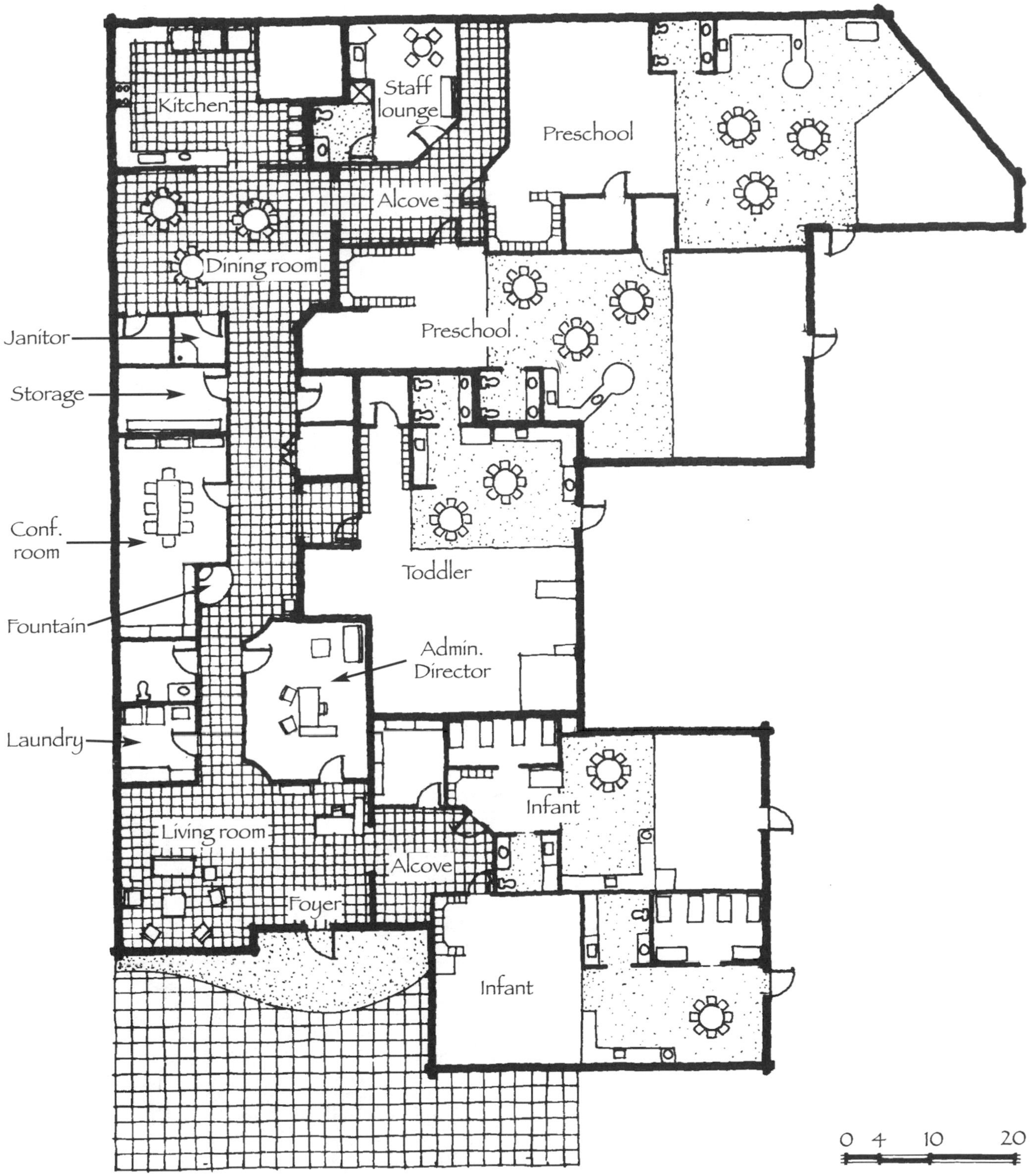

Figure 6.15
This center, built partially inside and partially outside a multistory Social Security Administration building in order to provide natural light and outdoor play space to every group room, features a modified residential core; alcoves marking clusters for infants, toddlers, and preschoolers; a fountain and unique ceiling treatment to break up its corridors.

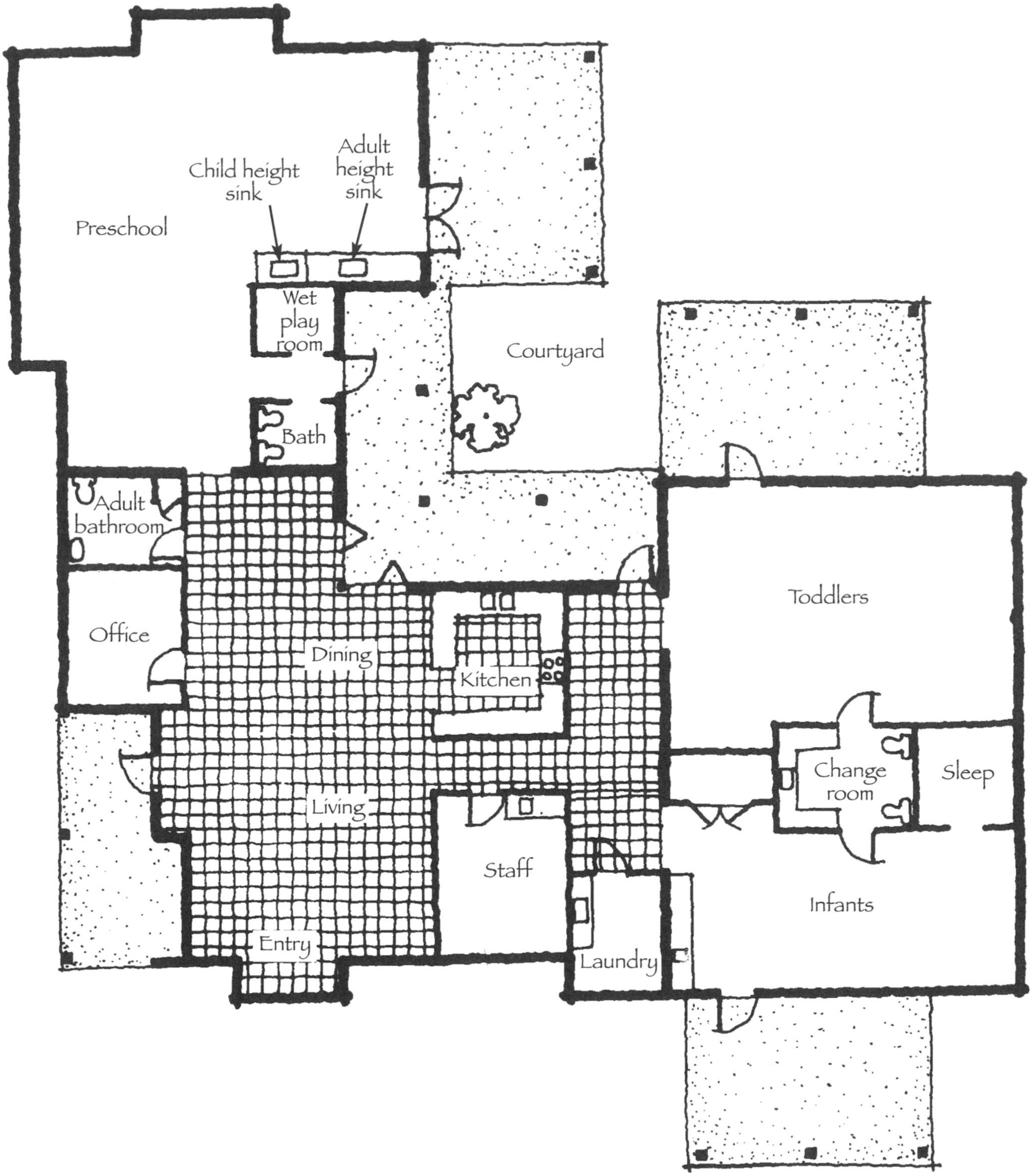

Figure 6.16
The residential core model is featured in this space-conserving L-shaped plan in which group rooms wrap around a large outdoor courtyard for dining and play in a temperate climate.

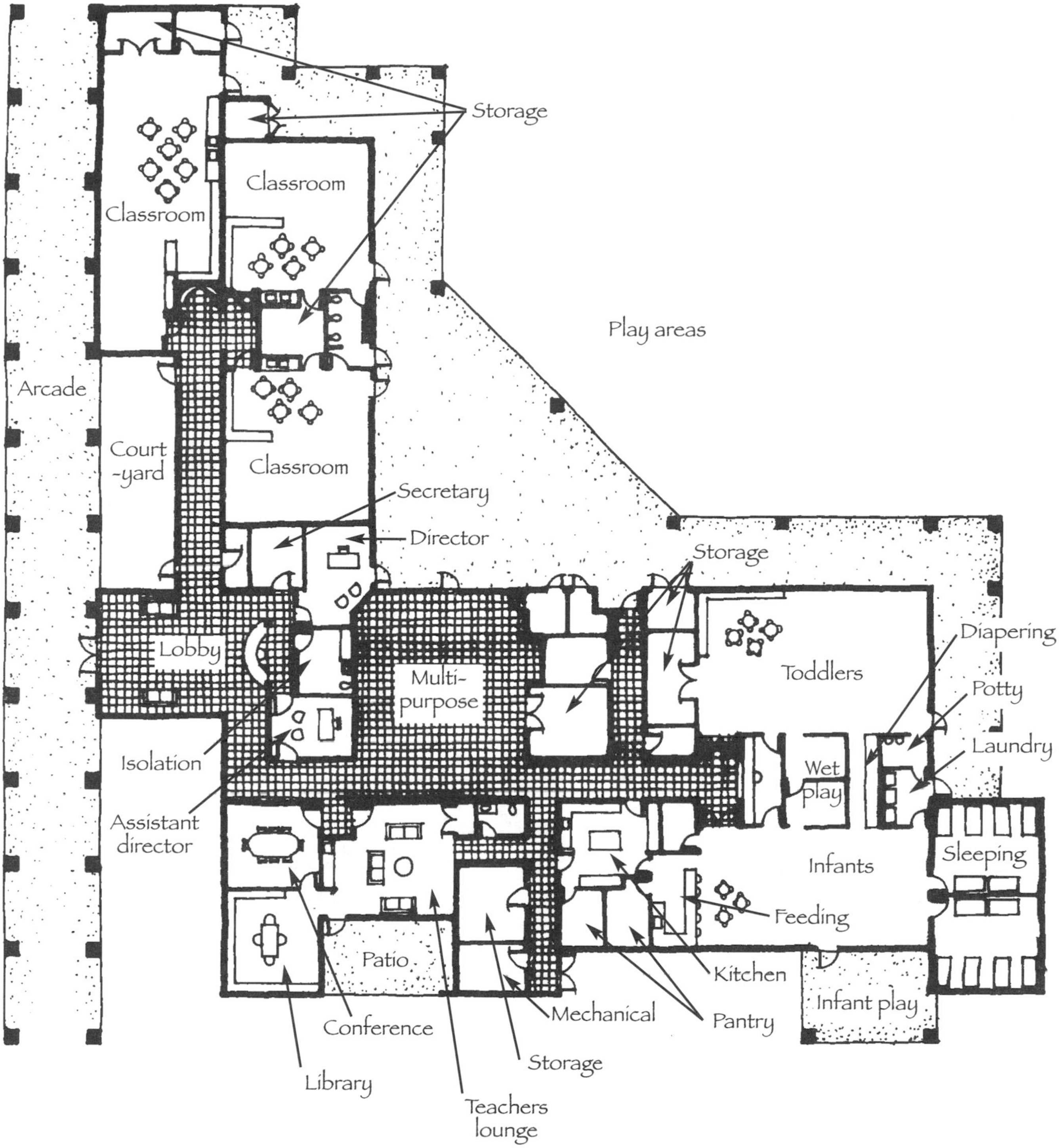

Figure 6.17
This L-shaped double-loaded corridor plan wraps around a partially covered courtyard and extensive preschool yard. Centralized staff and administrative facilities, plus a large multipurpose room, place infants and toddlers in one wing, preschoolers in the other.

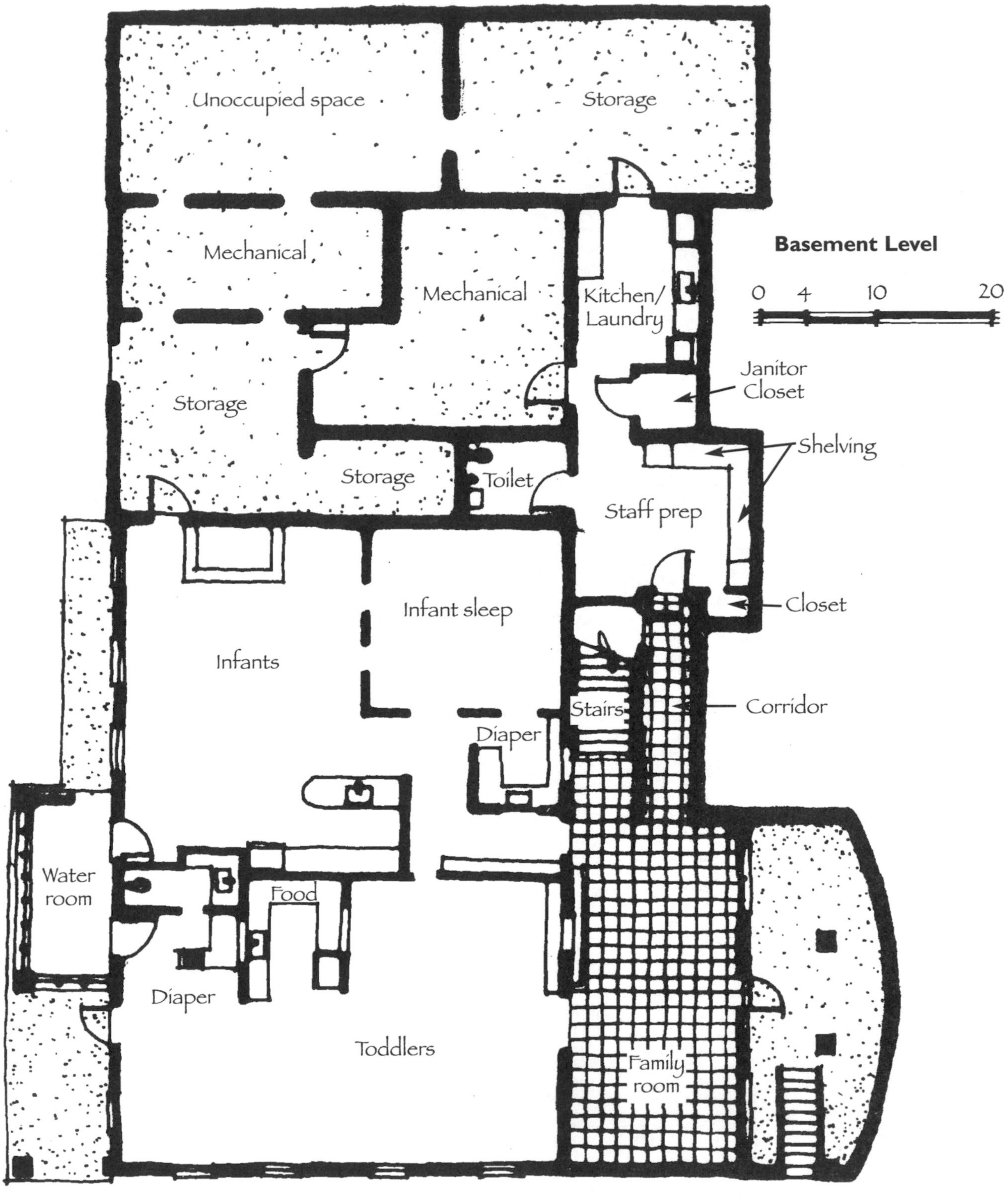

Figure 6.18 (Basement Level)
By excavating out a play yard for infants and toddlers, and relocating the building's entrance, a former church/parish house was renovated to create a child care center on the first floor and basement levels. Features include a family room on each floor, a music/movement space, and a projected glass enclosed wet play bay to be shared by infants and toddlers.

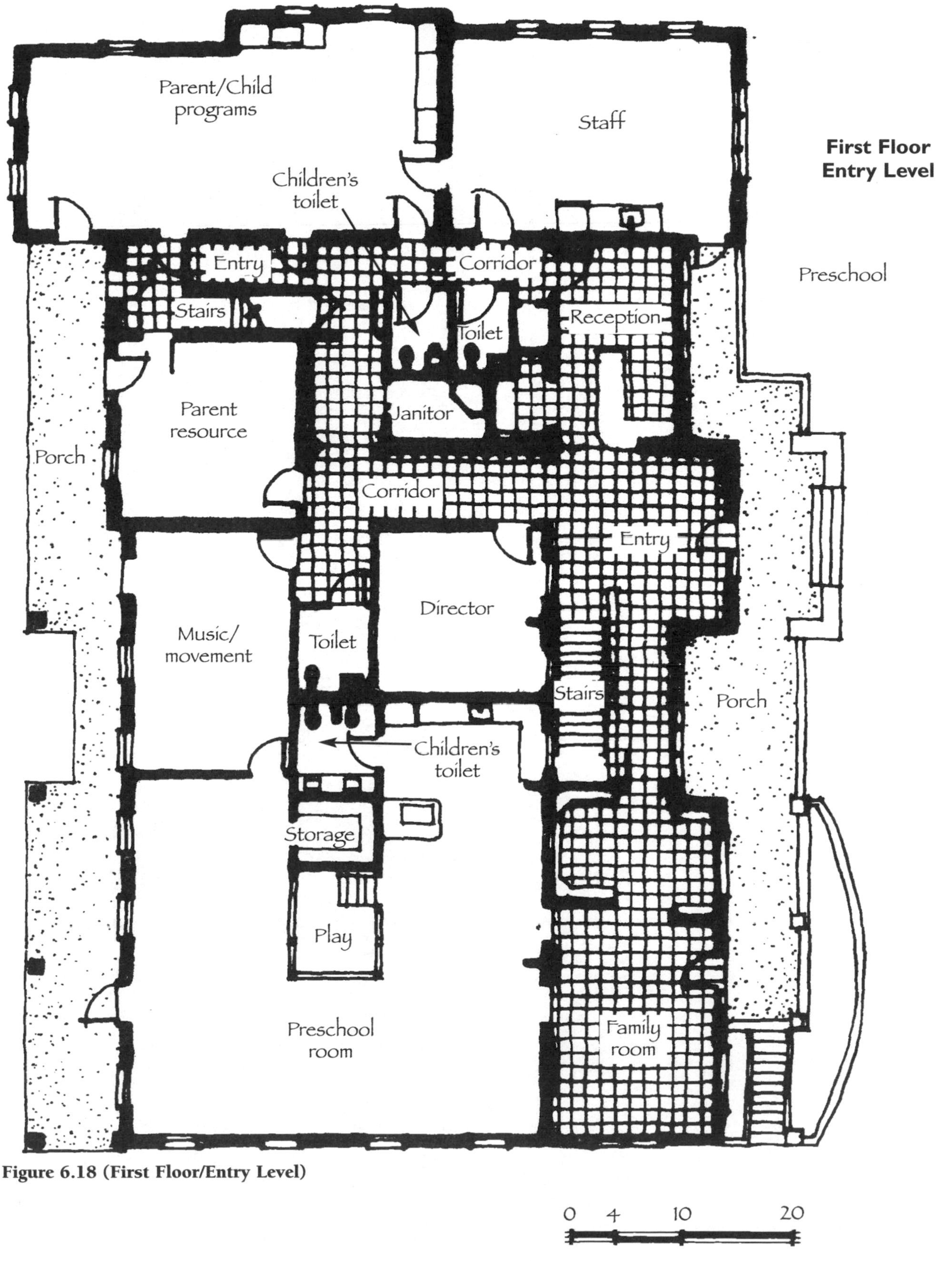

Figure 6.18 (First Floor/Entry Level)

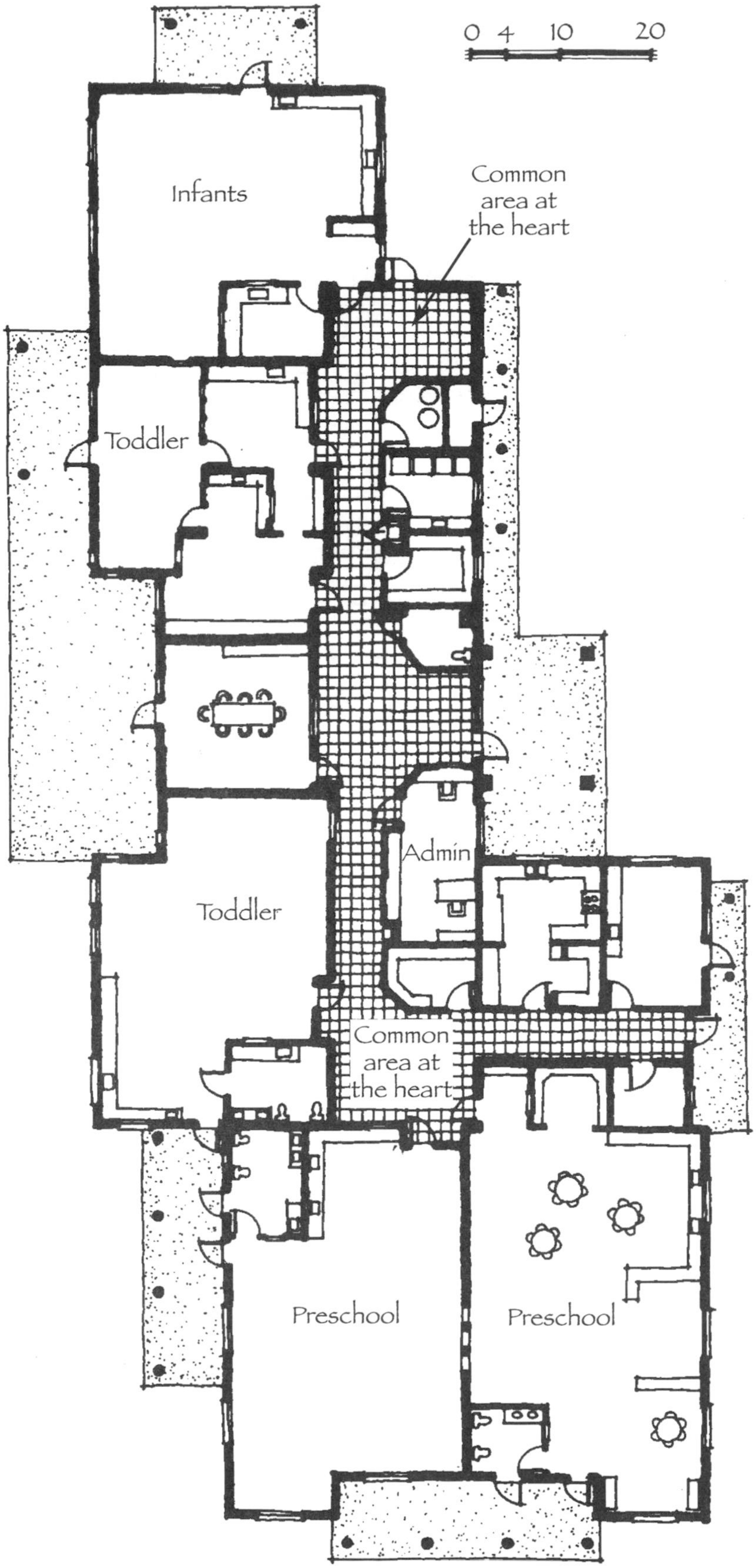

Figure 6.19
A modified double-loaded corridor plan provides natural light to every space, skylights in the darker portions of each group room, and a small common area at the heart at each end of the building.

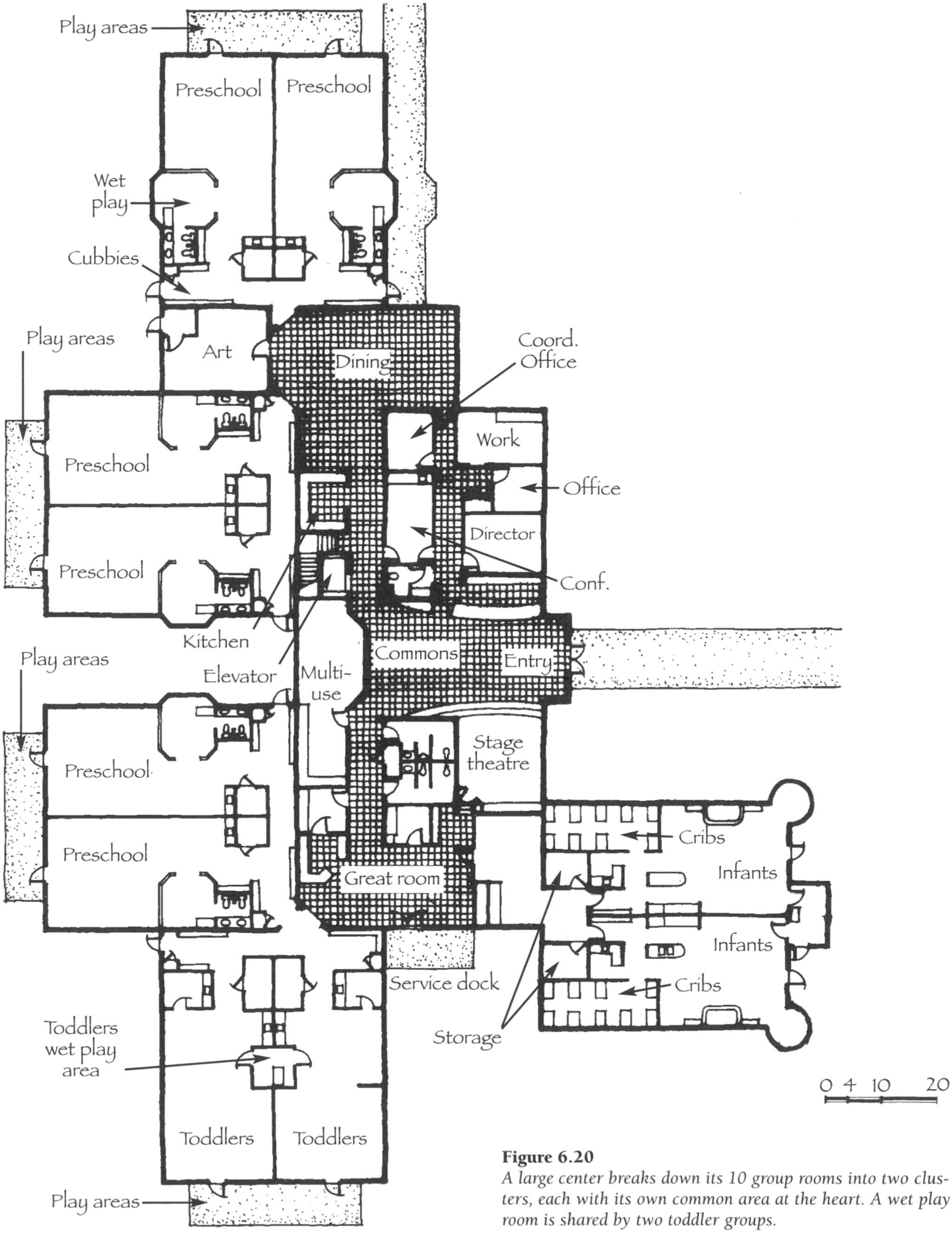

Figure 6.20
A large center breaks down its 10 group rooms into two clusters, each with its own common area at the heart. A wet play room is shared by two toddler groups.

Figure 6.21
A center built from prefabricated modules, fits onto a very constraining site by separating infants and toddlers from preschoolers, and by putting the director's office and the staff areas on the second floor, shown on the next page.

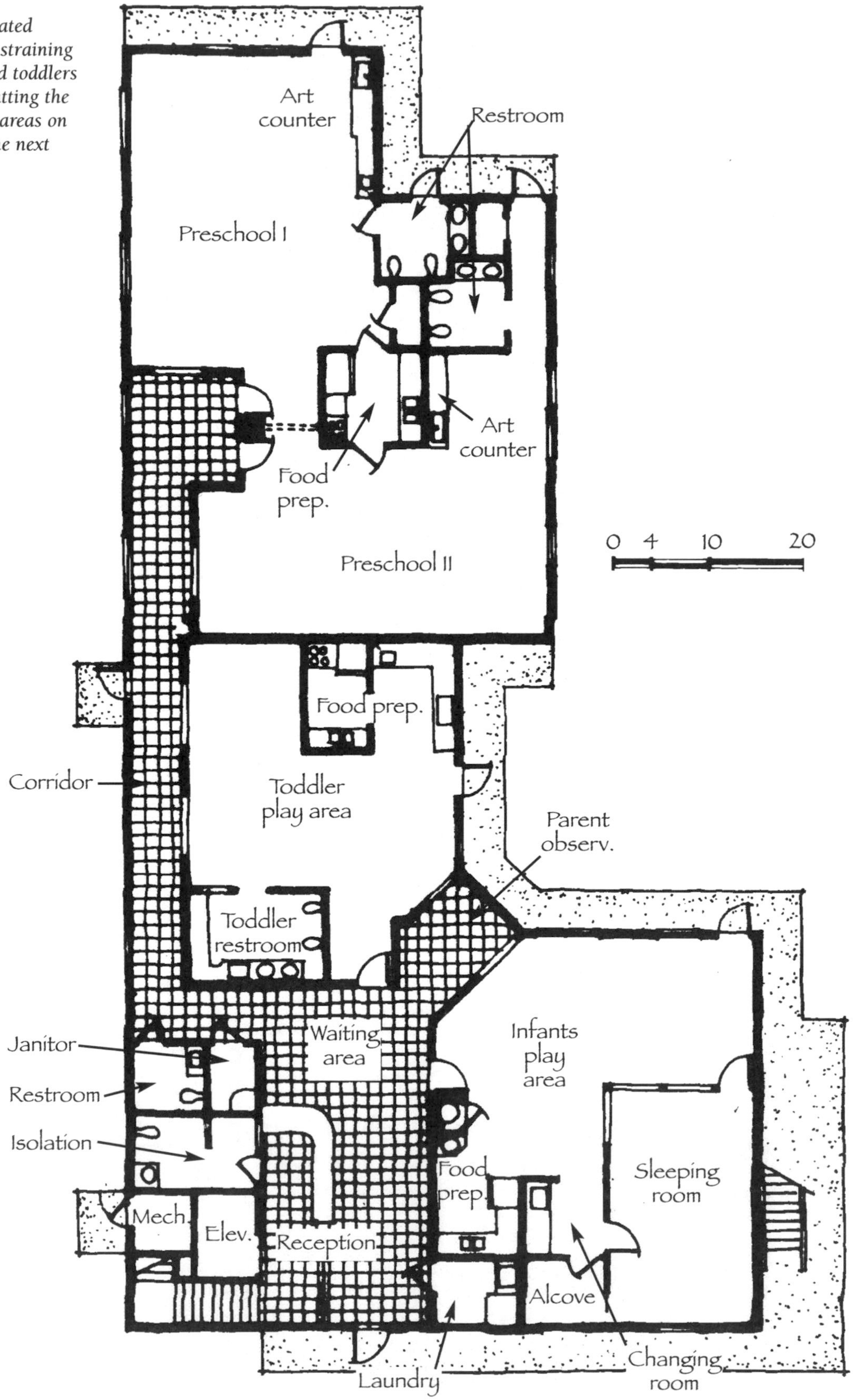

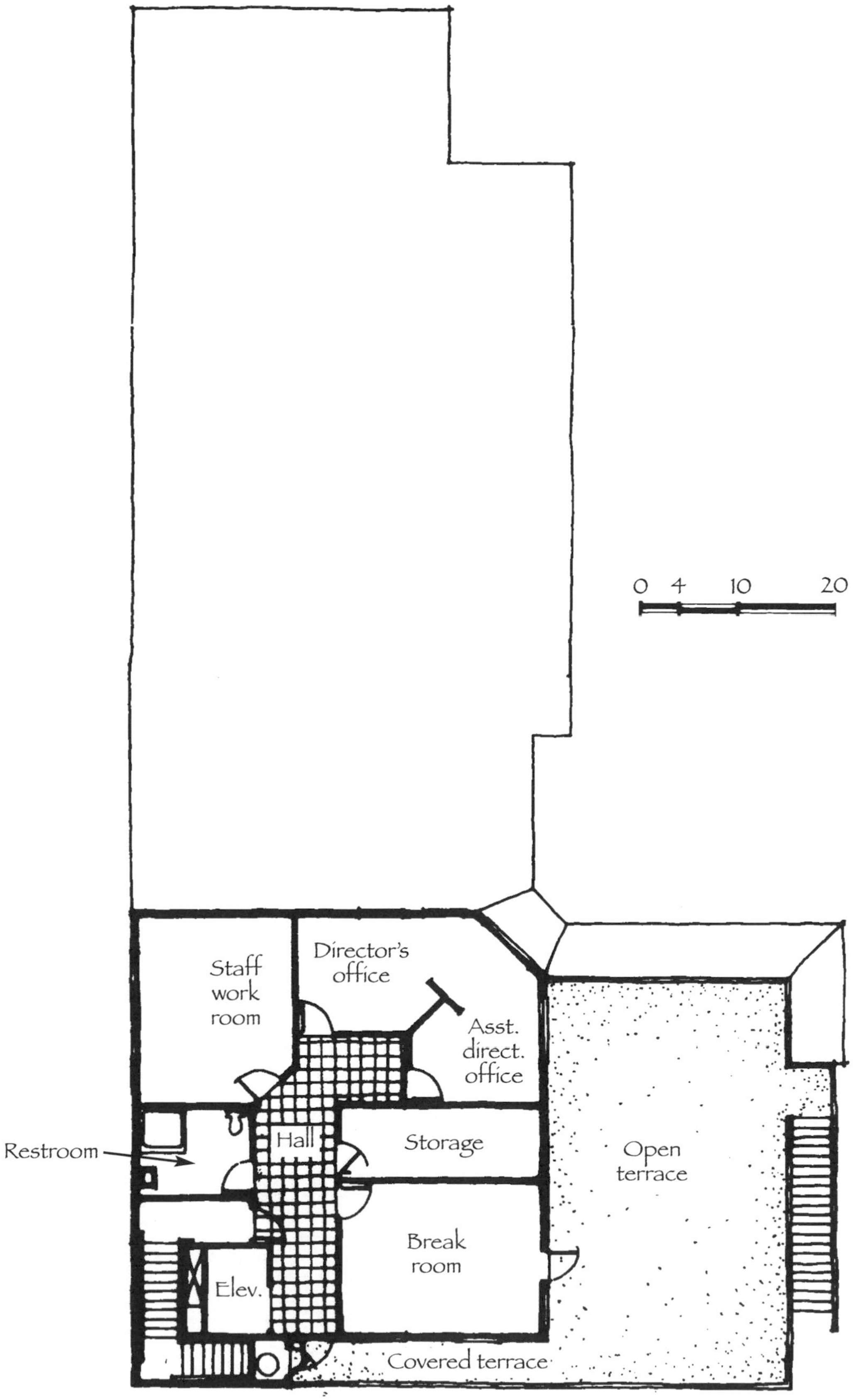
0 4 10 20
Staff work room
Director's office
Asst. direct. office
Restroom
Hall
Storage
Open terrace
Break room
Elev.
Covered terrace

CHAPTER SEVEN

ZONING A GROUP ROOM

No building ever feels right to the people in it unless the physical spaces (defined by columns, walls, and ceilings) are congruent with the social spaces (defined by activities and human groups).

—CHRISTOPHER ALEXANDER

The design of children's group rooms is the subject of this chapter and Chapters 15 through 18. Here we will look at the architectural parameters that create a good basic room structure and layout. Chapter 15 explores general principles of organizing and furnishing the group rooms, while Chapters 16–18 address specific requirements according to age. After presenting major principles of room layout, this chapter provides a 12-step process for generating a new layout, or evaluating an existing one, and concludes with three case studies where the principles are applied.

Group Room Layout: A Collaborative Process

As discussed in Chapter 6, it is possible to begin schematic design by first laying out the group rooms and then the building, or vice versa. But it is actually necessary to work at several levels of scale simultaneously, and to continually assess the appropriateness of group-room design as the overall building plan is taking shape. The center needs to be designed from the inside and the outside at the same time.

The complex functional requirements of children's group rooms are more likely to be fulfilled when architects seek caregivers' participation in exploring a room's full range of operational requirements. Collaboration is crucial at this stage of the process. But since it may involve extra time on the architect's part, a fee structure needs to be established at the outset (as noted in Chapter 3) to reflect this way of working. Architects and designers are urged to read this chapter and Chapter 15 carefully to gain insight into what makes child care rooms "work."

Honoring the principles of zoning, which this chapter addresses, helps to eliminate many of the design barriers with which caregivers contend daily. In zoning a room properly, architects can make a significant contribution to the lives of children and staff. Before renovating or simply rearranging a group room, child care professionals can employ these concepts to know better where to begin.

Identifying Functional Requirements

The first step in designing a room is to determine what activities and events the room will be used for. These are called its functional requirements. In child care, a group room's activities are quite numerous and diverse, creating a rather complex pattern of behaviors occurring within its four walls. Thus the team will want to begin by identifying and listing all the developmental, educational, and caregiving activities staff wish to have occur in the room. Functional requirements include *activities* (eating, sleeping, crawling, cuddling, reading, painting) and *equipment* (refrigerator, chairs, cribs, closets), and may also include *lighting* and *acoustic* requirements needed to support these functions. The names and number of functional requirements should reflect both what children require and what each caregiver wishes to make available, based upon his or her unique interests and abilities.

All functions of merit need to appear on the list at

BOX 7.1

Typical Functional Requirements by Age Group

Infants

Caregiving	Physical Movement/ Active Play	Quiet Play	Messy Play
diapering: storage of clothing and diapers	rocking	reading	water
sleeping (1 crib/child)	swinging	listening	sand
cooking/food preparation	crawling	manipulatives	painting
nursing, feeding, self-feeding	bouncing	dolls, stuffed animals, wheeled toys	
infant coats/personal storage	pulling-to-stand	passive observation of activities, events, light and nature	
staff coats/personal storage	cruising		
parent sign-in and notice board	music and movement		
physical contact with adults: cuddling, carrying			
massage and gentle exercise			
equipment/materials storage			
group meeting space			
private spaces			
one-on-one spaces			

Toddlers

Caregiving	Physical Movement/ Active Play	Quiet Play	Messy Play
diapering and toileting	rocking	reading	water
storage of clothing and diapers	swinging	listening	sand
napping (1 crib or cot/child)	crawling	manipulatives	painting: finger and easel
cooking/food preparation	bouncing	dolls, stuffed animals	coloring
feeding, eating	pulling-to-stand	passive observation of activities, events, light and nature	clay/play dough
parent sign-in/notice board	toddling	simple puzzles/constructions	collage
toddler coats/personal storage	spinning	cardboard blocks	
staff coats/personal storage	"plopping"/tumbling		
physical contact with adults: cuddling/carrying	balancing		
massage and gentle exercise	sliding		
equipment/materials storage	running		
group meeting space	pulling and pushing toys		
private spaces	riding wheeled vehicles		
one-on-one spaces	music and movement		
	hammering		

the outset so they can eventually be provided for in the design. Do not exclude something (for example, gross motor play), because there is no obvious way to make it happen or because the room appears too small. Similarly, for remodels, do not limit the list solely to those activities for which the room already has supports and materials (for example, using the room only for tabletop activities because it has six tables and 30 chairs). An activity rejected at this initial stage may be lost forever. When something is of genuine value, there is usually a way to make it happen, provided it remains a priority.

BOX 7.1

Typical Functional Requirements by Age Group *(continued)*

Preschoolers

Caregiving	Active Play	Quiet Play	Messy Play
toilets	climbing	reading	water
preschool coats/personal storage	crawling	listening	sand
staff coats/personal storage	swinging	manipulatives	clay
parent sign-in and notice board	sliding	small unit blocks	paint
napping (1 cot/per child)	balancing	writing	collage
cooking/food preparation	music and dance	math/science	cooking
physical contact with adults: cuddling, wrestling	storefront		woodworking
	puppets		science/animals/ nature study
equipment/materials storage	dress-up clothes		
group meeting space	house play		
private spaces	dramatic play themes		
one-on-one spaces	large hollow blocks		
	miniatures		

School-Age Children

Caregiving	Active Play	Quiet Play	Messy Play
afterschool coats/personal storage	running	reading	arts and crafts (ceramics, leather, knitting, sewing)
staff coats/personal storage	climbing	listening	
parent bulletin board	sliding	homework	
toilets (age segregated)	swinging	puzzles and games	clay
cooking/food preparation	music and dance sports	rest/lounging	painting
equipment/materials storage	games		woodworking
group meeting space	theater		photograph
private spaces			
one-on-one spaces			

Because children and staff are always growing and changing, expect the nature and number of functions to change over time. However, a room design based on the principles discussed here usually can graciously accommodate most changes.

Box 7.1 suggests a range of typical functional requirements for the different age groups, organizing them into four general categories: caregiving, active play, quiet play, and messy play. Additional categories—therapeutic, for example—are possible. Three of these categories—active, quiet, and messy play—relate specifically to physical zones in the room; the fourth category—caregiving—occurs throughout the four zones.

Fixed Features

Once a room's functional requirements have been identified, you will want to begin to create or shape a space to accommodate them. The structural or architectural elements that create and contribute to a room's form—walls, doors, floors, ceilings, windows, lights, outlets, heating and air conditioning units, sinks, bathrooms—are known as its *fixed features*. When you design a room from scratch, you create fixed features. When you renovate a room, you must grapple with the composite of fixed features that already exists. In either case, the fixed features eventually become the building

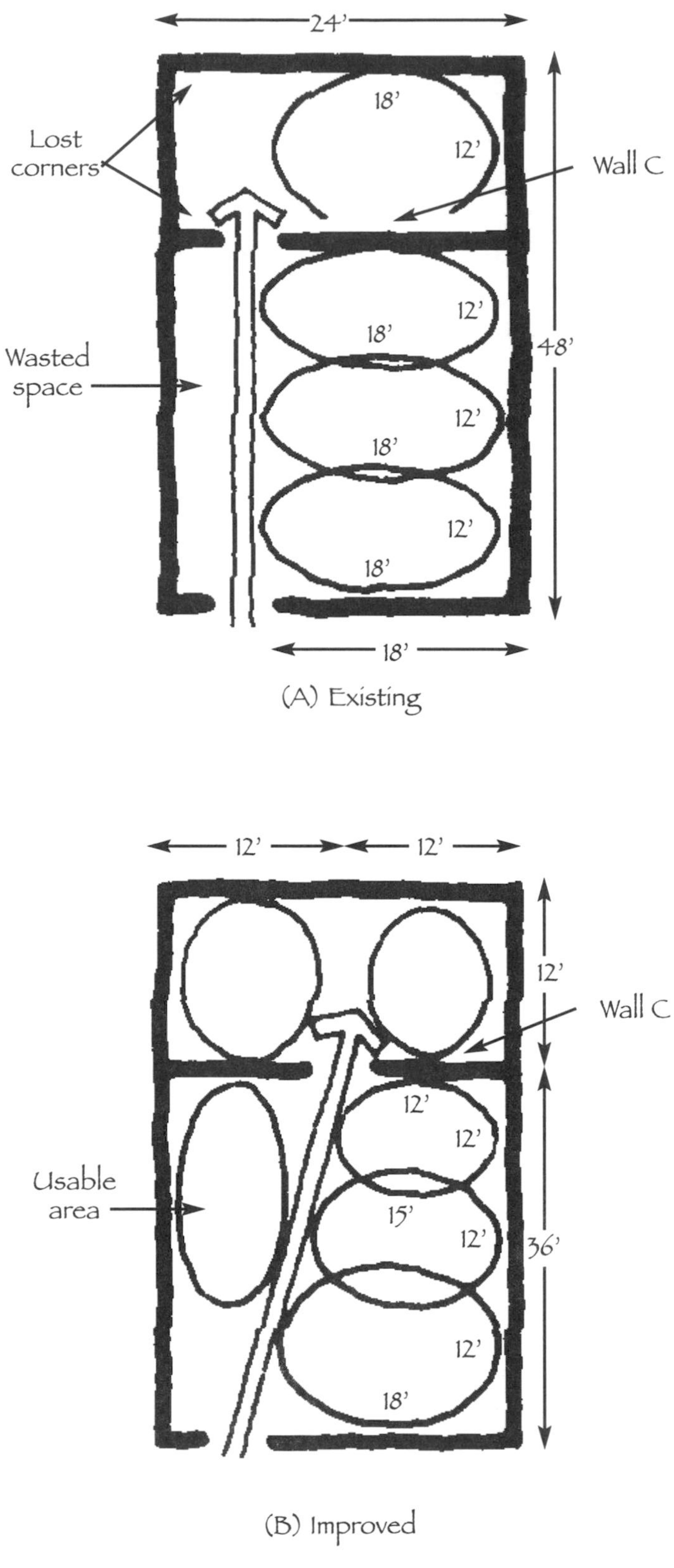

Figure 7.1
(A) Existing, (B) Improved

elements least amenable to change. Although most fixed features can later be modified in some way, the expense of such structural modification fosters a tendency to see them as unchangeable. In new construction, this means that it is important to try to get them right at the outset. With renovations, on the other hand, the design team will want to be open to changing fixed features where doing so will produce invaluable improvements in a room's overall layout—despite the fact that such changes might be costly.

> ***Example:*** In the room illustrated in Figure 7.1a, the location of the doorway to the small room at the rear, directly opposite the main entrance to the room, creates several problems:
>
> - It makes a long, narrow "runway" for children.
> - It creates space that is too narrow to be very useful.
> - It leads to the loss of two corners and makes wall C so long and deep that the areas created off of it are impractically large for most activities.
>
> Moving the door to the middle of wall C, (Figure 7.1b) alleviates all these problems and allows the room to more readily adapt to its needed functions.

Two factors related to a room's fixed features are the room's sun orientation and its relationship to or connection with outdoor play space. As you create your room, you will want to note the sun's path on your plan and therefore where it would be most desirable to have windows. Also create a bubble diagram indicating the closest outdoor space to this room, and an arrow from the room suggesting where an indoor/outdoor connection might occur. You will want to strive for a good indoor/outdoor connection from each group room. If this is not possible, then the connections that can occur need to be identified early on, including how the children will get outside and how they will be supervised in transit and while outdoors.

The Power of Fixed Features

Fixed features determine a room's shape and form. The messages they convey are extremely important in two respects.

First, fixed features "speak" to us, affecting our perception of space. The height of a ceiling may suggest that we stretch and jump, or crouch and con-

BOX 7.2

Sensing the Messages of a Room's Fixed-Feature Constraints

Stand and walk in the empty room, or imagine yourself present in one on paper, or in model form. Consider how the space might feel at different times of the day and under different light. Allow its subtleties of character to be revealed to you. Notice the position of its doors and corners. Where are you drawn to be sociable and active? Where would you prefer to sit to eat and draw, or to solve a puzzle and read a book? Listen for as long as you need to. Let your intuition be your guide.

tract. An area's patterns of light and shadow invite or dissuade us from approaching. Walls, floors, and ceilings create spatial limits. Most of us, *especially children,* instinctively respond to a room's inherent messages. (Notice how children race around exploring every nook and cranny of a new space, wondering: *How big is this space? How did I get into it? How can I get out?*)

An effective room layout depends upon working with rather than against the room's messages. For example, a door (even one that is locked and never used) broadcasts an implicit message of "opening" and "transit." A cozy area created by placing pillows on the floor in front of such a door will never feel as protected as one located in a corner without a visible doorway. *Ignoring or overriding fixed-feature messages*—such as placing high-energy activities in zones suggesting tranquillity (or vice versa)—*always involves some cost to people's sense of peace and well-being in a space.* Thus, it is important to honor what any room's fixed features—especially its doors and corners—are, or will be, communicating. For help in identifying and appreciating the messages a room's fixed features present, try the exercise in Box 7.2.

Second, fixed features create the regions of transit and protection in a room—the two most important factors in locating activities. Doors automatically "tell" where the areas of exposure lie; corners communicate the places of protection. A successful layout depends upon recognizing that certain activities and functions (art, sinks, climbers, storefronts) work well in exposed places, whereas other activities (small unit blocks, manipulatives, reading) require protection.

Regions and Zones

For efficient space use, activities with different physical requirements need to be segregated within a group room. The goal in designing the room is to arrange its fixed features to create two main regions—wet (exposed) and dry (protected)—and four major zones—entry, messy, active, and quiet—within it.

What Are Regions?

Group rooms need to have two regions: one for wet activities and another for dry. Wet activities are those that involve water or other messy materials (such as sand, paints, clay) or heavy foot traffic to and from the building or outdoors, and that therefore need a washable floor surface. Because the position of an activity sink typically determines where the room's wet region will be, proper placement of the sink is critical. The wet region usually comprises about half the room. The dry region comprises the remaining half of the space and is generally carpeted.

What Are Zones?

Within these two regions, regardless of age group, four general categories of activity normally take place: entry, messy, active, and quiet. Rooms function best when the architecture allocates locations—or zones—for these activities. The wet region typically encompasses the entry and messy zones; the dry region the quiet and active zones (Figure 7.2):[1]

- Wet region = entry zone, messy zone
- Dry region = quiet zone, active zone

It is desirable to locate the entry and messy zones near one another because they are both high-use areas involving a lot of movement of people on their feet. At the same time, it is essential that any quiet zone be as remote and separate from the entry and

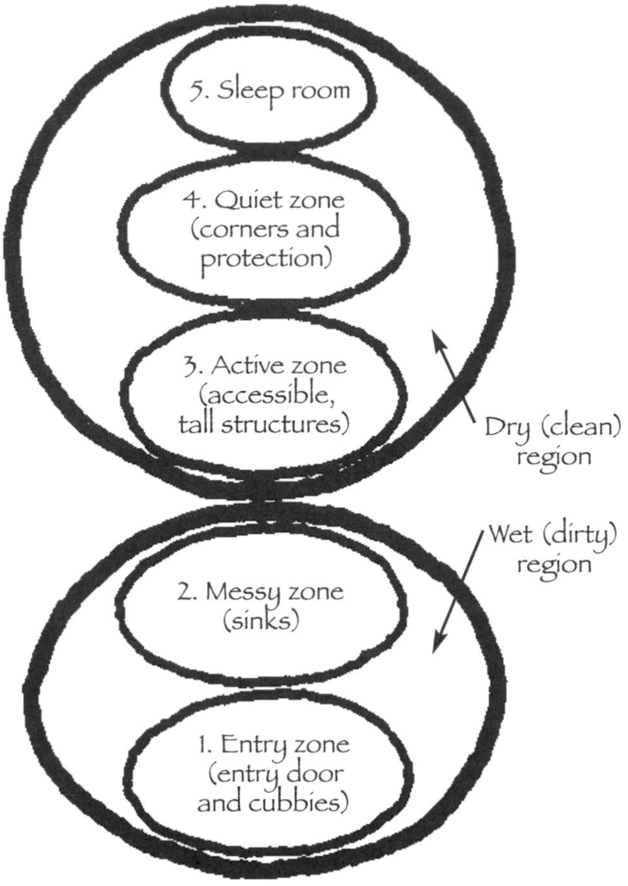

Figure 7.2
A room's wet region is comprised of an entry and a messy zone; its dry region of an active and a quiet zone; there may be a fifth zone—a sleep zone in infant and sometimes toddler rooms.

messy zones as possible. Since many quiet activities involve use of the floor, carpet is especially appropriate. Carpet also provides padding under active play equipment where children might fall. Hence, the quiet and active zones naturally belong as part of the room's dry region.

A Fifth Zone: Infant Sleep

Infant rooms, and sometimes toddler rooms, require an additional zone for cribs and sleeping. This zone needs to be a separate room or partitioned space near the quiet zone and furthest from noise and activity. Ideally, it is also located in the part of the group room that receives the least amount of natural light.

Activities that Occur in the Four Zones

To help you better understand the functions of the four zones, activities that typically occur in each one are described below. The number of activities and their locations are intended to be suggestive; specifics will vary from program to program.

Activities in the Entry Zone

Every group room needs an entry or "vestibule" near its entrance doorway to provide a place of transition. An entry zone:

- Allows parents and visitors to pause and be greeted before being thrust into the midst of activity
- Provides children with a point of approach, greeting, and separation from parents in the morning and a point of leave-taking at the end of the day
- Provides children playing in the room some protection from unexpected intrusion and distraction
- Provides a clearly demarcated location for taking off and putting on outer clothing, for containing the dirt from footware, and for acknowledging a distinction between indoor and outdoor behaviors
- Ideally provides direct access to the outdoors

Box 7.3 lists the activities and supports that typically occur in and around a room's entry. You will want to add your own requirements to the list.

Activities in the Messy Zone

The activities that typically occur in the messy zone involve tables and chairs; a lot of free flow around easels, woodworking benches, and water, sand, and clay tables; and back and forth trips to a sink. Ideally, there is also an outdoor play yard connection from the room's messy zone. Box 7.4 on page 144 describes these in detail.

All these facilities need to be arranged near one another. This usually necessitates a washable floor surface of considerable size, typically about half of the room. A washable floor surface that is too small to accommodate the full range of messy activities severe-

BOX 7.3

Typical Activities, Facilities, and Supports in the Entry Zone

Dressing/Undressing/Storage

- Children's personal storage—coats and materials, portfolios, art work
- Staff personal storage—coats, handbags
- Places to sit and assist children with dressing/undressing
- Sufficient floor space for toddlers to spread out clothing

Greetings/Farewells/Oversight Activities

- Sign-in/sign-out procedures
- Parent notice board
- Lost-and-found box
- Greetings, farewells between children, parents, and staff
- Information exchange between parents and staff
- Observation
- Door to play yard

Dirt Control

- Floor surface that absorbs dust, dirt, and moisture from shoes
- Storage of visitors' shoes (infant room)

Storage

- Adjacent storage for carriages, car seats, wagons

ly compromises the educational program. Alternatively, one which is too large limits the amount of carpeted area for tranquil activities. Err on the side of too much washable surface since it is easier to lay carpet over a washable floor covering than to do the reverse.

Activities in the Active /Dramatic Play Zone

Generally speaking, the spaces not occupied by the corners, the entry, and the messy zone are most appropriate for movement, climbing, and dramatic play.

Box 7.5 on page 145 lists some typical activities that occur in the active/dramatic play zone. (Refer to Chapters 16–18 for more age-specific information about recommended supports for the active zone.)

Activities in the Quiet Zone

Many quiet activities involve small, loose materials with which children create their own structures (blocks, manipulatives, construction toys) or in which they discover an inherent structure (puzzles, books, games). These materials are often best used on the floor, provided they can be protected from transit and passersby. Hence the need to locate them in an extremely protected place. Quiet activities can also include resting, cuddling, daydreaming, and just plain hanging out.

Box 7.6 on page 145 lists some of the typical activities that occur in the quiet zone. (Refer to Chapters 16–18 for more age-specific information about recommended supports for the quiet zone.)

Creating Wet and Dry Regions

Improper zoning of group rooms and inappropriate placement of fixed features create the kinds of problems typical of many new as well as old centers:

- Too many doors for getting in and out of the room
- Sinks in corners, encroaching on quiet zones
- Doors in all four corners so there is no place of protection
- Wall space consumed by doors, cabinets, and windows

BOX 7.4

Typical Activities, Facilities, and Supports in the Messy Zone

Personal Hygiene/ Diapering/ Food Preparation/ Water and Sand Play

- Washable floor surface
- Toilets and handwashing sinks (toddlers, preschool)
- Diaper-changing sink (infants, toddlers)
- Adult-height sink and counter for food/art preparation and cleanup
- Optional child-height sink for cleanup/water fountain
- Water play trough (built-in faucets and drain)
- Sand play trough (sometimes)

Arts and Crafts/Eating

- 2–4 child-size tables and chairs for collage, crafts, snacks, eating, cooking activities
- Child-accessible storage for crafts materials
- Low table for clay and playdough use
- Bins for holding clay; storage of tools
- Projects
- Door to play yard

Painting

- Wall-mounted or freestanding easels
- Walls, racks, shelves for drying children's paintings and art work
- Wall-mounted display surfaces for children's art work, other visual images, hooks for smocks
- Storage for easel paper (tube)

Woodworking

- Woodworking bench with vise
- Bins for wood scraps
- Peg-board panels for displaying tools
- A tree stump for hammering nails

Nature Study

- Science/nature/animal display and work surfaces

Cooking Projects/Eating

- Separate table for open, ongoing snacks (seating 4–6)
- Storage/display of snack supplies (food, juice, cups, napkins, etc.)
- Storage/display of cooking supplies (staples, utensils, dishes, pots, oven, refrigerator) and/or cart

Storage

- Storage for children's works-in-progress
- Trash baskets
- Storage for bulk crafts supplies

- No entry zone off the entry door, so visitors and cubbies spill into the room's activity
- No access to the outdoors, or play yards in shadow

All of these problems can be remedied by creating wet and dry regions and the four activity zones.

The order of the zones—from entry and messy to active and quiet—reflects a public (more active) to private (more tranquil) progression, which is desirable to honor in every room's layout. Here is the reason. Unlike a home, which has bedrooms, a study, and a family room where people can retreat if they want some privacy or peace and quiet, a group room is a single space which many people share. There are no ancillary spaces where someone can go to get away from the group. By subdividing the room, it is possible to create opportunities for individual and small group retreat. However, full-height walls are not the tools for doing this. Instead, the definition of public versus private, or exposure versus protection, must be achieved through

BOX 7.5

Typical Activities in the Active Zone

- Climbing/large motor play
- Costumes and dress-ups
- Dramatic play/fantasy
- Wheeled vehicles
- Fantasy house and doll play
- Large unit blocks
- Puppet play
- Music and movement
- Storefront
- Cot storage (sometimes, for some age groups)

BOX 7.6

Typical Activities in the Quiet Zone

- Reading
- Resting, hanging out
- Small unit blocks
- Listening
- Math
- Manipulatives
- Group meeting
- Writing
- Private and semiprivate spaces

the room's architecture and its ability to create wet and dry regions.

Unless a conscious effort is made to protect a substantial portion of the room from foot traffic, people's movement and activity will take over, eliminating potential places of retreat. Thus the first goal of any room layout is to separate the wet and dry regions and to concentrate the room's doors and activity sinks in its entry and messy zones, so as to protect a substantial portion of the room—not just a corner—for quiet play. This alone will make an enormous contribution to the functionality of each room.

The Wet Region: A Place of Exposed Spaces

In order to create protected spaces, the exposed spaces in the room must be minimized and concentrated in one location, namely the wet region consisting of the entry and messy zones.

The Entry and Messy Zones

Since exposure is created by doors, especially those leading in and out of the room, all or at least most of the room's doors need to be located in the entry and messy zones. The room's doors include its entry door off one of the building's corridors; its emergency exit and play yard door(s); doors to bathrooms; and doors to storage closets. Concentrating the doors in these two zones also has the advantage of increasing the amount of unencumbered wall surface in the room, leaving more space for windows, for display, or for a climber for active play. Figure 7.3 illustrates good and poor door placement in a room.

The Main Transit Path

Ideally a room should have only two doors connecting it to the exterior: one serving as its entrance/exit from the building corridor and the other as its emergency exit and exit to the play yard (Figure 7.4). (Two doorways are sufficient to meet the fire laws in most states. Check local building codes for the number required in your area and the required distance separating these doors.) Having only two entrance/exit doors minimizes the amount of space lost to transit and the confusion generated by people entering or leaving from many different parts of the room. Where more doorways exist (as in Figure 7.5a), try to eliminate or relocate those that are unnecessary, (as in Figure 7.5b)

Figure 7.3
(A) Too many doors usurp valuable protected floor space.
(B) Consolidating storage and relocating the doors and sinks gives this room a dry region even though the emergency exit door could not be relocated.

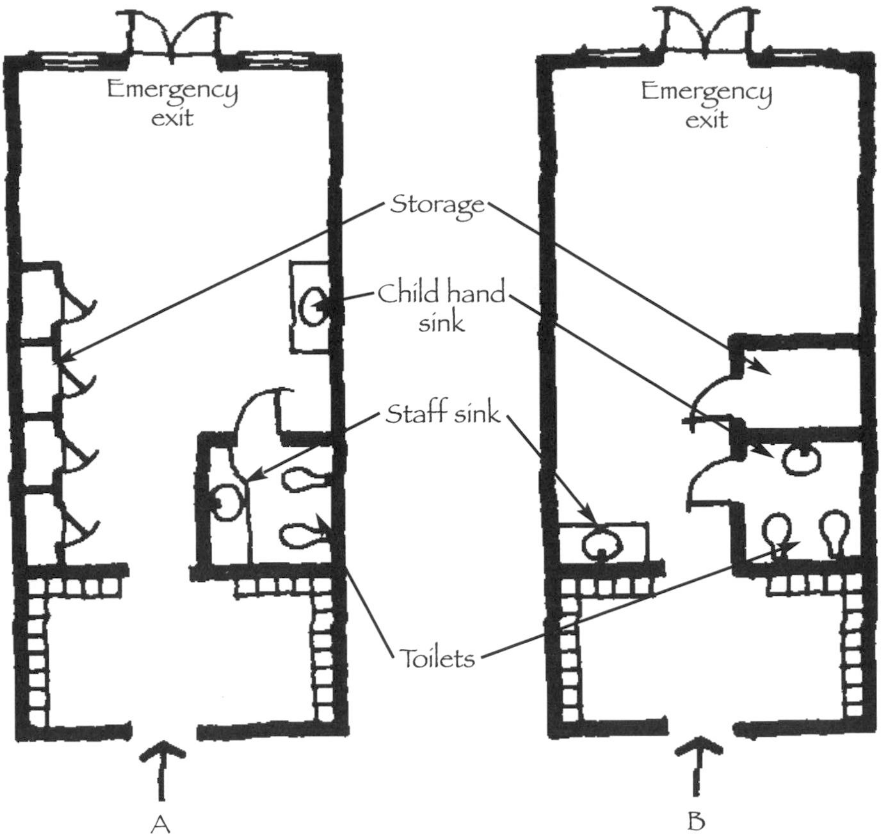

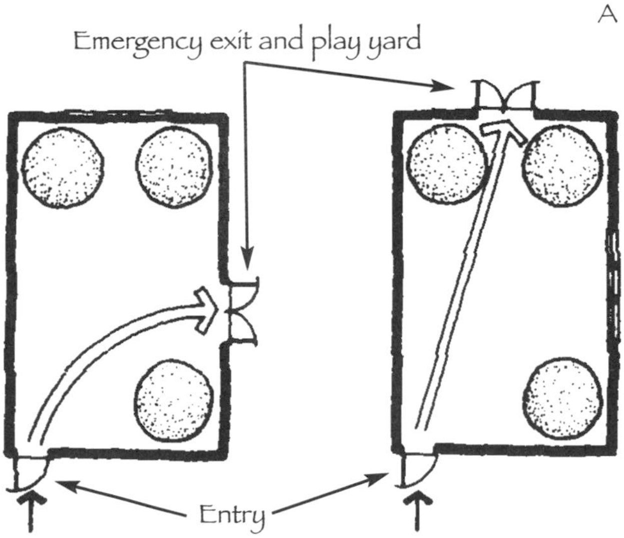

Figure 7.4
The room's main path of transit lies between its main entrance and its emergency exit/play yard doors.

especially those that force traffic to intrude upon corners and the quiet zone.

The path between the two doors—entry and emergency exit— creates the room's primary path of transit. To honor fire codes, this path will need to be kept free of furniture and activity.

Activity Sinks

Activity sinks are defined as either teacher-height or child-height sinks used for curricular activities. These are distinguished from handwashing sinks, which are normally placed in or near bathrooms. Just as the room's entry door tends to define its entry zone, a room's activity sinks tend to define its messy zone.

The location of activity sinks and the space around them affects:

- The room's circulation pattern
- The ability to sequester corners and protected zones for more tranquil activities
- The ease with which people can access water and clean up
- The staff's ability to supervise the entire room while working at the sink(s)
- The number of messy-type activities the room will accommodate

Because there is so much foot traffic around sinks and the activities they support, locating them in the messy

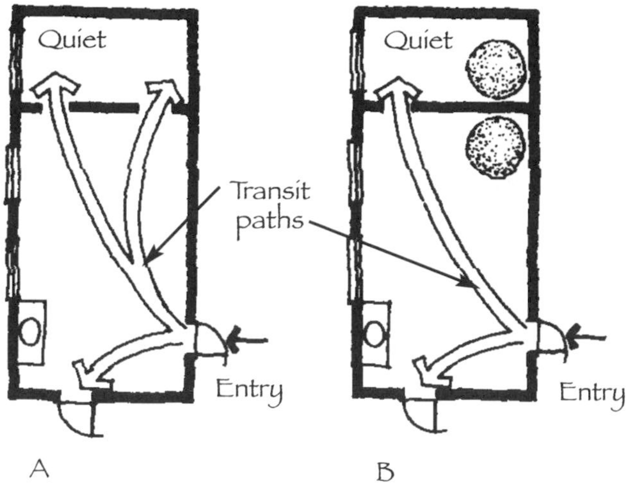

Figure 7.5
(A) The two existing doors into the quiet room limit the available corners for protected play.
(B) Eliminating one doorway into the quiet room adds two additional protected corners.

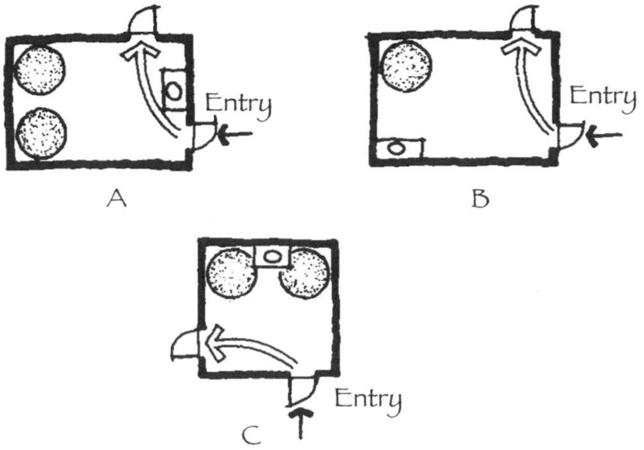

Figure 7.6
(A) Do: Locate the sink near the primary path of circulation and far away from the protected regions of the room.
(B) Don't: The sink is poorly placed in the protected region of the room. It is too remote from the entry.
(C) Don't: The sink is poorly placed in a protected corner. It is too remote from the entry.

zone helps to concentrate movement in the wet region. Figure 7.6 illustrates dos and don'ts of sink location.

Ideally, each group room will have two activity sinks: an adult-height sink in a teacher preparation counter 6–10 feet long, with cabinets above and below; and a child-height water play table that is either built in or placed under a built-in faucet and drain.

Incorporating a Water Play Table

Water fascinates young children, and exploring its properties is one of their prime learning activities. Since most centers do not have ready access to creeks, streams, lakes, rivers, and oceans, plentiful opportunities for water play need to be provided inside as well as outside the center.

The expense involved to add a built-in water play table or a freestanding water faucet and drain (Figure 7.7) is minor compared to the benefits these elements will provide over the life span of the facility. Built-in water troughs—or a faucet and drain for a trough on wheels—can:

- Spare staff much time and effort required to fill and empty water play tables.
- Offer children more frequent and varied water play opportunity—soapsuds, colored water, etc.

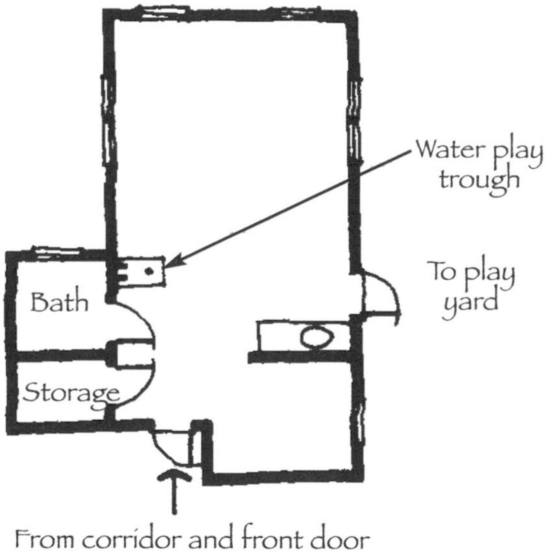

Figure 7.7
Adding a separate drain and faucet for a built-in (or portable) water play trough contributes immeasurably to the ease and joy of playing with water.

- Promote sanitation since the water can be changed easily and often
- Sometimes serve as a child-height cleanup sink

Staff and architects are strongly urged not to eliminate this option!

Room Shape, Doors, and Zones

It is easy for bubble diagrams to express a desired spatial relationship between a room's wet and dry regions. This is because they illustrate ideal configurations, which are most easily achieved when a room stands on its own and its walls can be pushed out, or doors located, as desired. Part of the challenge in laying out a group room is that such ideal relationships are rarely achievable in the real world. Instead, the room's shape will depend, in part, upon how it must be coordinated with the site and with the building's circulation paths and other rooms. Thus it is unlikely that rooms in any two centers will be alike.

This discussion cannot address all the room shapes and challenges that are likely to arise. Nor does it wish to present any single layout as the ideal. Rather, it is hoped that considering the pros and cons of the following two configurations can guide your own inquiry.

Let us assume—as is typically the case with a compact building design—that the rooms will be rectangular in shape, not square. Whether the entry door is placed on the long or short wall of the rectangle determines the room's orientaton as either long and narrow (Figure 7.8), or wide and shallow (Figure 7.9). These two particular layouts honor most of the zoning principles discussed so far. However, they do so in two different ways.

In Figure 7.8, the entry door is in the corner of one short side of the room. Doors and sinks are concentrated in the wet region, leaving a large portion of the room, and its two deepest and most remote (from the entry) corners, intact. There is a door from the messy zone to the play yard, allowing free movement between indoors and out, especially in nice weather. In inclement weather, when children are likely to be wearing raincoats, snowsuits, and boots, they can come and go between the room and the play yard through a door in the entry zone, thereby tracking less dirt through the room itself. The possible disadvantage of this layout is that the active and quiet zones are next to one another. However, they often can be separated by partitions, dividers, and the design of furnishings within the areas themselves.

In Figure 7.9, the entry door is in the middle of one long wall of the room. Doors and sinks are concentrated in the messy zone, which lies between the active and quiet zones, which it separates nicely. The quiet zone benefits from good definition and two deep corners. There is a door from the messy zone to the play yard. The bathroom could also be placed at the play yard end for access from outdoors, or it can be placed next to the entry zone as shown. The disadvantage of this plan is the limited amount of wall space available to the messy zone for sinks, above-counter storage, easels, and display. This is not easily rectified.

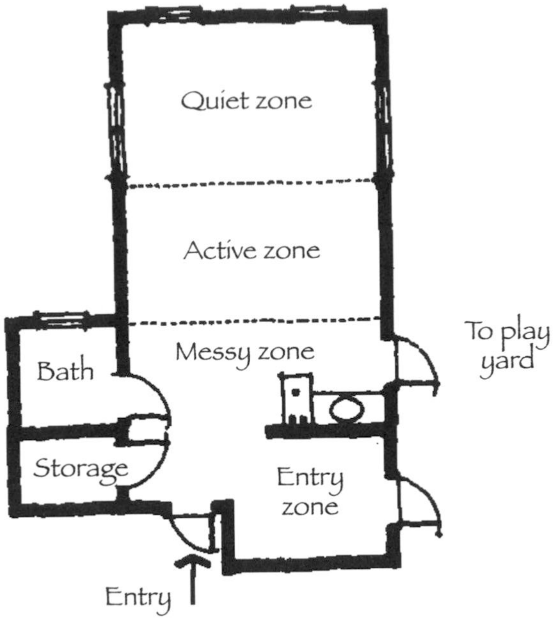

Figure 7.8
A rectangular room with its entry door in the corner of one of the shorter walls.

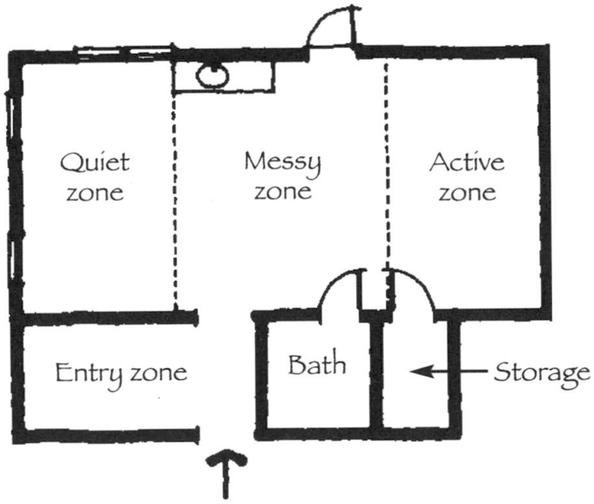

Figure 7.9
A rectangular room with its entry door and emergency exit door in the middle of its longer walls.

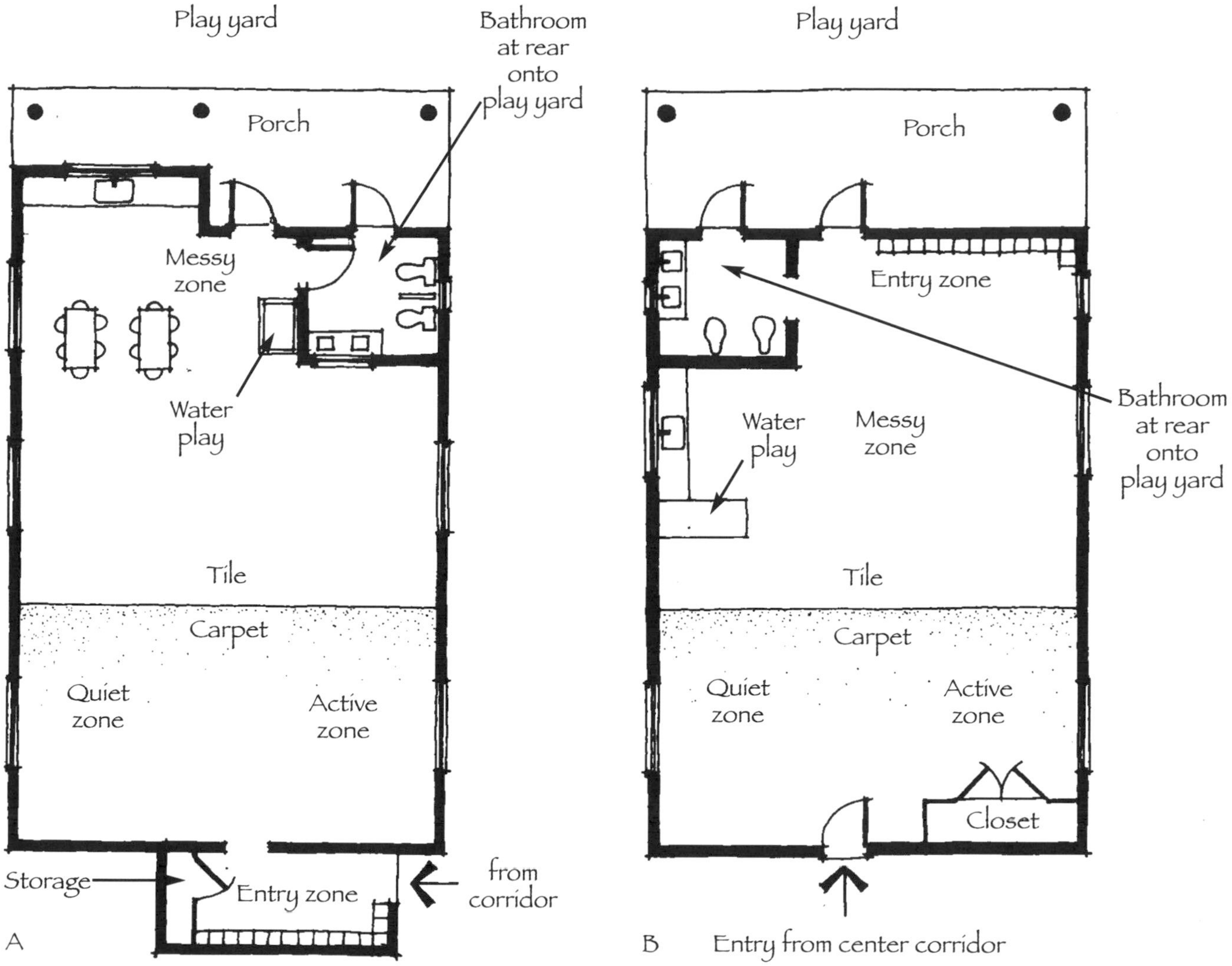

Figure 7.10
(A) The children's bathroom is located on the play yard side, across the room from the entry and cubbies.
(B) The children's bathroom and cubbies are located on the play yard side, across the room from the entry.

As you create a new plan, or evaluate one that exists, explore ways in which entry and exit door locations—relative to the room's shape, site and building connections, and the placement of sinks—can be concentrated to leave protected corners remote from traffic. Strive to create truly separate wet and dry regions.

Locating Entry and Messy Zones in Warm Climates

In warm climates, where children spend a great deal of time outdoors and need to flow freely between indoors and out, a question often arises as to where to develop the entry zone with the children's cubbies, and where to position the bathrooms. Should the cubbies and bathrooms be close to the room's door from the building's corridor, or should they be close to the play yard?

Figure 7.10 illustrates two possible ways to handle this. In Figure 7.10a, the entry zone where children store their belongings is kept near the room's entry from the building's corridor, where parents arrive and leave, read the notice board, drop off their children's apparel, and pick it up at the end of the day. However, the bathroom, and the messy zone with the sinks, have been placed at the opposite end of the room closer to the play yard. This arrangement works well since the heaviest foot traffic is concentrated where it most often occurs, i.e., between the room and the play yard. The entry zone is really a convenience for parents and visitors and is used less frequently.

In Figure 7.10b, the entire entry zone and messy zone have been located at the play yard end. Often, in this arrangement, parents and children actually enter the room through the play yard rather than through the building's lobby and main corridor. This works better in small centers than in large ones where surveillance, safety, and control are more complicated. Also, the room needs to be sufficiently wide (26–28 feet) so that transit from the building corridor down its middle is less likely to disturb activities occuring on either side of the transit path. Even if parents and children enter through the room's corridor entry door, the entry and messy zones are concentrated where they are used the most.

The Dry Region: A Place of Protected Spaces

As doors create a room's exposed areas, corners create its protected spaces. Although access to and from the room is essential, as are bathrooms and sinks, what designers often fail to recognize is that a truly protected and tranquil zone in the room is no less important. This protected space needs to be of substantial size, and not just a corner.

The Quiet Zone

Take time to identify all the corners and protected spaces of the room being designed or renovated, making particular note of the one or two that seem most remote from the doorways and most secure. If you are uncertain, imagine yourself choosing a place on the floor to build a big structure with lots of little blocks. Which corner feels least vulnerable to intrusion, and disruption of your block structures or your body?

If a room has doors in all four corners, it is necessary to create protected areas by eliminating some doors. Alternatively, it may be necessary to abandon such a room as a group space for child care, reserving it for assembly or some type of active play.

Recognizing the Most Protected Corner

Generally speaking, a room has at least one corner that can be considered to be its "most protected" space. Most occupants of a room identify this corner instinctively. It is usually filled with furniture belonging to the person who controls the space—the teacher's, doctor's, or therapist's desk, Dad's favorite chair, or even storage. *The most protected corner is generally furthest from, and often diagonally opposite, the entry door* (Figure 7.11). Examine rooms with which you are familiar. Sense where the most protected corner is and note what furniture is placed there. (As discussed in Chapter 15, in group rooms this corner is often the best location for small unit block play.)

Identifying the most protected corner is important in two respects:

- We feel most secure when our bodies are oriented with a solid surface at our backs. Thus we instinctively place our backs, chairs, and desks against a wall or in the room's most protected space.
- We experience the most control of a space when this protected corner is far from the door, giving us more time to prepare for and respond to an unexpected visitor. It enables us to both comfortably scan all areas of the room and monitor intrusion through the entry door.[2]

Honoring the messages of the most protected corner is critical in child care group rooms to give children relief from the multiple comings and goings that easily disrupt their play, to help them feel in control of the room, and to give them a place of genuine retreat. *It is particularly important to carve out a substantial amount of protected floor space—including, but not limited to the room's most protected corner—so that small groups and individuals can sit, lie, or work on the floor without being stepped on or interrupted by transit.*

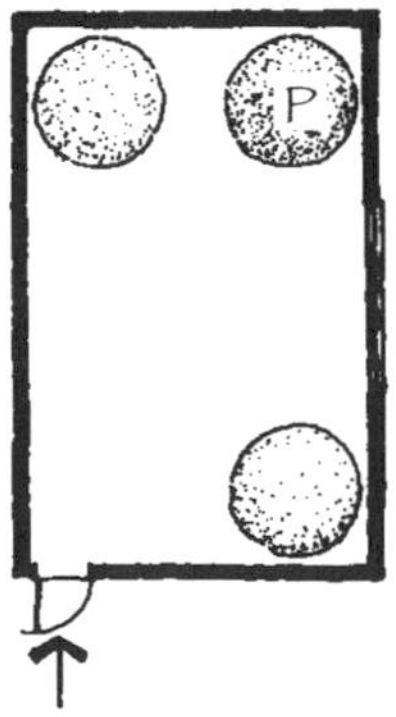

Figure 7.11
This room's most protected corner.

The Active Zone

The activities listed in Box 7.5 as occuring in the active/dramatic play zone are intermediate in their need for protection and exposure between quiet and messy play activities. For example, any play using dolls, doll houses, small trucks and cars, or a pretend kitchen, needs a fair amount of privacy and protection. However, climbing on a climber needs space and access, while selling produce in a pretend store, or putting on a puppet show both benefit from exposure to "customers" and an "audience." Thus, active play is ideal alongside a room's major pathway, provided it can also receive some protection either through the room's architecture, or through the use of multileveled structures, lofts, and partitions.

In the messy zone, the activities themselves usually involve quite a bit of free flow, and tables and chairs protect the play materials and children's bodies from the movement of people on their feet. In the active zone, on the other hand, activities either tend to be more circumscribed and benefit from enclosure (i.e., a play house), or need to be contained so they do not get out-of-bounds and create too much noise and confusion.

The two factors that influence the location of the active zone are:

- Proximity to the room's main circulation route—which facilitates children's access to a climbing structure and to certain forms of dramatic play. Being close to the path also makes the zone appear larger, and saves space, because the path can accommodate movement, such as getting on or off a climber, that may "spill over" from the zone.
- Relationship to the room's walls and overall pattern of visibility—for placement of the tall structures usually included in the active zone.

Active play usually occurs best on carpet. However, whether to use carpet or washable flooring for this zone is ultimately a matter of personal choice, based somewhat upon the activities there.

Locations for Tall Structures

Since the active zone ideally includes a multileveled structure or climber, location of the zone also involves height and visibility considerations. Appropriate locations for tall structures are often few and always need to be carefully determined. Here are some guidelines for locating tall structures:

- Do not place a tall structure in the middle of the room where it will block visibility.
- Try not to place a climber in a corner because it generally requires access on three sides.
- Do not place a tall structure in front of a window, where it may block light and be dangerous should children fall. However, it may be appropriate under a high window, especially if it provides children the opportunity to look out, or next to a low window to light a play area inside the structure.

Examine the room for locations for tall structures where they will not visually block areas requiring continual surveillance.

Example: In Figure 7.12, A, B, and C represent three possible locations for a climbing/dramatic play structure. Any other location either blocks the entry, the windows, access to the sink, or usurps a protected corner.

- Location A is very close to the entrance and would take up valuable space in what is most naturally the messy zone.
- Location B is possible but limits the overall size of the quiet area because it is so close to the most protected corner.

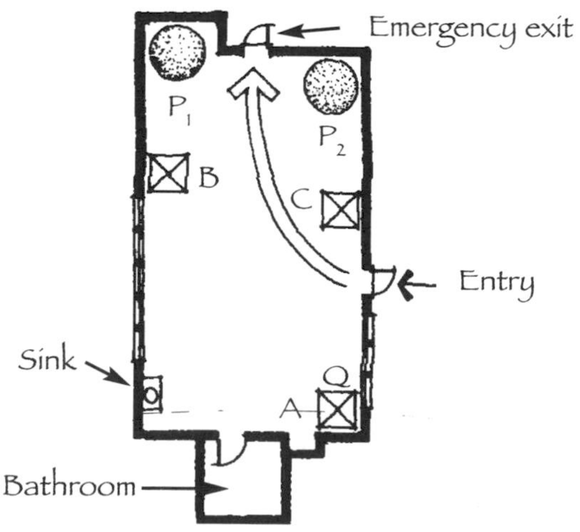

Figure 7.12
Of A, B, and C, location C is the best placement for a tall structure in this room.

- Location C is ideal, except that the structure would block a staff member standing at point Q's ability to observe the quiet-zone corner P2. Since children in the quiet zone tend to sit on the floor, to work independently, and to be more reserved, this area requires the least supervision. Moreover, if the adult moves a few feet toward the sink, the structure is no longer in the way. Staff supervising messy play are usually moving about on their feet. Thus the possibility of passively attending to events in the quiet zone is assured. Location C is also best because it is close to the main path of transit through the room.

The message that children receive when they first enter the room is another factor affecting location of a tall structure. First impressions are ideally clear and simple, revealing some of the options in the room. Tall structures automatically command visual attention. When a tall structure is too large, or dominates the view from the door, it may overpower all other options, suggesting that climbing is the most important activity. This tends to raise the level of activity and tension in the space. Ideally, the structure's visual prominence should not exceed that of any other of the room's valuable offerings.

The sketches in Figure 7.13 indicate where multilevel structures might go in rooms with different fixed-feature constraints. The circled X marks the best location.

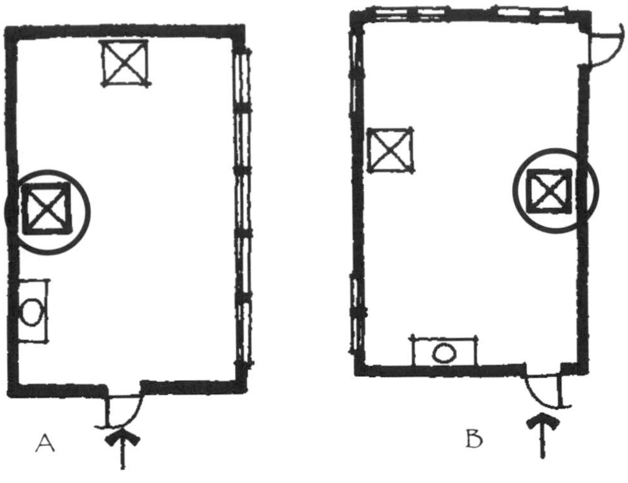

Figure 7.13
Possible (X) and best (circled X) locations for tall structures in rooms with different fixed-feature constraints.

Marking the Boundary Between Wet and Dry

Architectural treatments such as varying ceiling heights, lighting, window size, and color are particularly powerful ways to mark the boundary between the wet and dry regions. Ideally, every group room has two to four different ceiling heights—one for each region or one for each zone. Windows in the messy zone may be larger to let in more light for art work, while those in the quiet zone may be lower and closer to the floor where children are playing. Colors in the quiet zone may be more subdued than those elsewhere. Softer artificial light, and more task-specific lights in the quiet and entry zones, may be complemented by more ambient and vivid light in the messy and active zones.

Strive to introduce fixed feature changes such as these into both new construction and renovations to support the zoning that is occuring at floor level. Chapters 10, 11, and 12 discuss these treatments in greater detail.

At floor level, the separation between the wet and dry regions is signaled by the line between the carpet and the washable floor surface (to be called the carpet/tile line for simplicity). Once the location of the regions and zones has been established, it is time to make a preliminary decision about the location of the room's carpet/tile line. The exact placement of this line is likely to shift slightly as the activity areas in the two regions become more firm—after you have applied the information provided in Chapter 15. It is generally nice to carpet as much of a room as possible. However, carpet's most important use is to cover the protected and tranquil portions of the room. Whether or not to carpet the entry zone is a matter of climate, preference, traffic, aesthetics, and cost.

Generally, a room with a single washable floor region and a single carpeted region is easiest to clean and maintain. It is also best if the carpet/tile edge separating the regions is straight or slightly curved, but not irregular. A straight line will be less expensive in both materials and labor. A clearly predictable difference in floor surface assists children in distinguishing appropriate activities, behavior, and energy levels.

In determining the carpet/tile line, also take note of the room's shape. In Figure 7.14 the rectangular room is distinctly longer than it is wide. In principle, the tile/carpet edge could lie either perpendicular to the longer axis of the room (A), or parallel to it (B). When

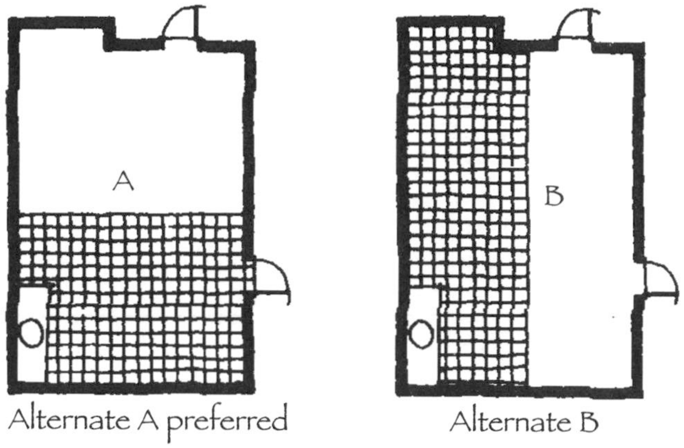

Figure 7.14
Placing the carpet/tile line perpendicular to the room's long axis makes a narrow room appear balanced (A). Orienting the carpet/tile line parallel to the long axis overemphasizes the room's narrowness.

the line is oriented perpendicularly (A), it tends to divide the room into two approximately equal squares, and to make it feel wider. The parallel orientation (B) accentuates the linearity of the room, as well as the "line-up" effect of the areas that are produced as a result. Aesthetically, the more balanced layout (A) is preferable.

Twelve Steps to Room Zoning and Layout

The 12 steps presented in Box 7.7 on pages 154–156 summarize the main points discussed here concerning zoning and suggest a strategy for designing a room from scratch, or attempting to rearrange and improve an existing one. For purposes of illustration, a simplified room layout with several constraints is used as the example. *This is not a floor plan that should be copied.* Nor does this example claim to cover all the complex circumstances that can arise. Rather, it is intended to provide a set of tools with which the design team can assess its own situation.

Case Studies

The following three case studies of renovated spaces provide real-life examples of the kind of creativity and compromise required in turning an existing building into a child care facility. Each one describes how the fixed-feature constraints, messages, conflicts, and trade-offs were all considered in the process of locating each room's wet and dry regions, and entry, messy, active, and quiet zones. Room plans at the end of Chapters 16, 17, and 18 also provide many examples of ways in which group rooms of different sizes and configurations were zoned and developed.

Case studies begin on page 157.

BOX 7.7

Twelve Steps in Laying Out a Group Room

Step 1: Identify the Room's Functional Requirements

List *all* the developmental *activities* and caregiving *functions* that will occur in the room you are designing.

Step 2: Draw the Room's Fixed Features

Draw a scaled floor plan showing all the *fixed features* of the room you are designing or one you are renovating (Figure 7.15). Note the sun orientation on this layout and plan for light and windows accordingly. Locate related outdoor play space as its own bubble and plan for connection from the start. One-quarter inch per foot is a useful scale for this phase of design development. Take time to sense where the most protected and exposed portions of the room lie.

Step 3: Identify the Protected Regions

On your floor plan, place large circles ("bubbles") around the substantial corners of the room. Put a "P" inside the bubble(s) marking the one or two corners that seem the most *protected.* Protected corners are generally 7'x 7' or larger and at some distance from a doorway (Figure 7.16).

Step 4: Identify the Exposed Regions and Main Transit Path

Identify the room's entrance and emergency exit doors and draw the main path of transit through the room on your floor plan (Figure 7.17). If there are other doors, draw secondary paths from them to the main path. Notice the pattern of foot traffic. Relocate or eliminate the doors as desired and feasible to concentrate them as far away from the corners as possible, so as to maximize the room's protected space.

Step 5: Locate the Wet and Dry Regions

Based on information you have gathered in steps 1–4, draw two large bubbles on your floor plan to represent the *wet* and *dry regions* of the space (Figure 7.18).

Step 6: Locate the Entry Zone

Within the wet region of your floor plan, draw a bubble indicating the approximate location and size of your *entry zone* (Figure 7.19). Keep in mind the functions outlined in Box 7.3 for this zone.

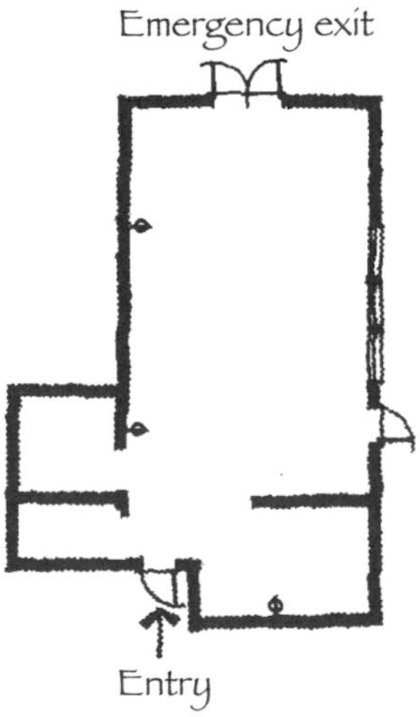

Figure 7.15
Fixed features.

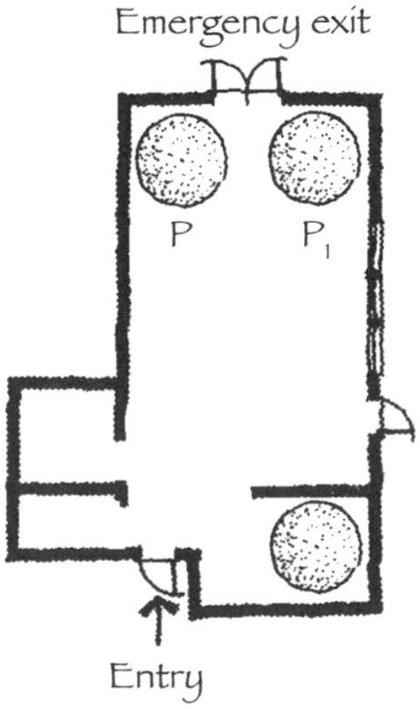

Figure 7.16
Protected corners.

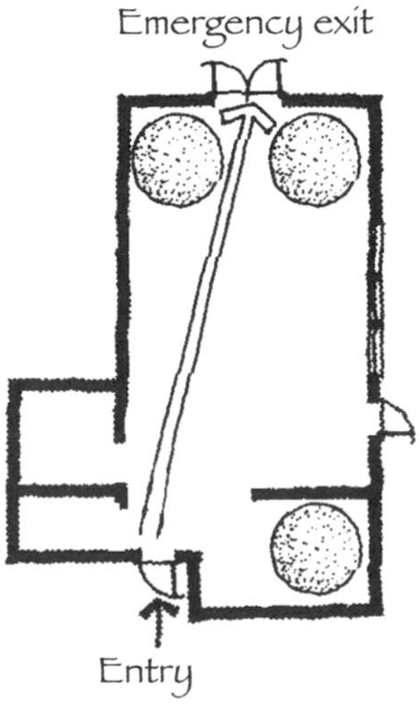

Figure 7.17
Main transit path.

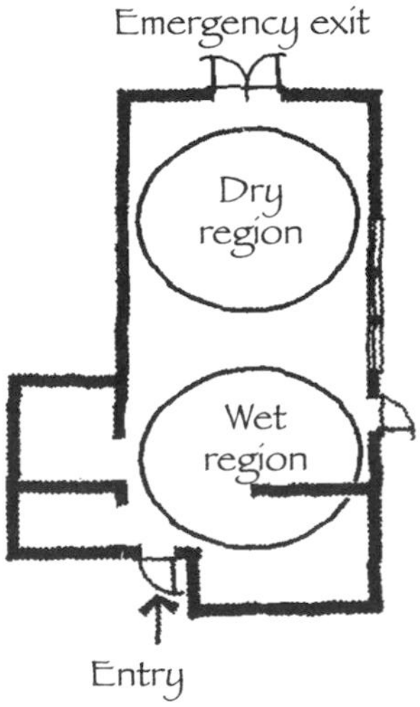

Figure 7.18
Wet and dry regions.

BOX 7.7

Twelve Steps in Laying Out a Group Room *(continued)*

Step 7: Locate the Messy Zone

Within the wet region of your floor plan, draw a large bubble representing the approximate size and location of your *messy zone* (Figure 7.20). Keep in mind the functions outlined in Box 7.4 for this zone.

The bubbles you have drawn for both the entry and messy zones should lie inside the larger bubble representing the wet region of the room. If you find, after reviewing the activities in the entry and messy zones, that your initial "wet" bubble is too large or too small, adjust it accordingly.

Step 8: Locate Sinks/Bathrooms in the Messy Zone

Within the messy zone, locate *sinks, bathrooms,* and other *high-use facilities* near the entry and/or primary path of circulation. Draw the *secondary transit paths*—as short and direct from the main transit path as possible—that will be required to access these facilities (Figure 7.21). Use the following guidelines:

- The primary circulation path can pass *through* the messy play zone, provided the path is at least 3–5 feet from the sink and has sufficient space on each side so that those passing through will not interrupt messy play activity. The tributary from the primary circulation route to the bathroom and sinks should be as short and unobstructed as possible. It will be traversed three or more times a day by each of the room's occupants.
- Never locate sinks in the room's most protected corner(s).
- The expense of moving an existing sink to a more desirable location is always worth it. Designing a room around a poorly placed plumbing source reduces staff efficiency and burdens staff with extra labor.

Step 9: Locate the Quiet Zone

Within the dry region of your floor plan, draw a bubble representing the approximate size and location of your *quiet zone.* Place it in the most protected part of the room, usually the part furthest from the entry (Figure 7.22). Include the protected corners you identified in Step 3. Plan to carpet this zone.

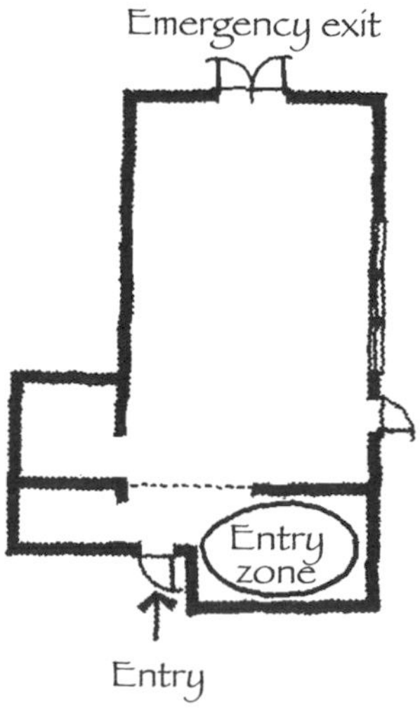

Figure 7.19
Entry zone.

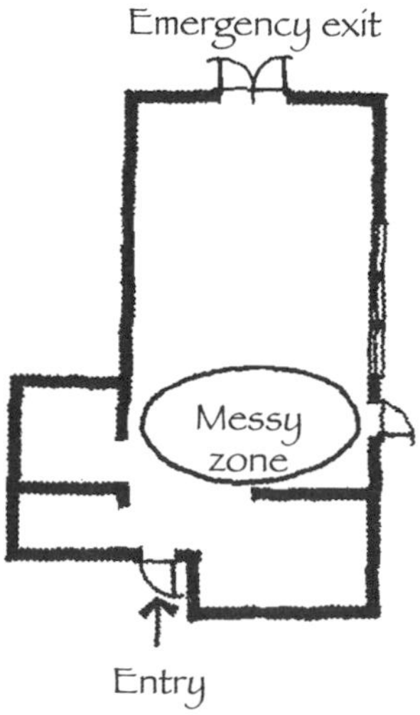

Figure 7.20
Messy zone.

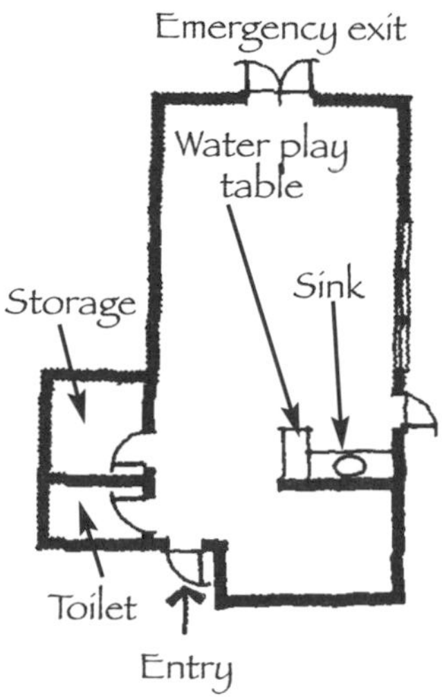

Figure 7.21
Sinks, bathrooms, and storage.

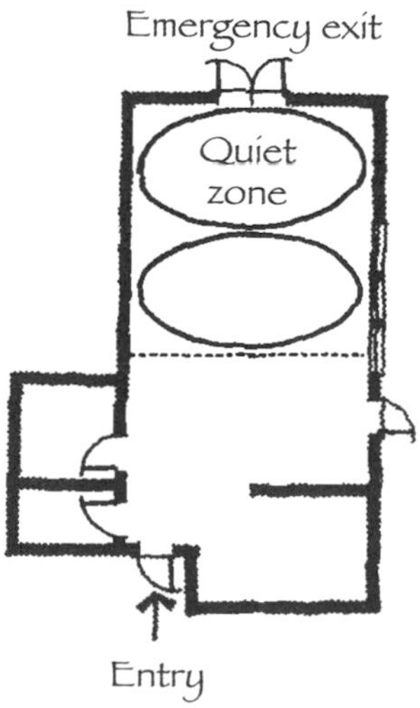

Figure 7.22
Quiet zone.

BOX 7.7

Twelve Steps in Laying Out a Group Room *(continued)*

Step 10: Locate the Active Zone

Within the dry region of your floor plan, draw a bubble representing the approximate size and location of your *active zone* (Figure 7.23). Make sure the zone is accessible to the room's main transit path and permits placement of a tall structure inside it. Also keep in mind that active play can get out of hand in a space that is too large and unbounded.

As you work, adjust the size of your active and quiet zone bubbles so they both fit within the dry region, or adjust the dry region accordingly.

Step 11: Finding a Location for a Tall Structure

Within the active zone, mark the best location for *a tall structure* with a circled X (Figure 7.24). Place it close to a solid wall that it can stand against, preferably not in a corner, and not where it blocks visibility to the room's active areas. Placement close to a main path of transit or under a high window is ideal.

Step 12: Mark the Boundary Between Wet and Dry

Draw a line separating the wet and dry regions to indicate the approximate *demarcation* between the room's carpeted and washable floor areas (Figure 7.25). Consider ways of highlighting this boundary with changes in ceiling height, lighting, windows, or color.

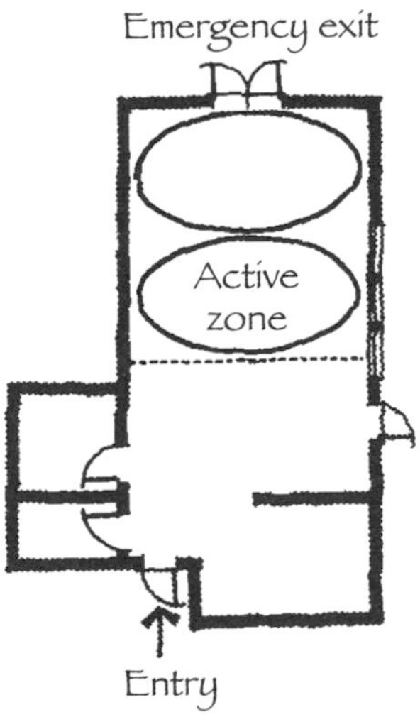

Figure 7.23
Active zone.

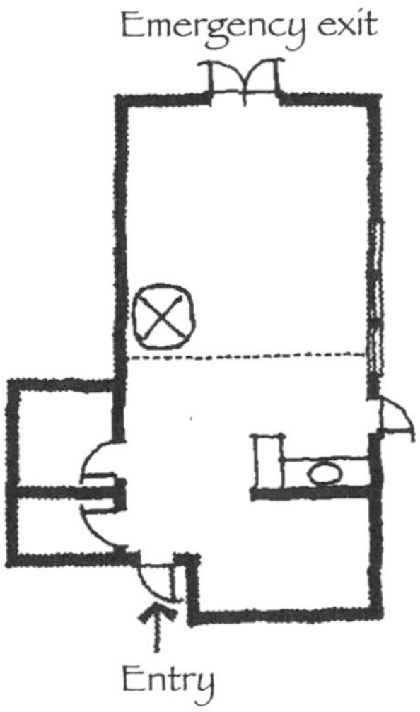

Figure 7.24
Tall structure.

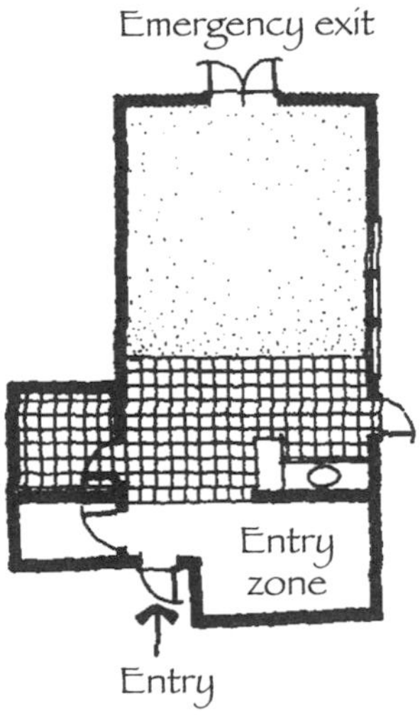

Figure 7.25
Carpet/tile line.

Case Study 1: A Preschool Room

Existing Conditions. This remodel space for 17 three-to-five-year-olds, located on the first floor of a 30-story building, is twice as long (48′) as it is wide (24′). It has an existing entry area at one end, and a kitchen, bathrooms, and space for the director's office at the opposite end of the room, which also serves as the emergency exit and access to the play yards. Note the major transit pathway from entry to exterior play area. The room is surrounded on three sides by windows and on the fourth side (transit region) by closets for electrical and mechanical equipment (which cannot be relocated) and storage. There are really only two useful corners (circled), P1 and P2. Although P2 is the most remote from the entry door, its seclusion is violated by the heavily used door at the rear and by proximity to the kitchen.

The space is punctuated by two rows of large concrete columns that prominently divide it into three parts. Two of these parts, at either end, are equal in size. The middle portion is twice the size of the end portions. Since the entry zone is already dictated by the architecture, the primary question is where to locate the messy, active, and quiet zones within the three prominent divisions (1, 2, and 3) created by the fixed-feature columns.

Design Solution. The ideal room layout—according to the principles outlined in this chapter—would be to place the messy zone near the entry. Doing that in this case, however, would place the messy zone furthest from the existing water source and access to the play yards, and in the area with the most protected corner. It was not possible to relocate the plumbing, nor was it possible, due to exterior conditions, to relocate the entry or the exit doors. Thus, *it makes most sense to dedicate Area 3 to messy play, where it will be accessible to sinks, water, bathrooms, the kitchen, and the transit to the director's office and playground.* Fortunately, the 12′-x-24′ space demarcated by the columns, plus the kitchen area, are sufficient for the full range of messy play activities. Column (B) also forms a natural boundary for an edge between tile and carpet.

The next question is where to locate the quiet and active zones. Area 1 contains the most protected corner in the room, but, being closest to the entry, its tranquillity could potentially be disrupted by numerous comings and goings. Area 2, on the other hand, has virtually no existing corners and its greater size naturally suggests expansiveness and movement. It would be difficult, and counter to the fixed-feature constraints of Area 2, to place the quiet zone there. It would be possible, on the other hand, to create a barrier between the entry zone and main transit path and Area 1, to protect its integrity as a place of tranquillity. *Thus, while some compromise is necessary, the fixed features clearly suggest that Area 1 be the quiet zone and Area 2 the active zone.*

The next question is where to locate a multi-level structure within Area 2. Clearly, the structure cannot go against the windows or the closets. The two possibilities are against the existing columns (a) or (b). Both of these have the advantage of proximity to the primary transit pathway. Being furthest from the quiet zone, all else being equal, (b) is preferable.

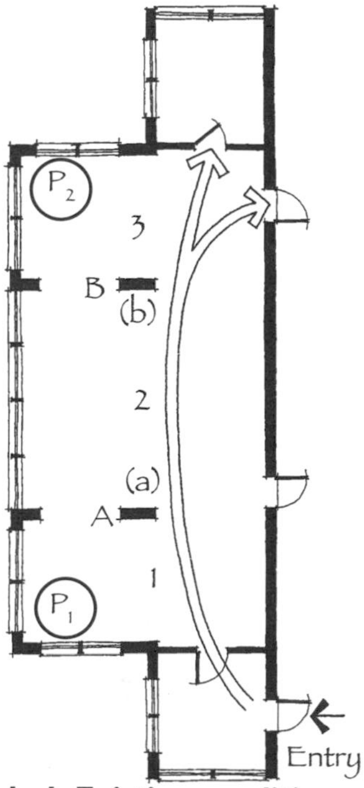

Case Study 1: Existing conditions

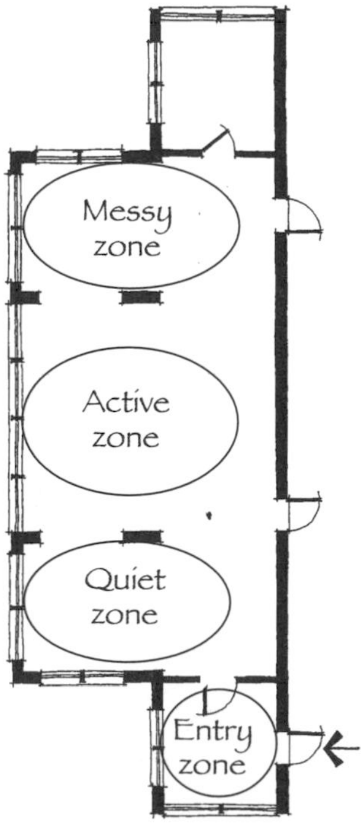

Case Study 1: Zoning diagram

16

15

8

7

4

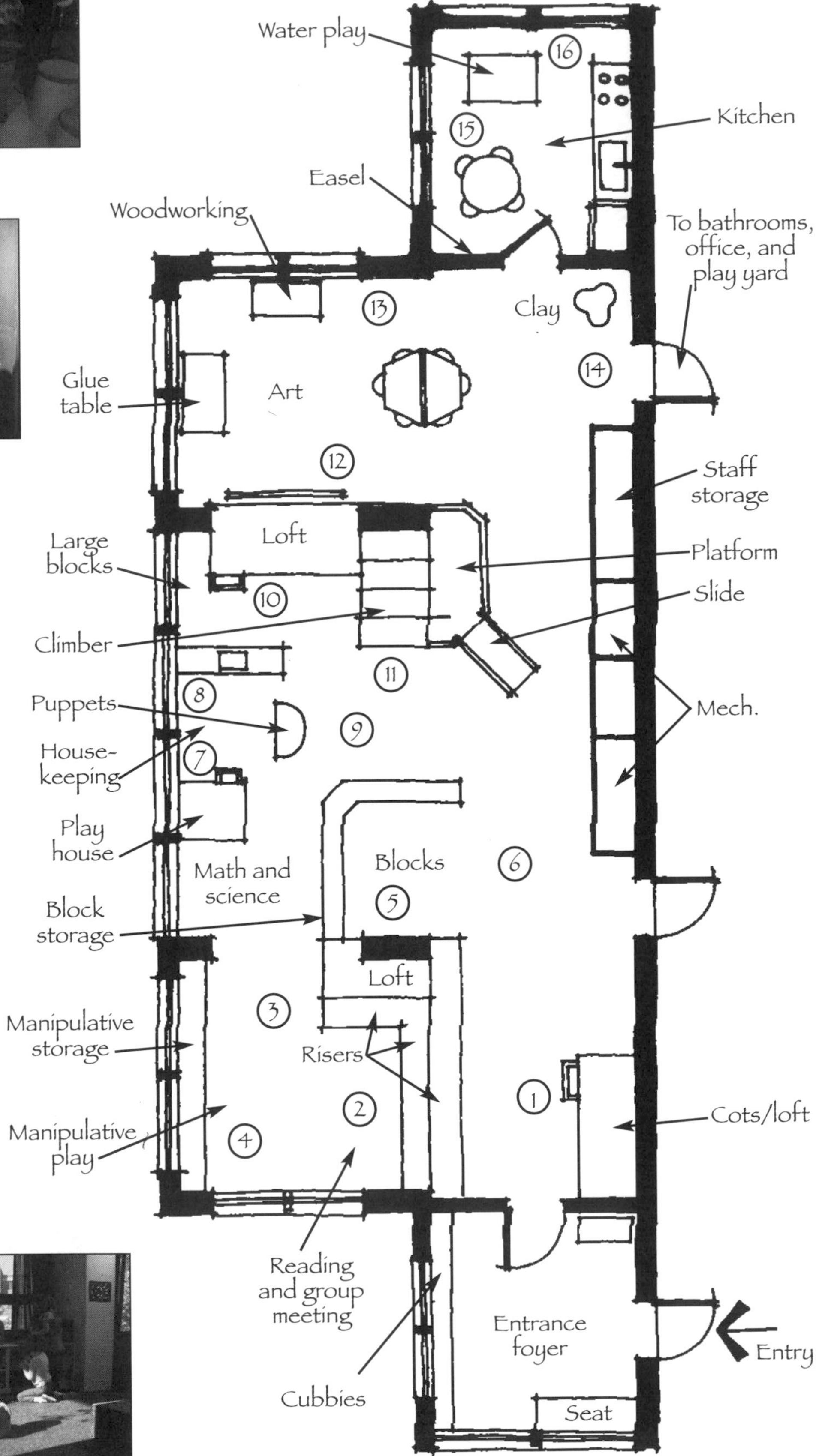
Water play
16
Kitchen
15
Easel
Woodworking
To bathrooms, office, and play yard
13
Clay
Glue table
Art
14
12
Staff storage
Loft
Large blocks
Platform
10
Slide
Climber
11
8
Puppets
9
Mech.
House-keeping
7
Play house
Math and science
Blocks
6
5
Block storage
Loft
3
Manipulative storage
Risers
1
2
Cots/loft
Manipulative play
4
Reading and group meeting
Entrance foyer
Entry
Cubbies
Seat

Case Study 1: Design solution

12

13

14

9

10

11

5

6

3

2

1

Case Study 2: A Room for Three-Year-Olds

Existing Conditions. This room for 16 three-year-olds in a renovated supermarket is approximately 23′ x 34′. It has large windows flanking the emergency exit and extending from 2 feet above the floor to the ceiling at one end of the room. It also has a small window located 6 feet above the floor on the one long, otherwise uninterrupted wall (C). The emergency exit, which leads directly to the street, is never used as an entry. Children get to the play yard on the other side of the building via the room's entry door.

Design Solution. Due to existing conditions, plumbing had to be located more or less in the middle of Wall B, a somewhat awkward location. The main transit path does, however, go alongside the sink/bathroom area.

There are three corners in the room, with P1 and P2 the most protected, and the most removed from the entry. Although a portion of P3 is extremely protected due to the protrusion of the staircase, the staircase also limits P3's depth to about 4 feet. An entry zone would most logically be located near the room's entry door, assisted by the structural "L" created by the sink wall. Despite the emergency exit, the far end of the room has the lesser amount of foot traffic and is therefore the most protected space overall. It would seem preferable for quiet play. However, this is also where the best natural light, desirable for arts and crafts, is located. The question therefore arises: *where to locate messy, active, and quiet zones, given the central location of the plumbing and the fact that the room's most tranquil portion is located in front of its only large windows?* The zoning diagrams in Figure 7.26 on page 162 express three alternate ways of zoning the room, in addition to the way that was eventually chosen.

Many activities in the messy zone involve artistic expression, which benefit from proximity to natural light. However, placing arts and crafts tables and messy play near the windows has two unfortunate consequences: It makes messy play somewhat remote from the sink, and more important, it destroys the protectiveness of the room's two best corners by filling them with tables and opening them to traffic and movement. Corners P1 and P2 are best reserved for peaceful play. Although it would be nice for art work to have natural light, *heeding the room's fixed-feature messages and providing places of genuine tranquillity are more important overall planning considerations than the single consider-*

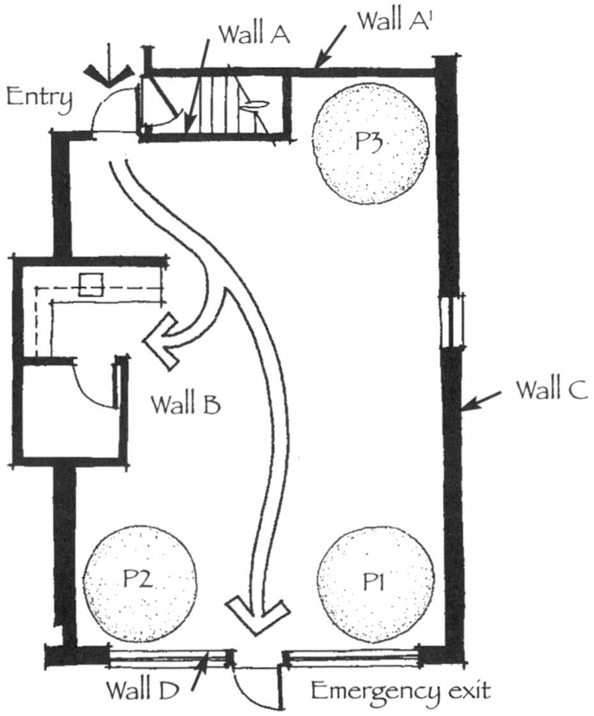

Case Study 2: Existing conditions

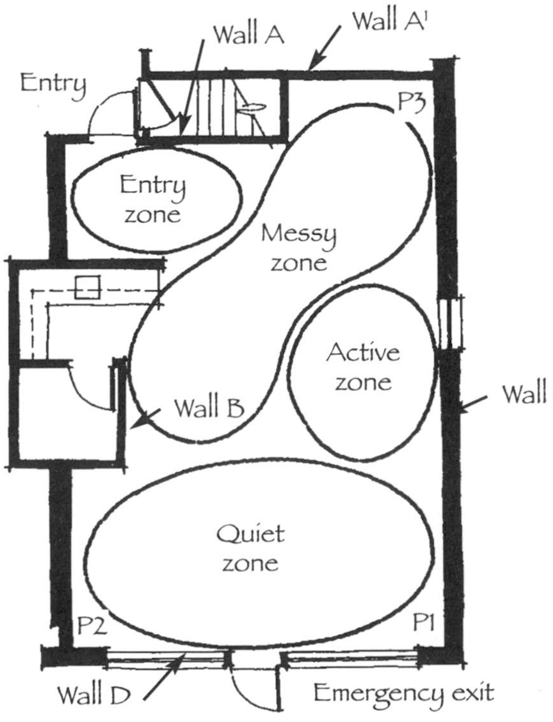

Case Study 2: Zoning plan used

1

2

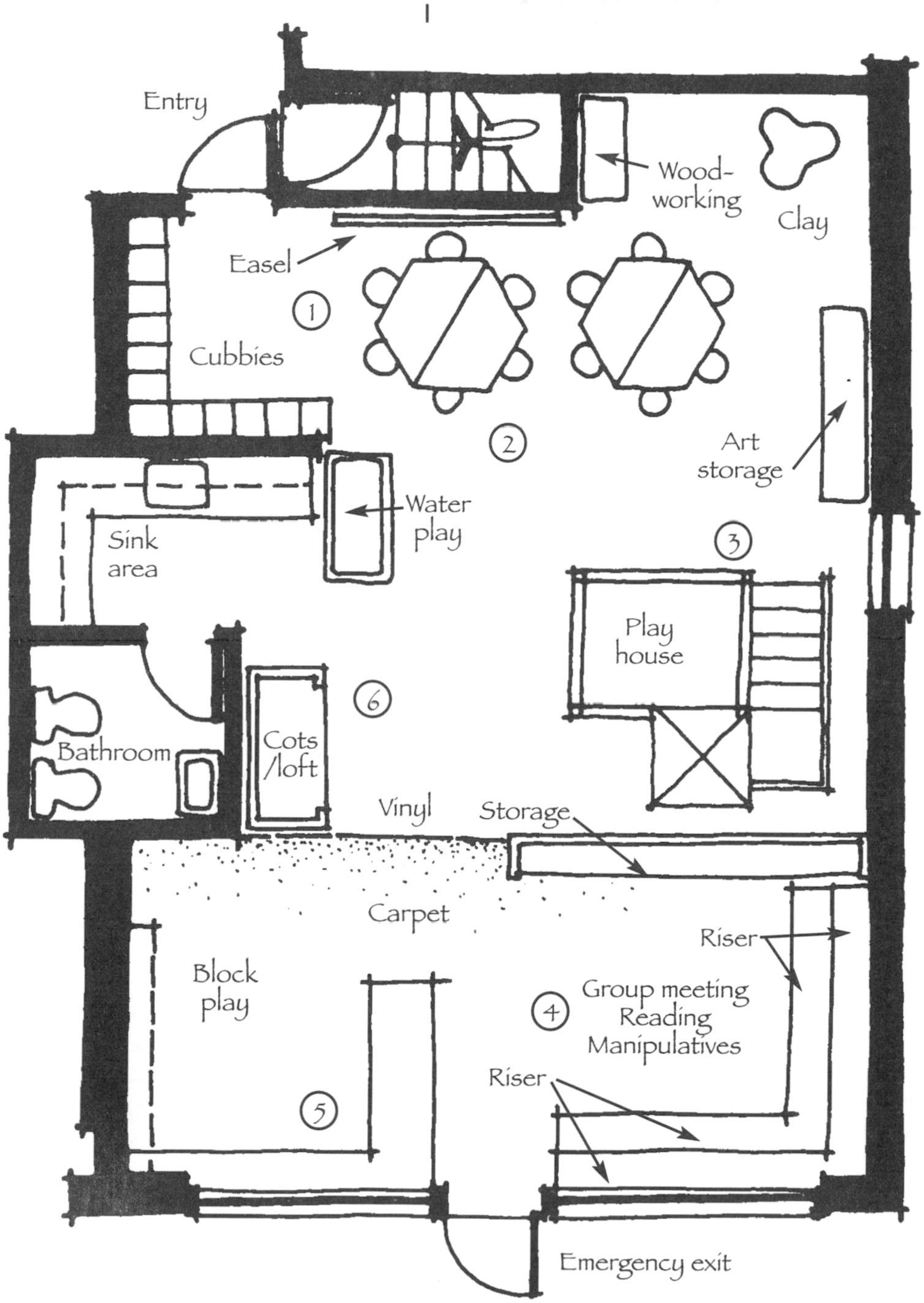

Case Study 2: Design solution

3

6

4

5

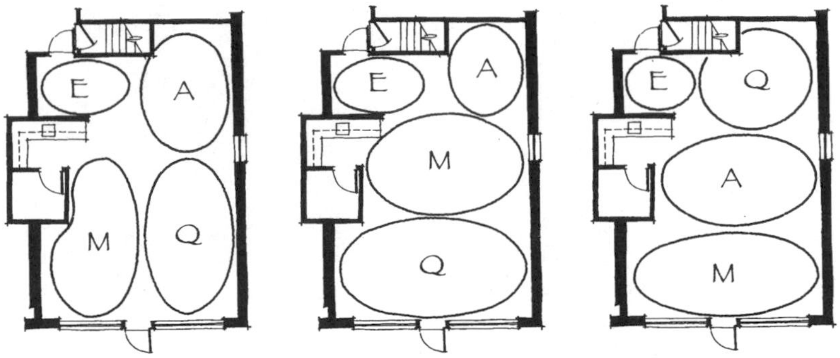

Figure 7.26
Case Study 2: Alternate zoning plans

ation of windows for art activities. In this instance, it is more appropriate to use the corners for quiet play and locate the tables for art in a messy zone near the sink and entry. The height of any dividers in a quiet zone is usually quite low, therefore, as much natural light as possible will be able to cross to the messy zone. Electrical lighting in the messy zone also can be improved (full-spectrum lamps).[3]

A further consideration in deciding how to use the portion of the room remote from the emergency exit concerns the carpet/tile line. The edge between carpet and tile could lie perpendicular to walls B and C, helping to balance the two portions of the room. If, on the other hand, corner P3 were to be part of a quiet zone, the carpet might have to run perpendicular to walls A and D, accentuating the room's longer dimension. Obviously, the former is preferable, as was illustrated in Figure 7.14.

The next question is where to locate the messy and active zones within the remaining 50% of the room. If located in the middle of the room, messy play would be closest to the sinks. Then the active zone could possibly be near the front door without conflicting with entry. However, if the size of the entry zone "forces" activity toward corner P3, such activity and a climber could be constrained.

To resolve this issue, a final factor needs to be considered: Where in this room is a tall structure best located? The three options that do not interfere with the quiet zone, the windows, or the entry zone, are locating it at Walls A, B, or C.

- A tall structure in and around Walls A/A[1] would be a bit confined by P3 and possibly by the shortness of Wall A.
- One at Wall B could work, but the area would be limited in size due to the short length of wall B and the fact that a climber of any depth would be right in the major transit pathway.
- Wall C is the most ideal location, especially if the structure is placed under the high window, which would give children the opportunity to climb up and look out. Active play at C is also in the middle of the room where, according to the fixed-feature messages, there appears to be the most space and opportunities for expansive movement. The messy zone might then go from the sink back to walls A and A[1], including corner P3, which can give valuable protection for a low clay table, science, or woodworking.

Putting a tall structure in location C does have the disadvantage of blocking visibility across the room for a staff member standing at point P3 trying to observe the corner P1. However, since staff supervising messy play are generally moving about, they can get an unobstructed view of the quiet play area just by moving a few feet toward the entry. Also, children engaged in quiet play generally require minimal active supervision.

Case Study 3: An Infant/Toddler Room

Existing Conditions. This space for ten infants/toddlers (ages birth to 30 months) consists of two rooms: a larger room of irregular shape approximately 20′ x 21′ on its longest dimensions, and a smaller 9′-x-14′room remote from the entry. The larger room has light on two sides—one large window that comes down almost to the floor, with a view to the tot lot—and two other windows at 4 feet above the floor. The smaller room has one small window 4 feet above grade. The emergency exit goes directly to an outside parking lot. A similar exit was added to the back room for safety.

Design Solution. The remoteness of the back room, and its smaller size, suggest it as the space for cribs and napping. The wide corridor directly outside the larger room's entry is a convenient place to create the entry/transition zone, thereby preserving space in the room itself, which is small. The triangular room therefore needs to accommodate messy, active, and quiet zones. It also needs to be plumbed for a staff prep sink, a diaper-changing sink, and a low water-play trough.

This larger room has only two real corners, P1 and P2. While being areas of the room least vulnerable to traffic and intrusion, they are not, however, as protected as some of the corners in Cases 1 and 2. The major transit path runs from the entry to the emergency exit and across to the sleep room located at the rear. The area receiving the greatest foot traffic should be the messy play zone. The territory that includes the two corners could then be devoted to quiet and active play. Of these two, P1 seems most suited to quiet play, cuddling, and toddling because it is "behind" the door, and the diagonal room entry "directs" traffic flow towards P2. Corner P2 may be a place for a raised loft/climber/playpen that could place babies at adult eye-level and enable them to look out the 4′ high window. Alternatively, a raised structure could go against walls A and B.

The next step is to locate the sinks and plumbing. Wall E—near but outside the main transit path—is considerably longer than Wall F. Wall E could best accommodate two sinks and a water-play trough and leave adequate accessible space around the sinks for diaper-changing, cleanup, and prep. An added bonus is the proximity of the diaper-changing area to the sleep room.

The edges of the entry and emergency exit doors "suggest" a line between carpet and tile flooring. Exactly where this line belongs will depend upon the required size of the active, quiet, and messy zones.

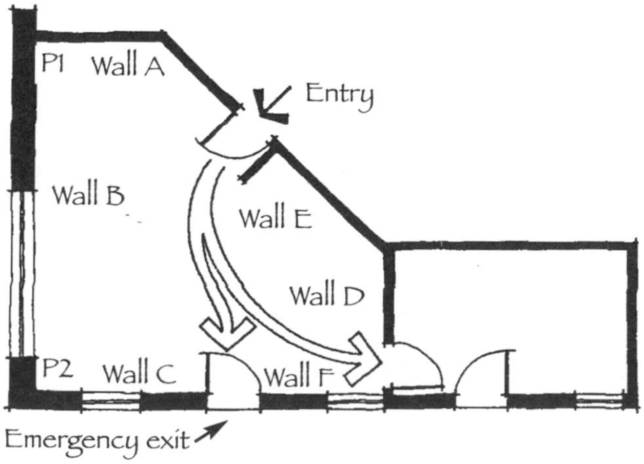

Case Study 3: Existing conditions

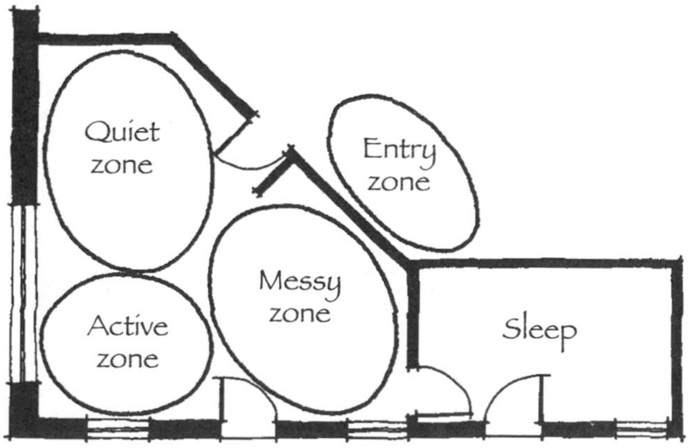

Case Study 3: Zoning diagram

1

2

3

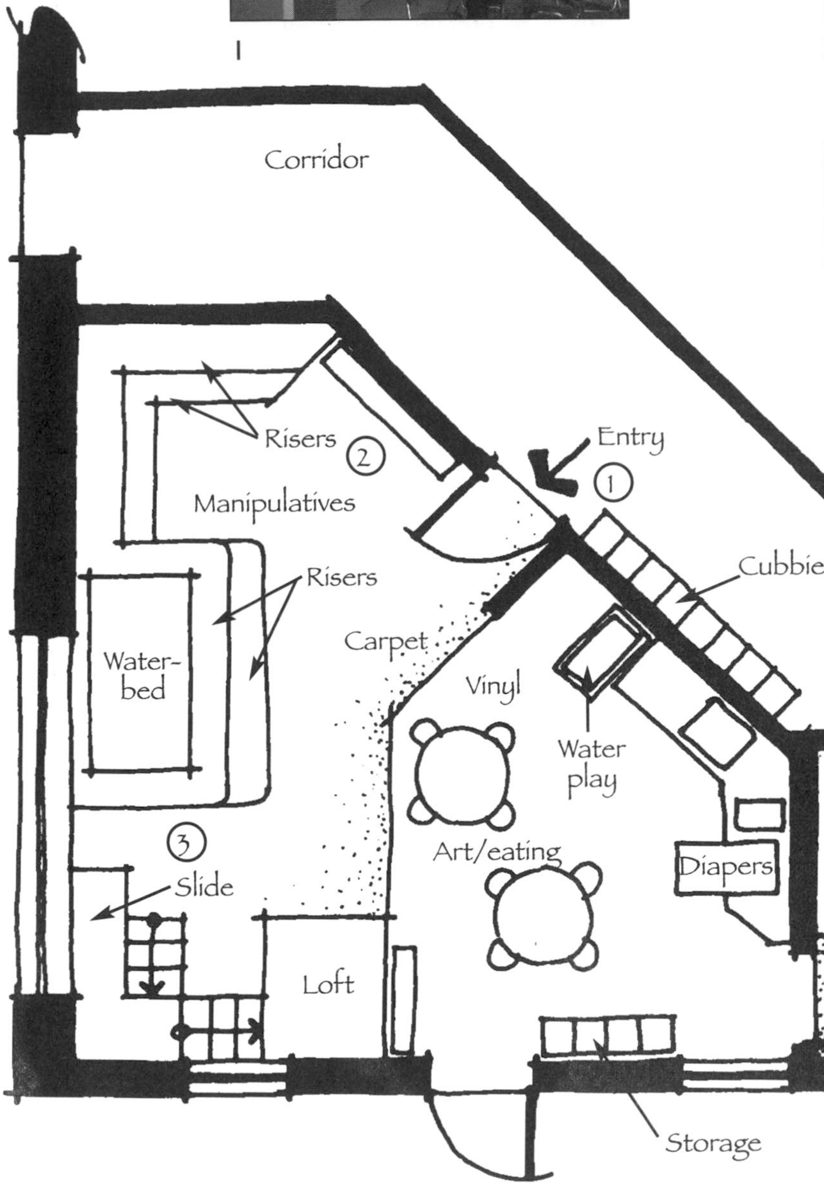
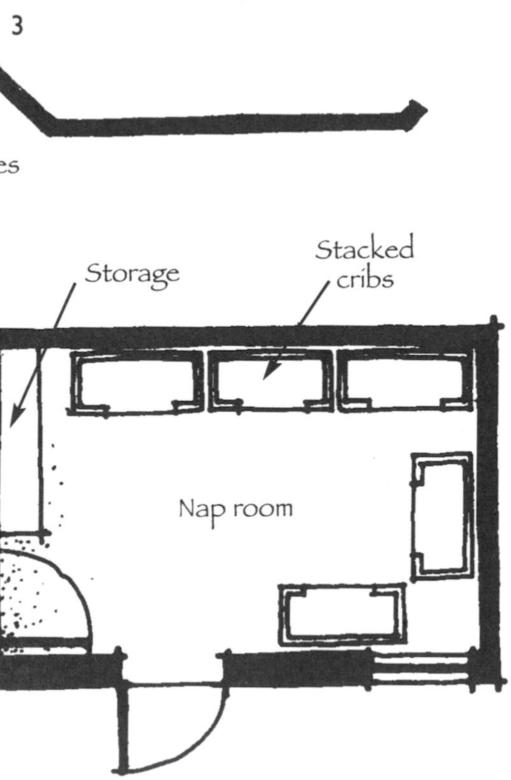

Case Study 3: Design solution

Conclusion

Congratulations! You have completed the most important tasks in laying out a room that will be harmonious and highly functional for years to come. You now have a list of the room's functional requirements and a plan of the room showing:

- Its fixed features
- Its protected and exposed areas
- Its entry/exit and emergency exit doorways
- The major transit path between its entry and exit
- Its wet and the dry regions
- Its entry, messy, quiet, and active zones
- The dividing line between the carpet and washable flooring in the room

In addition, you have made progress in giving more specificity to the location of bathrooms, sinks, water play troughs, and multileveled structures.

As you review the plan, once again take time to "listen" to the room's fixed feature messages. Does the plan you have made for your room create places of protection as well as exposure? Have you located the quiet zone in the most tranquil portion of the room? If not, why not? What can be done to make the layout more harmonious?

Once you are satisfied with the room's zoning, you are ready to locate all the activities on your list of functional requirements and design/choose the specific furnishings and equipment that will support them. Then you can give precise dimensions to facilities and to finalizing the carpet/tile line. Chapter 15 provides guidelines for developing your room's activity areas.

Notes

[1]In homes, the four zones might be represented by the entranceway, the kitchen/bathroom, the living/family rooms, and the bedrooms or study.

[2]According to feng shui, the most peaceful night time rest occurs when the bed is oriented diagonally away from but facing the bedroom door. Placing a bed right next to or directly opposite the door is a poor location. In hospital rooms, the preferred bed location is in the corner furthest from but facing the door.

[3]In cases (Case 2 was not) where buildings are one story, consider adding skylights.

PART THREE

INGREDIENTS OF GOOD DESIGN

CHAPTER EIGHT

HEALTHY BUILDINGS

Our present systems of design have created a world that grows far beyond the capacity of the environment to sustain life into the future. The industrial idiom of design, failing to honor the principles of nature, can only violate them, producing waste and harm, regardless of purported intention. If we destroy more forests, burn more garbage, drift-net more fish, burn more coal, bleach more paper, destroy more topsoil, poison more insects, build over more habitats, dam more rivers, produce more toxic and radioactive waste, we are creating a vast industrial machine, not for living in, but for dying in.[1]

—William McDonough

This chapter looks at the impact of a building's materials, systems, and location on the health of the children it serves and on the environment in which it exists. In the process it makes a case for the necessity and importance of ecologically sound, sustainable design practices.

Building Ecology and Sustainable Design

We stand at a critical point in history. Increasingly, the delicate balance between our desire to build and mold the environment to our wishes, and the effect of such practices on the inherent harmony and regenerative capacities of the earth to sustain itself and living beings, is becoming apparent. Along with explosive growth and the degradation of natural systems has come the production of synthetic materials, processes, and products that create greater efficiency for the building industry and for our lives, but which are known in many instances to be toxic to living forms and to the environment. New evidence links many diseases to toxic chemical exposure, water and air pollution, processed foods, and soil-depletion. With our survival hanging in the balance, we cannot afford to assume that the world will somehow solve its problems.

Fortunately, however, appropriate technologies and sustainable design solutions are available and becoming more so. *Sustainable practices* are those that meet the needs of the present without compromising the ability of future generations and other parts of nature to meet their own needs, now and in the future. Design is at the root of our problems: products and processes that deplete natural resources and create toxins and waste. But design is also at the root of the solutions. We are capable of creating approaches that are nontoxic, use mainly renewable energy sources, produce wastes that become food for some living system, and produce durables (such as TVs and cars) which, although they do not decompose, can be returned to their producers to be disassembled, remanufactured, and continuously reused.

Many of the alternative approaches suggested here require no added costs or effort; they simply require

. . . our source of survival

attention in the placement and design of the building. Other suggestions may increase initial costs or effort—locating and using nontoxic adhesives, for instance—but will reward you with reduced maintenance, a more healthful setting, greater durability, and a longer lifespan. You will want to look carefully at the costs and benefits of each choice over the long term. Striving to lessen the negative impact of the materials and methods we do employ moves us, little by little, in the right direction. Even small steps toward resource conservation and avoidance of toxic substances can have far-reaching effects on the center's users and on the world in which we live.

Design teams are therefore encouraged to at least become more conscious of the potential impact of the materials and systems they will use in building a child care center, for three reasons:

- Children's health is more profoundly affected by toxins than is that of adults
- Our practices affect children's awareness and their willingness to embrace more eco-friendly options
- The health of the planet and our survival depend upon sustainable design solutions

Children and Toxins

In previous eras, buildings were ventilated naturally and building materials and furniture were made from natural substances: wood, clay, cotton, wool. Today our buildings and their occupants sometimes suffer from "sick building syndrome," the consequence of inadequate ventilation systems, combined with synthetic interior finishes and furnishings, which often exude minute quantities of noxious gases.

Toxins are a far greater threat to young children than to adults because children have proportionally less internal tissue to absorb pollutants. A child's liver detoxifying system is small and immature. Asymptomatic buildup as a result of excessive exposure to toxins and poor air quality during the most vulnerable period of childhood can result in dysfunction in later years. Children—unaccustomed to monitoring their health—may not realize how unwell they feel until the effects reach major proportions. Thus the more children can avoid small and unnoticed toxic exposures early in life, the less likely they are to become sensitized to chemically related substances and reach the overload stage. It is in everyone's best interest to use natural fabrics and substances wherever possible.

Appendix III provides toxicity ratings for some of the more common exterior and interior building materials. *This information is not prescriptive, but is intended to indicate places where caution and awareness are advised, and where choices, if possible, can be made.*

Teaching Environmental Awareness

Rather than being raised in buildings that desensitize them to nature, or give them few opportunities for seeing the effect of their actions upon the environment, children need to learn environmentally conscious ways of living. For example, at the Boyne River Ecology Center in Ontario, Canada, visiting groups of elementary school students are taught how much energy various electrical appliances will consume (hair dryer, TV, computer). They are then taught to read the amount of energy—generated by windmills on the hill above the center—that is stored in batteries, displayed in a case inside the building. In order to not run out of energy before their visit ends, the children must decide together which appliances to use, and for how long.

Exposure to such lessons, and to ecologically sound solutions in youth, hopefully will prompt preferences for sustainable solutions throughout life: passive and active solar heating rather than furnaces; biological waste treatment systems rather than sewers; photovoltaics and windmills rather than transformers and generators. With a little extra effort, designers can begin to create a better world by intentionally choosing approaches that set the best examples for future generations.

Ecological Materials

In choosing structural materials for a building, one aim is to protect children from harmful toxins and the global environment from further depletion of natural resources. Using local materials wherever possible conserves resources within a community and strengthens its local economy. Ideally, the choice of materials is based not only on traditional criteria such as performance, durability, appearance, and cost, but also on such environmental factors as the effect of the material on:

- *Embodied energy* (the energy required to extract the raw materials, manufacture the product, transport the raw materials and finished product, apply materials on the job site, and demolish and dispose of building debris)
- *Contribution to pollution* (the amounts of CO_2 and toxic emissions generated in production, use, and disposal)
- *Effect on indoor air quality*
- *Contribution to resource depletion*
- *Solid-waste generation and disposal*

Ecologically sound materials produce low waste and are nonpolluting, energy efficient, durable, long-lived, and easy to repair. They are also capable of being reused or recycled, are renewable and have low impact on the environment, and are produced in socially equitable ways for the workers involved.

Some questions that architects and clients can ask suppliers about building materials follow.

QUESTIONS FOR MATERIAL SUPPLIERS[2]

1. Are renewable or sustainable energy sources used in manufacture of this material?
2. Are any environmentally significant hazardous solid, aqueous, or gaseous wastes produced during manufacture of this material?
3. How much energy is required to manufacture this material?
4. How much energy is used to transport this material from its source to the project site? Are local sources for this material available?
5. How much embodied energy is involved in this material or the building over its lifetime?
6. Are there less energy-consuming, longer-lasting alternatives for the same application?
7. Do different construction systems offer better alternatives for resource recovery at the end of building life?
8. Can this material be easily recycled or reused?
9. How much maintenance does this material require over its lifetime? How energy-intensive is the maintenance regimen? Are waste by-products produced during maintenance?
10. Does this material require special coatings or treatments that could present health or safety hazards?
11. How is indoor air quality affected by any off-gassing of this material during and after installation?

Becoming Informed

There is a rich and growing body of knowledge—both in other countries and our own—of ecologically sound products, building materials, and approaches. Especially noteworthy is Germany's *Bau-biologie* (meaning "building biology") movement started by medical doctors 20 years ago. These researchers have conducted a comprehensive reassessment of every aspect of building and design, which combines scientific information with a holistic view of the relationship between people, buildings, and nature.[3]

Some information pertaining to sustainable building practices is acknowledgably technical for the lay person. However, the general principles can be easily grasped by most. While cost, availability, and suitability factors affect the selection of all materials, teams designing child care centers are encouraged to also become familiar with the increasing number of environmentally friendly "green" building materials, and the nontoxic water-based resins, adhesives, paints, stains, natural wood waxes, natural fiber carpets, carpet underlayments, organically grown cottons, and natural plant-dyed fabrics, on the market.[4]

GUIDELINES: SUSTAINABLE DESIGN[5]

- Strive to use sustainable design practices wherever possible, or at least to lessen the negative impact of products and materials known to cause harm to the environment and living beings. Many of these practices add no extra cost.
- Locate buildings to minimize environmental impact and to preserve open space, wildlife habitats, and wetlands.
- Design energy-efficient buildings by using high levels of insulation, high-performance windows, and tight construction. In southern climates, choose glazing with low solar gain. Orient buildings to facilitate passive heating and cooling.
- Choose building materials with low embodied energy.[6] One estimate of the relative energy intensity of various materials (by weight) is: Lumber=1, Brick=2, Cement=2, Glass=3, Fiberglass=7, Steel=8, Plastic=30, Aluminum=80.
- Use building products made from recycled materials. Some examples are: cellulose insulation, Homosote, Thermo-ply, and recycled plastic lumber.
- Provide for storage and processing of recyclables: recycling bins near the kitchen, buckets for compostable food waste, and composters outside.
- Avoid lumber products from old-growth timber. Use sustainably harvested timber. Determine or confirm sources via the International Hardwood Products Association (P.O. Box 1308, Alexandria, VA 22313).[7]

- Avoid any finishes containing urea formaldehyde resins. Phenol formaldehyde resins, as in exterior-grade plywood, are considered safer because they are more stable.
- Avoid chlorine bleach and allergy-forming ingredients found in permanent press, wrinkle-resistant, or shrink-proof fabrics, as well as foam-filled products.
- Minimize packaging where not needed to prevent damage, and by purchasing products in bulk.

Water and Plumbing

To protect a precious and limited water supply, purchase only water-conserving appliances (especially low-flow toilets, clothes washers, and dishwashers) for the center. A central water filter system is recommended to purify drinking, cooking, and bathing water that may contain residual chlorine. Where existing codes permit, make every attempt to recycle gray water. In addition to down spouts, rain chains (metal chains hung between the roof and the ground for channeling rain water) can visibly demonstrate water's life cycle to children.

Plumbing, typically needed in multiple locations, is one of the more costly aspects of outfitting a child care center. Since this system is unlikely to change for the life of the building, it is critical to get it right at the outset. (See Chapters 4 and 7 for details.) For easy clean-up and prevention of odors, be certain to provide floor drains around toilets and sinks where spills and accidents may occur (also see "Ventilation" section).

Figure 8.1
Flowforms circulate water in the figure-eight pattern in which it naturally flows, giving it increased energy and oxygen while humidifying the environment. Their rhythmic pulsation is particularly soothing to people and plants.

GUIDELINES: WATER AND PLUMBING

- Install water-efficient equipment such as low-flow toilets, showerheads, and faucet aerators to reduce water use and the demand on sewage treatment plants and septic systems.
- Install a central water filter system or separate filters on all sinks where water will be used for drinking and cooking.
- Gray water that has been used for bathing or washing dishes or clothes, can be recycled for flushing toilets or irrigation. Where current codes prevent such use, consider designing plumbing for easy future adaptation.
- Consider rooftop water catchment systems for outdoor watering, and/or oversized gutters which can capture rainwater in visible streams, or in cisterns, to be used for irrigation and nonpotable purposes.
- Install filters, which remove 90% of residual chlorine, on showers in staff areas and wherever children are bathed. Chlorine and residual chlorine in water can be harmful to hair, skin, eyes, nose, and mouth membranes and lungs.[8]
- Consider the use of Flow-forms to clean and humidify the air; make moving water visible to all, both indoors and outside (Figure 8.1).
- For safety, maintain tap water temperatures below 120–130 degrees Fahrenheit. Provide temperature-balanced valves at all areas serving children.
- Design water-efficient, low-maintenance landscaping by using drought-resistent native plants and perennial ground covers.

GUIDELINES: FAUCETS AND SINK HARDWARE

- Infrared faucets that turn on and off according to hand proximity are increasingly popular for water conservation and sanitary reasons. However, these automatic devices do not teach children conservation awareness. Use levers or faucet knobs instead.
- Foot-pedal hardware is difficult for children to operate while washing and may easily become a toy.
- For adults using diapering sinks, install foot-pedal or single-lever hand-operated hardware to reduce contamination.

Heating and Cooling

In some cultures, people's lives still revolve around variations in temperature and climate: gathering around a central fire or retreating behind thick walls in cold weather, or relaxing in courtyards with fountains and greenery in hot weather. Sunlight, firelight, blankets, and heavy clothing are symbolic of warmth, while moving water, cool colors, things blown by the wind, and shade symbolize coolness. Saunas, Jacuzzis, hot tubs, and Japanese baths, often considered amenities of the affluent in North America, nonetheless provide physical and social sustenance for entire cultures and communities. In our society, furnaces and air conditioners— supplemented by an occasional hearth—usually replace these experiences.

Because we tend to notice thermal qualities only if they are pleasant or unpleasant, the thermal constancy of our contemporary interiors frequently cuts us off from variations in temperature that could offer us life and vitality—the comfort of a balmy day or the invigoration of a cold, snowy one. Greater reliance on passive or natural methods of heating and cooling would not only conserve fossil fuels and reduce pollution, but re-establish our relationship with climatic cycles. Operating blinds, shutters, windows, vents, and other thermal-regulating devices also helps keep us in touch with our body's needs in relation to the exterior climate. Exposing children to these tools can deepen their connection with natural forces.

Recommendations for specific heating and cooling systems—which depend upon climate and locale—are beyond the scope of this guide. However, three factors affecting choice will be mentioned here.

- When selecting any heating or cooling system for a new or renovated facility, consider energy consumption, carbon dioxide emissions, and indoor air quality. Wasteful systems are environmentally harmful and educationally irresponsible. Utilize passive and active solar and natural methods of building design as much as possible. Forced-air systems tend to dry out the air and circulate allergens and irritants. Consider air filters and humidifiers.

- Design heating and cooling systems to provide choice at individual locations, especially the children's group rooms.

  Many child care buildings suffer from extremes of cold and heat as a result of a single, centralized thermostat. Always provide some windows that open, preferably offering cross ventilation, and doors that promote a relationship with the outside.

- Design room heating and cooling systems to affect children at their height, within 1–3 feet of the floor, not just taller adults (Figure 8.2). Since warm air rises, many systems create cold and drafts at floor level. Give serious consideration to in-floor radiant heat (which sometimes needs to be supplemented by convection systems), especially in spaces for infants.

Figure 8.2
Radiant floor heat ensures that children will be warmed at their level, 1–3 feet above the floor.

GUIDELINES: HEATING

Passive and Active Solar Energy

- Reduce operational energy use by using passive solar strategies such as heating with sunspaces, increasing thermal mass, daylighting, proper shading, use of high-performance glazing, operable windows positioned for cross ventilation, high levels of insulation, and exhaust air heat recovery.
- Orient new construction to make optimal use of passive solar heating, daylighting, and natural cooling (which can be incorporated cost-effectively into most buildings), as well as solar water heating and photovoltaics: or design buildings for future installation of panels.
- Use deciduous trees on the south and west sides of buildings (in the northern hemisphere) to dramatically reduce cooling loads. Trees, hedgerows, and shrubbery can block cold winter winds or help channel cool summer breezes into the building.
- Where appropriate, consider more active solar heating systems involving solar panels and rock and tile heat storage capacitors.

Room Temperature

- Provide adjustable thermostats within the building, especially in each group room, since heating/cooling requirements may vary with the age of the children, their activities, and the amount of sunlight striking the building at different times of day.
- Measure the temperature of the room at the child's level, within 1–3 feet of the floor. Maintain group rooms between 68–72 degrees Fahrenheit.
- Strive to use in-floor radiant heat and carpets wherever children will be playing on the floor.
- Because of the high rate of respiratory infections in child care, a relative humidity of 50–55% is desirable during the heating season. This has the added benefits of making the room feel warmer at lower temperatures, thus using less fuel and reducing the static electricity in the air. Humidity above 70% is conducive to mold growth.

Draft Protection

- Equipment that generates a great deal of heat, cold, or draft directly around it will make that portion of the room unusable.
- Hydronic baseboard heaters release no airborne pollutants or fried dust, are not noisy, and provide a steady heat with no drafts because natural air motion distributes the heat. They need to be shielded from children's touch, however.
- Children like sitting near windows to enjoy views of the outside, especially in winter when it is harder to get out. To prevent drafts, use double or triple thermopane windows, good seals and insulation around doors and windows, interior vestibules, and proper location of doors to the outside relative to prevailing wind directions.
- Design air locks (an enclosed space between an exterior door and the room beyond it), vestibules, and a shielded location for the receptionist in entry/reception areas at the outset. Remedial solutions, such as shields and radiant heating panels, ease the situation but never make it fully comfortable.

Equipment

- To reduce operating costs and produce less pollution during operation, install only durable high-efficiency furnaces, boilers, and air conditioners. Install equipment with minimal risk of gas spillage, such as sealed-combustion appliances.
- Avoid ozone-depleting chemicals (CFCs, HCFCs) in mechanical equipment and insulation.
- Screen or shield all heating and cooling elements from children's reach.
- Be certain to clean all heating and cooling ducts periodically.
- Consider using a geothermal heat sink to warm the building in winter and cool it in summer. While expensive to install, this system is highly ecological and economical in the long run.

Radiant Heating

- Radiant heat warms objects instead of air. It allows people to feel warm at lower air temperatures, increasing muscle tone and aliveness.
- Passive and active solar heating is the most clean and energy-efficient form of radiant heat. It produces no fumes, consumes no fossil fuels. However, rock beds used in active systems need to be checked periodically for mold growth and radon emissions.
- Polybutylene radiant-floor heating can be installed in a concrete slab or in a 1½-inch lightweight concrete topping over a wood floor, or below wood floor framing. The system is quiet, clean, comfortable, and doesn't blow air and dust around. The water circulating in the tubes can be heated in any manner: oil, gas, electricity, passive solar. Carpet, wood, linoleum, and ceramic tile flooring can be placed over radiant floor heat, provided the floor coverings and adhesives are nontoxic or will not volitize. Other benefits of this system include no sound, no dry air, and no circulation of allergens and toxins.
- Since infants are particularly vulnerable to heat loss, radiant-floor heating and careful zoning of HVAC systems are desirable. Large amounts of glass draw heat away from their bodies even if they are not near the window.
- Consider providing a radiant heat panel above the diapering station to keep undressed infants warm.

GUIDELINES: COOLING

- Consider orientation, exposure, trees and shrubs, and cross-ventilation as natural ways to help cool buildings in hot climates or seasons.
- Use awnings, roof overhangs, trellises, deep window reveals, ceiling fans, blinds, light-colored exterior walls, thick interior masonry, earth walls, screens, courtyards, and open towers to keep the interior cool in hot climates or intensely sunny areas. If possible, avoid tinted glass, which reduces the quantity and quality of natural light to the interior.
- Openings in cover guards for fans and vents must be small enough to keep little fingers out.
- For mechanical air-conditioning systems to maintain constant air flow at a median temperature, they need good filters; isolated motors, fans, and compressors that reduce noise; and drains that prevent mildew growth by removing collected water.

Ventilation and Air Quality

Unlike in the past, when the wind was relied upon to bring fresh air into buildings, and leaky building envelopes allowed indoor pollutants to move outdoors, today's buildings have become more tightly sealed, and mechanical cooling and heating systems are common in all climate zones. At the same time, thousands of new materials and products used as goods, finishes, and furnishings have increased sources of interior pollution.

Good ventilation systems depend upon air pressure control to balance building exhausts, air intakes, and air leakage sites in the building envelope. More air should be mechanically supplied to a building than is extracted under all operating conditions. Many HVAC systems themselves add to air quality problems because they may be contaminated with mold and bacteria, which they transfer throughout the system and to the building's occupants. Ducts and coils in HVAC systems need to be checked and cleaned regularly.

Indoor air quality depends upon the absence of pollutants, the power of ventilation systems to pump fresh air indoors, and the power of filters to remove polluting substances. The choice of ventilation system will affect children's current and future respiratory health and their environmental and chemical sensitivity. The incidence of asthma is rising in young children, partly as a result of poor ventilation systems coupled with toxic interior finishes, toxic cleaning products, and less time spent breathing nonpolluted outdoor air.

Areas Requiring Special Ventilation

In addition to its general ventilation requirements, three areas of a child care center need special ventilation: bathrooms, diaper changing areas, and kitchens. Since children under three or four are just learning bladder and bowel control and toilet use, many accidents occur. These may not be cleaned up immediately because staff are busy attending to the child, and toilets may not be flushed regularly. As a result, odors build up in the toilet area—a frequent complaint of users and visitors to centers.[9] Most bathrooms need supplementary exhaust systems, ideally under staff control, to help remove odors. An operable window in the area is also highly desirable.

Any diaper changing station not located in a bathroom needs its own exhaust system. Although diaper containers are sealed and odor-controlled, their frequent use, and the fact that diapers sit in containers for part or all of the day, prevents the complete elimination of smells. Additional ventilation at the source, and an operable window nearby, are both highly beneficial.

Since kitchen aromas bring joy to our senses and to our hearts, it makes sense to locate the kitchen so these can be appreciated. However, good ventilation and exhaust fans, especially over the stove, are also needed to eliminate undesirable odors, gas pollution, and stale air.

Severely Harmful Pollutants

In striving to provide good-quality indoor air, caution needs to be taken with regard to several severely harmful pollutants: carbon dioxide, volatile organic compounds including formaldehyde, radon, asbestos, lead, and bioaerosols.

Carbon dioxide affects the nervous system and slows down reactions. Carbon dioxide pollution in the interior can come from combustion processes in the building such as garages, water heaters, clothes dryers, and furnaces, as well as fax and copy machines, computers, televisions, and refrigerators. While some of these sources are minor and difficult to control, all appliance venting, flues, pipes, and welds need to be cleaned, sealed, and properly adjusted to keep carbon dioxide to a minimum. Gas stoves need to be pilotless.

Volatile Organic Compounds (VOCs) are organic substances that emit toxic gases: chlorine, toluene, ammonia, ethylene, glycol, turpentine, naphthalene, acetone, sodium hydroxide. Many paints, varnishes, stains, adhesives, air fresheners, polishes, hygiene products, pesticides, cleaning fluids, decorating compounds, and pet products emit VOCs, as do aerosols, which dispense chlorinated fluorocarbons (CFC's) that damage the ozone layer. The worst VOCs are formaldehyde (discussed below) and chlorine. Polyurethane foam also contains extremely toxic VOCs, emitted slowly over the life of the product, but especially if the foam is burned.

VOCs are known to cause headaches; skin, eye, nose, and throat irritation; nausea; central nervous system, liver, and kidney damage; and even cancer. If products containing VOCs must be used, always choose those which do not off-gas, or off-gas very little, and those whose decay rate is rapid (i.e., the gas diffuses over a short time frame). Petrochemical paints and related products should be avoided or used only under extensive ventilation, allowing the paint plenty of time to dry before the room is used. Be sure to consider nontoxic products.[10]

Although the newest carpets available have low

levels of VOC emissions that decay rapidly, most commercial carpet pads and adhesives will emit VOCs. Low-VOC-emitting products are identified by the Carpet & Rug Institute's IAQ testing label. Nontoxic adhesives and pads such as CFC-free foam pads, synthetic jute, and felted wool are increasingly available on the market. Typically, rooms containing newly installed carpets need to be aired out for at least a week prior to occupancy.

Formaldehyde is one of the most common industrial adhesives in timber and plastic products, and a VOC that typically occurs in two forms: urea formaldehyde and phenol formaldehyde. Phenol formaldehyde, used in exterior-rated building materials such as plywood, waferboard, and oriented stran boards, is usually considered safe for use because it is more stable and not water soluable. Urea formaldehyde, on the other hand, is water soluable, and off-gasses at room temperature and with increasing humidity and exposure to heat. It is typically used in particle board found as a floor underlayer material, cabinetry, furniture and veneers, synthetic and sheet floors, siding, vinyl wall coverings, fiberboard, permanent press fabrics, draperies, carpets, and as a common preservative especially in paper products. As potent human irritants, suspected carcinogens, and sensitizers (to itself and other chemicals) that lower the threshold for allergic reactions, products of urea formaldehyde should not be used indoors. If they must be used inside, they should be sealed, as by painting the exposed surfaces of cabinets and furniture made of particle board. New formalydehyde-free medium density fiberboards, which use lignin as a natural bonding agent, are also available.

Elimination of urea formaldehyde is possible only by removing and replacing the source with metal, hardwood, drywall, and plaster. In some cases, a water-based sealer or nitrocellulose-based varnish can be applied over formaldehyde containing materials. Seek professional advice for dealing with older buildings containing urea formaldehyde foam insulation (UFFI), an insulating material that is now banned. Indoor formaldehyde levels can be measured with a do-it-yourself kit or by the local health department.

Radon is a lethal gas that occurs naturally in some groundwater, rocks, and soil, as well as in some concrete, cinder block, bricks, and gypsum wallboard building materials, and in natural gas. Radon has been estimated by the EPA to be the leading cause of lung cancer in nonsmokers. Inexpensive EPA approved test kits can be used to test for presence and level. If possible, avoid constructing a new center in areas known to have high levels of radon present. Levels in existing buildings can be measured by your local EPA office or state agency and, under professional guidance, can be somewhat controlled by ventilation, drainage, filtration, removal, and sealing techniques.

Asbestos was once widely applied for fireproofing, decoration, and thermal, electrical, and acoustical insulation. It is harmless until its fibers are released into the air or water, where they can eventually lodge in the lungs or intestines, causing malignant tumors and an increased risk of cancer of the larynx, chest, or abdomen. Asbestos removal in an existing building needs to be handled professionally and in accordance with state laws.

Lead is now illegal as a paint component, but can be present in older buildings, where children may inadvertently eat cracked or peeling paint. No safe level for lead exposure has been demonstrated. Chronic exposure to low levels can cause brain damage, permanent neurophysiological defects and behavior disorders. Older buildings can be used for child care only if lead paint is removed and plumbing is checked for lead content. Precautions need to be taken against breathing dust contaminated with lead, letting the dust spread, or leaving residues that can enter food or the air. Old lead pipes, or newer copper pipes with lead-containing solders, can also cause lead to enter a building's drinking water. For new plumbing, utilize low-lead solder in the joints of copper pipe.

Bioaerosols are airborne irritants or allergenic materials (such as respirable particles and dust mites) that have grown or accumulated indoors over time, particularly in carpets. For control, periodic deep steam cleaning of carpets, and use of high-efficiency particle arrestance (HEPA) air vacuum systems, are recommended. Microorganism growth is usually not significant when relative humidity is below 65%. In areas of high humidity, the potential for mold growth is greater regardless of the floor covering.

GUIDELINES: VENTILATION AND AIR QUALITY

- Research indicates that many centers find it difficult to eliminate odors in bathrooms and diaper changing areas. Excellent ventilation and a drain in the floor for cleanup are recommended.
- Gas ranges require hoods vented to the outside, a powerful fan, and an operable window nearby. Cooking gas can have an effect similar to formaldehyde in some persons, especially those spending long hours daily over a gas stove.
- Install mechanical ventilation equipment to ensure safe, healthy indoor air. Heat recovery ventilators are preferred in cold climates for energy savings, but simple, less expensive exhaust-only ventilation systems can be adequate.
- Physical reactions to "tight buildings" occur where windows are sealed and ventilation systems filter only about 85% of the air. The result is that smoke, perfume, hair spray, body odors, and airborne bacteria and viruses, as well as small amounts of formaldehyde and other gases exuded by synthetic building and finishing materials, are recirculated and breathed by the inhabitants. Where existing HVAC systems are inadequate to support the volume of air that needs to be filtered and recirculated, the recommended solution is to redesign the system or outfit these buildings with windows which open.
- Provide plenty of operable windows for basic health and so people can control both the air and the full-spectrum light in the center. (See Chapters 10 and 11.)
- Avoid materials that off-gas volatile organic compounds into the air, particularly formaldehyde-based finishes, adhesives, carpeting, and particleboard.
- Introduce pleasant odors such as fragrant flowers, cookies baking, fresh air from open windows, and essential oils.
- Minimize the need for pesticides by designing insect-resistant detailing.
- Use only nontoxic cleaning products.[11]

Electromagnetic Fields

Electromagnetic fields (EMFs)—which are simply a form of energy like light—are created by every electrical device that operates either by battery or on current from a wall outlet. Radio and television towers, overhead power lines, and transformers radiate intense levels of EMFs. It is neither possible nor desirable to avoid EMFs, which are a by-product of the myriad benefits of electricity. Rather, it is the cumulative strength and duration of exposure to EMFs, not their existence, which is the object of concern.

No studies have ruled out exposure to EMFs as being a health risk. On the other hand, safe levels have not been established. Not everyone exposed to EMFs develops disease, and not all disease is attributable to EMFs. However, a large number of studies have shown that EMFs have profound effects on animal and human physiology, resulting in ill health, increased stress, and psychological and sexual dysfunctions, and that the incidence of cancer is greater among subjects exposed to long-term EMFs—especially children—and those individuals whose tolerance has been exceeded.

The human body is fundamentally an electromagnetic system which, to remain healthy, must vibrate at appropriate frequencies. Young children are especially vulnerable to distortion of these frequencies. Results of a Swedish study involving children exposed to elevated EMF levels from high-voltage cables revealed their risk of cancer was two times higher than normal. The incidence of multiple sclerosis and other serious diseases has also been linked to increased EMF exposure.[12] It therefore seems wise to err on the side of caution by not locating child care centers near powerful EMF sources such as broadcast terminals and transformers.

Although not conclusive, there is also growing evidence that long-term exposure to even low-level EMFs in our homes and workplaces can be harmful by triggering allergies, raising stress and blood pressure levels, and causing disturbed sleep. It seems only reasonable, then, to reduce long-term exposure to low-level EMFs as much as possible in child care centers. EMFs can pass through walls and floors, but do not build up, nor can they be transferred to another object. Prime sources are overhead power lines, metal pipes and radiators holding water, computers, stereos, microwave ovens, dishwashers, hair dryers, and cell phones. Even when appliances are unplugged, the wiring feeding the sockets is still "live" and generating EMFs. Gauss meters (specific to North America or Europe) can be purchased, or a local electric utility company can be hired, to measure EMF levels in a building.

Fields the size of those generated in small buildings can usually be corrected by incorporating shielding for cables and conduits, and even special supply-demand switches so that electrical current is present only when needed. Beds, particularly for sleeping children, should be located as far as possible from outlets, clocks, and other electrical devices, and not be made of metal.

GUIDELINES: ELECTROMAGNETIC FIELDS

- Avoid locating child care centers near transformers, power stations, and radio and TV broadcast terminals.
- Plan electrical wiring and placement of electrical equipment to minimize children's and staff's electromagnetic field exposure.
- Reduce the EMFs around electrical cables and conduits in the building by shielding or insulating them, and possibly by installing special supply-demand switches.
- Purchase shields available for equipment such as computers and microwave ovens to prevent artificial electromagnetic fields from negatively impacting children and adults.
- Measure EMFs in the building by purchasing an easy-to-use, affordable gaussmeter, or hiring a professional. Strive to limit children's exposure to levels characteristic of the average person's exposure in this society.

Notes

[1]W. McDonough, *Design, Ecology, Ethics and the Making of Things,* (the Centennial Sermon presented at the Cathedral of St. John The Divine, New York, N.Y., February 1993) 7.

[2]Adapted from the AIA's "Making a Difference: An Introduction to the Environmental Resource Guide," *Architecture* (May 1991).

[3]*International Institute for Bau-Biologie and Ecology*, P.O. Box 387, Clearwater, Florida 34615 (Tel: 813/461-4371, Fax 813/441-4373).

[4]An excellent and comprehensive guide for everyone is *The Natural House Catalog,* by David Pearson (Simon & Schuster, 1996). For architects, the *AIA Environmental Resource Guide* (ERG) is indispensable.

[5]Portions of the guidelines in this chapter were adapted from "A Checklist for Environmentally Sustainable Design and Construction," *Environmental Building News: A Bimonthly Newsletter* 17, no.1.

[6]See the AIA's *Environmental Resource Guide* (ERG) for Life Cycle Analysis of 28 categories of building materials.

[7]Pearson, *The Natural House Catalog.*

[8]Toxic by-products of cholorine called trihalomethanes have been linked to cancer and birth defects.

[9]Gretchen Lee Anderson, *Removing Barriers to Childcare Facilities Development* (California State University, Northridge, CA, 1993).

[10]Nontoxic paints are available from The Old Fashioned Milk Paint Company, Groton, MA; Auro Paints; and the Glidden Spred 2000 paint series, to name a few. Environmentally sound carpet adhesives are available from Envirotec (CA) and other companies. See Pearson, *The Natural House Catalog.*

[11]See Norma L. Miller, ed., *The Healthy School Handbook* (Washington, D.C.: NEA Professional Library, 1995) and Debra Lynn Dadd, *Home Safe Home: Protecting Yourself and Your Family from Everyday Toxics and Harmful Household Products* (New York: Tarcher/Putnam, 1997).

[12]A. A. Marino, "Electromagnetic Fields, Cancer, and the Theory of Neuroendocrine-Related Promotion," *Bioelectrochemistry & Bioenergetics* 29 (1993): 255–276; Rodney Girdlestone, "Electromagnetic Fields," *Mind Body Soul: The Alternative Lifestyle Magazine* (Sept/Oct. 1994): 21; and Rodney Girdlestone and David Cowan, *Safe as Houses? Ill-health and Electro-stress in the Home* (Gateway Books, 1994).

CHAPTER NINE

SOUND

The voices of the past do not sound the same in the big room
as in the little bed chamber and calls on the stairs
have yet another sound. . . .
Still further it is possible to recover . . .
the resonance of each room in the sound house.

—Gaston Bachelard[1]

We all have memories of the way things sound in particular places: the "creak" of a single staircase tread, the "catch" of the gate latch, the "thud" of the front door closing, the "hollow" of footsteps on the marble floor. The quality of sound in a space contributes significantly to its spirit of place. Yet child care centers are often built without sufficient attention to how sounds will be transmitted or reverberate in their spaces, or to the quality of the acoustic environment in general. This chapter looks at ways in which sound affects children's development and explores how design can influence a center's acoustic factors.

Sound and Sacred Architecture

Earlier civilizations understood that sound had profound impact on human well-being. Buildings—especially places of worship —were designed to incorporate specific geometric proportions known to affect their acoutistic properties.[2] The architecture of an Islamic mosque intentionally manipulates its acoustic environment to create harmonious sound patterns that balance the body's energy systems and help attain spiritual connections with God. The French Abbey of Le Thoronet, a simple stone vault considered the purest example of twelfth-century Cistercian monastic architecture, was designed as an immense musical instrument for enhancing the human voice, magnifying perception of the body's internal rhythms, and deepening the occupants' awareness of inner spiritual forces.

> . . . the Abbey does not promote a fundamental tone, but instead allows all notes to resound equally. . . . even a pin dropped at the end of the nave, some 40 meters away, generates a full range of harmonic overtones producing the mysterious character of a heavenly choir. Standing next to a certain pillar in the nave, one's hearing seems suddenly turned inside-out; the heartbeat and internal workings of the organs are magnified; even external sounds seem to originate from within. . . .
>
> . . . A large wood panelled Islamic ceiling found elsewhere . . . was found by acoustic engineers to be virtually soundproof, due not to its thickness, but to its particular carved geometric patterns, which set up a kind of interference grid effectively absorbing most external sound.[3]

Today's buildings, designed according to different geometrical principles, often fail to shield occupants from an onslaught of external noise, or they themselves produce enough internal sound pollution to induce discomfort, poor performance, and illness. Rarely are modern building designs or materials chosen for their sound-enhancing properties, except in the case of concert halls and acoustically specialized facilities. However, sound plays an important role in keeping the body balanced and healthy.

Sound Organizes Matter

Sound, light, and color, which comprise some of the many rhythmic vibrations in the universe, differ only in their vibrational frequencies.[4] The human body has rhythmic patterns of breathing, heartbeat, sucking, and movement that are the result of vibrational frequencies intrinsic to its different organs and tissues. While not necessarily audible to the human ear, these vibrations are, nonetheless, sound frequencies which maintain tissues in an optimum state of health. Sound actually organizes matter and gives it shape.[5] The sounds in our midst can literally nourish or debilitate us.

Research on the biology of sound by the French physician Alexander Tomatis, indicates that *every cell* in the body registers sound waves. Thus we actually hear with our entire bodies, not simply with our ears; we can react to sound even if it is below our level of conscious awareness (as when we are sleeping). Because of powerful links between audition and the senses of touch, smell, and vision, Tomatis considers the acoustic nerve the "major mechanism of reception and integration of perception."[6] He has identified three times as many nerve connections between the ear and the brain as between the eye and the brain.

The first human embryonic cells are sound-sensitive, and by the time the human fetus is four-and-one-half months old, the auditory system is virtually complete. By the seventh month in utero, precise fetal body movements synchronize with the phonemes of the mother's speech.[7] Such sensitivity and speed of auditory development even before birth undoubtedly assists in the rapid acquisition of language in the first three to five years of life.

We all know what it is like to use sounds to help us locate ourselves, others, and objects in space. Remarkably, some congenitally blind infants can accurately reach for and grasp objects in space based upon echoes they detect off the objects as a result of sounds they themselves emit (provided the environment is sufficiently echoic).[8] Lacking sight, children and adults use sound, and its relationship to touch, to create and verify their organization of space.

Collectively, these facts indicate that children are "wired" to respond to all the sounds they hear as a form of survival and adaptation to an unfamiliar world. Living tissue is particularly responsive to the organizing power of certain sound frequencies. However, it is also vulnerable to the disorganizing power of others.

The Effects of Noise[9]

As with all the senses, human beings are designed to detect changes in sound, but not to endure a steady onslaught of it. In preindustrial times, people lived and worked in acoustically unpolluted settings. The sounds they heard—a twig snapping, an animal's cry, or the clap of thunder—carried meaning for survival or provided pleasure. Church bells, ploughs, cowbells, and other man-made sounds were usually not physiologically stressful.

By contrast, consider a few of the sounds associated with modern urban life, many just outside the doors of most child care facilities: airplanes, highways, sirens, lawn mowers, snow blowers, sonic booms, fire alarms, street cleaning and repairs, and sometimes even construction. Indoors, there may be the perpetual background noise of heating and cooling units, ventilating fans, fluorescent lights, refrigerators, dishwashers, flushing toilets, running water, telephones, copy machines, and equipment moving down resonant corridors.

Studies document an accelerated rate of hearing loss in industrialized nations due to noise, i.e., an overabundance of loud, unwanted, and harmful sounds. While most adult city dwellers learn to "tune out" ambient noise to some extent, the relief experienced by escaping for a walk in the woods reveals the cost of such accommodation. Exposure to repeated loud noises induces a perpetual "startle" or "fight or flight" response in children as well as adults, leading to tensed muscles, fatigue, diminished reflex responsiveness, and accident proneness. Other physical responses to noise include headaches, tension, high blood pressure, hyperactivity, poor digestion, decreased immunity, and neurological disorders. Inability to concentrate, irritability, poor sleep, poor work performance, and reduced mental acuity can also result.[10, 11]

Sound in the Child Care Environment

Unlike adults, children have few habituated responses for lessening the impact of noise and virtually no control over what they hear. Since the sounds in their midst affect every cell of their bodies, their immature tissues are particularly vulnerable to the impact of intense vibrations, reverberations, and noise. Conversely, a harmonious acoustic environment supports good organ and tissue development. The potential for permanent health and hearing damage in young children, as a result of inappropriate or excessive sound, is quite real.

Sound is also an important source of orientation and security, especially for children. Many find the sounds of other children crying, of unfamiliar equipment, and even the experience of extreme quiet to be anxiety-provoking. On the other hand, familiar sounds—human voices, soft music, birds, and breezes outside—are comforting and reassuring, especially in a strange place.

Acoustic Goals for Centers

Because the acoustics of a child care center have a significant, although sometimes subtle, effect on everyone's well-being, the acoustic goals are twofold:

- To create a harmonious and pleasing acoustic environment
- To control, absorb, or dissipate unwanted noises (physical vibrations, high-pitched whines, reverberations, and echos)

Sound either supports or interferes with activities in a given environment. The spirit of a place is enhanced by moderate levels of acoustic variation or difference-within-sameness (see Chapter 1), where voices, activities, and sounds from the natural world create a nonintrusive backdrop to foreground events.

Achieving a Quality Acoustic Environment

Achieving acoustic quality in a child care center is a matter of incorporating into the center's design subtleties that are not commonly employed by the building industry. For this reason, it is advisable to include an acoustic engineer on the design or renovation team from the outset. The foundation of acoustic quality involves:

- The designer's awareness of and commitment to consider the appropriate acoustic atmosphere for each space
- A contractual agreement with the contractor to meet previously identified noise criteria ratings for each space
- Consistent attention to detail throughout the project, from selection of the building site and materials to acceptance testing of the finished facility

Ways to ensure acoustic quality include: (1) avoiding noisy locations, (2) use of appropriate construction and landscaping techniques, (3) use of indoor sound-absorption strategies, and (4) intentional introduction of pleasing sounds.

GUIDELINES: ACOUSTIC QUALITY AND LOCATION

- Sound has the power to organize and disorganize living tissue. Aim to create a harmonious acoustic environment and to reduce the sources and impact of noise.
- Avoid if possible the following acoustically negative adjacencies: highways, mass transit, railroads, major industries, fire stations and hospitals, shopping centers, fairgrounds, air bases, power substations, transformers, major transmission lines, and airports.
- Intermittent and irregular sounds, such as produced by the sources listed above, are the most annoying. Continuous featureless noise at low levels has little effect on performance. High-pitched noise is more irritating than low-pitched noise.

Avoiding Noisy Locations

The quality of the center's final acoustic environment begins with site selection (see discussion in Chapter 4). Careful investigation at the outset is vital. Since children will ideally spend 50% of their time outdoors, the acoustic climate of the play yards is perhaps one of the most important aspects of selecting a location for the center. Avoid noisy locations wherever possible.

Appropriate Construction and Landscaping Techniques

How a building is constructed, and what surrounds it, both affect its acoustic quality. Acoustic landscaping has the additional advantages of helping to cool and clean the air, visually screening noise sources, and attracting birds, crickets, and other pleasant-sounding creatures.

GUIDELINES: BUILDING AND LANDSCAPING FOR ACOUSTIC QUALITY ON ACOUSTICALLY CHALLENGING SITES

- Use concrete or masonry, rather than lighter construction, to form a massive partition that will limit penetration of exterior noise to the building's interior.
- Where light construction materials are employed, reduce transit of vibrations through the structure to the inside by: (1) staggering the studs in new construction, (2) adding a

second interior wall to an existing building with an airspace between the two walls, or (3) hanging the interior wall finish with resilient metal channels made for this purpose.[12] Such methods create structural discontinuity, reducing the ability of vibrations to travel to the inside.

- Techniques for blocking airborne noise from outside are similar to those used to conserve energy indoors: double and triple glazing; weather stripping on doors and windows; sealing air leaks in sill skirts, floorboards, ducts, electrical switches, and power outlets in outside walls.
- Dampen the sound around a building and its exterior play yards with landscaping in the form of earth berms, a dense barrier of trees and shrubs, a fence of concrete or masonry, or combinations of these (see Figure 5.7). The best plantings for absorbing sound are wide belts of tall trees or plants that have thick, fleshy leaves and thin stalks that can bend and vibrate.
- The lower the building relative to these screens or the earth (either by building into the earth or cutting back the earth and placing the building in a hollow), the better its acoustic shielding.
- The closer the planting screen to the actual noise source (street or highway), the more effective it will be.

Indoor Sound Control Strategies

Noise is transmitted in three main ways: through the air, by impact, and by flanking transmission. Airborne noise is best controlled by mass, using the construction and landscaping techniques just described. Impact noise—noise transmitted through floors and walls—is best controlled by absorbent surfaces, such as carpet, a "floating floor" (a separate floor resting on a resilient quilt above a structural floor), or a floating ceiling. Flanking transmission occurs when impact sound from plumbing, elevators, etc., travels along floors and walls to distant locations. It is best reduced by sealing cracks around electrical, mechanical, and plumbing equipment.

Every noise control problem involves three independent elements: the source (air, impact, flanking), the path (building exterior, building interior, room interior), and the receiver (adult, child). Some sounds can be controlled at their source; others need to be controlled along their path; and in certain cases the receiver may need to adapt. Each element must be evaluated independently and as part of the entire system. To give a room a more intimate and relaxed acoustic atmosphere, reduce its reverberent qualities by adding absorbent surfaces and by varying ceiling

Figure 9.1
Furniture, lofts, and platforms of varied heights help prevent sound from traveling across the room.

and furniture heights. A pleasing level of ambient or background sound also helps to offset noise and make the direct sounds from children and activities less noticeable. Ambient sound may come from the low "hum" of the people using the space, or through the intentional introduction of fountains, chimes, and music.

It is helpful to define what constitutes a satisfactory acoustic environment for particular areas of a building. Current standards, frequently based on Noise Criteria (NC) ratings established by the American Society of Heating, Refrigerating, and Air Conditioning Engineers (ASHRAE) and the American Society for Testing Materials (ASTM), give quantitative values that can be precisely specified for each area.[13] The Noise Criteria ratings also provide a firm specification against which the performance of building systems can be readily checked before final approval of the completed construction.

Because children and their furniture are close to the floor, often 50% of a room's volume is empty and over their heads. This permits sound to travel unimpeded across the room. Varied ceiling heights, and partitions, lofts, and climbers at different heights, can help to absorb and dampen ambient noise close to its source (Figure 9.1).

GUIDELINES: SOUND CONTROL STRATEGIES

- Early in the design stage, establish firm guidelines, perhaps based on ASHRAE and ASTM Noise Criteria ratings, for controlling noises and vibrations from mechanical systems.

- Because textiles are frequently scarce in child care centers (due to sanitation or fire considerations), architects cannot rely exclusively on their use to mitigate acoustically harsh construction. The building itself must have good acoustic balance.
- In spaces that are quiet and free of distraction, sounds made by occupants can be soft, or loud and harsh, depending upon the room's interior volume and the sound-absorbing properties of the finish materials. The reverberance of a space (the length of time that sounds persist in it after their source has stopped) increases as a room's volume increases and decreases as the amount of absorptive material increases. Variations in ceiling height improve a room's volumetric and sound control. Low ceilings (7.5–9 feet) are desirable in quiet areas, and higher ceilings (9–11 feet) in more active areas.
- With 50% of the space in a room above children's heads, and usually empty, sound travels easily from place to place. Prevent unwanted sound flow by creating a variety of vertical forms in a room—lofts, platforms, climbers, dividers, and ceilings at different heights. Sounds will be prevented from traveling further when they strike these structures (Figure 9.1).

Noisy printer, fax, and copy machines are close to, but shielded from, the reception area. (The Copper House)

Sources of Noise

- Usually, the heating/ventilation system is the dominant background sound source that needs to be controlled. Instead of laying ducts across rooms, consider having them feed into rooms from corridors. Heating/ventilation noise may be acoustically tolerable when it is continuous, bland, and unobtrusive.
- Consider running the structural components of walls up to a deck above, rather than simply to a dropped ceiling. When selecting wall materials and insulation, choose those with the most appropriate or higher Sound Transmission Coefficients (STC). Insulating wallpaper may be appropriate in some instances.
- Even the smallest cracks or open joints greatly reduce the sound-insulating value of walls. Back-to-back wall outlets, air ducts, and plumbing facilities can create small and easily overlooked openings through which sound can escape. Where locational separation is not possible, making such cracks airtight, and staggering receptacles are essential sound control strategies indoors.
- Fan equipment in ceilings requires more acoustic insulation than a thin layer of acoustic ceiling board.
- Evaluate sounds emitted by large and small appliances as a criterion of selection. For example, powerful flush mechanisms on toilets can be frightening to young children.
- Where possible, shield piping and duct work to minimize their vibrations and noise.
- Place photocopiers, fax machines, and other noisy pieces of equipment behind closed doors or in shielded and isolated areas.
- Lessen the buzz of fluorescent lamps by using high-quality ballasts or remote ballasts, and by immediate relamping when the bulbs begin to hum. (Longer-lasting full-spectrum bulbs need to be changed less often.) For more information on lighting, see Chapter 10.

Sound and Location

- Avoid locating incompatible spaces, such as children's spaces and mechanical rooms, adjacent to or near one another. Services better located at a distance or shielded from children's areas include elevators, furnace and utility rooms, trash chutes, and janitorial closets. Place storage and low-use facilities, rather than children's spaces, near mechanical and electrical systems. (See Figures 6.8 and 6.12.)
- Clustering group rooms around a multipurpose or gross motor area (a "core" space) is ill-advised because of the difficulty of preventing high-activity sound from infiltrating the surrounding rooms (see Figure 4.4). Instead, acoustically shield gross motor rooms and/or locate them in a remote part of the building where their sound and reverberation will not be disturbing.
- To help buffer sound transmission from room to room and from corridors to rooms, use the interior walls of rooms for closets or storage (see Figure 6.12). The resulting wall thickness creates a more distinct transition between rooms and corridors and a subtle "entry" space that makes the room more private. This treatment is especially appropriate for group rooms, offices, and spaces needing speech privacy.
- Locate spaces requiring speech privacy—director's office, conference rooms, children's rooms, staff areas, and telephones—remote from large public spaces and/or treat them with sound absorptive materials and added wall thickness.
- When zoning rooms (see Chapter 7), separate quiet and noisy areas. Use acoustic manipulation, i.e., a quiet lower-ceiling space for resting, and a more acoustically alive space for dramatic play, to create variety and heighten interest in activities.

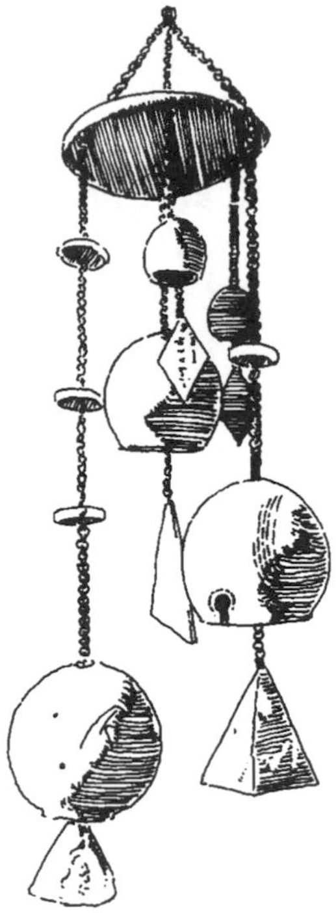

Figure 9.2
Wind chimes, birds and frogs chirping, small fountains, and gentle breezes add delightful sounds to a place.

Sound and Materials

- A predominance of nonporous, hard, and sound-reflective building materials—concrete, glass, plaster, and sheet plastics—account for the sterile and resonant acoustic quality of many child care centers.
- Use soft, porous, sound-absorbent materials, such as carpets, upholstery, drapes, textured wall hangings, ceiling banners, and ceiling acoustic panels and tiles (preferably inconspicuous) to dampen undesirable sound transfer. It is advisable to treat either the floor or ceiling or both acoustically, depending on circumstances.
- Chalkboards, dividers, tackboards, or storage units can provide places for attaching sound-absorptive materials. Homosote on the back of bookcases absorbs some sound while creating a useful display surface at child level.
- Consider adding carpet (with the appropriate flammability ratings) to an entire wall, or its lower portion, for added sound absorption, wall protection, and coziness (see page 234).
- Place sound-absorbing materials on the ceiling and walls of telephone alcoves, above table height.

Introducing Pleasing Sounds

We each carry memories of spaces and objects that have special meaning because of the unique sounds we associate with them. The acoustic spirit of a place can be unforgettable and awe-inspiring. What memories of acoustic delight can we create for children in child care?

GUIDELINES: INTRODUCING ACOUSTIC PLEASURE

- Attract song birds outdoors with berry-producing plants, bird feeders, and bird baths. Consider creating an outdoor aviary (see Chapter 21). Raise birds such as zebra finches, parrots, parakeets, and canaries indoors in large cages. The sounds of birds chirping often soothe and enchant children.
- Raise crickets and frogs in indoor terrariums or attract them by providing ponds and dense foliage outside. The sounds they make are pleasant and informative.
- Plant bamboos, reeds, and tall grasses outside to create resonant tones in response to air movement.
- Hang wind chimes, pinwheels, windbells, and flutes inside as well as outside an open window (Figure 9.2).
- Nothing matches the soothing sound of moving water in a natural stream, bubbling fountain, or splashing waterfall. Take advantage of such amenities at any center site that permits them.
- Indoors, consider recirculating fountains and small waterfalls, from table top versions to flowforms.
- Consider creating an acoustically shielded "sound room" where children can freely experiment with real instruments—drums, marimbas, cymbals, xylophones, etc.—without disturbing others. Design the room itself to be an instrument by creating the walls out of different resonant materials—woods, metals, plastics—that can be played at child level.

Notes

[1]G. Bachelard, *The Poetics of Space* (Boston: Beacon Press, 1969), 60–61.

[2]According to the principles of sacred geometry, specific geometric proportions (occurring in simple polygons and polyhedra) are also the basic consonant musical ratios: the octave, 1:2; the fifth, 2:3; the fourth, 3:4; and the major third, 4:5. The proportion 1:2, used to create a rectangle with length and width in a 1:2 ratio and a diagonal the value of the square root of five, is known as the "Golden Section." This proportion has been famous since antiquity for its aesthetic perfection.

[3]R. Lawlor, *Parabola: Myth and the Quest for Meaning,* Vol III, Number 1, (Brookline, NY, 1978), 12–19.

[4]As demonstrated by a color organ that simultaneously produces a sound and its corresponding color when a key is played: red corresponds to the vibration of the key of C; yellow to E, blue to G, etc.

[5]Hans Jenney, Cymatics: The Healing Nature of Sound, Vol II. MACROMEDIA, P.O. Box 279, Epping, NH, 03857. In the 1980s, Hans Jenney demonstrated the power of sound to organize matter. His experiments placed granular substances (such as sand, sugar, licopodium), emulsions, and colloidal particle suspensions in both liquid and air, on a vibratory plate through which he passed different sound frequencies. Specific auditory tones induced the randomly scattered substances to coagulate into specific geometric patterns, forms, and lattices. Human tissues and cells are almost entirely plasma, i.e., liquid particle suspensions. Thus, living tissue is especially responsive to the organizing/disorganizing power of sound.

[6]A. Tomatis, "Chant, the Healing Power of Voice and Ear," in *Music, Physician for Times to Come,* ed. Don Campbell (Wheaton, Ill: Quest, 1991).

[7]J. C. Pearce, *Evolution's End: Claiming the Potential of Our Intelligence* (San Francisco: Harper, 1992), 71.

[8]T. G. R. Bower, *The Perceptual World of the Child* (Cambridge, MA: Harvard University Press, 1977), 76–77.

[9]Some information in this section is adapted from Carol Venolia, *Healing Environments: Your Guide to Indoor Well-Being* (Berkeley, CA: Celestial Arts, 1988), 84–97.

[10]David Tame, *The Secret Power of Music* (Rochester, NY: Destiny Books, 1984). Tame reports that because shrill sounds will coagulate proteins in a liquid medium, teenagers in Great Britain created a fad of taking raw eggs to rock concerts. The intense energy of the rock music hard-boiled the eggs by intermission!

[11] Steven Halpern, *Sound Health: The Music and Sounds that Make Us Whole* (New York: Harper & Row, 1985), 70. Halpern reports that the standard rhythms of rock music, even at normal volume, have been found to weaken muscles, increase heart rate, and contribute to a loss of symmetrical functioning of the two hemispheres of the brain.

[12]Venolia, *Healing Environments,* 33–34.

[13]See ASHRAE Systems Handbook (American Society of Heating, Refrigerating, and Air-Conditioning Engineers) for NC (noise criteria) for a range of situations. Contact the American Society for Testing and Materials, 1916 Race Street, Philadelphia, PA 19103, for further information on their standards for noise and acoustics.

CHAPTER TEN

LIGHT AND LIGHTING

. . . Light is the most important environmental input, after food, in controlling body function.

—Richard Wurtman[1]

Despite its importance, light is the variable most sorely neglected by interior design practice. Because of cost, architects too often specify 2-x-4 fluorescent ceiling grids for child care centers without considering alternatives, treating lighting fixtures as unidimensional rather than task-specific, and as unrelated to the natural light entering through windows. Hence centers are often bombarded by waves of intense fluorescent light, interspersed with deep shadows, which are harsh and inadequate for the tasks at hand.

Electric lighting really needs to be designed in relation to the quantity, quality, and location of natural light entering each space. The best solutions employ a variety of artificial lighting forms to complement natural light and include task-specific as well as general-ambient requirements. Criteria developed for elementary schools are not appropriate since child care spaces function very differently. The costs involved to achieve a varied and satisfying lighting plan need to be part of the architectural thinking and budget from the outset.

Children tend to congregate near sources of natural light.

Natural Light

The spirit of a place depends more on the presence of natural light than perhaps any other factor. Like cats, people tend to go where the sunlight is and to prefer rooms with windows on at least two sides. Natural light changes slowly and continuously throughout the day and across the seasons, enabling us to experience objects and spaces under different conditions of illumination. Natural light helps the body maintain its circadian rhythms and influences many health-related factors and many psychological factors such as orientation, security, variety, motion, and change (difference-within-sameness).

Light affects our total body chemistry. Experiments demonstrate that different colors and intensities of light affect blood pressure, pulse and respiration rates, brain activity, glandular and metabolic functions, and biorhythms. Phototherapy is used to treat neonatal jaundice, psoriasis, and herpes sores. Medical science even has a special word—heliotherapy—to describe the salutary effects of sunlight. Insufficient exposure to sunlight can result in vitamin D deficiency, demineralizaton of bones and teeth, weakening of the body's immunological defenses, and increased stress and fatigue.

Recognized links between natural light deprivation and depression have led to "sunshine laws" in countries such as Canada and Japan, where designers are required to guarantee that a minimum number of hours per day of daylight are available to the occupants of buildings.

A well-documented malaise related to insufficient exposure to sunlight is Seasonal Affective Disorder (SAD). Sufferers of SAD, including children, can experience depression, lethargy, carbohydrate craving, and may even require hospitalization during the autumn and winter months as a result of increased time spent under artificial illumination.[2] Electric light, which is deficient in certain wave lengths of natural light energy, appears to suppress the secretion of the neurotransmitters serotonin and melatonin, both of which control the above emotional and physiological factors.

The most effective way to ensure that children receive sufficient exposure to natural light is *to provide readily accessible outdoor play spaces all year long.* This is one reason why the exterior space of a center needs to be large enough to permit all children to be outdoors at the same time, not just some groups on a staggered schedule (see Chapter 4). An open but covered outdoor area further extends use of the outdoors, especially in harsh climates.

Windows are the second best means of assuring that children experience natural light, particularly if they are operable, have low sills, and frame interesting views. Incredibly, child care spaces lacking any windows whatsoever are still being created! *A windowless space should never be used for full-day occupancy by children or adults.*

Many architectural features can assist in bringing natural light into child care spaces. A few to consider include greenhouses, balconies, courtyards, porches, window wells, atria, skylights, and light borrowed through clerestories and interior walls of glass.

GUIDELINES: NATURAL LIGHT
(Also see Chapter 11)

- *Maximize the presence of natural light—essential for good health—in all indoor spaces.* No room in which children spend several hours a day should be without windows.
- Provide windows on two sides of a room to balance light and reduce glare.
- Design "thin" buildings, when possible, to keep every part of a room within the sphere of a window's influence.
- Window wells, lowered window sills, porches, balconies, decks, atria, skylights, greenhouses, dutch doors, clerestories, and interior windows are all means of linking the indoors with sunny outside spaces.
- The best assurance that children will have sufficient exposure to natural light is to provide year-round easy access to outdoor play spaces from the group rooms. Include some covered outdoor areas for inclement weather and harsh climates. Porch roofs in glass or transparent plastic will not block the transmission of daylight through windows into a room.
- Ensure that art areas have plentiful natural light. Supplement with full-spectrum artificial lighting as necessary.

Porches make outdoor play possible in all kinds of weather, while roofs made of glass or transparent plastic allow full transmission of daylight to the inside.

Artificial Light[3]

Artificial or electrical light is needed to supplement natural light at night time, in winter, on gray days, and for indoor activities that do not take place near windows. Ideally, electrical light will be designed to create the same range of light qualities and variation found outdoors—shaded, filtered, directional, bright and general, warm or cool in tone—and will be controllable or programmable to suit the activities planned. The atmosphere of each space can be significantly changed by the ways in which it is lit.

There are two main considerations to weigh in selecting artificial lighting: lamp type (traditional; energy-saving fluorescents and incandescents; and full-spectrum), and purpose (ambient or task-specific). The purpose of the lighting in turn helps determine the type of light fixture most appropriate for the job.

Lamp Types: Traditional versus Full-Spectrum

Since the advent of the electric light bulb about 100 years ago, humans have spent increasing amounts of time indoors. As a result, we have been the subjects of an unprecedented experiment in the effects of electric lighting on our health. What we have learned is that the spectral curve of artificial lighting is deficient (compared with sunlight), especially in the near ultraviolet and infrared wavelengths. While overexposure to ultraviolet light has identified risks, studies indicate that a modest amount of near-range UV radiation is a necessity. The deficient spectra of most fluorescent and incandescent lights, coupled with the filtering effects of windows, windshields, computer terminals, eyeglasses, and sunglasses, are now known to affect the incidence of headaches, arthritis, SAD, stunted growth, tooth decay, low learning ability, poor calcium absorption, and numerous other conditions.[4] In young children, the effects of inadequate lighting can be similar to those of malnutrition.

> Those minerals and chemicals in the individual cells of our bodies that would normally be metabolized by the [missing] wavelengths . . . remain in the equivalent of darkness, even though other wavelengths are present. The end result is an incomplete metabolic or biological combustion process.[5]

Increased levels of cortisol (the stress hormone) and of ACTH (the growth hormone and source of adrenaline) have been found to account for the agitated mental and physical behavior of some children in school all day under standard fluorescents.[6] Although fluorescent lights give the illusion of continuous illumination, they actually emit 120 flashes of light per second. Evidence suggests that this flashing can induce hyperactivity in children and can trigger epileptic seizures in those who are seizure-prone. As a replacement, investigate the new energy-efficient fluorescent electronic lights.[7]

The effect of a light source on the color appearance of an object is indicated by the Color Rendering Index (CRI) and ranges from 0–100. Sunlight is rated 100. The higher a lamp's CRI, the more it renders colors as "true." Cool white fluorescents have a CRI of 62, warm white fluorescents 56, and some energy-saving lights 48. Full-spectrum lamps, on the other hand, are those with a CRI of 85–90. Full-spectrum lamps are available as fluorescent, incandescent, halogen, and reflector/floor bulbs for recessed and track lighting through most large-tube manufacturers. Full-spectrum bulbs cost more than most other fluorescent lamps and produce fewer lumens per watt, but last longer. Their extra cost is outweighed by their health benefits as well as their longevity.

> The rapidly developing scientific literature in the field of photobiology suggests that . . . without including some full-spectrum interior lighting, we may not be adequately supporting the health of the user population. Full-spectrum lighting means . . . any light source which closely mimics the spectral curve . . . as produced by the sun. It should include radiation in the near-ultraviolet band from 300–400 nanometers.[8]

Today, compact fluorescent bulbs, the most energy-efficient bulbs available, are increasingly replacing traditional bulb types. They save 70–80% of the electricity used per unit of light, thus being the most ecologically conscious and well as the most cost-effective form of light. They are available in full-spectrum varieties as well, known as high color-rendering triphosphor lamps, with an 85–89 CRI.

Children in full-day child care need full-spectrum light. Where possible, replace standard fluorescent and incandescent bulbs with energy-conserving full-spectrum fluorescent, incandescent, and halogen lamps. If it is not practical to use full-spectrum lamps throughout a center; they should be installed where their potential benefit is greatest, especially in children's rooms and offices.

Purpose: Ambient or Task

In addition to the type of lamp, it is essential to consider the purpose the lighting is to serve: general-ambient or task-specific. Different fixtures are appropriate for specific applications and vary as to aesthetic design and the type of light delivered. Use of different lighting types throughout a building, a room, and even the same area of a room, are essential in giving each space "atmosphere." For example, ambient light over a large area will encourage group activity. Adding a halogen spotlight to the area creates a small pool of light encouraging one or two children to use a portion of the space in a more focussed way.

Light sources can be direct (source visible), indirect (source concealed), or a combination of both (direct/indirect). Their beam spread can be wide to narrow, depending upon the type of bulb, the type of fixture, and its distance from the surface being illuminated. The newer, minihalogen fixtures can provide precise and powerful light from distant, sometimes almost inconspicuous, sources.

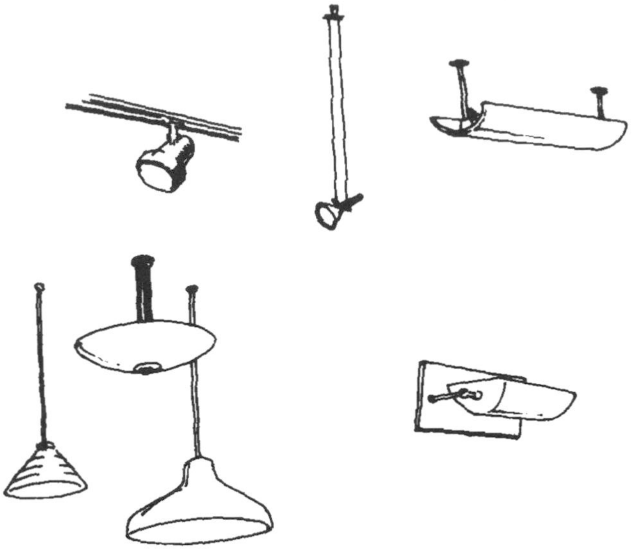

Figure 10.1
Options for ambient lighting abound to meet the wide range of lighting requirements that exist in child care.

Fixtures for General Illumination

Most of us would not light our homes the way offices, schools, hospitals and other public places are lit. Suspended ceilings with 2-x-2 or 2-x-4 fluorescent grids are a sure mark of an "institution." Where possible, strive to make lighting in child care centers homelike rather than institutional, especially in children's rooms and places where people gather. This can be done, even if fluorescents are employed, by using some of the fixture types described below and illustrated in Figure 10.1.

Ceiling-mounted direct fixtures with fluorescent bulbs are the least expensive, and therefore the most ubiquitous, form of ambient lighting, but the quality of the light they deliver is neither comforting nor homelike. Make every effort to minimize their use and to supplement them with other types of ambient and task-specific fixtures. Where there is no alternative to ceiling-mounted direct fixtures in corridors, placing them perpendicular to the length of the corridor will make the space seem shorter and wider. Design such fixtures to be as unobtrusive and nonglaring as possible. *Egg-crate parabolic diffusers,* which are more expensive than standard plastic diffusers, conceal the bulbs and thus reduce the amount of unwanted glare.

Ceiling-recessed can lighting, which uses incandescent spots and floods or halogen bulbs, is a softer, more residential, more streamlined and less obtrusive way to light most spaces than ceiling-mounted fluorescents. However, exclusive use of parabolic shielded fluorescents and/or recessed can lights can produce a claustrophobic effect.

Wall-mounted cove lighting fixtures with fluorescent bulbs, which "wash" light down a wall and/or up over a ceiling, are superior to overhead fluorescents as a means of simulating the experience in nature of being "surrounded" by light. Lit ceilings and washed walls create open and inviting spaces. Ideal for most spaces, cove lighting fixtures normally do not take up valuable wall space; can create a nice architectural detail around the room; leave the ceiling uncluttered; and can be switched to shine up, down, or up/down simultaneously. Up/down wall-mounted fixtures are also available as cans. *Pendant down linear fluorescent fixtures (tube lights),* suspended by slender poles or cables from the ceiling, function somewhat like cove lights. They are fluorescent tubes half-covered by a "housing" (available in playful colors), which provide a variety of lamp configurations—up, down, direct, or combinations of these. Other options include varying the quantity of lamps per strip and various lamp-shielding accessories.

Hanging fixtures need to be evaluated on their individual merits. Their effectiveness for general illumination can depend upon ceiling height. These fixtures may not always provide the quantity of illumination expected at floor level. Where many fixtures are required they can create a bevy of distracting objects overhead and prevent the ceiling from being used for other purposes. If made of inexpensive plastic, they may yellow with age. However, individual hanging fixtures used to create pools of light and direct focus over a table or area are highly desirable. Choose a unique design to make a powerful aesthetic statement.

Wall-mounted sconces, usually with incandescent bulbs, provide the softest light. Depending upon design, some can be switched up, down, or up/down like cove lights. These fixtures help to "break up" wall surfaces, thus increasing visual variety.

Track lights are extremely effective for both ambient and task lighting and provide the greatest flexibility for the money. They can be chosen to handle incandescent or the more powerful halogen bulbs (mini- as well as standard-size, which are close to the sun in brightness and tone), with spotlight or flood-light spread. Fluorescent wall wash units are also available. The cans can be turned up, down, and sideways for both direct and indirect illumination. Generally speaking, they are less obtrusive than other ceiling-mounted fixtures. For remodels, existing ceiling-mounted receptacles can be replaced with tracks.

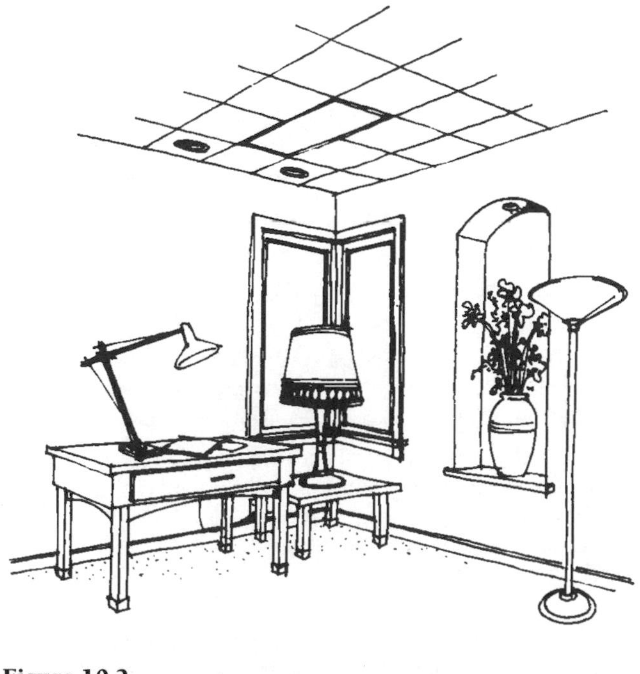

Figure 10.2
Some possibilities for task-specific lighting.

Wall-mounted fixtures (sconces, and cove lights) work especially well where children—particularly infants—will lie on their backs and look up at the ceiling; ceiling-mounted illumination lights may glare in their eyes. All ceiling-suspended fixtures chosen for infant rooms need to project the light upwards rather than down: saucer-shaped fixtures and indirect linear fluorescents are appropriate.

The fixture choice does not depend only on the quality, quantity, and spread of light produced; the aesthetics of fixture design also matter. Try to envision each potential fixture in the space where it will go. Consider whether its size, shape, lines, and color harmonize with the architectural elements of that space and contribute significantly to the qualities of place envisioned for it. Before making a decision, evaluate lighting fixtures in other settings. Working with a lighting designer or an electrical consultant can definitely help with what may seem like complex decisions.

Approaches to Task Lighting

General illumination is necessary but does not create effective "places." The play of shadows and the contrasts between light and dark created by using task-specific lights as a supplement to general ambient illumination are more interesting and comforting than uniform illumination. "Pools" of light facilitate spatial orientation, draw people together, and provide objects and people with definition and relationship. Pools of light affect people's attention and behavior, and their impressions of spaciousness or enclosure. Some task lighting is esential in child care centers. Choices are illustrated in Figure 10.2 and discussed below.

Sconces, tracks, and even *ceiling-recessed can downlights* can be installed as task-specific illumination in certain areas. (These lighting types can also provide general illumination, as discussed earlier.) *Under-cabinet cove lights* above work counters contribute immensely to efficiency and mood.

Table and desk lamps add a special touch to children's spaces. (The presence of plentiful outlets will ensure that unwieldy lamp cords do not have to run long distances.) Strings of tiny lamps (similar to Christmas tree bulbs), sometimes encased in plastic tubing, create *"little" lights* that have great child-appeal. Similarly, small glass *pendant lights* (see Figure 10.2) hung above children's heads, often in soft colors, can effectively lower a ceiling and gently illuminate a counter, a reception desk (see the photo on page 197),

GUIDELINES: ARTIFICIAL LIGHT

- Electric lighting, whether general ambient or task-specific, should be warm, natural, and homelike. Avoid suspended ceilings with 2-x-2 and 2-x-4 fluorescent grids, wherever possible, because they are institutional and create unwanted glare.
- Wall-mounted lights are preferable to ceiling-mounted fixtures for washing light up over the ceiling and down the wall, thereby "surrounding" the room with light, freeing the ceiling for other uses and from unsightly grids.
- Task-specific lighting is required to supplement general ambient illumination. Table, desk, hanging, and track lights enable varied types and levels of illumination.
- Create "pools" of light by placing lights low and apart to encompass the furniture comprising and defining each area. Pools of light can exist only if there are slightly darker spaces in between them.
- In most rooms, lighting needs to be flexible. Track lighting is the most adaptable.
- A tapestry of light and dark areas in rooms and buildings adds to their comfort, interest, and spirit of place. Use low illumination levels for less active areas and higher light levels for more active areas. Provide both general ambient and task-specific lighting.
- For their health-giving properties, use full-spectrum incandescent or fluorescent and high-color-rendering triphosphor bulbs wherever possible, especially in children's rooms and places where people gather.
- Bulbs with a warmer color rating, both incandescent and fluorescent, give more natural appearances to most skin tones. Oranges, pinks, and peaches are less pleasant under fluorescent lights with a cool rating.
- Limit the use of fluorescent lights wherever possible, especially if they are not high-color-rendering, because they make people look unnaturally pale and make objects and surfaces appear cold and sterile.
- Provide electronic ballasts on fluorescent fixtures to minimize their hum.
- Avoid fluorescents wherever there are epileptic or seizure-prone children. Replace them with energy-efficient electronic lights with 84 CRI.
- Use full-spectrum or triphosphor bulbs in light fixtures to supplement natural light in art areas because standard fluorescent lights distort colors.
- Since lighting affects the perception of form and color, always select textures and colors for walls, upholstery, carpets, and furnishings under the lighting conditions to be used in the space in question.
- Follow local building codes for emergency lighting requirements.

or a dining table surface. *Architectural lamps* with swinging arms are sturdy and useful for children at art and drafting tables, or where visual impairments require that children have some control over work surface illumination. *Wall-mounted snake- and goose-neck lights* are ideal for bulletin boards and art displays.

To avoid eye strain due to strong figure/ground contrast, task lighting need be only moderately brighter than the background (a difference of perhaps 35–45 foot-candles). The ideal ratio of task to background luminance is 3:1, meaning optimum visual comfort is maintained when task illumination is not more than three times the luminance in the areas adjacent to the task. A light-to-reflection ratio of 3:1 is also ideal so that the eye's pupil is not forced to undergo constant adjustment.

Room-by-Room Recommendations

Lighting should support the activities that occur in a space and the feelings desired for the space. The secret is to employ a variety of fixtures. For a general guide to the varied ambient and task-specific lighting requirements of different areas in child care centers, see Box 10.1.

Controlling Light Levels

Dimmers are ideal for varying both general ambient and task-specific light levels. To break down a bank of lights and relate their use to changes in activity at floor level, install *multiple switches*. See the guidelines below for other means of controlling light level.

GUIDELINES: CONTROLLING LIGHTING LEVELS

- Designing rooms with windows on two sides is the best way to control interior glare and create inviting environments.
- Use baffles, roof overhangs, awnings, deep window reveals, filtered glass, and exterior plantings to help control the brightness of unshielded natural light.
- During daylight hours, interior lighting can be calibrated to balance glare on window walls or around windows. Glare can also be controlled by installing curtains or shades. (For more information on window coverings, see Chapter 16.)
- Use dimmers on both incandescent and fluorescent (costly) light fixtures to provide opportunities for different levels of illumination and to offset the gloom of gray days.

BOX 10.1

Child Care Center Lighting Suggestions by Location

Room/Area	Recommended Lighting Types
Sleep Rooms	Sconces on dimmers; a bedside lamp on a dresser.
Sick Bay	Sconces, cans on dimmers, sufficient for a child to read; no overheads that glare into eyes; an adjustable gooseneck lamp for examining a child if necessary.
Infant Rooms	Ambient light from wall-mounted coves or sconces with direct/indirect distribution, saucer-shaped up-lights, track lighting, upward-facing tubes that do not glare into the eyes of babies lying on the floor.
Toddler, Preschool, and School-age Rooms	Ambient light from wall-mounted coves, cans, or sconces with direct/indirect distribution, spots and floods in recessed cans, halogens, tracks, or tubes. Task-specific light can include table and desk lamps, sconces, tracks, and hanging lamps.
Corridors	Wall-mounted coves, cans, or sconces, with direct/indirect distribution; ceiling recessed cans; snake lights to emphasize wall areas.
Offices	Wall-mounted coves, cans, or sconces with direct/indirect distribution; ceiling-recessed cans; tracks; task-specific desk, table and hanging lamps.
Staff & Conference Areas	Wall-mounted coves, cans, or sconces with direct/indirect distribution; ceiling recessed cans; tracks; task-specific desk, table, and hanging lamps.
Kitchens	Ceiling recessed cans and tracks; overhead fluorescents; under-cabinet task-lights.
Dining Rooms	Wall-mounted coves, cans, or sconces with direct/indirect distribution; ceiling recessed cans, tracks, hanging lamps above tables.
Gyms and Multipurpose Rooms	Fixtures that cannot be moved or damaged by balls and flying objects; overhead fluorescents or even light throughout.
Art work, Bulletin Boards	Wall-mounted goose-neck and snake lights, tracks, minihalogens, fluorescent wall-washing.

- Use dimmers in sleep rooms to permit children to sleep in near-total darkness while enabling the staff to illuminate the room when required. Some low-level illumination is necessary even in darkened toddler and preschool group rooms at nap time.
- In rooms with banks of lights, provide multiple switches to enable staff to vary the illumination.
- Use views of lighted landscapes or indirect lighting of window coverings to offset the coldness and darkness of window walls at night.
- Paint walls containing windows a medium-to-light color value to minimize strong contrast between the wall color and the entering sunlight. Either light the wall opposite a window, or paint it a medium-to-light value color, to prevent it from absorbing the daylight cast upon it.
- Choose matte wall finishes rather than highly luminous or polished surfaces for areas where reflected glare from sunlight is potentially likely.
- Under-cabinet lighting is desirable wherever there are work surfaces with cabinets above.

Above-counter lights and mirrors create the stage for beautiful displays.

Outlets and Switches

Walls are usually the repositories for the numerous outlets needed around every room, as well as for switches for light, ventilation, heating, and cooling systems. However, unless carefully planned in advance, the placement of electrical outlets and switches can compromise the use of walls for display and educational purposes (see Chapter 7). Evaluating the location of all outlets and switches is a task for the design team and/or child care professionals before the construction drawings are approved.

To provide multiple receptacles without destroying a wall's integrity, put outlets as low as permitted by local codes. At permanent work surfaces, place outlets just above the surface height. Make certain they meet code requirements by being the three-prong grounded variety. Cluster switches at code-required heights above the floor. Most important, position them at the perimeter rather than in the middle of walls. To make them easy to find but less visually obtrusive, locate switches at the entrance to rooms and choose switch and receptacle plates whose colors match wall colors, or can be painted to match (Figure 10.3).

Motion detector lights, which automatically go on or off when someone enters or leaves the room, can be installed in bathrooms, offices, kitchens, and other low-use areas of the building to conserve energy.

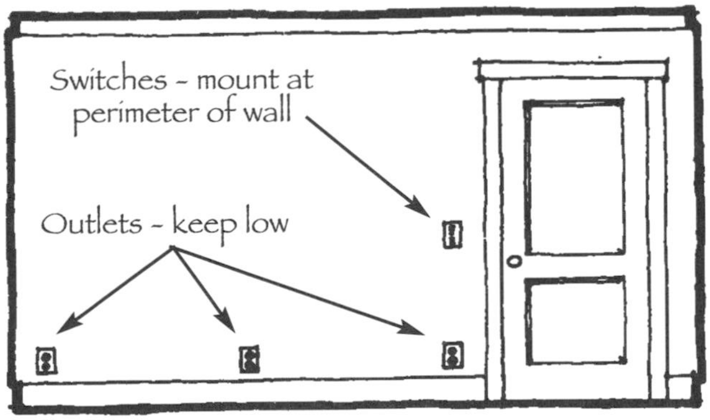

Figure 10.3
Wall space is valuable. Conserve it by placing electrical switches near the perimeter and receptacles low down.

GUIDELINES: OUTLETS AND SWITCHES

- Make electrical outlets plentiful. They can be at child height if safeguarded by covers or the three-prong grounded style.
- Erratic placement of switches can compromise the use of walls for display and educational purposes and also make a space difficult to use. These are best clustered together and located at a wall's edge. The design team and/or child care professionals need to evaluate the location of all switches and outlets, in advance, as part of the overall design plan.
- Consider double-pole switches that allow for multiple switching locations.

Children can operate the lights at the rear of this woodworking shed. (The Copper House)

- Consider motion-sensor switching (for bathrooms, offices, etc.) as an excellent energy conservation strategy.
- Consider locating switches at child level for lights inside such structures as playhouses, lofts, and woodworking sheds. This gives children some degree of control over the task-specific lights in their rooms.

Exterior Lighting

For safety and security, exterior lighting is needed in parking areas, walkways, paths, and at building entrances and exits. Options include overhead lights on poles, lights low to the ground, small lights encased in plastic tubes—all on timers or solar cells—and motion detectors, depending upon circumstance and distance. Some models are solar powered.

GUIDELINES: EXTERIOR LIGHTING

- Do not forget exterior lighting for parking areas, walkways, and entering and leaving the building at night: overhead lights and path lights on timers; motion detectors.
- Small white Christmas tree lights can be delightful on porches, balconies, and trees outside. Small lights encased in plastic tubing can span bridges and some pathway areas.

Notes

[1]Richard J. Wurtman, "The Effects of Light on the Human Body," *Scientific American,* Vol. 1, 233 (1982): 68–77.

[2]N. E. Rosenthal, et al., "Antidepressant Effects of Light in Seasonal Affective Disorder,"*American Journal of Psychiatry* 142, no.2 (1985): 163–170.

[3]Steven Rosen, Principal, *Available Light,* Boston, MA, provided invaluable assistance with portions of this chapter.

[4]J. N. Ott, *Health and Light* (New York: Simon & Schuster, 1973).

[5]Frank H. Mahnke and Rudolf H. Mahnke, *Color and Light in Man-Made Environments* (New York: Van Nostrand Publishing Company, 1987) 45.

[6]Fritz Hollowich, *The Influence of Ocular Light Perception on Metabolism in Man and in Animals* (New York: Springer Verlag, 1980).

[7]The energy-efficient fluorescent electronic lights from *Lights of America,* Walnut, CA (Tel: 800/321-8100; Fax 909/598-6732) are safe, cool-operating, and last 16 times longer than conventional incandescent bulbs. They are flicker-free, silent, and suitable for any climate and have an 84 CRI.

[8]M. Spivak and J. Tamer, *Light and Color: A Designer's Guide* (Washington, D.C.: AIA Press, 1983) 72.

P. C. Hughes,"The Use of Light and Color in Health" in A. C. Hasings, J. Fadiman, J. S. Gordon (eds.) *Health for the Whole Person; The Complete Guide to Holistic Medicine* (Boulder, CO; Westview Press, 1980).

CHAPTER ELEVEN

WINDOWS, DOORS, AND SECURITY

Emptiness and formlessness can only be won
by substance and order, darkness by light,
and depth by a solid ground.

–CHRISTIAN NORBERG-SHULZ

Chapter 10 addressed the importance of natural light to people's well-being. This chapter looks at how the shape, placement, and glazing of windows affects rooms; how the design and placement of doors affects communication and layout; and the security issues related to each.

Windows: Plentiful and Operable

Few things affect the feeling or spirit of a room as much as the sunshine it receives. As eyes are gateways to the human soul, windows can be gateways to the soul of a building. Beautiful windows, framing wonderful views, and gently modulating light from outside, are significant contributors to making rooms charming and unforgettable.

Windows enable children to:

- Follow the course of the sun through the day to establish a natural sense of time
- Experience the healthful and aesthetic benefits of natural light and, when open, of full-spectrum light, fresh air, and sounds
- Learn about the outside world—nature, streets, sidewalks
- Follow a parent after leave-taking; anticipate a parent's arrival
- Observe the weather, and the life of plants and animals
- Feel less confined indoors or in a small room

The quality of sunlight a room receives has a major impact on its mood and comfort level. (The Copper House)

The cardinal direction in which each room of a building faces affects the quality of sunlight it receives and therefore the number and location of windows it will need. The group rooms, where children spend most of their day, need to have the most comfortable and wonderful light. In the northern hemisphere, that light usually comes through south-facing windows.

Rooms with windows on at least two sides are preferable aesthetically and because they reduce glare. This may require the building to have staggered spaces and an irregular perimeter—often more costly financially but infinitely more satisfying for its occupants. Windowless rooms are to be avoided, especially in spaces children occupy for more than an hour a day. Ideally, a room's windows will also frame interesting views. Rooms without views can feel oppressive; "views" can be created with plants and vines around a window, and by the placement of objects outside.

Interior Windows

Interior windows between rooms, or between rooms and corridors, as well as clerestories, can help bring natural light to interior spaces that have no direct outdoor access; they also foster connectedness between spaces.

Kitchens are valuable sources of learning and pleasure for children and adults. But safety regulations often restrict children's presence in the kitchen. Therefore have at least one interior window through which children can observe the cook in action. The larger the window, the better—as illustrated in these two photographs.

Interior windows help connect corridors with rooms and children with cooks inside kitchens. (The Copper House)

From their dining area, these children can look through a large window directly into the kitchen. (Reggio Emilia)

Standardized panes are used for the operable elements in this unique window.

Window Design

> It may be ridiculous to make every window different just for the sake of being different, but it is even more so to make every one the same just for the sake of being the same, or to shape them just to impose an elevational pattern.[1]

The most appealing windows have graceful frames and panes of glass that glow in response to transmitted light. Such windows are not spaced according to a rigid construction system, but are shaped and scaled to suit the size and shape of the room, at heights framing and highlighting beautiful elements outdoors. Providing a room with at least one such window can transform it. Windows whose shapes follow or repeat a ceiling's unique form also contribute immeasurably to a room's spirit of place. Frames that vary in shape can utilize standard window sizes for the operative panes. Even if a room's windows do not have unique forms, ideally they can be placed to frame unique views.

Creating a Window "Place"

Regardless of the construction approach, strive to make one window in each room into a special "place." Alexander et al. argue that such a window place is a necessity for making a room feel truly comfortable because it allows the room's occupants to sit in the light to which we are naturally drawn.[2] A window that qualifies as a "place" is usually recessed into the wall, its sill low. It provides a view for the person sitting—either to the outdoors or to a special vista of the room. If its corner is too hidden or its built-in seat too narrow, hard, or stiff-backed, the special place may never be used. An armchair or couch that everyone finds comfortable can be the model for the cushioning and slope of built-in seats.

Here are some examples of special window places:

- A small window seat large enough for one or two
- A big bay window with a built-in seat or couches and chairs pulled up into it

. . . a window seat in the living room (The Copper House)

. . . a deep alcove with windows on three sides (The Copper House, preschool room)

- A deep alcove with windows on all sides, similar to a sun porch
- A window with a low sill built into a recessed area that invites sitting and cuddling
- Small, low windows, perhaps of colored glass, as part of child-sized niches and alcoves. Where these cannot be exterior windows, they can easily be part of interior partitions and dividers

Window Size

The amount of light and ventilation required from a window generally depends upon the size of the room, the level of the building it is located on, and the direction(s) it is facing.[3] Varying window size creates intrigue and delight, especially for children. Some considerations regarding window size:

- Smaller windows with higher sills (24–30 inches or higher) offer more psychological security to inhabitants of rooms higher off the ground (such as staff areas). Higher windows reveal more open sky and transmit more light, and can therefore be smaller.
- Large plate-glass windows are rarely used in child care centers, perhaps because they provide little sense of protection or enclosure.

. . . a window with a low sill, built into a recessed area (The Copper House, infant room)

. . . an interior partition with child-sized windows (alcove not shown)

- Windows divided into small panes (avoid artificial muntins), some no greater than one-foot square, help to put children more in touch with the natural world outside and at the same time to feel secure and protected inside.

Sill Heights

So that infants and toddlers can see outside, aim to have windows in their rooms start about one foot above the floor. Accessible and low windows need to be tempered or of safety glass. In preschool and school-age rooms, windows can begin at 24–30 inches above the floor, although some lower ones are desirable since these children also spend a great deal of time on the floor (see previous page).

In existing buildings, try to make high windows lower wherever possible. If existing windows are above children's heads and cannot be lowered, be certain to provide a loft under or near a window so children can see out.

Windows versus Wall Area

While plentiful windows are essential for providing each room with adequate natural light, punctuating walls with windows reduces the amount of space available for mounting educational materials, artwork,

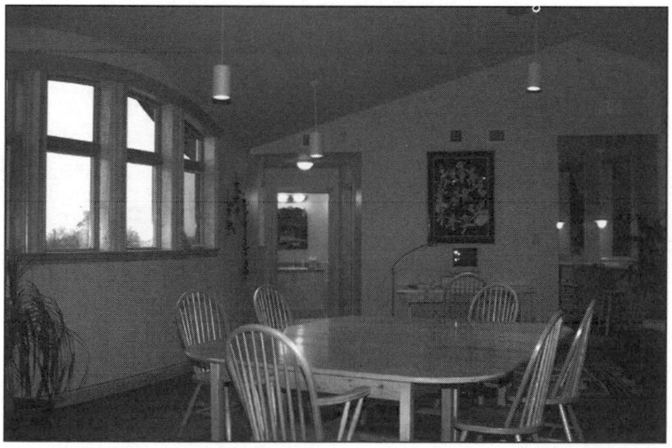

Smaller windows with higher sills lend psychological security to this second story room. (The Copper House, staff area)

A loft placed under a high window enables children to see out.

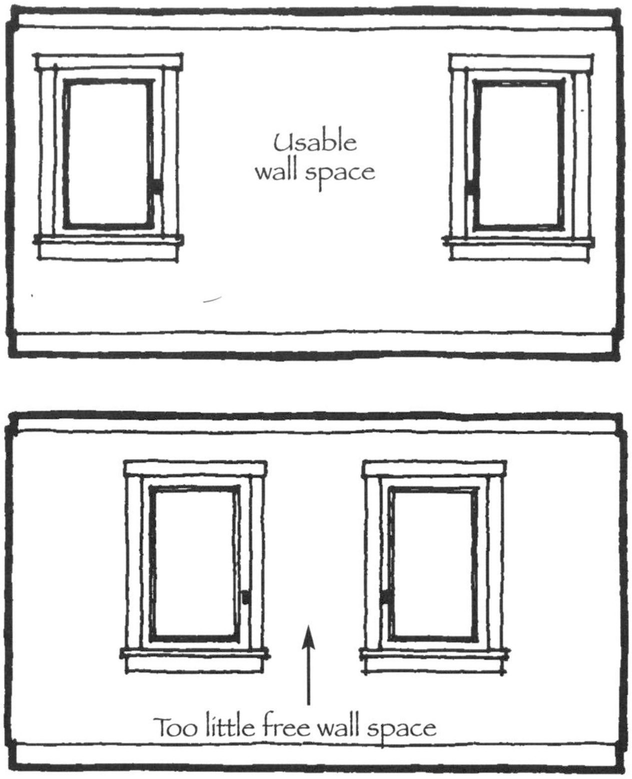

Figure 11.1
Place windows to preserve usable wall space for display.

schedules, and the heavy display requirements of the popular "project centered" curricula. The placement of windows in each room, and their number, therefore need to be planned to allow reasonable expanses of wall space to remain (Figure 11.1).

Windows that Open

Operable windows not only provide fresh air and full-spectrum light, they also contribute significantly to the homelike, nurturing spirit of a place. All operable windows in child care centers need screens. They also need to prevent children from climbing or falling out, either by the use of opening "adjusters" or "ventilating locks" that limit openings to 6 inches or less, or by a design that does not have the window opening wide.

Hopper windows (which open in from the bottom), or awning windows (which open out from the top) are less of a safety hazard than double or single hung windows because their openings are more restricted and less easy to access. Ventilating locks can be used to control how far either window will open. At child height, it is possible for fingers to get pinched when windows are not held open securely or not closed securely. Screen placement, either inside or outside the window, needs to be consistent for the windows selected for any single wall or room. See Figure 11.2 for various window types.

Where multiple panes are used, consider having only the middle ones operable, rather than the lowest ones at child height. Windows opening into the room or onto play areas need to be either quite low or high enough for children to not bump their heads.

Install any double-hung windows that are child-accessible to open from the top only, or equip them with "ventilation bolts" that prevent the lower portion from opening more than 6 inches so children cannot try to climb or fall out.

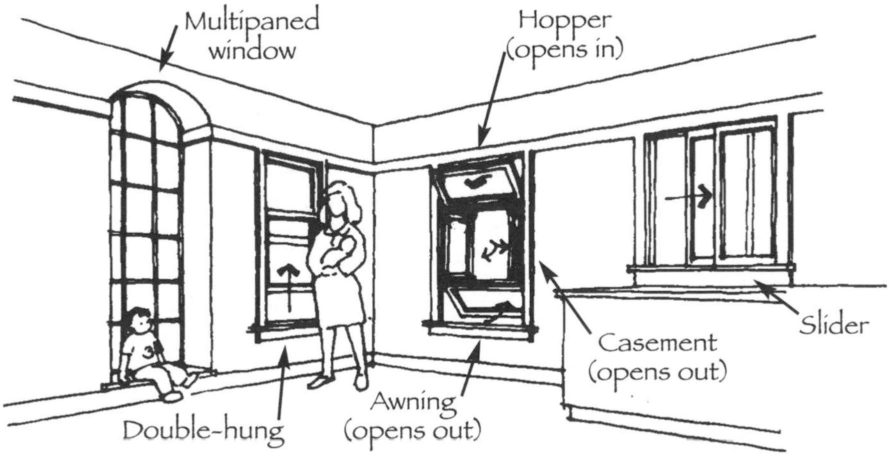

Figure 11.2
Some different types of operable windows.

Window Reveals

A window's "reveal" is the wall opening around it between the frame and the outer surface of the wall.[4] (Note the deep reveal in the photo on page 199.) Buildings constructed using modern technologies usually have reveals about 3–5 inches deep. A deeper reveal will, however, enhance a window's architectural and aesthetic presence. Window reveals reduce glare and gloom, reinforce an indoor/outdoor connection, contribute to a room and a building's spirit of place, and provide a homelike atmosphere. Deep reveals provide draft protection, and broad sills for displaying plants and objects, or for creating comfortable window seats. Most important, when they are 10–12 inches wide and splayed or lying at an angle between 50–60 degrees to the plane of the window,[5] they help prevent a harsh glare where the frame meets the wall.

Where windows are feasible on one wall of a room only, increasing the height and the depth of the windows' reveals can help to balance the inevitable glare; locating the windows near the wall's corners also helps. The nicest reveals are thickenings of the wall material, poured or built up in a manner that makes them continuous with the structure of the wall, as opposed to being elements inserted into wall openings (see page 199). These same wall thicknesses can also be used for shelving and display.

Framing Materials

A window's shape, reveal, and frame are what give it distinctiveness. Wooden window frames are the most residential but also the most expensive and high maintenance. Aluminum frames transmit cold or heat unless "thermally broken." Aesthetically appealing options include:

- Framing windows with aluminum on the outside and wood on the inside
- Softening full aluminum frames and giving them more "substance" by encasing interior windows with wood on all sides, including a wooden sill
- Providing a wooden valance across the top of an aluminum window to give it more "body" and presence in a room
- Adding wooden trim to the wall around the window. (See pages 197, 198, 200, and 201.)

Protection from Breakage

Double- and triple-tempered thermopane glass is difficult to break and is shatterproof. A large window comprised of a pattern of small panes minimizes the risk of large panes breaking, makes the view more child-scaled, and enables some panes to open while others remain shut. The use of plastic muntins to create a false sense of small panes is not recommended, as it provides none of the physical advantages of small panes and introduces artificiality. Any large plates of glass into which people might mistakenly walk (or birds fly!) will need to be made of shatterproof tempered glass and decorated with unobtrusive paintings or decals to signal their presence.

Protection From the Cold

Because young children—especially infants—frequently are unaware or cannot communicate that they are cold, in northern climates the best strategy for protecting against drafts is to use high-quality, tightly-sealed double or triple thermopane glass windows. Wood window frames transmit less heat or cold than metal frames that should always have a "thermal break." Window coverings also provide some draft protection, when drawn.

GUIDELINES: WINDOWS

- Consider the quality of sunlight for each room by determining—as the building is designed or the center's layout created—the cardinal direction each room is facing. In the northern hemisphere, south-facing light is warm and golden, light from the north cooler and more silver/gray. Children, especially infants, deserve the building's sunniest locations.
- Rooms with windows on at least two sides are always preferred and reduce glare.
- Children benefit from views as well as access to natural light. Design windows in infant and toddler rooms to start about one foot above the floor, in preschool and school-age rooms about 24–30 inches above the floor.
- When existing windows are above children's heads and cannot be lowered, place lofts under them to enable children to see out.
- Where possible, skylights can do wonders to introduce natural light. Light "tubes," applicable in some instances, can also bring natural light into windowless spaces.
- Make at least one window in each room into a special "place": a recess in a wall, with a low sill, that provides a special vista and comfortable seating for a few persons.

- Unique windows and doors designed on paper benefit from refinement of their dimensions during the construction process—by positioning each edge, mullion, and sill according to the "feel" of the window in relation to the room and the exterior it reveals.
- Without sacrificing valuable natural light, the number of windows in each room, and their placement, need to allow for reasonable expanses of wall space for display.
- In addition to standard-size windows, consider using large windows comprised of smaller panes, only some of which can open.
- Details such as beveling, prisms, etchings, and stained glass added to interior and exterior windows as ornamentation and as delightful interactive elements further refine the play of light on interior surfaces.
- Windows with deep reveals reduce glare where the frame and wall meet, provide draft protection and broad sills for display or window seats, reinforce the indoor/outdoor connection, and contribute to a room's spirit of place. Deep reveals are especially helpful in rooms with windows on one side only.
- Wooden window frames are the most residential and beautiful but can be expensive. Also, consider those with aluminum on the outside and wood on the inside, which may be more expensive but easier to maintain. Aluminum windows require a "thermal break" and can be softened with wooden casing and valences.
- Windows installed one foot above the floor can prevent drafts if made of tightly sealed, tempered, double- or triple-thermopane glass.
- If possible, place the main kitchen work counter on the room's south or southeast side, surrounded by big windows (except in hot climates). This benefits the cook, who will spend many hours there. Open shelves built across windows can still let sun in if wall space for storage is tight.

Windows that Open

- A reasonable number of operable windows, providing both fresh air and full-spectrum light when open, are essential in each room and should create cross-ventilation.
- Hopper, or awning, windows are the safest. At child-height, use a ventilation adjuster to limit their opening to 6 inches or less. Windows opening into rooms need to be quite low or above children's heads.
- Multiple-paned windows provide the option of making only the middle panes operable.
- Provide locks on all operable windows, especially if child-accessible.

Where wall space is tight, open shelves built across windows can still let sun in.

Window Coverings

Window coverings can be purchased in fabric, metal, plastic, or wood, depending upon budget and aesthetics.

Purposes

In child care centers, window coverings serve three purposes. They (1) help control glare, (2) darken a room at nap time, and (3) prevent outsiders from seeing inside, especially after dark. Window coverings may not be required if windows are double-paned and appropriately sealed, and if views in or out are not a problem.

Selection Factors

There are four factors to consider in selecting window coverings:

- The amount of light reduction or invisibility desired
- Children's access to the coverings
- Whether coverings will partially occlude a window when not in use, thereby reducing the light entering the room
- The aesthetic appropriateness of different styles and designs

Evaluate each room individually. Coverings are usually selected according to the amount of transparency desired. However, total darkness or total lack of visibility from the outside are rarely necessary. Instead, subdued light at nap time, and inability to see interior details from the outside after dark, are generally satisfactory. Below are some main points to consider.

Types and Applications

- *Drapes and vertical blinds* are *not* recommended in children's spaces because they usurp window space and because children invariably pull at or play with them.
- *Fixed continuous-bead roller shades* fulfill the window treatment requirements of child care centers well. These shades are sheets of fabric (similar to a hand roller shade), raised and lowered by pulling a chain of metal beads clockwise or counter-clockwise. The shades sometimes ride inside a small track on each side of the window. This type of shade is available in varied hues, and in varying degrees of opacity, depending upon the size and number of small "holes" built into the fabric. The chain can be cut quite short to be inaccessible to children. When not in use, these shades form tight rolls that are unobtrusive and usurp very little window space. They are also effective on interior windows where screening is desired, but where extremely shallow reveals expose the shade to the movement of every passerby. Although not typical of residential window treatment, their unobtrusive nature makes them aesthetically benign.
- To control both glare and light levels at nap times or at night, *minivenetian blinds* allow the greatest flexibility. However, their wands (preferable) or cords need to be kept short and/or tucked out of reach. Relatively unobtrusive when not in use, when fully extended they are irresistibly fun for children to play with and can be easily bent or misshapen.
- *Roller shades* occlude light well, do not obstruct a window when up, and have a cord problem only when they are down; however, they offer little flexibility with regard to light control.
- *Roman shades* also occlude light well but have no flexibility and tend to have long cords which need to be protected. Their heavy, scalloped form

Continuous-bead roller shades effectively screen light in an infant sleep area. (The Copper House)

obstructs light when not in use and can conflict aesthetically with thinly framed windows and rooms with straight lines.

- A *wooden valance* or *baffle* across a window, sometimes running around all four walls and connecting all the windows (when they are the same height), can effectively hide shades and blinds that are not in use. However, it will also prevent some light from entering the room.
- Light from *skylights* needs to be controlled during nap time. Consider the appropriate type of shielding, and its cost, when the skylight is selected.

Aesthetic Concerns

Choosing the color and pattern of window coverings is an important aesthetic consideration that depends upon a room's size, shape, and other patterned elements. Generally speaking, group rooms are visually chaotic. It is difficult to control the colors and patterns of the many materials and furnishings needed for the program. Since an aesthetic conflict can easily arise between the window treatment and the rest of the room's offerings, the safest course is usually to choose window coverings without patterns, in neutral hues that match the window frames or the neighboring walls. This will integrate the windows with the surroundings.

GUIDELINES: WINDOW COVERINGS

- Window coverings are needed to control glare, darken group rooms at nap time, and limit visibility to the interior after dark.
- Minivenetian blinds with wands and roller shades with a continuous beaded chain are recommended for child care; drapes and vertical blinds are not.[6]
- *Skylights will need to be covered when children are napping.* Explore shade options, ease of operation, and cost at the time the skylights are selected.
- It is often best to choose window coverings in neutral hues, without patterns, that match windows or walls, so as not to have them conflict aesthetically with other elements in the room.

Doors: Graceful and Glazed

Door Design

Some doors beckon and reveal; others intimidate or obscure. Some are new or designed to impress; others reveal the hand of a craftsperson, the wear of weather, the creak of old age. By their shape, materials, sound, weight, and operation, doors convey subliminal messages about a place and the people in it. Strive to make most doors welcoming and friendly. Doors with some variation in surface detail, with windows to the interior (some at child height), and with a handle one consciously grasps and manipulates, help to reinforce the memory of the entry experience.

A door that welcomes and reveals.

A front door with glazing enabling children and adults to see inside.

This gracious wood-framed glass door gives toddlers a preview of their room and of the adjacent living room. (The Copper House)

Door Functions

At least three types of doors are called for in child care centers: a *front door,* other *exterior doors,* and *interior doors.*

The Front Door

Ideally, the center's front door will look like a door to a house, with glazing at adult height, and side-glazing for children, so both can catch a glimpse of the interior. Wooden doors are friendlier than metal or glass ones. Fully glazed front doors, common to banks and other public facilities, tend to have an institutional tone. For the same reason, electronic eye doors are not recommended unless the center serves large numbers of individuals with physical disabilities.

Exterior Doors

Usually there are two types of exterior doors: those that are official exits and those that go to play yards. The former are often fire-rated and, if emergency exits, must follow Universal Building Code requirements. Glazing in both types of doors (where codes and cost permit), is desirable for the light it provides to the interior, as well as the information it gives users about where they are going. In small spaces, and at the end of corridors, glazing in exterior doors greatly relieves claustrophobia by adding light and life to a room.

Doors to play yards, if part of children's group rooms, are especially wonderful when partially or fully glazed.

Interior Doors

Aim to provide interior doors with glazing at both adult and child eye-levels. Then children can anticipate the space they are entering, and a small child seated or standing near a door is protected. Glazing on an interior door suggests a relationship between the spaces on either side of it. The residential tone of

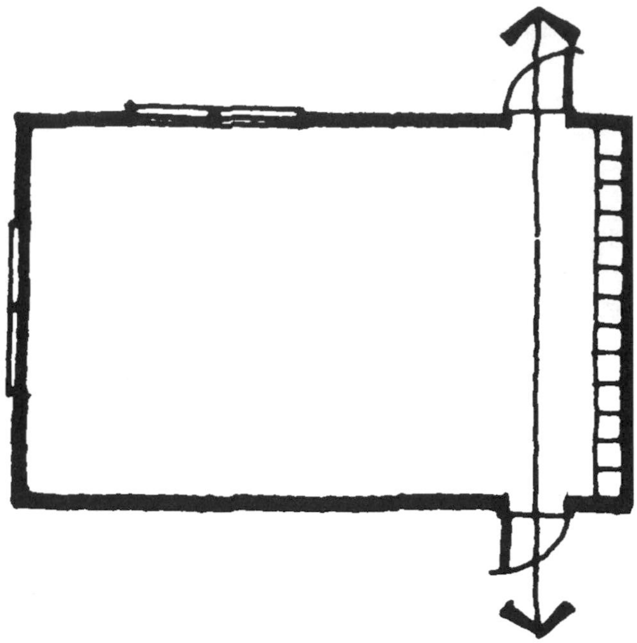

Figure 11.3
Locate doors at the narrow end of most rooms to concentrate foot traffic

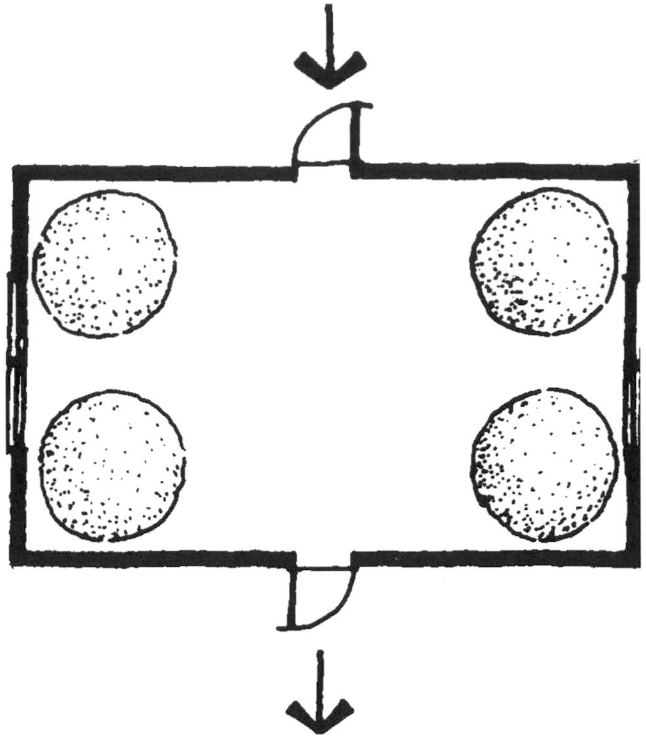

Figure 11.4
Locating doors in the middle of the longer walls of large rectangular rooms, preserves the four room corners.

wooden interior doors make them preferable to metal.

The design of doors to offices and staff areas needs to be evaluated individually. An absence of glazing ensures complete privacy. However, the door to a director's office, for example, needs a window (with optional coverings perhaps) for it to feel welcoming and permit tacit surveillance.

Generally, exit doors swing out, whereas interior doors swing in the direction of most frequent travel. Space inside rooms is conserved whenever doors can be made to swing out.

Door Location

In most rooms, especially small ones, the flow through the room works best if the door is located near the room's corner. While use of one corner will be usurped, this placement can maximize use of the other corners by keeping the walls as long and uninterrupted as possible. If the room is required to have both an entry and an emergency egress, place the two doors at one end, ideally the narrow end (Figure 11.3), to concentrate the foot traffic. Verify required separations between doors with the building code. (Also see Chapter 6 for the location of doors around common areas at the heart and informal gathering places.)

In large rectangular rooms, doors located in the middle of the longer walls work best, enabling easy access to all parts of the room and preserving use of all four corners (Figure 11.4). (See Chapter 7 for more on door placement in group rooms.)

Door Finishes

Whether to paint, stain, or simply varnish a door is an aesthetic decision affected by the door's material, its desired prominence, its amount of glazing, and how it relates to other elements in the room (windows, valences, trim). Evaluate the finish for each door independently. Varnished or stained wooden doors have the advantage of allowing the natural appearance of the

Painting a house facade on interior windows and doors is artificial. It tends to separate a room from an adjoining corridor or space rather than connect it to that space.

wood to show. Doors painted a different color from walls will stand out; those painted the wall color tend to "disappear." Painted interior doors can easily scratch and chip. Exterior doors often require paint for weather protection. Painted doors may need different colors on each side to correspond with the decors they connect. Colored door and window frames often draw attention away from what is most important in the room. (See Chapter 12, Color, for more information on selection of paint colors.)

Dealing with a Series of Doors

Corridors with many similar doors can benefit from the placement of a different sign, graphic, or color on each door to distinguish them. Better yet, the glazing on each can vary in size or shape, or the doors themselves can be of different but harmonious designs. Such variation is superior to assigning numbers or names.

A currently popular design treatment for dealing with a series of group rooms off corridors, is to outfit the corridor wall of each room with paned windows and doors to make it look like a "house." In some instances, this is successful. In many cases, however, the effect is forced and artificial, a cliche that actually separates the rooms from the corridor and each other.

GUIDELINES: DOOR DESIGN AND LOCATION

- Three types of doors are needed in child care centers: a front door, other exterior exits and entrances including doors to play yards, and interior doors.
- Doors can be metal, wood, glass, or combinations of these. They can be totally opaque or punctuated by windows of various shapes and sizes. Front doors and interior doors made of wood are the most residential.
- A glazed door, whether exterior or interior, is usually the most beautiful and satisfying because it creates a relationship between the spaces it also serves to separate.
- Solid doors are required for fire safety, for spaces such as storage, adult bathrooms (and janitorial closets where a view inside is undesirable) and sometimes for emergency egress. Some staff areas and offices may also call for complete privacy.
- Interior doors with glazing at both adult- and child-height protect a small child seated or standing near the door and help children anticipate where they are going.
- The most desirable doors are heavy enough to close with a "thud" and provide acoustic privacy, yet contain glass panes for visibility and light.
- Dutch doors are useful for controlling children's access while allowing light, sound, and connection between spaces.
- A child-height door somewhere in the building is always a delight. Child-height openings in low partitions, which adults can see over, have a similar kind of magic.

Child-height openings delight children and adults alike.

- A deep door reveal (as described for windows) reinforces the experience of transition from one space to another.
- Doors with large expanses of glass (and large windows) need decals or some artistic element to protect people from walking, and birds from flying, into them.
- In most rooms, especially small ones, the flow through the room works best if the door is located near the room's corner. In large rectangular rooms, locating doors in the middle of the longer walls preserves use of all four corners.
- Doors painted a color different from the walls will stand out; those painted the wall color "disappear." Varnished wood doors show the natural wood grain and are warm and homey. Colored door and window frames may draw attention away from what is most important in a room.
- When a series of doors exists along a corridor, aim to vary the size and shape of the glazing or the design of the doors themselves.

GUIDELINES: SECURITY

- Doorbells, buzzer systems, or electronic card or pad systems are effective ways to provide security at the front door. Glazing in the door is also recommended.
- Exterior doors that function as secondary entrances require security similar to the front door. This is especially true of the service entrance. They may also require panic and single-action hardware.
- All doors that children should not operate, or that teachers need to control from both sides, need locks, bolts, or hooks placed out of a child's extended reach.
- Provide locks on interior doors according to program needs. Any interior door giving children access to unsupervised public areas requires security similar to that for exterior doors.
- Locks on closet, bathroom, and other doors accessible to children but not intended for their use need to have an internal release latch so the door can be opened by any child accidentally locked inside.

Security and Locks

At the Front Door

Security at the front door is essential. It is assisted but not resolved by the presence of a receptionist or greeter inside the door. A doorbell is the easiest form of control, since it can be responded to in person or by someone "buzzing" the lock free. Many centers use electronic card or pad systems as the primary means of giving enrolled parents and staff unencumbered yet controlled access to the facility. A door with some glazing enables visibility in both directions, an added form of security.

To prevent children from leaving the building unattended, a buzzer system can be used after most parents depart in the morning. A heavy door, perhaps with a secondary knob located very high up, is difficult for children to operate. If the front door must remain open to the public, another point of security, perhaps on a card system, will be needed closer to the children's areas.

At Other Entrances and Exits

Exterior doors that function as secondary entrances and exits for the general public, and especially the service entrance, require security similar to the front door. However, no lock or fastening should be installed that prevents free escape from the interior in case of emergency. Panic hardware and single action hardware (that allows a door to open either way but keeps it from swinging back past the center point) may be required on exterior doors.

At Play Yard Doors

A lock or deadbolt is required on all play yard doors for security at night and on weekends. With play yards enclosed, indoor/outdoor flow is facilitated when both children and teachers can operate the play yard door; a compression hinge can allow it to remain open at times. However, care-givers will need to control children's use of the door from either side. Locks, bolts, or hooks placed up high can serve this purpose, as can an electronic card system.

For Interior Doors

Locks (which can be keyed, pushed, slid, turned, or electronically controlled) are required on any door to which children should not have access, ideally placed quite high and out of extended child reach. As the proverbial "locked in the bathroom" tale indicates, children manage to operate all kinds of locks both intentionally and accidentally. Ensure that doors can be unlocked from both sides. Security similar to that at the front door is necessary on any interior doors giving children access to unsupervised public areas. Ability to lock each group room door at night may also be desired.

Hardware—Knobs and Levers

A well-designed door knob or handle, with a distinctive shape, weight, and texture, gives the hand that turns it a conscious bodily experience of opening or closing a door. In the past, door knobs, as well as door hinges, were important design elements. Standardiza-tion has forced latch and hinge design to become lost arts. Door levers now replace knobs, and most hinges are barely visible. Where it is possible to individualize these elements, the experience of passage is the richer.

It is important to distinguish between hardware that will be operated by children and that which will not. For safety and control, adults often prefer to operate the doors, especially exterior doors. But door levers that are simple to operate, and designed with safety in mind, give children opportunities for learning and self-sufficiency. Evaluate the appropriate hardware for each door by charting the route to and from it to determine the consequences were it to be child operable.

GUIDELINES: HARDWARE

- Mount door hardware for children at 24–30 inches.
- Scale hardware for children to a child's hand. Ensure that it is free of sharp edges and protrusions, and easy to repair and maintain.
- Render a door child-operable by using appropriate hardware that assists in balancing the door's weight with its ease of swing.
- Ensure that all locks can be unlocked from both sides (in case a child gets locked in).
- Doors with slow-closing devices and/or rubber gaskets on the edges prevent finger pinching.
- Doors requiring panic hardware, or electronic eyes for those with disabilities, often appear institutional. They can be "softened" by color and by glazing if permitted by code.

Notes

[1]Christopher Day, *Places of the Soul: Architecture and Environmental Design as a Healing Art* (San Francisco: Harper, 1994), 90.

[2]C. Alexander, et al., *A Pattern Language* (New York: Oxford University Press, 1977), 837.

[3]Ibid, 892. The authors suggest that, depending upon climate, the total window area of a room should comprise 25–50% of its floor area.

[4]Also called a "jamb."

[5]Alexander, et al., *A Pattern Language,* 1055.

[6]Window treatment cords are a leading cause of strangulation among young children. Use wands or short chains. Spring-mounted cord tenders, or breakaway endings, can be purchased for older shades at nominal cost per shade. Consult the Window Covering Safety Council hot line: (800) 506-4636.

CHAPTER TWELVE

COLOR

Color is a living force that
directly influences the soul.

—KANDINSKY

How bleak our world would be without color! By helping us identify living forms, the state of our health, the ripeness of produce, or the time of day, color adds dimension, meaning, and beauty to life. An integral part of the designer's job is to address the physiological, psychological, aesthetic, and technical aspects of color.

Changing a center's interior color scheme is one of the easiest and least expensive ways to transform a child care setting, especially when the building's design is sterile or institutional. The approach to color presented here encourages conceiving of color as a means for creating a palpable "atmosphere" comparable to being outdoors in nature amidst trees, water, earth, and sky.

Children respond to balanced, nurturing environments, just as adults do, with a sense of peace and well-being. As in nature, which tends to mix many different colors together so each is distinct but none is out of place, the best approach is to create fields of color within which almost any combination of children, adults, toys, and furniture can function in pleasant harmony.

While this approach requires a few skills and attention to detail, the outcome is perceptibly enlivening. You are encouraged to embrace the challenge of understanding and working with the full-spectrum system presented here. Because the use of color in child care centers is relatively unexplored territory, about which very little has been written, this chapter covers the topic in considerable detail. It outlines a systematic process for making functional, beautiful, and nurturing color environments for children. This process is based upon the author's own experience, guided by the work of Goethe, Itten, colleague and color/style specialist Carla Mathis, and colorists Donald Kaufman and Taffy Dahl.[1] Even if you choose not to take this extra step, the general considerations and guidelines will aid you in getting the maximum benefit from standard commercial paints.

It is important to emphasize that selection of color should be an integrated process—one intimately influenced by the type and amount of light a space receives, as well as by the textures and patterns of the materials in the space. When choosing colors for child care spaces, supplement the guidelines in this chapter with the information on light in Chapters 10 and 11, as well as with that on finishes and furnishings in Chapters 13 and 14. Similar to a home, the aim is to create a *fully integrated interior* where all the colors, forms, and patterns harmonize with one another.

The Power of Color

Our response to color is total. As a form of energy, color affects our physiology as well as our mind and emotions. Exposure to the warmer colors (red, orange, and yellow) has been shown to excite the body, while exposure to the cooler colors (green, blue, violet) calms it. Subjecting a person to a given color for as little as five minutes changes his muscular as well as mental activity. (For example, bright bubble gum pink has the effect of subduing violent prisoners in seconds, reducing their muscle strength at the same time.) Color can alter the apparent size and warmth of a room; influence our estimation of volume, weight, time, temperature, and noise; encourage introversion or extroversion; induce anger or peacefulness. Color affects the autonomic nervous system, respiration, blood pressure, muscle tension, eye blinks, cortical activity, enzymatic and hormonal secretions, and many other body functions.

Reactions to color, as to light, are deeply ingrained in our nervous system. Most people prefer colorful surroundings to bland ones. Birren maintains that one of the greatest healing effects of color may be its power to relieve anxiety by drawing us outside ourselves and away from self-preoccupation.[2]

What Is Full-Spectrum Color?

Every color we see outdoors actually has within it small amounts of all the colors and is enhanced by the presence of the color at the opposite end of the spectrum. When mixing colors, this natural effect is achieved, regardless of color, by adding a little pigment of all the colors to the paint in question, as well as small amounts of the particular colors present in the architecture, art work, furniture, upholstery, and wood surfaces of the room.

> For either a painting or a room, the atmosphere binds all other elements. In either case, the approach to color is the same: leave out nothing that nature includes.
>
> For architectural spaces, this means employing the artist's approach—mixing each color with all the hues inherent in light. This has not been the standard practice of paint companies, whose color formulas usually consist of only two or three pigments. Any color, even gray, may be made up of a dozen or more hues. Instead of following the usual paint formula and adding black to the mix, a rich gray can be created by combining all of the primary colors. The result is a neutral whose composition ranges across the spectrum. Every other mix destined for the same space should be just as complex. The actual amount of the pigments will vary with the requirements of the space and its illumination, but *every color in the palette should include some of every other color.* [Emphasis mine.]
>
> Such complex formulas not only enable a wide variety of hues to harmonize as they do in nature, but they establish an equation: full-spectrum colors equal light. The room's atmosphere becomes a dynamic process of colors interacting under different conditions. Even if the conditions themselves cannot be controlled, such as the available sunlight, they can be observed and then interpreted through color to realize the space as a luminous and beautiful whole.[3]

It is important that creating a harmonious color environment be a focus of the architectural planning from the outset.

Understanding Color

The following discussion of color terminology and principles is a helpful prerequisite to understanding the color selection and mixing process described below.

The Properties of Color

The three basic properties of any color are its hue, saturation, and value:

- Hue: the name of a color or specific pigment
- Saturation/Intensity: the purity or strength of a color; amount of pigment present; colorfulness or brightness
- Value: a color's lightness or darkness; the amount of gray added to the basic hue.

White, gray, and black are perceived as "colorless"—as having neither hue nor saturation (intensity), but only value.

The Color Wheel

Colors fall into three main categories: primary, secondary, and tertiary (Figure 12.1):

- Primary colors = red, yellow, blue. The three basics from which all other colors can be mixed.
- Secondary colors = orange, green, purple. The colors obtained by mixing two primary colors together (red + yellow = orange).
- Tertiary colors = colors made when a primary and a secondary color are mixed (yellow + green = yellow green).

"Temperature"

A color's "warmth" or "coolness" is determined by which half of the color wheel it falls on (Figure 12.2). The hues of longest wavelength—red, yellow, orange, and some purple derivatives on the left half of the color wheel—are considered warm. Blue, green, purple, and some yellow derivatives of shorter wavelength on the right half of the wheel are considered cool. Within any

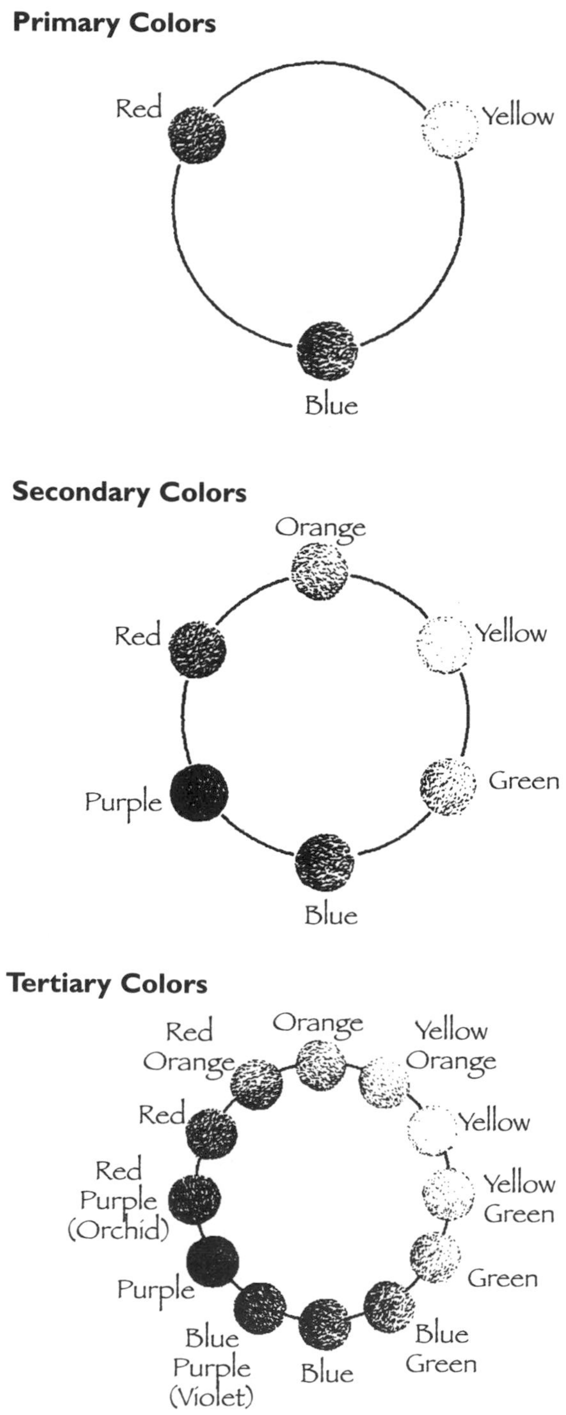

Figure 12.1
Primary, Secondary, and Tertiary colors.

hue, some values will be warmer than others. For example, while blue is a cool color relative to red, manganese blue (which appears greenish) is warm relative to ultramarine blue. Warm colors, which tend to be more arousing, are most appropriate for child care set-

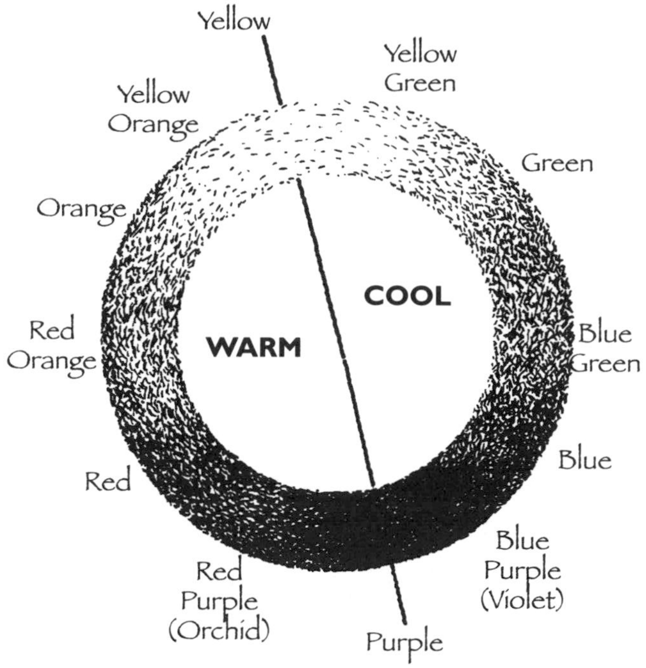

Figure 12.2
Warm and cool colors.

tings, provided they are not pure pigments. They direct attention outward and are conducive to muscular effort, action, and cheeriness. Cool colors foster an inward orientation and are appropriate for sedentary, restful activities. Because of their coldness, pure pigment cool colors should be used sparingly in child care settings.

Resonance: Working with Color Tonality[4]

Although saturation seems most to affect people's color preference, it is really variations in color tonality, or resonance, which create interesting and satisfying interior design effects. A particular hue is said to have different resonances depending upon what is used to alter the original pigment. The five simple resonances, as described by Mathis,[5] are as follows:

- *Tinted:* obtained by adding white, cream, or unbleached titanium to a color; colors are lighthearted, innocent, and/or sweet.[6]
- *Shaded:* obtained by adding black or Payne's gray to a color; colors are serious, profound and/or mysterious.[7]

- *Washed:* obtained by adding water or a clear thinning agent to the basic hue; colors are clear, crisp, and/or pretty.
- *Toasted:* obtained by adding brown (raw or burnt umber, raw or burnt sienna, or both) to the basic hue; colors are warm, nurturing, and/or luscious.
- *Muted:* obtained by adding the complement (the opposite color on the color wheel); colors are soft, gentle, and/or subtle.

When more than one method of altering a hue is used, the results are a pleasing complex resonance. An example would be

Tinted + Toasted + Muted.

For example, adding both white (*tinted*) and raw sienna (*toasted*) to red gives a milky terracotta. Add a bit of the complement—green—and the terracotta becomes *muted* to a soft, warm hue that blends with natural wood tones and suggests the warmth of a mother's skin.

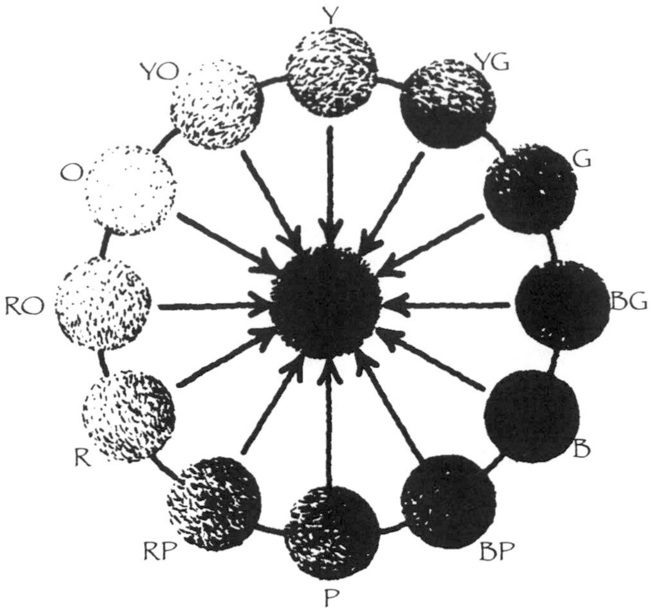

Figure 12.3
Complementary colors.

Harmonies, or Color Schemes

Harmony refers to the way colors work together in various combinations under varying circumstances. While color in a tube or on a paint sample chip appears a certain way, how it will look on a wall or canvas can only be determined by its situation relative to the accompanying colors, to light, to the expanse covered, and to the surface texture onto which it is applied. Thus, in addition to hue, saturation, and value, it is important to understand principles of how colors interact with one another, and of color extension, described below.

Mathis and Conner describe five color harmonies (also called color schemes) as follows:[8]

- *Neutral:* A neutral color scheme involves the use of two or more neutrals (e.g., brown, black, white, gray). The effect is stable, sophisticated, restful.
- *Monochromatic:* A monochromatic color scheme uses the same hue in gradations of value from light to dark: for example, pale green, with pure green, and dark green. The effect of this scheme is restful, expected and/or elegant, but it can also become monotonous. With interiors, it may work best as a background for brighter tones of other colors.
- *Analogous:* An analogous color scheme is created by a harmony of two or three hues that are side-by-side on the color wheel, which support and enhance one another (e.g., red-purple, blue-purple, or orange/red/purple). The effect is calm, friendly. Analogous schemes offer more variety than monochromatic schemes, but neither type satisfies the problem of the *afterimage* phenomenon described below with direct complements.
- *Complementary:* A complementary color scheme involves a harmony of two hues that are opposite each other on the color wheel (Figure 12.3). If colors of equal saturation and value are used, the effect is balanced, stimulating, dramatic and/or intense. Complementary colors balance the warm and the cool, the active and the passive. They are often found in nature, such as in violet flowers with yellow centers, bluebirds with orange-yellow highlights in their wings. Any pair of true complements contains all three primaries (red, yellow, and blue) which, when present in suitable proportions, will create gray if mixed. Careful handling of value and intensity is necessary to ensure the success of complementary color schemes.

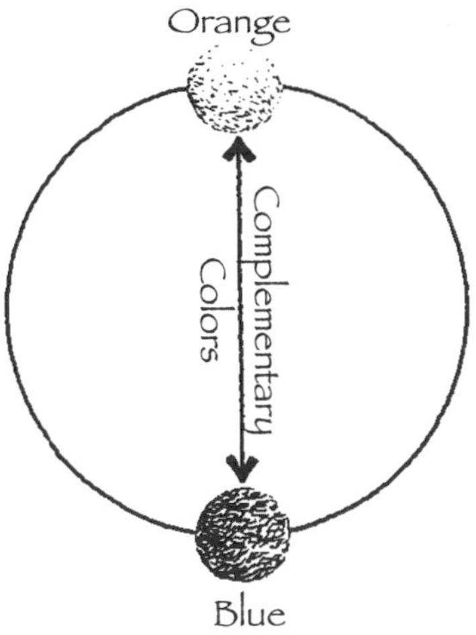

Figure 12.4
Direct Complements.

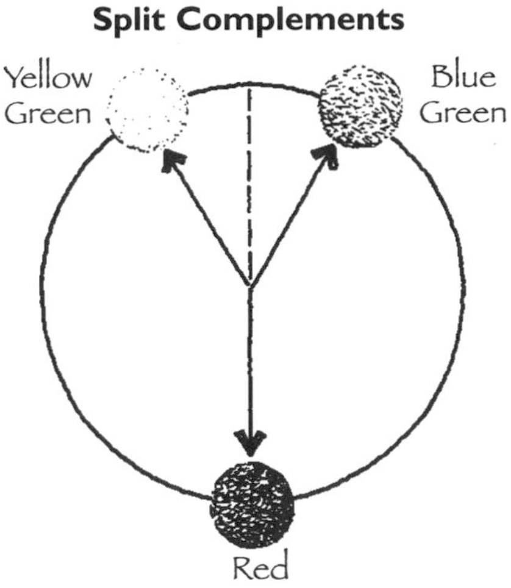

Figure 12.5
Split Complements.

Here is where the afterimage effect comes into play. Physiologically, the eye requires any given color to be balanced by its complement, and will generate it if it is not present. Thus, if you look at a red wall and then turn to a white wall, you will see green. When used side-by-side in a color scheme, complementary colors provide balance because when they are placed next to each other the afterimage of one enhances the other. This effect—the *afterimage phenomenon*—is both stimulating and calming.

There are three variations of complementary color schemes:

Direct (or true) *complements* are the colors directly opposite each other on the color wheel, such as red and green, orange and blue, or purple and yellow (Figures 12.3 and 12.4). They create pleasing semineutrals (when mixed in equal proportions), and ideal optical color balance.

Split complements are created by first drawing a straight line across the color wheel between two true complements. Then from the center of the wheel, draw arrows to the next lighter color on one side and the next darker color on the other (Figure 12.5). Because they are "off" balance, color schemes that employ split complements are active and stimulating; they can even be unsettling.

Example: Red-orange and red-purple are the split complement of green. Without careful balancing of resonance, saturation, and, value, this harmony could create a high-energy "fiesta" feeling that may result in fatigue for children and caregivers over a full day.

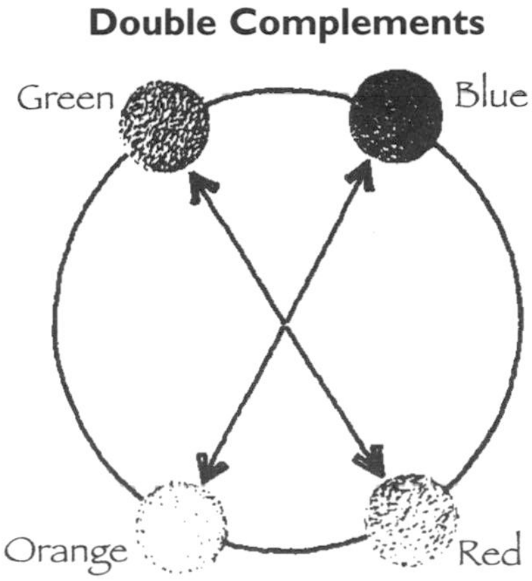

Figure 12.6
Double Complements.

Double complements are two sets of true complements that are spaced at least one color apart on the wheel (Figure 12.6). Double complements yield four colors, which tend to create an extremely active, pulsating context.

Example: Red-orange and red-purple split the complement of green, and when in harmony with yellow-green and blue-green (which in turn split the complement of red), create a pulsing color rhythm that stimulates without rest. Nature rarely has such intensity. Although a color scheme of double complements can be harmonious, it may be somewhat like caffeine: Continuous exposure can be exhausting and frenzied.[9]

- *Triadic:* A triadic color scheme is a harmony of three contrasting hues that are equidistant from each other on the wheel, and far enough apart that the semineutral created (if they are mixed) is not muddy: reds/yellows/blues or greens/oranges/purples (Figure 12.7). None of the three colors in the triad is analogous (side by side on the color wheel), allowing for more variety of color than any of the other schemes. A triadic color scheme is cheerful, active, and energetic. Because it is balanced and easy to live with, many designers believe triadic color schemes work best for living spaces.

Note: Colors are considered "harmonious" if their mixture yields gray. Those which do not yield gray are termed "expressive" or "discordant." All complementary pairs, all triads whose colors form equilateral or isosceles triangles in the color wheel (red/yellow/blue or green/orange/purple), and all tetrads forming squares or rectangles (i.e., double complements) are harmonious.

Extension

Color extension refers to the relative sizes (areas) of two or more color patches used in a given space, a contrast of proportion between much and little. It also refers to how the afterimage phenomenon affects the colors present, relative to one another. For example, if a chromatic hue such as green is placed next to an equivalent area of white, the eye will spontaneously generate green's complement, which is red. This afterimage will be projected by the eye onto the neutral, making it appear pink or reddish. The greater the amount of green relative to the quantity of white, and the more that green surrounds white, the stronger this effect. Similarly, where small amounts of one hue are surrounded by, or scattered in a larger field of its complement, the small amounts of color will have a more scintillating and powerful effect than if they were imbedded in white or a neutral. "The minority color, in distress, as it were, reacts defensively to seem relatively more vivid than if it were present in a harmonious amount."[10]

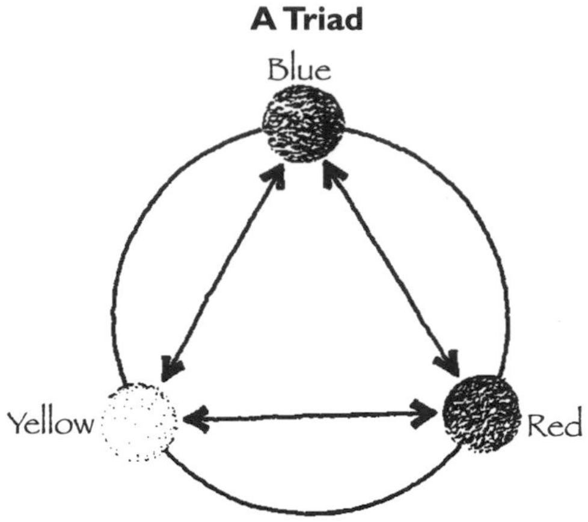

Figure 12.7
A triad.

The Psychology of Color

Let us now look at what different hues communicate psychologically. Phrases such as "feeling in the pink," being "red with rage," or "green with envy" abound in every culture, and tell us something about a color's characteristic effects. Most colors have both positive and negative connotations, depending upon their intensity or degree of saturation. A few of the familiar associations are listed in Box 12.1 along with each hue's most appropriate uses.

General Considerations in Color Selection

The following factors need to be taken into account when planning the center's overall color palette and selecting individual colors.

The Relationship Between Color and Light

Color and light are inseparable. Our perception of color is influenced by the intensity, direction, and sources of light falling upon it, and by the quality of the surface textures to which it is applied.

BOX 12.1

Hues: Their Associations and Uses

Red. Exciting and stimulating. Suggests energy, power, passion, fire, life, but can also connote blood, aggression, and rebellion. Stimulates the body to respond with direct action; therefore good for physical exercise, or to stimulate initiative.

Generally best used in small amounts as a highlight color. Avoid where rest and calm are desired. Variations such as rose, maroon, coral, and pink, which turn red feminine, gentle, and acquiescent, are more suitable for child care spaces. Deeper derivatives of red (terracotta) work well on floors.

Orange. Exciting, optimistic, expansive, confident, social, and festive. Easier to live with than red. Normalizes the body, replenishes depleted vitality, is an appetite stimulant, and a universal healer.

Good for social and eating spaces (warm pumpkin for a dining room). Pure pigment hues may appear garish while muted hues are warm and luscious on walls, ceilings, and floors.

Yellow. Cheerful, sunny, radiant, warm, inspiring. Represents the intellect, enlightenment, and communication. Raises blood pressure, heart and respiration rates. As the happiest of all the colors it can relieve depression, tension, and fear. Good for concentration, clarity of thought, conversation, counseling, well-being. Pervades the atmosphere like sunlight, being the brightest and easiest color to perceive when fully saturated. Cool yellows may have a greenish, bilious appearance, especially under cool fluorescent lights.

A good color for ceilings and walls but will show the dirt if used on floors. Wood flooring with a clear finish is a form of yellow.

Green. Retiring, relaxing, tranquil, refreshing. Represents new growth, rejuvenation, birth, death and transformation, balance, harmony, healing, purification. But, when dulled by gray, can become the color of envy, mold, sickness, and decay. The most restful color for the eye, it is the only natural neutral incorporating both the heat of yellow and the coolness of blue. Has a sedative effect on the nervous system, making it good for areas of rest and relaxation.

Various derivatives work well on walls, ceilings, and floors.

Blue. Serene, relaxing. Represents the spiritual intellect, intuition, inner peace, transcendence, heaven, and living out one's ideals. As the antithesis of red and orange, it chills rather than warms; reduces pain, blood pressure and pulse rate; soothes the nervous system. Due to its intrinsic coolness, blue can be cold and bleak in large areas, symbolizing sadness and depression.

Should be used sparingly, because of its coolness. Its warmer shades, tending towards green, are the easiest to live with on walls, ceilings, or floors.

Purple. Subduing, dignified, calm and joyous. Represents nobility, inspiration, but its darker tones can be mournful, lonely, conceited. A blend of red and blue, the two colors most opposed physically and psychologically, all tints of purple represent the brighter aspects of life; all shades the dark and negative forces.

Red/purples can work well in child care settings, but blue/purples are to be avoided as too dark and cold. Light blue/purple (violet) bedrooms induce a deep, relaxed sleep. In general, lighter tones work well for walls and ceilings; deeper hues on floors can deplete the body of energy.

White. Purity, perfection, cleanliness, coolness and extroversion. Contains all the colors and can represent both life and death.

Is too sterile and harsh in its pure form. Best for walls and ceilings when creamed, toasted, or mixed with small amounts of all the hues.

Black. Mystery, the unknown, introversion, strength, but also negativity and death. Absorbs and restores energy, restricts, and protects.

Appropriate for child care spaces only as an accent in small amounts.

Brown. Represents balance and the earth. Aids concentration but can have a heavy effect. Especially good for floors, walls, and furniture when present as wood tones.

Gray. Represents persistence and spiritual struggle, death, and rebirth.

Generally not a good color for child care. In the tropics, light values of warm grays, contrasted with creamy white, can be effective in restful areas.

Gold. Color of the sun, rich and warming. A delightful accent color.

Silver. Color of the moon, cool and delicate; peaceful. As an accent, can aid creativity.

When selecting color (and texture and pattern), work with large samples of paint colors, floor and wall coverings, upholstery materials, and other textiles. Try to view them under the lighting conditions of the spaces for which they are intended, and in combination with one another to ensure coordination of color, texture, and pattern.

Always choose colors in relation to their surroundings. To judge the effect of natural and artificial light, it is crucial to examine all the proposed colors in situ. Changing the color of the lighting (fluorescent, halogen, incandescent, natural light) will change the colors of dyes, finishes, and furnishings. The more chromatic the lighting, the more it will modify the intrinsic colors. The whiter the lighting, the purer the intrinsic colors appear. Warm colors are experienced more intensely under high illumination than under low illumination. The restfulness of cool colors is increased by low illumination. Full light whitens the intrinsic color, while shadow obscures and darkens it.

Over the course of a day, morning light is faintly chill (palish yellow or a flat grayish-white on a cloudy day). Afternoon light is a rich gold. Midday light is a white light that makes a room look most like the color it is painted—more so than at any other time of day. Winter light is grayer, bluer, and cooler; summer light is more yellow and warm.

Colors will be perceived differently under each of these circumstances. Glare and dazzle can be as harmful to eyes as insufficient light. A pleasant pastel with good reflectance may be less fatiguing than plain white, while a high-reflectance paint can increase light levels in dull environments by about one-third. Try out your samples under all the different lights you have in the room. If you must work off-site and cannot simulate the real conditions, it is best to make color choices under northern daylight, which has the least yellow in it.

The Effect of Sample Size on Color

Because color, light, and pattern are so affected by context, it does not work to base choice of hues upon small samples laid out side by side on a presentation board, as typically provided by interior designers. Paint colors need to be observed in samples at least 18″ x 24″, in relationship to the other colors in the room, to the floor coverings, and to the changing light conditions. Colors on sample boards should carry right to the edge and completely cover the board.

When choosing floor coverings, a pattern at one-inch square may look vastly different filling a 15-x-30-foot room than in a small sample. A texture perceptible 8 inches from the eye may wash out when held 6–10 feet away. A lavender that looks pleasant when held up to the window may appear cold under fluorescent light.

The best way to "try on" a floor covering color in a room is to get a large sample—at least 4′ x 4′—of the material, place it in the room, and observe it from various locations, under different light conditions. If you do not have access to the room, be certain to observe samples on neutral backgrounds from the heights and distances at which they will be experienced.[11] This will indicate how the tones and weave appear in large quantities and at distances greater than arm's length. Do not be surprised if the colors and patterns change under these conditions, and you are forced back to the drawing board! Many carpet colors take on a grayish hue from a distance.

Using the same color on the shelving, table, and chairs helps define this area's boundaries.

The Effect of Volume on Color

A room's volume radically influences the appearance of its chosen color—almost as much as the light it receives. The color of a paint chip will be about 50% lighter and brighter when it is applied to four walls and a ceiling. So, to achieve the same effect on the wall as on a chip, a darker and duller paint will be required.

Color As a Visual Organizer

Any discussion of color in child care settings needs to recognize that children's spaces are as a rule visually chaotic! As our most powerful visual organizer, color has an important role in helping a room's occupants deal with visual overload. For this reason, it is important that the background colors of the walls have a luminous rather than an imposed effect—achieved with full-spectrum color—so they function as a non-intrusive backdrop rather than a focal point for the room. Then color and texture can be used on play and seating surfaces, and storage and display units at child height, to create valuable definitions within a room.

As discussed in Chapter 7, every group room is typically organized into four major zones. Within each of these zones there may be several activity areas. (For example, the messy play zone may include areas for water, sand, painting, and woodworking.) Color can denote the perimeter of a zone, such as messy play, whose boundaries need to be fluid. Using different hues on the walls that create different zones demarcates their different functions.

A group room composed entirely of light-colored wooden bookcases, tables, and chairs can appear homogeneous and undifferentiated. When there are few level changes in the room helping to differentiate spaces, different hues placed at a child's level on play surfaces, partitions, and shelving units (as opposed to walls), can help cue where areas begin and end. A child standing in the room can see different (but harmonious!) tones (e.g., a creamy yellow space, a soft blue-green space, a subtle, toasted peach space) and know that the colors delimit areas and activities. To achieve this effect, it is sometimes necessary to apply color or paint to new furnishings, or at least to the backs of some units.

Suiting Colors to Age Groups

Any color can be appropriate for any age group, depending upon its brightness, lightness, amount, and the other colors present. For example, green can be a good color for an infant room. But if the green is too gray it may be somber and, if too bright, it may be overly stimulating. Thus, it is the particular tint or mixture of a color with its complements that determines whether a specific color works well for a specific age group.

Since color selection is more art than science, allow your own sense of the spirit of respective age groups to guide you in choosing wall colors. Following are some thoughts about possible wall colors for different ages that guided the color palette for the Copper House.

Infants. The infant's experience revolves around human flesh—nursing at the breast, being clothed and unclothed several times daily, being touched, and cuddled. Infants not only see but feel every vibration of color around them. *Colors like pink, peach, and salmon seem appropriate for infants, as do creams, tinted, washed, and toasted hues.* To honor diverse ethnic groups, choose a middle value that is neither pink nor dark chocolate. Then add touches of brown, yellow, and red to reflect the skin tones of different races.[12]

Toddlers. Toddlers are always on the go. Learning to use their newly found motoric abilities, they vacillate between independence and returning to a secure nest, between "do it self," and needing to be cuddled and assured. They can tolerate more stimulation than infants—therefore hues that are warmer and richer—but benefit from colors that are also relaxing and soothing. *Balanced colors like greens, blue-greens, or those with slightly more spark or calmness, such as mellow yellows and purples, seem to match their mood.* Triads, split complements, hues of middle value that are neither neutrals nor pure pigment, match their sense of adventure and their vulnerability.

Preschoolers. Preschoolers are an independent lot, eager to learn and to do, better able to regulate their own pace and to rest when necessary. Curiosity, creativity, and imagination blossom from ages three to six. *Touches of bright, energetic hues such as yellows, oranges, and purples can support the preschooler's inquisitiveness when played against a calming backdrop of soft warm colors.*

School-Age Children. In their younger years, these children are like preschoolers, and as they approach 10, 11, and 12, more like teens. A typical afterschool group may encompass 5–12 year olds, whose energy levels, powers of concentration, needs for connectedness and solitude, desires to be physically active or sedentary, can vary tremendously. *As a result, a neutral backdrop of complex warm whites and beiges sometimes works best,* with highlight colors coming from the furnishings and the colors chosen by children for their own extensive artwork.

Using the Spatial Effects of Color

Warm colors advance; cool colors recede. Lighter, less saturated, cooler hues therefore make a room appear larger. This is often a necessity in child care spaces where rooms are small and ceilings low. However, to avoid the chill of cool colors, especially blue, it is important that all the hues be toasted, and less intense saturations of the warm tones be used to achieve the appearance of enlargement desired. Dark ceilings appear weightier and lower; light ceilings appear higher and give a room more volume. Similarly, small fabric or floor patterns enlarge space, while large patterns reduce it. If the walls of a low-ceilinged room are painted a medium value tint, and its ceiling is a very light value tint, a deeper value carpet, such as a soft forest green or deep teal blue-green, can give the room greater height.

> Color need not be noticeable to have a noticeable effect. All that is needed to create a harmonious atmosphere is the interplay of warm and cool, sunshine and shadow. Two colors can be only subtly different, but still make a powerful duet. Even one hue can be made to play many roles. Sometimes texture itself produces enough visual variety to give the impression of a full spectrum of light.[13]

A space with little architectural detail can often tolerate more intense color than spaces with elaborate moldings, wainscoting, and woodwork that naturally draw attention to themselves.

Color can mask or accentuate a room's length, width, height, volume, warmth, and brightness, depending upon the function of the space and the users' needs. Box 12.2 contains some suggestions.

Working with Colors Already Present

Color deliberations need to take into consideration what is already in place. Choose wall colors that take their lead from the color of the flooring, furniture, upholstery, and major architectural features in the room (windows, fireplaces), as well as the landscape and natural materials visible outside the windows. A particularly beautiful art work that is visually dominant can also serve as the catalyst for color decisions.

Where wood surfaces are plentiful, add colors representing the various wood tones—burnt umber and raw sienna, occasionally burnt sienna—to "toast" the

BOX 12.2

Using Color to Affect Spatial Perception and Mood

To make a room larger: employ "toasted" hues using less intense saturations of warm tones.

To create depth: use cool, receding colors.

To foreshorten and make distant walls seem nearer: use medium-bright, intense warm colors.

To widen a narrow corridor: (1) paint the two walls different colors, or (2) add a vertical band of a contrasting color on one wall, repeating with a similar band further down on the opposite wall.

To shorten a long corridor: use a warm, bold, dark color or a graphic at its end.

To unify a room and enlarge a space: use hues similar in saturation and value, but avoid monotony.

To enhance concentration (as in offices): use subtle hues and soothing neutrals, e.g., soft yellow, sandstone, pale gold, soft peach, pale green, soft olive tones, beige, pale or light green, and blue-green.

To keep people moving in corridors and stairwells: use vivid colors.

In corridors where light is dim: use lively hues of high reflectance (light, toasty yellows).

In corridors where art is displayed: use restful, neutral colors.

paints. Mathis represents the various wood tones in the following way:

maple, oak, birch	=	raw sienna (teaspoons to 1 tablespoon/qt)
ash, oak tree bark	=	raw umber (drops to teaspoons/qt)
walnut, walnut-stained oak	=	burnt umber (drops to teaspoons/qt)
mahogany, cherry	=	½ burnt umber + ½ burnt sienna (drops to teaspoons/qt)
redwood	=	burnt sienna (drops to teaspoons/qt).

. . . and Two Caveats:

Beware of Personal Bias in Color Choice

Familiarity, convention, and personal preference are often the bases of color choice in child care. When people feel insecure in the area of color design, they tend to make choices that are "safe" and familiar, such as beige or off-white, or bright primaries corresponding to the toys and materials on the market. A less obvious basis of choice is the fact that many of the forms and colors we prefer correspond to our own natural coloring and personally unique color palette, and physical form. While choosing colors that satisfy personal taste is fine for individual expression, for child care we need to put personal preferences aside and consider the collective community.

A Caution About Using Primary Colors

Preschool children are generally extroverted by nature and particularly responsive to color. In fact, prior to age five or six, children are more likely to remember color than form. Thus the usual architectural cues used to delineate form may be imperceptible to children or superseded by color.

Young children generally prefer bright colors, especially red and yellow, to more subdued tones. However, the fully saturated primary hues of most plastic toys are not the best choices for the interior walls and furnishings of a center. Unlike at home, in child care centers many children are using numerous colored materials at the same time. The presence of too much bright color in an environment can have deleterious effects—making children hyperactive, agitated, and exhausted, or causing them to shut down their senses in order to block out the intensity of the stimuli. The cold fluorescent lights typically employed in child care centers, aggravated by the sheen and glare from brightly colored plastics, substantially contribute to the "high pitch" of these settings, creating eyestrain, headaches, nausea, nervousness, and stress in children and adults alike. In addition, since bright colors make the environment visually demanding, children have difficulty concentrating on any one thing.

Choosing Exterior Colors

In selecting colors for the building's exterior, consider the climate (temperate, tropical), geographical location (desert, forest, seaside, plains), and locale (urban, suburban, rural) of the center. Warm, saturated, intense hues tend to work well in temperate and tropical areas, as evinced by the bright oranges, blues, and purples of African, Mexican, and southern dwellings surrounded by dense vegetation, brilliant flowers, and intense sunlight. Cool, light tones and neutrals are more common in northern climates characterized by rain, snow, and blustery gray days, and in urban areas without vegetation.

In particular, take note of the vegetation and natural colors appearing in the land around the center. Are these primarily green or brown or both? The exterior of the building will harmonize with its setting to the degree that some pigment equivalent to the hues of the natural earth materials is present in whatever color is chosen. This factor should influence the general resonance level of the interior spaces as well.

Choosing Interior Colors

We can start with two assumptions: (1) the colors in the children's group rooms are the most important interior color choices, and (2) it is best if the colors vary from room to room, or at least from one age group to another. Children spending three to five years in a center deserve some variety of experience. Moreover, since they "read" color more readily than form, children's comprehension of different groups and spaces is assisted by color coding.

At this point, it helps to imagine the finished room:

1. Write down adjectives that describe the mood you intuitively feel each age group's space should have. For example, you might decide that warm, soft, cuddly colors are appropriate for babies; that rich, more stimulating hues—still with some element of calm—are appropriate for toddlers; while bright, energetic hues are suitable for preschoolers.

2. Take time to sit in or imagine each room being designed. Feel its energy and spirit of place. Pay careful attention to the qualities of natural and electrical light in that room, and how these vary during the day. Note the physical relationship between the windows and sources of electrical light and the floor coverings.

Colors for Floors

It is wise to begin by selecting floor coverings for each room. Selecting floor coverings is the most important interior design decision you will make, well worth the time and effort required to get it right. The room's color scheme takes its directive from the floor's colors and harmonizes with them. Be warned, however, that finding flooring in your chosen colors can be frustrating. It is not unusual to have to search among several manufacturers before finding a carpet, linoleum, or tile line with good colors. For a discussion of the several interrelated factors in addition to color affecting flooring choices, see Chapter 13.

Keep in mind that extremely dark colors can make a floor appear heavy, draining energy from the body and causing the room to feel smaller. Yet very light tones show the dirt easily. Solid colors are not advised, as they show stain and dirt more readily than carpets or tiles with flecks and mixed hues. So-called "learning" carpets with games and symbols designed specifically for children are too colorful and too visually busy to be tolerable in an all-day setting. Commercial carpets designed for offices and public facilities have the required durability, but often come only in muted grayed-down tones that fail to have sufficient vigor for children. Mixed-hue carpets with analogous colors are better. Be careful that mixed-hue carpets are not created with complementary colors since, on the floor, the eye blends the complements and the carpet appears gray or taupe.

Colors for Walls

Once the floor colors for the group rooms are selected, it is time to consider the wall colors. Keep in mind the general considerations in color selection outlined earlier as you choose the color schemes for your rooms.

In general, choose the dominant colors for children's spaces from the warm side of the palette, for energy and youthfulness. Then they can be slightly toasted with earth tones (burnt umber, burnt sienna) for richness and to make them complement the wood, and tinted with white or cream for lightness. Key subordinate wall colors (used as accents or to distinguish an area of a room), to water and growing things: blue/greens, green/blues, and red/purples (however, avoid blue/purples). Also avoid grayed, muted, shaded, darkened and shadowy hues, pure pigments, and clear thin colors with a sharp edge. Pure pigments such as red, yellow, and blue can be used in small quantities as accent hues, provided they are in a matte finish to subdue their intensity.[14]

Some colorists recommend a maximum of three colors in a room, with highlights of an additional single bright color. Variety can also be produced by changing a color's intensity, value, and texture. It is not necessary to resort to white and beige walls to create a neutral backdrop. So long as the wall colors are toasted, creamed, and kept light in saturation, they will have the effect of creating an "atmosphere" rather than a pronounced color palette.

Where the room has architectural definition in the form of subspaces, alcoves, or bays used for different functions, it is good to distinguish these spaces by different but harmonious wall colors. These might be termed the room's secondary hues. Consider warmer, more intense resonances for active areas and as the room's primary hue; cooler resonances and hues (blue-greens, red-purples) for quieter areas. Avoid any large expanses of true blue or blue-purple.

> ***EXAMPLE:*** In the infant room of the Copper House, the basic room color is peach. To create a triadic harmony, the small, adjacent food prep area is a lively violet, and the lower half of the sleep room is a soft, creamy teal green, which is repeated in the wet play bay on the opposite side of the room. (See floorplan, Chapter 16).

Paint Finish

A flat or matte paint finish, which shows the dirt more readily, and is more difficult to wash or clean than a glossier finish, might be appropriate for staff and administrative areas. In areas that children will use, it is preferable to use an intermediate eggshell or satin finish, which has a bit more reflectance value than matte, but nothing comparable to semigloss or high gloss paint. The latter are excellent finishes for woodwork and for areas where walls can get splashed or wet. Semigloss and high-gloss paints may also work well where high reflectance can add luminosity to a space, such as a dark corridor. Generally, the brighter the color, the more matte the finish called for.

> BOX 12.3
>
> **The Concept of Lazuring a Wall**
>
> With special brushes (available through Waldorf Schools), a thin layer of varnish is applied over a thin layer of paint. Alternate layers of paint and varnish are continuously applied, similar to the way a painter builds up paint on a canvas. Light falling on a lazured wall's surface is reflected in myriad ways, giving the wall great life and luminosity.

Texture

Because textural irregularities reflect and partially transmit light in various ways, any color will appear different on different textures. For example, a rough piece of unfinished wood will have color variations across its surface, while its porosity will make the color applied to it appear darker. For this reason, all colors should be tried out on the particular surfaces to which they will be applied. Natural full-spectrum colors have some of the same effects as texturizing a wall in that they make the color appear more in the material than on it.

Special effects can be achieved using Zolotone (a paint mix containing particles of different pigment), or by wiping, sponging, and staining, which allow the surface and texture of the underlying material to shine through. These techniques are labor-intensive, however, and their appropriateness needs to be carefully evaluated in each instance.

Rough plaster walls need very little color to bring them to life and are often best in neutral and soft hues that better allow the play of natural light to color their surface. "Lazuring," a technique popular in Waldorf Schools, whose founder Rudolf Steiner was influenced by Goethe, aims to give walls added texture (Box 12.3).

Where there is an abundance of both sunlight and texture in a room, the use of a variant of white can work well, allowing the wall's own texture and the room's natural light to play with one another. The effect is to cast subtle shades of rose, blue, violet, and gold upon the walls over the course of the day. This will work only if an abundance of greenery and natural features are visible outdoors. Generally, creamed or tinted warm whites are preferable in child care. Pure white is stark, cool, and glaring.

. . . and Two Cautionary Notes

Painting Window and Door Frames

Painting window and door frames (especially aluminum ones) in contrasting colors is a popular interior design technique that attempts to provide color in an otherwise bland and texturally sterile environment. Rather than being applied across the board, this approach deserves assessment in each situation. Outlining a window or door with a color different from that of the wall causes the window or door to compete for visual attention with educational materials and play surfaces. If the window or door is architecturally beautiful, the eye will be drawn to it naturally, regardless of its color. If the opening is not particularly distinctive, it is perhaps best to allow the quality of the light entering the room, or the protective effect of the door to speak for itself, and to use color to draw the child's attention instead to the room's offerings. Generally speaking, varnished wood doors are preferable to painted ones which easily chip. Where prominent doors and frames break up small walls, it is preferable either to paint these the same color as the walls to enlarge the space, or to paint them a separate color but in a similar or slightly lighter value than the walls.

A Word About Toys

In most child care centers, as well as homes, the toys are predominantly made of plastic and colored in pure pigment primary hues. Americans have a great deal to learn from the Europeans, whose wooden toys and furniture are rarely in primary colors but in softer, more complex hues that exude real beauty and design integrity. A few U.S. companies have recently created separate toy and furniture lines using muted and pastel tones, but the grayed-down nature of these colors makes most of them dull and unappealing. Until such time as American manufacturers produce fewer plastic materials in more appropriate hues, designers face a dilemma. Bright primary toys scream out for visual attention, and they rarely harmonize with other color schemes. The procedures recommended in the following section for color mixing can assist in creating balance without the need to resort to walls in white or primaries. However, because of their negative impact, it is also helpful to encourage staff to cut down on the number of bright, primary plastic toys and/or to cover these with fabrics or paints in hues that match the chosen color scheme.

Mixing Full-Spectrum Colors

Are you ready to try your hand at becoming a master paint mixer? The process described here for mixing your own paint to incorporate full-spectrum attributes departs from the standard procedure of just choosing chips from the local paint store, but it works with them. The goal, which the author shares with Kaufman and Dahl, is to create the same harmonious atmosphere we experience in nature in the interior color schemes. Full-spectrum color brings a sense of luminosity to a space, and aliveness to its walls, without the background overpowering or drawing attention away from the activities of the children.

The creation of full-spectrum paints takes time, experience, and slightly more money than using commercial paint colors. However, the unforgettable dimension and luminosity that complex colors give a space can make the additional effort more than worthwhile. Natural, full-spectrum color appears almost to be intrinsic to the surface material rather than applied to it, thus making it particularly powerful in offsetting the bland, institutional feel of many child care facilities. Full-spectrum paint is especially important when working with neutrals and/or primary colors.

For a description of the procedure for creating full-spectrum paints from scratch, readers are referred to Kaufman and Dahl, pages 216–218. For those who do not choose to involve themselves with that level of complexity, a simplified approach to custom-mixing commercial colors, developed by Carla Mathis, is outlined in Box 12.4. This approach allows you to create a complex resonance for any and all colors of choice. It begins with commercial paint colors that are then custom-mixed, ideally on site, and tried out on large sample boards placed on various walls to see how the colors interact under existing illumination. The custom-mixing continues until the desired resonance is achieved. Then it is taken to a custom mixing supplier who will create a written formula for your one-of-a-kind color. This formula can then be reproduced in quantity by most paint suppliers.

B O X 1 2 . 4

How to Mix Your Own Paint Colors

- After arriving at a "felt sense" of the preferred wall colors for a room, begin by selecting a commercial paint chip that approximates the major wall color desired. Purchase a quart-size can of this color. *Be sure that this color does not use black in its formula.* Ask the paint store to use Raw Umber in place of black.
- Also purchase a plastic squeeze bottle of each of the following widely available Cal-Tint Universal Tinting Colorants: Raw Umber, Burnt Umber, Raw Sienna, and Burnt Sienna, Bulletin Red, Orange, Interior Yellow, Thalo Green, Thalo Blue, and Violet. These may be added to any brand or type of paint (i.e., latex or oil).
- Add small amounts (four to six drops at a time) of Cal-Tint Burnt Umber and Raw Sienna pigment to your quart of color, taking care to stir the tints thoroughly into the base. The Burnt Umber relates to most warm brown furnishings and the earth outside; the Raw Sienna relates to the color of natural maple, pine, birch, and other "yellow" woods. If the woods in your furniture or architecture are actually more redish, instead use only a few drops of Burnt Sienna, to soften and enrich your color. These tints will automatically cut the sharpness and blandness of the commercial product, making it more livable and akin to the colors in nature. In addition, add as little as one drop of each of the Cal-Tint basic hues, or at least of those that come closest to the colors in the flooring material. If your paint gets too dark, add white or cream for the desired intensity.
- When the color has the degree of toasted lusciousness you prefer, paint it on an 18″–24″ square of poster board or cardboard, including all the edges. (Painting directly on the wall will require priming later on.) Allow the sample to dry, or dry it with a hairdryer. (Dried paints are rarely the same as the color in the can—some darken, others pale.) Place the painted square in different lights and spaces in the room to evaluate the resonance. Keep working with this quart of paint until you achieve the resonance desired when the paint is dry.

  As noted earlier, a room's volume radically influences its color. A paint chip's color will also appear about 50% lighter and brighter when applied to four walls and a ceiling. So, if the chip gives the desired effect, a darker and duller paint will be required to replicate that effect on the walls. Glare and dazzle can be as harmful to eyes as insufficient light. Since paints now have numbered reflectance levels, these should be selected in relation to existing light conditions. A pleasant pastel with good reflectance may be less fatiguing than plain white, while a high reflectance paint can increase light levels in dull environments by about one-third.
- If you want to use other colors on other walls, proceed to mix these as well. (See also *Working with Colors Already Present*, page 146.)
- Now take your paint to a custom mixing place, which will create written recipes and formulas to match your samples. Give instructions to the mixer to avoid black and to put in tiny amounts of all hues. These written formulas can then be taken to most paint suppliers (those who have the pigments available). This must be a custom match. Be careful of computer matching, which tends to identify the closest paint chip formula in the particular brand of paint.
- Once all the wall colors for the room have been prepared and purchased, for example peach and soft teal blue, add ¼ cup of peach to the gallon of teal and vice versa. (Subsequently, it will be necessary to add ¼ cup per gallon [for deeper and cooler hues] and up to 1 cup per gallon [for lighter and yellow-based hues] to every other color used in rooms adjacent to the space in question; see "*Unifying the Building's Colors*" on the next page.)
- If even the above seems daunting, Carla Mathis has created the following formula for creating a warm creamy white using the Benjamin Moore color system of 32 increments in an ounce (identified by double letters), and the Universal Tint system of 48 increments in an ounce (identified by single letters), which an ordinary paint dealer can add with an increment dispenser to one gallon of # 1 light tinting base. Colors will vary with other brands and darker tinting bases. The recipe aims to attain a full spectrum within the white color range. Additional formulas for some child-appropriate colors using Benjamin Moore paints, and selected child-appropriate Donald Kaufman colors, can be found in Appendix IV. Even if you use only these formularized colors, still attempt to unify the different wall colors in the building by following the directive in the preceding paragraph.

Creating a Cream With Your Paint Dealer

OY (Oxide Yellow)	20
GY (Gray)	12
OG (Orange)	2
MG (Magenta	1
I (Burnt Umber)	1

Shortcut version: Kaufman and Dahl suggest that improved results can often be obtained from commercial formulas just by providing a small amount of the missing part of the spectrum (often the complementary color). The amount required to achieve a complex full-spectrum effect is frequently so small as to seem inconsequential. They cite the case of a pink that became less strident by adding the barest trace of thalo green, or a commercial beige whose dullness was transformed by a mere 1/64 of an ounce of Thalo blue, blue being the pigment most often missing from the warm neutrals many people prefer.[15]

Unifying the Building's Colors

People occupying a building want to be able to experience it as a whole, even if they spend time primarily in one room. This means that although color can be used as dramatically or subtly as one chooses in a given space, it is also important that there be a coherence and harmony in terms of the resonance, temperature, and saturation of the colors used throughout a structure. Good design conveys a sense of seamless integration as one glances through an open door or moves from one room to the next. Visual spaciousness increases when colors of similar resonance are carried from one room to another.

> . . . the placement of color is as critical to the atmosphere as the hue's composition. Each color should somehow serve form, whether it is to enhance the architecture's existing shapes, or to disguise them in favor of new ones that color creates. This idea of a hierarchy of forms expressed by a complete spectrum applies not only to an individual space, but to the aggregate of spaces. Juxtapositions of warm and cool color, and the luminosity they create, should carry over not only from wall to wall, but room to room.[16]

To complete the color palette for the rest of the building, continue the process described above. Begin by selecting the floor coverings for the other spaces, applying the same principles discussed above for the children's group rooms. Covering different areas of the center with differently colored carpet or floor tile can help orient people to the layout of the building.

> *Example*: The Copper House has a pale green carpet for infants, a blue-green and purple carpet for toddlers, a red-yellow and purple carpet for preschoolers, wood for school-age children, and a teal green carpet with an orange fleck for the public and administrative areas. In addition, area rugs and terracotta tile were used in various places.

Placing a different color inside each room on the wall opposite the room's door aids both orientation through the building and room identification. Color can be used to differentiate corridor walls when they form a wide angle; to camouflage certain areas (e.g., framing and doors) by painting them the color of adjacent walls; and to accentuate certain areas by selecting contrasting hues. Bands of color can be used to direct children to different locations. Placed at child height (below three feet), color bands are especially effective if they also have tactile properties.

GUIDELINES: COLOR

- Visually demanding colors make it difficult for children to focus or concentrate on any one thing. Although young children tend to prefer bright colors to more subdued tones, inundation by bright primary colors can make children hyperactive and exhausted, or cause them to shut down their senses against the intensity of the stimuli.
- Attempt to create an "atmosphere" and fields of color within which almost any combination of children, toys, furniture, and adults can function in pleasant harmony.
- Familiarize yourself with the psychological effects of different hues and match these with the respective functions and age groups in each space.
- Since children "read" color more readily than form, a color-coding scheme based upon a different dominant hue for each room will assist their comprehension of different groups and spaces.
- It is not the hue itself, but the particular tint, shade, or mixture of a color with its complements, that determines how well a specific wall color or floor material works for a specific age group.
- Assess colors in relation to their surroundings. Aim to use use large swatch and sample sizes. To judge the effect of natural and artificial light, be sure to examine all proposed colors at the site itself (not only in the store or on an interior designer's presentation board).

Floors

- Begin by selecting floor coverings and carpet for each room. Choose mixed hue carpets with analogous colors. Extremely dark colors can make a floor appear heavy and cause the room to feel smaller, while very light tones show dirt too easily.

Ceilings

- In rooms with 8-foot ceilings or lower, lighten the ceiling color by at least half by adding 50% white or light cream.

Walls

- Full-spectrum-color paints—achieved by adding small amounts of all the colors, plus small amounts of all colors existing in the exterior environs, and of the colors in the rest of the building, to any single can of paint—can help to offset the bland, institutional feel of many child care facilities.
- In general, have the dominant colors for children's spaces be "warm" for energy and youthfulness—earth tones slightly tinted with white or cream for lightness. Key sub-

ordinate wall colors to water and growing things—blue/greens, green/blues, and red/purples. Avoid blue/purples and muted, shaded or shadowy hues, pure pigments, or clear thin colors with a sharp edge, e.g., a sharp lemon-yellow or a clear blue or violet.

- Pure pigments (such as red, yellow, and blue) can be used in small quantities as accent hues, provided they are applied in a matte finish to subdue their intensity.
- In general, the brighter the color, the more matte the finish. A flat or matte paint finish, harder to wash, might be appropriate for staff and administrative areas. In children's areas, an intermediate eggshell or satin finish (more reflectance value) is preferable to matte.
- Semigloss or high-gloss finishes are excellent for woodwork or areas where walls can get splashed or wet. These finishes can also work well where more luminosity is needed, such as a dark corridor.
- A room's length, width, height, volume, warmth, and brightness can be masked or accentuated with color. Hues similar in saturation and value can unify a room and make a space seem larger. But avoid monotony.
- Bright colors and intense, warm colors foreshorten and make distant walls seem nearer. Pale colors and cool, receding colors create depth.
- Choose or mix full-spectrum background wall colors for their luminous rather than imposed effect, so they function as a nonintrusive backdrop.
- If fluorescent lighting is used in bathrooms, avoid paint or wall coverings in the medium-value yellows, greens, and blues. When these hues are reflected onto skin, they make people look pale, jaundiced, or cyanotic.
- Once all the colors for the building have been selected, add a small amount of each color (see Box 12.4) to every gallon of every other color. This ties them together and creates harmony throughout the building.
- Once all the colors are mixed for the building, be sure to save some amount of each for touch-up jobs and future reference.

Exterior

- When selecting exterior colors, consider the climate, geographical location (desert, forest, seaside, plains), and locale (urban, suburban, rural). Take special note of the vegetation and natural colors appearing in the land around the center. Add drops of corresponding colors to the exterior (and interior) paints.

Notes

[1]Johann Wolfgang von Goethe, *Theory of Colours* (Farberwehre), trans. Charles Lock Eastlane (London: John Murray, 1980).

Johannes Itten, *The Elements of Color* (New York: Van Nostrand Reinhold, 1970).

Carla Mason Mathis and Helen Villa Conner, *The Triumph of Individual Style* (Menlo Park, CA: Timeless Editions, 1993).

Donald Kaufman and Taffy Dahl, *Color: Natural Palettes for Painted Rooms* (New York: Clarkson Potter/Publishers, 1992).

[2]F. Birren, Light, *Color and Environment* (New York: Van Nostrand Reinhold, 1982).

[3]Kaufman and Dahl, *Natural Palettes*, 12–13.

[4]Carla Mathis has been an invaluable contributor to many portions of this chapter.

[5]Mathis and Conner, *Triumph of Individual Style*, 118–119.

[6]When creating a tint, it takes a large quantity of white to lighten a color even slightly. Therefore, always add colors to white; never add white to colors. Because adding white to a color may change its hue slightly, also add a touch of the color above that hue on the color wheel to make the color fresh and never chalky. As described in W. F. Powell, *Color and How to Use It* (Walter Foster Publishing, Inc., 1984), 18.

To create creams, which are considered tints, mix equal quantities of pastel yellow and pastel pink. Creams can be colorful, light, subdued, or grayish, depending on the proportion and nature of the hues present. It is good to toast them a little by adding burnt umber or raw sienna.

[7]Darken colors for use in child care centers by toasting (adding raw umber), never by shading (adding black). To darken a color, add dark to light. Also add a touch of the color below the hue on the wheel so that the new color remains fresh and never muddy (Powell, *Color and How to Use It*, 18). Any mixture will be darker than its lightest contributory color.

[8]Mathis and Conner, *Triumph of Individual Style*, 148–149.

[9]It is also possible to achieve an analogous complementary color scheme by choosing two colors next to each other and combining them with the complement of one of the two: yellow-red and yellow combined with blue, the complement of yellow-red. (W. F. Mahnke and Rudolf H. Mahnke, *Color and Light in Man-Made Environments* (New York: Van Nostrand Reinhold, 1987), 31.

[10]Itten, *Elements of Color*, 62.

[11]Some paint stores also have "light boxes" that can be used to replicate certain light conditions.

[12]A concept developed by Carla Mathis.

[13]Kaufman and Dahl, *Natural Palettes*, 53.

[14]Mathis, personal communication.

[15]Kaufman and Dahl, *Natural Palettes*, 218.

[16]Kaufman and Dahl, *Natural Palettes*, 13.

CHAPTER THIRTEEN

INTERIOR FINISHES

Whether people are fully conscious of this or not,
they actually derive countenance and sustenance
from the "atmosphere" of the things they live in or with.

—FRANK LLOYD WRIGHT[1]

This chapter addresses the nature and design of the interior materials used on floors, walls, and ceilings in child care facilities, and of the visual enhancements (signs and artwork) employed for information and decorative purposes. Though often given only routine consideration, the choice of interior finish materials can more powerfully affect the ambience of a child care center than any other single factor. All subsequent colors, textiles, furniture, and accessories will need to be selected in relation to these initial interior choices, if a fully integrated interior is to be achieved. They are the critical backdrop against which everything else happens.

The interior surfaces are the close-at-hand aspects of a center that children contact the most. Since the skin is the largest organ of the body, we receive vast amounts of information and stimulation through our sense of touch. For children under three or with a special need, touch is the most critical of all the senses. Texture and feel are the primary ways they learn about the physical world and their own bodies. In fact, giving children with learning disorders increased tactile stimulation has been found to improve their form and space perception. Interior finishes, as well as furnishings, therefore affect children as profoundly if not more so than overall building design. It is important that cost estimates for a building include projections for interior materials at the outset so these will not be shortchanged at the point of selection.

Materials convey messages to which children and adults respond: Hard and indestructible finishes convey "hands off" messages and expectations that children will act inappropriately and destructively towards their environment. By contrast, a setting that is inviting, soft, and sensitive to people's needs (with

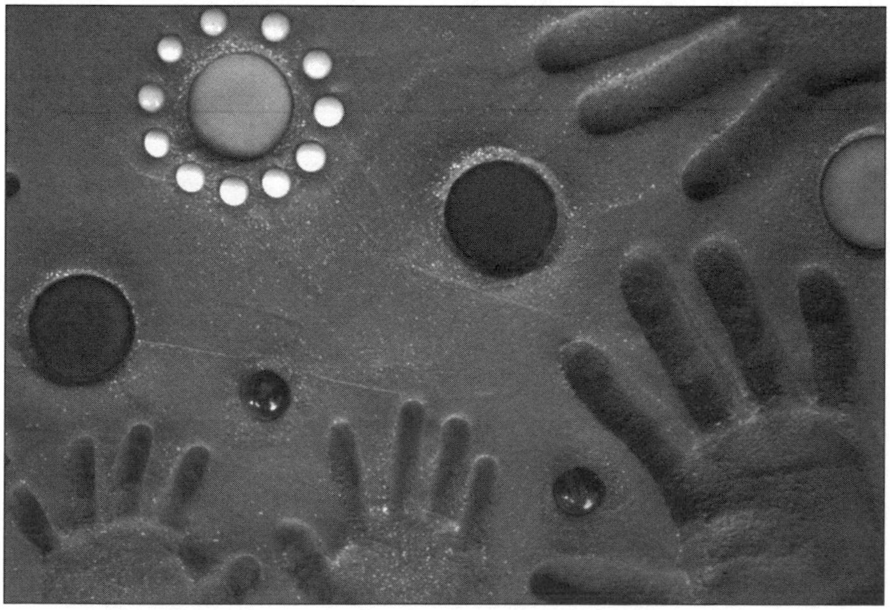

Touch is the most important sense for young children.

carpeting, wood paneling, and padded surfaces) expresses respect for the user, which in turn leads children to respect the center. Research has shown that the presence of "softness" in child care centers (carpets, pillows, cozy furniture, and malleable materials such as water and sand) is predictive of center quality.[2]

By affecting what people see, hear, touch, and smell, finishes directly impact how people feel. The textural qualities of materials and finishes are also vital for children's cognitive and physiological development. When they provide difference-within-sameness and variety, finishes are one of the most important means designers can use to help keep the nervous system healthy and alert; when bland and homogeneous, they contribute to sensory deprivation.

Texture

The experience of texture results from a complex interaction of the material—its structure, tactile properties, depth, color—with our skin and with the light sources around it. Everything has texture; when we speak of wanting "more texture" somewhere, it is usually because the existing surfaces all have a similar flat, smooth quality. The view that child care facilities should be antiseptic and childproof, and therefore replete with smooth, washable surfaces, deprives children of the textural richness they enjoy and deserve. Instead, we need to employ a variety of textures, especially in group rooms, appropriate to the use and desired mood of particular spaces.

Man-made materials such as plastic tend to show wear and tear and do not age gracefully. Natural substances, on the other hand, such as wool and unpainted wood, show the marks of use and time in ways that enrich and mellow them. And they are nontoxic and healthful. Finish materials chosen for newness and efficiency are best balanced by materials that convey a sense of naturalness, history, and maturity. No material is right or wrong; rather it is variety that is desired.

Textural Authenticity

Perceptual distortions result whenever an object or a surface is given a camouflaged or superficial finish at variance with its true nature. Thus, artificial plants rarely pass for real ones up close, and hefty metal doors covered with imitation wood grain reveal their true nature by their sound, weight, and thermal conductivity. Because the integrity of materials and finishes contributes significantly to a healthful environment, to the capacity of children to learn about materials, and to learn about truthfulness and honesty, the use of imitations and substitutes is discouraged in child care settings.

Maintenance and Upkeep

Because everything in a child care center is subject to intense use, the maintenance requirements of different finishes are an important factor in their selection. Since low-maintenance materials are often the most hard and cold, a balance needs to be struck between upkeep and aesthetics. All interior finishes need periodic maintenance, as well as frequent renewal, especially if the quality of the materials is only modest to begin with. In the long run, it is always most cost-effective to purchase products of better quality from the start.

Safety

Selected materials need to be in accordance with local fire and building safety standards. But code requirements should not become an excuse for eliminating textural variety from a room. An increasing number of attractive carpets, fabrics, and finishes—in a variety of colors and textures—are available commercially. Originally designed for health care settings, these items are cleanable, antimicrobial, and meet class A ratings for smoke and flammability. Local architectural or interior design firms are generally familiar with commercial-grade sources.

GUIDELINES: FINISHES

- The quality, design, and aesthetic appeal of finish materials profoundly affect a building's spirit of place and the way people feel in it. "Softness" is predictive of child care center quality.
- Touch is the most important sense for children under three or with special needs.
- Use finish materials with different textural qualities to provide varied tactile experiences and difference-within-sameness in a space.
- In choosing finish materials, balance aesthetics with maintenance requirements. Low-maintenance materials are often the least friendly and appealing.

Floors

Since the floor may be the single most important surface in the child care center, it is good interior design practice to choose the texture, finish, color, and pattern of flooring material first, and to base all other interior design decisions on this factor. (See Chapter 12 for considerations in selecting floor color.)

Functions of the Floor

Through design, the floor not only functions as a circulation platform, but also as a play and sitting surface, a definer of activities, an object of exploration, and a stage for all manner of events. The ideal floor is warm to the touch, skidproof, easily cleanable, moisture resistant, antimicrobial, nontoxic, and does not generate static electricity.

Children use the floor as furniture.

In a child care setting, the floor is considered furniture. Children much prefer playing on floors to sitting on chairs, provided the floors are comfortable and not blocked by furniture; they find floors more touchable than walls. Allocate available funds first for the purchase of good flooring materials; tables and chairs are easily improvised at lower cost. Using the floor as furniture has the following advantages:

- **Movement and Control.** Encouraging children to use the floor as a sitting and play surface is a critical means of controlling their movement and effecting a successful room plan: On the floor children's energy is reduced. Because they are not traversing space, their actions are less distracting and perceptible. The energy expenditure required to go from floor-sitting to standing as opposed to chair-sitting to standing means that once children are down low, they tend to stay there.
- **Flexibility.** Use of the floor as a play surface reduces the amount of furniture required, especially chairs, and makes an area more flexible. It allows children to expand or contract space at will; and they need not shout across furniture to communicate.
- **Broadened Field of Vision.** Playing on the floor enables children to adjust their viewing height and field of vision by sitting or kneeling. Since young children focus more on parts than on the whole, a broader field of vision enables them to take in more at a glance and overcome a developmental limitation.
- **Productivity.** The floor helps create a more tranquil, productive group room—especially for playing with small unit blocks, small construction toys, and manipulative materials—so long as physical boundaries (such as storage units and partitions) control circulation across the playing surface.
- **Versatility.** The floor plane can be manipulated to create pits, platforms, wavy floors, ramps, and steps, all of which increase area definition and provide opportunities for movement. Floors and other horizontal surfaces can be lowered or raised; hard or soft; textured or smooth; solid or slatted; flat, inclined, or undulating. They can be made of natural or man-made materials, including water and air mattresses, sacks of beanbag pellets, trampolines, nets, suspension bridges, etc. (See also Chapter 15.)

The floor can also provide:

- **Spatial Definition:** Since child-sight lines are close to the floor, children experience the greatest definition and organization of space at floor level. Changes in the level, and in the color and texture of flooring materials help to define circulation paths, zones of the building, and zones within the group rooms.
- **Varied Textures:** Hard and soft flooring materials provide experiences with different textures. However, all changes in texture need to be seamless and smooth, to eliminate possibilities of stumbling. Surface changes must not impede the movement of wheelchairs, wheeled and pull toys, and other devices through the room, across the different floor surfaces.

Carpet on platforms and walls adds coziness and sound absorption to a unit block area. (The Copper House)

- **Changes in Level:** Changes in floor level such as platforms, risers, and lofts are valuable for the spatial-definition and varied movement opportunities they provide. (See Chapter 15.) Most platforms require boundaries: storage units, rails, walls. Platforms 4–6 inches high involving only one step need a clear demarcation of level change where the child steps off, such as a different texture or color at the edge.
- **Sound Absorption and Resilience:** Because group rooms are active places, sound absorption is highly desirable, especially in quiet areas. Carpet serves this functon well. The thicker the carpet and pad, the more the acoustic benefits achieved. Carpeting (provided it meets code), can also be placed on walls, and/or extended up walls from the floor, to increase sound absorption and feelings of coziness, particularly in quiet play, small block, and reading areas.
- **Warmth:** Radiant-floor heat (which is not blocked by most carpets) is the best way to ensure that floors are kept warm at the level where children spend most of their time. This is especially true for infant rooms. (See Chapter 8.)
- **A Surface for Wheeled Toys:** Where there is likelihood of children using wheeled toys indoors, it is best to provide a smooth, hard floor surface: vinyl, linoleum, wood, tile, or sometimes low-pile carpet.

Choices of Flooring Material

Interior flooring materials fall into five general categories: carpet, vinyl resilient flooring and linoleum, ceramic tile and concrete, wood, and area rugs. The choice of material depends on the activities it needs to support and whether children will sit on the floor surface.

Carpet

Carpet, especially if it has some depth or tuft, is one of the primary ways to ensure there is softness in a room and to make it comfortable for children to sit on the floor. As discussed in Chapter 7, children's group rooms are best zoned for quiet and active areas, both of which benefit from a carpeted surface. The carpet can be a large loose piece (bound and tacked down at the edges), or it can be permanently installed.

Carpeting allows infants to learn skills safely and comfortably.

Installed carpet is sometimes the only way to guarantee some soft floor surface in a room.

Carpeting is especially important in infant rooms, where babies spend a great deal of time on the floor learning to sit, crawl, and walk. With a thick pad, it is also valuable in cushioning the falls of young toddlers. The greater probability of food and urine spills does not rule out the use of carpet in infant and toddler rooms, provided it is a good-quality carpet that cleans easily.

Factors to consider in selecting carpet include fiber type and durability, pile, backing, padding, glues required for installation (see Chapter 8), color (Chapter 12), weave, pattern, stain resistance, ease and type of cleaning required, ability to lessen static electricity, moisture and mildew resistance, antimicrobial properties, ability to minimize friction of wheeled vehicles, and ability to support small building materials.

Carpet Fiber.[3] Carpets vary in durability based upon their fiber content. One hundred percent olefin-based carpets are soft but do not hold up well; the friction of just dragging items across the floor can sometimes cause them to melt. One hundred percent polyester carpets tend to "pill" and do not hold up well in heavily trafficked areas. Nylon carpets, blends with a predominance of nylon, and natural fibers are the most durable. Nylon carpets should have a minimum of 26-ounce face weight and should have a "continuous filament" to avoid the fluffing off of fiber.

Pile. Generally speaking, carpet with a cut pile, or a cut and loop pile, is more desirable than carpet with a loop pile because it is softer and more residential in appearance. The pile needs to be dense enough to minimize the degree of "smiling"—exposure of the backing when the carpet is bent. This is especially important where carpet will be used to wrap risers, steps, and platforms.

Because of cost and cleanliness, there is an unfortunate tendency to use very flat carpets in child care. This reduces the carpet's softness and touchability and adds an institutional quality to the space. Good-quality, thick, dense carpet is well worth the investment. It will not have to be replaced as frequently, will better withstand wear and tear, and responds as well as thinner carpet to cleaning,[4] provided the appropriate machine—dry or wet vacuum—is used. Children can build with blocks and manipulatives on a thick carpet, so long as it is dense and firm. Although expensive, wool carpets are preferable to synthetics because they are more durable and do not off-gas. However, many new synthetic carpets are now being controlled for off-gassing and soil resistance.

Construction

Carpets are generally constructed in one of three ways: woven, tufted, or fusion-bonded (Figure 13. 1). Woven carpets may offer greater styling latitude and

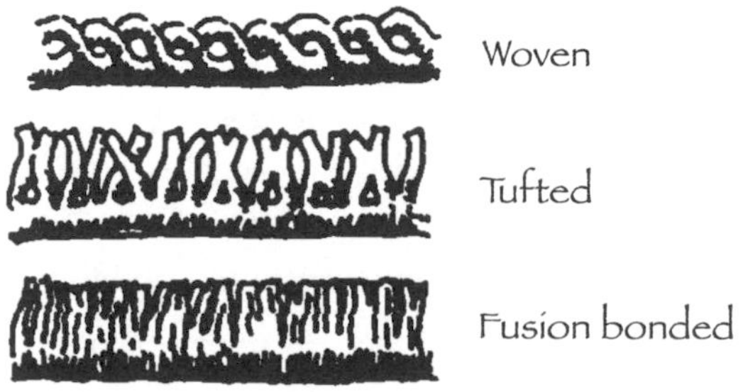

Figure 13.1
Three common types of carpet construction.

increased stability, but they are usually more expensive. Good-quality tufted carpets also provide excellent performance. Fusion-bonded tiles are made by fusing the pile tuft into a resinous compound. This results in a greater percentage of the pile yarn being exposed on the wear surface rather than tufted into the backing, so the carpet is likely to wear out faster.

Backing/Padding/Glues. A carpet's backing and padding are as important to consider as its pile. The glues used to lay most carpets are a latex-based product the emits fumes and can be quite toxic; investigate products that are water-based.[5] Newer vinyl cushion-backed, moisture-resistant carpets requiring no glue or pads because they are self-adhesive, are often excellent; many of these are washed in the same way a vinyl floor is washed, using a wet vacuum cleaner. They are extremely stain-, germ-, and mildew-resistant.[6]

Carpet laid over concrete without sufficient padding is a real danger to children, as it provides practically no resilience or protection in a fall, while the softness of the surface leads them to expect to be cushioned. Make sure that pads are of natural materials (CFC-free foam pads or recycled pads, felted wool, jute or synthetic jute) free of pesticide residues. Avoid synthetic foams because of their toxicity if burned.[7]

Squares versus Sheet Goods. Where a high degree of soilage is expected, carpet squares may be preferred to sheet goods because individual squares can be replaced. However, squares must be carefully laid to assure that their edges do not show or start curling—a great temptation to tiny fingers!

Natural Fiber Floor Coverings. Also consider natural-fiber floor coverings such as coir, sisal, and reed for areas of the building such as hallways and staircases where durability, but not softness, is desired.

Vinyl Resilient Flooring and Linoleum

Toilet areas and messy zones, which involve the use of paints, water, sand, etc., call for an easily cleanable floor surface that is not slippery when wet. Most vinyl resilient flooring, in the form of sheet goods or tiles (VRT)—10 or 12 inches square—meets this requirement well, especially if it has a matte finish. Vinyl tiles vary in hardness, resilience, and durability. Inquire about the adhesives required to lay particular products and the extent to which these may off-gas. Since red paints stain the most, consider testing flooring samples with that color.

An alternative to VRT is linoleum, a natural material made from linseed oil, cork, tree resin, wood flour, clay pigments, and a jute backing, now available in attractive colors and patterns. Linoleum floors are extremely comfortable underfoot but may require unique maintenance.[8]

As discussed in Chapter 12, always select flooring materials with some mottling, stippling, or fleck, rather than solid colors, which show every stain, scratch, and scuff mark. Subdued patterns that do not draw attention to themselves are preferable to dominant and geometric designs, which add visual confusion and tend to make a room appear smaller.

Ceramic Tile and Concrete

In some locations harder, more water-impenetrable flooring materials than VRT and linoleum may be desirable.

Small Ceramic Tiles. Because of their high grout-to-tile ratio, 1-inch-square ceramic tiles are not very slippery, and may be desirable in wet play bays, which need a more water-impenetrable surface than do table-top art activities, which can take place on VRT or linoleum. These tiles, frequently used around swimming pools, come in a wide variety of colors, with a matte (less slippery) or glazed finish. More affordable neutral colors can be interspersed with chromatic tiles for a pleasing and colorful effect.[9]

Large Ceramic Tiles. Large (12–14 inches square) tiles in terracotta and earth tones make excellent flooring for heavily trafficked areas, such as corridors and a building's entry, where their effect is more residential and durable than VRT. In a matte finish, this tile usually is not too slippery for children wearing wet boots down corridors. However, it is much too slippery around water-play areas. (See Chapter 21.)

Concrete. An interesting and less expensive alternative to large ceramic tiles is poured, colored, and scored concrete. Amenable to a variety of finishing techniques, concrete:

- Can be scored in custom patterns, as opposed to uniformly shaped tiles
- Can be embedded with stones, mosaics, and other materials
- Can be scored and sanded to make it more slip-resistant
- Lends itself to having paths and patterns designed into it. This might be appropriate where one wish-

One-inch square chromatic tiles scattered among neutral-colored ones provide an attractive nonslip surface for bathrooms and wet play areas. (The Copper House, toddler room)

es to denote a special entry—say, to the children's spaces—or to create an enticing path through a larger space for children to follow.

Wood

Natural Wood. Wood floors are resilient, residential, easy to clean and maintain, sanitary, and beautiful. However, they are expensive. They may also not be the best choice of material for messy play zones where the object is to allow children to experiment and make a mess rather than constrain them for fear of damaging the floor. Wood floors are highly appropriate in communal areas, living rooms, offices, staff areas, and indoor gymnasiums. Wood floors need an impermeable polyurethane finish, and some require waxing or refinishing from time to time.[10] Ideally, use wood from sustainable harvests.

Synthetic Wood. There is a certain attractiveness to the newer vinyl-impregnated wood floors which are more maintenance-free, without splinters, and unlikely to warp. But, because of their synthetic surface, they do not feel or sound like wood when walked upon, especially those of inferior quality. The desirability of having a floor that looks like wood needs to be weighed against the lack of authenticity of synthetic materials that do not perform like "the real McCoy."

Area Rugs

Area rugs are unattached carpets laid on top of wood, vinyl, tile, or larger wall-to-wall carpet surfaces. Generally, area rugs are textured or patterned, or both. Many require pads, and they must be secured by double-sided tape if they slide when stepped upon. Area rugs are an effective and delightful way to define space, and add visual variety and softness to rooms and corridors.[11]

Ceilings

What's up there refers to fire, smoke, bad air, loud noise, theft, accidents, and the repairman. It's a covering for wires, cables, tubes, ducts, immediately accessible for maintenance. . . not for pleasure of use, but for occasions

Area rugs help define space while adding softness and visual appeal. (The Copper House, school-age room)

GUIDELINES: FLOORING MATERIALS

- The floor is furniture in child care centers. Making floors warm and inviting has many physical and programmatic benefits.
- All flooring material and carpeting must meet local fire codes. Class A ratings meet the most stringent standards.
- Purchase flooring materials in sufficient quantities to have a backup supply for replacing damaged areas, and for covering surfaces such as platforms and risers, which may be added later.
- Carpet is a valuable means of introducing softness (a prime indicator of center quality) into children's spaces.
- Good-quality, thick, dense carpet is more durable and responds better to cleaning than thinner carpets of lesser quality. Cut piles are more residential than loop piles.
- Vinyl-backed "peel and stick" carpets, which are 100% washable, are ideal for children's group rooms. Installation of carpet squares, as opposed to sheet goods, sometimes facilitates replacement of heavily soiled areas.
- Installed carpet assures some softness in a room. Large remnants of scrap or mill-end carpets, bound at the edges, can be used to delineate areas in the quiet and active zones, if installed carpet is not desired.
- Consider both vinyl resilient flooring (a synthetic material) and linoleum (a natural material) for messy play zones.
- One-inch-square ceramic tiles can create a nonslippery, water-resistent surface in wet play bays.
- Large ceramic tiles (12–14 inches square) are slippery in wet areas but excellent for high-use entries and corridors. Scored and colored concrete is equally durable, resists slipping, and lends itself to custom artistic treatment.
- Ensure that any adhesives used for laying flooring materials, and any scotch-guarding or stain-resistant surfactants applied to carpeting, are nontoxic.
- Always choose a carpet, tile, or linoleum that is mottled or flecked, since solid colors reveal every stain, scratch, and scuff mark. Subdued patterns and colors are preferable to dominant and geometric designs.
- Wood floors—resilient, residential, beautiful, and easy to clean—are often ideal in common areas, living rooms, offices, staff areas, and indoor gyms.
- Identify places in corridors and rooms where area rugs of unique pattern and texture can help define a space, add softness, and distinction.

> of breakdown . . . You do not want to raise your eyes to look into fluorescent fixtures or the bright bulb in the track lighting can. You keep your head down—a depressive posture, an outlook limited to the horizontal, the downward stare.[12]

In ancient architecture, ceilings were given as much attention as walls, floors, and doors. Their height and contour symbolized upliftment of the human spirit and connection to the divine. Only in modern institutional settings has the ceiling's aesthetic and symbolic significance been ignored.

Planning Ceiling Treatments

Suspended ceilings with synthetic grids and fluorescent lights are a sure mark of an institution. Since ceilings are often tied into the mechanical and electrical systems for the entire building, if a residential feel is desired, the finish and shape of the ceilings will require special consideration early in the design process and some major design decisions. When wiring and ductwork can be placed in the walls rather than the ceiling, the ceiling can be designed as a pleasing feature of the environment. Where budgets, codes, and fire-regulations permit, the homelike feel of plaster and wood ceilings, and exposed beams, is far preferable to suspended ceilings with grids. (For an example, see Chapter 2, page 22).

An octagonal-shaped ceiling is graced by wood detailing and recessed lighting. (The Copper House, infant room)

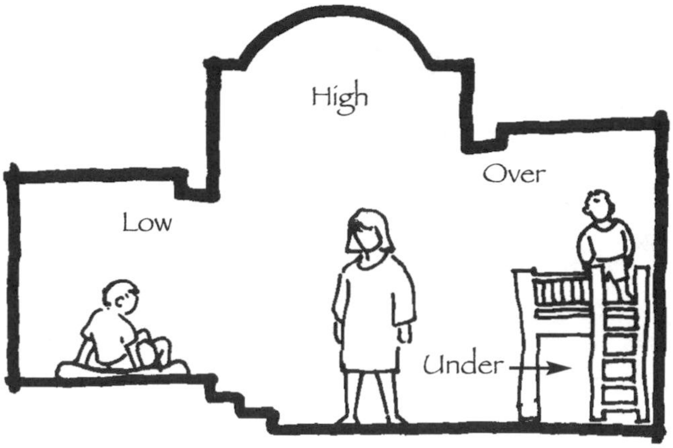

Figure 13.9
High, low, over, under: variations in ceiling and floor height provide different perspectives, levels of intimacy, and spatial relationships for children.

Ceiling Height Variation

Conventional wisdom suggests that low ceilings make for intimacy, high ceilings for formality. But what matters more than absolute height is some ceiling height variation within the child care center and its rooms to vary the quality of children's experience (Figure 13.2). Varying ceiling heights also helps modulate a room's acoustics.

The height of a ceiling should support the desired social distances between the people using the space. The higher the ceiling, the more distant people seem from each other. Therefore, ceilings might be higher in very small rooms or narrow corridors, and lower in places where more intimate social interaction is desired. In the group rooms, three or four ceiling heights, corresponding to the social interactions and energy levels of the four zones (Chapter 7), are desirable. For example, the entry zone might be around 8 feet high, the messy and active zones 9–12 feet high, the quiet zone 8–10 feet high. Small alcoves without doors might have ceilings as low as 6–7 feet.

Ceilings can be especially useful in child care centers to suspend play devices, swings, trapezes, mobiles, decorations, banners, and basket chairs. As shown on the next page, a ceiling of wooden slats 6–8 inches apart extending over a portion of the room or over specific play areas can facilitate suspension of objects where they are desired. An alternative is to mount a single beam, in an appropriate location, to support some of these needs (see beam locations on floorplans of the Husky infant and school-age rooms in Chapters 16 and 18). In spaces without much floor-level variation, being able to suspend fabric, plants, and art work from the ceiling can have strong aesthetic and acoustical impact on a room (page 240).

The ceiling height over the messy play zone (left, not visible) curves from 9 to 11 feet; that over the quiet area (right) is at 10 feet.
(The Copper House, preschool room)

Wooden slats spaced at 6–8 inches over part of the ceiling, permit suspension of objects and equipment.

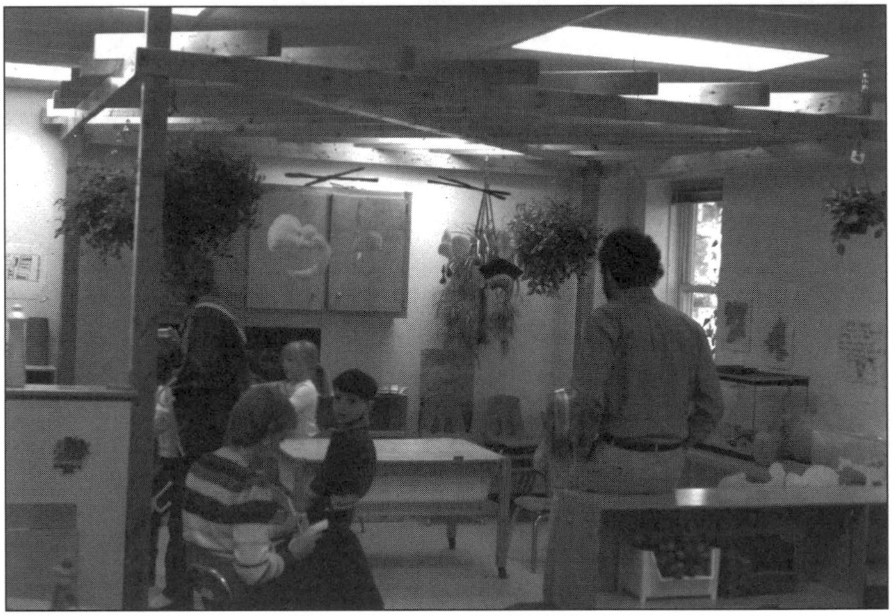

A wood trellis adds beauty and spatial definition to a large preschool room.

Walls

Walls play an important role in the function and beauty of a child care center. In addition to providing visual and acoustical separation, walls need to work as storage, display, write-on, and interactive surfaces. Interior walls that are thin or poorly insulated reduce both the acoustic privacy of adjoining spaces and the sense of secure enclosure they are meant to provide. Where appropriate, explore ways to enliven walls by varying their thickness, shape, and surfacing with materials such as wood, brick, tile, stone, and stucco, or special artistic treatment. In contrast to the flat, nondescript quality of the drywall often used in modern architecture, varied materials and detailing can give walls liveliness. Hand-plastering creates a beautiful, uniquely hand-crafted effect (page 242). Tints can be added to the wet plaster before application, to preclude surface painting and papering. (See Chapter 12 for a discussion of wall color.)

Although the presence of children's messy hands demands that walls be cleanable, not all wall surfaces need to be flat and shiny. Give careful consideration to the sheen of wall surfaces and to ways in which walls

A tie-dyed banner lowers the ceiling over a quiet area.

GUIDELINES: CEILINGS

- Ceiling design is an important contributor to the spirit of a place. Suspended ceilings with 2-x-4 grids are rarely used residentially; they are a sure mark of an institution.
- Wherever possible, vary ceiling heights to signal changes in space use and different levels of intimacy, to provide variety and area definition, and to vary the quality of light and sound. In narrow corridors and small rooms, a high ceiling can minimize feelings of entrapment. Group rooms benefit from two to four different ceiling heights corresponding to the activity levels of the four zones.
- Shaping the ceiling can help to define the space below. A vaulted ceiling creates a "center" and "edges" to the activites which lie below it.
- The number and style of ceiling apertures—skylights, clerestories, balconies, mezzanines, and overhangs—also can be varied.
- Consider varying ceiling materials—for example, using plaster, wood, mosaic tile, stucco, and stained glass. Ceiling treatment is especially important where children are lying down and looking up (infants).
- If using acoustical tiles, carefully consider their texture in relation to the size of the room. Highly stippled surfaces can make small, low ceiling spaces feel claustrophobic.
- A change in ceiling height coupled with a change in ceiling material is particularly powerful in creating a unique "place."
- Where cost is a factor, creative use of banners can vary ceiling heights and afford aesthetic interest (see left, and also page 234).

can enliven a space by reflecting, shadowing, or playing with the light cast upon them. However, too many flat, shiny surfaces create an unpleasant, institutional feel.

Simple treatments applied to the edges and boundaries of walls, corners, door frames, and windows can help to unify an entire facility. Interesting effects can also be achieved by running floor materials, especially carpet, up walls, or by placing wall materials, such as wood paneling, over ceilings to integrate horizontal and vertical surfaces.

Wall Finishes: Paint versus Vinyl

Designers often debate whether paint or vinyl wall covering is the best surface treatment for turning standard gypsum wallboard into an appropriate surface for child care. Each has virtues and disadvantages. It is also possible to combine the two—i.e., paint above, and a more durable finish on lower, more vulnerable wall areas.

Attributes of Paint

- Economical, easy to apply, simple to change.
- Generally not toxic once dry.
- Reasonably washable in eggshell, semigloss, and gloss finishes; flat or matte paint finishes should not be used in areas where hands might touch a wall.
- Easily chipped and marred by movable equipment (carriages, strollers, carts). Can be "touched up," but time is rarely available. Some extremely durable new paints are offered in a variety of colors and textures.[13]
- Infinite variety of color choices (see Chapter 12).

Hand-plastering gives walls a uniquely textured, vibrant, and appealing effect.

Attributes of Vinyl

- Somewhat costly and complex to install initially (requires wall preparation), but its durability may make it less expensive in the long run.
- Manufactured in varying grades of thickness and durability, in a wide range of colors, with varied textures and surface patterns.
- Usually washable, regardless of surface texture.
- Can be coated to resist ballpoint pen, crayon, lipstick, and other indelible substances.
- Vinyls and their adhesives off-gas; vinyls contribute to a synthetic, inauthentic, institutional atmosphere.
- Difficult and costly to remove.
- In locations receiving repeated abuse, even heavy vinyl wall coverings usually last only slightly longer than paint. Preferable are more durable surfaces such as wood, brick, or carpet.

Bumper Guards, Corner Moldings, and Rails

Bumper guards, corner moldings, and/or rails may be needed in high-use areas. As visually prominent institutional elements, they need to be attractive and will appear more integral to the entire design if made to coordinate with other horizontal elements in the architecture. Some points on their use:

- Make guards of wood rather than metal, for a more residential feel.
- Place bumper guards at floor level to be less conspicuous.
- Use handrails, with their surfaces scored for grippability, for greater protection. These can double as handrails for children with disabilities and people in wheelchairs.

Walls as Program Supports

There are many ways to use a room's existing walls as truly functional supports for a child care program (see Chapters 15–18).

Building off walls horizontally, at different heights and depths, can create seats, tables, counters, shelving, high and low platforms, and sloping work surfaces (Figure 13.3).

Figure 13.3
Seats, tables, counters, platforms, and sloping work surfaces can be created by building horizontally off walls or partitions.

A "functional" wall separating an infant and a toddler room.

Resilient sheet materials can create display walls even on curved surfaces. (The Copper House, preschool room)

In some instances, instead of building a gypsum wall to separate two spaces, it may be worth considering making the wall "functional" by incorporating structures and changes in level such as platforms, stairs, slides, diaper-changing tables, and interactives into the wall on both sides.

In addition to full-height walls, partitions two-to-three-feet high can also provide children with a sense of protection and enclosure, while not interfering with adults' ability to see into the area. Similar to walls, properly designed partitions can support play panels, vertically mounted toys, grab bars, textures, display and write-on surfaces, easels, mirrors, and reflective materials at varying heights.

Walls for Display

There is a great need in child care for walls that can display children's work, documentation, educational materials, signs, notices, interactives, fire and safety information, etc. Large expanses of display surface—literally, entire walls—in corridors, group rooms, and staff areas are preferable functionally and aesthetically to traditional bulletin boards. Some recommended surface materials include Forbo, Homosote, and cork:

- **Forbo:** A natural, nontoxic, self-sealing, resilient linoleum sheet material available in many attractive colors. Costly initially, but cost-efficient in the long run because of its durability and self-sealing properties when tacks and staples are removed. Impact-resistant, with excellent acoustical properties, and easy to install even on curved surfaces.
- **Homosote:** A recycled paper panel that comes in 4-x-8-foot sheets. Some varieties are fire-rated. Provides acoustical insulation. Can be painted and sealed with polyurethane, purchased with a burlap finish, or placed under vinyl wall covering to create a longer-lasting tackable wall surface. Needs periodic replacement due to tack and staple holes which remain (see page 244). (Also works well on the backs of storage units.)
- **Cork:** More expensive than homosote. Available in sheets or tiles in different textures, thicknesses, and colors. Provides acoustic insulation.

Tackable surfaces the size of full walls are very useful.

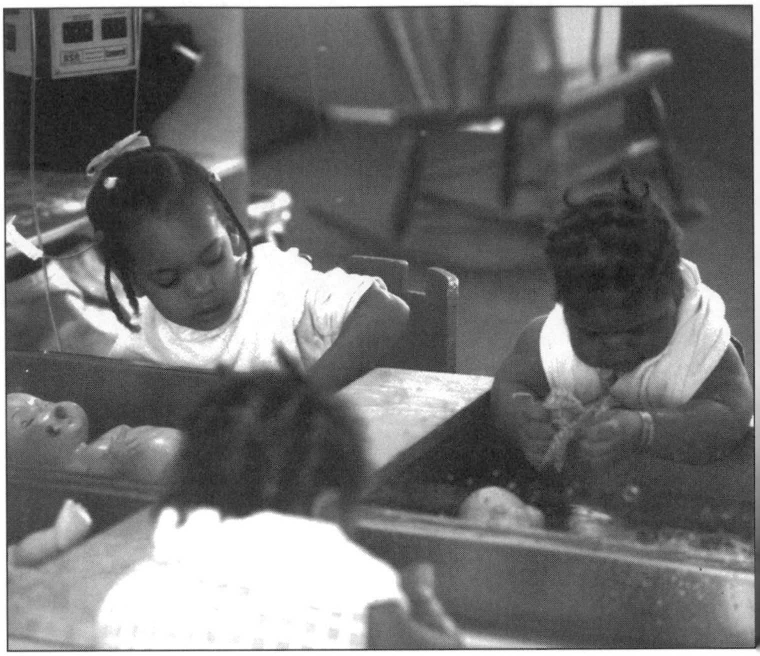

When children face a wall to play, mirrors can make them feel more secure by revealing what is going on behind them.

These display surfaces will accept tape and staples, which are preferable to tacks for children's safety. Velcro and felt-type materials, and self-adhesive products with soft textures are also useful. Magnetic boards are appropriate for certain purposes but can be cold if used over large areas.

Mirrors

Mirrors of various sizes and shapes are educational and intriguing for children. They can add depth to a wall or space, and assist with transit down long corridors. Every group room benefits from some mirrors at child height for fun and to assist in the development of self-concept.

- Mirrors of tempered glass are best. These provide a true image, do not scratch, and are durable and shatterproof.
- Plastic mirrors are not recommended.[14] They are difficult to hang flat without distortion, and they scratch and cloud easily, becoming unattractive over time.

Mirrors can be educational and fun.

GUIDELINES: WALLS

- Consider enlivening walls in selected locations by the addition of wood, stucco, tile, stone, carpet, cork, and brick to enhance their color and tactile qualities.
- Consider glass and glass block walls, in limited quantities, where acoustic, but not visual, separation is desired.
- Textures on walls help control sound, clue boundaries, assist in way-finding and area definition (as do texture and color changes on floors).
- Cinder block walls are discouraged because of their abrasiveness, unfinished feel, and institutional look.
- Curved walls or curved portions of a wall can break the monotony of straight lines and invite people into a space. This is especially effective in public areas: corridors, stairwells, entrances, and around corners. Use of curved walls in group rooms needs to be carefully evaluated because rectangular furniture does not easily fit against a curve.
- Wood, carpet, handwoven rugs, mirrors, and mosaic tile can be added to architectural elements, such as protruding and freestanding columns, to give them softness and added interest.
- Very hard plastic surfaces[15] are sometimes useful in select areas where children will be writing, painting, or playing on walls, but are not recommended as a general surfacing material.
- Consider using wood in a variety of forms for wall surfaces, baseboards, bumper guards, and handrails.
- Cove bases at the juncture of walls and floors are another prominent design element. Choose colors and materials that match the walls to make them less prominent and reduce the institutional feel of a space.
- Half walls and partitions in children's spaces can do most things a full wall does: provide platforms, tables and seats, plant ledges, display surfaces, and facades for dramatic play. Partitions need to be stable and nonflammable and should not block any means of egress. Some states require them to be screwed or otherwise affixed to the floor. It is helpful if they have some acoustic insulation properties as well.
- A "functional" wall that incorporates changes in level and interactives is sometimes advantageous.
- Use eggshell and semigloss paint on walls children will touch. Use gloss finishes on moldings and woodwork. Reserve flat paints for adult spaces.

Hand-woven rugs add softness and interest to a structural column.

- Painted walls are inexpensive, easy to apply and change. Vinyl-covered walls provide a slightly more durable surface at greater cost and with less flexibility.
- Bumper guards, corner moldings, and rails (preferably in wood to be more residential) can protect walls that receive repeated abuse from carts and carriages.
- Provide plenty of display space in group rooms and corridors by covering large portions or entire walls with materials such as forbo, homosote, cork, velcro, or fabrics capable of receiving tape and staples.
- Mirrors of tempered glass, but not plastic, located at child-height, resist scratching and clouding.

- Where mirrors are installed to prevent collisions around corners and difficult-to-see places, plan their location in advance so they become integral to the architecture.
- Commercial curved and domed mirrors are less appealing than custom ones because of their association with antitheft precautions in retail stores.
- Use "fun" mirrors advisedly and only with staff assistance. Certain distortions can confuse young children, especially those with special needs.

Signs and Art

Signs and artwork are usually affixed to walls and so are discussed in this context.

Signs

Because the presence of signs clearly denotes an institution, the fewer the signs, the more residential and intimate the setting. As prominent visual elements, the design of signs needs to be part of the entire interior plan, not an afterthought. Signs can powerfully convey information beyond their literal message, and thereby enhance moods the center wishes to encourage: efficiency, uniformity, playfulness, welcome, surprise, or originality.

Mechanized sign production has made us forget the powerful way in which hand-constructed signs of wood, rope, glass, etc., create personalized images. If custom-design is not possible, signs can still be made more aesthetically appealing and effective through choice of typeface, size, and material contrast (wood on wood, metal on brick, paint on wood).

The number of signs often increases in proportion to the size of a facility, and the absence of architectural way-finding cues. The need for signage is minimized when the building is easy to read—i.e., its physical spaces (identified by landmarks, columns, walls, and effective use of lighting) are congruent with its social

Interactives at child-height help children to feel welcome.

A hand-constructed sign gives this center a personalized and memorable image.

spaces. Strive to incorporate code-required signs, such as "Exit," with sensitivity.

Since young children often do not respond to the same cues as adults, orientation devices at child height are desirable. Objects to spin, buttons to push, something to touch, a sequence of photographs of children or animals, all help to welcome and orient young ones.

GUIDELINES: SIGNS

- In a well-designed facility, architectural and interior design treatments support way-finding and a sense of place. Users need not rely on signs and artwork alone for orientation.
- Minimize the use of signs. Place them perpendicular to the line of transit, at predictable intervals, so newcomers quickly become oriented in the building and stay "on course."
- Signs hung from above create the illusion of a lower ceiling, serve to break up a long corridor, and are easily seen by adults. (See page 101).
- Poor lighting, excessive glare, and competing colors and finishes nearby reduce sign effectiveness.
- Children can interpret signs employing logos and symbols, such as a crawling baby, a preschooler catching a ball, or the outline of a boy or girl.
- Where possible and appropriate, make signs visible to children as well as adults.
- Signs with friendly wording—in more than one language in centers used by multiple ethnic groups—make people feel more welcome.
- Use a unique sign or logo to distinguish children's areas, particularly in multiuse facilities, or to mark routes to designated children's activities.

Art

The role of art is to complement and enhance an already beautiful and varied building by deepening its character and aliveness. The use of graphics "palliatively"—to camouflage an unattractive interior—is recommended only as a last resort. Large painted murals depicting popular children's characters tend to be "cutesy"and not really child-oriented. They lock a space into a particular style and eliminate flexible use of its walls.

Graphic art can definitely assist with orientation in corridors and public spaces. Since people tend to establish temporary "goals" or landmarks as they traverse a given path, a graphic can serve this purpose and reinforce existing architectural markers. By identifying these places early in the design process, ceiling heights, lighting, and furnishings can be further coordinated with the graphics to maximize their impact.

If located on walls parallel to the user's line of movement, large, unique graphics with very little detail (such as a large cat or flying bird) have the greatest orientational power. (See page 100, top).Those who become lost in the building will recognize the territory because of the graphic's boldness and uniqueness. Distinctiveness can be achieved using any medium: traditional paintings, mosaics, banners, three-dimensional art, or photographs (perhaps depicting the history of the building or community, and activities and persons within it). A variety of media and shapes is desirable.

Thoughtfully framed and mounted artwork reflects a center's attention to detail and commitment to care. (The Copper House)

Wall niches can hold artifacts for people's enjoyment. (The Copper House)

This graphic promotes anticipation of the corridor's change in direction.

The aesthetics and symbolism inherent in art can nourish children's souls by providing them with images of wholeness, community, and self-worth. A child care center need not acquire a collection of master works, but rather provide a consistent and well-planned approach for exposing children to inspiring works of art: lithographs and silkscreen prints; original oil, acrylic, and watercolor paintings; fabric and soft sculpture; photographs; mosaics; sculpture; metal work; and other art forms. Thoughtful display of children's own artwork also is important.[16]

To display art requires planning and intention. Giving each piece appropriate mounting and its own mat and frame, however modest, reflects a center's overall attention to detail and commitment to care. As the interior is outfitted, wall areas that can benefit from artistic treatment will become apparent. Art can then be selected in themes, sizes, and hues to complement the interior color scheme. Even buildings of rather standard design can be transformed by beautiful artwork.

GUIDELINES: ART

- Graphic art can be whimsical and appealing without being childish. Avoid Disney, TV, and standardized fairy tale characters, which tend to be "cutesy" and are often used to make a place appear child-oriented when everything else is not. Adult attempts to make something childlike are never the same as children's own artwork.
- Movable graphics allow for flexibility. "Supergraphics" painted directly on walls lock the center into a particular image.
- Rhythmic or wavy patterns may cause perceptual confusion and should be avoided.
- Unique orientational graphics, which create strong identification images and assist in way-finding can enhance and bind together the aesthetic appearance of a building. Artwork that begins on the outside of a building can continue inside: for example, wall motifs and banners on the exterior might be repeated, perhaps with different details, down an interior hallway.
- Graphics placed perpendicular to the flow of traffic, which are approached head-on or where people can pause to study them, can be less bold and more detailed. A particularly effective means of foreshortening a long, monotonous corridor is to place an eye-catching graphic at its terminus. If the corridor turns a corner, a graphic at the intersection helps people anticipate the change of direction.
- Mirrors, alone or in combination with other elements, can be effective graphic devices.
- Reserve a portion of the architectural and interior design budget for artwork.

Interactive art at child-height.

- Complement the beauty of artwork with properly focused lighting for an effective display.
- Emphasize variety, flexibility, and forethought in the choice of decorative art. Art can be two- or three-dimensional, textured or smooth, interactive or abstractly decorative. Display it respectfully—i.e., appropriately mounted, framed, and hung.
- Mobiles, kites, banners, tapestries, and soft sculpture hung from the walls and ceilings provide wonderful visual interest.
- Ethnic art and craft have high child-appeal, great educational value, and honor diversity in a simple way.
- Art that portrays nature and animals appeals to everyone.
- Include works created by the children. Consider enlarging some of these by projecting a slide of a child's drawing on a large piece of paper, tracing it, and then recoloring it. Also have children decorate removable panels with chalk, magic markers, or paint.
- Consider interactive art or works with various textures.
- Framed posters and prints of important artists (Matisse, Picasso, Cassatt) can introduce great art at modest cost. It is also possible to rent or borrow works of original art from local museums or art galleries.
- Give spaces that children frequent on a regular basis a sense of change and renewed interest by periodically rotating, or even temporarily removing, the artwork.

Children can be introduced to great art at modest cost with posters and prints.

Notes

[1]Quote taken from A. Lawlor, *The Temple in the House* (New York: Tarcher/Putnam, 1994), 135.

[2]Elizabeth Prescott and Thomas G. David, "Concept Paper on the Effects of the Physical Environment on Day Care" (Pasadena, CA: Pacific Oaks College, 1976).

[3]Cindy V. Beacham of Odyssey Design Group provided invaluable assistance with portions of this chapter.

[4]Gretchen Lee Anderson, *Removing Barriers to Childcare Facilities Development* (California State University, Northridge, CA, 1993). She reports that worn-out carpeting, needing to be replaced after only two to three years, was a problem in many centers.

[5]For sources see: David Pearson, *The Natural House Catalog* (New York: Simon & Schuster, 1996).

[6]Such carpets, manufactured by Collins and Aikman, were used for the Copper House. The thick backing can make the carpet difficult, although not impossible, to wrap around risers.

[7]Also consider 100% hair underfelt, available from Colin Campbell, Vancouver, which is thermally efficient and flame-retardant, suitable for any surface and for both residential and industrial applications.

[8]DLW linoleum, PA was used in all the art areas of the Copper House.

[9]This approach was used in the wet-play bays of the Copper House.

[10]Consider nontoxic *Os* natural oil-based, microporous waxes from Germany, sold throughout North America.

[11]In the Copper House, a 9-×-12-foot Gabbeh area rug was used as the carpet for the living room. A similar rug was used for the quiet area of the school-age space, and in the sitting area of the lobby. Smaller, inexpensive area rugs from India and Scandinavia, ranging from 2-×-4 to 3-×-8 feet, were used as highlights in each of the children's group spaces, as part of a sitting area in the corridor, and as runners in heavily trafficked portions of the hallways.

[12]James Hillman, "One Man's Ceiling is Another Man's Horror," in *Utne Reader* (Feb/March, 1985), 104–107.

[13]Zolotone.

[14]Lexan mirrors and panels are more durable and scratch resistant than Plexiglas.

[15]Such as *Acrovyn* and plastic laminates.

[16]The Italian schools of Reggio Emilia, which specialize in having children work in a variety of media from a very young age, are replete with extraordinary examples of children's representations.

CHAPTER FOURTEEN

FURNISHINGS

Consciously and unconsciously, expressing ourselves in our environment lets us see who we are and helps us shape who we become. Our choices and arrangements of furniture, the things we put on our walls, the music we play, the colors we select, and the ways we use each room all give us messages, reinforcing our beliefs about ourselves.

—CAROL VENOLIA[1]

Appropriate furnishings—furniture, fabrics, cabinetry, and accessories—can soften and personalize an otherwise institutional design. Inappropriate furnishings, on the other hand, can detract from even an excellent design. Since children, staff, and families come in contact with furnishings more directly than with any other element of the child care environment, their importance cannot be overstated. Budget sufficient funds for furnishings and accessories at the outset.

Furnishings in child care centers are often ordered at intermittent intervals from catalogs, or obtained as hand-me-downs from a variety of sources. Attention may not be paid to their aesthetic qualities, so long as they are functional. However, in a truly integrated design, the building and its furnishings have an apparent harmony. Frank Lloyd Wright understood this so well that in some instances he designed not only the building but also the furniture, light fixtures, fabric patterns, ashtrays, and dishes that went in it.

Fully equipping a center requires much more than furniture: waste baskets, dishes, pots and pans, utensils, small and large appliances, cleaning equipment, lamps, window treatments, artwork and decorations, vases, plants and planters, umbrella stands, coat hooks and hangers, bottle warmers, bibs and bumpers, etc. A truly harmonious setting is achieved when the forms, colors, materials, and textures of all these elements, big and small, are selected in relation to one another and to the overall spirit one wishes to express.

When it comes to design, every detail matters. Child care centers do not often receive, but certainly deserve, the same attention to detail given our homes, for centers are indeed homes to hundreds of children each day. An aesthetically integrated environment—one in which color, texture, form, and light complement one another—assures children and adults that they are worthy of beauty and the finer things in life. While each staff member must be able to personalize and take ownership of his/her own group room, there also needs to be a sense of integration and unity to the center as a whole. This comes from a certain measure of uniformity of the accessories and details used throughout.

Getting Started

As discussed in Chapter 6, it is best if a preliminary furniture plan for each group room occurs at the beginning of the design process. Knowing the sizes and space requirements for all the furnishings and equipment a room needs to accommodate will help in creating the room's size, shape, adjacencies, and separations. The following suggestions are intended to help you early on and as each plan is refined and implemented.

Listing all the functional requirements (activities desired) for each room will begin to reveal the furniture and accessories needed to support those activities. For example, the activity of "painting" requires a painting surface (sloped or flat or both); a child-accessible place to store supplies of paper, paints, brushes, aprons; water for diluting paints and cleaning up; a way to secure the paper or object being painted; a place to dry and/or display the completed painting; and possibly chairs. (See Chapter 7.) Children with special needs may have additional requirements.

Once your list of functional requirements is complete for the entire room, you can use the room layout generated according to the guidelines in Chapters 7 and 15 to draw a furnishings layout on the room's plan.

The participation of staff, who can clearly delineate the full range of items required to execute a task, is crucial when designers are planning a room layout or equipping a center.

Creating an Interiors "Bible"

The furnishings layout will show the approximate location—and also the dimensions—of each item desired. In some cases, you may have a specific item in mind. In others, you may need to search for the appropriate source. In either case, once you've created a basic floor plan, use it to generate a comprehensive master list or "bible" of everything the room requires. (You may need to work back and forth between the list and the plan.) This bible is indispensable. It is the "program" for the interior's design. A sample bible page is shown below. Give each item in the bible an identification number, based perhaps on the room and areas within it. For example, IA-2 might indicate Infant Room, Art Area, item #2.

It is helpful to create two bibles: one generated by staff for learning materials (books, toys, supplies, etc.), and one for furnishings and accessories, prepared in a collaboration between staff and designers. Also create a separate binder consisting of "cut sheets" that display a visual image (sketch, catalog cut-out, or photograph) of each item, along with the item's number. The cut sheet shows the precise product to be purchased or built: its dimensions, design features, source, and cost. An example of such a cut sheet is shown on page 253. Once an approximate cost is applied to each item, the furnishings budget will be clear and priorities can be set.

The "Facilities Lists" in Chapters 16–18 identify generic furnishings for the different activity areas in group rooms, according to age.

Furnishings, Fixtures & Equipment List

Location	**Item**	**Quantity**	**P / C**	**Comments**	**Price**
Infant Room Art Area					
IA-1.	art storage unit	2	P	*Community Playthings* KA30 Multistorage Unit 14″D × 36″H × 45″L; with castors and 6 bins; 6 additional bins @ $7 ea, all bins "clear"	$470 ea
IA-2.	light table	1	P	*ABC* #067-80061 31″L × 23″W × 24″H (cut to 20″H)	$360 +$15 labor
IB-2 &3.	tables & seats		P	*see bottle prep area*	
IA-3.	messy play trays	2	P	*find source*	
IA-4.	shelves	2	C	above art storage unit; for stereo; 36″L × 14″D with turned-up ends	
IA-5.	plant container	1	P	wicker, metal, or terracotta	$50
				TOTAL	

Note: ***P****= purchase;* ***C****=custom build*
Items in ***bold*** *are to be custom designed.*
Another column may be added at right indicating who is responsible for procurement (architect, client, interior designer, etc.).

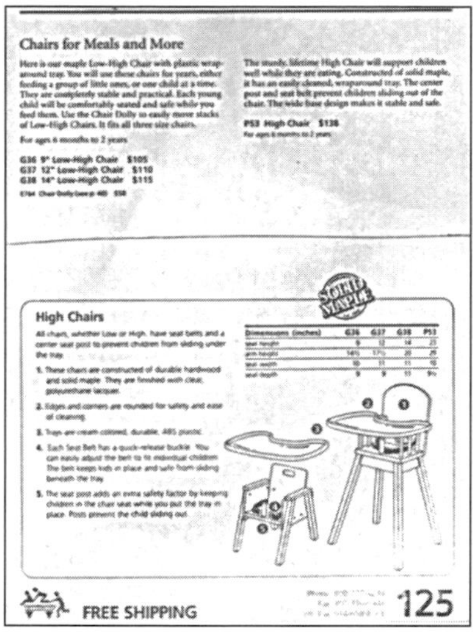

A supplier's "cut sheet" for infant feeding chairs.

The Art of Placing Furnishings

Because the success of a child care facility stands or falls on the appropriateness of its rooms' layout, Chapters 7 and 15–18 address the complexities and nuances of layout at length.[2] The following general principles, applicable to all spaces, will help to create harmony in a room:

- **Contrast:** Juxtapose opposites such as: light/dark, high/low, concave/convex, protected/exposed, plain/patterned, machine-made/hand-made, dull/shiny, hard/soft, masculine/feminine, etc. (See the six dimensions of contrast in Chapter 2, pp. 27–31.)
- **Spaciousness:** Aim for a sense of spaciousness, especially if a room is small. People and activities will easily fill it up. Emptiness gives the eye, mind, and heart an opportunity to rest. Spaciousness is achieved by keeping the furnishings small in scale, while varying their size and placement so that, similar to a composition on a canvas, there is a balance of large and small, fullness and emptiness, something and nothing, throughout the space.
- **Balance:** Introduce some balance of high and low furnishings: lofts, platforms, interior roofs, banners, cabinets, etc. Having all furnishings at child-height creates boredom and leaves the 50% of the room over children's heads empty, which in turn creates acoustic problems.
- **Parallel Placement:** For optimal use of space, place most furniture parallel to the walls; as an alternative, arrange it diagonally to the axis of the room.
- **Definement:** Place furniture on or off, but never straddling, a carpet.
- **Coordination:** Hang pictures, mirrors, bulletin boards, display frames, etc., on walls at levels that *coordinate with critical architectural lines in the room: window sills and frames, door frames, wainscoting.* Locate furniture between two window frames, never across any one. Position items to be hung on walls within the visual boundary created by the upper and lower portion of the window or door frames; or hang items consistently around the room at some height between these extremes. Design drapes, curtains, or blinds to come to the bottom of window sills, otherwise to the floor.

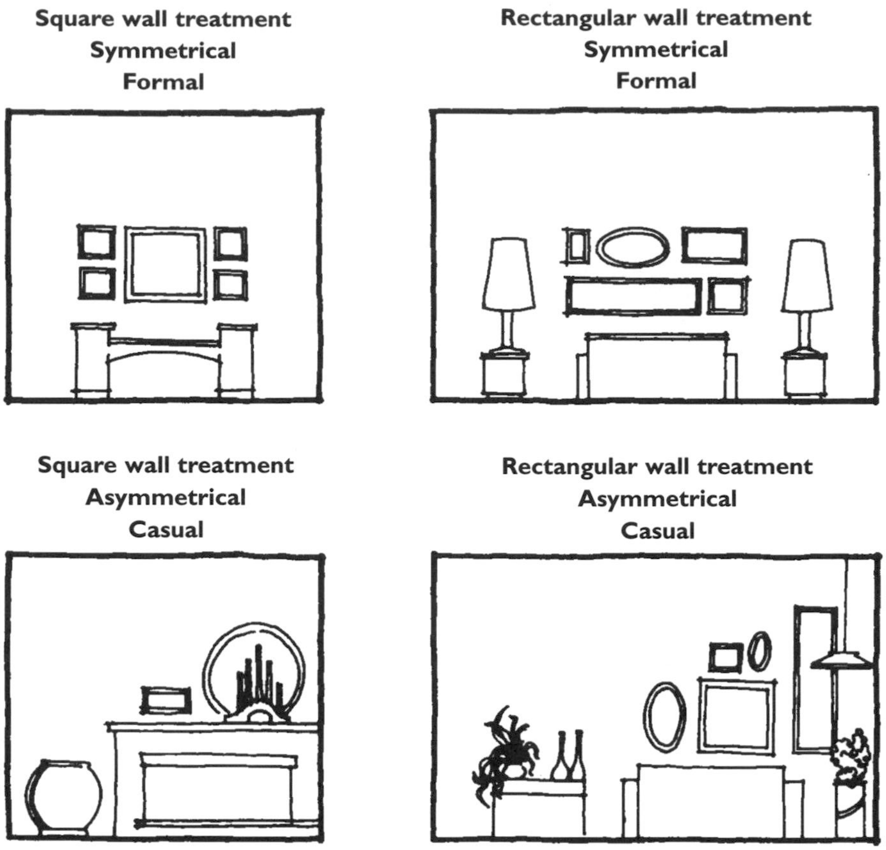

Figure 14.3
Place furniture and hang pictures and wall decorations to coordinate with the room's critical architectural lines.

- **Scale:** Furnishings that obviously dwarf the size of children, or intrude because they are too high or large, should either be modified or replaced by items of more appropriate scale. Sometimes *the placement of an object can help to minimize or magnify its size,* making it compatible with the space—e.g., placing a large cabinet against a wall makes it less obtrusive than putting it in the middle of the room. Painting an object the same or a similar hue to the wall will further diminish its optical appearance.
- **Odd Numbers:** Too many pairs make a room appear formal and rigid. This applies especially to furniture in adult spaces.
- **Variety:** Provide both flexible/movable pieces and stationary ones.
- **Subtle Color:** Because of the high level of activity in children's rooms, keep furnishings simple and subdued. Dramatic treatment is appropriate in rooms with less action, where less time is spent. (See Chapter 12 on Color.)

Furniture

Anyone who has shopped for a chair is aware of the range of choices and seemingly infinite number of options available. Aside from its appropriateness as a seat, each piece communicates a different mood and message, a unique character and spirit of place. Some invite sprawling and sinking; others demand attentiveness and rigidity. Some command; others retreat; still others are barely noticeable.

Choosing the right chair is no small matter! Chairs can be made of wood, metal, plastic, bamboo, cardboard, canvas, leather, and combinations thereof; painted or with a natural finish; with or without padding, backs, arms, legs, and sides; on wheels, rockers, three legs, four legs, or a base. Each fine point of the design merits evaluation in relation to the size, age and agility of its users, and the context in which it will be placed. Direct experience sitting in it and, ideally, the chance to examine it in the space for which it is intended, are desirable. A harmonious design, which truly honors the intended spirit of your place, calls for similar selectivity with every item of furniture.

From an aesthetic standpoint, the best way to choose new or replacement furniture is to first sit quietly with your eyes closed and envision the space in question. (VF) Allow both an image and a word or phrase to come to mind that embody the mood and spirit you wish the room to have. Then, in your mind's eye, see each piece of furniture the room requires. Allow a word or phrase to come to mind that describes the qualities of each piece. Sizes, shapes, perhaps even colors and patterns, may emerge as a "felt sense" or as complete designs. Subsequent browsing through catalogs or furniture and second-hand stores can be helpful in putting flesh and bones on these initial images and descriptions. If the room's main pieces of furniture express the intended mood, then the smaller items can be filled in gradually.

Types

Child care centers generally employ three types of furniture:

- **Commercial children's furniture.** Ready-made items such as tables, chairs, and bookcases available primarily through catalogs. Although this industry is exploding with suppliers, there is little variety in design. For ergonomic and design considerations pertaining to different ages, see the furniture specifications for each age group in Chapters 16–18.
- **Custom children's furniture.** Refers to items built to fit a specific space or situation, such as risers, waterbed platforms, and lofts. Examples created by the author, who has specialized in this area for 30 years, are explained and illustrated in Chapters 15–18. Whereas commercial suppliers usually produce "one-size fits all" items, custom design enables the scale and shape of the furnishings to fit the dimensions of a given space—a frequent necessity because child care rooms are often too small or too oddly shaped to otherwise accommodate the full range of activities desired.
- **Adult furniture.** Used mainly in the offices and staff areas, but also in the public (lobby, vestibule, corridor) and parent areas. Some adult furniture—usually a couch, arm chair, or rocking chair—will be needed in each of the children's group room.

Quality

Furniture in child care settings receives approximately 10 times the wear and tear of pieces in an average home. It is always cheaper in the long run to purchase moderate- to high-grade equipment that is solid, well-engineered, and built to last. The joints, hardware, and finish are particularly important. For wood furniture, the least stable joint construction is side-to-end construction. Most stable are: (1) peg, glue, and screw, (2) dado and screw, or (3) glue and screw, in that order. Manufacturers who have perfected these aspects will gladly educate you on the fine points of construction and design.

It goes without saying that everything in a child care center—including the furniture—needs to be safe, sturdy, easily maintained, easily cleaned or disinfected, and capable of looking good after repeated washings. This is especially true of fabric used on upholstered furniture (see section on Fabrics, later). Pay particular attention to the size of furniture for the ages intended (see Chapters 16–18) and for the scale of the room. Splayed legs on tables and chairs will make these items extra sturdy. Tables and chairs need to have weight for stability yet be light enough that children can move them easily. Check that legs do not scratch the floors or create noise.

Materials

Although slightly more expensive than plastic, wood furniture is preferable because it lasts longer, is more attractive, more residential, and helps to create a neutral backdrop. It also has 30 times less the embodied energy of plastic. Some additional benefits of wood, compared with plastic:

- Is easy to clean, shows less soil, does not fade with washing
- When covered with a durable finish, ages more gracefully
- Permits the room's color and excitement to come from the walls, equipment, children's clothes, and toys
- Introduces variety and warmth as a contrast to the majority of children's materials made of plastic

Butcher block and Baltic birch plywood furniture can be extremely durable without appearing institutional. Bamboo and rattan are often more durable than wood.

Man-made materials such as plastic, vinyl, and steel often scratch, fade, and look dingy after only brief use. Not only does plastic not necessarily withstand children's abusive treatment better than wood, its ubiquitousness in contemporary children's lives sometimes invites ill-use, whereas wooden furniture asks for respect and care.

Aesthetic Qualities

More difficult to discuss generically—but important in choosing furniture that will add to a space's spirit—are furniture's aesthetic qualities. Is the piece homelike or institutional? Will its color, size, and shape add to or detract from the room's overall design?

Mass

An object's mass is the volume of space taken up by its height, width, and depth. In addition to ergonomics and durability, furniture choices need to be based on the feeling of spaciousness desired in a given location—i.e., the amount of space the furniture appears to occupy and the amount of negative space or emptiness that is part of its design. For example, an open director's chair appears less bulky and more movable than an upholstered armchair of the same dimensions. A dark object will appear weightier and seem to take up more space than a light one. Since children's rooms generally pack much furniture and equipment into a small space, the mass of each element is critical in creating a sense of spaciousness overall.

Line

An object's line—straight, curved, or rounded—refers to its outline or the shape of its form. Straight lines represent efficiency, sternness, accuracy and symbolize the masculine. Curved and rounded lines create restfulness, gracefulness, and softening, and symbolize the feminine. Because young children need and respond to a predominantly feminine environment, it is preferable that most major furnishings have at least some suggestion of curved lines. In good design, balance and harmony result from a combination of curved, rounded, and straight lines.

Blending Old and New

A space equipped solely with new wooden furniture can appear as bland and undistinguished as one filled with plastic. Varied furnishings are essential to a sense of being nourished in a place. Commercial children's furniture can be nicely offset by the inclusion of some older, mellowed items—acquired from second-hand stores or parents' attics—which differ in style and

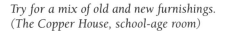

Try for a mix of old and new furnishings. (The Copper House, school-age room)

speak of longevity. Try to include at least one such piece in every room. Make sure that older pieces do not look dingy and uncared for, and are refurbished as appropriate. Nothing reproduces the beauty of an old, worn, hand-waxed chest, trunk, or cupboard.

Table and Chair Sizes

Chair and table heights and sizes appropriate to different ages are discussed in the chapters for each age group (Chapters 16–18). The general rule of thumb is a 10-inch difference between the top of a table and the top of the chair seat. (The differential can be as little as 8 inches for toddlers.) If the table has an apron (a band around the top of the legs), this difference will need to be measured from the bottom of the apron, making the seat heights lower. Where there are mixed-age groupings, several heights of tables and chairs may be needed.

Furniture for Sleeping

Children napping two to three hours per day in a child care center deserve the same feeling of comfort and territoriality as they would have in their own beds. Cribs for infants come in at least three sizes: full, small, and porta-crib size (see Chapter 16). Those made of wood (as opposed to plastic), standing at least slightly above the floor, help make the sleep room appear more like a bedroom at home. In Reggio Emilia, beautiful large baskets placed on the floor, lined with bumpers and sheets, are used for infants. Many of these have a cutaway portion that enables babies to crawl in and out as they choose.

In this country it is customary for toddlers and preschoolers to sleep on vinyl-covered mats that may fold, in molded plastic bins which stack, or in stacking cots of mesh vinyl with metal or plastic legs. (See also page 159, photo 1.) These are space-efficient but, even with the necessary bedding added, they are somewhat institutional. Note the beauty and comfort of the stacking wooden children's beds, with foam mattresses, used in Germany. (See Chapters 16 and 17 for more on sleeping equipment for toddlers and preschoolers.)

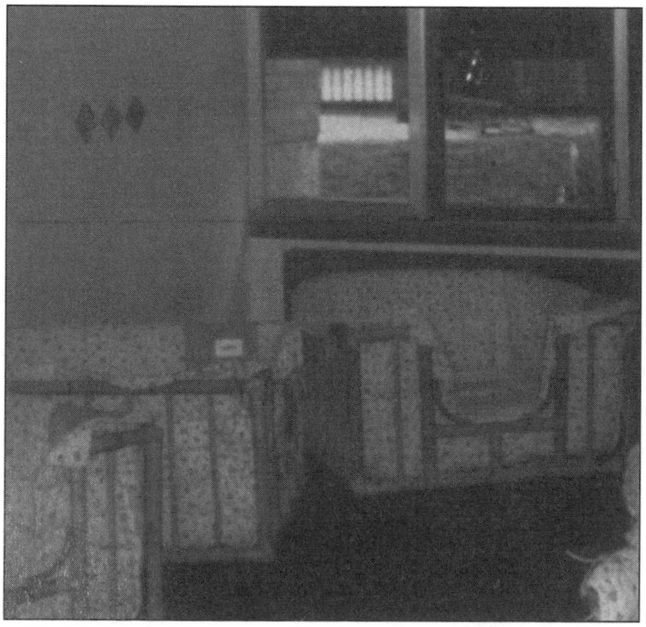

Baskets are used for infant sleeping in the Italian schools of Reggio Emilia.

For naps, the Germans use beautiful wooden beds with foam mattresses, that stack.

GUIDELINES: FURNITURE

- All furniture must meet fire codes, but aesthetic qualities—such as color, line, mass, construction, and design—are also important considerations.
- Wood furniture is generally more neutral, more durable, as easy to maintain, warmer, more pleasing, and more cost-effective in the long run than plastic furniture.
- Aim to include at least one older piece of furniture with some character and history in each group room and in some of the public spaces in the building.
- Conserve space by using furniture, such as chairs and stools, that stacks.
- The floor is major furniture for children. Level changes, mats, cushions, seats without legs, and other floor features can constitute a majority of the required seating.
- The most stable joint constructions for wood furniture, in order, are: (1) peg, glue and screw; (2) dado and screw; and (3) glue and screw. The least stable is side-to-end construction.
- Make sure that furniture is built or made to be untippable; is free of sharp edges or rough surfaces; resists splintering and cracking; has safe, durable ornaments and protrusions, and no lead-containing paint finishes.
- Critical for safety are rounded corners, beveled edges, counter-sunk screws and bolts, and nontoxic finishes.
- Beds, cots, and mats for napping need to be cleanable and labeled or identifiable as each child's own. Use cots where floors are cold or damp. Cots that stack can retain each child's bedding. Mats need less storage room but require additional storage space for bedding.
- Though it is desirable for children to be able to move some of the furniture, space can become destabilizing and disorienting when *everything* can be moved easily.
- Any castors on movable storage units need to be lockable and sturdy.
- Since the offerings of commercial sources change constantly, use the most recent catalog when ordering. More expensive companies often ship free of charge, making their prices equivalent to those who do not.
- Better-quality commercial furniture is always cheaper (and usually more harmonious) in the long run.
- Adding some custom-designed furniture optimizes space usage in the group rooms.
- Provide each group room with at least one seat that is comfortable for an adult.

Cabinetry

As noted in Chapter 4, plentiful storage space is the item of highest priority for staff but is often the first thing that gets cut when the budget is limited.[3] Cabinets, counters, and shelving are needed not only in the children's group rooms, but in kitchens, bathrooms, conference, and many other areas of the building. Children's cubbies are sometimes considered part of the cabinet budget, especially if custom-made. Cabinets are usually custom-built to fit a particular space, although some commercially available modular units[4] may be adaptable to your particular space.

Cabinets, open shelves, and closed closets with interior shelves for materials, supplies, equipment, toys, and cots used on a daily basis are needed in every group room. Well-thought-out storage helps with organization and reduces clutter; poorly dimensioned storage adds to it.

Sizes of Cabinets and Counters

Every group room needs at least one bank of cabinets above and below a counter containing a sink, for storage of staff supplies and things to be kept out of children's reach. Recommended cabinet and counter dimensions are listed below:

counter length (with a sink at one end)	6–10 feet
counter height (cabinets below)	36 in high, 24 in deep
cabinet height (upper)	30–42 inches
cabinet inner depth	12 inches
cabinet height above counter	18 inches

Where wall height permits a taller cabinet, extending the cabinet the room's full height will not provide additional accessible storage, and the cabinet is likely to appear out of scale with the room. Instead, decorative placement of items atop a lower cabinet will add grace to the room.

Make cabinet shelves adjustable in height. Shelves deeper than 12 inches require that some items be stashed behind others, making retrieval difficult.

Closets

Most group rooms need a minimum of 40–60 sq ft of closet space, in addition to cabinets and other shelving.

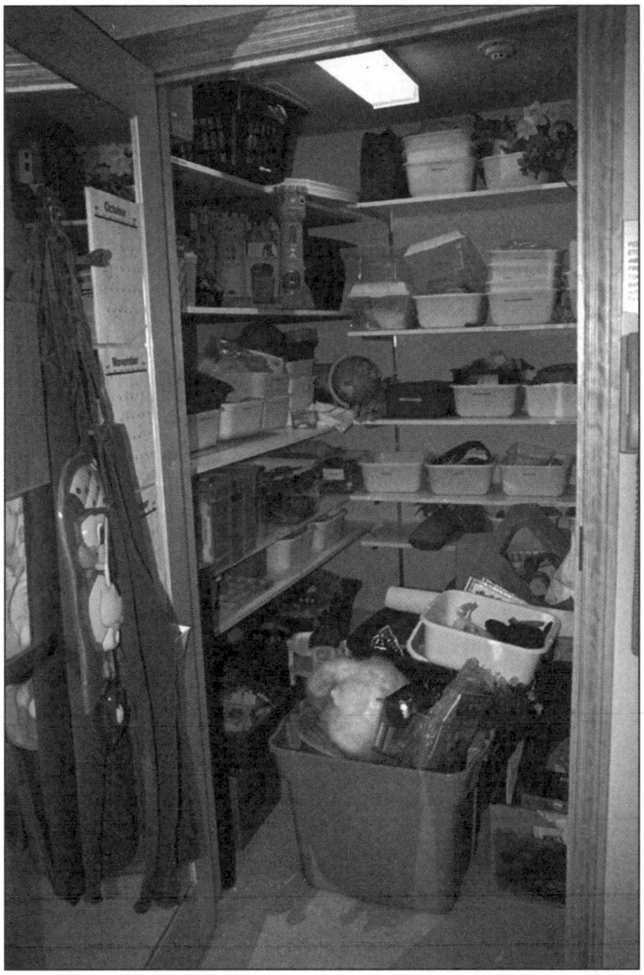

There is never too much closet space. Provide at least 40–60 square feet per group room. (The Copper House, toddler room)

Shelves in closets can vary in depth from 12–24 inches and generally need to have some real depth in order to hold large bins and toys, jars of paint, reams of paper, and other bulk supplies. Some floor space needs to be available for big balls, wheeled toys, large muscle equipment and items not safely stashed on shelves. Cots [approximate dimensions: 24″W × 53″L × 6″H (preschool) or 22″W × 40″L × 4¾″H (toddler)] will need to be stored in the main closet, in a separate closet of their own, or under a loft in the room. (See also page 159, photo 1.)

Cabinetry Materials

Cabinets can be made of laminate or wood. Consistent with the residential approach espoused in this guide, wood and wood-veneer cabinets are recommended for their soft and warm look. Although painted cabinets may also be appropriate in some circumstances, good-quality wood with a durable clear finish is preferable.

Newer centers often invest a great deal of money in laminate cabinets in colors chosen by the architect or designer. While this color adds interest to an empty room, it often does not work well once the space is occupied. Rather, it forever forces the center to adjust its color choices to that of the built-in items. In addition, it adds unwanted visual intensity and confusion to rooms already replete with colorful activities, clothing, and materials. Although easier to live with, neutral

A reading loft and cot storage (behind the curtain) are combined. (The Copper House, preschool room)

laminate colors (light beige and off-white) tend to be cold and institutional.

Counter Tops

Counter tops do need to be made of laminate to withstand water and extensive use. Neutral-colored laminates permit changes in the room's color scheme and give the counters a subdued appearance.

Fabrics

The three places where fabrics are likely to be used in a child care center are as: (1) upholstery; (2) bedding, pillows, and other accessories; and (3) wall hangings. Upholstery, bedding, and pillows are the items most apt to receive human touch. They may therefore require the most frequent change and replacement over time. Budgeting for periodic refurbishment or replacement can ensure greater use of fabrics overall. Consider hiring a parent or professional seamstress to assist in making pillows, covers, and other fabric items.

Upholstery

Cushioned and upholstered furniture is more inviting than unadorned plastic and wood, although each has its place. Upholstered furniture usually costs more to purchase and maintain than unupholstered pieces. However, it adds softness to a space and communicates a palpable message of caring.

Material Choices

Using a range of upholstery textures and materials, appropriate to the activities of each area, increases a room's sensuousness and tactile variety. Patterns can be introduced to further impact the interior's design. Ordering two sets of slipcovers simultaneously increases the longevity as well as the cleanliness of upholstered furniture.

Vinyl fabrics (such as naugahyde) declare a space an institution. Though frequently used, they are cold to the touch in winter, warm and sticky in summer, do not wear well, can fade and crack, be torn or punctured. Many other durable and more tactile fabrics (denim, corduroy, velour) meet fire ratings and can be Scotchgarded and antimicrobially treated. A number of these have been developed specifically for the healthcare and corporate office markets.

Couches and chairs in lobbies and in spaces receiving intensive use and exposure to children's sticky hands will be cheaper in the long run if upholstered in leather.

Fabric Textures

Different textures are appropriate for different activities and uses. Light textures and warm colors communicate affection, while textures with depth and a rich pattern make a statement of security. Children especially enjoy textures that are soft, perhaps with some nap, but rarely with slickness.

Woven fabrics such as weaves, twills, loop, and cut piles have a stable structure. Nonwoven fabrics such as knits, lace, net, braid, or crochet most often added as decorative trim, are easily damaged. While of great appeal to children, they are best used only on replaceable accessories. Nonfabric items (metals, wood, glass, bone, shells, pearls, semiprecious stones, ceramics, plastic, paper flowers, etc.) used as ornament or trim need to be evaluated for safety and durability.

Bedding and Fabric Accessories

Being able to lie down and rest in one's own bed, or wrapped in a throw on a couch or large chair, is one of life's pleasures offered by homes. Ideally, centers can find creative ways to give scheduled nap times, on cots, surrounded by one's peers, similar tender and memorable qualities.

Bedding

Fabrics for beds, with appealing textures and patterns, enhance children's nestling instincts. We certainly consider these features important in a child's bedroom at home. Why not in the center as well? If the center, rather than the parents, provides the bedding, coordinate bedding with the room's color scheme and vary the color by age group. Consider creating duvet or blanket covers in two or three different colors or patterns from which children can choose.

Pillows

An effective and inexpensive way to soften a center's ambiance is to add cushions to unupholstered furniture

Pillows of different sizes and loft, including some of rigid foam such as the one the girl is sitting upon, transform a window bay into a comfortable place for nestling. (The Copper House, infant room)

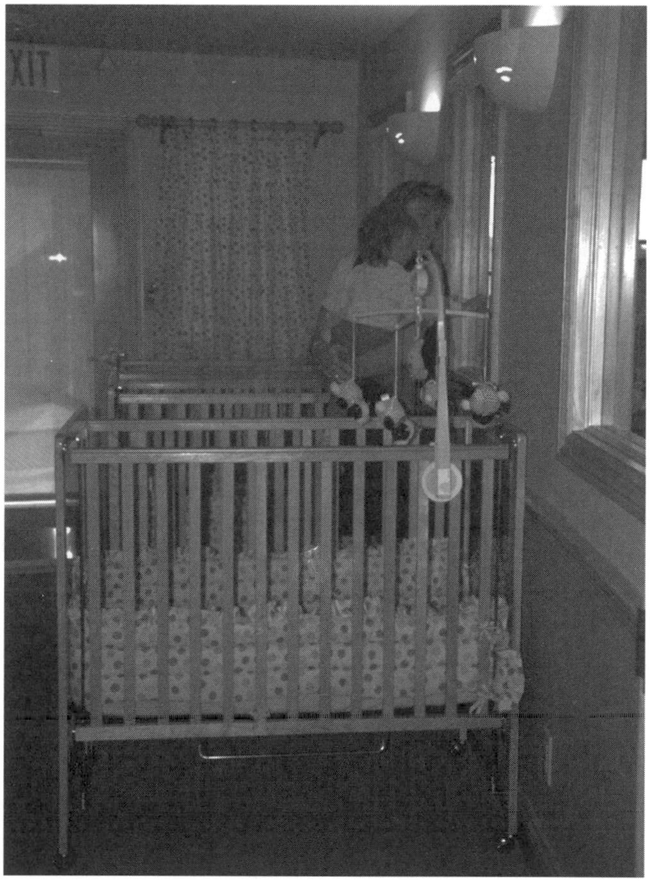

Coordinated crib bumpers, curtains, and blankets create a sense of calm in this sleep space. (The Copper House, infant room)

(such as wicker and wood chairs and benches), and throw pillows to the couches, chairs, risers, quiet areas, and lofts of the room. Pillows are light, movable elements that children can hug, transport, and use to create places of nestling and privacy. If two sets of covers are made or ordered simultaneously, it may be possible to introduce two totally different color schemes into a room—adding yet another dimension of variety—as well as ensure that covers can be cleaned easily.

Pillows in many shapes and sizes are desirable:

- 12-to-18-inch throw pillows
- 24-inch soft, stuffed pillows
- Velour-covered bean bag chairs
- Pillows that double as puppets
- Large stuffed mats
- 24-inch-square foam pillows (approximately 6 inches high) serve as occasional seats for adults and children. They also serve as material for building impromptu forts and hideaways.

Fabric Accessories

The choice of fabrics for accessories such as bibs, bumpers, tablecloths, place mats, and napkins merits careful consideration for color, pattern, texture, style, and washability. An infant sleep space with many cribs acquires a sense of calm and design integrity when all the bumpers and curtains coordinate.

Children deserve to experience the "good life." Meals take on an entirely different tenor when eaten on colorful, washable tablecloths and place mats. Cloth napkins, perhaps made by cutting standard terry cloth hand towels in half to create child-sized, washable napkins, conserve paper.[5]

Wall Hangings

Wall hangings—in the form of fabric stretched across canvas or as appliquéd, woven, or crafted forms of fabric art—can add distinctive and varied decoration to child care spaces. The molas of the South American cultures, depicting domestic and agricultural scenes, are particularly charming and educational.

GUIDELINES: FABRICS

- All fabrics must meet fire codes. Class A and B rated fabrics are readily available at design centers and through commercial suppliers.
- Cushions and pillows with two sets of zippered covers permit easy change for cleaning and repair, as well as enabling introduction of a second, coordinated color scheme.
- Loose cushions sometimes need to be equipped with Velcro or other restraining devices to prevent shifting and pilferage.
- Cushions and pillows are versatile elements that children can sit upon, hug, transport, and use to build impromptu hideaways and structures.
- Parents often enjoy creating pillows, cushions, and bedding for the center. This eliminates labor costs while giving parents a sense of investment in their child's room. Hiring a professional seamstress may also be appropriate.
- Fabrics for bedding—sheets, blankets, comforters—whether brought from home or purchased by the center, are most attractive when they coordinate with a room's color scheme, while still being individualized.

To ensure coordination of color, texture, and pattern work with the actual furnishings and fabrics intended for use.

Accessories

Accessories are generally smaller items that can add zest and fun while supporting activities in a room. In addition to the fabric items discussed above, they include:

- Lamps
- Baskets, bins, and wastebaskets
- Dishes and flatware
- Artwork, sculpture, mobiles, and prisms
- Plants and containers
- Knick knacks and other decorative items

While accessories are often acquired "catch as catch can," the fact is that their presence is keenly felt. Their ability to harmonize with other elements in the space can make or break the integrity of a design. They need to be chosen with attention to functionality, size, design, color, and ability to coordinate with the rest of the room's interior colors, finishes, and furnishings. For example, the black metal trash baskets characteristically used in a corporate office may be far too chunky and sterile for a children's living room. Decals of Sesame Street figures in bright primary colors may clash with the room's more toasted and creamed hues, as can commercial children's aprons, dishes and cups, and plastic bins in bright primary colors.

Finishing Touches

Once construction or renovation is complete, and the furniture is in place, it is time to "dress" the building. At that point, take a close look at each room to see what can be added to bring its spirit to life. Perhaps a wall calls out for a painting or piece of three-dimensional art, an area of ceiling asks to be lowered with banners, a corner would be graced by big stuffed pillows, an activity area by an area rug, mobiles, and hanging plants. Let your intuition be your guide as to what is missing or needed. Working with accessories is more art than science. Allow yourself to experiment, try out unusual combinations, discover that an item intended but inappropriate for one room works brilliantly in another. Once again, the aim is to create a fully integrated interior where all the colors, textures, patterns, and shapes complement and harmonize with one another.

Notes

[1]Carol Venolia, *Healing Environments: Your Guide to Indoor Well-Being* (Berkeley, CA: Celestial Arts, 1988), 33–34.

[2]Readers are also encouraged to explore the many books available on *feng shui*, the Chinese art of placement. This ancient art has devised guidelines for arranging furniture, objects, colors, textures, and other elements to affect their energy or *chi*, thereby bringing the inhabitants prosperity, good health, restful sleep, and harmonious relationships.

[3]Gretchen Lee Anderson, *Removing Barriers to Childcare Facilities Development* (California State University, Northridge, CA, 1993).

[4]Available from IKEA and similar outlets.

[5]An idea provided by Carla Mathis for the Copper House.

PART FOUR

THE FUNCTIONAL SPACES

CHAPTER FIFTEEN

DESIGNING GROUP-ROOM ACTIVITY AREAS

People need
an identifiable
spacial unit
to belong to.

—Christopher Alexander

Chapter 7 presented procedures for identifying a group room's wet and dry *regions*, and then for subdividing those regions into entry, messy, quiet, and active *zones*. After a group room is zoned, the next step is to take its functional requirements and locate them in *activity areas* so that every cubic inch of the room counts. This chapter explores the general concept of creating activity areas, while Chapters 16–18 address the specific concerns of activity areas for particular ages.

What Is an Activity Area?

An activity area is a special place that has at hand all the tools and supports needed to fulfill that area's function. Well-designed activity areas evoke their own spirit of place, such as the attraction of a potter's studio, a woodworker's shop, a photographer's darkroom, or a personal library. When a room has a variety of spaces—each of which supports a different function—activities can develop to their fullest. The idea is to begin by listing all the functions or activities the room is intended to accommodate (as explained in Chapter 7), and then to create activity areas for each of these functions. There is no ideal number of activity areas. Highly developed rooms may support as many as 15–20. Small spaces may have fewer areas or some that double in function. Lists vary across time, available space, and children's and teachers' interests, reflecting the diversity of each group of children and caregivers.

Box 15. 1 on the next page suggests activity areas, organized by the four major zones (entry, messy, active, and quiet) that might be present in each group room.

Organizing a space into activity areas has many advantages and serves many purposes. Here are a few:

- **Improved utilization of space.** When children occupy several areas simultaneously, most of the facilities available in the room are used for most of the day. This prevents the congestion and tension that arise when everyone tries to use the same materials at the same time.
- **Regulation of behavior.** Well-organized activity areas regulate behavior and the use of materials by providing places where, within clear physical limits, things can be found, explored, and put away.
- **Promotion of children's independence and educational process.** When areas provide the materials and supports children need to engage in activities safely on their own, teachers can be more confident in trusting them to work things out for themselves. With well-designed activity areas, teachers need not try to be everywhere at once—handing out materials and overseeing their use. This frees staff to be available for the extended dialogs with children that lead to true inquiry and experimentation.

Play/Educational Experience Types

In order to meet the varied developmental needs of any age group and the requirements of children with disabilities, strive to have enough activity areas to

BOX 15.1

Possible Group-Room Activity Areas, by Zone

Entry/Transition Zone
- Children's personal storage area
- Staff personal storage area
- Parent Sign-in/Communication area

Quiet Zone
- Sleeping/Napping/Resting area
- Reading area
- Listening area
- Manipulatives area
- Writing area
- Small-Block area
- Math area

Messy Zone
- Toileting/Diapering/Bathroom area
- Feeding/Eating/Snack area
- Water area
- Sand area
- Clay area
- Painting area
- Collage area
- Woodworking area
- Cooking area
- Science and Nature area

Active Zone
- Large-Block area
- Dramatic Play area(s)
  - Housekeeping area
  - Doll Play area
  - Puppet Play and Storefront area
  - Costume and Dress-Up area
  - Fantasy Themes area
  - Miniatures area
- Music and Movement area
- Gross-Motor area

Additional Spaces Required
(room location may vary)
- Large-group meeting area
- Private and semiprivate areas
- Staff work area and telephone

make the following six categories of experience available to children at all times:

1. **Quiet activities:** listening, viewing, meeting, reading, cuddling [quiet zone].
2. **Structured activities:** puzzles, construction toys, small unit blocks, manipulatives, games [quiet zone].
3. **Craft and discovery activities:** paint, clay, collage, water, sand, woodworking, science, animals and plants [messy zone].
4. **Dramatic play activities:** puppets, store, fantasy themes, masks and dress-ups, kitchen and doll play, miniatures [active zone].
5. **Large-motor activities:** climbing, sliding, swinging, crawling, hanging, tumbling, rocking, balls, ring toss, large blocks, punching bags [active zone].
6. **Therapeutic activities:** inflatable and foam equipment, water bed, air mattress (in every zone where appropriate).

All six categories may be present in each group room or particular functions may be placed in separate rooms—an art room, a climbing room, or a dramatic play room. The latter option works well where multiple small rooms exist near one another. But it is problematic if it forces the need to schedule groups of children for a particular resource.

Activity-Area Attributes

Contrary to common practice, a table and chairs arranged in a space or corner do not make an activity area. An activity area has five defining attributes (Figure 15.1):

1. A specific physical location suited to the activity
2. Visible boundaries
3. Play and sitting surfaces
4. Provisions for storage and display of materials specific to the area's function
5. A mood that distinguishes it from contiguous spaces

Well-planned activity areas visually entice children to explore and use the materials placed there. Most of

This game area has a location, visible boundaries, play and sitting surfaces, storage/display of the games, and its own mood.

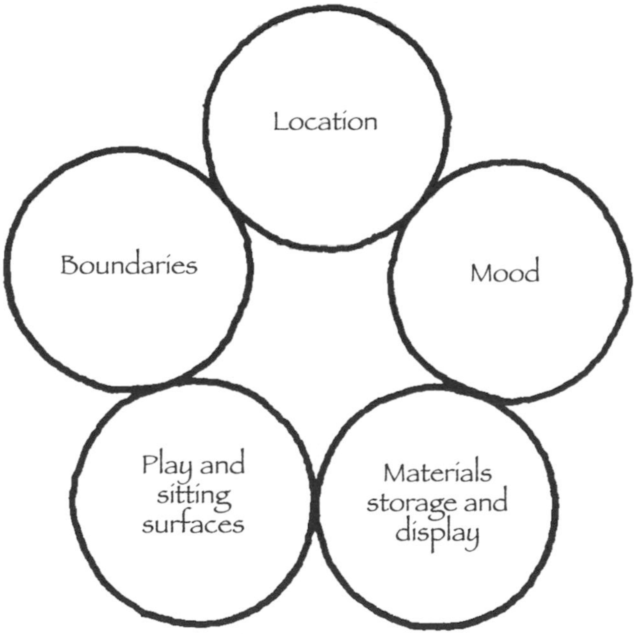

Figure 15.1
The five attributes of an activity area.

this chapter examines ways to design activity areas so that they incorporate these five essential attributes. Although the chapter addresses location first—and treats it as the key attribute in designing activity areas that function well—you may wish to vary the sequence in which you address these attributes to suit your own situation.

Locating Activity Areas In A Room

The key to locating activity areas rests upon understanding that some activities work well in exposed spaces and others in protected spaces. Good room layouts make an appropriate match between the activity and its location.

Using Protected Regions

As discussed in Chapter 7, the first priority in developing a room plan is to use the room's protected regions and its corners well. Protected regions are best for quiet activities and places of rest and retreat, and for building activities such as small unit blocks, construction toys, and manipulatives that need to be safeguarded from intrusion by traffic while being played with.

Of all a room's activities, small unit blocks benefit most from a corner's protection, or from the protection offered by being placed on a platform. Too frequently, a small unit block area is placed near a doorway, because entry areas often have free space around them. However, blocks located near entries are rarely used, since no child wants to build something that may be trampled. The only transit acceptable in areas where children use unit blocks and small construction toys is that of children going to and from the shelves where these materials are stored. Activities such as reading, listening, writing, and group meetings also require

A protected corner provides a haven for building with small unit blocks and construction toys.

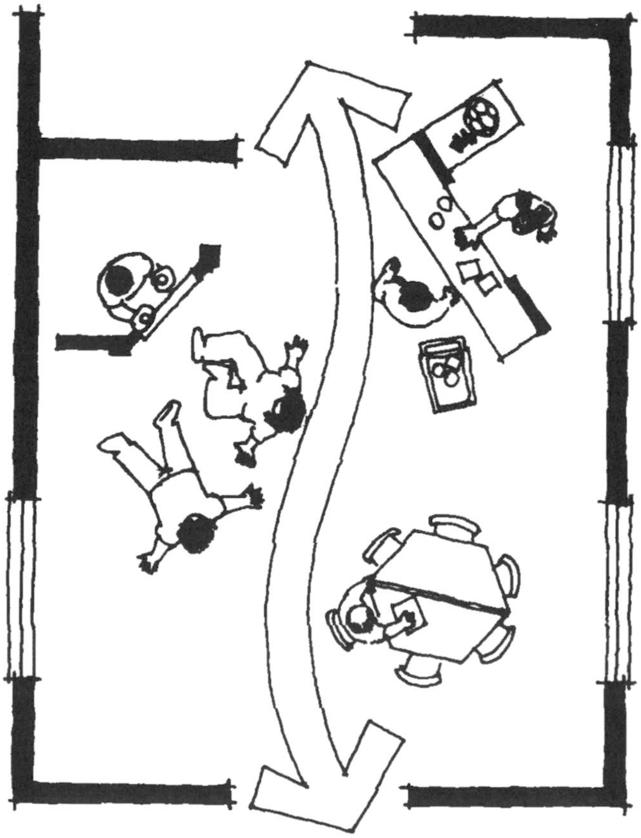

Figure 15.2
Storefronts, puppet theaters, and some tables are best located near the room's major pathways.

physically protected regions but can tolerate some exposure because the child's body can protect the book, earphones, etc., while engaging in the activity.

Using Exposed Regions

Activities involving tables (art, science, sand, water, woodworking) or the motion of people on their feet (storefronts, puppet theaters, climbers) work well near pathways and in open, busy spaces (Figure 15.2). The movement involved in these activities is then incorporated into the general transit in the area. At the same time, the play materials are protected by furniture, equipment, or the table surface, and children's backs act as barriers to the movement around them.

Other Locational Factors

In addition to identifying the best uses for protected and exposed regions, also consider these factors in locating activity areas:

- Separate conflicting activities (quiet and noisy, messy and clean, expansive and contained).
- Locate messy activities near sinks.
- Place platforms near high windows so children can see outdoors.

- Place reading, art, or writing areas close to sources of natural light, as long as doing so does not compromise the overall room plan (see the floorplan and discussion for Case Study 2 in Chapter 7).
- Locate areas requiring electrical appliances (fish tank, cooking) near outlets. If this forces undesirable compromises in layout, consider rewiring.
- Capitalize upon any unique architectural feature—a beautiful view, a niche, a fireplace, or a change in ceiling height—by making it a salient and functional part of an activity area.

If, after you have applied these tactics, some spaces remain unassigned and/or some activities are still unaccounted for, consideration of the other four attributes of activity areas—boundaries, play and sitting surfaces, materials display and storage, and mood—can help you achieve a workable layout. Floor plans illustrating how the five attributes of activity areas can be incorporated into specific group-room designs are shown in the case studies in Chapter 7 and, for specific age groups, at the ends of Chapters 16–18.

GUIDELINES: LOCATING ACTIVITY AREAS

- Place quiet and retreat activities in the room's protected region(s).
- Place activities using small building materials, especially unit blocks, in protected regions where the floor can be used as a playing surface.
- Place activities involving tables, crafts, movement, and foot traffic in the messy and active zones, where the work surfaces and children's bodies will protect the play materials and foot traffic will be absorbed by the room's main path of transit.
- Also review Chapter 7 for hints for identifying a room's regions and zones.

Creating Boundaries for Activity Areas

Once activity areas for all a room's functional requirements have been mapped in the room, boundaries will be needed to signal where each area begins and ends. Boundaries—usually furniture, partitions, or low walls and dividers—reduce disruptive behaviors by distinguishing activities, limiting the number of participants in an area, and physically separating tasks. Failure to provide appropriate boundaries for areas can weaken a room's design.

Considerations in Boundary Design

Boundaries can vary in height, mass, penetrability, transparency, and rigidity. Each of these factors affects children's ability to feel safe and to see caregivers and others at play, and adults' ability to keep an eye on all activities. Boundaries designed as interactive surfaces, such as risers and play panels (see pages 274 and 284 later in this chapter), can function as seats and encourage gross and fine motor actions.

For stimulation, and to facilitate communication and supervision of children, keep boundaries low, child-scaled, and/or varied in height and penetrability. Boundaries that enable visibility across areas:

A wall of plastic cubes open randomly on one or both sides serves as a divider, display unit, and crawl-through space in an infant room.

A free-standing A-shaped divider provides a book rack in the reading area and an easel in the crafts area.

- Promote "contagion," or the cross-area effect that activities initiated and sustained by some children can have upon others. This is a necessary ingredient of an active group room. When children can look across to or hang out at the edges of an area watching others at play, their boredom or confusion about what to do next is relieved.
- Aid children in transitions, especially transitions from independent to whole-group tasks (from clean-up to a group meeting, for example).
- Enable staff to more easily observe all events, although they may not participate directly in each one.
- Promote feelings of safety and security, which depend upon environmental predictability and access to information.

High or cluttered boundaries (paper bags and boxes stored on top of shelves, etc.) are distracting. Boundaries that vary in fluidity, scale, and color introduce diversity, making rooms appear spacious and less congested. Be certain to secure tall free-standing boundaries, dividers, and cubbies against tipping and falling.

Solid versus Fluid Boundaries

Boundaries can be as solid as four walls or as fluid as taped lines on the floor. Solid boundaries, such as those provided by encircling a space with bookcases, storage units, furniture, or low dividers, are appropriate for most activities using the floor. However, softer and more fluid boundaries are needed where children are moving on their feet—as in the messy zone. Use of only solid boundaries in a room creates discrete boxes and defined pathways that ask children to move somewhat like rats in a maze. Moreover, using only firm boundaries makes a room appear cluttered, fails to visually entice children into activities, blocks visibility across areas, and inappropriately confines activities requiring freedom of movement.

Using Floor Level, Ceiling Height, and Light to Create Boundaries

Fluid boundaries can be created by employing changes in floor level, floor material (carpet to wood), ceiling height, and lighting as illustrated below:

- Raise the floor level onto a platform 4 inches to 5 feet high, so the perimeter of the platform delineates the activity area's boundaries and any area underneath. The photographs on page 273 provide some examples of raised areas. For more illustrations see pages 305 and 357.
- Lower the level of the floor (an alternative not often available), or achieve this effect by enclosing a

A four-inch-high platform incorporating storage makes an excellent manipulative area.

A large 12-inch-high platform places children counter-height to an adult counter, and serves as a play and sitting surface in its own right.

The unfinished struts of this dramatic play loft encourage children to embellish the "house." Cots are stored underneath.

Two well-defined activity areas: A dramatic play loft suspended from the rafters and an open woodworking area underneath.

A manipulative area enclosed with 12-inch-high carpeted risers.

space with an L, U, or rectangular arrangement of low carpeted risers, so the internal floor level appears lower than its perimeter.

- Change the height of the ceiling with eaves, canopies, trellises, and mobiles, as was shown earlier on pages 239 and 240.
- Create pools of light using spotlights, floodlights, subdued lamps, etc., so the space under the light appears and feels distinct from surrounding areas.

Advantages of Raised Levels

Changes in floor level offer many economic, educational, and therapeutic advantages:

- Since 50% of a room's space is over children's heads, making effective use of cubic footage can add considerable usable space to a room.
- Having a few children up on a platform greatly reduces the commotion at floor level caused by many little bodies moving about on their feet.
- Children practice eye-hand coordination and large muscle movement in climbing up to and down from high platforms.
- Similar to viewing New York City from the World Trade Center, being up high enables children to survey the room and understand its spatial organization.
- Raised levels provide options for privacy, small groups, territoriality, personalization of space, and retreat.
- Going under, over, across, inside, and upon different surfaces, and perceiving the world kinesthetically and visually from a variety of spatial vantage points, teaches children important spatial relationships, which may be a critical means of preparing them for reading and symbol decoding later on.[1]
- Platforms of varied heights reduce the amount of sound that travels across a room (see Figure 9.1 on page 182).
- The security and back protection offered by raised levels help children focus and concentrate.

Level changes can be permanent installations, or they can be designed to be rearrangeable, an option provided by "kits" composed of modular parts.

Using Color to Define Boundaries

Another powerful way to demonstrate boundaries is through the use of color. Color is an excellent visual organizer, and busy group rooms are visually chaotic places.

Using color to define boundaries does not mean painting the door and window frames one hue, the walls another, and the ceiling a third. This effect draws the eye to inconsequential features of the environment. Instead, it means placing particular colors on the work surfaces, display and storage units, cabinets, area dividers, etc., of a specific area to signal where the space begins and ends. These visually perceptible differences within the room—a yellow space, a blue space, a green space—delimit the activities to which they pertain. To achieve this effect, it is sometimes necessary to paint even new furnishings. For more on color as a visual organizer, see Chapter 12.

Using Boundaries to Vary the Size of Areas

Rarely are so many people placed together in such confined space, with so few options for withdrawal, as are

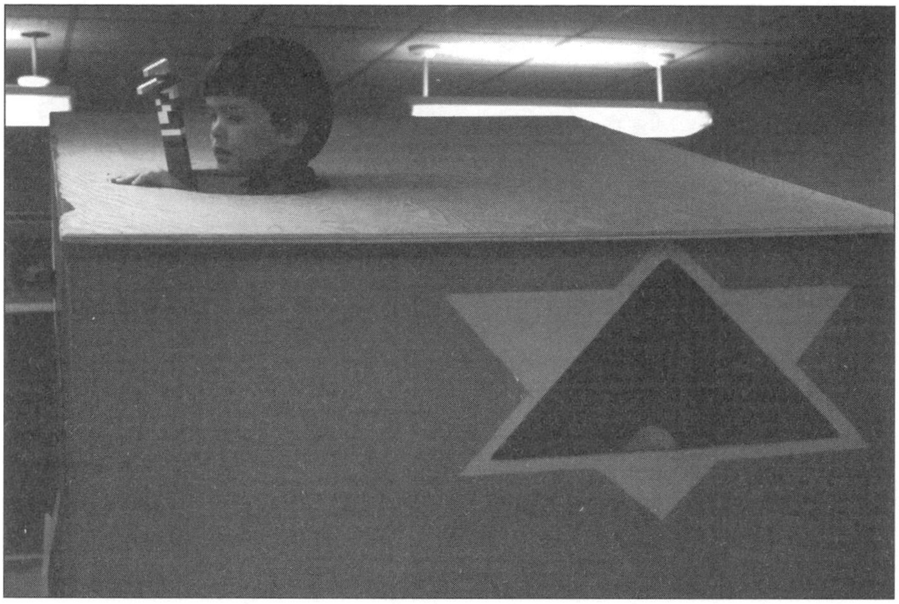

High perches offer a bird's-eye view of the room and teach important spatial relationships.

Commercially available kits containing panels, uprights, and props (such as the one shown here from Quadro) can be rearranged to create a variety of levels and equipment.

children in child care centers. In seeking places of retreat, it is not uncommon for children to hide in their cubbies. Boundaries that vary the size of areas in a room help to provide options for privacy, for small groups, for a whole-group meeting, and for one-on-one interactions.

Many activity areas work best if they accommodate about four children comfortably. Physically limiting the number of children an area can accommodate:

- Supports quiet, cooperative play and discourages leader-dominated behavior.
- Minimizes congestion and enhances positive participation by encouraging children to use all the facilities in a room.
- Increases the opportunity for children with disabilities to interact with peers and to form friendships with children whom they may invite home or visit, thus enhancing and broadening their social experience.

Activity areas large enough for about four people work extremely well.

Creating Boundaries for Private Spaces

Children have significant needs for privacy, which are often overlooked in group care settings and can be especially hard to honor in light of increasing concerns about possible abuse. A balance between children's need for privacy and their need for supervision can be achieved when it is understood that privacy is broader than total aloneness. In fact, it is possible to distinguish four types of privacy:[2]

- **Auditory privacy:** controlling access to information/being able to tell secrets
- **Visual privacy:** being free from the visual distraction and bother of others
- **Territorial privacy:** controlling access to spaces/having a place of one's own
- **Total privacy:** being alone or by oneself

Manipulating the height, transparency, sound absorbency, and other parameters of boundaries can ensure that all four types of privacy are provided in each room. (See Chapter 7, page 161.) In addition, small window seats, platforms, cubby holes, soft enclosed seating, and spacious stair landings can create places of retreat, rest, observational learning, and preparation for new situations that are crucial to the development of self-concept and personal identity. These photographs show some of the types of "private" spaces designers can create for children.

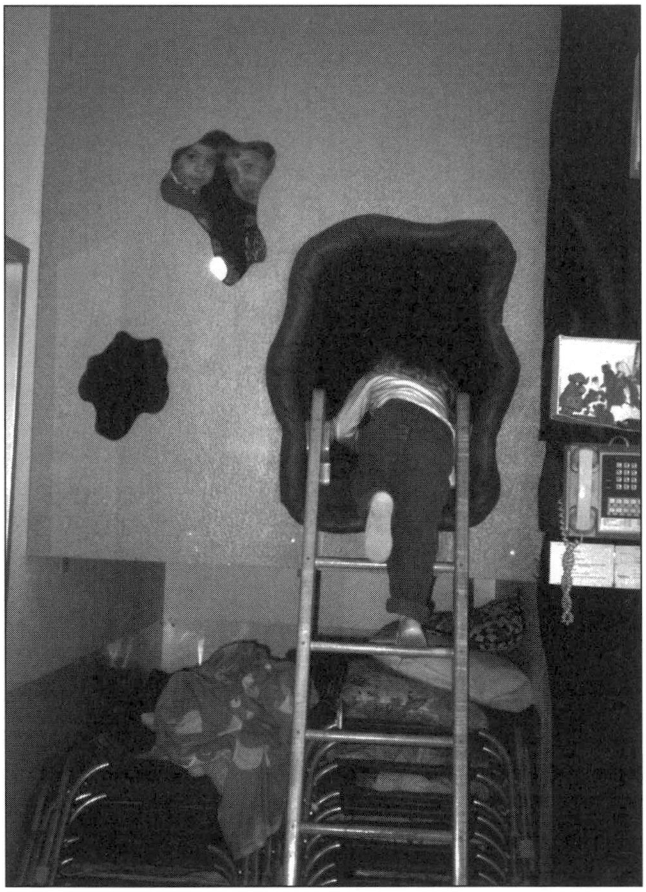

A "bear's cave" built in the space above a cot alcove is lined with carpet-covered foam. Cut-outs enable good staff visibility yet children feel hidden. A removable ladder places access under staff control.

Space explorers enjoy a quiet moment on a wide stair landing.

From a six-foot-high perch it is possible to observe anyone entering the room without interacting.

Children deemed this crow's nest, hanging from the rafters in a corner, an appropriate hideaway for 3 or 4.

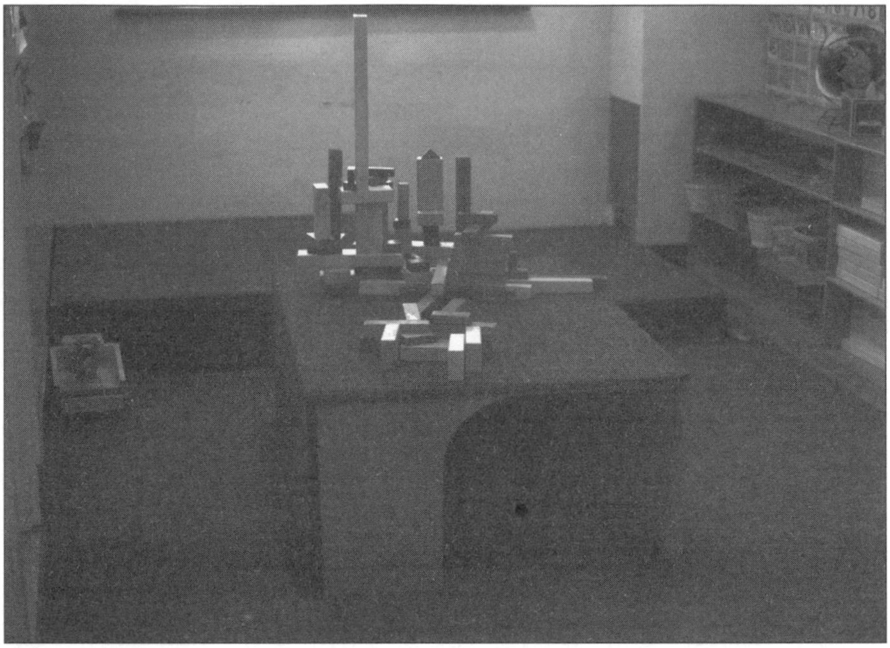

Platforms (and lofts) can be shaped and structured to create private spaces.

Fiberboard barrels with specially cut entryways, make bubbles that can be moved about easily.

Private spaces in a room:

- Provide shy children with opportunities to explore feelings and inner turmoils that are not easily exposed to public surveillance
- Allow those who occasionally may not feel like working with peers to retreat and behave according to their mood
- Provide time-out spots from the fast pace of a group program

When building platforms and lofts, look for ways to incorporate small, semienclosed spaces for one or two children to be alone.

Fiberboard barrels, obtainable without charge from chemical companies and hospitals, make easily transported private bubbles for resting or getting away from it all. The barrel may be cut with varied openings, decorated, and lined with foam, Mylar, or fake fur to give it interesting textural qualities. Bored and distressed children often spend as long as an hour in one of these barrels, seemingly unengaged. However, they tend to monitor and assess ongoing activities, emerging from the barrel when calm or energized and better prepared to join their peers.

Children also need private settings or activities that allow them to express and release anger or frustration by being able to build, knock down, throw, kick, or punch away violent and angry feelings. Therefore, pro-

GUIDELINES: CREATING BOUNDARIES

- Define each area with boundaries that signal where the area begins and ends.
- The activities within a given area usually determine the degree of firmness or fluidity its boundaries should have.
- Use walls and furniture to create firm boundaries for tranquil and floor-based tasks.
- Vary an area's floor height, ceiling height, or perimeter lighting to create more fluid boundaries for active and table-based activities.
- Consider marking the extent of areas by changes in color. Color is a powerful visual organizer and an effective way to indicate a fluid boundary.
- Also consider the height, mass, penetrability, transparency, and rigidity of each boundary. How does it affect the room's spaciousness, feeling of order, and overall visibility? How does it affect children's safety and options for privacy?
- Vary the physical parameters of boundaries to provide four types of privacy: freedom from auditory and/or visual distraction, the ability to establish personal territories and occasional control over spaces, and total aloneness.
- Use boundaries to vary the size of areas. Design most areas for about four children and an adult.
- In addition, provide at least one space for a whole-group meeting; spaces for one-on-one interaction; and private places for children to rest, observe others, release emotional anxieties, and cry.

vide places to let off steam, run, fall, and jump, as well as soft areas for retreat.

Selecting Play And Sitting Surfaces

The topic of play and sitting surfaces often conjures up images of tables and chairs which, at a child's eye level, can make an environment appear more populated with legs than any other feature. Given the freedom to choose surfaces for executing tasks, children often prefer floors, storage unit tops, chair seats, and platforms to tables. In addition to the following suggestions, see Chapters 14 and 16–18 for more ideas on play and sitting surfaces at each age level.

Floors

In protected regions, it is often best to use the floor as a play or sitting surface in order to structure and moderate children's movements and effect a functional room plan. Some of a floor's many virtues are listed below:

- **Once on the floor, children tend to stay there.** They may still move about, but they are not causing commotion by traversing classroom space.
- **The ability to play on its floor makes a space more flexible and reduces the amount of furniture required.** When children play on the floor, they can spontaneously adjust their distance from one another so they need not shout across furniture to be heard.
- **Children on the floor can adjust their viewing height by sitting or kneeling.** A wider field of vision lets children take in more at a glance and overcome a developmental tendency to look at details rather than the entire array.

For further information on floors and suitable floor coverings, see Chapter 13.

The floor is "furniture" and a valuable play and sitting surface.

Tables

To conserve floor space, introduce variety, and increase safety, strive to minimize the number of tables in a room. Also use a variety of table sizes and shapes to maximize the chances of providing surfaces that are appealing and useful to children of different ages and physical capabilities. Small tables (for four to six) are especially useful in reducing the space between children who are working together, lowering the room's noise level, and promoting conversational intimacy. Many tables at manufacturers' recommended age-specific heights (see Chapters 16–18) are too large and too high. They place great stress on a leader to keep a large group intact, and raise noise levels by forcing children to yell across the table to be heard.

Here are some recommendations for the use of tables:

- Rather than crowd a room all day with tables used by everyone for 30 minutes at lunch time, consider multiple-use furniture: tables that stack, or flip up or down; counters with stools; or platforms that double as play and eating surfaces. (See also page 273.)
- Covers placed over water and sand troughs (especially if built 6 inches wider on each side for knee clearance) can transform them into tables. Alternatively, the covers can be used on their own, mounted on suitable supports (cinder blocks, etc.) to raise them off the floor.
- Vary table heights by providing at least three choices: 10 inches high, at which children kneel, sit, or squat without chairs; regular child-scaled height (approximately 14–20 inches); and child counter-height (approximately 20–24 inches). Children love the 10–12 inch-high tables, at which they can kneel or sit on the floor. These low tables give them increased visual command over their materials and the freedom to put the full force of their bodies into their play, especially when working with clay and construction materials (Also see Chapters 16 and 17 for more information on tables.)
- Because casual conversation occurs most readily when people are at right angles to one another, small round, square, rectangular, and trapezoidal tables (Figure 15.3) promote verbal interaction—provided their diameter is not too great. Large tables can pull people apart.
- For activities such as art and science, where children are on their feet and moving about, child

Covers transform water (and sand) troughs into tables.

This counter on the back of a storage unit flips down when not in use as a writing area.

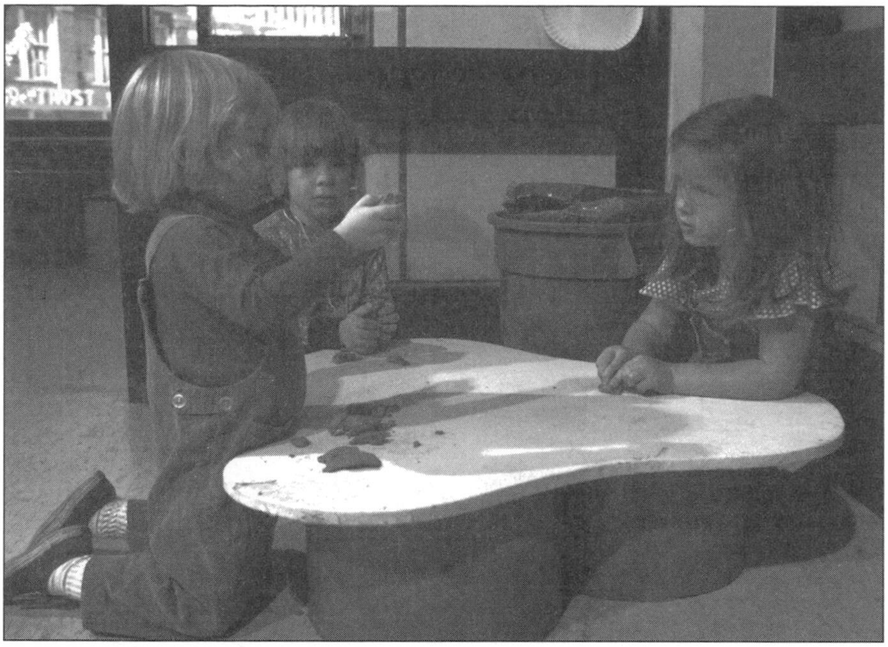

A 10-inch-high table increases children's visual command and freedom to put the full force of their bodies into their work.

Counter-height surfaces can be well-suited to certain types of activities.

counter-height surfaces (20 inches for toddlers, 24 inches for preschoolers) are ideal and often preferred to sit-down tables. (Also see pages 158–159, photos 13-16, and page 273.)

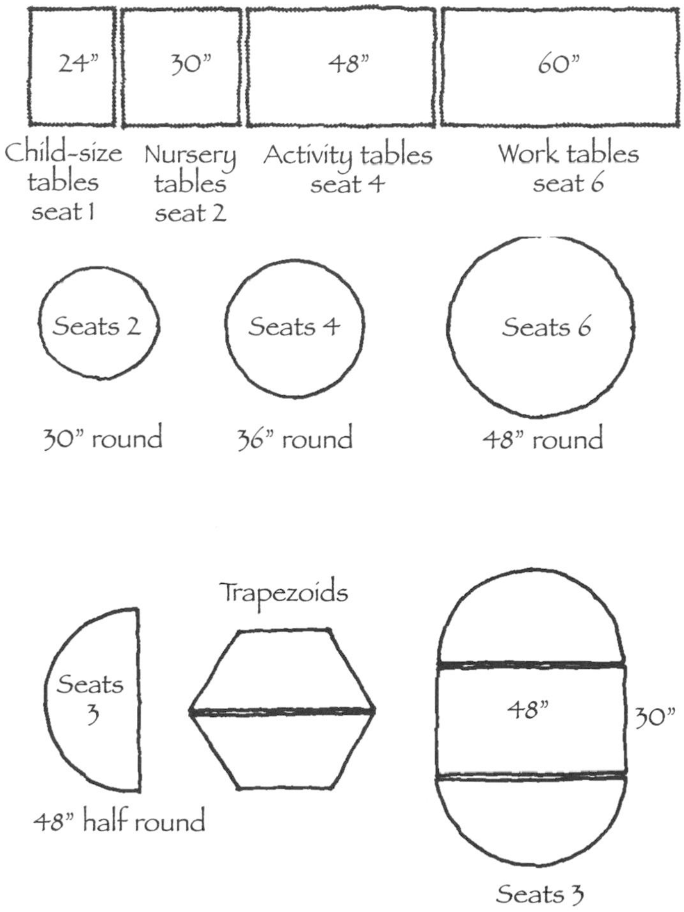

Figure 15.3
Small tables provide versatility in use and can be combined for various purposes.

Figure 15.4
Horseshoe-shaped tables lack versatility and may take up a lot of space.

Figure 15.5
Trapezoidal tables are versatile and space-conserving.

- The horseshoe-shaped table with a cut-out for the teacher is a frequent, though not always wise, purchase. These large tables usurp much space and cannot be used flexibly in combination with other surfaces (Figure 15.4). They reduce the opportunity for children to interact with one another and instead force the orientation toward the teacher. Unless teacher control is truly desired, avoid these tables in favor of smaller square, round, rectangular, or trapezoidal ones that support intimacy and can be joined to form larger surfaces.
- Trapezoidal tables are ideal for the average group room (Figure 15.5). When placed with their long sides together, they approximate the intimacy of a round table. When pulled apart, 5 children can sit at each trap (10 in all) for lunch or a snack. Three or more tables can be variously arranged to accommodate different types of activities.

Chairs and Other Sitting Surfaces

Young children rarely choose to sit and, even more rarely, to sit still. Seating options responsive to their frequent change of body posture tend to work best. Chairs are only one possibility. Sitting surfaces can vary in the presence and height of backs, arms, padding, and possibilities of reclining.

- In addition to standard straight-backed wooden and plastic chairs, inflatables and bean bag chairs can be excellent resting and holding surfaces.
- Armchairs, couches, risers, waterbeds, pillows and cushions, mattresses, net and swinging chairs, and hammocks encourage cuddling and allow children to fully settle in with books and toys.
- Stools are often preferable to chairs with backs because children working at tables tend to lean forward over their work and rarely use a back support. Stools slip easily under work surfaces when not in use and, if made from fiberboard tubes with round bases, cause fewer problems with tripping and unbalancing than four-legged chairs.
- Fiberboard tubes can be used to make chairs with backs cut in fanciful designs. Tubes can also be adapted to the support needs of a child with

Inflatable (as well as bean bag) chairs are fun.

Hammocks encourage cuddling and rest.

Stools provide a sturdy but movable seating surface around a snack table.

Figure 15.6
A rocking chair two can share.

disabilities. Retaining straps or belts can be added if desired. (See page 159, photo 12.)

- Rocking chairs, both adult- and child-scaled (Figure 15.6), encourage physical contact between adult and child, help caregivers comfort tired or ill children, and give energetic ones constructive opportunities for movement.

Options for Stimulating Movement

Children learn primarily by moving and using their bodies in space. The predominant use of tables and chairs in childcare—probably a carry-over from elementary school practices—creates a lack of alternative play and sitting surfaces in many settings. Listed below are some suggestions for stimulating movement and satisfying children's motoric needs (see Chapter 16–18 for age-specific recommendations):

- Use walls to support play panels, vertically mounted toys, grab bars, textures, mirrors, and reflective surfaces at different heights.
- Build off walls and vertically mounted play panels to create seats, tables, counters, high and low platforms, and sloping work surfaces. (See page 243, Figure 13.3.)
- Consider varying floors and horizontal surfaces by making them lowered or raised; hard or soft; textured or smooth; solid or slatted; flat, inclined, or wavy. Incorporate resilient natural or man-made materials, water mattresses, air mattresses, sacks of beanbag pellets, trampolines, and net or suspension bridges into floors and platforms.
- Use carpeted risers as boundaries, objects to climb and crawl over, play and sitting surfaces (for both adults and children), or supports for toddling.

Low wavy walls assist toddlers and children with disabilities and support interesting interactivities.

A single dowel, mounted at any height desired, holds changeable household and houseware items for exploration.

A carpeted wavy floor made of ¼ inch Masonite over fiberboard tubes challenges all ages.

A net bridge 5½ feet above the floor can hold a 250-pound man and delight a child with disabilities.

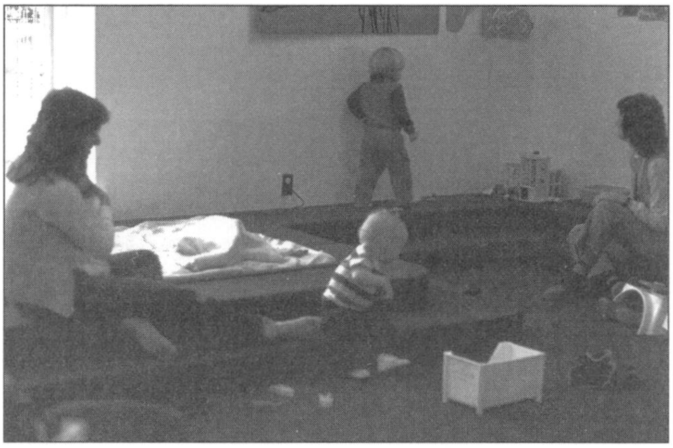

Tiers of carpeted risers serve as boundaries, objects to climb and crawl over, play and sitting surfaces, and supports for toddling.

Play equipment can be suspended from a beam spanning a room's narrowest dimension.

Using Ceilings to Support Play

Ceilings are invaluable for suspending movement apparatus and interactives, provided the ceiling is sturdy, within adult reach, and low enough to limit the torque of swinging objects. Try to design a portion of every group room's ceiling as a grid of wooden slats 6 inches apart, over a floor area where suspended items are likely to be used (see page 240). Or include a single beam, spanning the room's narrowest dimension, from which you can hang a swing, birdcage, punching bag, or swinging basket chair.

GUIDELINES: SELECTING PLAY AND SITTING SURFACES

- Children do not necessarily gravitate toward tables and chairs. The ages and physical needs of the children working in an activity area, as well as the activity itself, help determine the most appropriate type and height of play and sitting surfaces.
- Think first of children's characteristic movements and postural needs—not just of standard furnishings—when designing play and sitting surfaces.
- To increase spatial versatility, strive to minimize the number of tables in a room.
- Scale tables for four to six persons to promote conversational intimacy.
- Provide tables of various heights: 10 inches (good for clay and construction); child counter-height (good for science, art, water, sand); regular child height (good for eating, collage).
- Experiment with having a drafting-type table with an inclined surface.
- Tables with cut-outs usurp valuable space and limit children's ability to interact. Small round, square, rectangular and trapezoidal tables, which can be joined to form surfaces of various shapes and sizes, are more useful.
- Stools, couches, beanbag chairs, waterbeds, pillows, hammocks, net and swinging chairs, rockers, platforms, and risers are excellent alternatives to regular chairs in many instances.
- Consider ways that walls, floors, dividers, platforms, and ceilings can be designed to provide varied play and sitting surfaces within each room.
- Consider ways to use vertical space more effectively for storage, or as climbers and lofts for children's use.

Orientation of Play and Sitting Surfaces

In arranging sitting and play surfaces, strive to honor children's orientational needs for physical security at their backs and for monitoring surrounding areas. (See Chapter 1.)

Physical Security. Since people lack eyes in the backs of their heads, they feel most secure when their backs are protected and when they can monitor what approaches them head-on. Sitting and play surfaces need to be oriented so that children's backs are against or perpendicular to the wall and so that they face into the room. Do not force children to expose their backs to the room.

Ability to Monitor Surrounding Areas. Physical security also entails having some contact with events beyond one's immediate sphere. Too much protection can be as unsettling as too much immediate physical or visual input, especially if children feel cut off from things around them and cannot predict what might interfere with their activity or position. The orientation of play surfaces, as well as variations in the height and penetrability of boundaries, should enable a child seated in an area to have outward visibility on at least one side. As long as sufficient space exists between the child and the potentially distracting events, external activities will not impinge on the child's play. The option to visually "monitor" other areas of the room is comforting because of the background information it provides.

Adults instinctively position their backs against walls or in the most protected corners of the room, leaving children, especially if seated in a circle on the floor at group-meeting times, vulnerable with their backs exposed. When children's needs for back security and visibility are not met, behavior problems are the likely result. If it is impossible for both children and adults to have protection at their backs, children need access to the corners, walls, and spaces of greatest protection.

Group meetings are noticeably more congenial when conducted in an L-shaped seating arrangement, such as two tiers of risers nestled into a corner (Figure 15.7). The security provided by the walls and the right-angled orientation:

Figure 15.7
Two tiers of carpeted risers built into a corner make group meetings more intimate and congenial.

Materials for use in a given area need to be stored and displayed so that they are accessible to children's play and sitting surfaces.

- Allow children to make eye contact with one another
- Promote intimacy by reducing the territory the group occupies
- Eliminate the "Teacher, I can't see" complaint
- Place all children equidistant from the caregiver (sitting at floor-level in the middle of the L)

Rather than being a distraction, the opportunity to scan the entire room while sitting on the risers keeps children awake and attentive.

Providing Materials Storage and Display

As discussed in Chapter 4, child care spaces never seem to have enough storage space. While staff need storage for bulk supplies and for materials that require adult supervision or are subject to rotated use, much of the storage in group rooms needs to be accessible to children's play and sitting surfaces. Then children can see what is available, where it is to be used, and where it belongs. Otherwise, adults spend too much time transporting items from large locked supply cabinets, and being purveyors of materials rather than facilitators of learning. Materials accessible to children need to be displayed as much as to be stored.

Importance of Attractive Materials Display

A child's invitation to play is communicated by the visual presence of play materials, not by furniture, play platforms, and work surfaces. For example, cushions on the floor next to an empty bookcase do not make a reading area. However, an attractive display of shelved books clearly indicates that the cushions are to be sat upon while reading, rather than used as a "landing pad" for jumping off the shelves. A puzzle can be irresistible when placed invitingly on a wide counter, but will generate little interest piled haphazardly on a shelf. Similarly, locked cabinets and empty shelves proclaim: "Hands off. These materials are too precious to be put out for your use. You can have only what the teacher chooses." But the message of well-stocked, child-height shelves is: "Look at our beautiful wares. Come touch them, use them, and learn from them."

Massing color, height, and quantity are display tactics that caregivers, as display artists, are called on to employ continually for the effective functioning of their rooms. Good display of materials is one of the two activity area attributes most often overlooked by designers. (Boundaries are the other.) Clear, visible storage and display provide children with unambiguous physical surroundings for orientation and limit-setting, capture their curiosity, entice them into an area, and enable them to find and replace the materials they need for activities.

Quantity of Materials on Display

The quantity of materials displayed affects their perceptibility, accessibility, and use. Too few materials make a place uninteresting, as if there is nothing to do;

Choose bins that fit the items they hold and display them distinctively.

too many materials make it appear chaotic and also make it difficult to know where to begin. Provide different types of materials involving varying degrees of complexity[3] and requiring differing numbers of cooperative users to:

- Allow each child to feel competent at something
- Ensure that the unique interests of individuals will be met
- Ensure that children at different stages of development will be challenged
- Encourage cooperative play

Instead of making everything available at once, rotate the supply of materials put out for use. Also, periodically change the display location of materials that are available continuously, to renew children's interest. Infants and toddlers cannot tolerate as many exposed items as older children. (See Chapter 16.)

Organization

It is important that caregivers take the time to organize and set up the room prior to the children's arrival. Once the desire to do something is initiated, a child finds it hard to wait for the activity to be "set up" or to maintain interest while someone searches for the necessary tools. The full, constructive execution of an activity requires that all the props necessary for performing it be near at hand, in sufficient supply. Time spent after-hours setting up a room frees caregivers to be facilitators rather than custodians of learning, and supports children's basic needs for self-sufficiency and independence. Good basic design and room organization enable caregivers to prepare the environment with a minimum of effort and additional time—critical concerns given the long hours of child care.

Types of Storage Containers

Storage shelves and bins need to fit the items they hold and display them distinctively. Proper containers hold all the pieces at once, show their contents clearly if stored above children's eye-level, and yet are light enough to carry and small enough not to usurp all the work surface. Children will be encouraged to care for and put things away if there are cues, such as images, by which to do so. Placing storage units right beside the play surfaces where the materials are to be used minimizes transport, loss, and extraneous movements through the room.

Works-in-Progress and Personal Treasures

To ensure that children are encouraged to take their time and expand upon unfinished projects, provide protected places for the storage and display of works-in-progress. These need to be out-of-the-way shelves and surfaces open to view and to air circulation for drying. Vertical tack surfaces that display children's work throughout the room reinforce a sense of belonging, enrich communication, and stimulate an interest in symbols. Paper and writing materials in every activity area will encourage children to draw and write about their activities. The visible display of children's unfinished and completed work, and of written and graphic materials throughout the room, stimulates talking about what one is doing. This in turn serves to strengthen vocabulary and communication skills and generate feelings of mutual pride and respect for work well done.

A child's willingness to risk bringing personal treasures from home to the neutral territory of the child care center is confirming evidence of a room's supportive design. It is best to give personal treasures proper display and safety. Applaud these items as children's desire to affirm their presence in the room and to have a stake in its composition.

Storage and Cleanup

The easiest way to encourage proper respect for materials, as well as a cooperative spirit of cleaning up, is to have the room's attractiveness convey such respect. Participation in cleanup allows children to learn basic self-help skills and to see the way others have used and combined the materials available in the room. While sweeping, washing, and storing things away, children practice primary motor skills, learn to be useful contributors to the room's maintenance, and gain information about creative possibilities.

GUIDELINES: PROVIDING MATERIALS STORAGE AND DISPLAY

- Emphasize the display of materials. The presence of play materials, not furnishings, communicates to children what there is to do. Children want to know what play materials are available, where they are to be used, and where they belong.
- The best way to store/display materials in an activity area is to place them right next to the children's play and sitting surfaces.
- Staff need additional storage space—above child height or elsewhere—for bulk supplies and items not in use, especially with infants and toddlers.
- The arrangement of individual items on a shelf affects how each is perceived. When planning displays, consider the items' color, size, quantity, and the amount of storage required.
- Select storage bins large enough to hold all the pieces of a play material, yet light enough to lift and small enough for the play surface. If storage bins are stored above children's eye level, they need to be transparent or labeled with an image or icon.
- Organized storage encourages children to keep the activity area clean and to replace materials.
- Too few materials make a place seem drab and uninteresting; too many make it appear chaotic. Appropriate quantities vary over time and situation.
- Provide space to store and display unfinished "works-in-progress."
- Vertical tack or display surfaces encourage sharing and communication.
- Having safe places to keep children's personal treasures from home increases children's sense of belonging and desire to personalize the room.

Varying Mood

Maintaining the same level of alertness all day places internal stress on children's bodies, even if the stress is not perceptible to the adult eye. Options for different levels of engagement help people to feel comfortable and remain alert over long periods of time. Many centers suffer from either blandness or overstimulation, with insufficient variety of mood. (See also "Children's Four Basic Environmental Needs" in Chapter 1.)

Aim to match the mood of each area to the physical energy children expend in performing its activity. For example, tranquil activities occur best in warm, soft, textured spaces; expansive activities require spaces that are cooler, harder, and more vibrant in tone. The ultimate goal is a room with multiple activity areas, each of which has a unique spirit of place. Then, as children go from place to place within the room's four walls, they can experience spaces that are soft and hard, dark and light, cold and warm, colorful and bland, large and small, noisy and quiet.

Differentiation in the *physical space* can be provided by varying:

- Floor height (raised or lowered levels, platforms, lofts, pits)
- Ceiling height (canopies, eaves, trellises, skylights)
- Boundary height (walls, half-height dividers, low shelves)
- Lighting (natural, fluorescent, incandescent, local, indirect)

GUIDELINES: MOOD

- Within each room, create areas with different moods—soft, hard, dark, light, cold, warm, colorful, bland, etc.—so that children will have choices and thereby be able to maintain their energy and attentiveness over the course of a long day.
- The mood of an activity area is created by personalized decorative techniques (pillows, color, textures, fabrics, knickknacks, and furniture design); by varying the physical parameters of space (floor height, ceiling height, boundary height, and lighting); and by varying the visual, auditory, olfactory, textural, and kinesthetic qualities of a space.
- Quiet, tranquil activities call for warm, soft, textured spaces. Expansive activities call for spaces that are cooler, harder, more vibrant in tone.
- Research indicates that the degree of "softness" in a room is predictive of the quality of care. The primacy of touch for young children, coupled with the fact that the skin is the largest organ of the body, make the presence of a variety of touchable textures critical to children's psychological and physiological well-being. Pillows, cozy furniture, wall hangings, carpets, and malleable and messy play materials (water, clay, paint, and sand) can effectively soften institutional blandness.

Mood is also created by decorative techniques that make a space sensorially rich and varied—plants, pillows, colors, textures, fabric, knickknacks, etc. Anything that moves, grows, changes shape (mobiles, wind chimes, fish, animals, plants), or reflects movement (mirrors) adds visual interest and excitement. Tablecloths, flowers, subdued lighting, and candles in nonbreakable jars at meal times create delightful atmospheres that are part of the good life children are entitled to share.

Sensory variety can be provided by varying:

- Visual interest (wall murals, classical art, children's paintings, views to trees and sky, color)
- Auditory interest (mechanical gadgets, music, voices humming, gerbils scratching, children laughing)
- Olfactory interest (cookies baking, fresh flowers, plants in the earth)
- Textural interest (wood, fabric, fur, carpet, plastic, laminate, glass)
- Kinesthetic interest (things to touch with different body parts; things to crawl in, under, and upon; opportunities to see the environment from different vantage points)

Mood is set by aesthetically pleasing spaces. "Beauty is as beauty does" in designed and constructed environments as well as in the social world. A beautiful space acts as a mirror of the well-being desired for all children and their caregivers.

Modifications for Children with Disabilities

Children with disabilities—physical, learning,[4] or perceptual—deserve plentiful opportunities to move and to interact with materials in the environment so that muscles and faculties do not weaken or atrophy with disuse. By age three or four, many children with disabilities are burdened with feelings of mistrust about their world, doubt about their abilities to affect that world, and shame and guilt about their behavior in the eyes of others. These feelings of inadequacy are issues that can be affected by a room's design.

The Role of the Caregiver

Only by risking, doing, failing, redoing, and succeeding can each child grow optimally. Overprotective caregivers who, in the presumed interests of safety or to avoid legal culpability, prevent a child with a disability from experiencing the risk-taking essential for normal development, simply retard and prejudice that child's chances for a positive developmental outcome. The challenge should always be to enable children to move with and even without their mechanical supports, in order to maximize use of both their stronger and weaker capabilities. Out of the freedom to explore, to experiment, to make mistakes, and to master new skills comes the self-confidence of knowing they can succeed, which is the best guarantee that they will be able to succeed in years ahead.

The Hyperactive Child

It is usually argued that hyperactive children suffer from overactive nervous systems that need to be calmed by reducing environmental stimulation. An alternative interpretation,[5] although speculative, argues that the prescriptive to strip environments bare for hyperactive children only serves to exacerbate their problems because it reduces environmentally derived

Free-standing play structures allow children with disabilities to experience the tactile properties of rough barn wood, operate door latches, and lift the lid of a mailbox (not shown).

sources of stimulation, and forces them to rely almost exclusively on their own activity to energize their nervous systems. If the physical environment is rich and varied, hyperactive children may be able to find outside themselves the stimulation needed to settle into activities for sustained periods of time.

Special Design Features

The following general concepts are intended to highlight design features that can augment a basic room plan where children with disabilities are integrated with more typical children. Space does not permit coverage of the extensive recommendations for clearance, transfer, height, width, reach range, maneuverability, etc., of children under age five with disabilities. Readers are encouraged to consult the Universal Building Code as well as the proposed ADA accessibility guidelines for play areas.[6] Because adaptive equipment for specific needs is not always available, it is also helpful to consult national and local parent groups organized for particular disabilities—spina bifida, multiple sclerosis, cerebral palsy—which sometimes informally distribute useful designs and adaptations of standard equipment that members have created.[7]

Exploring and doing builds self-confidence.

A ramp with cleats enables children with physical disabilities to pull themselves up to a sandbox at a higher level.

Mobility and Transport

The greatest environmental barrier for a child with a physical disability is lack of access to desired spaces and facilities. Children wearing crutches or braces and those in wheelchairs require extra-wide, clear transit pathways through the room and wide entrances to boundaried areas. Sufficient floor space in each area is required for the child's wheelchair or crutches. Expandable metal grips can be fastened to the sides of chairs, tables, and storage units, or onto walls to hold crutches upright and out of the way. Sometimes, a tummy board on casters, which the child lies across and propels with his or her arms, can be used as a substitute for braces and wheelchairs.

Do not eliminate raised levels in a room simply because children with physical disabilities will use the area; changes in height frequently challenge them to exercise limbs and faculties that can benefit from use. Following are some guidelines for appropriately modifying the height and design of raised levels so that they can be accessed by those with physical disabilities:

- Platforms less than 1 foot above the floor may require a gradually sloping ramp at the entry.
- Lofts and structures 2 or more feet higher than the floor will need a ramp supplemented by cleats, ropes, or grab bars on the ramp surface or sides, by which children can pull themselves up to the higher level.
- A wheelchair or walking ramp with handrails on both sides needs to project 12 inches in length for every 1-inch rise in height (known as a 1–in–12 slope), potentially usurping floor space and getting in the way of children's movement. (Without handrails the slope is 1 in 20.) Therefore, establish a reasonable balance between the height of a structure and the length of the ramp required to get to it. In the case of high structures, the ramp can double back on itself to conserve space. A minimum 5-foot-diameter landing is required for wheelchairs.
- Provide a seat and storage space near the ramp's entry for a child who needs to remove braces in order to climb the ramp. Design the storage space so as not to interfere with any child's movement around the structure.

Sitting Surfaces

Children with physical disabilities need:

- Considerable back support
- The ability to have their legs in line with their bodies (standing or lying) or hanging straight down from their knees

Sitting on the floor or on stools or risers without backs may be uncomfortable for them. Following are helpful alternatives:

- Seats with backs, especially in self-help areas (coat cubbies, toilets), maximize the independence of children with physical disabilities. These seats can be outfitted with casters for the mobility of children with braces, to reduce their need to shift from sitting to standing in order to get about.
- Places to lie down and stretch out, such as platforms, water beds, and modular foam furniture that open to form a bed, greatly relieve muscle tension and encourage relaxation. (See page 235.)

In quiet areas, a wheelchair potentially violates the protection from transit which floor-based activities need. When a child with a physical disability cannot get down on the floor to play, a small table with several chairs (for friends)—placed near the storage units at the edge of such an area—can enable the child to participate in the activity without infringing on the area's security. Miniature block sets are an attractive tabletop alternative to unit blocks on the floor.

Play Surfaces

Tables/Wheelchair Trays. A child in a wheelchair usually sits too high to reach the surface of a table at standard child-height. Higher tables with cut-outs clearly expand work surfaces for children in wheelchairs or with restricted torso mobility but tend to be higher than a standard chair and quite large, thus quickly overpowering a space. A viable alternative is a *wheelchair tray*, which most manufacturers produce in a variety of sizes and designs. Despite appearances, trays usually do not isolate the child from peers any more than large tables with cut-outs do, and they conserve space.

Sand Tables. Tables at which children with disabilities may stand to work, such as a sand table, may need to be higher than tables for children who are not disabled and may require a semicircular support to brace the child's body.

Water Tables. In contrast, a water table may need to be lower, to both support the body and free the child's arms to reach over and into the water. Since spilled water underfoot is dangerous, a nonskid surface should always be provided under the trough. Children in wheelchairs at outdoor sand and water tables require sun and wind protection.

Workbenches. Workbench activities can throw the body backwards, making children with disabilities lose their balance. Bracing, by means of sturdy chairs, body straps, or placement of the workbench parallel to a nearby wall, may be helpful.

Drafting Tables. Consider providing a surface with variable angles of inclination, such as a drafting table (at which a child may sit on a high stool, feeling important). Children with special needs, or with visual impairments, may better perceive symbols viewed at an angle they can control, than in a predominantly horizontal or vertical orientation.

Other Play Facilities. Other types of play facilities that children with disabilities can share with those who are not disabled are shown here and on page 294.

Storage and Display Units. In most cases, it is not necessary or advisable to change the height of storage and display units for the child in a wheelchair. Doing so can interfere with the accessibility, visibility, and design of boundaries for the other children. However, the tops of storage units, especially if widened, can become good work and display areas for children in wheelchairs.

Infants can spin a "magical" marble embedded in a bench at infant height.

A vertically mounted xylophone makes it possible for a child in a wheelchair to compose a tune.

A fiberboard tube mounted on a lazy susan and enclosed with plastic makes an inexpensive marble spinner.

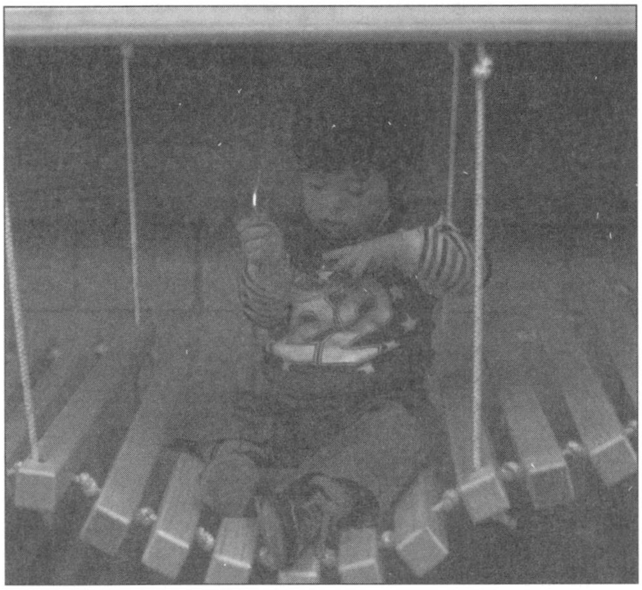

Inexpensive and easy-to-build suspension bridges promote sensori-motor integration whether walked or sat upon.

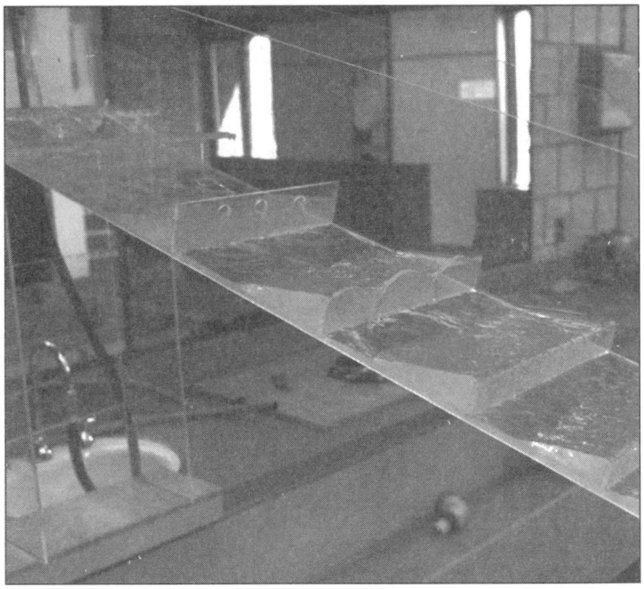

Even when children can't play with water, they still can see and hear it running down an acrylic/plastic sluice.

Modifications for Deaf Children

Good visibility into and out of areas increases the contact of deaf children with ongoing events and the ability of others to engage them from a distance. Materials and surfaces that transmit vibrations, especially wooden platforms and lofts, are useful ways to increase a child with a hearing impairment's awareness of ambient movements and sounds. Lofts are valuable for enabling children to see what they cannot hear.

Modifications for Blind Children

Even children who are legally blind frequently have some minimal vision and light sensitivity. Provision of good lighting—without glare—can definitely assist children with minimal vision, especially where there are floor, wall, and table lamps they can adjust to their own needs.

Most blind children are fearful of moving through space. Since they tend to be light on their feet and tense in their upper bodies, they need help in lowering

Children unsteady on their feet are held securely as they "bounce" between two vertical sheets of rubber.

their center of gravity and moving on their feet, especially when weight shifts are involved. Comfortable, soft furnishings will help their muscles relax and help them gain confidence. Large-muscle equipment such as swings, tumblers, and rockers—designed to hold children securely while encouraging them to move their bodies in different directions—are invaluable therapeutically.

Raised areas can be accessed by blind children, providing the areas have no protruding, irregular edges. Keep dividers and boundaries to areas free from clutter, so children with visual impairments can use the edges of these spaces as tactile orientational guides. Textural changes (wood, carpet, Formica, brick, etc.) in floors, boundaries, and levels can provide significant clues for orientation and mobility. Research suggests that blind children can utilize echoes in detecting environmental features. The sounds emitted off certain materials may assist them in orientation, provided not all surfaces in the room are sound-absorbing.[8]

Changing and Maintaining a Room's Layout

Ideally, a room's design can change as its functional requirements change. Its activity areas should not be seen as unalterable. However, three concerns about modifying a room's layout are worthy of mention:

Textural variations in floors can provide blind and sighted children with cues for orientation and mobility.

1. When a room is poorly planned, staff may rearrange it frequently in an attempt to find a workable solution. This is extremely time-consuming for staff and unsettling for children, particularly those with disabilities, who require predictability about their world. Instead, ensure that the room's basic plan is sound from the outset (see Chapter 7).
2. Many group rooms, especially small ones, often can be laid out in only one way to accommodate the broad range of functions required. This means that the room's layout cannot be changed without sacrificing something.
3. The fact that a room's layout cannot or does not change is not a detriment. The basic functions of rooms in a house (kitchen, living room) usually remain the same. It is important not to compromise the principles of activity-area location simply for the sake of change. Instead, consider changing the design and development of the other four attributes of an area—boundaries, play and sitting surfaces, storage and display, and mood—as time and the program progress. The areas themselves, rather than the room's overall layout, are really the locus of the room's educational program.

Once a comfortable, well-functioning room layout has been achieved, take steps to see that it is maintained. Custodians can cooperate in this process if they are given clearly labeled floor plans and explanations for a room's arrangement so they are not tempted, by force of habit, to simply push all the furniture back against the walls.

Summary

The design of an activity area is based upon:

- Its function or the nature of the activity it supports
- The number of users
- The body postures assumed in performing the activity
- The protective supports the activity requires

To complete the layout of a group room, consider the five attributes of activity area development:

1. *Locate* each activity area according to the degree of protection or exposure it requires and in its appropriate zone within the room.
2. Give each area *boundaries* with the appropriate degree of firmness or fluidity to optimize children's comfort, visibility by staff, and the safety of the materials being used in the area.
3. Provide appropriate *play and sitting surfaces* for the activities performed and materials used in the area.
4. Provide appropriate *storage and display* for materials used in the activity.
5. Give each area a distinct *mood* or *spirit of place*.

In order to meet the varied developmental needs of different age groups, and the requirements of all children, including those with disabilities, strive to make at least the following six categories of experience available at all times in every group room: quiet, structured, craft/discovery, dramatic-play, large muscle, and therapeutic.

Notes

[1]For example, the only difference between the small letters b and d, both of which consist of a circle and a line, concerns the spatial orientation of the line as either to the right or left of the circle.

[2]Adapted from M. Wolfe and R. Laufer, "The Concept of Privacy in Childhood and Adolescence," in *Man-Environment Interaction*. ed. D.H. Carson (Milwaukee, WI:EDRA, 1974).

[3]See S. Kritchevsky, E. Prescott, and L. Walling, *Physical Space: Planning Environments for Young Children* (Washington D.C.: National Association for the Education of Young Children, 1977).

[4]The manifest problems of learning-disabled children, most of whom have difficulty dealing with symbols, may stem from immature or improper development of their sensorimotor systems. J. Zeller, 1985 *A Methodology for the Identification of Specific Motor Deficits*, Harvard University: Doctoral Dissertation, found that 98% of the 500 learning-disabled children she tested were characterized as being physically "clumsy." Others have demonstrated that learning-disabled children learn symbols more readily after being trained to use fundamental motor patterns such as crawling, falling, rocking, spinning, etc. See A. J. Ayres, *Sensory Integration and Learning Disorders* (Los Angeles: Western Psychological Services, 1973).

[5]J. H. Satterfield et al., "Response to Stimulant Drug Treatment in Hyperactive Children: Prediction from EEG and Neurological Findings," *J. Autism Child Schizo*. 3 (1973): 36–48 offer an alter-

native interpretation of the hyperactive syndrome: Because amphetamines, which energize the average adult or child, tend to slow down hyperactive children, they hypothesize that these children's nervous systems may be asleep or underactive. Such children move excessively in an attempt to provide themselves with the sensory stimulation they need to stay alert and able to function at levels similar to their classmates. Amphetamines thus make the hyperactive child appear calm because, consistent with their effects on normally active individuals, they heighten the child's arousal levels in ways similar to their own bodily movements.

[6]Federal Register 1998, *ADA Accessibility Guidelines for Buildings and Facilities: Rules and Regulations*, Vol. 63, No. 8; *Proposed Rules*, Vol 63, No. 83.

[7]See also equipment designed by *Rifton*, P.O. Box 901, Rifton, New York 12471-0901.

[8]T. G. R. Bower (1977) *The Perceptual World of the Child.* Cambridge, MA: Harvard University Press.

CHAPTER SIXTEEN

SPACES FOR INFANTS AND TODDLERS

Remember as children our easy innocence
when alive with the new ability to see
we devoured a many faceted world.
Our unfettered imaginations
explored the mysterious corners
of small-scaled universes,
followed the paths of radiant lights
and joyous colors.
Harmony among many things
was so apparent then—
We had frogs as friends.
Our hearts were ever open
to continued discovery and surprise.

—BENJAMIN THOMPSON, *excerpt from unpublished poem*

This chapter addresses considerations specific to the design of activity areas in infant and toddler group rooms. It is intended to be used in conjunction with Chapter 7, Zoning a Group Room, and Chapter 15, Designing Group-Room Activity Areas. Through the use of questions, the chapter encourages you to create personalized solutions. Through the use of facilities lists, it outlines the basic supports for each area, and through the use of guidelines, it suggests design possibilities. Because many design considerations are similar for infants and toddlers, most are discussed together. However, where requirements clearly differ, they are addressed independently.

Program Considerations

First we need to consider several factors pertaining to the overall program of infant and toddler spaces: group sizes, ratios, and square footage; infant and toddler developmental capabilities; and what children at these ages need most.

Group Size, Ratios, and Square Footage

Every major study of infant and toddler care has shown that quality depends upon small group sizes, high staff-child ratios, stability of child care providers over time, and continuity of caregivers. As discussed in Chapter 4, consistent with good developmental practice, this guide espouses caring for:

- Infants from birth-to-15-or-18 months in groups of preferably 6 and no more than 8 babies with two caregivers
- Toddlers from 18-to-30-or-36 months in groups of 8 to no more than 10 with two caregivers

Smaller group sizes are always preferable (see Table 4.4). Maintaining caregiver continuity for the first three years is essential. Vulnerable infants and toddlers depend upon a primary, consistent, and stable adult with whom they feel bonded and intimately connected during the long hours of child care. Having one caregiver over an extended period of time, rather than switching every six to nine months, is important to a child's development during the radical changes of the first three years. Without continuity of care, infants and toddlers have to establish new primary relationships over and over again.

Although infant and toddler groups are small, the group room must support a full range of activities. This need for flexibility, as well as the use of bulky equipment, calls for generous amounts of storage and floor space. Because of these requirements, infant rooms need more square footage per child than do rooms for other ages[1]: about 90–100 square feet per infant, including sleeping, food prep, diapering, entry, parent areas, storage, and play. Toddler rooms need about 65–75 square feet per child for the same range of activities, excluding a separate sleep space (see discussion following Table 4.5).

Developmental Capabilities[2]

During the first 18 months, a child moves rapidly from being relatively stationary and unable to sit without support to crawling, sitting upright, pulling to stand, and walking. Each infant's cycle of sleeping, eating, playing, and maturing is unique.

Children 18–36 months progress from uncertain balance on their feet to being agile runners and climbers. Toddlers are continuously on the move and function best in an environment that protects them from straying too far, yet gives free reign to their inquisitiveness and desire to practice a full range of movements.

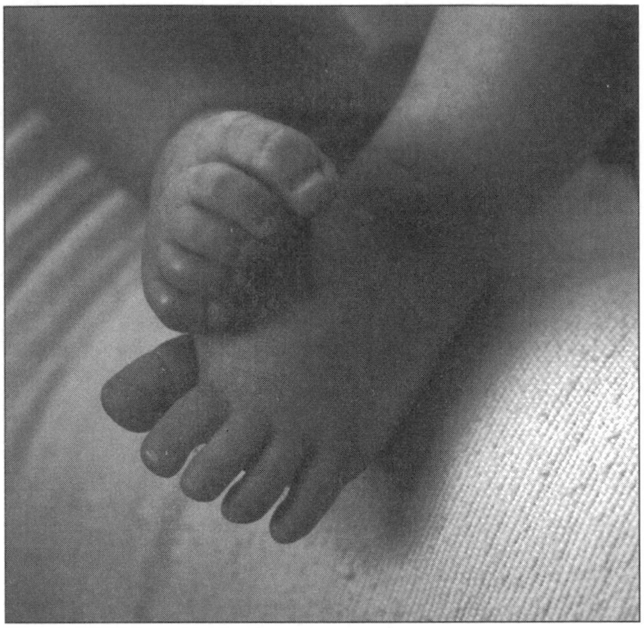

Box 16.1 summarizes some of the developmental landmarks of children between birth and 36 months of age.

What Infants and Toddlers Need

The needs of infants and toddlers can be most easily discussed in three separate areas: the need to be held and carried, the need for sensation, and the need for movement.

The Importance of Being Held and Carried

Infants are born expecting to be held and loved. For millennia newborns were carried by their mothers as they worked. (The Balinese, for example, consider it dangerous and sacrilegious for babies to touch the ground before 105 days of age.) They were jostled, slung, and balanced against the flesh of human beings engaged in the natural motions of living. Infants absorbed great quantities and varieties of experience through their adventures in the arms and on the backs of a busy person. The devices of modern Western babyhood—carriages, infant seats, cribs, playpens—were unknown.

BOX 16.1

Mastery of Developmental Tasks Birth to 36 Months

Developmental Task	Beginning Age
What Infants Can Do	
roll over	2–5 months
reach for toy	3–5 months
bring toy to mouth	3–5 months
sit up alone	6–10 months
turn towards soft sounds	6–12 months
play peek-a-boo, patty cake, hide objects in fist, look at books, talk	6–12 months
pick up objects with thumb and finger	7–10 months
bang 2 blocks together; clap hands	7–15 months
crawl	8–11 months
stand holding on	8–12 months
hold cup and drink	10–17 months
walk alone	11–15 months
fill molds with sand; pots/pans as drums	12–18 months
roll and catch big soft ball; pull toys; build towers with small boxes and knock over; stack two blocks	12–20 months
say 3–10 words; mamma, dadda	12–21 months
scoop up water and pour it out; nest cups; take off own clothes	14–22 months
What Toddlers Can Do	
take off clothes and shoes	14–22 months
follow two directions	14–30 months
point out body parts	18–24 months
say two words together	18–24 months
use playdough or clay	18–24 months
pretend play with dolls, stuffed animals, adult clothes, tricycles, toy vehicles	18–24 months
put on clothes, shoes	20–36 months
climb up and down stairs	24 months
hop 2–3 steps on one foot, jump	24 months
kick a ball	24 months
use cup and spoon	24 months

In a trend-defying book entitled *The Continuum Concept,*[3] psychologist Jean Liedloff argues for the importance of returning to this "in-arms" phase of child-rearing during the first six to eight months of life because such continual contact provides most humans with the basic experiences of safety, security, and being unconditionally loved. This, in turn, leads to trust in life, in others, and in one's self. Liedloff believes that current practices that regulate infants' rhythms and place them in physical contact with inanimate holding devices deny infants an essential opportunity to know their own inherent goodness, right to life, and place in human society. As a result, she hypothesizes, we have the malaise, abuse, addiction, violence, social pathology and "longing to be loved" so characteristic of contemporary culture.[4] By contrast, the children and adults in the indigenous culture she studied (a carrying rather than a cash society) exhibited a joy, self-reliance, social responsibility, and contentment glaringly absent in our own.

Consistent with Liedloff's hypothesis, worldwide cross-cultural studies of childhood physical affection and adult violence by neuropsychologist James Prescott, Ph.D. and geographer James DeMeo, Ph.D. indicate that cultures with high levels of physical affection or body pleasure for their infants and children also have low levels of adult violence; cultures with low levels of physical affection and body pleasure were observed to have high levels of adult violence.[5]

Infants thrive on being held and carried "in arms."

Liedloff's "in arms" premise may not prevent every societal or individual wound. However, its implications are profound and not ones we can afford to ignore. Both mothers and their infants grieve when separated while a baby is young. Often, child care center caregivers grieve when brought an infant as young as three weeks or three months for full-time care. As noted in Chapter 1, enabling mothers to remain at home with their infants for the first six weeks to six months can help to promote (although it cannot guarantee) care that is more likely to result in physical contact and carrying.

But if infants in child care need to be "in arms," how many can one adult hold at a time? Mothers attest to the all-consuming needs of even one infant, and to the juggling act required to care for two. Yet most states decree that one caregiver is capable of managing a minimum of three or more babies single-handedly and that two caregivers can handle seven or more! When one caregiver changes a diaper, answers the phone, prepares food, or goes to the toilet, the other caregiver is responsible for the entire group. This almost superhuman task imposes great strain on staff and the infants in their care.

Although no panacea, design can ameliorate the realities of group care, especially if it facilitates physical contact between infants and adults and provides movement opportunities to supplement experiences of being held. Keeping group sizes small, and providing

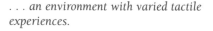

. . . an environment with varied tactile experiences.

different types of slings and backpacks to suit varying caregiver sizes and comfort, can also increase the potential for infants to be carried and held.

The Importance of Sensation

Infants and toddlers are sensorimotor beings. Being sentient more than conscious, their bodies soak up the rhythms and patterns of sound, light, movement, temperature, texture, and form around them. Life is experienced through the body, as a whole. Nothing is irrelevant or neutral.

This calls for an environment filled with sensory delights: pleasant aromas; delightful sounds; interesting colors, plants and live moving creatures (fish, pets); changing light and shadows; and wonderfully varied tactile experiences. Since the skin is the largest organ of the body, and touch the most critical of the senses for children under three[6] or with a special need, it is vital to ensure that textured elements—cozy furniture, carpets, pillows, wall hangings, malleable and messy play materials—are plentiful in infant and toddler spaces.

The Importance of Movement

Infants and toddlers spend much time mastering movements involved in body control, object control, and control of self in space: sitting, swaying, crawling, grasping, bending, turning, walking, climbing. They need to learn to move, and they learn by moving. To encourage this learning, the environment must be designed to foster safe movement. When spaces for infants and toddlers are not designed to promote safe and stimulating movement, children will find unsafe ways to move and caregivers will constantly be saying "no" and demanding restraint. "Sculpting" the entire space as a landscape for interaction, makes it possible to both nourish children's senses and encourage the movement they require. Chapter 15 suggested some options for stimulating movement (see especially page 285).

Thus, a nurturing environment for children under three:

- maximizes children's physical and emotional contact with adults
- facilitates custodial tasks to increase caregivers' availability to children
- provides a varied, nurturing, and sensorially rich context for children's earliest, most impressionable interactions with the nonhuman world
- encourages children to learn to move and to delight in practicing and achieving new physical skills

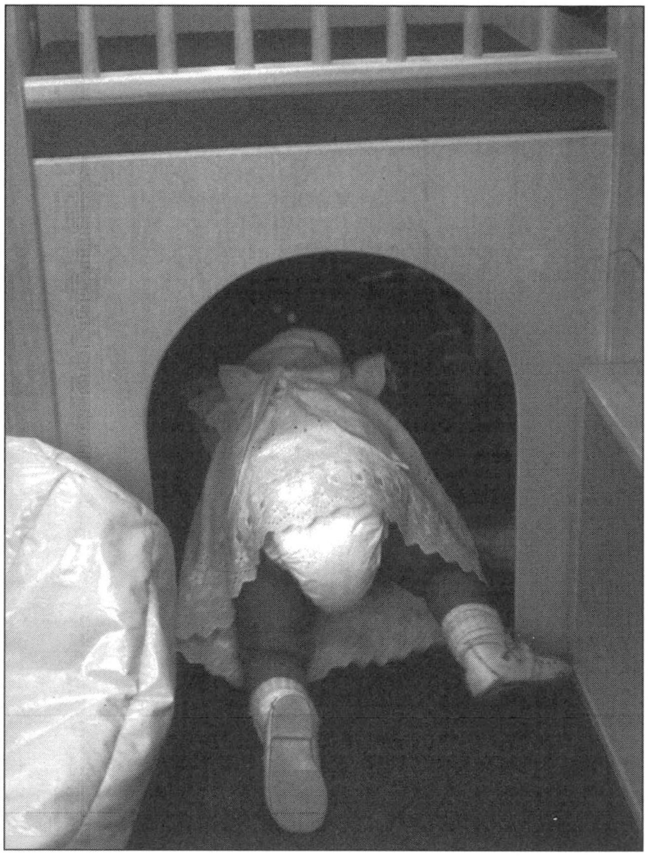

. . . an environment that encourages movement.

Design Considerations

In addition, infant and toddler spaces benefit when the team keeps in mind the following general considerations related to room layout and design for these age groups.

Organization: Zones and Activity Areas

Every infant and toddler room needs to have the four zones—entry, messy, active, and quiet—described in Chapter 7. In addition, infant rooms also need sleeping, nursing, and food preparation space, and both infant and toddler rooms need to provide the six types of play experiences described in Chapter 15.

Research indicates that small babies are highly sensitive to the appearance and organization of their surroundings.[7] They can remember physical landmarks (such as the location of windows) as well as bodily cues (when mother unbuttons her blouse I can nurse). In progressing from sitting to crawling to walking they use spatial features such as boundaries, shapes, and mass to navigate. Clear, stable room organization assists them in learning basic cause-and-effect relationships involving objects and people.

Orientation to Light

Because of their limited mobility and limited ability to get outdoors, infants and toddlers need the sunniest locations in the building, and the easiest, most direct access to outdoor play yards. (For the importance of light, see Chapters 10 and 11.)

Parent Interaction

The physical presence of parents and extensive parent-staff communication are indispensable for infants and toddlers. Creating informal places for parent/staff and parent/child interaction—alcoves, partially enclosed areas—promotes interaction. Thoughtful design treatment of the entry zone (discussed later in this chapter) can help to ease separation anxiety.

Staff Concerns

Minimizing the physical and emotional stress on caregivers is an important priority in designing rooms for infants and toddlers. Lifting and carrying children weighing 20–35 pounds, and repeatedly getting up from or down onto the floor can be physically demanding. Providing at least one adult-height chair helps to ease these burdens. A small, low couch where an adult and children can sit together promotes physical contact, especially if it is sturdy enough for infants to pull up on and toddlers to climb. An ordered environment with good sight lines and uncluttered floors that can be traversed quickly enables staff to easily supervise the group while interacting with a single child. Settings that keep children both safe and occupied help staff relax their vigilance, so they can be more playful and attentive to the needs of individuals. (See also Child/Caregiver Interaction later in this chapter.)

The Floor

In infant and toddler spaces the focus is on the floor; it therefore needs to be soft, warm, and without drafts. Visual and auditory communication from the center of the room to the periphery needs to be unobstructed so that adults can move quickly to the periphery for any child requiring attention, and so children can keep an eye out for caregivers as they roam and explore. One way to accomplish this is to keep the room's center empty for transit, and to place changes in level on the perimeter. Depending upon the height and transparency required, boundaries to areas on the perimeter can then be designed as play and sitting surfaces. When level changes are built into a corner, walls constrain the activity on two sides, so fewer built boundaries are needed.

Keeping the center of the room open and free of furniture (assuming it is of reasonable size) enables it to function both for transit and as a hub or a changing stage that can be set for spontaneous events. Here, children may receive special attention from adults. Portable equipment stored elsewhere—such as mats, swings, parachutes, and air mattresses—can be set up to provide varied play experiences.

Infant Spaces

Infants need broad horizontal surfaces with minimal boundaries. Since floor areas in infant rooms may contain little furniture, *play spaces can easily fuse with or turn into transit zones.* Three ways to protect infants playing on the floor are to: 1) provide nooks and alcoves for play, 2) have ample square footage to separate play from transit, and 3) use some platforms and changes in level as play and sitting surfaces (Figure 16.1).

Every infant room needs a "plopping" place, both easily accessible to and somewhat protected from traffic across it, where adults can comfortably make physical contact with several babies at once (see the suggestions in *Changes in Level*, below).

Toddler Spaces

Toddlers, on the other hand, need opportunities to roam freely, over an "up and down" scape of subtle 3- to 6-inch changes in level that satisfy their relentless desire to perfect balancing and walking skills. (Level changes can also be used for quiet rest and cuddling.) Toddlers benefit from open space with defined boundaries, somewhat like a "corralled open range."

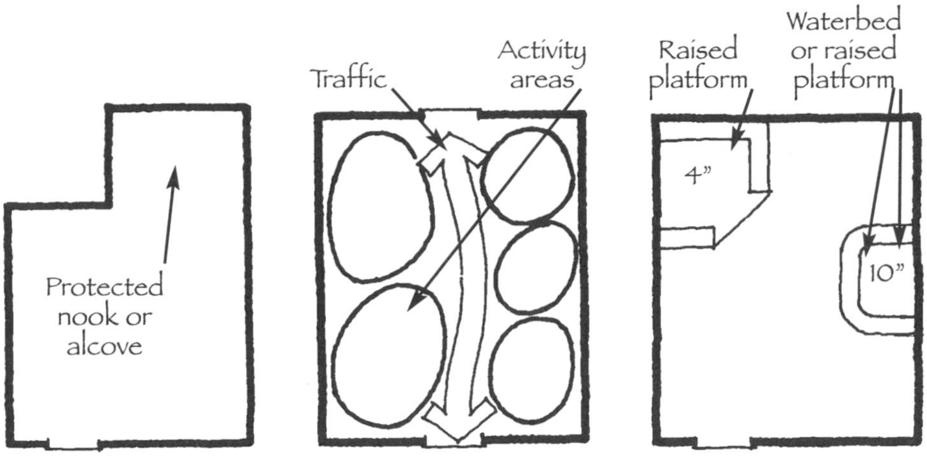

Figure 16.1
Protect infants playing on the floor by providing alcoves, ample square footage to separate traffic from play, or raised areas in the room.

Changes in Level

Platforms, risers, and lofts can function as "furniture" in infant and toddler rooms to provide protected, varied floor surfaces and places for exploration. Level changes may appear fixed but actually can be part of a "kit" of rearrangeable components. (See pages 275 and 328.)

- *Platforms 4–10 inches high* and at least 2–4 feet deep can be useful "plopping" places that offer physical protection and increase caregiver ease in getting up and down. They can incorporate water mattresses or other resilient surfaces.
- A crib- or twin-size water-mattress, surrounded by 5- and 10-inch high risers on which infants can crawl, stimulates sensorimotor integration while providing a safe place for several to cuddle and rest. (Also see pages 235 and 325.)
- *Carpeted risers 4–12 inches high* can serve as boundaries, play and sitting surfaces, objects to climb and crawl over, supports for pulling to stand, and for toddling. (See page 285.)
- *Surfaces raised 2–4 feet above the floor* provide children with a bird's-eye view of the world vital to cognitive mapping, exercise limbs, and add valuable square footage. The *spaces underneath* can be enclosed to varying degrees, and their ceilings and

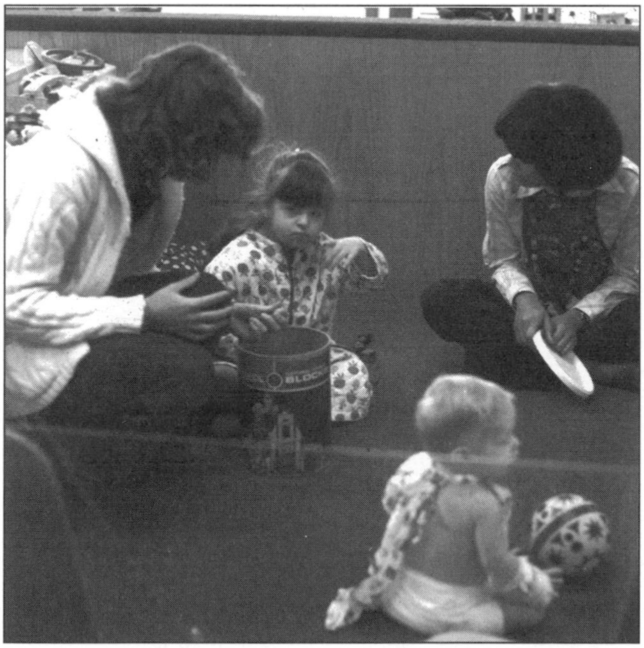

A 4-inch-high platform is comfortable for adults and children.

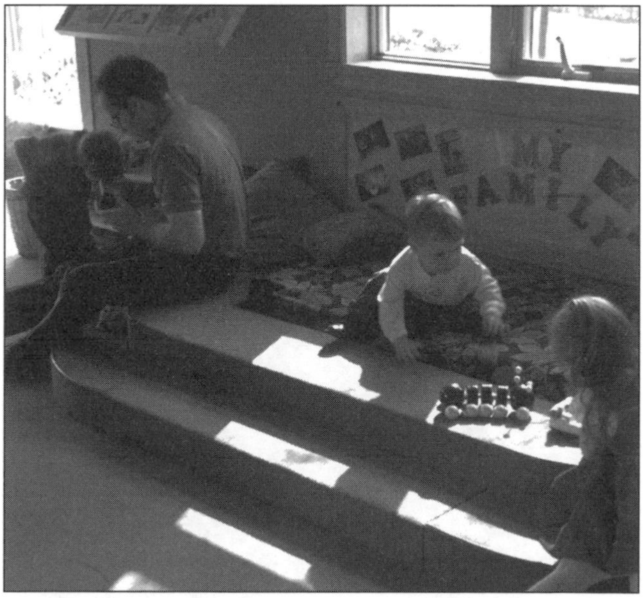

A regular or water mattress area makes a perfect "plopping" place for adults and infants to cuddle, play, and rest. (The Copper House)

Decorated spaces underneath lofts provide interesting places to explore.

Thirty-six-inch-high platforms make it possible for infants to be eye level to standing adults.

walls can be decorated with mirrors, Mylar, mobiles, graphics and varied textures as shown in the photo at left. (Note: children under 18 months do not like totally enclosed, womblike spaces.) An L-shaped loft creates at least two distinct zones above and below, as shown on page 324 later in the chapter.

As a platform's level rises, the height and rigidity of its boundaries need to be manipulated to prevent children from climbing over them or falling out, while still allowing them to watch or be watched by others. Visibility and safety are ensured when rails, cutouts, or Plexiglas panels are added.

- *Platforms no greater than 36 inches high* enable caregivers to lift infants and toddlers comfortably and relate to them at standing adult eye level. However, such spaces should not be used to "park" infants if they are confined areas where exploration is limited.
- *Props* can be built into levels to challenge balance and coordination. Some examples of such props might include regular-, water- and air-mattresses; sacks of beanbag pellets or varying densities of foam; trampolines; horizontal nets; mats; suspension bridges, and other resilient materials.

Accessible Toy Storage

In addition to plentiful closed storage, accessible toy storage is needed at child and adult levels. The tendency for infants and toddlers to gather, stack, dump, and knock down materials often results in piles of toys cluttering the floor. Manipulatives work best in bounded floor areas or on platforms surrounded by built-in storage that can contain the toys when they are pulled off shelves. (See pages 273 and 274.)

Safety

Safety precautions for infants and toddlers include warm and resilient flooring to cushion falls, rounded corners, no sharp edges, nothing children can accidentally pull down on top of themselves.

Furniture Dimensions

Recommended dimensions for infant/toddler furniture are indicated in Table 16.1.

Program-Specific Decisions for Infants/Toddlers[9]

In designing activity areas to support your infant and toddler programs, the following basics need to be considered:

- Arranging the entry zone to provide transition and support
- Facilitating interaction between child and caregiver
- Providing for sleeping/napping/rest
- Handling diapering/toileting
- Providing for feeding/eating
- Developing spaces that support a rich range of child-focused activities

Entry Zone

The general functions of the entry zone and the importance of transitions to children are explained in Chapter 7. The entry zone to an infant or toddler room is a place for:

- Welcoming parents and encouraging them to visit the rooms
- Storing children's outer clothing and staff belongings
- Removing adults' shoes to reduce dirt on floors where children crawl
- formal or informal check-in
- parents to observe children at play

Children from 3–36 months need to see their parents as often as possible, especially while still nursing. Often, infants and toddlers experience separation anxiety when parents depart and stranger anxiety in the presence of unfamiliar others. A well-designed entry eases the parents' transition and lets them informally observe their child without being seen, to ensure that their child has calmed down after he or she thinks they have left. Ideally, the design should also discourage children from going into the entry zone, where they might wander out the door or be overwhelmed by someone coming through it.

Table 16.1 ***Recommended Furniture Dimensions: Infants and Toddlers***

	Seat and Table Height[8]			
Age	Seat Height	Av. Seat Width	Av. Seat Depth	Table Ht.
6–18 mo	5″	11″	6.5–7″	12″
12–30 mo	6.5″	11″	6.5–7″	14″
24–36 mo	8″–10″	11″	6.5–7″	16″

Shelf Height	
Infants	12–15 inches
Toddlers	12–28 inches
Adults	4 feet above the floor, out of child reach

Water and Sand Play Table Height	
Infants	12 inches
Toddlers	18 inches

QUESTIONS: ENTRY ZONE

1. What images do you have of the entry to your infant or toddler room?
2. How many people are apt to occupy the entry at one time?
3. What activities must the entry accommodate?
4. How do you wish to handle observation of the group room from the entry?
5. How do you wish to handle check-in?

GUIDELINES: ENTRY ZONE

- Use gates, dutch doors, plants, or low dividers to set off the entry zone and create a protected space to which infants and toddlers have limited access.
- If possible, design the entry zone at an angle to the room, or with a large plant or semitransparent divider so that parents can observe children without being easily seen.
- Provide a couch, love seat, bench or carpeted riser where adults can sit to remove children's outer clothing and their own shoes.
- Provide a shelf, box, or designated floor space for storing adult shoes and boots.
- Provide a bulletin board for parent notices.
- Provide floor coverings that limit the transference of dirt to the group room.
- Provide storage for children's and staff's personal effects.

Low gates keep infants from crawling into the entry zone.

Child Personal Storage

Each infant and toddler needs storage space for outer garments (especially in wet climates), diaper bags, personal supplies, toys, and things they make to take home. The best place to store most of these items is near the room's entrance (or playground exit). However, storage for diapers and extra clothing is best located near the changing area.

QUESTIONS: INFANT/TODDLER PERSONAL STORAGE

1. Where do you want storage cubbies for outer garments? What size and design of cubby will work best?
2. Do you wish to store diapers and extra clothing near the changing area, or elsewhere? How much space is required for each child? What size and design of bin will work best?
3. What large items will you encourage/discourage parents from bringing/leaving at the center? Do you want to store these in the entry, the room, elsewhere?
4. Where will you store extra clothing for *toilet-training toddlers?*

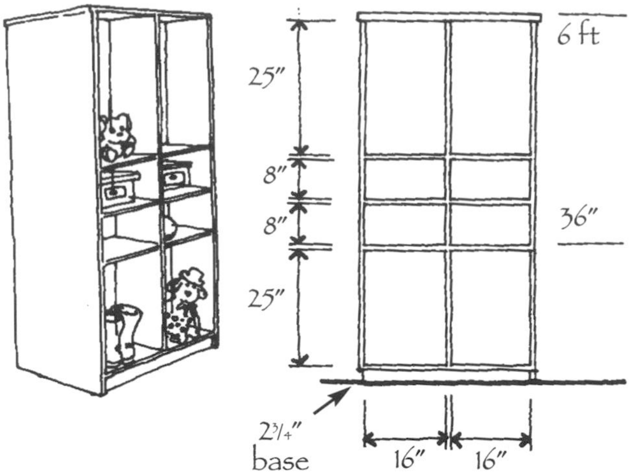

Figure 16.2
One possible design for an infant cubbie.

GUIDELINES: INFANT CUBBIES

- Provide each infant with a cubby approximately 16″ wide x 12″ deep x 32″ high to hold snowsuits, hats, mittens, favorite toys and large diaper bags of personal belongings. A shelf with a removable bin labeled with the child's name is also helpful (Figure 16.2). Since infants normally do not access their cubbies, a door or textile curtain on the front of each hides excessive paraphernalia, making the entry more visually appealing.
- If you wish infants to access their cubbies, the lower portion might contain a basket for toys and a blanket, while the upper portion is concealed behind a door.

GUIDELINES: TODDLER CUBBIES

- To facilitate self-dressing and a sense of ownership, design toddler cubbies so that children can access them (Figure 16.3). Provide separation of boots from coats. Supply rods or racks for drying mittens. Hang hooks at child height.
- Place a board in front of the lower portion of the cubby so that boots can be easily "stuffed in" and to catch clothing that drops from hooks.
- Mount a round of 4-inch PVC pipe on each cubby to store rolled paintings going home.
- Include a bench and *plenty of floor space* in the cubbie area: toddlers often lie on top of their snowsuits and jackets to get into them!
- Arranging cubbies in an L or a U shape can create an entry zone.
- Secure all free-standing units from tipping and falling.

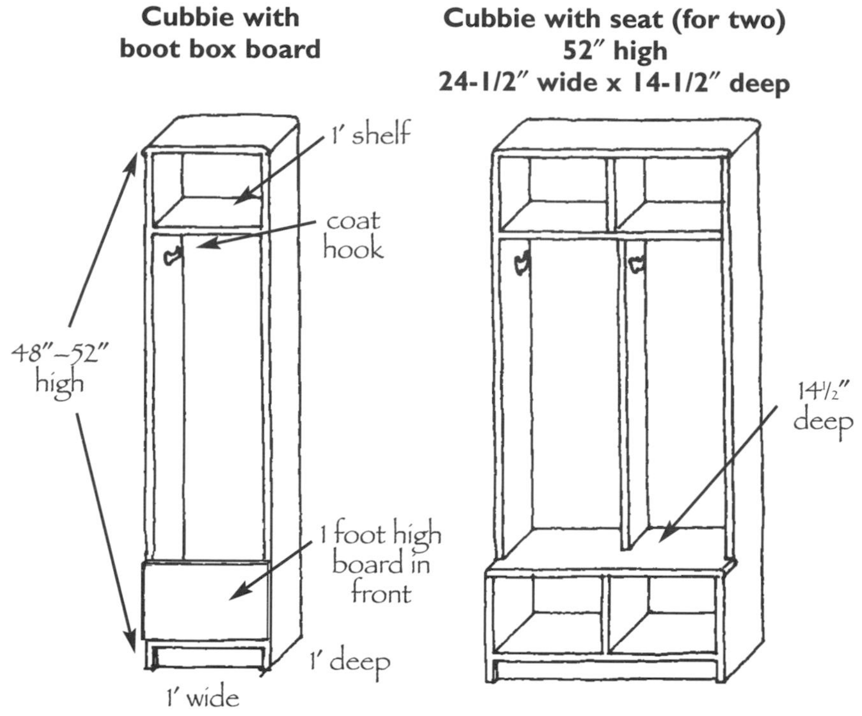

Figure 16.3
Two possible designs for a toddler cubbie.

Staff Personal Storage

Staff require storage for coats and purses, personal belongings, files and work materials.

QUESTIONS: STAFF PERSONAL STORAGE

1. What types of personal storage do staff want in the group room? Elsewhere?
2. What size is best for storage units? How might they look?

GUIDELINES: STAFF PERSONAL STORAGE

- Provide a coat closet in the entry zone for staff. Include a shelf, a rod and hangers, and floor space for shoes and boots.
- A mirror on the outside of this closet door can assist children as well as adults who are dressing or undressing.
- Provide appropriate secure storage for additional staff personal effects and files.

Carriage and Car-Seat Storage

Storage, convenient to the entry or exit, is needed for bulky equipment such as carriages, strollers, and car seats.

QUESTIONS: CARRIAGE AND CAR-SEAT STORAGE

1. What are the local codes concerning child transport and evacuation?
2. What equipment is needed to transport infants through the center, and outdoors? Where is this best located (at the entry to the building, near the infant/toddler rooms, in the play yard, elsewhere)?
3. What equipment is required for emergency evacuation of infants and toddlers—i.e., carriages, cribs on wheels, etc.?
4. Will parents leave car seats for someone else doing pick-up? If so, how many do you anticipate and where are these best stored?

GUIDELINES: CARRIAGE AND CAR-SEAT STORAGE

- Provide storage for carriages, carts, and car seats near the entry zone, but preferably not in it. These items are large and bulky! A stroller for three is 6 feet long x 30″ wide x 3′ high; carts which transport six are 5 feet long x 30″ wide,

Space underneath a staircase is perfect for storing infant carriages for three. (The Copper House)

A wagon for six.

with a 39″ high handle. Car seats measure approximately 18″ x 25″.

- Some considerations in locating transport storage: (1) place storage as near to the group room as possible to minimize staff absence from the room; (2) infants need to be carried to vehicles and cannot be left unattended; toddlers can walk in groups to get there; (3) large vehicles can be unwieldy to maneuver through the center and through average-sized doors.
- Ensure adequate planned storage space for carriages and carts so that they need not be stacked in corridors.

Other Storage

In addition to toys, books, and art supplies, infant and toddler programs require an astonishing amount of large, bulky equipment—swings; infant seats; feeding tables; foam mats, balls, etc. When not in use, these need to be stored away to free floor space for play.

Provide a consistent, clearly identified location for first aid equipment in every group room. The entry zone or a cabinet above the staff sink often works well.

QUESTIONS: OTHER STORAGE

1. What type, quantity, and size of items will require storage at some time? List these and list their dimensions. Custom-tailored storage for large items is more efficient.
2. How much shelf space, floor space, and other space is required to store these items? Provide dimensions wherever possible.
3. Where will you locate emergency first-aid equipment in each group room?

GUIDELINES: OTHER STORAGE

- Provide *large* amounts (40–60 sq ft) of enclosed storage space (closets) for bulky equipment and activity supplies. Locating closets near the entry reduces the chance they will block visibility.
- Place emergency first-aid equipment in a cupboard or in its own labeled cabinet in a visible, easy-to-reach location.

Parent/Staff Communication

Direct verbal and written communication between parents of infants and toddlers and staff is essential. Encourage parents to convey what has happened at home, and staff to convey what has happened at the center, daily. It is important that parents always feel welcome and have easy access to staff. Parent-to-parent contact is also desirable.

QUESTIONS: PARENT/STAFF COMMUNICATION

1. How and where do you envision parent-staff communication occurring—i.e., near the entry, throughout the room, special seating corner, etc.?
2. What supports do you wish for parent-staff exchange—i.e., mail boxes, notice board, coffee area, other?
3. How do you plan to encourage parents from different families to meet?
4. What types of environmental supports will encourage all of a child's significant adults to come frequently and to linger?
5. How do you intend to keep daily records of infants and toddlers and how/where do you wish to share these with parents?

GUIDELINES: PARENT-STAFF COMMUNICATION

- Provide obvious *informal* places where parents and staff can linger and chat.
- Provide ways for staff and parents to leave written notes (child's cubby; parent mail boxes, wall hangings with individual pockets, etc.).
- Provide a place (preferably private) where parents can review and respond to records of their child's daily eating, sleeping, and elimination patterns. The area shown later in food prep (page 319) might work well for this type of communication.

Child/Caregiver Interaction

Infant caregiving is physically and emotionally demanding and deserves utmost support from the environment. Since diapering and feeding occupy 50% of caregiver time, efficiency and ease in performing these functions are essential in maximizing the adult's ability to devote attention to children while performing these routine caregiving tasks. Well-designed environments facilitate supervision, lots of physical contact between adults and children, and primary caregiving.

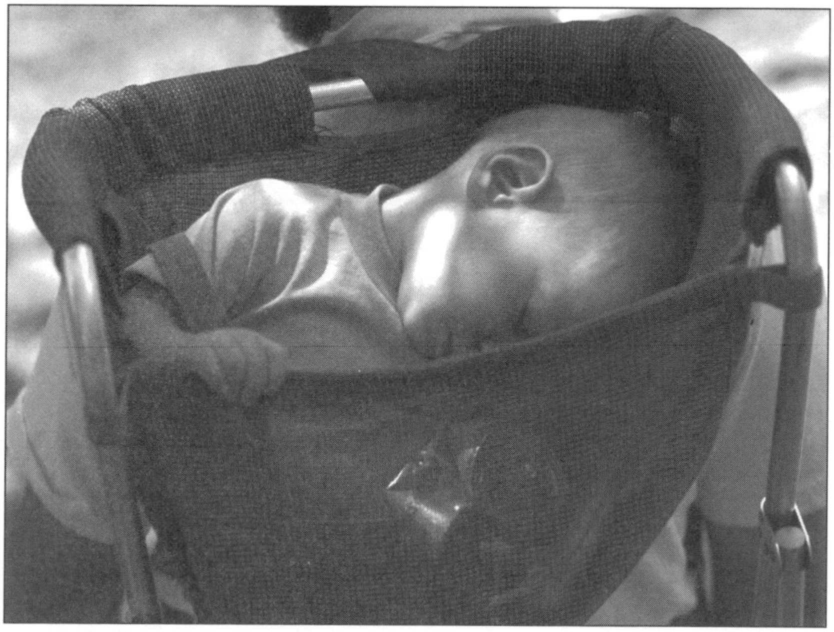

A variety of infant carrier styles ensures caregiver comfort.

The increased mobility of older infants and toddlers, coupled with their greater body weight, inquisitiveness, and poor impulse control, places great physical demands on staff. A well-defined environment provides safe and stimulating ways for children to move about while reducing custodial burdens.

QUESTIONS: CHILD/CAREGIVER INTERACTION

1. How can the environment and program encourage extensive physical contact between caregivers and infants/toddlers? Which staff supports can promote closeness?
2. How will you create warm, draft-free floors—the prime location for child/caregiver interaction?
3. What other supports would assist staff in their caregiving?

GUIDELINES: CHILD/CAREGIVER INTERACTION

- An ordered environment with good sight lines and uncluttered floors enables staff to maintain constant awareness of the group while focusing on a single child.
- Provide a range of slings, backpacks, and infant carriers that are comfortable for individual caregivers to wear.
- Provide at least one comfortable adult-height seat.
- Provide ways for adults to be comfortable sitting on or near the floor. Options include: stacking "back" seats; beach and canvas sling chairs; 6–12″ high boxes or foam cushions; mattresses (regular or water) and futons on the floor; platforms 4 to15 inches high (at least 2 x 4 feet) on which staff and infants can sit.
- Provide seating that adults and infants or toddlers can share: rocking chairs and gliders, hammocks, net, and wicker swinging chairs, large beanbag chairs, arm chairs, couches.
- Caregivers holding infants for feeding may be most comfortable seated on an adult-height couch or chair.
- *For toddlers:* Stairs that let toddlers climb onto changing tables reduce caregiver back strain (see the pull-out stairs in Figure 16.5 on page 316).
- Platforms 36 inches above the floor place children at standing-adult eye level.

Sleep Spaces

See Chapter 14 for general information on furniture and bedding for both age groups.

Infants

Infants spend many hours sleeping and benefit from a sheltered area where each baby has a separate crib in a space that feels like a bedroom at home, not like a "gang" room of cribs.

Choose crib styles and sizes early in the process and design the size of the sleep space around them. Small cribs are generally preferable because most states require a 2- to 3-foot separation between them, which means allocating 30 square feet per crib. (See Chapter 4, Table 4.5.) When adequate space is not allocated in advance, infant rooms easily become overrun with cribs and lack room for much else, especially safe places for babies to crawl about. This situation is untenable and detrimental to infant development.

In instances where, even with the use of small cribs, most of the room's square footage will be occupied by cribs, stacking units should be considered. Infants suffer far more from lack of space in which to move and explore than they do from being in snug bunks only while they are sleeping. The adult perception that stacking cribs look like "cages" is not borne out by the response of babies, who go to sleep faster and sleep longer in them. Indeed, all cribs are a form of cage.

QUESTIONS: INFANT SLEEP AREA

1. What images do you have of the sleep area in the infant room?
2. What size and type of sleeping equipment do you prefer? Given available square footage, how will you conserve floor space for play?
3. How do you prefer to group the 6–8 sleeping units, i.e., all in one large room, in 2 alcoves, other?
4. What form of separation do you envision between the activity area and the sleep area: (a) no wall, (b) half wall, (c) glass wall, (d) regular wall with windows?
5. What local codes for spacing, style of equipment, visual and acoustic access, and emergency evacuation must be honored? Are stacking cribs permitted?

GUIDELINES: INFANT SLEEP AREA

- Create a separate sleep area for 6–8 cribs, separated by walls, half walls, planters, or dividers, to which caregivers have visual, auditory, and quick physical access. Give it a homelike appearance, like the area that was shown earlier on page 261.
- Select either full-sized (52″ long by 27″ wide) or small (40″ x 27″) cribs, one for each child, with firm mattresses. Rails

"Ganging" cribs gives an infant sleep space an institutional appearance.

Instead, create a bedroom feeling by organizing cribs . . .

. . . into small clusters, with a dresser and lamps, a glider, and homey touches, (The Copper House) (See Figure 16.8 for the location of this sleep space within the group room.)

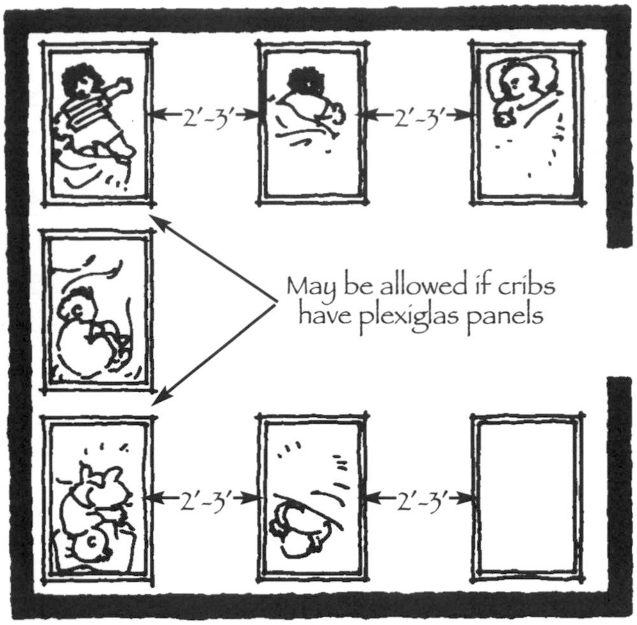

Figure 16.4
A two or three foot separation is required between cribs with railed sides.

can be no more than 2⅜ inches apart. Plexiglas ends are sometimes desirable.

- Unless codes allow cribs with Plexiglas panels in the ends to be placed end to end, allot 30 sq ft of crib space per child to ensure 2–3 feet between cribs or cots on all sides (Figure 16.4).
- Equip at least one crib—one that will *fit through doorways*—with special casters for evacuation. A large carriage kept in the sleep area can also serve for evacuation.
- With three solid sides, stacking cribs provide light and sound attenuation, reduce the spread of airborne germs, minimize adult back strain, limit use of cribs to their intended purpose—sleeping, and take up much less space than traditional cribs. Caregivers report that infants feel safer, fall asleep faster, sleep longer, and disturb each other less in them. Free-standing units can be arranged to form an enclosed sleep area. The use of diapers, mattresses, and washable liners prevents any possible contamination by feces or urine from the upper to lower crib.
- Commercial stacking cribs[10] measure 24¼″deep x 42″ long and 72″ high, and hold a small crib mattress (3″ x 23″ x 40″). Stacking cribs also can be custom-designed with varying ceiling heights, numbers of cutouts in the sides, and to accommodate different size mattresses. For ease of lifting children in and out, make sure the second level does not exceed 36″ high; place heavier babies and toddlers on the bottom.
- Sleeping arrangements popular in other countries that might be considered include hammocks and, in New Zealand, a carrier on springs.
- An emergency exit door from the sleep area—which may need to be fire-rated—is desirable, and required by some states. Check local regulations.
- Where possible, create outdoor sleeping porches or terraces. Even in winter, Scandinavian infants are placed outdoors in carriages when they sleep, to expose them to fresh air and full-spectrum light.
- Provide some natural lighting that can be controlled, and *artificial lighting on a rheostat*, so caregivers can perform their functions without disturbing sleeping children. Wall sconces and a dresser-top lamp are excellent.
- Provide a dresser to store clean linens, a hamper for dirty linens, a rocker or glider, and space for caregiver circulation.

Commercial (left) and custom-designed (right) stacking cribs help preserve open floor space when square footage is tight.

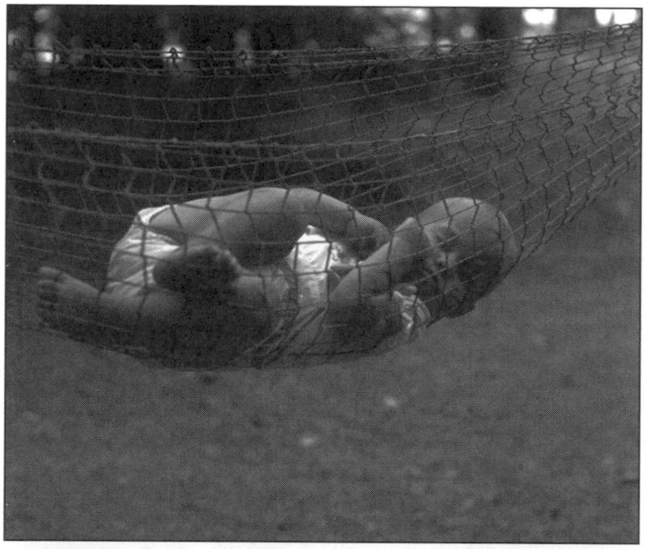

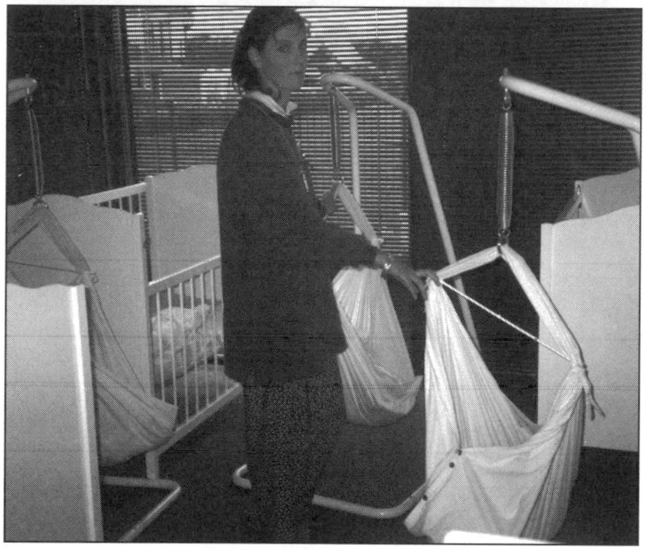

Hammocks and a textile "basket" on springs (New Zealand) provide beds for infants in other cultures.

- Provide adequate ventilation and fresh air, ideally from windows that open.
- Provide mobiles above the cribs, wall decorations, and equipment (tape deck, CD player) for playing soothing music as children awaken or drift off to sleep.
- Older infants who are beginning to walk can sleep closer to the floor on cots, small beds, or in baskets similar to those used in Reggio Emilia (see page 257).

Toddlers

Unlike infants, toddlers take long naps and, if distracted, may resist sleep. It is ideal if they can have a separate rest area, similar to a bedroom at home, in which to retreat. However, to conserve space, toddler rest usually occurs on portable cots, beds, or mats (see Chapter 14) dispersed throughout the group room. (Some states prohibit use of padded mats for children under three years.) Since toddlers' sleeping patterns are irregular and highly individual, those children who sleep longer require some protection from the others. Visibility of sleeping children is essential.

QUESTIONS: TODDLER SLEEP AREA

1. What images do you have of toddler sleep arrangements? Do you prefer a separate toddler nap room, or sleeping within the group space?
2. Do you prefer cots, mats, beds?
3. Where can children play so as not to disturb longer nappers, or where can long nappers be located?
4. What local codes for spacing, style of sleeping equipment, and emergency evacuation need to be considered?
5. Can bedding be located near the sleeping area?

GUIDELINES: TODDLER SLEEP AREA

- If a separate toddler sleep space is not provided, do a room plan overlay of cots/beds to ensure they all will fit: toddler cot size is approximately 22″ x 40″ x 5″ high.
- See also Furniture for Sleeping in Chapter 14.

Diapering/Toileting

Infants

Diapering is a major source of infant-caregiver interaction, and, because caregivers usually talk to infants while changing them, helps promote language development. When the diapering area is efficiently planned, with conveniently located supplies, caregivers can provide children with individualized attention (Figure 16.5). Locating the changing table so that caregivers need not turn their backs to the room and can see the group easily while diapering is an important consideration. The sink in the changing area must be separate from that used for food preparation and other purposes. Tightly sealed containers are needed for soiled diapers, and sometimes a toilet or industrial sink for feces disposal.

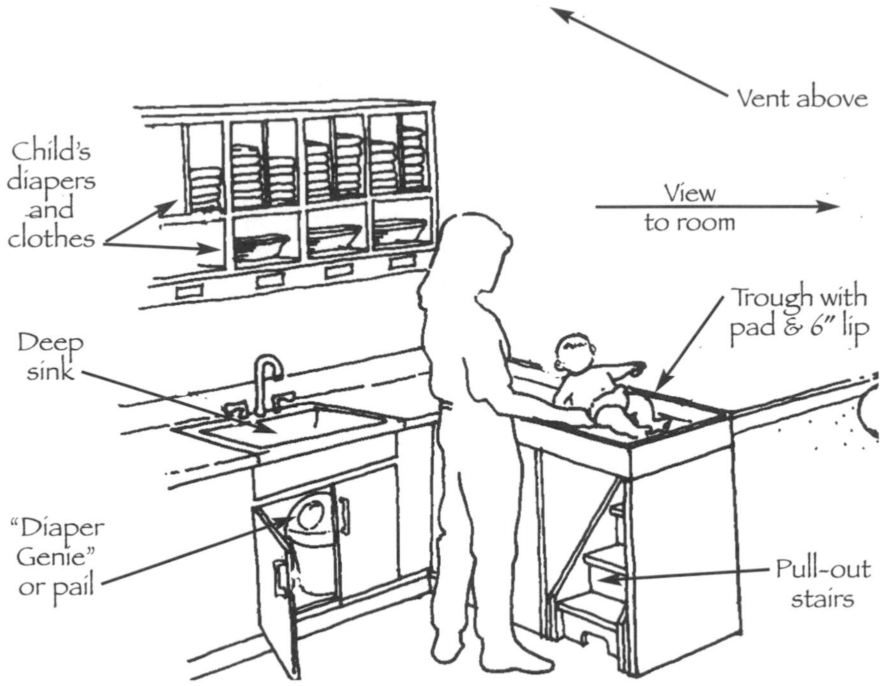

Figure 16.5
A well-designed diapering area.

QUESTIONS: INFANT DIAPERING

1. What images do you have of the diaper changing area in the infant room?
2. Will one changing table suffice? Would you like a second one—adjoining the first, or near the sleep area?
3. Can the sink adjacent to diapering be large enough to bathe an infant?
4. What types of diapers (cloth, disposable) will you use? Who will provide them? How will soiled ones be handled?
5. Do you plan to have a washer and dryer in the center? How far from the infant and toddler rooms will they be?
6. How will you handle children's soiled clothing?
7. What local codes apply to diapering areas?

Toddlers

Toddler rooms need to be designed with both toilets and a diaper changing area. If the changing table includes pull-out steps (see Figure 16.5), toddlers enjoy climbing up on their own. The diapering area can be similar to that for infants, or it can be a low platform where the child stands. Make it easy for toddlers to "help" with their diapering by enabling them to get their own clean diaper, make an X on a chart after changing, wash their own hands, etc. Toilets need to be

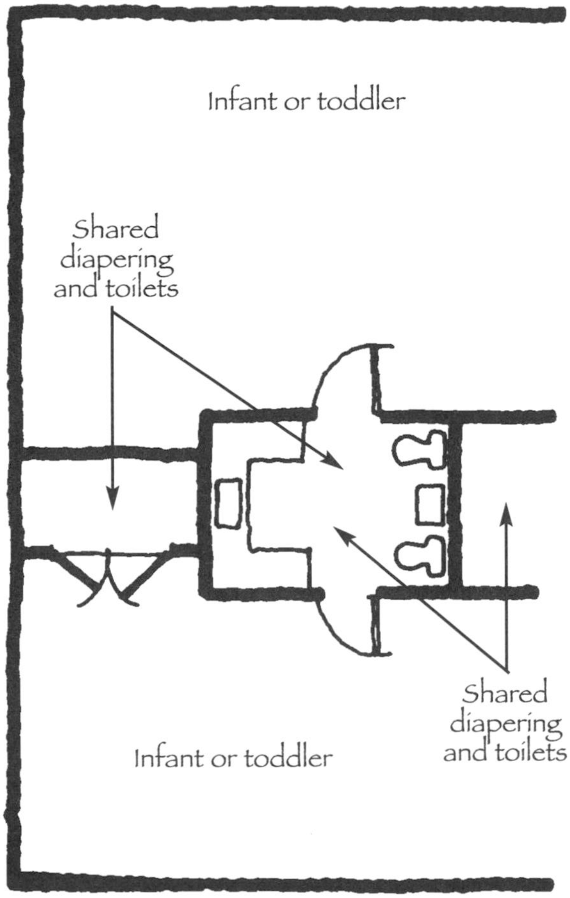

Figure 16.6
A diapering area and toilets can be shared between two infant, two toddler, or an infant and a toddler room.

accessible and located so children can "sit" watching others at play rather than feeling isolated or pulled away from group activities. Suggestibility is enhanced when two can "sit" together.

QUESTIONS: TODDLER DIAPERING/TOILETING

1. How many toilets do you want for 8–10 toddlers?
2. Will these toilets be toddler height (11 inches), or do existing conditions require use of full-size toilets with booster steps?
3. Do you want the toilets in a "bathroom" or in a more open, accessible place? If open, how will you handle odors and mess?
4. Do you prefer the diapering surface to be counter height (36″ high) or quite low so toddlers can stand upon it?
5. Will two rooms share a diapering and toilet area (Figure 16.6)?
6. What local codes apply to toddler toileting?

GUIDELINES: INFANT AND TODDLER DIAPERING/TOILETING

- Locate diaper changing areas away from food preparation and provide a different sink, possibly color-coded, for each area.
- Orient the changing table so caregivers can view the group.
- Adequately sized diapering and toilet areas, accessible from two group rooms, can be shared.
- Provide a changing surface approximately 36″ high x 24″ wide by 42″ long for diapering and dressing, with a 2–3 inch pad. Build a raised edge which sits 6 inches above the pad, around 3 sides of the surface, or a trough 9 inches deep with a 3″ pad, to prevent children from rolling off. A strap is considered unsanitary by public health authorities. Moreover, the child should never be left without the touch of the caregiver. Make the pad nonskid, nonporous, washable, and warm to the touch. Pads will need to be scrubbed down with soap, water, and disinfectant between each use, or supplied with a disposable covering material. Vinyl-covered pads work well.
- Near the changing surface, provide a sink large enough to bathe a child. Sinks with elbow-operated handles or foot pedals reduce contamination. Allow for counter space next to the sink on which to place supplies and children's clean clothing. An L-shaped configuration of sink and changing surface is efficient and intimate enough to enhance interaction between caregiver and child. Allow 60–100 sq feet for the diapering area.
- Some centers prefer to have 2 changing surfaces for each infant or toddler group. The two might be parallel to one another with a sink in between, or one might be located near the sleep area. However, two caregivers should not change children simultaneously.
- If cloth diapers are used, a toilet or industrial sink for feces disposal may be required, in addition to a sink for hand washing. Check local codes.
- In addition to changing tables and sinks, the area will need:

  —a large, lined foot-pedal operated container for diaper disposal, or alternative hands-free container.[11] The container can be placed inside a lower cabinet convenient to the changing surface.

  —a laundry hamper or individual children's bags for soiled clothing

  —pull-out stairs for older infants and toddlers

  —rheostatic lighting that shines upwards, not into eyes

  —a paper towel dispenser, liquid soap, hand lotion, rubber gloves

  —accessible storage for children's diapers, clothes, and any supplies brought from home (see dimensions below)
- Each child needs an individual storage space, approximately 5″ wide x 14″ deep x 1–2 feet high, for a personal supply of diapers plus a space approximately 10 inches wide x 14 inches deep x 6 inches high for changes of clothing, etc. Plastic bins or baskets in individual compartments work well. Locate these on shelves above or below but within arm's reach of the changing surface so the caregiver can be in contact with the child at all times. (See the diapering area in the floor plans on pages 330 and 332.)
- Provide shelves for storing all supplies: wipes, salves, paper towels, etc. Shelves should be easy for caregivers to reach but out of the reach of children.
- Provide a supply of clean toys, hooks over the changing table to suspend mobiles, or pictures or a mirror pasted on the ceiling or the underside of an overhead shelf to occupy children and provide a basis for infant/caregiver conversation while diapering. A mirror placed along one side of the changing surface also adds educational value.
- Provide additional ventilation for the changing space so odors do not penetrate other areas.
- Protect the diapering area from drafts. Increase the area temperature 2–4 degrees. A radiant heat panel suspended over the changing surface is a nice way to warm a naked child.
- *Toddlers* being toilet trained may use 11-inch-high toilets or an adult-height toilet made accessible by steps and an adjustable seat. Two toilets per group will prevent accidents and enable two to "sit" at the same time.
- Locate *toddler toilets* so that children can observe activities while "sitting," and adults can observe children.
- Some toddlers and children with disabilities may benefit from a potty chair.
- Provide quiet or silent toilet plumbing; many children fear the "roar" of the flush mechanism.

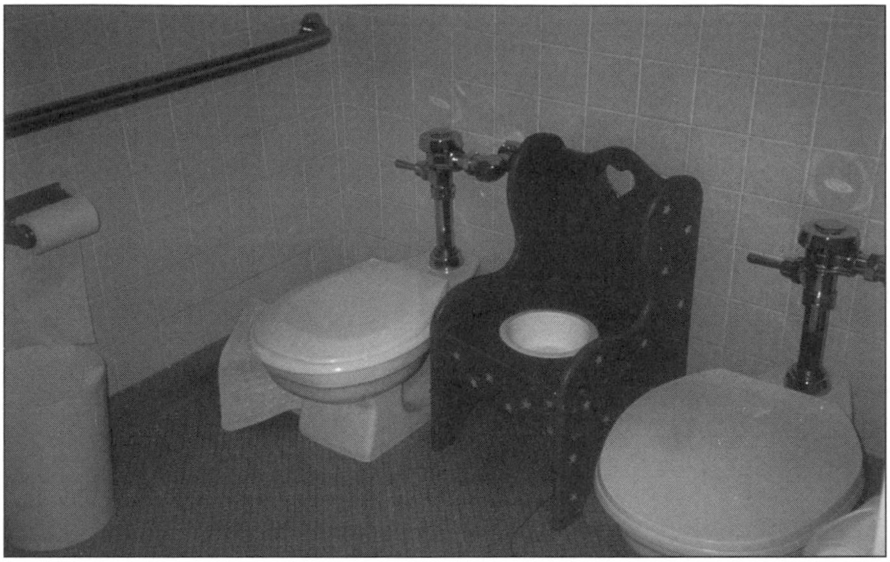

A potty chair may be appropriate for some toddlers and children with disabilities.

Washer and Dryer

A washer and dryer convenient to the infant and toddler rooms are highly recommended for cleaning sheets, blankets, bibs, wash cloths, towels, and smocks. A dryer is handy for wet snowsuits and clothing. Send soiled personal items and cloth diapers home for laundering.

GUIDELINES: WASHER AND DRYER

- Purchase a full-sized washer and dryer unless there is no adequate space. Smaller stackable units have insufficient capacity for most centers. Depending upon the items laundered, one washer and dryer may be needed for every 30 children.
- Create a small lockable laundry room or pullman closet with appropriate ventilation, electricity, floor drain, and laundry tub for soaking. Include some shelves for supplies, space for folding, and an area for storing clean and dirty linens.
- Have children help with folding laundry in their rooms, or in the residential core, if there is one.

Feeding

Infants

Encourage mothers to breast-feed their babies or at least to provide breast milk in bottles[12] by supporting them logistically. Breast milk contains essential nutrients—especially the amino acid tryptophan, which is necessary for brain serotonin development—that are absent in formula. Depression, poor impulse control, and violent behaviors have been linked to deficits in brain serotonin.[13] Breast milk also provides essential antibodies that stimulate the immune system. These antibodies are especially crucial for infants and toddlers in group care, where exposure to infection is constant.

QUESTIONS: INFANT FEEDING

1. How do you envision supporting mothers who wish to breast feed? What types of seating and provisions for comfort and privacy will you supply?
2. What images do you have of the infant feeding area? How can it be given a homelike atmosphere?
3. What sizes and types of appliances are needed in the food preparation area: refrigerator, hot plate, crock pot, bottle warmer, blender, other?
4. What are your furniture preferences for infants who can sit unassisted to be fed: low stackable seats with trays, feeding tables, high chairs, low tables and chairs, other? How many of each type will you need?

As infants mature from 6 weeks to 18 months they move through different types of feeding arrangements: from breast feeding and being held for bottle and soft food feeding, to being fed solid foods while seated in a low chair with a tray, to self-feeding at a low table. Low chairs in which children sit with their feet touching the floor are preferable to high chairs because they

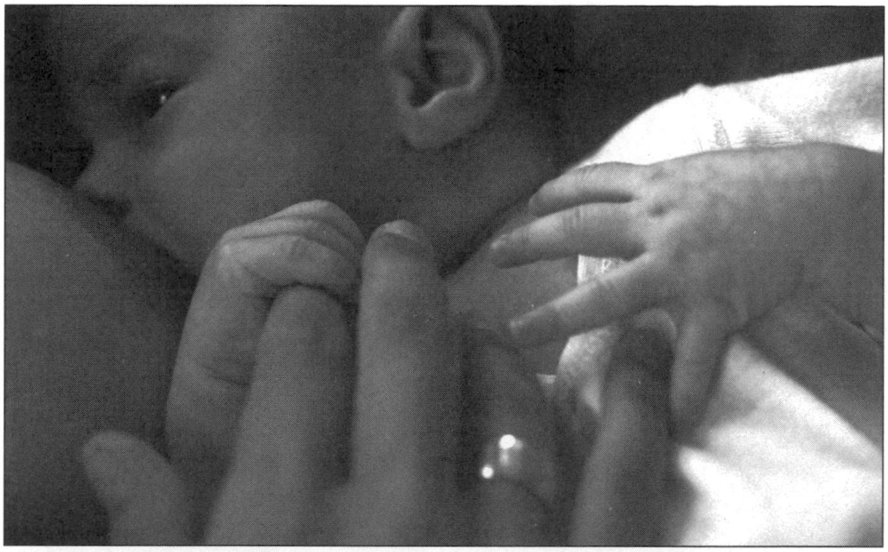

This 10′ x 10′ L-shaped bottle and food preparation area in an infant room includes a wide counter with stools where parents and staff can sit to make notes in children's log books. (The Copper House) (See Figure 16.8 for the location of this food prep area in the group room.)

increase the child's control and reduce the sense of being strapped in and imprisoned.

Early experiences with food affect later attitudes toward the social aspects of eating. It is important that feeding be a quiet, enjoyable time when babies can feel close to and be nurtured by their mothers or caregivers, can experiment and "play" with foods, and can learn simple self-feeding skills. Honor individual schedules and the need for individualized care by feeding only a few seated infants at a time.

Because of the time involved in these tasks, caregiver comfort in preparing meals and feeding infants is essential. Even with a main kitchen in the center, a food preparation area is needed in the infant room.

GUIDELINES: INFANT FEEDING

- Rockers, gliders, or chairs with wide seats and arms (or no arms) are recommended for mothers nursing or caregivers bottle-feeding infants. Locate this furniture in a quiet area.
- Providing mothers with a pleasant area, such as space near a window with a view, will encourage them to nurse. A secluded area for breast pumping may also be needed.
- Avoid overhead lights that shine into the eyes of supine infants.
- If given solid foods, infants not yet able to sit are best fed on an adult's lap with a counter or table surface nearby to hold the food. If infant seats are used, they should be placed on the floor or on a deep platform 10–15 inches high, with sufficient space for food jars nearby.

A 12-inch high "table" with cutouts to hold infants securely can be used for feeding and other activities.

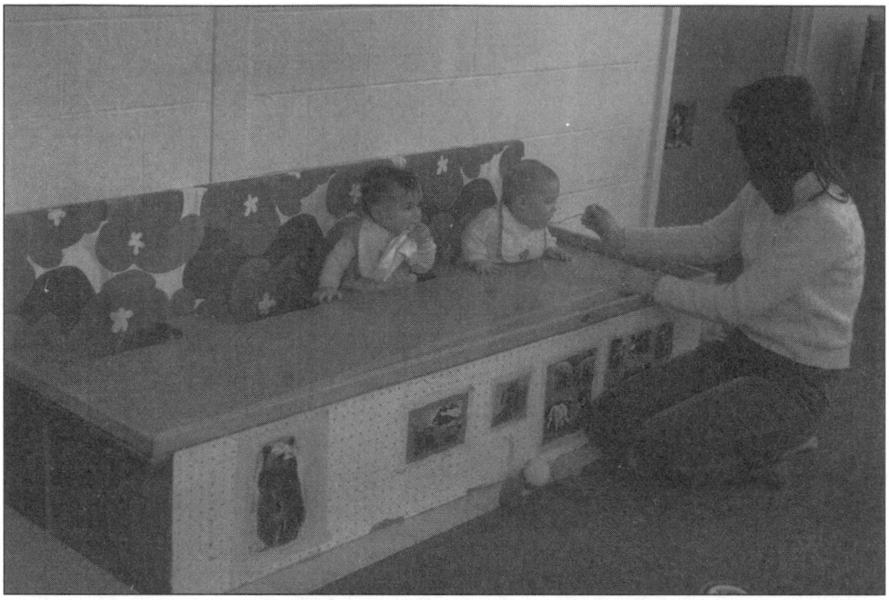

Low tables and sturdy cube seats, or chairs with sides enable older infants to feed themselves and eat together.

- Because feeding furniture takes up a lot of floor space, decide in advance what styles are preferred and how many children will be fed at one time. Ensure that surfaces and seats are washable, sturdy, and secure, with no sharp edges or protruding parts.
- Avoid large space-consuming tables.
- Infants able to sit up on their own can be fed in child-height feeding chairs with trays, which stack when the trays are removed (see page 253). High chairs are less desirable: they confine the child, take up much space, and do not stack. Collapsible models tend not to be folded away on a daily basis.
- Seat older infants (and toddlers) who can feed themselves in groups of 3 or 4 with one adult at small, low tables (12–14 inches high), in sturdy chairs with sides (5–6½ inch seat height) or in cube seats that offer two heights.
- Even if the center's main kitchen is near the infant room, a minikitchen (with no child access) is needed in the group room so staff need not leave the room to prepare food. Provide a sink, refrigerator (preferably full-sized) with bins for each child's milk and food, food-warming appliances, and storage for juices, crackers, bibs, utensils, etc. A crock pot is excellent for bottle warming. Avoid microwave ovens that destroy the nutrients in breast milk and can heat milk hot enough to scald a baby!
- A plastic-lined hamper for soiled linens—perhaps with sections for wet and dry items—is helpful near the eating area.

This space-saving "kitchenette" in an infant room includes cupboards, an undercounter refrigerator, and a countertop that pulls out for more working space. (See Figure 16.10 for its location in the group room.)

Toddlers

Toddlers are able to feed themselves with finger foods and will advance to using eating utensils by the time they enter the preschool group. Toddlers are active and easily distracted; spills, crumbs, and dropped foods are to be expected. They need sturdy seats that will not tip, and a congenial atmosphere with adults and peers at meal times. Since they are no longer on individualized feeding schedules, they are mature enough to eat as a small group at a table for four with lots of caregiver support, in their room or in a dining area.

QUESTIONS: TODDLER FEEDING

1. What images do you have of the toddler feeding area?
2. How do you wish to feed toddlers—i.e., low high-sided chairs with trays, low tables with chairs or cube seats, other? How many of each kind of seat will be needed?
3. Will toddlers eat in a common dining area?

GUIDELINES: TODDLER FEEDING

- See Table 16.1 for table and seat heights. Choose seats without straps that provide good back support and keep children's feet firmly on the ground. Cube chairs that have two seat heights when reversed are excellent at this age. Square, rectangular, and hexagonal tables are the most versatile and can be used for eating, art, and table activities.
- Toddlers can eat in a central dining area, provided the setting and group size are small and intimate. Consider providing a low counter where older toddlers might serve themselves.

Typical Infant/Toddler Activity Areas

The discussion that follows describes typical activities and their supporting spaces in group rooms for infants and for toddlers. These descriptions are intended to get you started thinking about your program needs and wants. Be certain to incorporate your own ideas and visions!

QUESTIONS: INFANT AND TODDLER ACTIVITY AREAS

1. What images do you have of the infant or toddler room as a whole, and of the play areas and activities in particular?
2. Can you list all the major activity areas, furniture, and equipment you hope to have in each room? Can you list all the toys, objects, etc., you wish to purchase, store, and display to support children's activities and caregiving? Have you collected images from catalogs and magazines showing all these items? (See "Creating an Interiors Bible," Chapter 14.)
3. How will you promote closeness between children and staff?
4. How might you reduce the physical demands of caregiving?

Infants: Infants spend much time mastering movements involved in body control and object control: sitting, swaying, crawling, grasping, bending, turning, pulling to stand, walking, and climbing. Quiet play on soft furniture close to adults is as important as active movement. Exploration with light, water, sand, paint, clay, and natural materials is also to be encouraged.

Given the right supports, infants are capable of far more than imagined. It is important that the environment be responsive to their abilities while lying on their backs, crawling with eye level at 6 inches, and standing unsteadily with eye level at about 20 inches.

Toddlers: Toddlers vacillate between new-found physical independence and a desire to remain close to primary caregivers. An ordered environment that defines options and sets limits can assist adults to gently cooperate with these vicissitudes rather than being controlling. Compared with that for infants, the toddler environment includes more highly developed activity areas, with a wider assortment of materials: books; blocks; props for pretend play; water, sand, paint, mud, and clay for discovery play; materials for fine-motor activities. Ensure that the supports for these activities are small-scaled and safe. The range of activity areas and materials in a toddler room is not dissimilar to that for preschoolers (see Chapter 17), but areas need to be less enclosed and toys provided on a rotated basis. Toddlers tote things between areas, often leaving a jumble of toys to be sorted.

GUIDELINES: TYPICAL INFANT AND TODDLER ACTIVITY AREAS

Review the general guidelines for zones in Chapter 7 and for activity areas and 6 types of play in Chapter 15.

- Use walls to support play panels, toys, grab bars, textures, mirrors, and reflective surfaces at different heights. Play panels, if sturdy and interlocking, can function as "walls" and low dividers; or they can be hung on brackets so that they are interchangeable. (See page 246.)
- Make mirrors of all shapes and styles available to lying, crawling, and standing infants and toddlers. Place mirrors on the wall space under windows, on the walls and ceilings of "caves," and on play panels and lofts. (Also see page 244 for mirror placement suggestions.)
- Instead of using a standard gypsum wall to divide a large space into two group rooms, consider a functional wall that might provide crawling, climbing, sliding, observation, and hiding spaces on both sides. (See page 124 and the dividing wall on page 337.)
- Toddlers are consumed with learning the properties of containers—opening things and putting things into and out of containers to discover and rediscover hidden objects and relationships. Toys, furniture, and spaces can be designed to support this learning by including enclosures, doors, panels, and openings.
- To assist children with visual and hearing impairments, be sure that some surfaces in the room do not absorb sound.
- Avoid walkers: they are dangerous and inhibit children's movement and development.
- Doors with glass panels near the floor enable children, especially if hearing-impaired, to see what is coming toward them, and those approaching to be aware of children on the other side.
- Provide storage at child height, and additional storage above 4 feet for adult access to supplies that can replenish items at child level.
- Consider the spirit or mood of each area in the room. Provide places of real beauty and aesthetic value.
- Provide direct access from the group rooms to covered outdoor areas and separate infant and toddler play yards.

Messy Play

The delight that infants and toddlers take in the sensorial and tactile properties of materials calls for plentiful opportunities to "mess about" with malleable substances such as sand, water, paint, and clay. Ideally, the abandon generated by the abundance of sand and water on a beach would somehow be matched by the child care environment. Providing sufficient space for these activities—on easily cleaned surfaces with good drains—is essential if staff is to be receptive to "mess making." An enclosed, tiled "wet" room with a hand-held shower to wash down walls, floors, and children allows infants and toddlers to indulge their senses in body-painting and other messy play activities and staff to easily clean up after them. (See Figures 17.13, 17.15, and 17.16 for illustrations of a "wet" room.)

For a comprehensive list of messy play activities and supporting facilities, many of them appropriate for infants and toddlers, see Chapter 7, Box 7.4.

GUIDELINES: MESSY PLAY FOR INFANTS AND TODDLERS

- Use small tables. To conserve space, provide only as many as are really necessary. Vary table shape and height for different kinds of play. Counters that flip up or down, platforms and risers that double as play, sitting, and eating surfaces, and covers that transform water and sand troughs into tables all help conserve floor space.
- To conserve space, use stacking chairs or feeding seats with trays.
- Most older infants and toddlers do not want to sit in chairs—they prefer to stand, sit on the floor, or climb, climb, climb.
- Malleable materials such as water, sand, paint, and clay are essential tools of discovery play and experience at this age. The area for their use needs to be sizeable, washable, well-ventilated, and well-drained.
- Much custodial work is eliminated if the water play trough—12″ high for infants, 18″ high for toddlers—is mounted onto its own drain with a cleanout trap, under a plumbed faucet. The trough itself can be portable or permanently installed (see page 331). Heights for sand play troughs for infants and toddlers can be the same as for water play.
- Infants not yet able to stand can engage in messy play with paint, water, and sand containers placed directly on the

Infants can make a mess on a tiled floor with a built-in drain. Mirrors mounted on the foot of wall space between the floor and the windows add sparkle and interactive possibilities.

Plexiglas mounted in front of a window makes an interesting painting surface for seated or standing infants. Paper can be clipped to the "easel" if desired.

floor, provided the floor is waterproof, ideally with a built-in drain.

- Consider creating a fully enclosed tiled "wet" room, with sloping drain in the floor and hand-held shower, that allows children to apply water, paints, etc., to walls, floors, and even their own bodies.
- A good surface for infant and toddler art, especially clay, is a table 10 inches high at which children can sit, kneel, or even stand without chairs.
- Create an easel by using a wall- or A-frame-mounted sheet of fire-rated homosote 4 feet high and 4–6 feet long. Sealed with semigloss paint and polyurethane, the homosote is completely washable. (See pages 333 and 351.)
- Alternatively, create an easel of Plexiglas, either free-standing or mounted in front of a window. If placed near the floor, even seated infants can paint.

Quiet Play

The younger the infant, the more blurred the distinction between quiet and active play, due to the child's immobility and need to be held and carried. However, rapid developmental changes during the first 18 months, and care in groups, necessitate tranquil spaces conducive to cuddling, nestling, experiencing delightful sensations, and being able to explore materials at one's own pace. Quiet activities for both infants and toddlers may include looking at books and being read to, listening to music, playing with manipulatives, emptying and filling containers, resting, socializing, and just plain observing the sights, sounds, shadows, lights, and colors in the setting. Ideally, the area for quiet play features plants, mobiles, and prisms, and is near low windows that offer views of outside vegetation and flowers.

FACILITIES LIST FOR QUIET PLAY

(can be separate from or combined with manipulative play)

- Couches, arm chairs, carpeted risers
- Hammocks, net chairs, beanbag chairs
- Water bed and risers, futons, mattresses, mats
- Carpeted floor surface
- Place for everyone to gather
- Books
- Low reading loft
- Tape deck, record and/or CD player, audio and video tapes, records, CDs, VCR
- Soft toys
- Private spaces

FOR MANIPULATIVE PLAY

- Platforms
- Low shelves, milk crates, and boxes to hold:
  –Puzzles, games, pegs, beads, lottos

Chatting and playing peek-a-boo in a quiet play area under a loft.

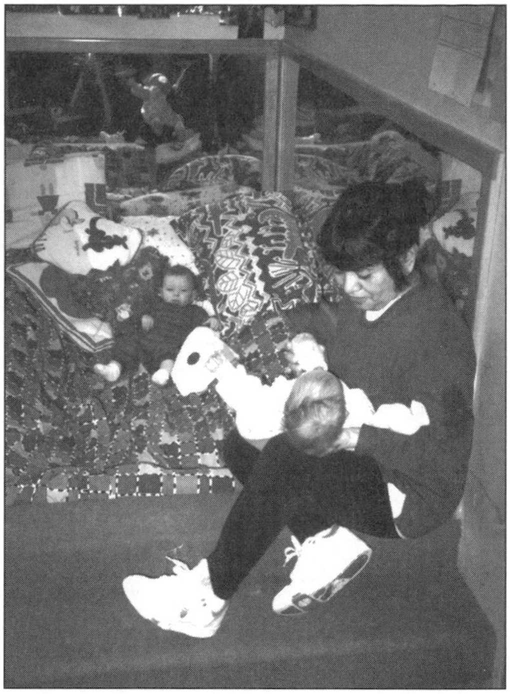

(Above) Five- and ten-inch-high risers enclose a twin-size water mattress that can be replaced with foam wedges (right).

–Small construction toys

–Small cars and trucks

–Small soft blocks

–Lock boxes, busy boards, lacing cubes

–Wind-up toys

GUIDELINES: QUIET PLAY

- Small window seats, soft enclosed seating, and low platforms are valuable for rest, observational learning, and preparing children for new situations.
- Beanbag chairs, arm chairs, couches, risers, pillows and cushions, low mattresses, futons, hammocks, and net chairs encourage cuddling, rest, and muscle relaxation. A modular foam couch or chair that unfolds to form a "bed" is a space-saver.
- Rocking chairs encourage physical contact, calming rhythms, and constructive opportunities for movement. They are also lovely in sleep rooms and for nursing mothers. However, they are dangerous to crawling babies. For this reason, gliders are often preferred.
- A soft Yucatan hammock (without rods) suspended from permanent hooks provides a place for an adult and several children to relax together, as long as sufficient space is allotted for it during planning. (See page 283.)
- As the "plopping" place in infant rooms, consider a twin- or crib-size water mattress surrounded by low risers (5–10 inches high), with an optional cover. A regular crib- or twin-sized mattress is less interesting but also works well, as does a carpeted platform 10 inches high.

A manipulative platform with built-in storage. (The Copper House) (See Figure 16.9 for its location in the toddler room.)

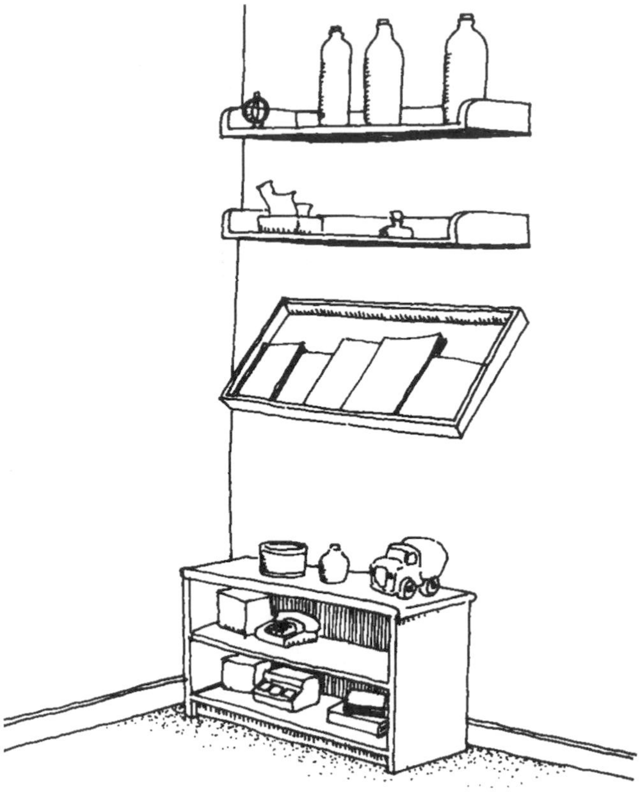

Figure 16.7
A one-inch lip around low bookcases, shelves with turned-up ends, and shelves on angle brackets make appropriate storage for infants.

- A light table 10–12 inches high can provide fascinating sensory experiences for infants and toddlers.
- Carpeted risers 10–12 inches high are good for pulling-to-stand and holding-on while learning to walk, and for creating "play pits" and boundaries to quiet areas. (See page 274.)
- Create low platforms with built-in perimeter storage—or floor areas bounded by storage units—to store, display, and "contain" toys and children in traffic-free zones and to enable pulling-to-stand. (Also see pages 273, 274, and 337.)
- Design low shelves with a ¾- to 1-inch lip around the top and along the front to prevent toys from falling off.
- Also consider low, angled shelves for displaying 10–20 books with their covers outward.
- Keep toy boxes small and without lids. Large toy boxes and milk crates ease the task of picking up loose items but encourage "dumping" and can lead to broken materials and lost pieces.

Active Play

The more mobile infants and toddlers become, the more insatiable their desire to move and practice their new-found skills. Adults may find it quite taxing to support exploration while still protecting children of this age from injury. The environment must therefore

(Above) An infant loft creates a raised playpen with a view out a high window, and a crawling space underneath. (Right) The loft includes low stairs and a slide. (See Figure 16.10 for the location of the loft in the group room.)

be both challenging and safe. Design the space to provide opportunities for every major form of movement: bouncing, climbing, rocking, tumbling, rolling, hiding, kicking, pulling, pushing, and dancing. Changes in level, small stairs, platforms, slides, ramps, lofts, mats, large foam bolsters, rocking toys, and different types of responsive and resilient surfaces can assist in achieving this goal.

FACILITIES LIST FOR ACTIVE PLAY

- Stairs to climb
- Foam mats, wedges, bolsters
- Slide
- Swing
- Ball crawl
- Changes in level
- Ramps
- Rocking toys: boat, horse
- Tunnels to crawl through
- Balance beams
- See saw
- Riding toys and wagons
- Pull toys
- Minitrampoline
- Suspension, net, or toddle bridges
- Small climber
- Low hand-over-hand bars

GUIDELINES: ACTIVE PLAY

- Create an overhead grid of wooden slats 6–8 inches apart, that can be stored 7–9 feet above the floor and lowered as needed, for hanging wind-chimes, mobiles, "trapezes," etc., over the floor area where they will be used. (See page 240.) Check local fire codes; do not block sprinkler heads or fire detection systems.
- Alternatively, provide a beam spanning the room's narrowest dimension—ideally within its active zone—at 7–9 feet high, to suspend swings and other equipment.
- Slight changes in level challenge the crawling, climbing, and balancing skills of children with and without disabilities.
- A series of boxes 3–18 inches high can be arranged to create an infinite number of landscapes for children to crawl, walk, sit, or lie upon. Tops for the boxes, embellished with different materials, can be rearranged, like the bases, to vary the horizontal/tactile playscape.
- Large-muscle equipment (swings, hammocks, rocking toys, minitrampolines) has great developmental and therapeutic value.
- Provide ways for older infants and toddlers to go safely up and down stairs: tread depth: 9″ for infants, 8″ for toddlers; tread height: 5″ for infants, 6″ for toddlers. (See the discussion of lofts under dramatic play below.)
- Textural cues at level changes (from wood, to carpet, to rubber) can be helpful and intriguing, but need to be seamless.
- Place commercially available large cardboard blocks in their own area or combine them with manipulatives (quiet play area) or with materials in the dramatic play area.

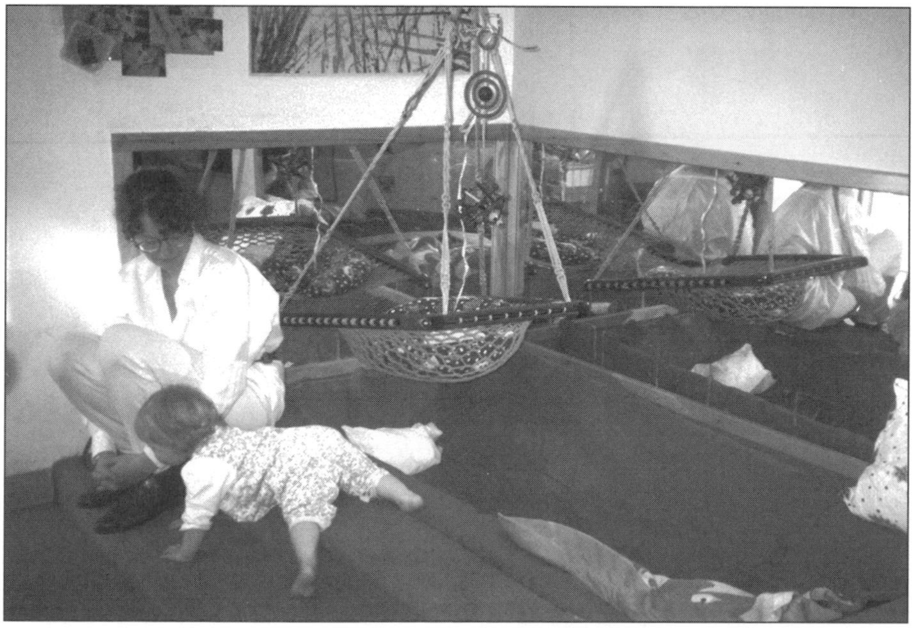

Small changes in level challenge balancing and climbing skills.

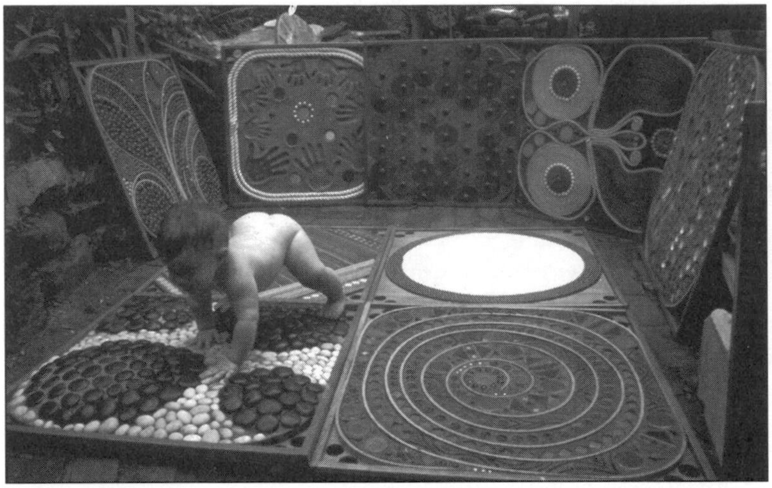

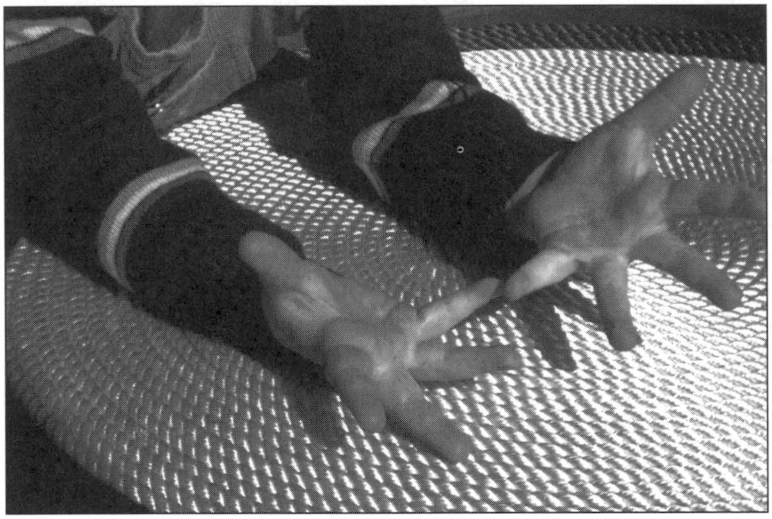

Tops for boxes of varying heights, embellished with a variety of materials, can be arranged to vary the tactile landscape.

Dramatic Play

Interest in imaginative and pretend play increases as infants and toddlers mature; this type of play is a primary way for them to learn about the world of animals and people. While infants under 18 months shy away from fully enclosed spaces, toddlers find them intriguing. To stimulate the urge to pretend and mimic, try to make available: places to crawl into; screens, panels, fabric to hide behind; doors to open and close; hand and finger puppets; and simple but attractive dress-up clothes and props.

FACILITIES LIST FOR DRAMATIC PLAY

- Hand and finger puppets
- Small puppet theater or window
- Miniatures
- Dress-up clothes
- Dolls and stuffed animals
- Doll bed, carriage
- Toy brooms, iron, dusters
- Sturdy child-size sink/stove/ refrigerator combo
- Small but real dishes, pots, pans
- Playhouse or cardboard box houses
- Doors and drawers to open and close
- Play loft
- Tent
- Mirrors

GUIDELINES: DRAMATIC PLAY

- Panels with openings and interactives can create beginning pretend and house-play settings for older infants.
- For *toddlers*, arrange house play equipment to form a fully enclosed space simulating the 4 walls of a room; a "roof" reinforces the house mood. Provide real pots, pans, dishes,

brooms, and recycled containers, and simple props such as ties, scarves, purses, and shoes.

- *Toddlers* enjoy both operating doors and drawers and climbing in and out of enclosures. Make sure all hardware is extremely sturdy. Otherwise, provide equipment with operable doors that are intentionally too small or too high to climb through. Ensure that hardware and door weight prevent injuries due to slamming on fingers.
- A loft/climber with stairs, a slide, and places above and below to explore are ideal for infants. *For toddlers,* provide a larger version with extensive active and dramatic play features such as a playhouse, a steering wheel, and movable cloth panels to enclose areas and to hide behind. (See pages 332–333.)

Illustrative Floor Plans

Pages 330–339 display scaled floor plans for different infant and toddler rooms. The plans identify many of the commercial and custom-built furnishings that were used to develop the activity areas in each room. Photographs accompanying some of the plans illustrate selected elements more fully.

Notes

[1]Many states acknowledge this need by setting the minimum available free play space for infants at 50 rather than 35 square feet per child.

[2]Arlene Uss provided valuable assistance for material in this section.

[3]J. Liedloff, *The Continuum Concept.* (New York: Addison-Wesley, 1977).

[4]Joseph Chilton Pearce makes a similar argument concerning the relationship between hospital practices that separate infants and mothers at birth and the high rates of delinquent and sociopathic behaviors in our culture: *Reaching Beyond Magical Child, Pregancy Birth & Bonding,* 1994, "Touch the Future," Video series.

[5]J. Prescott and J. DeMeo.

[6]A. Montagu, 1971. *Touching: The human significance of the skin.* New York: Harper & Row.

[7]L. Acredolo and D.Evans. Developmental changes in the effects of landmarks on infant spatial behavior. *Developmental Psychology,* 1980, 312–318.

[8]Adapted from *Community Playthings* catalog, Rifton, New York.

[9]Jennifer Kagiwada, Child Care Specialist for the General Services Administration, San Francisco, provided invaluable assistance with this chapter.

[10]One source is Nursery Maid, P.O. Box 922, Dinuba, CA 93618, (800) 443-8773.

[11]i.e., a "Diaper Genie"

[12]Breast-feeding for 2 years or beyond is recommended by the World Health Organization and UNICEF, and for at least one full year by the American Academy of Pediatrics. *Pediatrics,* Dec. 1997.

[13]J. W. Prescott, "Transforming the American Family," *Touch the Future* (Winter 1997/1998):10.

Figure 16.8
The Copper House Infant Room

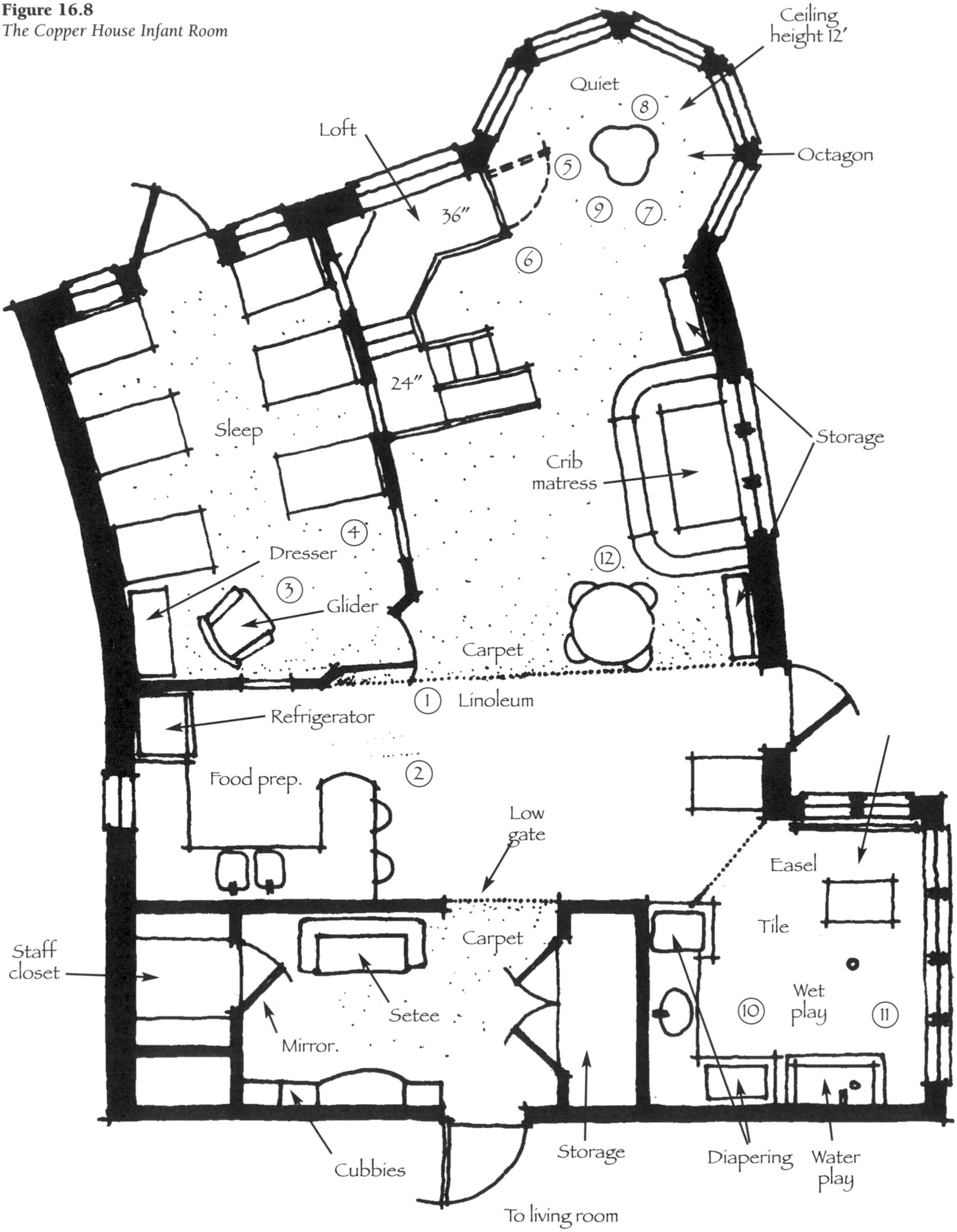

1. *Infant-room active area (left), mattress area (right), and quiet octagon (rear).*

2. *L-shaped bottle/food prep area for staff and parent use.*

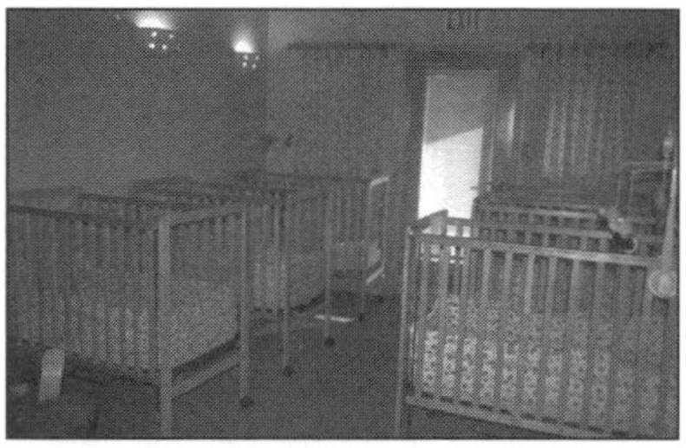

3. *Sleep room for six with sconce lighting on rheostats, a door and windows to the outside, and windows into the group room (not visible at right).*

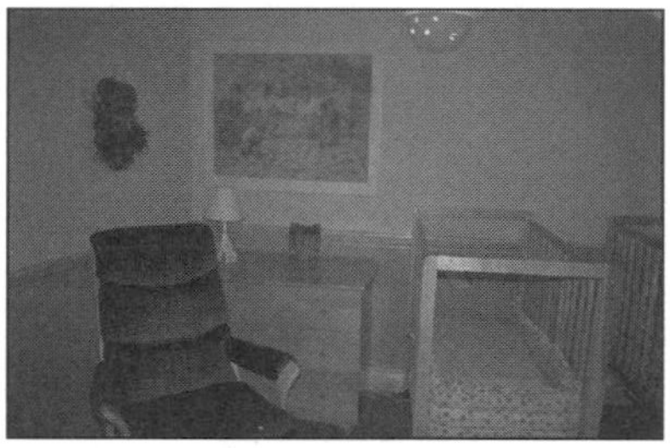

4. *Glider, dresser and lamp. and wall decorations in infant sleep room.*

5. *Climber includes stairs and a slide, platforms at three levels, a raised "playpen," and a fishtank and places to explore below.*

6. *Plexiglass-covered hole in platform lets infants see what is happening in crawl space below.*

7. *Octagon alcove: a special place for quiet activities.*

8. *Even crawling babies can look out windows one foot above the floor.*

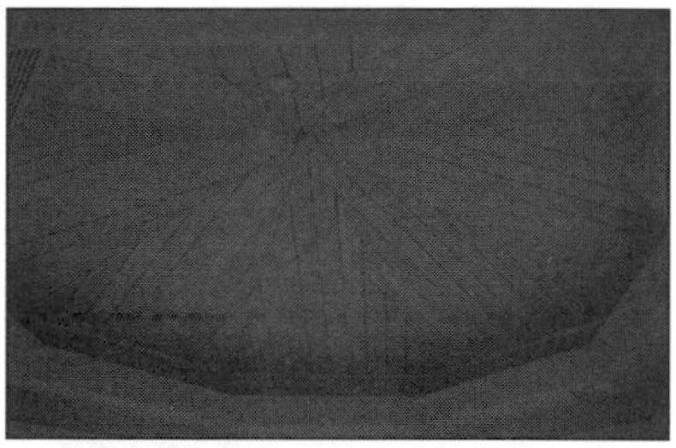

9. *The ceiling in the octagon.*

10. *Diapering area with two changing stations in wet play bay.*

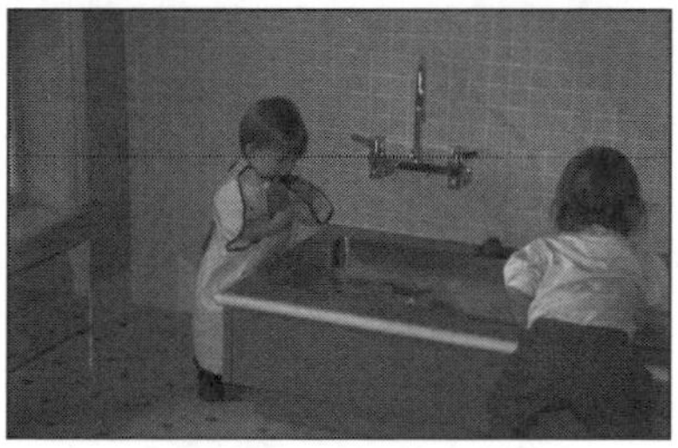

11. *Water play in a built-in trough 12 inches high.*

12. *Crib-size mattress surrounded by risers 5 inches and 10 inches high.*

Figure 16.9
The Copper House Toddler Room

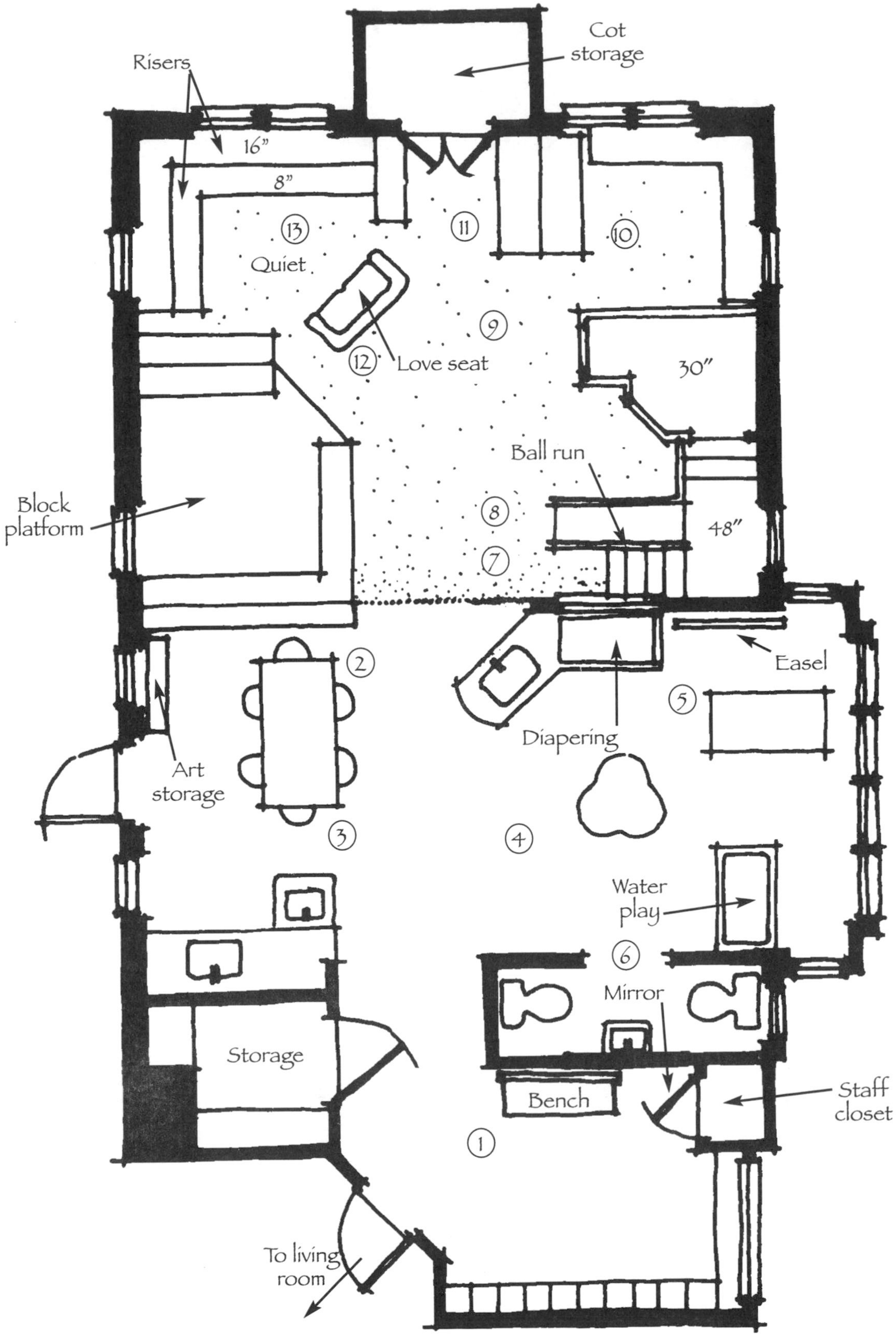

1. *Staff coat closet with mirrored door, bench, and plenty of floorspace in toddler's cubby area.*

2. *Sink, counter and cabinets for staff, and a sink at toddler height in art area. The door to the play yard is on the right (barely visible).*

3. *Delightful animal images greet handwashers.*

4. *The toddler wet play bay.*

5. *Free-standing easel 4 feet long.*

6. *Bathroom off the wet play area.*

7. *Dramatic-play loft with stairs, a slide, and a ball run; dress-up and storefront below; and a steering wheel behind the star, which spins when the wheel is turned.*

8. *Racing the ball down the slide.*

9. *Housekeeping area on other side of loft includes a moveable "playhouse."*

10. *This 2 foot x 4 foot "playhouse" embellished with tree limbs can be a bedroom, car, train or anything that suits your fancy.*

11. *One wall of the "playhouse" holds a busy board.*

12. *A manipulative play platform, with its roof aligned at the height of the window. Part of roof can be raised to ease access for adults*

13. *Risers and a book rack in the quiet area.*

Figure 16.10
The St. Louis Infant Room

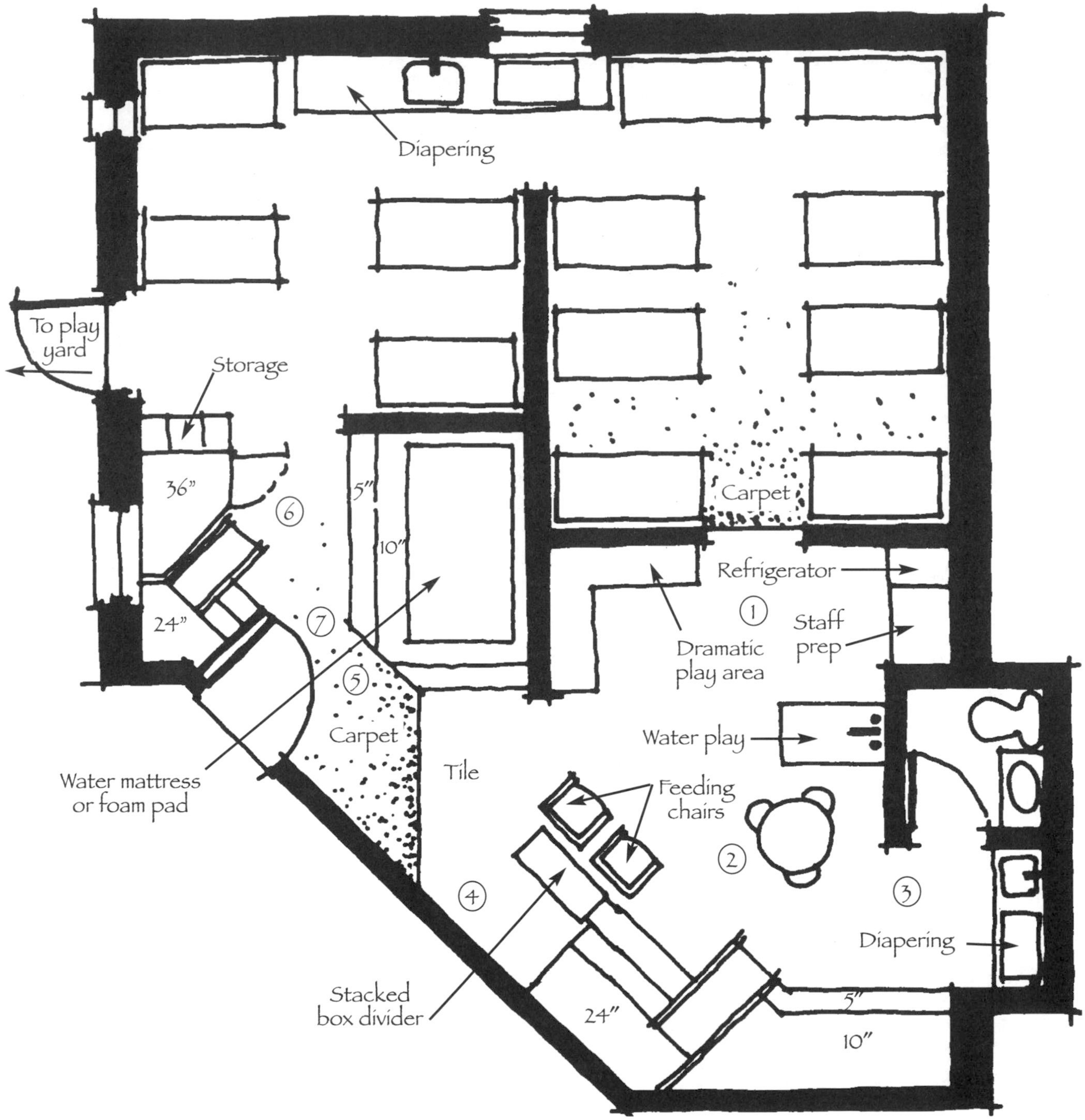

1

2

3

4

5

6

7

Figure 16.11
The St. Louis Toddler Room

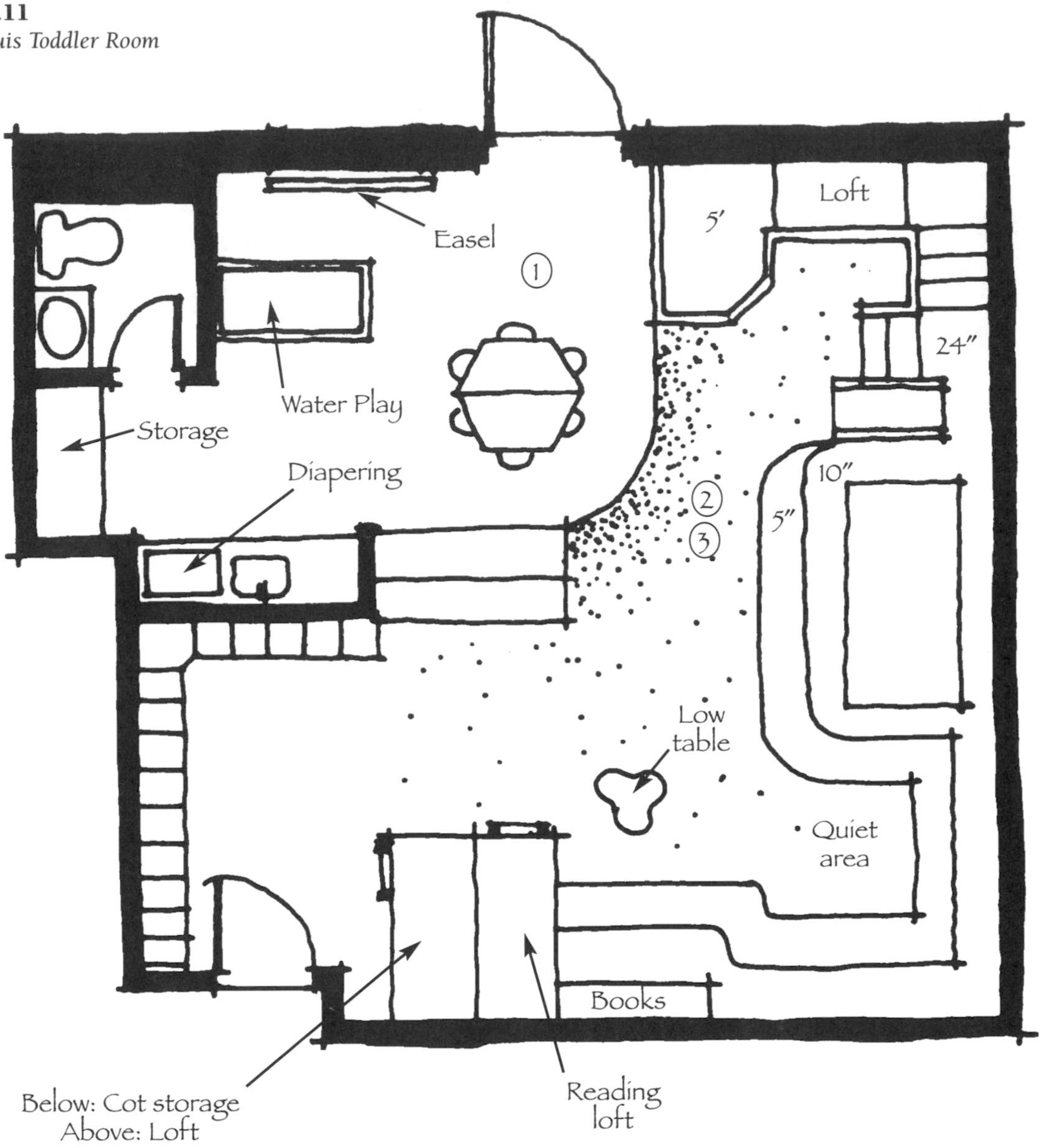

1

2

3

Figure 16.12
The Rindge Infant/Toddler Room. A "functional" wall divides a large space into an infant and a toddler room.

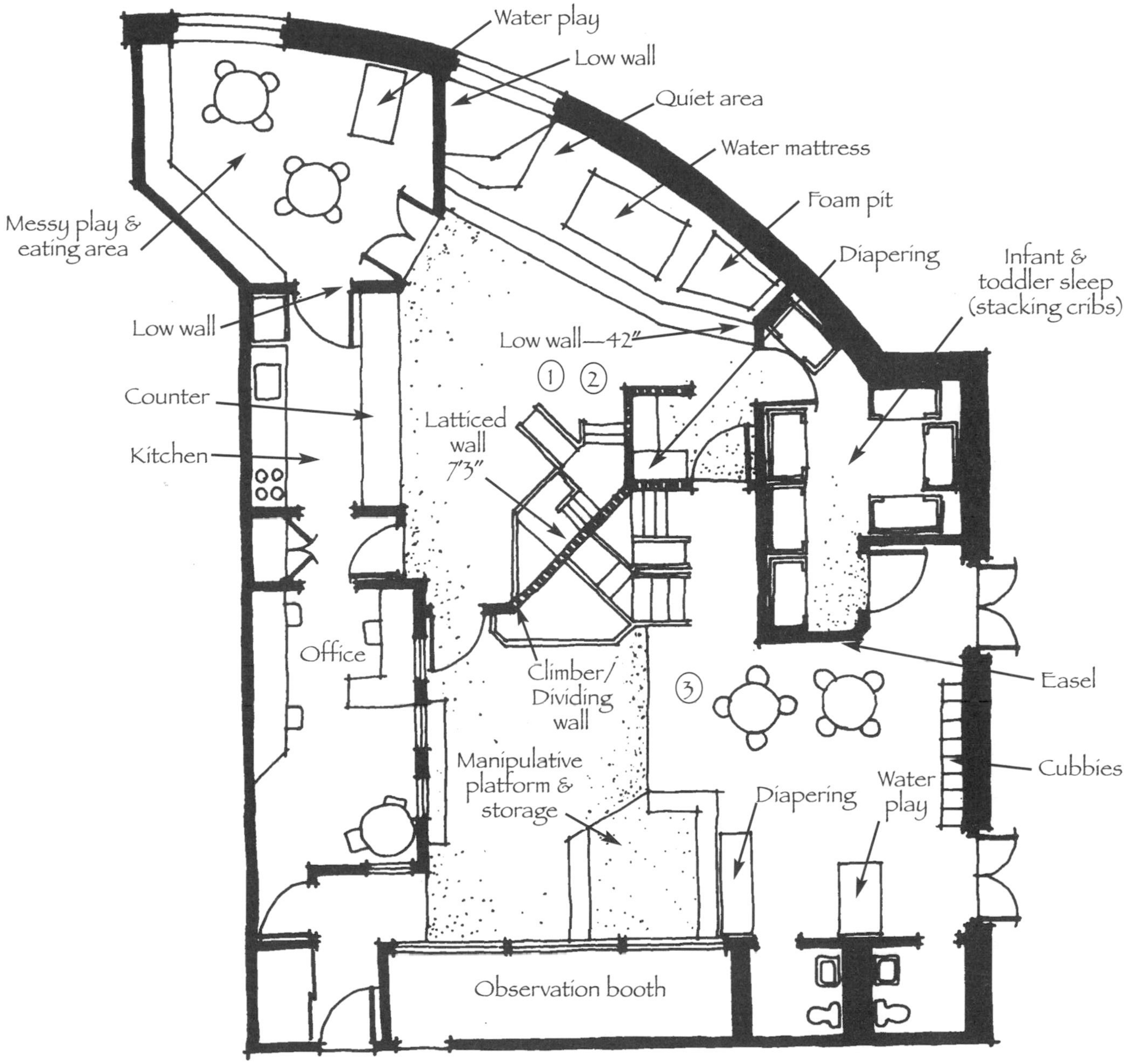

1

2

3

Figure 16.13
Small infant and toddler rooms benefit from a compact design which includes an adjacent family/living room, and a shared wet play area.

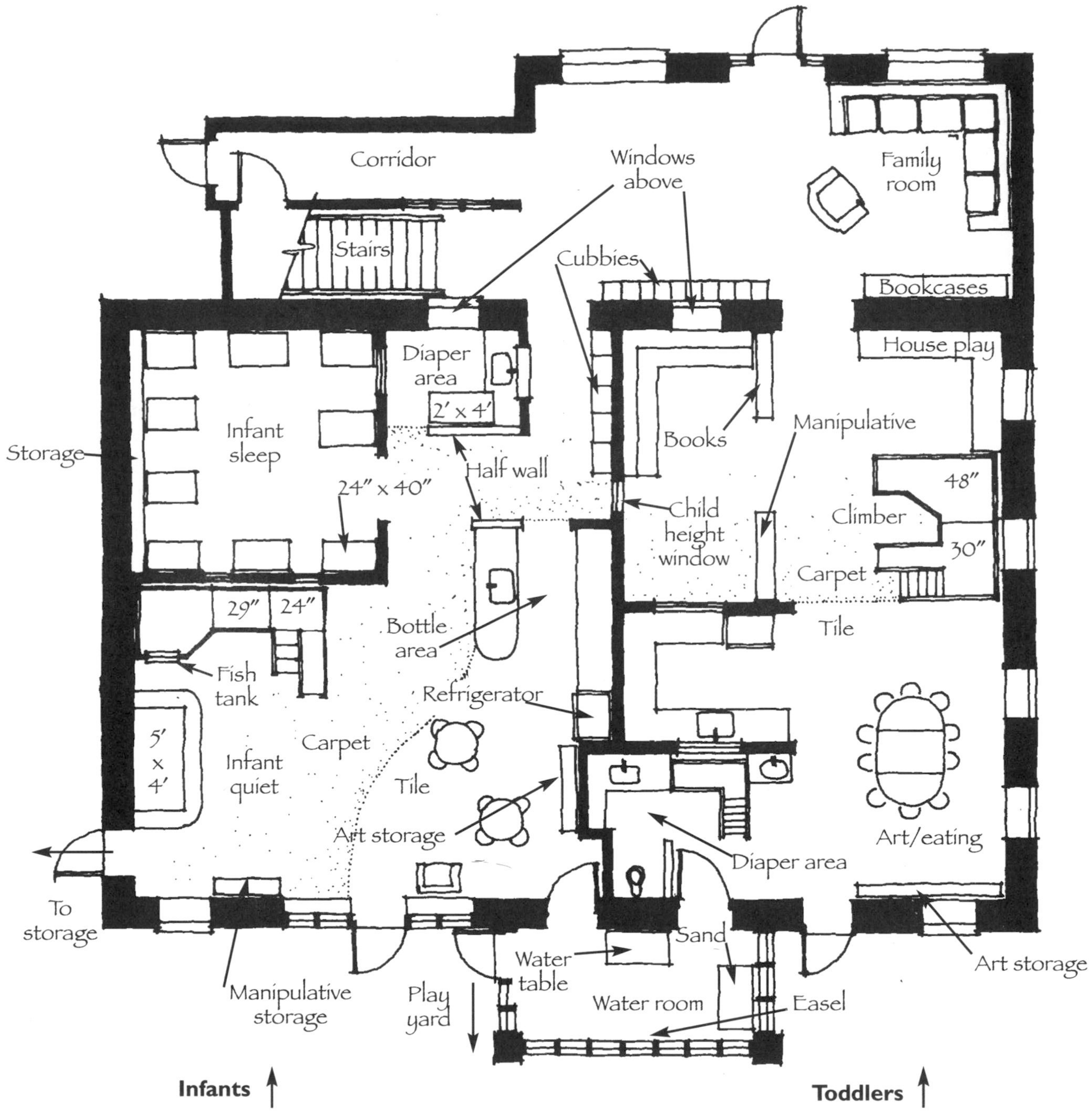

Figure 16.14
This design features an 8′ x 8′ wet play room shared by two adjacent toddler rooms

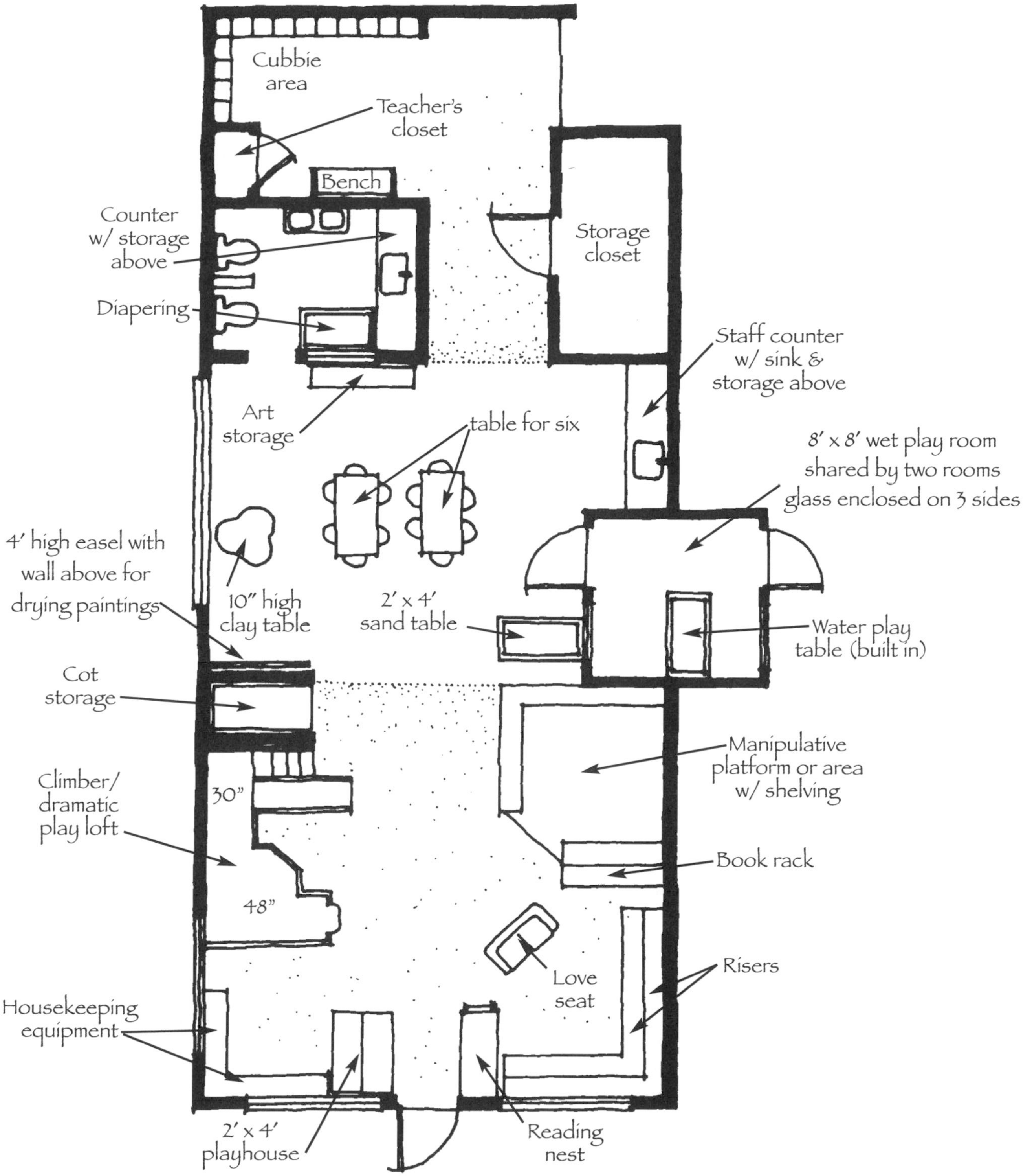

CHAPTER SEVENTEEN

SPACES FOR PRESCHOOLERS AND KINDERGARTENERS

Be aware of wonder.
Remember the little seed in the styrofoam cup:
the roots go down and the plant goes up,
and nobody really knows how or why,
but we are all like that.

—ROBERT FULGHUM

This chapter addresses the design of group rooms for preschoolers (ages three to five years old) and kindergarteners (ages five to six). The chapter's questions, facilities lists, and guidelines are intended to be used in conjunction with the zoning recommendations in Chapter 7 and the suggestions for developing activity areas in Chapter 15.

The chapter focuses mainly on preschoolers because kindergarten programs vary widely. Some centers do nothing special for five-year-olds; others provide five-year-olds with several hours of enrichment activities; still others segregate five-to-six-year-olds into a special class which emphasizes table-top and school readiness exercises with symbols and numbers. Considerations for the entry zone and for napping, bathrooms, and eating/dining are usually the same for kindergarteners and preschoolers, unless you wish to make distinctions (such as separate bathrooms for kindergarten boys and girls). In general, a kindergarten program will have the same broad range of activity areas, and the same six basic types of activities as the preschool room. It is usually the emphasis and use of materials, rather than the areas per se, that distinguish kindergartens from preschools.

Program Considerations

Before addressing design factors, a brief review of the overall program goals of preschool and kindergarten rooms may be helpful.

Group Size, Ratios, and Square Footage

As discussed in Chapter 4, and consistent with good developmental practice, this guide espouses caring for 3–5-year-olds in groups of 14–16 with 2 caregivers and kindergarteners in groups of 16–20 with 2 caregivers. The preferred average room size for these age groups is between 1,000 and 1,200 square feet. Because preschoolers and kindergarteners can climb and use vertical space, lofts and multilevel structures can be incorporated to compensate for limited square footage.

Developmental Capabilities

Preschoolers and kindergarteners grow at a relatively calmer and more steady pace compared with the rapid changes they experienced during their first three years of life.

Preschoolers

Preschoolers are avid learners, eager to master skills, agile on their feet, able to manage tools and implements, and beginning to show interest in child-to-child social life and play. Stories, make-believe, games with some structure, imitative play, and vacillation between cooperation and bossiness characterize their social life with peers and adults. They take great pride in constructing and building things from raw materials such as water, sand, wood, clay, and paint; love celebrations, ritual, and ordered events; and are beginning to draw distinctions between boy and girl play.

Kindergarteners

Kindergarten children are more capable than three- and four-year-olds of using symbolic language. They are also extremely dexterous on their feet and at small motor tasks. And they have a lot of energy and an enormous need to get along with other children. They love fairy tales, cartoons, power heroes, and stories—especially of success and victory where they can pretend to be more powerful than they feel. They have reached an age for making rules but don't have the logical grasp to make them consistent. They love improvisations such as playing school, ghosts, ninjas, and playing different roles within games involving chasing and escaping, attack and defense, acceptance and rejection, where there is one leader and others who follow. The average five-year-old can hop and stand on one foot briefly, walk with alternating feet on a balance beam, and catch an 8-inch ball with elbows near the body.

What Preschoolers and Kindergarteners Need

Preschoolers and kindergarteners are developing independence and self-control and expanding their horizons to include others outside their family. They still need loving contact with a few consistent adults with whom they are bonded and from whom they receive primary care. They also need the four factors discussed in Chapter 1 in equal quantities: movement, comfort, competence, and control.

Design Considerations

Preschool and kindergarten spaces can accommodate many changes in level and the broadest range of activity areas. The room should lend itself to accommodating a wide range of interests where, ideally, many areas are used simultaneously to explore a given topic. For example, the study of fish might include an undersea station on a loft; making fish prints, two and three dimensional representations at the easel, craft, and clay tables; reading about sea life; building a sea capsule in the block area; studying damming and streaming at the water and sand tables; listening to sea sounds; and moving like sea creatures. Most materials and toys can be accessible to children so they may obtain, use, clean up, and store items on their own.

Furniture Dimensions

Recommended dimensions for preschool/kindergarten furniture are outlined in Table 17.1.

Program-Specific Decisions

In designing activity areas to support your preschool and kindergarten programs, the following basics need to be considered:

- Arranging the entry zone to provide transition and support
- Facilitating interaction between child and caregiver
- Providing for napping/rest
- Handling toileting/bathroom functions
- Providing for eating/snacking

Table 17.1 *Recommended Furniture Dimensions: Preschoolers and Kindergarteners*

	Seat and Table Height			
Age	Seat Height	Av. Seat Width	Av. Seat Depth	Table Ht.
3 years	10″	11.5″	9.5″	18″
4 years	12″	12.75″	11″	20″
5–6 years	12″	12.75″	11″	20″
	Shelf Height			
Preschool			37–40 inches maximum	
Kindergarten			40–48 inches maximum	
	Water and Sand Play Table Height			
Preschool			24 inches	
Kindergarten			24 inches	

- Developing spaces that support a rich range of child-focused activities

Entry Zone

The importance of transitions to children and the general functions of the entry zone are explained in Chapter 7 and Box 7.3.

Child Personal Storage

Each child needs a place to store his/her extra clothing, outer wear, treasures from home, and objects made at the center. One storage unit can serve all these functions or clothing can be stored separately. The location of coat cubbies will greatly affect ease of parent/staff communication, ease of child/parent separation, tracking of dirt, etc. The activity of helping children on and off with clothing is a social event for parents and a demanding task for staff. Location, design, and adequate space in the cubby area is critical in supporting both these concerns, as well as children's ease in learning to dress themselves. The cubby area can also double as a place to communicate with parents via parent mail boxes, notice boards, etc.

QUESTIONS: CHILD PERSONAL STORAGE

1. What images do you have of the entry to your preschool or kindergarten room? How many people are apt to occupy it at any one time?
2. Do you prefer one cubby per child to serve all functions, or some other arrangement?
3. What size and design of cubby is ideal for the kinds of gear children wear in your climate (i.e., bulky snowsuits, rain gear)? Remember: Cubbies can be custom-designed; do not limit yourself to commercial models.

Cubbies arranged in a U create an entry zone.

The backs of a small group of cubbies (in Figure 17.1) face the front door and support a bulletin board greeting those who enter. A box with a lid doubles as a seat and stores lost-and-found items for parents to retrieve.

Figure 17.1
A preschool cubbie.

4. If you prefer to separate clothing from other storage, what design would you like for nonclothing items, i.e., tote tray, bin with door, open box, other?
5. If space is limited, can two children share a cubby?
6. Where is the best location for the coat cubbies—i.e., the corridor outside the room, inside the room near the entrance door, inside near the playground door, other? Where is it best to locate the nonclothing cubby, if you want these?
7. How do you wish to handle parent check-in?

GUIDELINES: CHILD PERSONAL STORAGE

- Allow enough space for most of the group to put on their coats in the entry zone at the same time (approximately 100 square feet).
- Cubbies can be arranged in L- and U-shaped configurations to create a transitional entry zone to the group room.
- Place benches and storage boxes (with lift-up seats for lost and found items) near the coat cubbies so children/adults can sit as they dress or undress (also see page 371).
- Cubbies require a minimum of one lineal foot per child. Where floor space is at a premium, consider placing cubbies in the corridor (if acceptable to fire marshals), or having two children share a cubby.
- A board placed across the lower front of the cubby creates a "box" for stuffing boots and catching clothing that falls.
- Provide a bulletin board for parent notices and a shelf, clipboard, or other arrangement for parent check-in.

Staff Personal Storage

The personal storage requirements of preschool and kindergarten staff are the same as those for infant and toddler caregivers. See the discussion in Chapter 16.

Other Storage

Provide a closet at least 40–60 square feet for storing bulk supplies, toys, and equipment. (Also see Other Storage, Chapter 16.)

Parent/Staff Communication

Despite the relative independence of preschoolers and kindergarteners, their parents still need daily contact with teachers to bridge events between home and center. It is important for parents to feel welcome at any time, to feel they have easy and immediate access to staff and can chat with them freely. Parent-to-parent contact is also desirable. The design of the environment needs to support parental presence and leave-taking as natural and easy events.

QUESTIONS & GUIDELINES: PARENT/STAFF COMMUNICATION

- See the same topic, Chapter 16.

Child/Caregiver Interaction

Preschoolers and kindergarteners still require much love and attention from adults as they confront their physical and intellectual limitations, their frustrations in dealing with peers, and their fears about the many unfamiliar aspects of life now opening up to them. Be sure that the environment continues to support close relationships and physical contact between children and adults.

QUESTIONS: CHILD/CAREGIVER INTERACTION

1. How can you promote continued closeness between preschoolers/kindergarteners and staff?
2. What suggestions do you have for reducing the physical demands of child care upon staff?

GUIDELINES: CHILD/CAREGIVER INTERACTION

- Provide at least one comfortable seat at adult height.
- Provide a couch, large chair, loft, or platform where a child can share private time with an adult.

Napping

Cots or mats can be set up in the group play environment or in a separate napping area. Make cot or mat storage, as well as storage for bedding, convenient to where beds will be set up. To prevent the spread of lice and disease, children's bedding must be kept separate either on a cot labeled with the child's name, in the child's cubbie, or by being washed daily. Consider

Preschoolers and kindergarteners thrive on love and attention from adults.

using the common area of a cluster of group rooms as the swing space for either long nappers or quiet play, so as not to disturb children who sleep longer. (See Chapter 14 for information on bedding.)

Rest for a Sick Child

Creating a separate alcove, niche, or place where a cot can be set up makes it possible for a child who is feeling unwell to remain in the preschool or kindergarten room until a parent arrives (Figure 17.5). Keeping the child in the familiar surroundings of the group room is preferable to sending him or her to the sick bay (see Sick Bay, Chapter 19).

QUESTIONS: NAPPING

1. Do you prefer a separate nap area, or cots set up in the group room?
2. What size and style of beds, cots, or mats will you use?

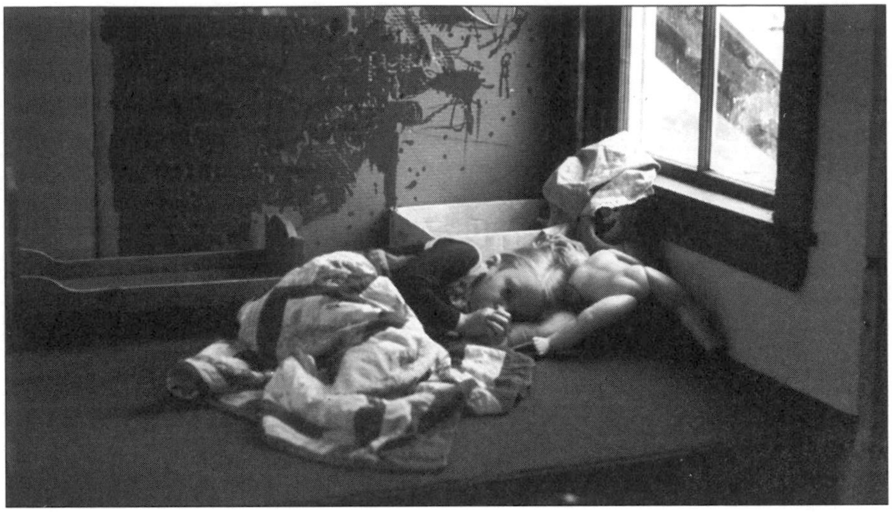

A low platform in the dramatic play corner becomes a "bed" for a sick child waiting to go home.

3. How will you deal with long sleepers versus "players" during nap time?
4. Are there loft, platform, and custom-built spaces which can serve as sleeping areas for some children instead of a mat or cot?
5. Where will you store each child's bedding? What amount and type of space is required?
6. Would you like to create a loft within the room that can store cots in the lower portion and is child-accessible in the upper portion (see page 273)? Or do you prefer to store cots/mats elsewhere? (See pages 158–159.)
7. What local codes or regulations apply to sleeping areas?

FACILITIES LIST FOR NAP AREA

- Cots (above floor, no drafts), mats, or beds
- Storage for cots or mats
- Storage for bedding
- Bedding
- Lights on dimmers
- Window coverings
- Soft music

GUIDELINES: NAPPING

- Provide each child with a separate cot, mat, or bed that can stack (see page 257) or be folded out of the way if you do not intend to have a separate sleep room.
- Do a room plan overlay of cots, mats, or beds to ensure they all will fit: a preschool cot is about 22″ x 52″ x 5″ high.
- Control natural light with shades (see Chapter 11 for information on window coverings), and electrical light with rheostats, to minimize disturbing sleeping children when light is needed.
- Provide adequate ventilation and fresh air, ideally from windows that open.
- Provide bedding that is washable, comfortable, of appropriate warmth, and coordinated with the room's color scheme. Give children options for coverlet design if bedding is not brought from home.
- Allow space in an out-of-the-way area to set up a cot or resting place when a child is unwell. A fish tank, bird, or gerbil cage nearby is often comforting.

Toileting

Bathrooms for preschoolers and kindergarteners need to be accessible; be relatively open; have a pleasant, homelike atmosphere; and include child-sized fixtures or easy ways for children to use adult fixtures. Provide 1 toilet and 1 sink for every 10 children over three years. Separation by sex is not necessary for preschoolers but is sometimes desirable at the kindergarten level. Design the room so that it can be cleaned easily but without an institutional appearance. (Most preschoolers are toilet trained but can have accidents.)

QUESTIONS: TOILETING

1. Do you envision a toilet area for each group room, or one that is accessible to several group rooms? With or without partitions? Child-scaled or adult-scaled? With sinks near the toilets or in the group room?

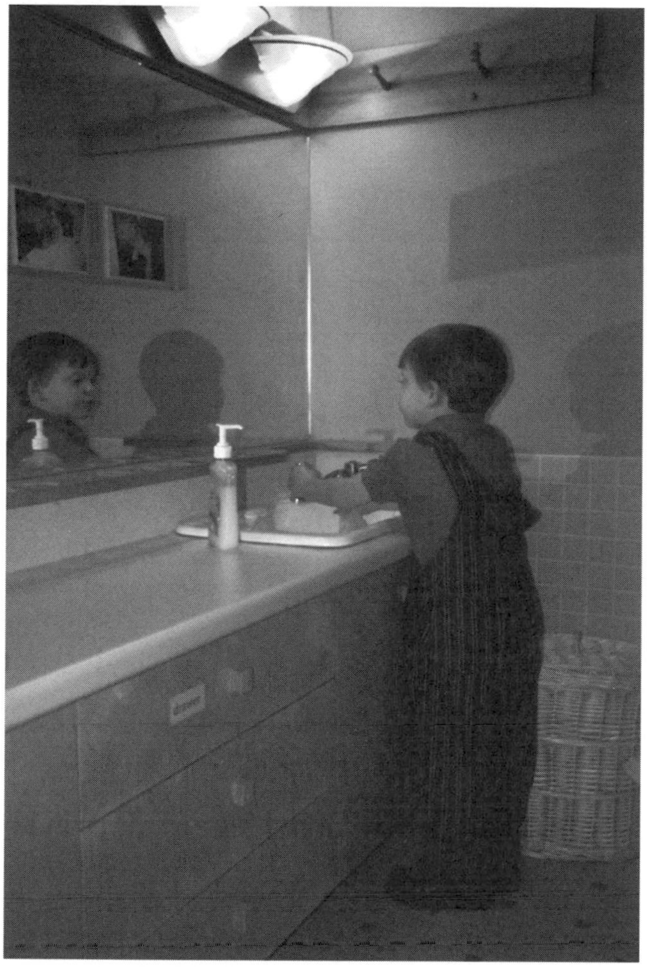

This preschool bathroom feels quite residential with wood cabinets, soft lighting, and a large mirror. (The Copper House)

2. Would you consider a greenhouse window or area as part of the bathroom space? What other ideas might make the bathroom pleasant and special—-windows with a view, small fountain, art work, other?
3. Is one toilet per 10 children (2 per class of 14–18) adequate?
4. What local codes apply?

FACILITIES LIST FOR BATHROOMS

- 11-inch-high toilets
- Storage for toilet paper
- Blackboard or other interactive surface on 24-inch-high stall partitions
- Handsinks 22–24 inches high, in bathroom or immediately outside
- Individual hand towels, paper towels, or air-dryer
- Soap dispenser
- Individual cups, toothbrushes, and holders
- Trash basket
- Bins for extra clothing (or stored in cubbies)
- Floor drain
- Hamper for soiled clothing
- Overhead shelves for storage (to reduce clutter)
- Soft lighting
- Large mirror
- Pleasant art

Fabulous seashells embedded in the partition between the toilets add to this bathroom's appeal. (The Copper House)

GUIDELINES: TOILETING

- See Plumbing, Chapter 4.
- Soft lighting and a large mirror over the sinks make the room more residential.
- Mount sinks in a counter with cabinets below or, for more flexible use, consider one large sink with two faucets.
- Provide special ventilation, and ideally an operable window, to eliminate odors when children have accidents or forget to flush.
- An electric hand dryer conserves paper and promotes sanitation.
- Low stall partitions—about 24 inches high—decorated with things for children to touch and observe—a planter, blackboard, Etch-A-Sketch, sea shells, etc.—increase the residential tone.

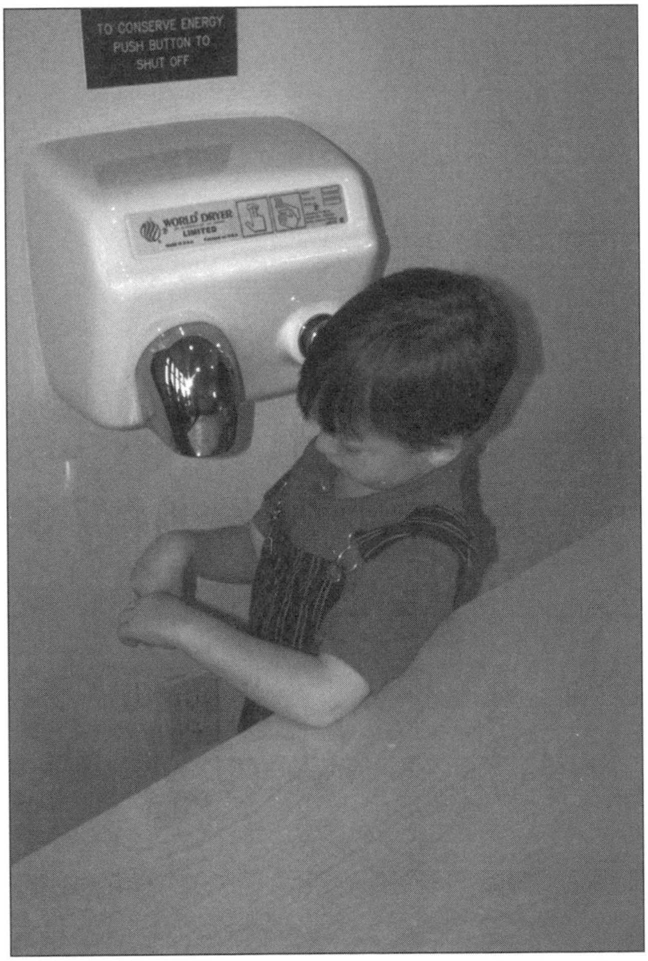

Preschoolers can use an electric hand-dryer and help to save paper.

Washer and Dryer

Use the washer and dryer provided for infants and toddlers (see Chapter 16), or install separate ones if the preschool and/or kindergarten population is large. It is helpful to be able to dry children's clothing after they play with water and snow.

Eating/Dining Areas

Strive to make mealtimes leisurely events during which children can feed themselves, talk, and feel close to adults and one another, similar to the experience of a family eating dinner together. Window seats, pleasant views, and an outdoor terrace in good weather add to the attractiveness of the experience. Transporting food is easiest if the eating area is close to the preparation area.

Snacks

Preschoolers and kindergarteners eat several snacks each day. An open snack table where children serve themselves is often preferable to a group sit-down. It avoids cluttering a room with too many tables and enables children to eat when they are hungry and to meet in small groups. Because of the profound human connection between eating and talking, more conver-

When only 4–6 preschoolers share a table, conversation flows and mealtimes are most pleasant.

An open snack table for 4 invites sharing, conversation, and independence.

sation occurs around small snack tables than elsewhere in the room. For ways to create additional eating surfaces without adding tables to the room, see Chapter 15, Selecting Play and Sitting Surfaces, and page 280. Also see The Cook, Chapter 19.

QUESTIONS: EATING/DINING AREAS

1. Does your program specify a central kitchen, minikitchens for several rooms, a food preparation area in each room, other? If there are minikitchens, do you want preschoolers to eat nearby, or do you prefer them to eat in their group room? How will you transport food and dirty dishes between the kitchen and eating areas? Would a warming cart for transporting food from the central or minikitchen to the group room be desirable?
2. Where and how will you provide for cooking activities? Would a cooking cart, holding a portable oven and supplies, be handy to share among several rooms?
3. How would you like to handle snacks, i.e., everyone sitting down at once, or an ongoing snack table? Would you have this in the preschool room or elsewhere?
4. Can the tables used for art activities serve for eating as well?
5. If there is a dining area, might you use these tables at the start and end of each day for quiet activities and cooking projects?

GUIDELINES: EATING/DINING AREAS

- Decide whether children will eat in their group rooms or in a separate dining area.
- If children will eat in their rooms, specify the number who will eat at any one time and identify sufficient eating surfaces. Remember to minimize the number of tables by using art tables, tops on water and sand troughs, low stackable tables, and tables/shelves that flip up or down. (See page 280.)
- When children eat in a separate dining area, ideally close to the kitchen/servery, maintain intimacy and reduce confusion by having no more than 14–18 children eat around four or five tables at one time.
- Store dishes, flatware, and linens at child height so children can set the tables themselves (see page 350).
- Consider a separate, ongoing snack table for four. Locate snack supplies nearby (cups, juice, crackers, baskets, napkins) so children can serve themselves. Bins of soapy and clean water, and cup hooks, enable children to wash their own cups and put them away, and avoid the use of paper products.
- See Table 17.1 for table and seat heights.

Typical Preschool and Kindergarten Activity Areas

A well-developed preschool or kindergarten space provides a broad range of experiences with different materials organized into discrete activity areas—perhaps as many as 20—within one group room (see Chapter 15). Materials within each area can be varied to include simple, complex, and super units,[1] some materials usable by

This dining area includes a hutch where children can get dishes, flatware, and linens to set the table themselves. (The Copper House)

one child alone, and others requiring that two or more children work cooperatively. So that children maintain their equilibrium over a long day, ensure that activity areas have qualitatively different moods, such as being messy, clean, active, passive, private, and social.

Because of kindergarteners' developing and expanding capabilities, you may find that you want to stress language arts games, listening and writing areas, math and science/nature areas, and an unstructured, theme-related dramatic play space in the kindergarten program. In addition, provide good opportunities for gross motor play both outdoors and inside.

Despite adult needs to be aware of each child at all times, every child deserves the right to privacy within the group setting and to some territory they can call their own. (See Chapter 15 for a discussion of private spaces.)

QUESTIONS: TYPICAL ACTIVITY AREAS

1. What images do you have of the preschool or kindergarten environment as a whole, and of its activities?
2. What are your priorities for activities and physical supports from the environment?

GUIDELINES: TYPICAL ACTIVITY AREAS

- Follow the general guidelines for activity areas in Box 15.1, for zones in Chapter 7, and for the six types of play in Chapter 15. Also see this same section in Chapter 16.
- Provide private spaces where children can pause or retreat. These might include crow's nests; peep holes; fiberboard barrels lined with different textures and shaped cutouts; platforms and lofts; spacious stair landings; a bench, couch, armchair, or window seat (see pages 276–278).
- Consider an emotional release area within or outside the room where a child can safely express frustrations and enthusiasm: throw, kick, run, fall, using mats, foam, mattresses, pillows, punching bags, etc.
- Consider the spirit or mood of each area in the room. Provide places of real beauty and aesthetic value (a beautiful display; a fish tank, bird, or animal cage, etc.).
- Provide direct access to outdoor play yards.

The discussion that follows describes typical activities and their supporting facilities in a preschool or kindergarten group room. These descriptions are intended to get you started thinking about your own program needs and wants. Be certain to incorporate your own ideas and visions!

Messy Play

For a comprehensive list of messy play activities and supporting facilities appropriate for preschoolers and kindergarteners, see Box 7.4 and The Wet Region, Chapter 7.

The messy region of the room generally supports

activities involving water, paints, clay, food preparation, etc., which require access to a sink and easily washable floor surfaces. Refer to "Selecting Play and Sitting Surfaces" in Chapter 15 for specific suggestions on how to minimize the number of tables, which usurp much floor space in this area. Discussed below are specific considerations for water and sand play, cooking, woodworking, and science and nature activities.

QUESTIONS: MESSY PLAY

1. Which of the activities/facilities in Box 7.4, if any, do you not want to include? What activities/facilities would you like to add?
2. How much table surface will you need? For which activities? Would 2 trapezoidal tables (4 units), seating five children at each when separated (20 total), and four at each when together (8 total) suffice for crafts, eating, and other table activities? Can an open snack table, tops on water and sand tables, and a clay table suffice for additional eating and work surfaces? Will eating, snacks, and cooking activities occur elsewhere (e.g., a shared minikitchen/dining area)?
3. Do you want a large (6′–8′ wide) easel on a wall as shown here or as a divider (see page 272)? Or do you prefer standard small A-frame easels or some other design?
4. How do you wish to handle drying of children's paintings: standard aluminum racks; tack board surface up high or on a wall; flat stacked planks or shelves; other?
5. What kind of storage do you envision for protecting children's works-in-progress (clay or wood creations, collages, etc.): high shelves, cubbies, shelves under work tables, other?
6. Where do you envision storing bulk craft supplies that are not displayed for children's use—in each group room closet or staff prep area, in central storage for a cluster, in the staff resource room? How much of this storage is needed, and of what type? Possible items may include large jars of paint, colored paper, newsprint, clay, playdough, scrounged materials, magic markers & crayons, and . . . (It is important to specify all the items that may require storage!)

GUIDELINES: MESSY PLAY

- See the guidelines in Chapter 16.

Water Play and a Wet Room

Water play is an essential activity for preschoolers and kindergarteners. Dedicated faucets and a drain facilitate filling, emptying, and varying the contents of water play tables. (For more information, see Incorporating a Water Play Table, Chapter 7, and the three case studies that conclude Chapter 7.)

A fully enclosed wet playroom with a hand-held shower to wash down walls, floors, and children,

A 4′ high by 8′ long easel made of homosote is washable when covered with semigloss paint and polyurethane. Homosote above the easel serves as a display/drying board for paintings.

A 6′ x 8′ glass enclosed wet play room, similar to a giant shower stall, is a safe place to make a mess.

Sand and water tables can be brought into the classroom.

Using brushes, rollers, and buckets of paint, children can paint the walls and their own bodies.

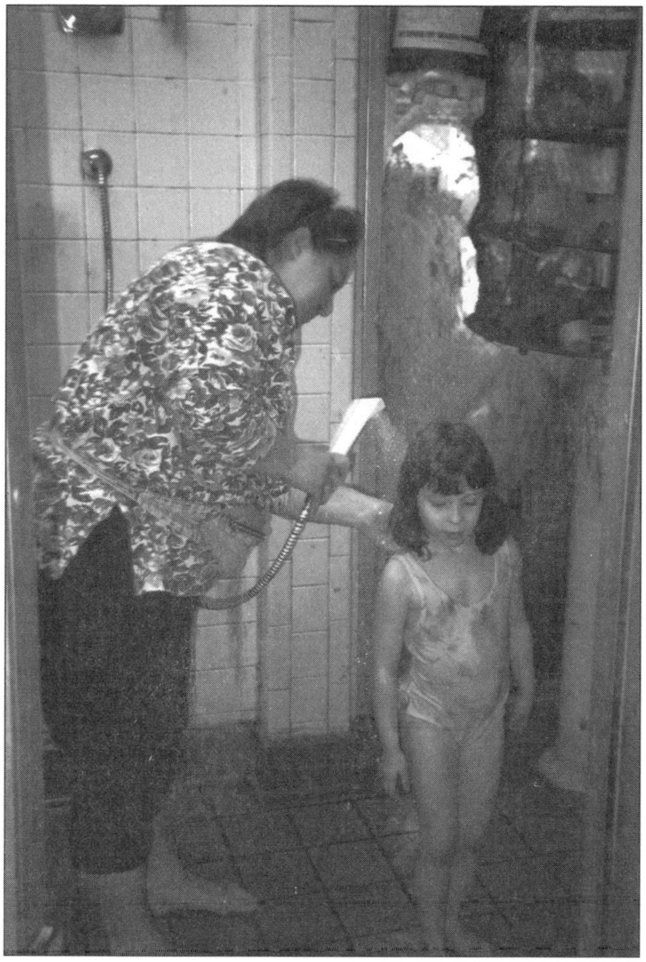

A hand-held shower facilitates cleanup of children and the room.

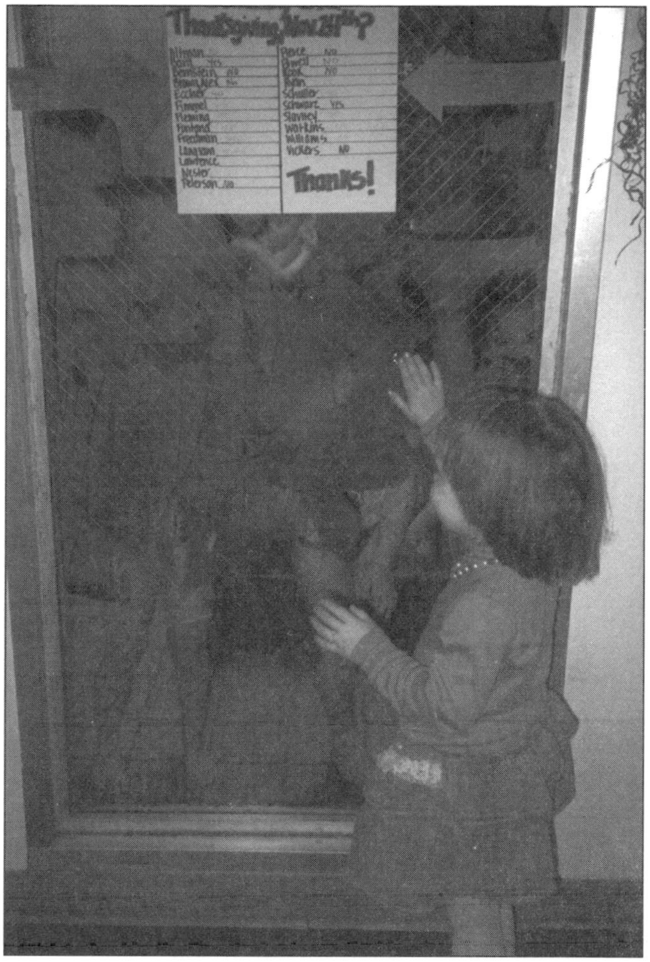

Looking in on the wet room from the group room.

allows preschoolers and kindergarteners to experiment freely with messy materials and staff to easily clean up after them. (Also see page 371.)

QUESTIONS: WATER PLAY/WET ROOM

1. Would you like a built-in drain and faucet to support a free-standing, commercial water play table, so the table can be easily filled and emptied and moved around? Would you prefer a permanent (built-in) water table?
2. *Specialty item:* For the center as a whole, or preschoolers specifically, is it a priority to have a fully tiled "wet" room, with shower, for body painting and messy exploration?

FACILITIES LIST FOR WATER PLAY

- Water play trough
- Faucet and drain (or other means of filling and emptying)
- Cold and warm water (temperature control valves)
- Water play toys (funnels, tubes, containers, dolls, etc.)
- Bins, baskets, hooks, shelves for toys
- Aprons on hooks nearby
- *Optional*: fully enclosed wet play room 6′ x 8′ or larger

GUIDELINES: WATER PLAY

- Locate water play on washable flooring with a built-in drain.
- Provide a trough that is at least 2′ x 4′ x 6″ deep at 24″ high for each preschool and kindergarten group. It is preferable to plumb this trough, which might be a large ceramic sink or a stainless steel liner fabricated by a restaurant supplier.
- Orient the water trough so children can play around three sides.
- Provide storage for water play toys adjacent to the trough.
- Provide hooks and waterproof smocks for 4–6 children.

Sand Play

Sand is most easily cleaned from a carpeted surface that can be vacuumed. Consider placing an area rug under the sand play trough or locating it on carpet near, but not directly in, the messy play area. Because of the developmental value of sand and water play, make every attempt to have both available at all times. However, to prevent clogging of drains with sand or too much water in the sand trough, keep the tables reasonably distant from one another, except when supervised. Troughs can vary in size and generate different types of play depending on their dimensions. Sit-in sand boxes indoors can be unwieldy unless well-bounded so the sand remains contained and is shaken off children's clothing before they go elsewhere. Sandboxes or mounds of sand outdoors may need to substitute for indoor sand play if space is at a premium.

QUESTIONS: SAND PLAY

1. Where would you like to locate a sand table? Is there enough space indoors for the size table you prefer?
2. What surface do you prefer under the trough (washable flooring or carpet)?

FACILITIES LIST: SAND PLAY

- Sand play trough
- Sand play toys
- Bins, baskets, shelves, hooks to hold toys
- Access to water

GUIDELINES: SAND PLAY

- Provide at least one trough 2′ x 4′ x 6″ deep at 24″ high for sand play. Trough size and height will determine the type of sand play children engage in.
- Orient the trough so children can play on three sides.
- Provide nearby storage for sand play toys.
- Make sure water for wetting down the sand to make it malleable is available nearby.

Cooking

Unlike in the United States, where children are typically forbidden from being in the kitchen, German regulations require a child-size kitchen, equipped with an operative sink, stove, refrigerator, and cabinets, in every room for children four years and older! Ways to give our children opportunities to prepare food might include: helping the center's cook in a room or at a table near the main kitchen (see page 198); preparing food at a space near a servery or minikitchen; cooking in the group room using portable appliances (stored there or on a moveable cart that can be transported throughout the center).

Woodworking

Learning how to represent ideas with wood and to use simple hand tools to build is highly educational for preschoolers and kindergarteners. Many teachers shy away from this activity because they feel it is dangerous and/or noisy. How and where the area is set up makes all the difference, as explained in the guidelines below. (See pages 158, 195, and 273, for some woodworking ideas.)

QUESTIONS: WOODWORKING AREA

1. Will you provide a woodworking area in your preschool/kindergarten room?
2. How would you like the area to look?
3. What tools, work surfaces, and storage options do you want to provide?

FACILITIES LIST FOR WOODWORKING AREA

- 2′ x 4′ x 22″ high woodworking bench with vise
- Bins for storing wood of different sizes
- Real tools, hung on pegboard panels
- Shelves or surfaces for storing works-in-progress
- Table with a washable surface nearby for gluing
- Tree stump of soft wood
- Optional: shedlike enclosure for workbench and tools

GUIDELINES: WOODWORKING AREA

- A safe, woodworking bench accommodates only 2–3 children at a time and is accessible from three sides only.
- Locate woodworking in the messy play area where a staff person is almost always apt to be present.
- Provide storage both for wood scraps and for works in progress.
- Make the bench surface as thick as possible (like a butch-

er's cutting block in an old-fashioned meat market) to reduce noise.

- Have a laminate-surfaced table nearby for gluing constructions when children tire of saws and hammers. (See page 158.)
- Display small (but real) lightweight tools on pegboard panels.
- A tree stump of soft wood makes an excellent (and quiet) block for children learning to hammer nails on the head. When the block becomes a "porcupine" replace it with another. (See pages 158 and 371.)

Science and Nature

Experiences with plants and animals encourage an appreciation for the care of living creatures. Indoor nature areas are intended to supplement, but never replace, experiences in the natural world of woods, fields, ponds, rivers, mountains, and gardens.

Ample working surfaces and storage are important in nature and science spaces. Other items in the science area might include magnets, magnifying glasses, microscopes, thermometers, batteries and bulbs, color wheels, animal hatching kits, discovery boxes, shells, nests, pods, fossils, rocks, etc.

QUESTIONS: SCIENCE AND NATURE

1. What types and numbers of items do you wish to have in the science/nature area?
2. What amount and types of storage space will these items require? What amount and types of display and work surface space are desired?
3. What animals do you hope to have in each room? How and where would you like to raise these animals?
4. Other considerations not mentioned above?

FACILITIES LIST FOR SCIENCE AND NATURE

- Storage and display shelves for collections, plants, and animals
- Child counter-height surfaces for working with materials
- A table and seats for 4–6 for group activities
- Good light, preferably natural
- Sink nearby
- Teacher storage for items not currently on display
- Notice or bulletin board
- Back or white board for sketching

This counter-height table and its display divider create a place for exploring science- and nature-related materials.

A large science area includes plenty of storage, counter, display and work space.

One day, children witnessed a mother gerbil give birth to 3 babies in this chicken wire "gerbil run" spanning a room's math to reading areas.

GUIDELINES: SCIENCE AND NATURE

- Locate the science area near a sink and include extensive counter/work space; storage for seeds, tools, supplies; display walls and shelves for collections of rocks, leaves, shells, etc.
- Give the area plenty of natural light and provide tables for all-round viewing.
- Place fish tanks lower than child eye level to prevent children from trying to reach the fish and pulling the tank down on themselves.
- Since animals do not do things "on command," consider locating cages for gerbils, mice, fish, birds, snakes, etc., in the midst of the group room, rather than in a designated science area. The desirability of such a location needs to be weighed against children's capacities to care for and protect the animals. (Hamsters might be in an open cage in the reading area. A fish tank placed in the lower shelves of a bookcase is fun to view while lying on the floor.)
- Small animal display areas, with a cozy seat nearby, can also be set up in niches and bays as "time-out" or semiprivate spaces. A cot could be located near such a niche, for a child who is unwell.

Quiet Play

Activities such as reading and listening, writing, manipulatives, small unit blocks, and math are quiet activities appropriately located in the more tranquil portions of the room.

Reading and Group Meeting

A comfortable reading area that allows preschoolers and kindergarteners to assume a variety of sitting and reclining positions, stocked with a wide range of books, assists in the rapid development of language. This area often works well as the space for storytelling and for meetings of the entire group once or twice a day. It may include listening and manipulative activities, or these may each have an area of their own. Risers, cushions, and small couches and lofts work extremely well in this area.

QUESTIONS: READING/GROUP MEETING

1. What activities, materials, and supports do you want in the reading/meeting area?
2. How and where do you envision conducting meetings for the whole group of 14–18? Do you wish an L-shaped arrangement of two tiers of carpeted risers (steps) to support group meeting time and quiet play? Are there other supports for these activities that you prefer or wish to add?
3. Since couches and armchairs can take up premium floor space, would it suffice to have these items in a family living room (if there is one) and to use risers and smaller items in the group rooms?
4. Do you want manipulatives to be included in this area?

A small wicker settee and gauzy curtain canopy create a cozy reading area.

FACILITIES LIST FOR READING/GROUP MEETING AREA

- Couches, armchairs, carpeted risers, hammocks, beanbag chairs, waterbed with risers
- Carpeted floor surface
- Books and book display
- VCR and TV
- Soft toys
- Reading loft
- Private spaces
- Display and bulletin boards

Here or elsewhere:

- Manipulatives
- Storage and display of manipulatives
- 10-inch-high tables
- Tape deck, record and/or CD player, audio tapes, records, CDs, earphones

Tiers of risers set into a large bay window create a beautiful place for reading, group meeting, and playing with manipulatives.

GUIDELINES: READING/GROUP MEETING

- Two tiers of carpeted risers in an L or U formation are excellent for reading and group meeting activities. (See Orientation of Play and Sitting Surfaces, Chapter 15.) Build each tier out of plywood with a seat height of 8–9 inches, and a seat depth of 12–15 inches maximum.
- In addition, a reading loft (see page 159), raised platforms and perches, small lofts and alcoves, and built-in or designed "bays" work well for this area. Choose seating that provides good back support.
- The reading/meeting area is best located near other quiet activities, with good task-specific lighting, and some natural light if possible, and with proper acoustic control.
- Provide space to display 20–25 books (20–25 lineal feet) at one time with their covers outward.

Ample storage for manipulatives is built at child counter height for working and display. A large amount of protected floor space is available nearby.

A 3′ x 4′ platform, 12 inches high, enclosed on two sides, makes a perfect protected place for one or two children to play with manipulatives

- Provide outlets for tape players, ear phones, and other electrical equipment.
- If manipulatives are included in the area, provide adequate shelving or consider storage bins on wheels located under the lower tier of risers (see page 371).

Manipulative Play

The floor, risers, or low platforms are nice surfaces on which preschoolers and kindergarteners can play with puzzles, games, and construction toys, provided the area is well-bounded and protected from traffic. Low tables that do not require chairs also can be added.

QUESTIONS: MANIPULATIVE PLAY

1. How do you envision the manipulative area? List what it will contain.
2. Where will you store the manipulatives not accessible to children at a given time?
3. List and cut out images of toys, materials, and all storage units you intend to use. Can you specify the amount and nature of the storage needed in the room and elsewhere for this area? (See Interiors Bible, Chapter 14.)

FACILITIES LIST FOR MANIPULATIVE PLAY

- Puzzles, games, lottos
- Small construction toys (Legos, flexi briks, snap blocks, etc.)

This beautiful fireplace was transformed into a small writing area.

- Miniature dramatic play toys
- Peg boards, lacing cubes, form boards, alphabet boards
- Child-accessible storage for manipulative items
- Optional low table (10″ high) without chairs; and/or table with chairs at edge of area
- Pillows and cushions
- Wall display surface for visual images

GUIDELINES: MANIPULATIVE PLAY

- Arrange 24″–30″-high storage shelves to create transit-free floor space in front of the shelves. Children tend to use materials close to where they are stored.
- Make sure that storage shelves are well-organized, labeled, and contain bins that hold all the parts to any given toy.
- If manipulative play is combined with reading and group meeting, consider storage bins that pull out from under the lower tier of risers (see page 371).
- Tables usurp floor space for play. If a table is desired, use a low one without chairs or place one with chairs at the edge of the space.

Writing

Preschoolers and kindergarteners have a great interest in learning to communicate with peers and adults through words and images on paper, as well as learning to copy letters and numbers. While this activity can take place at art tables, locating it in a separate area gives it added value. A writing area might involve a table and several seats, even cushions at a low table on the floor. Writing is also stimulated when children can sit up on a platform or loft 3–5 feet above the floor, removed from—but able to survey—the entire room. Clipboards or low tables not requiring chairs can be used as supports.

QUESTIONS: WRITING

1. Do you wish to have a dedicated writing area in your preschool room?
2. How and where do you envision it? On the floor or on a platform? Close to what other activities?
3. What features might you incorporate in the writing area?
4. Can you specify the equipment, storage, and amount of space required for this activity?

FACILITIES LIST FOR WRITING

- Small table
- 2–4 seats
- Storage shelves for paper, letters, and writing implements
- Nearby display wall for written work or suggested activities
- Optional platform or loft

GUIDELINES: WRITING

- Similar to the science area shown on page 355, a sheet of homosote tacked to the back of a table can form a boundary and display surface for a writing area.
- Display paper, writing implements, and cut-out letters invitingly.
- Add small "mailboxes" for each child to the area to encourage correspondence and communication.
- Combine writing with listening activities, if desired.

Listening

Although listening activities can be included in the reading/meeting area, it is sometimes desirable to have a dedicated place for listening to records, CDs, and tapes, usually with earphones that children can access at will. (See page 387.) The player (turntable, tapedeck, or CD player) needs to be on a secure shelf, but the area can be quite cozy with carpet, cushions nestled into a small niche, under or on top of a platform. One to four children, at most, would be there at the same time.

QUESTIONS: LISTENING

1. Do you wish to have a separate listening area in your preschool room?
2. What images do you have of its design?
3. Can you specify the equipment and storage space you will need?

FACILITIES LIST FOR LISTENING

- Record, CD, tape player for child use
- 2–4 sets of earphones
- Sturdy display shelf for equipment and storage
- Records, CDs, and tapes
- Carpet
- Soft seating, cushions, beanbags, couch, etc.
- Optional platform or loft

GUIDELINES: LISTENING

- Listening can occur at a table, while sitting on the floor, or on or under a loft. Make the area inviting and display some tapes or CDs with their covers outward so children can see the picture.
- If space is limited, consider a mobile listening cart, available commercially.

Small Unit Blocks

Small unit blocks—usually used while children sit or kneel on the floor—help children discover basic mathematical relationships, principles of weight and balance, and small-scale construction techniques in the design of miniature scenes for role-playing and fantasy. Small unit blocks work best in a *well-protected location* in the room so passersby cannot inadvertently knock over constructions. Miniatures (cars, people, animals) are a nice addition to the area. To reap their full educational value, sets of at least 200 blocks are desirable. (See pages 158–159, 234, and 373.)

QUESTIONS: SMALL UNIT BLOCKS

1. What images do you have of the unit block area?
2. How many blocks will you provide in each group room? What size and height of shelving will be required to store them?

An area for unit blocks, displayed with their longest dimensions visible, and accompanied by miniatures.

3. What size unit block area is desirable?
4. What other ideas do you have for this area: miniatures and vehicles, risers for building on, using the area as a group meeting space, etc.?

FACILITIES LIST FOR SMALL UNIT BLOCKS

- 1 set of small unit blocks, preferably 200–400 blocks
- 30″–36″-high storage shelves to store the blocks lengthwise
- Carpeted floor surface
- Highly protected space enclosed by storage shelves, elevated platform, other

GUIDELINES: SMALL UNIT BLOCKS

- Do not place small blocks near a doorway unless the area is enclosed or on a raised platform.
- Allow at least 8 x 10 feet, including storage, on a carpeted surface for this activity, and locate it near other quiet activities. Small areas encourage vertical structures; larger areas foster horizontal constructions as well.
- Blocks are best displayed with their long dimensions visible, embellished by outlines painted or pasted on the shelves to assist children in clean-up, so children can match the 3-dimensional forms to their 2-dimensional representations.
- Add storage for miniature cars, trucks, people, and other props used with the blocks.

Math

Preschool-age children and kindergarteners enjoy learning simple processes related to numbers. This may include informal counting, arranging items in sequences, measuring, weighing, making dimensional comparisons, etc. It is helpful to have a designated place where materials that support such activities can be stored and used.

QUESTIONS: MATH

1. Do you wish to have a separate area in your room for number-related activities? If so, how large should it be?
2. What materials and supports do you want in the area? How do you wish to store and display items?

FACILITIES LIST FOR MATH

- Table or counter top
- Open shelving for bins of materials
- Cubes, small blocks, number games, etc.
- 1-yard measuring rods, tape measures, rulers
- Bathroom scale, balance scale, other

GUIDELINES: MATH

- Design the area to accommodate the specific materials used for number activities. Generally, this would include shelves for bins of materials, a large counter or table for spreading out items, floor and wall space for scales, growth charts, number lines, etc.

A math area includes bins of items to weigh, sort, and count, and lots of counter surface.

Active Play

The preschooler's and kindergartener's need for vigorous movement should not be relegated exclusively to the playground; make indoor expression available throughout the day. Such play builds coordination and balance, breath and stamina, and provides basic orientational experiences in space which are prerequisites to deciphering symbols on a page. In addition to any indoor gross-motor room, specific equipment can be set up in the group room for climbing, crawling, sliding, swinging, hanging, etc. Moreover, lofts and platforms designed for a variety of purposes can provide ways for children to use their bodies. The possibilities for active play are infinite and will depend upon the amount of space available, the design of the structures, and the overall program. Some options are suggested in these photographs and in the facilities list that follows. See also Chapter 4, Multipurpose/Gross-Motor Rooms and Inclusion of Multipurpose Rooms in Primary Space Calculations and Chapter 15, Advantages of Raised Levels.

QUESTIONS: ACTIVE PLAY

1. What images do you have of a climbing structure or supports for large motor play?
2. Can you identify those items of equipment for large motor play that you definitely want to include in your rooms? Which ones are optional if space and money allow?
3. How much storage space, and of what kinds, will be needed for equipment? Be as specific as possible about sizes, numbers, and space needed.

FACILITIES LIST FOR ACTIVE PLAY

- Climber
- Slide
- Tire or monkey swing
- Punching bag
- "Bird cage" climber
- Overhead bars and rings
- Collapsible fabric tunnels to crawl through
- Minitrampolines

Left: A 4′ x 6′ free-standing climber includes graduated rungs, two platforms children can relocate, and a beam for suspending varied large muscle apparatus such as a punching bag, a monkey swing, tire swing, or the "birdcage" shown here.

Above: The slide. mounted by a single dowel, can pivot. Easily removed, it frees its supporting platform to become a stage or surface for interactive play.

After climbing this ladder, children know in their muscles and bones how high they have climbed, and how much energy it took to get there.

This large indoor climber includes spaces to crawl through and places to climb to.

- Foam mats, wedges, bolsters
- Ball crawl
- Ramps
- Changes in level
- Rocking toys, boats, horses,
- Balance beams
- See saw
- Riding toys and wagons
- Suspension, net, and toddle bridges
- Rope, net, chain, and wood ladders
- Firefighter's pole

GUIDELINES: ACTIVE PLAY

- Because young children learn primarily by moving and using their bodies in space, ways must be found to support large muscle play within the group room, unless the climate permits year extensive play time outside.
- Illustrations throughout this guide, and in the illustrative floor plans that conclude this chapter, suggest ways to make active play available in group rooms.
- A beam installed across the narrow dimension of the room makes suspension of portable apparatus possible.
- Many active play supports are moveable items that can be shared among group rooms. However, they can be large and do need adequate storage space.

An autoharp on display is irresistible.

Music and Movement

Activities involving rhythm, music, playing instruments, and learning to move the body with coordination and balance are instinctive and fun for preschoolers and kindergarteners. The group room ideally will have an area with sufficient clear floor space to allow a group to move and dance together spontaneously. As an alternative, consider ways to clear an area for this purpose. Even if floor space is at a premium, make music from records, tapes, or CDs available in the room at all times, located where sound will be appreciated and not disturbing. Speakers can be ceiling-mounted to conserve space.

QUESTIONS: MUSIC AND MOVEMENT

1. What images do you have of the music and movement area?
2. How large an area will you provide for music and movement? Will the area be in the group room or elsewhere?
3. Can you specify the musical instruments, tapes/CDs/records, and sound equipment you will need, and the ways in which you wish to store and display these for children's use?

Well-displayed musical instruments encourage spontaneous jamming.

FACILITIES LIST FOR MUSIC AND MOVEMENT

- Floor area at least 8'x10' for small-group movement
- Carpeted floor surface
- Tape/CD/record player—child accessible
- Storage for tapes, CDs and records—child accessible
- Display of musical instruments
- Display of scarves, banners, props to wave, etc.

GUIDELINES: MUSIC AND MOVEMENT

- Instruments are irresistible when accessible and beautifully displayed.
- If space is limited, consider a commercial mobile instrument cart.
- A large, carpeted, dedicated space available to the entire center for music and movement is a superb complement to more limited experiences in the group rooms.

Large Riding Toys

Preschoolers and kindergarteners take great pleasure in riding and operating large wooden, metal, or plastic trucks, cars, tricycles, wagons, etc. Play with such toys often occurs best outdoors, because it requires space for use and storage and is most enjoyable when the safety of others is not an issue. Where possible, however, it is desirable also to designate an indoor space for this purpose.

QUESTIONS: LARGE RIDING TOYS

1. Do you wish to have and can you find sufficient indoor space for using large riding toys?
2. Can you specify the toys, their sizes, the amount of storage space they need, and the amount of floor space to be allocated for this activity?

GUIDELINES: LARGE RIDING TOYS

- Large riding toys work best in a corridor or portion of it, in a little-used room, or in another space outside the group room.
- For safety and child access, store riding toys at floor level, perhaps in a small closet or behind a low wall.

Dramatic Play

Preschoolers and kindergarteners generally engage in at least five types of dramatic play:

1. **House play** involving child-sized equipment and furnishings. This might include an enclosure that functions as a "bedroom" or hideaway for dolls or for children themselves. Always arrange playhouse equipment to form a space or enclosure that is roomlike; never just line it up against a wall. Adding a roof is nice. (Pages 158–159, 160–161, 332–333, and 373 also show various types of house play facilities for children.)

(Top) Space under a staircase accommodates a play kitchen and a bedroom loft. (Bottom) Playhouse equipment arranged to form a convincing kitchen.

Dressing up is lots of fun.

Soapsuds from the water play table help to complete these outfits.

2. **Dress-up play** involving dress-up clothes, hats, and masks, and perhaps face painting.
3. **Play with puppets and a puppet theater or a storefront**. (Also see pages 158–159 and 393.)
4. **Play with miniatures** such as dollhouses, model horses and barns, etc. (This type of play can also occur in an area of its own; see the discussion of miniatures in the next section.)
5. **Theme-related dramatic play** in which preschoolers and kindergarteners enact the many themes—particuiarly of power—that fascinate them at this age: Batman, Spider man, Ninjas, Power Rangers, comic book heroes and space explorers, doctors, hairdressers, cooks, mail carriers, firefighters, etc.

QUESTIONS: DRAMATIC PLAY

1. How do you envision the dramatic play area?
2. What types of structures, platforms, and enclosures do you envision for the area? A playhouse? Structures to support other dramatic-play themes?
3. Are there commercial structures you might purchase? Would you prefer structures custom-designed for your space?

FACILITIES LIST FOR DRAMATIC PLAY

- Playhouse enclosure or panels
- Separate stove, refrigerator, sink, or a combo
- Dolls, doll bed, doll carriage
- Brooms, ironing boards, mops
- Pots and pans, dishes, milk and cereal cartons, fake food, etc.
- Enclosures for resting, hiding, putting dolls to sleep
- Dress-up clothes, hats, masks
- Storage for dress ups
- Mirrors; "dressing room"
- Puppet theater/store front, with puppets and store props
- Dramatic play platform for theme enactment
- Storage for props used with dramatic play
- Miniature dollhouse, barn, garage, etc.

GUIDELINES: DRAMATIC PLAY

- Generally speaking, different areas are needed for the five types of dramatic play, although they may be located near one another.

Dress-up clothes stored in the wooden chifferobe can be tried on in the circular "dressing room," which contains three full-length mirrors.

- These activities benefit from custom-designed structures and supports that are enticing and suggestive without specifying one type of play—i.e., a loft that can be variously decorated, rather than one permanently outfitted as a pirate ship.
- A loft can combine house and puppet/store play on the bottom with thematic play on the top, or vice versa. (See designs in the photographs accompanying the floorplans at the end of this chapter.)
- Thematic play calls for an identifiable area, ideally a raised platform 3–5 feet above the floor, which teachers and children can embellish with props to create whatever theme is being explored. (See pages 158–161 and 373.) If such a place is not provided, children tend to play in the room's circulation space, creating confusion.
- To set limits and maintain safety, lofts are best if no more than six feet deep and 7–8 feet long.
- Locate store fronts and puppet theaters along a main path of transit in the room to attract customers and an audience.
- Consider locating large hollow blocks near the dramatic play area so they can be used to extend dramatic play.

Miniatures

In addition to large toys, preschool- and kindergarten-age children are fascinated by miniatures such as dollhouses, barns, garages, hospitals, animals, and people. Sometimes these items are placed in the manipulatives

Making a purchase at the local store.

area or included with small unit blocks. Alternatively, miniatures can be set up in a dedicated quiet nook in the room for use by one to four children. Or children can transport a collection of miniatures to a protected place as desired. A carpeted floor and cushions are generally ideal supports.

QUESTIONS: MINIATURES

1. What miniatures do you anticipate using in your preschool/kindergarten room? Where do you wish to locate them? How much floor space and storage space will they need?
2. Are there special miniatures (such as an antique dollhouse) which can be available to children if given the right supports and protection?
3. What images do you have of how the room can be designed to support miniature play?

FACILITIES LIST FOR MINIATURES

- Miniatures (dollhouses, farm buildings, garages, animals, people, etc.)
- Carpet
- Chairs, cushions, low seats
- Storage bins and units for props
- Protected floor area
- Optional low table

GUIDELINES: MINIATURES

- Doll houses and certain miniature buildings may benefit from being placed on a low (10″ high) table.
- Many miniature buildings are large and need deep shelves when stored.
- Good-quality miniatures are expensive and need to be displayed in appropriate containers.
- Small cars and trucks are best used on protected floor spaces, low tables, and risers.

Large Hollow Blocks

It is generally advisable to separate large and small blocks because they are used so differently. Large blocks facilitate the development of muscular coordination and balance. Children tend to use them to build "rooms" and enclosures, while standing on their feet being very active, even aggressive. Large blocks require plenty of open space to build and often work well near dramatic play areas. When large hollow blocks are combined with small unit blocks, the small blocks are used to fill in the holes in constructions made with the larger ones, and the inherent mathematical principles in the small ones are overlooked.

Large hollow blocks, from which children build "forts" and enclosures, demand plenty of space.

QUESTIONS: LARGE HOLLOW BLOCKS

1. Do you wish to have a separate area for large blocks?
2. How large a set do you anticipate having?
3. If you cannot have a sizable set for each group room, do you plan to have a good-sized set for several groups to share? Where will you keep the set: multipurpose room? other?
4. Do you want to store these blocks on a cart so they can be moved outdoors or elsewhere? Do you prefer other kinds of storage for them?

Becoming computer literate.

FACILITIES LIST FOR LARGE HOLLOW BLOCKS

- I set (preferably 50 or more blocks) of large hollow blocks
- Storage shelves or a cart on wheels
- Carpeted floor surface

GUIDELINES: LARGE HOLLOW BLOCKS

- Large hollow blocks are a superb material for stimulating imaginative and cooperative play.
- To reap the full benefits of large hollow blocks, at least 50 are needed, plus plenty of space in which to build.
- It is rewarding to build outdoors as well as inside. Storing the blocks on a mobile cart makes transport easy.
- A large-block area works especially well if located near or as part of dramatic play facilities.

Other Activities

Provision of the activity areas outlined above constitutes the basis for a developmentally rich program. There may be numerous other materials, activities, and areas—such as computers—that you wish to include in your rooms. An alive environment is constantly changing and responsive to the interests of children and staff as they arise.

QUESTIONS

1. What other areas, activities, items of equipment not mentioned above do you want in your rooms?
2. What images of these do you have? Into which major activity areas might they be incorporated; or do they merit areas of their own? What other activities would be located nearby?
3. How often will these be used? What types of long-term and short-term storage and display do they need?

Illustrative Floor Plans

Pages 370 through 375 display scaled floor plans for four different preschool rooms. The plans identify the room's zones and all the commercial and custom-built furnishings that were used to develop the activity areas in each room. Photographs accompanying some of the plans illustrate selected elements more fully.

Notes

[1]See S. Kritchevsky, E. Prescott, and L. Walling, 1977. "Planning environments for young children." *Physical Space.* Washington D.C.: National Association for the Education of Young Children.

Figure 17.2
The Preschool Room of the Copper House.

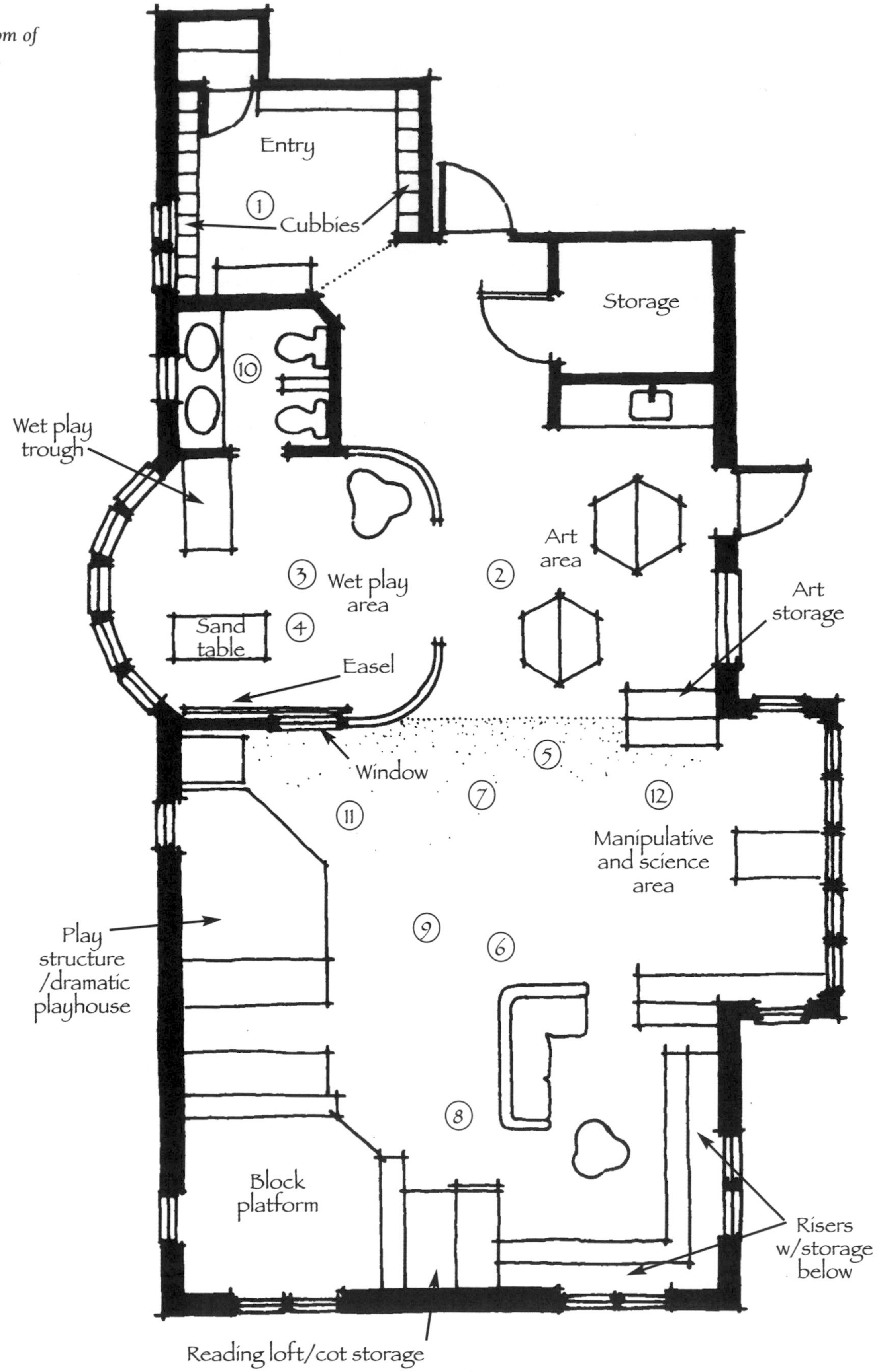

1. *Cubbie area.*

2. *The curved walls, ceiling, and windows of this wet play bay create a giant "hug."*

3. *Water play at a built-in trough with a hand-held shower at adult height.*

4. *A seven foot long painting easel.*

5. *The arts and crafts area including tables, storage, a staff-prep counter and door to the outside porch.*

6. *The reading/group meeting/ manipulative area. Bins on castors store manipulatives under the lowest tier of risers.*

7. *Panning two walls of the room (left to right): Next to the risers is a reading loft/cot storage unit, then a block platform, then a woodworking shed, and a dramatic play climber.*

8. *The reading loft with cot storage behind the curtain.*

9. *The dramatic play climber with a pulley and basket for hauling things up top.*

10. *A partial view of the bathroom.*

11. *Having tea under the loft, with a nice view to the play yard.*

12. *The project bay with windows on three sides.*

Figure 17.3
The preschool room for four- and five-year-olds at Developmental Child Care, St. Louis, features a wet play room (pages 352–353) shared by the entire center.

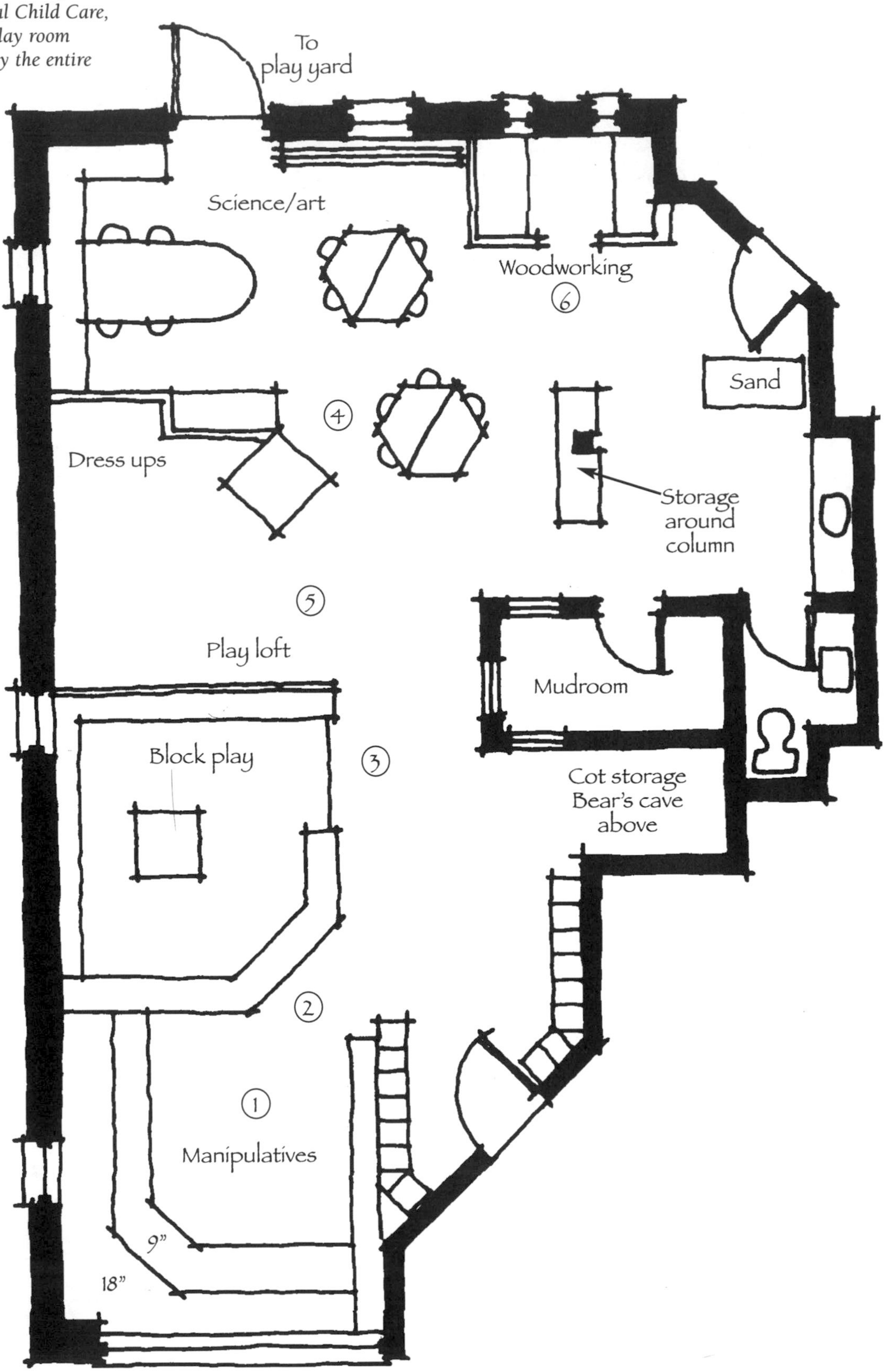

1

2

3

4

5

6

Figure 17.4
This small preschool room at the Eliot Pearson Children's School, Tufts University, still has space for a well-used dramatic play structure.

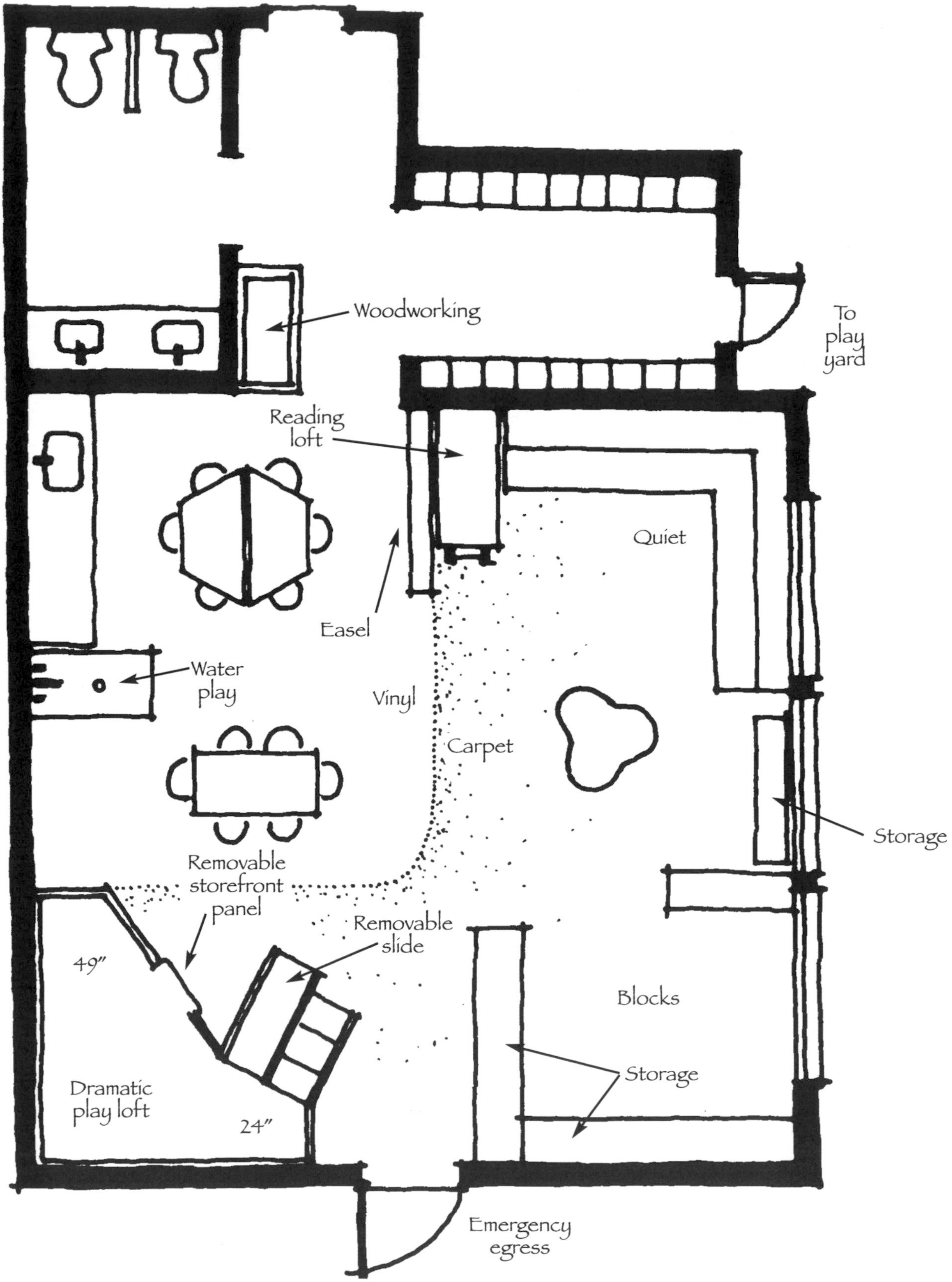

Figure 17.5
The conceptual plan for this preschool room features a family/living room, a music/movement room, and a central elevated covered platform for creative and dramatic play projects.

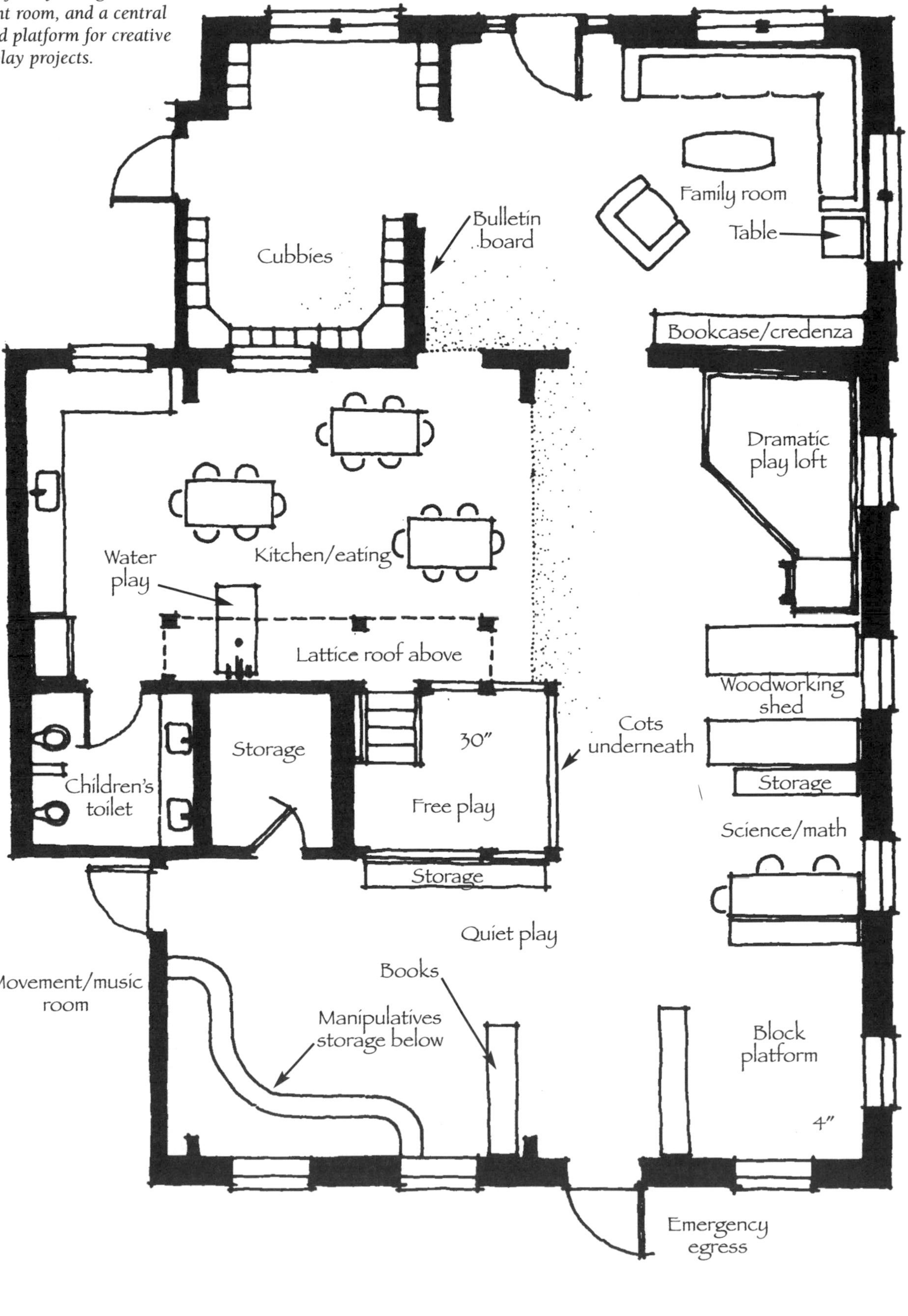

CHAPTER EIGHTEEN

SPACES FOR SCHOOL-AGE CHILDREN

There was a child went forth every day,
And the first object he looked upon, that object he became,
And that object became part of him for the day or a certain part of the day,
Or for many years or stretching cycles of years.

—WALT WHITMAN

School-age groups often span a wide and developmentally diverse range of ages. This chapter focuses on the activity and care needs of children six to ten years old who come to the child care center either before (6–8 a.m.) or after (2–6 p.m.) attending elementary school. (Five- to six-year-olds may also come to the center for the half-day—morning or afternoon—when they are not attending kindergarten.) The chapter does not address the design of elementary school classrooms for child care centers that are incorporating grades 1–6 into their programs. To create spaces that will challenge and support school-age children, use the questions and guidelines outlined here in conjunction with the zoning recommendations in Chapter 7, the activity-area design suggestions in Chapter 15, and for half-day kindergartens, the issues addressed in Chapter 17 for preschool/kindergarten rooms.

In the summer, a school-age program can become a day camp for the children who attend the center before or after school during the school year, especially if the size, location, and outfitting of the school-age space is designed with this use in mind at the outset.

Types of Programs

Programs for school-age children consist of three types: before-school, half-day for kindergarteners, and after-school.

Before-School Programs

Children whose parents start work early or have a long commute to work often need care before the school day begins. Increasingly, centers that are open early for full-day child care are also responding to this before-school demand. A pleasant, sunny place to eat breakfast; cozy chairs and couches to nestle into; places to play games, read, do homework, or talk are reassuring and comforting to children who may have to rise early and hurry out of the house before their schools open. The child care center can help to set the tone for the child's entire day.

Half-Day Programs for Kindergarteners

Sometimes half-day kindergarteners come to the child care center for the entire morning or afternoon when they are not in school. The recommendations for kindergarteners in Chapter 17 can apply for these children as well. In addition, coordination with the child's kindergarten teacher can help the center provide activities that complement rather than repeat what occurs in school. Children who attended the center as toddlers and preschoolers for full-day care but who are assigned to afternoon kindergarten may be energetic in the morning and wish to maintain some sense of continuity with their previous child care experience. Those who arrive at the center following a half day at school usually need a chance to switch gears (and peers!) by letting off steam or having some quiet "down" time.

After-School Programs

Children who have spent five to seven hours seated at desks in a large group, focusing on symbolic material, with little time outdoors, need real contrasts in experience, activity level, and environment during at least a portion of the after-school program. For the first part of the session, children generally prefer one of two opposite options: vigorous physical activity outdoors or quiet, passive, retreat activity inside. After this initial change of pace, school-age children especially enjoy cooking, games, crafts, music, and theatrical experiences. Intimate, relaxed time with sympathetic adults who can listen to the day's successes and failures is also very important. Some children may want to do homework. Children this age also enjoy taking responsibility for the care and maintenance of plants and animals, provided this is not overly burdensome or difficult. Experiences with farming, gardens and orchards, animal and pet care, and field trips to nature areas are invaluable. Because after-school programs involve the broadest range of activities, this chapter emphasizes the needs of these programs.

Program-Specific Decisions

In designing activity areas to support your school-age program, the following basics need to be considered:

- Arranging the entry zone to provide transition and support
- Facilitating interaction between child and caregiver
- Providing for rest
- Handling toileting/bathroom functions
- Providing for cooking/eating/snacking
- Developing spaces that support a rich range of child-focused activities

Furniture Dimensions

Recommended dimensions for school-age furniture are outlined in Table 18.1.

Entry Zone

See Chapter 7 for a discussion of the importance of transitions to children and the general functions of the entry zone.

School-age children welcome sharing quiet, intimate moments with an adult.

Table 18.1 ***Recommended Furniture Dimensions: School-age Children***

Age	Seat Height	Av. Seat Width	Av. Seat Depth	Table Ht.
	Seat and Table Height			
5–6 years	12″	12.75″	11″	20″
6–8 years	14″	14.5″	12.75″	22″
8–10 years	16″	16″	13.5″	26″
adult	18″	18″	14.5″	28″
	Shelf Height			
5–6 years			40–46 inches maximum	
6–8 years			48–54 inches maximum	
8–10 years			48–60 inches maximum	

Child Personal Storage

School-age children need a place to store their outer clothing and boots, school books and homework, and any objects and projects they create during the after-school program. Standard preschool cubbies, open or closed lockers, coat hooks, and personal bins are all options for fulfilling these needs. Since school-age children are in communal situations a large part of the day, having some protected, secure, private storage is very important.

QUESTIONS: CHILD PERSONAL STORAGE

1. Do you wish to separate children's clothing cubbies from storage for personal effects?
2. What design of cubby/storage unit/bin do you prefer for each type of storage?
3. Where might these be located in the room?
4. What size is best for these storage units and how much space will be needed for the entire group?

GUIDELINES: CHILD PERSONAL STORAGE

- See these same Guidelines, Chapter 17.
- Provide sufficiently large cubbies for the heavy and over-stuffed book bags and backpacks many school-age children carry.
- If your program offers extensive craft and music options, be certain to provide enough storage space in cubbies and/or in the work area, for works-in-progress, completed projects, and instruments.

Staff Personal Storage

Supervising staff will need storage for their coats, purses, and personal belongings. Staff may include full-timers, part-timers, and specialists who come on occasion. In addition, staff may need a work or preparation station; storage for resources, files, and other records, and a telephone.

QUESTIONS: STAFF PERSONAL STORAGE

1. What supports do staff want specifically in the school-age space? Elsewhere?
2. How many staff and specialists may be involved? How much storage space will they require?

GUIDELINES: STAFF PERSONAL STORAGE

- The personal storage requirements of school-age staff are similar to those of staff for other ages. See the same guidelines in Chapter 16 and the general guidelines in Chapter 19.
- Allow enough space for locked storage of special personal items and equipment staff may bring for specific projects.

Parent/Staff Communication

Parents of school-age children still require and appreciate contact with the adults who work with their children. Staff also benefit from the input and perspective of parents on issues that arise. Because parent/staff contact is apt to occur at the end of a long day, when people are hurried and tired, it is important that the design of the space and its informality foster this interaction as much as possible.

QUESTIONS: PARENT/STAFF COMMUNICATION

1. How/where do you envision parents and staff meeting and making contact with each other on a daily basis?
2. What supports do you wish to have for this—i.e., parent mail boxes, notice board, coffee area, comfortable seating, other?
3. How might you encourage parents from different families to meet?
4. What environmental supports can make parents feel more a part of the program—i.e., large display walls of children's work, shelves with children's projects near the door, a plate of cookies or snacks inside the room, etc.?

GUIDELINES: PARENT/STAFF COMMUNICATION

- See the same Guidelines, Chapter 16.
- Consider providing drinks and snacks (which children help to prepare) on a handy counter or table to refresh parents and encourage them to linger at the end of the day.

Rest

Children who have been at school all day need a change of pace. Sometimes this involves vigorous play outdoors, sometimes a quiet place to stretch out, daydream, do nothing, and just watch the world go by. While children this age do not generally nap, the opportunity to lie down informally, to curl up on a couch or pile of pillows, even to take a few winks without being noticed, is desirable, especially for children who are not feeling well. Provide one or more places of retreat, on a carpeted floor, loft, or platform, with pillows, comfortable seats, pleasant views, tranquil things to watch, security and comfort.

QUESTIONS: REST

1. What images do you have of ways to give tired, cranky children the opportunity to rest and rejuvenate after a day at school?
2. What supports will you require?

GUIDELINES: REST

- See discussion of Typical School-Age Activities: Quiet Play, later in this chapter.

Bathrooms

Most states require separate toilet facilities for boys and girls over five years of age. Handwashing sinks can be in the bathroom or outside. One toilet for every ten children is recommended.

QUESTIONS: BATHROOMS

1. How many toilets will your school-age program need? Where would be the best location in relation to the school-age space (in the room, outside the room, down the hall)? Do you need hand sinks inside or outside the bathrooms?
2. What amenities, if any, do you wish for these bathroom areas?

GUIDELINES: BATHROOMS

- See the Facilities List and toileting Guidelines in Chapter 17 with the fixture height modifications noted below.
- To make the room more child-friendly, keep the scale of fixtures and partitions somewhat lower than standard adult height.

Relaxing after a long day at school.

A school-age bathroom is softened by the addition of sconce lighting and playful art. (The Copper House)

- For children five to ten years old, sink heights can vary between 24 and 32 inches (standard adult height). Toilet heights can be between 11 and 16 inches (standard adult height). If the program serves large numbers of children at different ages, consider fixtures in two sizes, or at the size appropriate for the largest age group. Otherwise, use standard-height fixtures and provide booster steps for the younger children.
- Provide urinals in the boys' bathroom.
- If possible, provide stall partitions around five feet high, in keeping with school-age children's reduced stature.
- Electric hand dryers, and low built-in trash containers and paper towel dispensers, can help to keep the rooms tidy.

Eating/Snacking

Children who have been at school all day look forward to snacks, drinks, relaxing conversation over food, and opportunities to cook things they like. Since mealtimes in many schools may be quite chaotic and institutional, and since children in school-age programs have limited opportunity to hang around the kitchen at home, ways of supporting eating and cooking play a vital role in making the after-school room a place where children want to be. A minikitchen or an area with portable appliances is ideal. (For more on facilities for school-age children, see Messy Area for Cooking/Arts and Crafts later.)

QUESTIONS: EATING/SNACKING

1. What images do you have of a homelike setting for eating and snacking?
2. How many children will the area need to accommodate, at how many tables and chairs?
3. Can you identify the types and sizes of all equipment, storage, and work surfaces you will need?
4. What special touches and features do you wish for this area, such as flowers on the table, placemats, cloth napkins?

FACILITIES LIST FOR EATING/SNACKING AREA

- Tables and chairs
- Sink and counter space
- Cabinets for storing food and dishes
- Stove (or equivalent)
- Refrigerator
- Blenders, juicers, toaster ovens, popcorn poppers, etc.

GUIDELINES: EATING/SNACKING

- See similar Guidelines, Chapter 17 and the Messy Area for Cooking/Arts and Crafts below.

Typical School-Age Activities

School-age children are capable of practicing and perfecting skills in a wide range of areas: art, science, mechanics, sports, gymnastics, dance, music, drama, animal husbandry, computer science, etc. A well-designed environment gives them the opportunity to seriously explore these areas in depth by providing music and practice rooms; crafts, woodworking and photography studios; a hardwood floor gymnasium for dance movement and sports; a stage and small theatre; game and computer areas, etc. However, more modest facilities can also be satisfying, especially if flexible enough to respond to the varying interests of different ages and groups.

The discussions below provide suggestions for the types of activities children especially enjoy after school. In addition, this is the age when apprenticeship to people with unique skills, and hands-on learning of how to do things, is very important. Bringing in skilled volunteers, speakers, and unique equipment for children to work on, or conducting field trips and excursions to places of interest can deeply enrich the program. The possibilities are limitless and largely dependent upon both the space and the adults available to offer their skills and experience. Take advantage of community resources. Where space is tight in the school-age room, go beyond it.

Since children this age can get supplies on their own, there will be many people accessing and handling things. The efficiency of storage systems is therefore important, as well as security for costly equipment not easily replaced. Staff may also bring personal equipment and supplies to supplement the program's offerings.

Where the age spread is wide, the environment needs to both encourage interaction of younger and older children and be sensitive to the possibility for age-segregation at certain times and places.

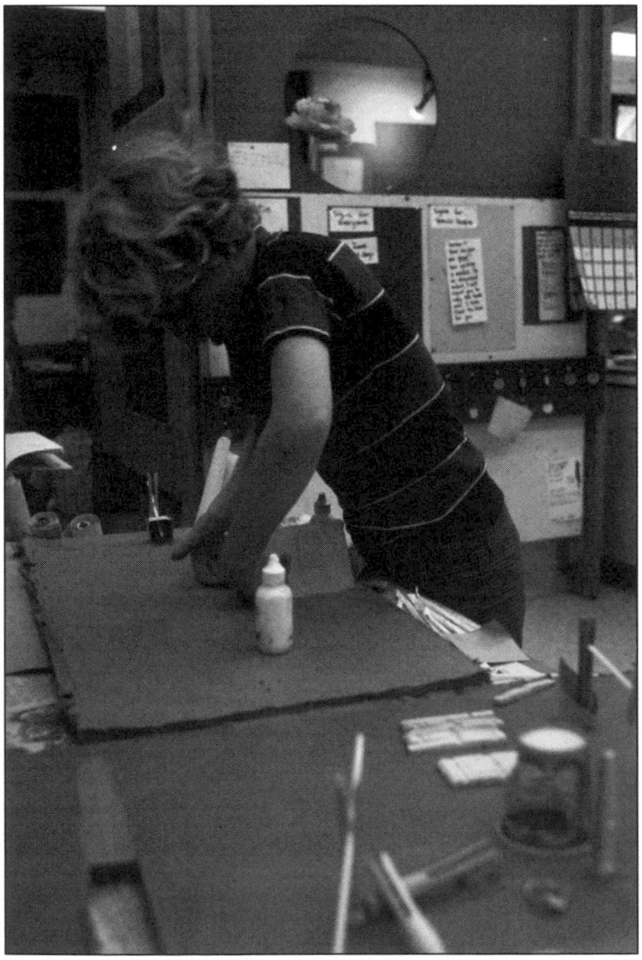

School-age children delight in building and making things.

QUESTIONS: SCHOOL-AGE ACTIVITIES

1. What images do you have of the school-age room and outside territory? What mood/feeling do you want the indoor and outdoor space to convey?
2. How will you ensure an atmosphere that brings staff and children close to one another, makes children feel secure to reveal their feelings about events at school, allows children to relax and let go, gives them privacy and quiet time alone?
3. Can you provide sufficient space outdoors and indoors for vigorous physical activity and sports?
4. How would you like children to be involved in the running and maintenance of the indoor and outdoor space? What chores and responsibilities might they be given as part of the curriculum? Is there room for raising plants, animals, ecological projects?

GUIDELINES: TYPICAL SCHOOL-AGE ACTIVITIES

- See similar Guidelines in Chapter 17.
- Depending upon staff and space available, the home base room might be a quiet place for snacks, resting, and homework while a wealth of activities take place elsewhere in the building or community.
- At these ages, it is important that staff know the population of children well and find creative ways to complement their experiences at school and at home.
- Unlike preschool children, who experience continuity of care throughout the day, children in before-school, half-day,

or after-school programs may experience stress due to the long day and many changes of personnel and location. The child care environment needs to simultaneously offer opportunities for nurturance, recreation, and challenge.

Messy Area for Cooking/Arts and Crafts

Meals, snacks, and cooking can provide much comfort and enjoyment for school-age children. This is also an activity in which children of different ages can participate easily. Having a minikitchen is ideal, but portable appliances, along with a small refrigerator and sink, can work well.

All kinds of arts and crafts activities are popular at these ages, including serious painting and clay work (ideally with a wheel and kiln), beading, leather craft, jewelry making, graphic arts projects, sewing, knitting, video, and photography. The availability of knowledgeable adults with the skills to guide these explorations, as well as the availability of equipment, will determine what options you can offer and how you design the space to support them. (See also "Additional Supports for the Messy Zone" in Chapter 7 and "Typical Preschool and Kindergarten Activity Areas: Messy Play" in Chapter 17.)

QUESTIONS: COOKING/ARTS AND CRAFTS

1. Will you have a minikitchen in the school-age room or elsewhere? How would you like to handle cooking and snacks?
2. What are your images of the craft area(s) in this room?
3. What craft activities do you definitely want to provide now? In the future? What special supports are needed for the craft activities you wish to feature?
4. How many tables and seats will you need? What design and height would be best?
5. What types of storage and display will you want for bulk materials, equipment, children's works-in-progress, display.

Learning to use a potter's wheel.

Increasing one's skill with woodworking tools.

Learning to use a sewing machine.

Using familiar media in new ways.

FACILITIES LIST FOR COOKING/ARTS AND CRAFTS

- Sink and counter for preparation and cleanup
- Stove, refrigerator, blender, oven, toaster, etc.
- Storage/display of supplies for snacks and cooking
- Child-accessible storage for crafts materials
- non–child-accessible storage for bulk supplies and equipment
- Washable floor surface
- Tables for crafts, snacks, cooking activities
- Separate snack table
- Chairs or stools
- Storage for children's works-in-progress
- Wall-mounted or freestanding easels
- Places to dry children's paintings and artwork
- Wall-mounted display surfaces for children's artwork and other visual images
- Smocks, paper storage tubes, trash baskets

- Sand and water troughs
- Painting: temperas, acrylics, oils, watercolors
- Clay: kiln, oven, potter's wheel
- Drawing and sketching supplies; drafting table for drawing/sketching
- Papier-mâché supplies
- Woodworking: workbench, hand and power tools, etching, sculpture
- Photography: cameras, darkroom, developing and printing supplies
- Jewelry-making supplies
- Bead and shell work supplies
- Leather craft supplies

GUIDELINES: COOKING/ARTS AND CRAFTS

- A complete residential kitchen with a homey table and chairs nearby is ideal for cooking and snacks. Alternatively, school-age children can use the cooking facilities in the residential core, if the center has one.
- If a wide range of ages is present, tables and chairs of different heights may be needed. See Table 18.1 for recommendations.
- For a basic list of craft activities also appropriate for school-age children, see Box 7.4 and The Wet Region, Chapter 7.
- Provide a sink with above- and below-counter cabinets for staff food preparation and storage. If possible, provide a sink at 24" high within the room, for child use.
- Extensive crafts options benefit from separate rooms, or well-divided spaces in the school-age area, such as a clay space with wheel and kiln; a darkroom; a woodworking shop; large tables for crafts; and artists' easels for work on canvas and paint boards.
- A child care center with an atelier[1] can arrange its schedule to make this space available to the school-age program.

Quiet Play/Homework

School-age children often like the opportunity to lounge around together—chatting, playing games, watching a video. At the same time, many become overwhelmed by being with peers all day and need some time and space to be alone or to pursue solitary activities. Lofts, niches, or platforms designed for one or two complement a quiet area furnished with armchairs, couches, carpet, and large pillows for a small group. (See also the examples of quiet spaces in Chapters 15 and 17.)

Children who do homework while at the center will need tables, desks, and/or computer space.

QUESTIONS: QUIET PLAY/HOMEWORK

1. What mood do you want the quiet play area to have?
2. What supports will it need?

A free-standing loft provides 8 places to spend quiet time alone or with a friend.

Large pillows convert a carpeted platform into a place to lounge and play cards.

3. How will you provide additional private areas and places of retreat in the school-age room? (See Chapter 15, Creating Boundaries for Quiet Spaces for suggestions.)

FACILITIES LIST FOR QUIET PLAY/HOMEWORK

- Soft seating and pillows
- Carpet
- Places to stretch out
- Pleasant views
- Some privacy and seclusion
- Books
- Fish, animals, plants, and views to watch passively
- Table and chairs or other supports for doing homework
- Computer(s)

GUIDELINES: QUIET PLAY/HOMEWORK

- See Typical Preschool and Kindergarten Activity Areas: Quiet Play and Guidelines for Reading/Group Meeting in Chapter 17 for activities and facilities that may also be appropriate at the school-age level.
- Provide some comfortable space large enough for the entire school-age group to meet once or twice a day. Risers, couches, armchairs, and carpeted areas are appropriate.
- Consider the homework needs of older children. These photos illustrate various options for collaborative and independent study.

A small niche under a loft just big enough for two.

Science and Nature Activities

School-age children learn important skills of independence and responsibility, as well as appreciation for nature, by being able to grow and care for plants and animals. In addition to opportunities for raising plants and other living things indoors, consider an organic garden and a small animal shed outside, especially for use during summer camp. School-age children also love to take apart and repair gadgets and build and

A table surrounded on two sides by 4′ high partitions and shelves makes an ideal listening "booth."

A standard table enclosed by partitions and shelves becomes a homework booth for one or two.

A custom-designed work station can make you feel special.

Doing homework side by side

Lofts create spaces for socializing and for being alone.

The fascination of starting an aquarium.

make things related to scientific inquiry. Flexible areas allow the program to be responsive to individual interests as they arise.

QUESTIONS: SCIENCE AND NATURE

1. What types and number of items do you wish to have in the science/nature area?
2. What amount and type of storage space will you need? What amount and type of display and work surface space do you desire?
3. What animals do you hope to have in each room? How and where would you like to raise these animals?
4. What other ideas would you like to incorporate?

FACILITIES LIST FOR SCIENCE AND NATURE

- Storage and display shelves for collections, plants, and animals
- Child counter-height surfaces for working with materials
- A table and seats for 4–6 for group activities
- Good light, preferably natural
- Nearby sink
- Teacher storage for items not currently on display
- Notice or bulletin board
- Black or white board for sketching

GUIDELINES: SCIENCE AND NATURE

- Locate the science/nature area near a sink and include extensive counter/work space; storage for seeds, tools, supplies; display walls and shelves for collections of rocks, leaves, shells; places to leave machines and gadgets being worked on.
- Give the area plenty of natural light and provide tables for all-round viewing.
- Consider locating cages for gerbils, mice, fish, birds, snakes, etc., in the midst of the group room, rather than in a designated science area. This needs to be weighed against children's capacities to care for and protect the animals.

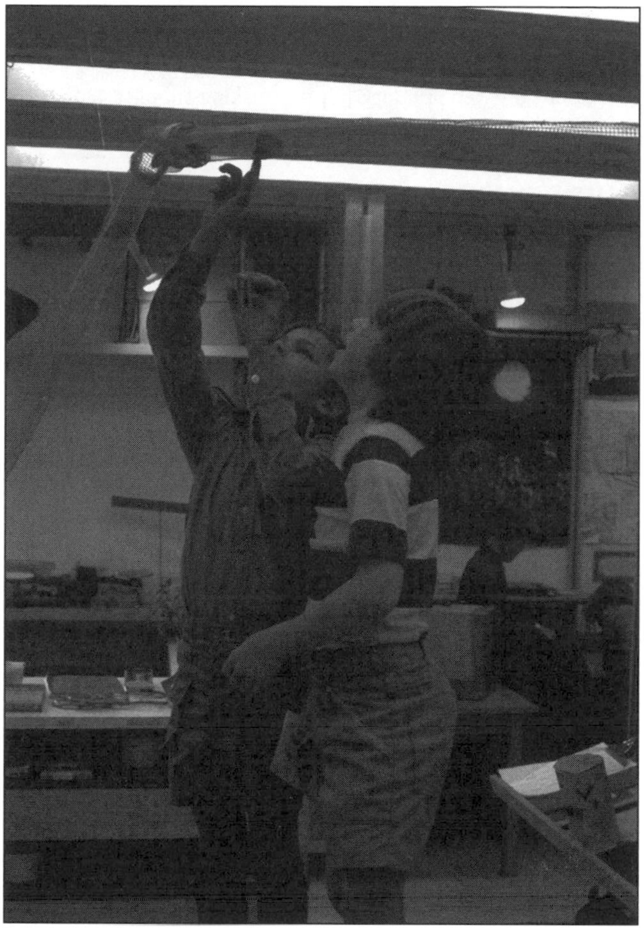

Gerbils amidst the life of the classroom.

- Small animal display areas, with a cozy seat nearby, can also be set up in niches and bays as "time-out" or semiprivate spaces.
- If possible, expand the plant and animal possibilities by having an organic garden, composting facilities, and an animal shed outdoors. Try to find a retired farmer or gardener who is willing to oversee these facilities.

Active Play

In addition to group sports and games, school-age children enjoy other forms of strength- and skill-building: ropes and exercise courses, indoor suspended equipment, trampolines, bikes, and skates. How and what to provide depends upon the ages and interests of the children, the climate, the topography of the site, and the resources available.

QUESTIONS: ACTIVE PLAY

1. How will you ensure sufficient space indoors for vigorous physical activity?
2. How will you ensure sufficient space outdoors for vigorous physical activity?
3. Can you specify all the activities you want to provide, the equipment required, and how and where it will be stored?

FACILITIES LIST FOR ACTIVE PLAY

- Climbing structures (indoors and outdoors)
- Swinging and hanging equipment
- Slides
- Tree houses, forts, hideaways
- Small-structure construction projects
- Bikes
- Skateboarding, ice skating, and roller skating facilities (onsite or in the community)
- Spaces for movement and dancing (outdoors and indoors)
- Tobogganing and sledding hills

GUIDELINES: ACTIVE PLAY

- A separate room or gymnasium for games, exercise, strength and skill building, movement, and dance is ideal. Where space is not available in the child care center, consider sharing such a space with a local school or community organization.
- Provide a range of loose props that can be suspended (with appropriate ceiling and wall mounts), and sufficient storage for these items, to offer varied experiences in limited space.

Sports Activities

Many school-age children enjoy competitive and group sports, especially as an antidote to sedentary school activities. Since this is an age when children are building skills and establishing control of their bodies, encouraging these activities on- or offsite is important.

QUESTIONS: SPORTS ACTIVITIES

1. What outdoor playing space is available to your program, either on-site or nearby? Can you transport children to sites at a distance?
2. What sports options do you wish to feature?

3. What are the storage, use, maintenance requirements associated with these sports?
4. What indoor playing space for group sports is available at the center or nearby?

FACILITIES LISTS FOR SPORTS

- Outdoor fields for soccer, basketball, volleyball, baseball, tennis, etc.
- Swimming pool
- Indoor gymnasium or large space for basketball, volleyball, dancing, movement

GUIDELINES: SPORTS ACTIVITIES

- Where outdoor space for sports is limited, children may need to be transported to local parks and playing fields.
- Facilities do not need to be full-scale at this age. A basketball hoop outside, and some open field space can permit many sports and games.

Dramatic Play

Participation in theatrical productions is extremely satisfying for school-age children, especially if they can help to write the script, handle the lighting, costumes, music, etc. They get to express nascent talents, learn new skills and ways of working in groups, and try on different roles and personalities. Under proper supervision, they are also capable of helping to build sets and props to suit whatever space is available. As is the case with preschoolers, smaller-scale exploration with puppets and role playing is still appropriate. (See pages 392–393.)

QUESTIONS: DRAMATIC PLAY

1. What are the best ways of supporting theatrical experiences for school-age children? Is there a large multipurpose room where they can rehearse and perform, or a corner of the school-age space?
2. What props, equipment, storage will be needed for your program?
3. What other forms of dramatic play do you want to offer?

FACILITIES LIST FOR DRAMATIC PLAY

- Stage for rehearsing and performing theatricals
- Costumes
- Make-up
- Stage props and lighting
- Puppet theater, puppets, puppet-making supplies

GUIDELINES: DRAMATIC PLAY

- For basic ideas, see Dramatic Play and Miniatures Guidelines, Chapter 17.
- More elaborate theatrical and musical productions, under the guidance of a skilled director, have enormous appeal at this age. A set of rearrangeable wooden platforms, boxes, and planks can be used to form a stage and props. Alternatively, a school or community center theater can be used for performances. Children often become completely absorbed in building and making all that is needed for a production, including the script, set, music, props, etc.
- Building forts, tree-houses, and hideaways of scrounged materials is another extremely popular form of dramatic play at these ages.

Music

Music is the glue that cements social exchange for school-age children. CD or tape players with headphones, or a separate listening room are the best ways for them to enjoy music without disturbing other aspects of the program. Children at this age are also learning to play instruments, making one or more practice rooms very desirable.

QUESTIONS: MUSIC

1. How will you provide options for children to listen to music in groups and individually?
2. Do you want to make it possible for children to study and practice instruments? Are separate rooms for this purpose possible?
3. What safeguards are needed for storing electronic and other music-related equipment?

GUIDELINES: MUSIC

- See the Guidelines for Listening (under Quiet Play) in Chapter 17.
- Strive to create at least one small, acoustically shielded room that can be used for instrument practice.

Games

School-age children love games with rules and those requiring skill, whether solitary or involving two or more players. Computer games may also be appropriate under some circumstances. Board games call for small, low (10" high) or standard-height tables that can seat four to six, or the use of the floor. Many electronic games (foos ball) and pool tables need a great deal of space for the equipment and the players around them. A separate area, alcove, or niche is beneficial for noisy and active games, so they do not disturb other activities.

The fun of playing games together.

QUESTIONS: GAMES

1. Can you specify all the games you hope to provide and the types of playing surfaces, supports, and amount of space they will need?
2. Where should these different types of games be located in the room?

FACILITIES LIST FOR GAMES

- Board games for 2-6 players
- Card games
- Electronic games
- Rhythm and movement games
- Markable space for 4-square, hop scotch, tag, etc. (ideally outdoors)

GUIDELINES: GAMES

- It may be helpful to categorize the games you will provide according to size and use: floor, table top, counter top, large surface (pool and electronic games), outdoor area. Carpet and 10-inch-high tables work well on the floor. Some games are best played at counter height (approximately 26–32 inches) rather than table height.
- For large jigsaw puzzles and games that may be played over a number of days, provide a protected niche or corner so the pieces and board can remain accessible.

Storage

Extensive storage is needed for the wide range of equipment and materials used in school-age programs. Some equipment is apt to be bulky, and some will need to be locked up. Many items may be seasonal, especially if the program becomes a summer day camp. It is important to identify and thoroughly think through all storage requirements.

QUESTIONS: STORAGE

1. Can you specify all your storage needs for equipment, supplies, activities, display? Determining the size of items is critical, as is specification of open versus locked storage, shelves versus closets, with or without doors, etc.
2. Can you predict future and summertime storage needs so that provision can be made for them now?

ITEMS REQUIRING STORAGE

- Crafts equipment and supplies
- Audiovisual equipment
- Sports equipment
- Games
- Tools
- Works-in-progress

GUIDELINES: STORAGE

- See considerations for Storage in Chapter 4 under Key Secondary Space Requirements.

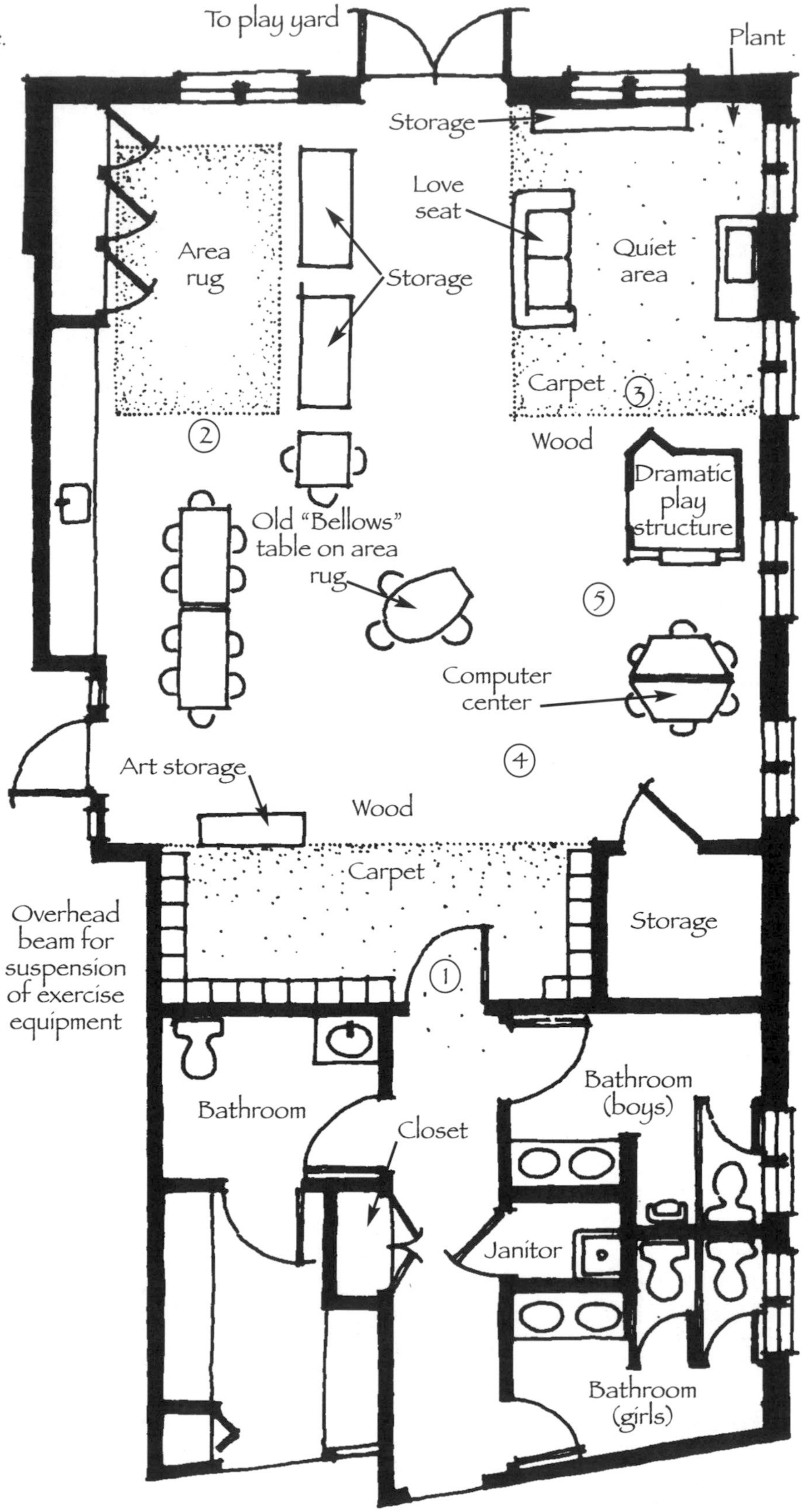

Figure 18.1
The School-age Room of the Copper House.

Illustrative Floor Plan

The floor plan for the school-age room of the Copper House is shown in Figure 18.1, along with some illustrative photographs of the space. This room is used by up to sixteen 5-year-olds in the morning, by 5- to 10-year-olds in the afternoon, and by similar ages during a summer camp. Programs that serve more children, and that can devote multiple roomsto the school-age group, benefit from assigning one or two separate functions to each room and developing the allotted room areas as activity areas, as explained in Chapter 15.

Notes

[1]An atelier, a key space used in the Reggio Emilia schools, is a large "studio" equipped with a wide array of materials for children to explore different media in depth. In Reggio, the atelier is staffed by a full time facilitator called an *atelierista*.

1. *An overview showing the art and staff prep areas (left), the door to the play yard (rear center), the quiet area (rear right), and dramatic play area (front right).*

2. *An area for blocks and miniatures.*

3. *The quiet area for games, manipulatives, reading, and resting.*

4. *Exploring computers alone and in groups.*

5. *A store front/puppet theatre complete with mirrored face painting station inside and an Indian mirror cloth tent roof.*

CHAPTER NINETEEN

SPACES FOR STAFF AND PARENTS: BUILDING COMMUNITY

How can we discover a genuine appreciation for the world around us?
How can we preserve our children's sense of wonder,
and how can we recapture it ourselves?

—JOHANN CHRISTOPH ARNOLD

Despite the undisputed roles staff and parents play in the lives of children, physical spaces to support adult needs are often limited or absent in child care centers. However, centers have the potential to create a large, extended family; to act as a hub of resources and support for parents and staff; and to become an educational collaborative for adults as well as children. This chapter addresses both the needs of the adults and the possibilities for building community in child care settings.

Child care is a burnout profession involving long, physically and emotionally demanding hours, poor wages, exposure to contagious diseases, and an average annual staff turnover rate of forty-two percent. As an antidote to such stress, every center needs at least one room where staff can have some privacy and take a real break. Parenting can be a burnout occupation as well, especially if you work eight to ten hours a day (not including travel time) to make ends meet, have to provide for the needs of children of different ages, and try to have a life in the few nonworking, noncaregiving hours that remain. Parents need help in getting to know the center's staff, and other parents benefit from being honored by staff as their children's primary caregivers.

For optimum functioning, a center needs many supports for adults: offices, lounges, conference and meeting rooms, resource areas, observation and therapeutic spaces, training facilities, kitchen and custodial facilities, adult bathrooms, storage, and amenities. Finding space for all these functions may not be easy given the demands of complex programs, limited square footage, and tight budgets. Therefore, each program will need to determine exactly what it can accommodate from the variety of potential facilities discussed in this chapter. In some programs, spaces may have to serve overlapping functions, or do double-duty. For example, a resource room may have to serve both staff and parents or may need to contain workstations for visiting consultants; conference rooms may have to serve as meeting rooms and training facilities. Your unique situation requires your own creative solutions to these challenges.

Staff

Staff refers to all the individuals employed by the child care center: teachers, administrators, program specialists, therapists, cooks, and custodians, as well as to unpaid individuals such as volunteers, student-teachers, and researchers.

What Staff Need

In addition to a pleasant work environment in which they can perform their responsibilities efficiently and compassionately, staff need one or more places where they can temporarily escape direct responsibility, to

Figure 19.1
The staff areas on the second floor of the Copper House.

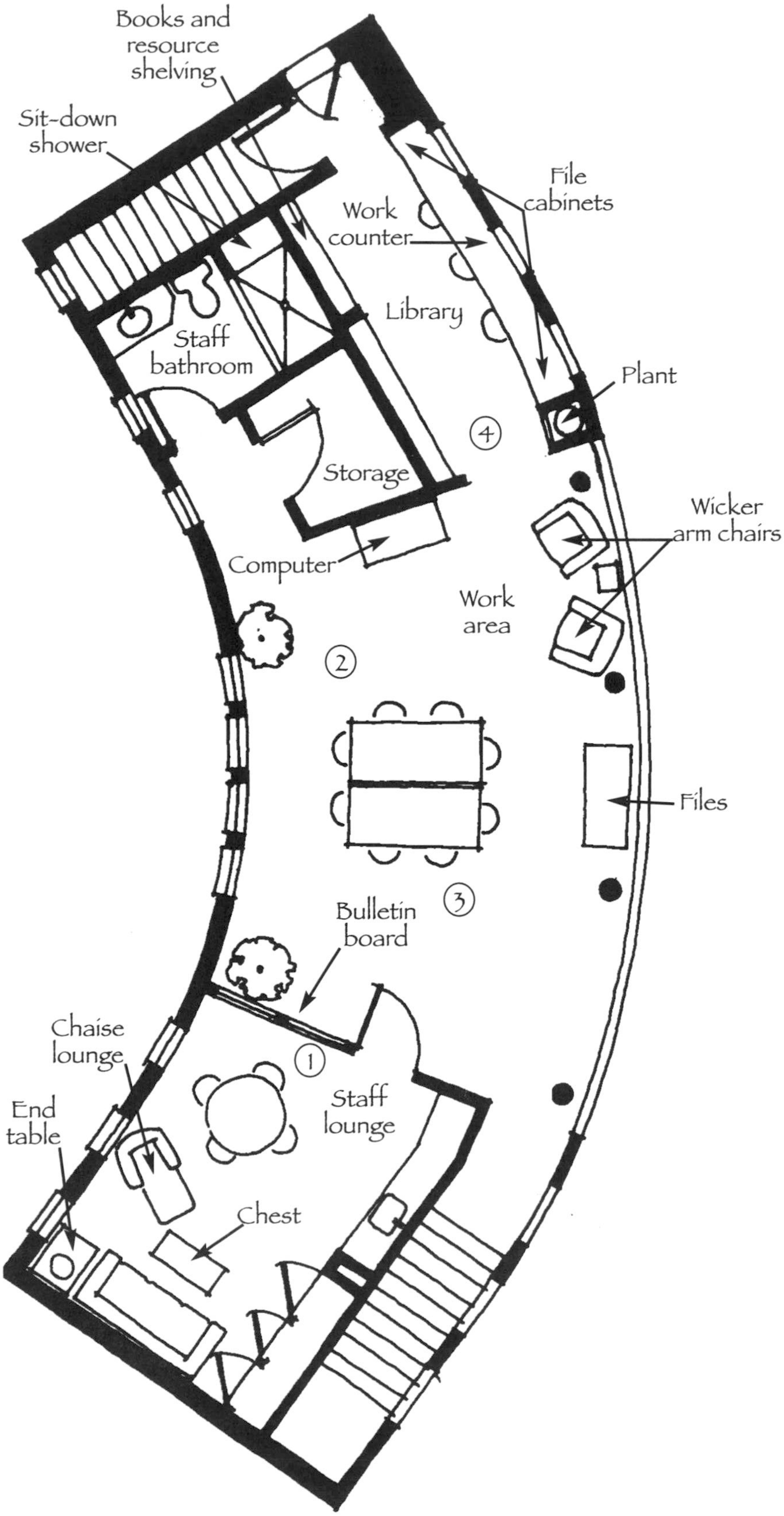

1

2

3

4

think, relax, and confer with one another. Such places help them better meet the rigorous challenges of their work. Places of comfort and beauty can be an asset to staff retention, even helping to compensate for low salaries. The second story of a building is often a good location for many staff functions, as the floor plan and photographs in Figure 19.1 illustrate.

Just as group rooms require a variety of zones and areas to meet children's developmental needs, staff members need a variety of spaces for:

- Resting and being alone (lounges, personal work stations)
- Working and personal storage (desks, offices, lockers, closets, etc.)
- Showering and grooming before, during, or after work
- Meeting, planning, and creating materials with colleagues (lounges, conference rooms, workshop spaces)
- Maintaining close contact with parents (conference rooms, workshop spaces, offices)

Small-group settings help staff to connect with one another so they can work out problems together and be more flexible in responding to individual family needs. In large centers, the establishment of physically identifiable subunits benefits staff, and in turn, children and parents.

Administrative Spaces

A director who is involved in the center's program, as well as accessible to parents, children, and staff, is more valuable than one shut away from the mainstream. In small centers, locating the director's office and related administrative areas near the center's entry can accomplish both of these aims. In large centers, it may be necessary for one member of the administrative staff to have greater public accessibility, while another is located closer to the children's rooms to oversee the curriculum and assist caregivers.

Planning office space for the director and administrative staff requires a balance of privacy and connection. Offices that open off a comfortable common sitting space, rather than directly off a corridor, support interaction, reduce feelings of isolation, and also provide opportunities for privacy.

QUESTIONS: ADMINISTRATIVE SPACES

1. How many administrators will your center have?
2. Who will need enclosed offices? Who can/should be more visible to the public?
3. Who will monitor the entry and exits and control access to the building: secretary, receptionist, director, assistant director, other?
4. Can the center afford a full-time receptionist? Will this person double as a secretary, bookkeeper, other?
5. Can you specify all the supports the receptionist will need?
6. What other functions are best situated adjacent to the administrative spaces: lobby, sick bay, conference room, parent resource room, bathrooms, coat closet, etc.?

GUIDELINES: ADMINISTRATIVE SPACES

- Well-designed administrative spaces usually are visible from the entry and able to control it visually, while communicating an atmosphere of welcome and friendliness. They are also convenient to major circulation paths through the building.
- The location of the director's office, and the furniture and accessories within it, powerfully impact how welcome and free to communicate parents, children, and staff feel. A small, cluttered administrator's office suggests a center that is disorganized and without space for visitors.
- It may be helpful to locate administration areas near conference rooms, a parent room, a staff resource room, and spaces for specialists.
- Locate one or more adult washrooms accessible to those with physcial disabilities near the main administrative area. At least one of these might include a diaper changing station.
- Locate a coat closet near the administrative area for use by administrative staff and visitors.
- Other general adult supports near this area might include a clock; a beverage/snack station; a telephone booth; bulletin boards; a quiet sitting/reading area; the center's lobby.
- It is preferable that the director's office be separate from that of the secretary. The director's office needs to be large enough (approximately 150 square feet) to include a desk and computer support; a sitting area apart from the desk for meeting with 2–4 parents or visitors; bookshelves; locked storage for confidential records; a closet for coats and personal effects; and perhaps a small sitting/play area for children.
- When the conference room is located at some distance from the director's office or is likely to be heavily used, it is critical that a small sitting/conference area be an integral part of the director's office (see the next page).

A welcoming director's office. (The Copper House)

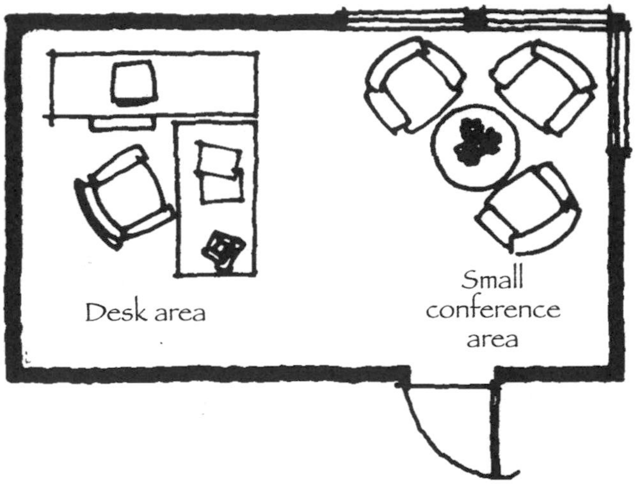

Figure 19.3
Strive to create a small conference area in the director's office, separate from the desk.

Supports for the receptionist, in the adjacent alcove, are visually- and acoustically-shielded. (The Copper House)

- A door with a window (with optional curtain or shade) balances the director's need for privacy with that for accessibility.
- The secretary, who often doubles as the center's receptionist, is usually more visible and accessible than the director. This person may need 80-150 square feet of space to accommodate: a desk; telephones; a computer and a fax; a copy machine; storage for office supplies; locked storage for confidential records; storage for personal effects.
- Give administrative offices, conference rooms, and work stations appropriate acoustic separation from noisy equipment and child spaces.
- Depending on where other caregiver supports are located, the administrative area may also need to accommodate staff mailboxes; first aid equipment; a safe place for keys for staff use; bulletin boards; beverages and snacks for parents, staff, and visitors; a parent sign-in station; and a sick bay for an ill child. (See the discussion that follows.)

Sick Bay[1]

Children sick enough to have to go home for care need a place to wait until a parent arrives. So long as the child is not in great distress, staying in a quiet area of the group room may be the best solution because of the room's familiarity and the fact that other children in that group have already been exposed to the illness.

When a child is vomiting, in pain, or has diarrhea, however, a space outside the group room, near a bathroom and a supportive adult, is needed. A small bay, near the receptionist, or the director—whoever is most likely to be available on a consistent basis—can be created for this purpose. The bathroom can be one that is available to the public, rather than a dedicated space, provided it is not heavily used and can employ booster steps to make adult-sized fixtures accessible to a small child. Make the sick bay a comfortable, restful, and inviting place.

This comforting sick bay is in an alcove right beside the receptionist. (The Copper House)

QUESTIONS: SICK BAY

1. Which adult in your center is most likely to be available on a consistent basis for a sick child—receptionist, director, other?
2. If you were sick, what type of a space would you like to rest in while you were waiting to go home? Describe it in as much detail as possible.
3. Who would you most want to have with you or nearby?
4. Can you create a sick bay near the appropriate adult, which has the qualities described in (2) above, as well as immediate access to a toilet and sink that a child can use?
5. What features and supports will your sick bay include?

GUIDELINES: SICK BAY

- Determine the adult most likely to be available to a sick child at all times.
- Create a cozy, inviting, child-appropriate space within view of that person, where a sick child can lie down while waiting.
- The bay/bed area might include child-appropriate artwork, washable stuffed animals; a few books and toys; sheets, pillows, blankets, and throws; storage for bed linens and extra blankets; an examination light. It is preferable for a sick infant to wait in his or her own crib with the usual caregiver.

- Provide a child-accessible toilet and sink, as well as paper towels and cleaning supplies, nearby. Booster steps to adult-height fixtures are acceptable.
- Provide lighting bright enough to examine a sick child, and dimmable lighting to encourage sleep.

Staff Lounge

Staff members need a lounge or place of retreat from the extraordinary physical and emotional demands of child care. Ideally, this place provides access to the outdoors, and some opportunity for recreation.

QUESTIONS: STAFF LOUNGE

1. How many staff will want to use a lounge at any one time?
2. Can the lounge be separate from a curriculum resource area, or must the space accommodate both functions?
3. Will staff eat in the lounge, or elsewhere?
4. If they eat there, what supports are necessary: table and chairs; sink, counters, and cabinets; stove and oven; microwave; refrigerator; coffee pot; other appliances; minikitchen?
5. Where is the best location for the lounge in your center so it is accessible to all staff, remote from child care areas, has views to the outside, and access to the outdoors?
6. Do you wish to provide a couch or screened area in the lounge for napping?
7. Can you provide staff with a residential bathroom complete with shower stall for after-work grooming?
8. Will staff need desks or work areas in the lounge, elsewhere?
9. Where can staff go to make personal telephone calls or have a private conversation?

GUIDELINES: STAFF LOUNGE

- Provide at least one visually and acoustically separate area for staff lounging, eating, resting, conversation, preferably with a view to the outside.. Equip the lounge with comfortable furniture, including a bed or couch for napping; soft, adjustable lighting; one or more telephones; a clock; a minikitchen for food preparation and snacks; a notice board; and storage/display for books, magazines, plants, and bric-a-brac. A space of about 250 sq ft is desirable for 15–20 full-time staff.
- Locate the lounge convenient to adult lavatories, circulation, and administrative areas, yet remote from child care responsibilities. If possible, create an exit from the staff lounge to an outdoor deck or patio for eating and sunning.
- As the staff lounge is a place of respite, try to keep it separate from staff work and resource areas used for program planning and development.

Staff Resource Area

Staff need a place where they can review literature and journals; store, share, preview, make, and test curriculum materials; access audiovisual aids; perform minor repairs on toys and equipment; and build furniture and equipment for their spaces. Keeping a centerwide

A large couch, chaise lounge, table and chairs,and minikitchen provide a place of respite in this staff lounge. (The Copper House)

rotating stock of curriculum materials, and bulk supplies of paints, paper, etc., in a central resource area, is extremely efficient. Temporary or permanent staff workstations can also be located in this area. Having a dedicated workroom for all these activities is desirable. However, depending upon the size and organization of the center, these activities also may overlap with the administrative spaces, parent participation areas, the conference room, or a central storage space.

QUESTIONS: STAFF RESOURCE AREA

1. Can you create a resource area separate from the staff lounge?
2. What activities and equipment do you want this resource room to accommodate: curriculum materials library; book and journal library; furniture building and curriculum-materials making; laminating and fax machines; computers; staff workstations; tables and chairs for meeting and training; parent resources; bulk storage; other?
3. Can you specify the types (closets, shelves, hooks, floors), and amounts of storage needed?

GUIDELINES: STAFF RESOURCE AREA

- Provide at least one room with work counters and plenty of storage space where staff can make a mess, use hand- and power-tools, glue, paint, etc., in connection with the development of curriculum materials and projects.
- Include sufficient power and electrical outlets for computers, tools, and audiovisual aids, as well as space for copy, laminating, and other machines.

Top: A staff conference/work area is adjoined by a staff bath with sit-in shower (left) and a resource library area (right). Bottom: The library has extensive storage and display for books, journals, and curriculum materials, and a counter with stools and file cabinets where staff can work. (The Copper House)

Hand- and power-tools and workbenches form a portion of this staff/parent resource room.

- Provide acoustical shielding, as appropriate, for noisy equipment used in the room.
- Include shelves and display racks for curriculum materials that can serve the entire center.
- Include shelves for display of professional magazines and books, as well as surfaces where such materials can be spread out and studied.
- Provide plenty of centerwide storage space for bulk and seasonal supplies. Be specific about the types and amounts of storage required: depth, height, and length of shelves, closets, and cabinets. (Also see Key Secondary Space Requirements: Storage, Chapter 4.)
- Provide some storage (perhaps lockable) for individual staff projects-in-progress.
- If group rooms do not have these, provide work surfaces for individual teachers to write, plan, read, and prepare their programs. (See Staff Personal Space and Amenities, below).
- A resource room for staff can sometimes double as an in-house and community teacher-training site, and a place where parents can make things for their children or improve their parenting skills.
- A sitting/conference area within the workshop space, for 5–10 people, may be desirable for meetings and trainings.

Staff Conference Areas

Periodic staff meetings—in both large and small groups—are essential for optimal operation of the center, and for creating a sense of unity and shared purpose. A large conference room and/or a resource room also often works well for ongoing staff development and training—one of the most important contributors to center quality.

Conference rooms of at least two sizes are ideal: (1) a large space that holds all the staff—perhaps 30–50; and (2) smaller conference areas for 2–4 adults (parents, colleagues, specialists) or for teams of 6–12 staff. Offices can sometimes double as small conference rooms for 2–4 people. When it is impractical to allocate space for a very large meeting room, a center can try to arrange for use of such a space with an organization in the community.

QUESTIONS: STAFF CONFERENCE AREAS

1. What is your total staff population? How often will this group need to meet and how large a room is needed?
2. Must the room be in the center, or can it be in a nearby facility?
3. What space is needed for in-service and/or community-wide training of caregivers? If you plan to offer on-site conferences, what amount and type of space is needed?
4. What subdivisions of staff will exist, and how many staff will comprise each subunit?
5. How close to the staff's base of operation should conference rooms be located?
6. Can you determine the number of small- and medium-sized conference areas desired and the furniture and equipment needed for each?

GUIDELINES: STAFF CONFERENCE AREAS

- Provide one space large enough to hold all staff members comfortably for periodic meetings and training of the entire staff. In large centers, where 40 or more adults may be involved, the conference space may need to be formed from two rooms with a removable divider, or it may need to do double duty as a space for some other function.
- Affiliation with a larger organization, (hospital, community center, college, corporation), may provide access to a large meeting space when it is impractical for a child care center to have one on its premises.
- Provide at least one conference area of approximately 200–250 sq ft for use by 2–12 persons.
- Locate conference areas convenient to circulation, but acoustically buffered from all other spaces.
- Locating it close to the director's and other administrative offices allows easy sharing and may encourage greater use. On the other hand, there may be advantages to locating it remote from the entry and closer to caregiving areas. (See Parent/Staff Conference Space, below).
- In large centers, disperse meeting rooms for 6–12 persons throughout the building for convenience.
- Equip conference areas with tables and chairs, bookcase/display shelves, a white board, a projector and screen, writing supplies, and rheostatic lighting. Smaller tables that can be arranged to form a large one, and stacking chairs, increase the room's flexibility. Round and oval tables afford all participants equivalent status.
- Provide beverages, lavatories, and telephones in the conference area, or nearby.

Staff Personal Space and Amenities

It is important to supply each staff member with: 1) storage for coats, purses, and other personal effects; 2) a personal workstation for doing paperwork, and for storing supplies and confidential files; and 3) access to amenities such as telephones, bathrooms, and showers,

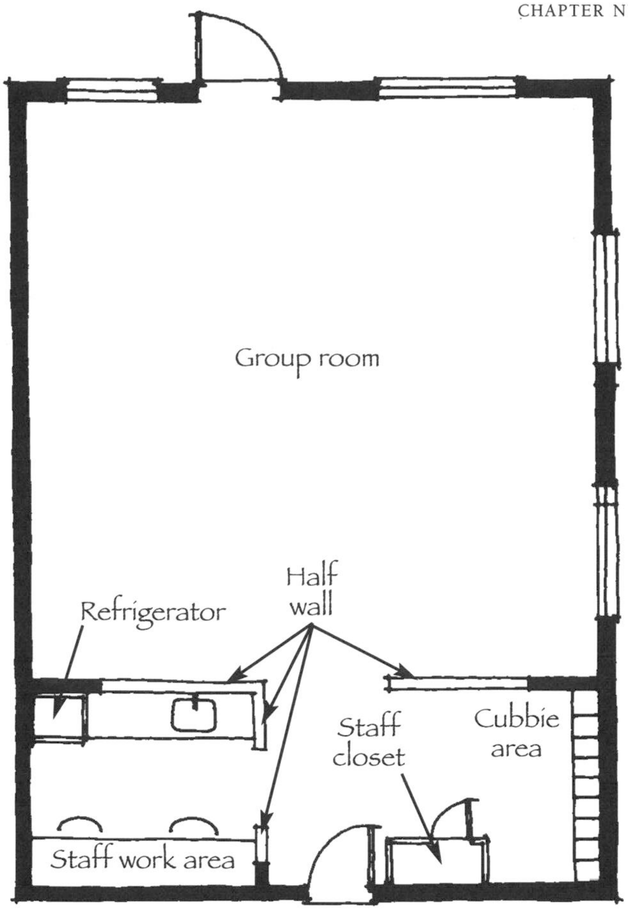

Figure 19.3
Sometimes it is desirable to have the staff work area as part of the group room.

snacks and beverages, mailboxes and message boards. These supports may be best located in the work areas or group rooms where staff are stationed, but many options exist.

QUESTIONS: STAFF PERSONAL AREAS

1. How many staff need personal storage and work space; which staff can share supports?
2. What is the best location (group room, office, lounge, resource room, other) for personal storage for each? Describe the types of storage needed in detail.
3. What is the best location for personal workstations for each? Describe the types of workstations desired in detail.

GUIDELINES: STAFF PERSONAL AREAS

- Provide each staff member with some lockable, out-of-children's-reach storage space for personal items and garments. A small coat closet is aesthetically more pleasing than a locker and works especially well if located in the group rooms or areas where staff work and will use it most (Figure 19.3).
- Provide telephones on which staff can have private conversations.
- Provide centrally located individual mailboxes, notice boards, and other means of intracenter communication.
- Provide easily accessible adult washrooms. A residential bathroom with shower is an amenity frequently used by staff to clean up and change for after-work engagements.
- Provide access to beverages and snacks.
- Many caregivers do not need a desk. Instead, the staff prep area in the group rooms—an adult-height counter with stools, and storage cabinets above and below—can often fulfill this purpose, as shown in Figure 19.3.
- For those full-time and part-time staff who need it (teachers, specialists), provide an acoustically buffered and visually sheltered personal work area. This might include desk and seating; shelves for books and resources; file cabinet; bulletin board for personal notices and displays; computer; telephone; and a chair for a visitor.
- Workstations can be clustered in a resource room, be placed in a separate staff office, or be part of each group room. Try to keep workstations separate from the staff lounge.
- Plan the design of individual staff work areas with an eye toward balancing privacy with accessibility both to other child care professionals and to parents.

Specialists

Psychologists, social workers, massage and physical therapists, speech and learning disability, and other specialists are often affiliated with a child care center on a full- or part-time basis. Accommodations that enable them to do their jobs well may include: (1) an office for paperwork and lockable file storage, and (2) a testing/therapy/meeting space. Additional supports may involve the need for unobtrusive observation of the testing/therapeutic space, electrical outlets, audiovisual aids, access to records, and storage of test and therapy materials. Consultation rooms usually need to be equipped with both child- and adult-sized chairs and tables.

QUESTIONS: SPECIALISTS

1. What specialists do you anticipate accommodating in your center? How often will they be present? Would you want to include a massage therapist for infants and children with disabilities?

2. What specific supports will each specialist require?
3. What adjacencies are most desirable for specialist spaces (near the director, administrative supports, the group rooms)?

GUIDELINES: SPECIALISTS

- Plan for the potential presence of specialists in advance. To conserve space, explore ways in which they can share office and treatment areas.
- Most specialists need a desk or work surface, storage for locked files, test and therapy materials, and a quiet place to plan and think.
- In addition, some or all may need a separate, cheerful therapeutic space to do testing, provide massage, conduct interviews, teach body movement and learning skills, etc. These spaces may need: child and adult furniture; electrical outlets; an unobtrusive means of observation; acoustic privacy; mirrors; large equipment like floor mats, massage tables, platforms, stairs, and large balls; and storage.
- Where appropriate, encourage specialists to conduct therapeutic activities in the group rooms so therapy becomes an integral part of children's play. Create permanent or portable dividers, equipment, and space in the rooms for this purpose.

Student-Teachers, Interns, Researchers

Child care centers sometimes serve as training sites for student-teachers, medical interns and residents, and researchers interested in child development. In addition to providing observation facilities (see below), giving these individuals clearly designated places to store personal belongings; compile notes; and meet with peers, staff, or trainers to reflect on their experiences will minimize disturbance to the children's program. Centers affiliated with educational institutions, or serious about staff-recruitment and development, may even want to have a separate wing or facility for ongoing staff training.

QUESTIONS: STUDENT-TEACHERS, INTERNS, RESEARCHERS

1. How many student-teachers, interns, and researchers do you anticipate accommodating in the center at any one time?
2. Where is the best place for them to store personal belongings?
3. What type(s) of workstations, if any, will each need? Where might these be located?
4. What size training groups might be involved? Where will they meet (staff lounge, conference room, resource room, parent room, other)?
5. Do you need/envision a separate wing or building for student and staff training?

GUIDELINES: STUDENT-TEACHERS, INTERNS, RESEARCHERS

- Plan for the potential presence of student-teachers, interns, and researchers in advance. Explore ways they can share office and meeting areas.
- Determine the best location for trainees to compile notes and observations: lobby, resource room, conference rooms, other.
- Determine where trainees can meet with staff and one another: conference room, small office, resource room, other.

Observation

Parents, staff, administrators, student-teachers, consultants, specialists, and residents-in-training may need to observe children at times. Observation works best when it is minimally disruptive to children's routines and does not usurp valuable wall space in the group rooms. Opinions differ as to the appropriateness of unobserved observers. Four options exist: (1) No special observation provisions—observers mix with children; (2) an unobtrusive observation area visible from child play spaces; (3) an observation booth with a separate entrance, using screens, windows, or one-way glass; and (4) a remote viewing area served by television cameras in the rooms.

QUESTIONS: OBSERVATION

1. What needs for observation do you anticipate in your center?
2. Who might these observers be (parents, students, therapists) and how many may need to be accommodated at one time?
3. What type(s) of observation facility do you prefer? (See the text that follows for options.)

Figure 19.4
Raised observation booths, whether open or enclosed, benefit observers while conserving a group room's valuable floor and wall space.

GUIDELINES: OBSERVATION

- Make observation minimally disruptive to children's routines.
- If observers mix with the children, provide low chairs or risers to place them at the children's level.
- Create unobtrusive observation areas by using plants, portable dividers, or high cubbies as screens and partial shields.
- Windows in the doors and corridor walls of group rooms enable unobtrusive visual observation without the need to add a booth and without usurping activity space. Windows are especially helpful for parents. However, observers usually cannot hear interactions.
- An observation booth shielded by fine-mesh screening is honest in that it makes observers somewhat visible to children, while creating a sense of separation.
- Use one-way glass advisedly: it is institutional in appearance; its mirrored surface creates distracting reflections in the group room; it makes the room appear hard and cold; and occupants never know when they are being observed.
- An observation booth raised 4 or more feet above floor level frees up wall and floor space in the group room. It can be enclosed or designed as an open balcony (Figure 19.4). Chairs, a writing surface, and provision for sound may be desirable.
- Design enclosed observation booths so that users can enter them without having to cross child-activity areas. Raised booths are preferable because observers need to be able to see and hear most areas of the room and because they conserve floor space. Usually, a booth size of 50–100 square feet is adequate.
- Where frequent observation by large numbers of observers is involved, the use of TV cameras operated and viewed from a remote location is advisable. This approach is frequently the least disruptive to children while giving observers the greatest opportunity to converse and compare notes. Viewing can even occur remotely, off-site.

The Laundry

At least one washer and dryer are useful for every center, and essential for programs serving infants and toddlers. Unless your center serves fewer than 30 children, invest only in full-sized appliances.

QUESTIONS: LAUNDRY

1. How many washers and dryers does your program need?
2. Where are these best located?

GUIDELINES: LAUNDRY

- Provide one full-sized washer and dryer for approximately every 30 children, especially if infants and toddlers are present. Use stackable units only if full-sized.
- Front-loading washers conserve water.
- For adequate disinfecting, maintain water and heat temperatures above 140 degrees F.
- Locate the laundry convenient to its point of greatest use or general access, but separate and secure from the kitchen and child care areas.
- An ideal laundry room is about 50–60 square feet and includes a deep sink for soaking, open shelves for supplies and folding, and floor space for baskets of clean and dirty items.
- Children can help to fold laundry as part of learning responsibility for themselves and the center.

The Custodian

Maintenance and janitorial areas are best located near the areas of the building to be serviced.

QUESTIONS: CUSTODIAN

1. How will maintenance of your center be handled: in-house custodian, outside agency, affiliated custodial care, other?
2. At what hours of the day/night will custodial personnel be on-site, and how might their presence affect the program?
3. How many workstations will custodial personnel require to service the building most easily? Where might these be located?
4. Will the custodian have duties other than cleaning the building—i.e., building and grounds maintenance, toy and furniture repair, other?

GUIDELINES: CUSTODIAN

- Provide a lockable janitor's closet with a minimum of 25 square feet of space, which includes a floor sink, and space for pails, mops, vacuums, and related supplies.
- If the janitor's duties extend beyond cleaning the building, a larger or a separate closet might be necessary for storing building and grounds- and maintenance-related tools; space and supplies for repairing toys and furniture; other. (Also see Chapter 4, Key Secondary Space Requirements: Storage.)
- Supplies for quick cleanup of children's activities are best kept in locked closets, out of children's reach, in or near the group rooms.

The Cook

A full- or part-time cook can be both an educator and a nurturer of good health for the entire facility. The odors of cooking make a place feel more comfortable and homey. Children and parents can learn important dietary and cooking skills, and have unique dietary requirements met by the cook. But, to do this job well, the cook needs an orderly and well-equipped kitchen, and some personal storage space, perhaps with a small office. Design the kitchen with viewing windows or other means of encouraging contact between children, staff, and parents and the cook.

QUESTIONS: COOK

1. Will you have a part-time or a full-time cook on staff?
2. How many meals and snacks will the cook provide? For how many children, adults?
3. How large will your kitchen need to be? What special supports might it require—i.e., walk-in freezer, multiple ovens, multiple sinks, commercial dishwasher, exhaust fan, other?
4. Since children are generally not allowed in the kitchen, how will you make it possible for them to interact with the cook—i.e., viewing-window, food preparation room nearby, child-sized kitchen nearby, other?
5. What amount of space is needed for food storage, bulk supplies, and recycling bins?
6. Can the kitchen be located convenient to a service entrance?

GUIDELINES: COOK

- Check local codes and licensing requirements concerning kitchen size, location, and requisite equipment.
- Depending upon center size, provide the cook with a kitchen of at least 150 square feet that can be protected from access by children, has adequate/appropriate storage for bulk and daily food supplies, space for recycling bins, convenient access to a service entrance, an operable window for ventilation, natural light, and a view to the outdoors.
- Provide space for the cook's coat, personal effects, menu and diet planning, a bulletin board, and telephone.
- Provide large, low viewing windows to enable children to watch the cook at work. Place the stove and preparation counters, rather than sinks, closest to these windows. (See page 198.)
- Consider providing a small room off the kitchen where children can work to help prepare meals. The room might even be equipped as a child-sized kitchen (see Chapter 17, Messy Play: Cooking) where children do some real cooking at their own level, under the supervision of an adult.
- Provide standard or heated carts for transporting food to the children's dining areas, and storage space for these carts in or near the kitchen.

Parents[2]

Two generations ago, the typical American family had an average of 2.6 children. Today the typical child probably has an average of 2.6 parents. The pressures on families to make ends meet while raising children alone far from family and friends, when parents are often young and have little or no training for this important job, make parenting very difficult these days. Child care centers designed to involve and support parents can:

- Facilitate parent participation in the care of their children
- Enhance communication between parents and staff
- Provide role-models, self-help, and parent training
- Help parents support one another
- Provide ways for parents to volunteer and support the center

The ideal building design enables parents and staff to rub shoulders with one another easily and informally in the course of their comings and goings. This is why living rooms, alcoves, livable lobbies and corridors, and informal gathering places in the building are so important. However, parent activities may also occur in spaces specifically designated for parents or in spaces—such as conference and resource rooms—shared by parents and staff. When using dual-purpose spaces for these purposes, remember that staff deserve a respite from all care-giving activities and that parents need to feel they are not intruding on staff when using shared spaces.

How to interest and involve parents in center activities is a question beyond the scope of this guide. However, *one powerful way to create a body of committed and caring parents is to enlist their help in building and making things for the center* or their children's group rooms. A periodic day of sewing or painting, cleaning, repairing, and building lofts, climbers, or even a playground will create community in a center as no other enterprise can.

Amenities and Supports for Parents

Parents are an essential part of a child care program and should feel welcome in the center at any time. Like their children, they often need support, nurturance, and training from the center's staff to feel good about themselves and more capable as parents. Ways to build community between staff and parents are the subject of the next main section of this chapter. Various design features can also help parents feel valued and invested in center activities.

QUESTIONS: PARENTS

1. What challenges do you face in getting parents actively involved in the center and their child's welfare (distance from the home, lack of time, ethnic diversity, language barriers, lack of after-hours child care, other)?

Parents form friendships while making a quilt for a water mattress.

Parents who help to create a center become deeply committed to it.

2. What physical amenities would truly nourish parents and make them want to spend more time at the center (snacks, quiet place to take a breather, chance to observe their child unseen, nursing area, washer/dryer, other)?
3. What aspects of the program would benefit from parental participation and support (curriculum and value-based decisions, fund-raising, field-trips, special events, other)?

GUIDELINES: PARENTS

- To ensure parent/staff contact, make it a rule that parents bring children to and pick them up in their group rooms. Provide short-term parking near the building, covered entries, and entry-transition spaces with benches and views that clearly invite parents inside.
- Parents often arrive at the center carrying numerous items. Create places to unload children and other paraphernelia and/or to store strollers, backpacks, and car seats convenient to the front door and to the group room entry zones.
- Consider providing "little red wagons" or carts near the front door for parents to transport children and their "gear" to their group rooms.
- Group room entry/transition zones at least six feet deep ensure that parents can be out of the main circulation path to meet or say goodbye to children, dress or undress them, wait for or observe a child at play, and confer with staff.
- Locate bulletin boards and parent mail boxes where parents are most apt to see them: the building entry, parent areas, and/or the group room entry zones. Add a few comfortable chairs to encourage parents to linger.
- Provide places in or near the group rooms for parents to put their outer apparel and personal belongings so they can participate in ongoing activities without adding clutter and confusion to the room.
- Provide clocks, telephones, and rest rooms with changing tables convenient to main circulation paths and/or children's areas where parents will be present.
- Provide a comfortable breast-feeding area in the infant room, or nearby, as well as a pleasant place for mothers to pump breast milk.
- Food is always an enticement to socializing. Setting out an inviting tray of refreshments at the beginning and end of each day encourages parents to snack and linger. (See Chapter 21, New Generation Childcare Centre, for the way one New Zealand center uses food as a parent amenity.)
- Where required, provide a daily sign-in book or counter in each group room entry zone.
- Create at least one place in the center where potluck dinners, workshops, and trainings for parents can occur on a regular basis. This might be the staff conference or resource room, the house living room, or a special parent space.

Parent/Staff Conference Space

For the child's welfare, parent and staff peace of mind, and parent confidence in the center, it is important that parents and staff be able to confer informally daily, and formally on a regular schedule. Informal conversations, often the most critical, occur most easily in the children's group rooms, or a nearby area.

QUESTIONS: PARENT/STAFF CONFERENCE SPACE

1. What design features will support daily informal contact between parents and staff in your program?
2. Where will you hold formal parent/staff conferences (office, lounge, conference room, staff area, living room)?

GUIDELINES: PARENT/STAFF CONFERENCE SPACE

- Informal parent/staff conferences most often occur in and around the children's group rooms, especially in an entry zone at least 6′ deep. (See Chapters 15–18.)
- Formal conferences or communications that children should not overhear should take place in a private office, conference room, or separate living room area, which is acoustically buffered, and convenient either to staff areas or to the children's group rooms.
- Design at least one parent/staff conference area of about 100 square feet that has a comfortable, informal atmosphere, soft lighting, and seating for three to five adults. The room might include information on parent education and child development.
- Locate the parent/staff conference area convenient to circulation, lavatories, telephones, beverages and snacks, coat racks, a clock, and water fountains.
- Because of the low frequency of parent/staff conference activity during most of the day, this conference area, if somethat larger (about 200–250 square feet) might double as a parent library/resource room (see below); a parent meeting room; a home-base for volunteers, student teachers, and part-time specialists; or a staff conference or resource room.

Parent Resource Room

In addition to interacting with their children and staff, parents are eager for information about child development, about parenting skills, about the pros and cons of their own behavior. They deeply appreciate access to educational materials that they have no time to track down in their busy lives. Creating a resource room and lending library for parents is a cost-effective way to make a wealth of books and audio-visual materials available to all. It also provides a place where parents can meet one another informally to chat and share experiences.

QUESTIONS: PARENT RESOURCE ROOM

1. Can your parent resource room be a separate space or will it be part of some other area (staff resource room, conference room, other)?
2. What resources will be especially helpful to your parent population: books, journals, magazines, video and audio tapes, toys and curriculum materials, sitting area, other? Will parents be able to borrow these and/or use them on-site?
3. Do you also wish to provide hand- and power-tools and space for parents to build and make things for the center, or for their children's use at home?
4. How much space will be needed for a parent resource room?
5. What types and amounts of work and display space do you want to provide?

GUIDELINES: PARENT RESOURCE ROOM

- At minimum, create a room, area, or alcove where books, videos, and audio tapes on parent education and child development are displayed for parents to borrow.
- Consider adding tables and chairs, audiovisual and computer supports, a comfortable sitting area, and a bulletin board so parents may use these materials in the center and meet others with similar concerns.
- Locate the parent resource room convenient to lavatories, snacks, telephones, water fountains, coat closets and circulation, to encourage parents to linger.
- Consider adding a children's book- and toy-lending library.
- Consider adding a workshop area to the resource room where parents can build and make things for their children or themselves, where local artists might teach crafts and handiwork skills, and where training programs of many sorts can be conducted. Facilities for making things are frequently a way to entice diffident parents, fathers, and grandparents to participate. This workshop might be shared by both parents and staff.
- Young parents often need help with meal planning and cooking skills. Trainings could be conducted in the center's kitchen, or in an appropriately outfitted parent or staff resource room.

Parents have fun and a sense of pride learning to make things for their children.

Building Family-Staff Community

Not so long ago, mothers who did not work outside the home met and compared notes at each other's homes, or while supervising their children on the playground. And trips to the supermarket, dry cleaner's, or pharmacy were as much for a child's education and entertainment as they were for the transactions involved. Today these events happen hurriedly, often in the evenings or only on weekends, or not at all. Harried working parents may not have time to fix breakfast or prepare a box lunch for their children; instead, they use the meal services provided by the child care center. They find it hard to meet and spend time with other families. Stress, isolation, and too-much-to-do prevail.

In the face of these realities, child care centers have the opportunity to be more than a place where children are cared for. They can also become a nexus of physical and emotional resources for staff and families.

On the physical level, by gathering a number of activities under one roof, some centers are becoming one-stop minimalls where parents can drop off and pick up dry cleaning; order take-home dinners in advance from a select menu; consult a dentist, nurse practitioner, or pediatrician on-site; leave siblings in a drop-in center while they jog, swim, exercise, or use work-out machines; exchange, sell, or rent the clothing and equipment that children quickly outgrow; and attend a variety of self-help, personal growth, and vocational skill-building seminars. Some centers offer swimming, yoga, tai-chi, foreign languages, music, dance, and theater classes for children and adults during and after regular child care hours, and on weekends. Some offer spaces for birthday parties and special individual family events.

By holding workshops and conferences on-site, some centers become an educational training base for parents and teachers in the broader community. Others provide housing for several teachers and students in order to have a resident caretaker oversee the facility at night. Some centers affiliate with senior citizens programs or create an intergenerational center, so that young and old can mix, enriching the lives of both. Still others, affiliated with industries that operate around the clock, provide 24-hour child care.

Many parents can manage the physical challenges of child rearing, provided they feel nourished emotionally and spiritually. Emotional support comes mostly from the attitudes of staff and their ability to create a place where parents are truly welcomed, respected, and heard. Creating dedicated spaces for parents is one tangible means of expressing care. So too is an open, informal building design that brings people in contact with one another, encourages spontaneity, and makes it easy for folks to pause and share common interests. Centerwide festivals, play days, barbeques, and special events always help to build community. When staff realize that they need parents as much as parents need the center's services, then true collaboration and community begin.

The needs are great and the possibilities infinite. The point is that every center has the opportunity to create community, to support busy parents, and to enrich everyone's life, including the elderly, while caring for children. Someday, child care centers may be as integral to a community's infrastructure as are its library, medical clinic, police, and fire stations. Meanwhile, we can create new and larger definitions of the enterprise so that the complexities of contemporary life do not outstrip our capacity to celebrate the gifts of families and our human need to cry and laugh with one another.

QUESTIONS: BUILDING COMMUNITY

1. What unique needs for physical and emotional support can you identify among your center's families, and which of these needs can the center begin to address?
2. What ideas come to mind for creating a greater sense of community among your center's families?
3. How can the design of the center honor these ideas?
4. What resources are available to make your ideas a reality?

GUIDELINES: BUILDING COMMUNITY

- Through brain-storming sessions, discussions, observations, and interviews, explore the needs, stresses, and dreams of parents in your center.
- Work together to cocreate a community of caring.
- Ensure that the design of your center reflects your visions for building community.
- For more ideas on involving the community in the center's activities and for using community resources to enrich the center's program, see Chapter 4, Preliminary Site Considerations: Relationship with the Community.

Notes

[1]This guide does not address the full-time care of sick children. Research (Gretchen Lee Anderson, *Removing Barriers to Childcare Facilities Development* (California State University, Northridge, CA, 1993) has shown such care to be extremely costly in terms of facility design and staff support because preschool children must be isolated from one another, yet cannot be left alone all day to play by themselves. The author favors federal and employer policies that enable the parents of children too sick to be at the center to care for them in the security and support of their own homes.

[2]"Parents" refers to grand-, step-, or foster parents and legal guardians, as well as to the child's biological parents.

CHAPTER TWENTY

OUTDOOR PLAY SPACES

For ourselves, and for our planet, we must be both strong and strongly connected—with each other, with the earth. As children, we need time to wander, to be outside, to nibble on icicles, watch ants, to build with dirt and sticks in the hollow of the earth, to lie back and contemplate clouds . . .

—Gary Paul Nabhan/Stephen Trimble

The hero who ventures forth in search of fortune or to achieve some superhuman or supernatural goal is a central mythological figure in most cultures. Armed with a talisman or valued object, he may cross a vast desert, crawl through a dark tunnel, hide in the branches of a tall tree, or climb a high mountain. However fanciful the tale, we can each relate to it in some way. The hero's journey may well be part of the collective unconscious memory with which children are born, a birthright 'driving' them—especially when supported by physical challenges outdoors—to practice hero behavior in play as preparation for adventures in later life.

Much of what children enact when playing outdoors might be seen as aspects of the hero's journey. Many a parent has watched, with bated breath, some heart-stopping feat of jumping, climbing, crawling, or hanging, and later, witnessed the child unload from jeans pockets the collection of "talismans" that made the feat possible. During the preschool years, feats of daring, power and control are paramount preoccupations, especially for little boys.

What more can we wish for our children than that they live self-confident in their ability to enjoy the mystery and fascination of conquering the unknown? A rich environment for outdoor play offers children the experience of venturing tentatively and then ever more sure-footedly, amidst the mysteries of nature while testing and honing physical skills.

The Importance of Nature

Movement, action and motion are essential to a child's development. Our senses operate on the basis of movment: The eye sees because it moves, and because it is sensitive to motion; hearing is the result of sound waves striking the eardrum; we smell scents carried on the air. Our senses operating by moving, being moved, or being in contact with stimuli that are in motion.

The natural world offers a perpetual play of sensory action and rhythm, in the movement of earth, air, fire and water—a feast for the sensorimotor apparatus of the human child. The original playscapes—before day care centers and playgrounds—were the fields, woods, paths, and streams near childrens' homes. Through experiences with nature's wonders in the form of sand, water, mud, trees, rocks, bushes, worms, butterflies, and birds, children received all the necessary motor stimulation.

These natural playscapes contrast sharply with the artifacts of modern urban development: hard-surfaced playgrounds equipped with mass-produced wooden, plastic, or metal play structures. According to Rudofsky:[1]

> . . . the average American city child . . . gets his first bad taste of the drearier forms of play in the confining space of a playground where so-called playground furniture has been set up for *taming* him. . . . He is expected to hop from rung to rung like a pet bird, or whiz among mazes that won't tax a mouse's brain.

Rural centers have the wherewithal to make childrens' direct experience with nature a priority, but urban child care centers need to make extra effort to provide experiences in nature. It is up to the design team to pay close attention to the qualitative aspects of a site—its landscaping, terrain, plant material, trees, and to do everything possible to preserve and utilize these essential play and sensorial experiences.

Site Planning Considerations

The success of any child care facility rests as much on the design and development of its outdoor play space as on the design of its interior. Although this guide is focused on bulding design, outdoor play ideally makes up 50% of the day care program. This chapter is intended only as an overview of the basic outdoor play issues design teams may want to consider. Many excellent and detailed sources treat this subject in greater depth.

Square Footage Requirements

Each child deserves enough outdoor space to play safely and exuberantly. Most states require—and NAEYC endorses—a minimum of 75 sq ft/child for all children outside at one time. However, 100–200 sq ft/child is preferable, especially in good weather.

Where outdoor space is limited, the APHA/AAP guide allows these exceptions: for infants, a minimum of 33 sq ft/child; and for toddlers (18–24 months), a minimum of 50 sq ft/child. Other options include staggering outdoor activity times, getting a waiver, or using parks and public spaces as alternate locations.

Alternate Locations

Where outdoor space is lacking or lackluster, alternative sites can be utilized. The most important criterion for an off-site outdoor play location is its proximity to the center. The shorter the walking distance, the more often the area will be utilized, helping to ensure that outdoor play remains a healthy one-half of the program, regardless of the local setting and climate.

Rural areas abound with stimulating outdoor sites that can complement or substitute for center-based play spaces: farms, greenhouses, woods, lake shores, and recreational lands. In cities, museums, parks, zoos, and places of historical or ethnic interest can serve a similar function.

Transitional Spaces Between Indoors and Outdoors

Children delight in hurrying outside to catch the first few drops of snow or to marvel at a fleeting rainbow. How easily they can do so depends upon how effectively an outdoor play space is linked to the indoors. For a full discussion of this subject, refer to Moving Between Indoors and Outdoors in Chapter 5.

When supplied with plants, places to sit, and play structures, a flat roof can serve as a valuable indoor-outdoor connector. Ideally, children can walk onto the roof from inside without using stairs. A portion of the roof can be designed to offer shelter from sun and wind. Rooftop playspaces require a lockable door, a safety fence at least 6 feet, and an approved fire escape leading to ground level.

Landscaping: Varying the Terrain and Elevation

Landscaping is critical to the success of an outdoor play area. An intriguing mix of trees, flowers, paths, inclines, hillocks, fences, and water can inspire children to engage in all sorts of creative explorations and make-believe. To achieve this, think of the outdoor space as a variety of spaces, each path and point it connects a "place" in its own right.

Use greenery of all sizes and shapes to delineate zones of play. Where possible, provide access to water (fountains, pools, ponds).

Varied elevation is of prime importance to play spaces. Flat sites can be modified to achieve a sense of varied terrain. Small hills or berms, either natural or constructed and covered with grass, encourage children to use gross motor skills while climbing, sliding, rolling, sledding, and playing "King of the Mountain" games. A minimum of one or two berms 4–5 feet high (200–400 sq.ft.) with slopes of 1:3, 1:4, 1:5 are recommended for a preschool area.[2] For additional discussion of this topic, see Sun/Shade, Wind, Water, and Plants in Chapter 5.

GUIDELINES FOR VARYING THE TERRAIN

- Preserve and incorporate all natural features, such as trees, ponds, rock outcroppings, and natural slopes.
- Plan landscaping that provides acoustic and visual separation between activities, facilitates interactions with the natural environment, creates private spaces, and adds aesthetic appeal to the play area.
- In northern climates, plan surface materials and ground-shaping to accommodate sliding, skating, sledding and snow-mounding activities in the winter.
- Create some terraces that follow the contour lines of naturally sloping land.

Shelter and Drainage

Every play area calls for a variety of exposure-and-protection combinations: sunny and shaded areas, breezy and wind-buffered terrain, wet and dry spots. Aside from the natural shelter of trees, bushes, mounds, and rocks—and in addition to at least one covered transitional space between the inside and outside—possible sheltered spaces include a covered or semicovered veranda, a porch, a gazebo or "band shell," a play shed, a hut, a lean-to, and a roofed activity space or play structure.

Be sure to consider drainage needs on a season-to-season basis. Play space that is fully usable in late summer and fall may be too wet for use in spring without the addition of proper surfacing and drainage mechanisms.

Proper drainage allows for quick use after rain or snow. Put the quickest drying surfaces closest to the building's entry and the slowest drying surfaces furthest away. Concrete curbs around sand areas are not appropriate because they prevent rainwater from escaping; wood is preferable. When altering the site with mounds, berms, or pits, ensure proper drainage. Use technical means when natural drainage does not suffice.

Bathrooms

Plan to have outdoor bathrooms and water fountains or to locate easily accessible indoor bathrooms adjacent to outdoor play areas. In warm climates where the outdoors is used continually, locate the indoor bathroom on the play yard wall, put messy play at that end of the room, and allow direct access to the bathroom from the outside. (See Locate Sinks in the Messy Zone in Chapter 7.) Locate at least one toilet and hand-washing sink within 40 feet of the door to the outdoor play area.

Environmental Hazards and Maintenance

Keep outdoor play areas clean and safe from debris, dilapidated structures, building supplies, sharp rocks, glass, and other injurious materials. For a complete list of environmental concerns, refer to Environmental Considerations in Chapter 4.

GUIDELINES FOR ENVIRONMENTAL SAFETY

- Remove all toxic plants. Children love to play with and eat plant material. Consult local sources for local plant characteristics.
- Ensure that equipment is neither corroded nor treated with toxic preservatives. Wooden equipment can be treated with CCA (chromated copper arsenate) to keep dislodgeable arsenic levels acceptably low.
- Separate trash areas from play areas to avoid contamination and stinging insects.
- Provide covered trash containers at convenient locations around the site.

Fences and Enclosures

Licensed child care facilities are required by law to provide outdoor enclosures that control access and that separate age levels, especially infant/toddlers from older children.

Group-dynamic considerations are also involved when planning effective fences and enclosures. While enclosures can separate activity zones (e.g., bike riding and sand play), where possible they permit all children to observe each other. This visibility helps younger children become attracted to, and more prepared to use, facilities beyond their present skills

Equally important are aesthetic considerations. The

A gate—always an invitation to enter.

design of the fences and enclosures will affect how inviting the play space is to use, how well it suggests a place for children, and how harmoniously it relates to the neighborhood.

Weigh all of these considerations when determining the appropriate height, depth, and degree of transparency for each fence or enclosure. Options range from a wooden, metal, or masonry construction to a planting or an earth berm. Ideally, various aesthetically pleasing forms of enclosure combine to create a secure, nonintimidating environment. For example, a combination of fencing, plant material, berms, low walls, seating, level changes, and material variety can make a tall concrete perimeter wall appear much less hostile, especially on the inside.

Children often prefer to gather around the edges of a space for privacy, fantasy play, or social interaction. Enclosures can enhance these functions by offering places to sit, climb, hide behind, or nestle into. Enclosures that jut forward into an open space help create attractive and compelling "edge" spots for children to rest or play.

GUIDELINES FOR FENCES AND ENCLOSURES

- Remember that fences intended to prevent vandalism can sometimes encourage it. Whereas a solid concrete wall may challenge an outsider to find out what lies behind it, a fence with well-spaced rails can show that nothing "valuable" exists on the other side.
- Place horizontal bracing above childrens' heads, so they can't step on those elements to hoist themselves up and over a fence.
- Make the exterior perimeter barrier at least 4 feet high, with the bottom edge no more than 3½ inches off the ground.
- Fences 8 feet high may be required for school-age children, or where complete visual screening is desired (e.g., for an adventure play area or for a site with high vandalism potential).
- To prevent head entrapment, make openings less than 3½ inches or more than 9 inches wide (and designed to discourage climbing).
- To prevent finger entrapment, openings should be between ⅜–1 inch.
- Provide the play area with at least 2 supervisable exits. Make the exit more remote from the building large enough to admit a maintenance truck.
- Where views beyond the area are desirable, use chain link, lattice, and other materials or plantings that maximize visibility. Where views are not desirable, use solid enclosure. Wood is preferable to masonry. Enclosures can be softened and reinforced with shrubs or vines planted on both sides, especially on the interior. Wood and wire fencing can be used to frame views.
- Use a variety of materials to maximize sensory experiences: rough/smooth surfaces; heavy/light, wet/dry, cool/hot, bright/dull, large/small objects; materials that make sounds independently, or when struck or walked upon; scented materials; materials that produce light and shadow effects.
- Think about ways to include sound exploration to outdoor play. Consider, for example, creating a "musical wall" by sus-

pending sound-making devices along a fence or other high enclosure.

- Use landscaping to provide acoustic and visual separation between activities, as well as opportunities for interaction with nature.
- Separate age-appropriate interior play spaces with fences at least 2 feet high.
- Create some enclosures that give children a sense of privacy but enable standing adults to see them.
- Locate storage sheds, swimming pools, and other large installations towards the perimeter of the yard in order not to block visual supervision of other areas.
- Ensure that any standing body of water is fenced. Check local ordinances about fence height requirements.
- Decks, balconies, terraces, and porches require enclosures or banisters at least 36 inches high. Ideally, such enclosures will permit visibility through some type of grid work (slats no further than 2⅜ inches apart). If it is unsafe for children to climb a barrier, use only vertical components and reduce or eliminate horizontal bracing at heights children can reach by foot.

Gates

As a portal from one space to another, a gate has a considerable subliminal impact on its user. Some cultures recognize this fact by giving certain gates a special significance.

GUIDELINES FOR GATES

- Gateways can be open arches as well as hinged panels of wood, metal, or wrought iron.
- Use large and small gates to demarcate major transitions and boundaries in the play yard.
- Ensure that gates functioning as barriers are self-closing and inoperable by small children.

Paths and Circulation

The paths on which young children move can offer engaging experiences of their own. Children delight in riding tricycles around and around in circles, crossing bridges, avoiding cracks in the sidewalk, examining the weeds that grow between bricks, and building mounds and castles with the sand and gravel under their feet.

Design a variety of circulation paths, covered and uncovered; curved and straight; wide and narrow; sloping and flat, in a variety of textures, colors, and materials (natural and human-made).

Design path surfaces to bring out the beauty of the surrounding vegetation and equipment. (Asphalt and concrete are relatively inexpensive and functional, but can detract from softer textures and more subtle elements in the yard.) Some paths can offer surprises of their own—herbs growing between bricks or flagstones, mosaic tile patterns, interlocking wooden shapes. There is something magical about encountering beauty unexpectedly as one moves through a space.

GUIDELINES FOR CIRCULATION PATHS

- Ensure that there is a hard surface dedicated to wheeled toys, so they do not interfere with general circulation.
- Occasionally vary the width of paths to form "bulges" where children can sit, play, rest, and observe.
- Add a trellis to some part(s) of the path to help shape it and the outdoor space on either side of it.
- Plan circulation paths as loops without long, straight stretches that might tempt children to run fast.

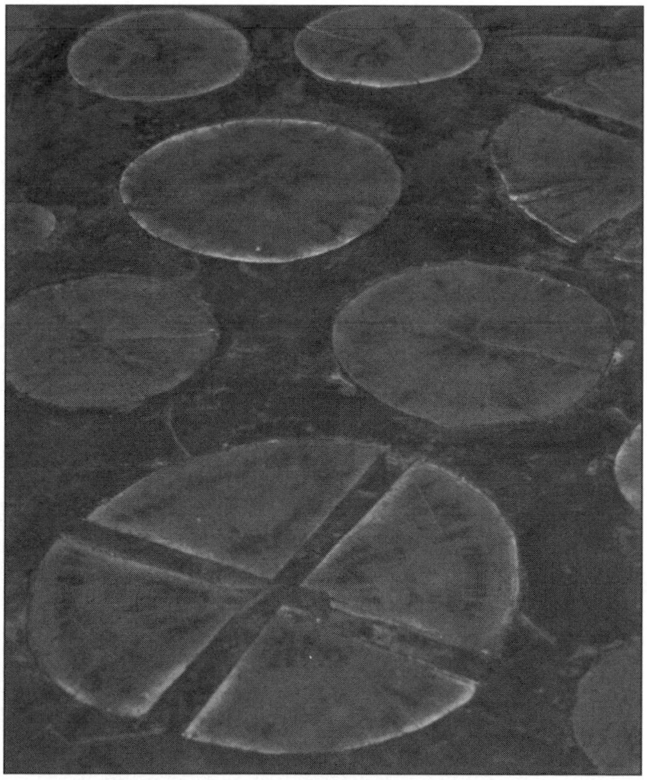

An imaginative path invites exploration.

- Separate main circulation paths from activity areas, but keep activity areas visible from these paths so that children can easily see and choose where they want to go.
- Create some paths with 1-inch cracks between their pavers where grass, moss, herbs, and small flowers can grow. Use no mortar or cement so the feeling is entirely natural.
- Create at least some paths out of soft tile and bricks—materials that are strongly connected to the surrounding earth and that show the mark of time and use.
- Create a "buffer zone" of at least 9 feet around all active areas (swings, climbers, bikes), so passing children are less likely to run in the path of activity.
- Consider the needs of differently-abled and wheelchair-bound children, with an eye to maximizing opportunities for action. They can derive special enjoyment from negotiating slight elevations or curves, or moving through an area with diverse structures, trees, flowers, ponds, and even small animals.

Landmarks

In laying out the play yard, choose an interesting landmark, ideally near the center, that functions as a reference point and that makes the yard as a whole more memorable. For example, a tree or a hill that is visible from a distance and that can be climbed to obtain views can fulfill this purpose admirably. Other possible central landmarks include a banner, flag, sundial, bird bath, gazebo, play structure, or fragrant garden. Elsewhere in the yard, entrances, transition zones, sitting areas, storage sheds, and other large play structures may serve as secondary landmarks or reference points.

Play Yard Design and Zoning Considerations

When it comes to providing outdoor space for each age group and for the many activities needed for each group, designers are again faced with the complexities of fair and best-use allocation. Many of the issues related to the planning of group activity rooms (Chapters 15–18) apply here, though the allocation of outdoor space is complicated by the absence of walls and partitions with which to clearly define and contain the designated activities.

Developmentally Appropriate Play Yards

Infant/toddlers, preschoolers, and school-age children have distinctly different motoric, social, and cognitive abilities. To keep younger children from being physically or emotionally hurt by stronger, more agile, and more sophisticated older children, divide the site into separate play yards for each group. Ideally, each yard will be contiguous with the respective group's primary interior space and linked by a covered transitional area. It is also desirable for the three yards to be interconnected, or designed so that the three groups can see and interact with each other to some degree.

It's especially important that designers create a well-organized environment for differently-abled and very young children. Make sections easily identifiable and assist orientation with clear cues and landmarks, both horizontal and vertical. Possible cues include distinctive colors, textures, changes in level, and repeated elements.

Play Zones

For all age levels, the outdoor space needs to provide:

- private places that are easily "owned" by a single child
- places for small groups of 1–4 children
- places for large muscle activity involving groups of up to 10 children
- places for games and sports involving more than 10 children
- plenty of free space for children to gather spontaneously

Designate separate zones for different activities in each age-appropriate yard so that compatible activities are close together and at least visually separated from incompatible activities. As with indoor activities, vary outdoor activity zones in size and location according to whether the activity is busy or quiet, structured or unstructured. Plan so that each zone has physical and visual links to the others so that children can see all the zones easily and move freely among them. Separate "minizones" may be required for individual play structures, berms used as play equipment, water play, animal areas, gardens, sand and dirt play, or retreat spots.

Play zones can be related to one another in one of three ways:

- separated by distance, landscaping, fencing, or enclosure
- linked (but not contiguous) to one another by convenient access
- contiguous to one another but well-defined.

Plan the creation of zones according to the developmental level of the age group and the nature of the activity. In general, it is helpful to locate quieter and easier activities in the middle of the yard or closer to the building, and more vigorous and challenging play at the perimeter.

Flow Between Play Zones

Design secondary circulation between play zones to create a sense of flow from one activity to the next. Flow between activities also encourages free play, exploration, decision making, attention span development, and spatial awareness. The bottom of a traditional slide, for example, rather than being a dead end, can provide an obvious option for further play: A child climbs a mound to cross a bridge to slide down a tunnel to go into sand or water, and so on.

Ideally, the flow will offer a series of graduated challenges and levels of skill development. It is important that each type of activity offer several skill accomplishment levels: e.g., for climbing—steps, a ladder, and a cargo net; for jumping—up and down, on a spring platform, and across some moving water. The flow can lead from one single activity to the next or, even better, provide multiple alternatives at crossing points. Plan so that children are able:

- to see the parts as well as the whole
- to easily determine alternative routes or movements
- to branch out either horizontally or vertically
- to withdraw, stop, rest, or go backwards, as desired (so they do not lose face or feel that they are quitting)

Providing the latter option means intentionally locating divisions or barriers somewhere between areas, as well as allowing for the flow to continue.

Offering a Full Range of Specific Activities

In addition to opportunities for expansive gross motor activity, outdoor play also provides cognitive, creative, and emotional learning experiences. An outdoor play space optimally offers six basic types of activity:

active	**creative** (sand, water, mud, gardening, building)
structured	**quiet** (story reading, crafts, nature study)
fantasy	**therapeutic** (for the differently-abled)

For most ages, strive to provide the following types of experiences in outdoor spaces, preferably on a four-season basis:

- *a mix of natural elements for observation and play:*

  water (fountains, pools, sprinklers, ponds)

  sand

  dirt mounds (for climbing and digging)

  a garden

  grass, trees, hills

  animals (and housing for them)

  areas that attract birds, butterflies, and benign insects

- *a mix of activities that develop skills and foster cooperation:*

climbing	rolling
hiding	ball play
sliding	play above the ground
hanging	woodworking and construction
crawling	arts and crafts

- *a mix of structures, surfaces, and objects for different purposes:*

  dramatic playhouses and imaginative play structures (car, boat, fire engine)

  hard-surfaced areas for wheeled toys and games

  informal paved areas for activities that are safe on pavement

  climbing structures (with room for more than one child and with a variety of entries, exits, and levels) low walls (for climbing and sitting)

loose parts (nets, balls, boards, blocks, ropes)

ambiguous objects (to stimulate creativity)

- *a mix of spaces for different purposes:*

  enclosed spaces

  emotional-release points

  private places

  places for retreat and quiet play

  places to sit (for children or adult observers/supervisors)

  places for picnics and cookouts

  sunny and shaded spaces and degrees of shelter

Infant/Toddler Play Yards

It is important that infant/toddler play yards offer a well-scaled series of spaces and experiences that cater to the respective motor and perceptual skills of different developmental stages. Such spaces might include soft crawling surfaces; warm materials; slight changes in level; and a variety of textures and interactive devices that provide interesting sights, sounds, scents, and surfaces. Separate equipment will be needed for crawling babies and for standing toddlers. Good options are infant and toddler swings, a porch swing where an adult can sit with one or two children, a play pyramid, soft surfaces for tumbling, a built-in slide.

GUIDELINES FOR INFANT/TODDLER PLAY YARDS

- Equipment needs to offer a range of increasingly more challenging tasks. Gradually sloping slides ramps, stairs, and platforms encourage crawling, pulling to stand, and toddling skills.
- Provide seats within close proximity for adult supervisors.
- Incorporate reflective surfaces, such as tempered glass mirrors (in locations where they will not get hot) to encourage recognition skills.
- Provide accessible and safe textures (grass, sand, stone, dirt and water) for infants to touch and explore. Check out durable ground covers of varying textures and scents that infants and toddlers might crawl and walk upon.
- Provide hard-surfaced area for wheeled toys or trikes.

Preschool Play Yards

Children 3–5 years old are agile and eager to explore and hone their physical abilities. They appreciate equipment with a variety of components or platforms with several ways to get on and off. Increasingly challenging ways of getting up and down from various heights help them develop age-appropriate motoric skills. For this reason, the components attached to platforms (ladders, ropes, chains, and tire nets) are often more developmentally valuable than the platforms themselves. Because preschoolers acquire skills more quickly for climbing up than down, it's important that climbing equipment offer a variety of ways to get down.

In addition to play structures, provide preschoolers with swings, slides, varied textures, scented materials, water, sand, paint, clay, some building materials such as large blocks, equipment for dramatic play, interactive equipment, soundmaking devices, small huts, and hideaways.

School-age Play Yards

School-age children respond less well to structured equipment and more to opportunities for using their bodies in space, for creative play, and for making their own spaces and structures. For younger children in this age group, loose parts (tools, bricks, boards, nets, toys, blocks—anything moveable) become accoutrements to play structures; for older children, loose parts become the structures per se. Thus huts, forts, and treehouses constitute the 'playgrounds' of the elementary school years.

Opportunities for active exercise, including both individual and team sports, are also essential for school-age children. Activities for older children who are only partially mobile, as well as for the able-bodied, include basketball, tetherball, shuffleboard, horseshoes, and ring toss. These activities, as well as many other games, require a hard surface.

A Word About Accidents: Challenge versus Hazard

To be a proper "hero" entails wildness and risk. Accidents on playgrounds attest to this fact. Although childrens' safety and a child care agency's potential liability are large concerns, cannot the risk be

Figure 20.1
The Husky preschool play yard.

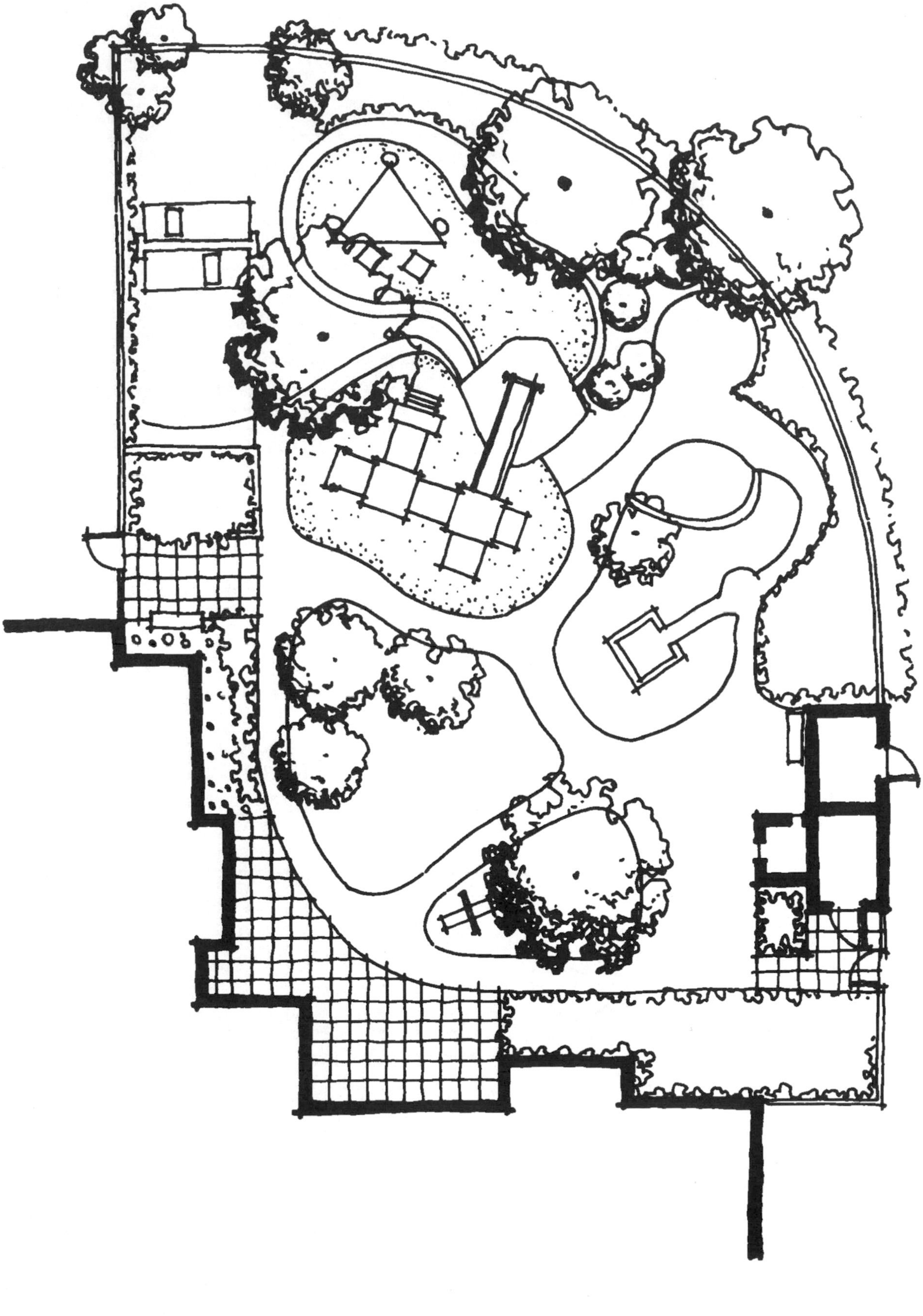

calculated? Too much safety is self-defeating. Children are not self-annihilative. For centuries they have climbed trees, forged streams, jumped from high places. It is important that an outdoor play area remain a place when children can experiment with risk and adventure.

> Children will use equipment in all possible ways, regardless of original design intent . . .—that is how they discover their limits . . . Playgrounds must be places where it is safe to stretch the limits of ability without the risk of serious injury. A hazard is the unforeseen consequence of a child's inability to handle a given challenge (a poor design feature, or poor maintenance) . . . A challenge is something the child can see and chooses to attempt. The playground designer's responsibility is to maximize challenge and minimize hazard.[3]

The majority of playspace injuries are caused by falls from equipment *to the ground surface below.* Other hazards involve: impact by swings and other moving equipment; collision with stationary equipment; protrusions, pinch points, sharp edges, hot surfaces on equipment; and playground debris. Fatal injuries can result from falls, entanglement of clothing, entanglement in ropes, head entrapment in openings, and impact from equipment tipover or structural failure.

A prime consideration is that all equipment arranged so that children playing on one piece of equipment will not interfere with those playing on or running to another. The APA specifies:

- 9 feet around fixed items.
- 15 feet around any moving part. Clearance space allocated to one piece of equipment must not overlap that of another.

Equipment Design

Play equipment alone does not make an adequate outdoor play yard. An assemblage of diverse play structures randomly dotting the landscape is a poor solution to providing an aesthetic and challenging environment.

Whether custom-built or commercial equipment is employed, it is important to make an effort to integrate it into the landscape, or add landscaping as a complementary component. In addition to providing challenge and complexity in the design of play areas, make sure to provide points that allow a child to rest or to leave an activity without feeling he has failed. Small watching places such as tree houses, forts, tower platforms, or large boxes can serve this function and give children the observational time which encourages them to join in again.

When designing play structures, or selecting commercial equipment, keep the following questions in mind:

QUESTIONS: EQUIPMENT DESIGN

1. Does the equipment provide motor challenge and complex patterns of activity? Possible large muscle play includes: climbing, swinging, bouncing, balancing, crawling, sliding, lifting, pushing, pulling, hand over hand, hanging by arms, spinning, jumping
2. Does the equipment allow for more than large muscle play?
3. Is the large muscle play at more than one level of difficulty, with paced alternatives?

Play Structures, Climbers, Platforms, and Raised Surfaces

Use fixed play structures only as part of an overall design and only if they are large enough to support creative activity zones.

Climbers are designed to present a greater degree of physical challenge than other equipment. Wood, rope, net, and tire structures usually feature platforms (sometimes covered) at several levels. These can double-function as hiding, retreat, and breakaway points, and as ambiguous settings for dramatic play.

Box 20.1 gives various play-structure dimensions that will prevent head and finger entrapment, discourage unnecessary falling, and provide for safer equipment overall.

GUIDELINES FOR PLAY STRUCTURES, CLIMBERS, PLATFORMS, AND RAISED SURFACES

- Plan a certain amount of repetition into the equipment and structural designs. Repetition assists cognitive learning and provides reassurance.
- Locate each play structure, activity site, and associated circulation area, to encourage movement through progres-

sively more difficult developmental tasks. Provide stop-off places for retreat if a child reaches an overly difficult challenge.

- Cover or recess all nuts and bolts. Bury anchors/footings for equipment, especially if concrete, below ground level or cover them with safety surfacing.
- If possible, place metal climbers (especially slides) in the shade or orient them in a north-south direction.
- Provide a means for children to display or announce the completion of a challenge. Possibilities include: platforms at the top of ropes and ladders; a bell to ring at the end of a complex route; banners to fly; adult seats nearby to call down to.
- Platforms over 30 inches (preferably 20 inches for preschoolers), require protective barriers at least 38 inches high, with no entrapments or footholds for climbing
- Play structures need to offer more than one access and exit.
- Vary the size, nature, and height of three-dimensional spaces. Variation assists in children's cognitive development and ultimately in symbolic learning and decoding.
- Provide variety in crawling spaces: wide and tight, with and without enclosure, long and short, a little or a lot of light at the end.
- Create ways for children to fall safely or jump some distance in space.
- Include depth cues such as textures or shadows in all portions of the environment.
- Provide some structures that allow children to be safely above ground, in groups, or alone. Provide variety in height and complexity by using houses, castles, towers, trees, platforms, nets, or ropes. Old-style jungle gyms are not sufficiently challenging.
- Platforms over 6 feet need an intermediary platform so children can halt and take an alternate route if desired.
- Ensure that climbing equipment has bars that stay in place when grasped, regularly spaced footholds from top to bottom, a safe way out for children when they reach the top, and a potential fall height of no more than 7½ feet.
- Consider installing wavy ramps and suspension bridges that provide a safe sense of risk-taking, especially for children in wheelchairs.
- Consider installing balance beams of varying heights, lengths, and inclinations. Beams offer wonderful skill-building activities for all ages and also make good informal seating, especially around sand pits.

BOX 20.1

Safety Dimensions for Climbers, Platforms, Stairs, Ladders, and Raised Surfaces

Platforms and Climbers

maximum height:[4]

children under 3	3 feet
children 3–6	5.5 feet
children over 6	6.6 feet

distance between stepped platforms:

preschool	12″
school-age	18″

Climbers, Steps, Ladders

spacing between horizontal bars:	3½–9″

Stairways

inclination angle:	35°
risers:	6–10″ high, uniform rise and run

Ladders

inclination angle:	75°
rungs, outside diameter:	no < 1⅜″
handhold and tread rungs:	no < 1⅝″

All Finger Openings	between ⅜–1″
diameter of rungs and hand-gripping components:	1–1⅝″

Movable Parts and Soft Materials

The best equipment possesses a large number of movable parts—suspension bridges, swings, etc. Injuries usually occur on traditional equipment because it is static. Children need to move; they get hurt when trying to make static equipment do something it is not designed to do.

All moving parts on play structures should be made of soft materials (tires, ropes, nets, wood, canvas) rather than metal, hard plastic, and chain. Traditional metal equipment—swings, slides, merry-go-rounds, seesaws, monkey bars—can be dangerous because

This page: The glider offers a secure but exhilarating ride.

Next page: An easily accessible, nonthreatening slide for toddlers.

metal is slippery when wet, hot in the summer, and cold in the winter. Rope climbers are typically safer than those built of metal bars. If traditional metal structures are unavoidable, combine them with natural elements such as wood, which fulfills a child's symbolic needs for warmth and protected spaces.

BOX 20.2

Safety Specifications for Swing Sets

Equipment Dimension	Minimum Distance
clearance in front of and behind swing set	9 feet
clearance between to-and-fro swings and their frames	27.5 inches
clearance between 2 tire swings and their frames	38 inches
clearance between bearing hangers	24 inches
clearance between bottom of swing seat (or tire) and the ground	16 inches
height between top of swing bar and the ground (to reduce torque and velocity)	8–9 feet

Swings

Can you recall the thrill of pumping high and seeing far out over the landscape, of feeling the wind blow through your hair? Swinging is akin to the hero's experiences of flying and free-fall. It also helps develop a young child's vestibular system (responsible for upright body balance).

A swing is the most popular piece of traditional outdoor equipment for all ages. Varying the styles, sizes, and heights of swings makes a play area more challenging and interesting. Choose among tire swings on swivels, belt swings, bouncing swings with rubber straps, 'horses' that two can ride, infant swings, and flat swings with rubber seats.

Careful design can reduce the likelihood of a child entering the path of a moving swing, or falling from a moving swing and being hit on its return. Box 20.2 below lists safety specifications for swing sets. Additional screening with hedges, bushes, low fences, and sitting walls may be desirable.

GUIDELINES FOR SAFETY: SWINGS, CABLE RIDES, AND SPINNING DEVICES

- Locate all swings and moving devices such as cable rides and merry-go-rounds at the edge of the yard, so the fence or enclosure forms a "back" to the swing area. This reduces the chances of collision behind the swings.
- Install swing seats made of rubber or approved impact-

BOX 20.3

Dimensions for Preschooler Slides (Unenclosed)

maximum height:	6′ 6″ (64″ PLAE)
preferable height:	4′ 6″ or less*
inclination angle:	30° or less
side rims	2.5"
guardrails:	23.5 to 27″ high
flat steps	7–11″ apart
tube slide: minimum internal diameter	23″

*Slides higher than 4′ 6″ require adequate enclosure with protective sides at the top.

absorbing material. Do not use wood or metal seats. Avoid rigid swing seats, which, unlike canvas or rubber belt swings, encourage standing.

- PLAE suggests calculating requisite, all-around clearance as two times the height of the swing beam. Therefore, less set-back is required for tot and tire swings with lower beams than for swings for preschool and school-age children.
- Place no more than 2 swings on any one apparatus. This reduces the collision risk for swing-users and passers-by.
- Place baby swings on a frame separate from swings for older children.
- Drill holes in all tire swings to ensure adequate drainage.
- Suspend swings by small linked chains rather than fiber rope, which can fray.
- For stability, suspend swings from A-frames that are designed so they can't be climbed.

Gliders

A cable ride or glider provides a superb swinging, free-hanging, movement activity for preschoolers and older children. It can be equipped with specially adapted tire swings and seats to hold an infant/toddler or differently-abled child securely. For safety, it is best located at the edge the yard, with appropriate launching and landing pads or platforms (according to its size and design).

Slides

Do you remember, as a small child, climbing the tall rickety ladder to a slide? At the top, the long, shiny surface lay before you, enticing but terrifying. How could you possibly go from standing to sitting without falling? The way down seemed endless and scary. With a pressing line of other children behind you, retreat was impossible.

Despite such anxieties, slides are the second most favorite equipment (after swings) for children under 6 years. The most exciting—and safest—slide, however, is not the type just described, but one that is built into a hillside or earth mound. This gives the user the feeling of gliding effortlessly without the fear of losing balance or falling. All along the way, the child can feel free to touch the grass, smell the wild flowers, or watch the sky. An earth mound can even have a crawl-through tunnel beneath the slide, and stairs, foot-holds, or hand-holds carved into its sides as ways to access the slide. Slides built into hillsides or mounds provide more challenging climbing and crawling opportunities than traditional, free-standing slides; there are no tall ladders from which to fall, and children can change their minds and retreat, if desired.

A variety of slides scattered in and about structures and landscaping make a play yard exciting. Slides can:

- be wide enough for two or three to slide together

This slide, by following the contour of the hillside, allows for a gradual descent.

- be curved, spiralled, or straight
- be constructed partially or fully as plastic tubes
- be of varying lengths and degrees of pitch

High-density polyethylene tube slides are particularly popular because they are safe (allowing for higher and steeper rides), easy to maintain, and colorful. Metal slides, by contrast, get can get too cold or too hot.

GUIDELINES FOR SLIDES

- Locate slides in an uncongested area of the yard. Ensure that a slide never shares landing space with another piece of equipment.
- Prevent accidents by ensuring that all slide bottoms:

  — have a smooth run-off parallel to the ground for 12–16 inches

  —are raised 7–12 inches above the ground

  —are followed by a clear, 11-foot run-off space
- Ensure that there is transition security at the slide's entrance.
- Generally, make the slide bed twice as long as the slide height, with no incline exceeding 40 degrees. Make sure that slides for 2 or more children do not exceed 12 feet in length.

Seesaws and Spring Rides

Children love the rocking motion of seesaws and spring rides. The fact that two people must cooperate to make a seesaw work is both its virtue and drawback. Because accidents can occur when one child is either "bumped" to the bottom or held suspended at the top, make every possible accommodation for safety.

SAFETY GUIDELINES FOR SEESAWS AND SPRING RIDES

- Spring-loaded seesaws are preferable to conventional ones.
- Ensure that seesaws have an enclosed fulcrum and a maximum height of 4 feet, 6 inches. Design so that each seat has a resilient block or half of a rubber tire protruding from the ground below it to cushion impact.
- Ensure that coil springs on spring rides are covered or designed to prevent pinching
- Ensure that seesaws and spring rides have handholds and footrests that encourage comfortable seating and give the child control over speed.
- Ensure that seesaws or spring rides have 39 inches of clearance in all directions.

Horizontal Ladders and Overhead Rings

For preschoolers, horizontal ladders and overhead rings are best used as a means of getting from one play structure to the next (rather than as free-standing elements). Make openings in exercise rings smaller than $4\frac{1}{4}$ inches or larger than 9 inches in diameter to prevent head entrapment.

Overhead bars help build upper-body strength and assist children in wheelchairs to cross terrain. Stationary bars are appropriate for preschoolers; suspended bars add more challenge for school-age children. Stationary hanging bars need to be less than 5 inches or more than 10 inches apart (smaller or larger than a child's head).

Loose Parts

Every outdoor area requires "loose parts"—ropes, balls, wagons, bikes, boxes and boards, ladders, pails, shovels, and nets—that children can use to create structures and games of their own. Some loose parts function as tools for working with certain materials (sand, water, clay); others are play or building equipment (balls, bricks and boards, wagons), requiring special space and storage for their use.

GUIDELINES FOR LOOSE PARTS

- Provide tools, storage, and an open area where children can build freeform structures by assembling various raw materials (tires, wood, boards, bricks, posts) in different ways.
- Provide opportunities for children to build with natural materials (sand, rocks, dirt, plants).
- Consider providing some manufactured kits such as tinker toys and Quadro™ for use as outdoor building materials. Children may need assistance in visualizing the finished forms of these projects before they are constructed.

Storage of Loose Parts

Typical loose parts that require storage include wheeled vehicles, sand- and water-play toys, wading pools, balls, ropes, boxes, blocks, and gardening tools. These items are best stored in an outdoor shed or in a part of the building accessible from, and contiguous with, the yard. Outfit the storage space with hooks, shelves, and bins, so that everything has its own place and is easily obtainable. Make some of the space child-scaled, so that children can access and put away play materials on their own.

GUIDELINES FOR STORAGE

- Materials are most apt to be used if stored close to their location of use.
- Consider designing storage sheds with flat or A-frame roofs. The exteriors can then serve as additional climbers and play equipment.
- Ensure that the shed's exterior is vandal-proof and weather tight.

Equipment for Differently-Abled Children

In providing for differently-abled children, the design challenge is to stimulate use of those faculties that are weak, as well as to challenge and strengthen those which are strong. Good design capitalizes upon every opportunity for movement.

As much as possible, make structures barrier-free for children in wheelchairs and adaptive equipment. Ramps, in conjunction with steps, can allow a wheelchair to climb to a platform. Design water- or sand-play troughs and tables for picnics or crafts at wheelchair height. All ramps, hills, and circulation paths need to have nonskid surfaces at least 4 feet wide. Ramps, equipped with handrails 16–24 inches high, must have 12 feet of run for every 1 foot of rise. Locate ample rest areas strategically along challenging routes.

Surfacing Around and Beneath Equipment

Because children's eyes rest first on the surfaces beneath their feet, especially when they are in motion, surfacing materials have strong psychological and aesthetic effects as well as safety implications. Where surfacing materials have stronger visual impact than the equipment on top of them, perceptual confusion can result. Alternatively, the appeal of certain surfacing materials can help to make otherwise stark or intimidating equipment more attractive.

Considerable evidence attests to the fact that falls from equipment are the most common cause of serious injury and death in outdoor play areas. Although climbing equipment is most often associated with injuries (most frequently lacerations of the head, face, and neck), the surfacing beneath them is responsible for the injury's severity. By covering surfaces in high-quality, impact-absorbing materials and minimizing heights, designers can substantially reduce injuries due to falls.

The wide range of childrens' activities requires a variety of surfacing material. The best choice depends upon a number of factors: safety needs, types of activities, climate/weather conditions, drainage, cleanliness and maintenance issues, cost, durability, and aesthetics. Sometimes, the surfacing material itself can be play equipment, whether it's human-made or natural (terrain, vegetation, landscaping).

Surfacing materials tend to be of four types:

- the ground itself (bare earth or grass)
- loose natural materials (wood chips, bark mulch, pea gravel, sand)
- hard materials (asphalt, concrete, brick, flagstone)
- human-made resilient materials (astroturf, commercial rubber sheeting, chopped-up tires)

Either unitary materials or loose-fill materials are acceptable under equipment. *Unitary materials* are typically rubber mats or rubberlike materials held in place by a binder that may be poured in place at the site (over dirt, asphalt, or concrete) and cured to form a unitary shock-absorbing surface. There are many different brands, with a range of shock-absorbing properties.

Loose-fill materials also have shock-absorbing properties when installed at a sufficient depth. (These materials should never be installed on top of hard surfaces such as asphalt or concrete.) Their shock-absorbing properties depend on their natural structure, depth, degree of compression, and the height from which a child might fall. Table 20.1 gives the critical fall heights for seven materials commonly used under and around play equipment. Recently synthetic resilients made from materials like urethane and polystyrene have become available, but in the interest of keeping the environment as natural as possible, they are not the preferred choice.

Extensive research suggests that all equipment be surrounded by a resilient surface to a depth of about 9 inches, extending beyond the external limits of the equipment for at least 4 feet beyond the fall zone.

GUIDELINES FOR SURFACING AROUND AND BENEATH EQUIPMENT

- Use soft surfacing materials such as sand, wood chips, pea gravel, or shredded tires wherever children might fall. There should be an 8–12-inch depth of shock-absorbency, especially under climbing equipment, under swings, and at the base of slides. *These materials need to be raked regularly to keep them soft and aerated.*
- Although sand is an excellent surfacing material, it can be abrasive to children and equipment. Use sand under climbers only if there is adequate drainage, because it can freeze in winter and become as hard as concrete.
- Ensure that all hard surfaces are nonabrasive.
- Select ground surfacing so that heat-collecting materials, such as asphalt and concrete, do not receive direct mid-day sunlight in hot weather. In very hot areas, even sand can become overheated.
- Do not double-function sand play and sand as a surface under active areas. Use boundaries to clearly separate these functions, possibly supplemented by putting wood chips over sand in active areas.
- Where sand cannot be utilized in certain intensive-use areas, pea-gravel may be a good substitute. Note that gravel other than pea-gravel may have sharp edges and is unsuitable for most play areas.
- Wood chips are excellent for high-impact areas and have a pleasant scent, but they crumble with use and require periodic replacement.
- Plain earth mixed with proper amounts of clay, sand, and silt makes an excellent surface for some activity areas and is more resilient than asphalt. Dirt is not appropriate material under active equipment, such as swings, since it can become extremely compacted and hard.
- Use grass in low-traffic areas but not under active equipment. Grass inevitably suffers from wear and tear and must be periodically renewed or relaid.
- As hard surfacing for wheeled toys and bicycles, asphalt is softer and preferable to concrete. Never use hard surfacing materials under equipment of any height.

Adventure and Creative Play

> A castle, made of cartons, rocks, and old branches, by a group of children for themselves, is worth a thousand perfectly detailed, exactly finished castles, made for them in a factory.[5]

The "creative" playground, an alternative to the traditional or adventure playground, is gaining increasing

Table 20. 1 ***Critical Fall Heights (in Feet) for Surfacing Materials Under and Around Play Equipment*** [6]

Material	Uncompressed Depth 6″	9″	12″	Compressed Depth 9″
Wood Mulch				
Double	7	10	11	10
Shredded	6	10	11	7
Bark Mulch				
Uniform Wood Chips	6	7	>12	6
Fine Sand	5	5	9	5
Coarse Sand	5	5	6	4
Fine Gravel	6	7	10	6
Medium Gravel	5	5	6	5

popularity with older preschoolers and school-age children. Creative playgrounds are constructed primarily from scrounged materials such as tires, lumber, telephone poles, railroad ties, cable spools, and scrap pipe. The construction often incorporates existing or purchased commercial equipment. Such a playground can include permanent equipment, sand and water play, an array of loose parts to accommodate all forms of play, and areas for art, gardening, and caring for animals.

An "adventure" playground, where children actively participate in the playground's construction, is especially suited to children over 5 years. Children are given tools for digging and gardening and loose parts for building structures. In the process, they are motivated to explore the playground environment and exercise their imaginations. Fire in barrels or in the form of well-contained bonfires can be provided to teach children how to use and control one of the four basic elements. This experience can serve as an excellent antidote to the sedentary, potentially enervating hours spent indoors.

Water Play

For children, nothing compares to the joy, fascination, and versatility of playing with water! Make opportunities for outdoor water play varied and expansive, with the water itself taking many forms: natural ponds, wading pools, fountains, hillside water slides, sprinklers, troughs of at varying heights with water "dropping" from one to another, and raised tables of water for children in wheelchairs or adaptive devices. Experiences with water include splashing, floating objects, streaming, and damming; they can be extended by the use of nozzles, faucets, valves, hoses, pumps, and brushes. Plan so that water play and sand play have appropriate points of connection as well as separation.

GUIDELINES FOR WATER PLAY

- Wading areas, especially combined with fountains, can occupy children indefinitely during warm weather.
- Use sprinklers and water slides as substitutes where standing bodies of water are a concern.
- Treat natural bodies of water respectfully by preserving the land along their edges for recreational and riparian use.
- Provide some running water. It fascinates children who use it to float sticks or boats and to stir up mud.
- Collect rain water in large barrels. Use chains for downspouts so children can closely observe water running off a roof.
- Avoid swimming pools with hard, abrupt edges. It has been shown that children teach themselves to swim when playing around pools that deepen gradually. Abrupt edges also impinge upon the peaceful, calming nature of water.[7]
- Water should be no deeper than 8 inches. Provide constant supervision wherever there is standing water, as children can drown in only a few inches of water. Be sure that standing water has no sudden changes in depth.
- Provide a concrete wall, wooden fence, or a side of the building on which children can "paint" with water.
- Plan storage for water play equipment next to the water play area. An outdoor drinking fountain, with a path for water to flow down steps or height changes, can be very exciting.
- Shallow dishlike depressions in the dirt or pavement, with drips and slight run-off channels, can provide puddles for play or for floating objects. Make sure the water does not become stagnant.
- Design surfaces near water play areas to minimize slipping.

Sand Play

Like water, sand play is an essential element of any play yard and can include a range of possibilities: sandboxes, raised troughs (especially for children in wheelchairs), and 1–6 tons of sand in a mound that children can climb upon and shape. A huge mound of sand is relatively inexpensive and can provide children with endless hours of activity.

GUIDELINES FOR SAND PLAY

- Locate sand play areas with maximum exposure to sunlight, because the sun effectively sterilizes sand, and because sedentary children can become chilled while playing with sand in cool weather. During hot summer months, however, the area may require a tent or awning to provide some shade.
- Ensure that sand areas have proper drainage and are protected from strong winds.
- Separate areas for sand play from those where sand is used as a landing surface for slides and other equipment.
- Contain small and large sand play areas with a barrier such as a tree stump wall or railroad ties. Concrete is not recommended as it is abrasive, and may prevent proper drainage. Children often use retaining walls as playing surfaces and as back supports—especially those who need assistance sitting. To keep sand within the area, design the retaining wall to include horizontal surfaces for sand play. Small, low tables within the sand play area are also desirable.
- Provide nearby storage for shovels, rakes, buckets, and toys; if possible, store equipment inside the sand play tables.
- Enhance sand play by locating it near elevated structures equipped with pulleys and buckets for hauling the sand up dumping and mixing it.
- Ropes suspended over large mounds of sand and dirt can provide older children with opportunities for swinging, jumping, or climbing.

Rocks, Boulders, Dirt, and Mud

A cluster of boulders and rocks (preexisting or brought to the site) makes a superb climbing and exploration zone. Mounds of dirt offer good, cost-effective environments for climbing and mud play, which is as creative and instructive as sand play (although mud on children's clothing may be a concern). Like sand, dirt requires periodic watering to keep it from being dusty, and regular inspection for glass, animal feces, or other debris. Other provisions for dirt and mud play are similar to those for sand play (see above).

Dramatic/Fantasy Play

As previously noted, dramatic or fantasy play is a favorite activity of preschool and school-age children. A variety of spaces (both specific and ambiguous) and props—a suitable site for a "playhouse," a steering wheel mounted on a post—for this type of play can be provided throughout the play yard. In a "creative" playground, where there is a varied landscape, as well as access to sand, water, and building materials, the potential for fantasy play is unlimited.

Develop one area as a stage for drama before an audience, at child scale. Private stages can be located behind bushes and under play structures. Allocate locked storage for costumes and props.

GUIDELINES FOR ENCOURAGING DRAMATIC/FANTASY PLAY

- Promote spontaneous fantasy play by providing, for 2–4 children, spaces that are within view but protected from direct scrutiny.
- Stimulate children's imagination by providing spaces that can be closed off or opened wide by sliding panels.
- Provide areas, props, costumes, and architectural stage elements that are ambiguous—i.e., not designed for explicit purposes—so that children can use them more creatively.

Gardens, Composting, and Vermiculture

On every play yard, and *at every age level,* set aside some territory as a flower or vegetable garden where children can grow and tend living plants. In urban areas, where experiences with nature are severely limited, a small garden can vitally enhance a child's sense of relationship to the earth. If necessary, the garden can consist of raised beds with soil imported from elsewhere. "Garbage gardens," consisting of seeds brought from food eaten at home, offer an exciting way to communicate life-cycle processes to small children, who generally take much pride and interest in nurturing tender seedlings.

At the other end of the life cycle is the proper disposal of organic matter, so that it can ultimately nourish new matter. Compost piles are easy to create and care for. They generally do not attract insects or varmints if enclosed in a wooden box or encircled with chicken wire and kept covered with leaves or yard cuttings.

Children can dispose of scraps from their meals and snacks and, over time, watch these scraps turn into soil.

An excellent companion to a compost pile is a

worm box, which provides "vermiculture" composting. By mixing in worms for decomposition and fertilization, garbage quickly turns into nutrient-rich soil. The redworm used in vermiculture composting eats its weight in discarded produce daily and can be enjoyed by children as a pet. By watching food scraps rapidly convert to clean-smelling, finely textured worm "poop," children learn a valuable lesson about the cycle of soil formation. Worm boxes can be easily built or purchased in various sizes.

GUIDELINES FOR GARDENING, COMPOSTING, AND VERMICULTURE

- Locate compost piles, which require periodic watering and turning, on the perimeter of a yard.
- Place worm boxes anywhere they are sheltered from intense heat and rain
- Somewhere within the garden, create a private, sunny enclosure with comfortable seating where one or two children can get a feeling of tranquillity
- Surrounding gardens by walls helps to create a peaceful haven from noisy traffic. The smaller the garden, the more firm its boundaries must be: walls, fences, hedges, or the building itself.
- Provide edible landscaping: berry bushes, herb gardens, fruit tree orchards.
- Consider adding a small greenhouse to grow flowers and vegetables year round.
- Allow the garden to have a quality of wildness, where plants grow as they do in nature: mixtures of plants with no barriers between them, no bare earth, and irregular boundaries. Edge the garden with stone, brick, and/or wood that can blend in naturally with the surrounding growth.

Birds, Butterflies, and Animals

Opportunities to care for birds, butterflies, and animals help children learn not to mistreat them—even unintentionally. Animals housed outdoors can be larger than animals housed indoors and are generally easier to care for. Possibilities include: ducks, birds (no parrots), rabbits, pigs, cows, ponies and horses, bees, chickens, geese, cats, dogs, goats, and lambs. (The allergies of individual children need to be considered in the choice of animals).

Every center's landscape plan ideally includes plant species or areas that attract local birds, butterflies, and wildlife (harmless ants, insects, and snakes) that children can observe in their natural habitat.

GUIDELINES FOR BIRDS, BUTTERFLIES, AND ANIMALS

- Keep in mind that animals can help "domesticate" children, so that they relate better to other human beings. Goats and rabbits have been successfully used as creatures of contact for disturbed children who cannot relate to people.
- Consider many types of bird feeders, both near the building (where they can be viewed close-up from inside) and out in the yard, to attract different varieties.
- Immunize animals for human-transmittable diseases and keep them in good health. Children require supervision in their proper care and litter areas need to be kept clean.
- Sweet-smelling flowers, herbs, grasses, and vines attract butterflies. Unlike butterflies, bees will not gravitate to flowers with wide and deep trumpets, such as honeysuckle or jasmine.

Quiet Play and Private Places

Every outdoor space calls for one or more spots for quiet play, often involving cognitive and manipulative materials such as books, small constructions, and toys. Design these areas as small enclosures (3–6 feet across), with a single means of access, for about 1–3 children. Inside, provide a dry sitting place (at ground level or easily accessed), convenient storage, and calming elements (greenery, shade). Ideally, only quiet-activity areas would be nearby. Low boundaries can help to make the space feel more secluded. Also provide a few private places that are easily "owned" by a single child.

Arts and Crafts Area

Where possible, include an outdoor arts and crafts area, preferably near an indoor space for ease of access. This space will require shelter, storage, water, and separation from circulation and high-activity zones.

GUIDELINES FOR ARTS AND CRAFTS AREA

- Include both horizontal and vertical work surfaces for drawing, painting, and construction.
- Nearby storage should include supplies, drying racks, and shelves for works-in-progress.

- Provide some display space for 2- and 3-dimensional work.
- Use floor and wall surfaces that are impervious to paint and clay.
- Offer protection from wind and strong sun.

Seating

Provide generous seating, scattered throughout the play area (including critical play zones) for adult supervision and for general observational participation. In addition to seats in the open, try to include child-friendly benches, logs, low walls, planter perimeters, elevated areas, and seats under trellises and roofs.

GUIDELINES FOR SEATING

- Provide seats for private reflection as well as seats for gathering in a group. Make both kinds of seating available in sunny and shaded locations.
- Arrange all seats so they face an activity or a view.
- Shield all seats from strong winds by their location, construction, or by a nearby barrier.
- Consider providing low sitting walls (16 inches high and at least 12 inches deep) as subtle boundaries between spaces

Recreation for Older Children and Adults

The outdoor spaces of a center can be designed to offer opportunities for rest, relaxation and activity to a wider audience—parents, older children, and the community. The more the community at large can utilize the day care facilities, the more it will value and support them. Within, or adjacent to, the outdoor day care space, consider offering outdoor recreational opportunities for older children and adults: walking, jogging, or biking trails; swimming or skating facilities; a specially-designed exercise course; a volleyball or basketball court.

Notes

[1](1964, pg. 328)

[2]Cohen et al (1979)

see Olds (1980)

[3]PLAE (1987, p. 66, *Consumer's Handbook for Public Safety*

[4]APHA/AAP [APA, 366-7]

[5]Pattern Language, p. 368.

[6]APHA/AAP(p.362) HPPS p. 21, *Playground Surfacing Technical Information Guide,* by the Consumer Product Safety Commission, Washington, D.C.

[7]A Pattern Language, p. 360–361.

CHAPTER TWENTY-ONE

CHILD CARE CENTERS OF THE FUTURE

All things change when we do.

—HOKOSAI

A Building Type in Search of a Model

It is indeed daunting to conceive of the ideal setting in which to raise future generations! Yet that is the challenge before us as children are being raised increasingly in organized facilities outside the home. The nature and design of these settings can no longer be left to happenstance. Rather, this is a societal issue requiring immediate attention. Child care centers are a new building type in search of models that not only provide for children's basic needs but that also honor them as the miracles they are by nurturing their spirits during the most formative and vulnerable period of their lives.

This final chapter presents one model for this new building type—the residential core concept posited in Chapter 4—using examples from two recently completed centers whose architecture and interiors significantly depart from customary child care design. After considering the advantages of this model for the total well-being of children, parents, and staff, you are encouraged to envision and create design models that reflect your own highest goals for children.

The Residential Core Model

Starting in 1994, the author had the opportunity to create two child care centers—one in Canada and one in New Zealand—using a concept envisioned some 20 years previously: to create a truly *homelike* environment for young children who spend 8–10 hours a day in a child care setting.

The essence of the model is to give a large facility an intimate presence by breaking down the center into small "houses," each of which features a "residential core." The residential core consists of a living room, dining room, and kitchen (servery) around which are located three age-appropriate rooms for infants, toddlers, and preschoolers, as shown in Figure 21.1.

The advantages of this model are many. In being able to freely use and move across the residential core, children have a "home away from home" throughout the day. Those who arrive early or leave late can relax in the living room, have a snack in the dining area, or engage in a cooking project in the kitchen without needing to be in their group rooms. Those who prefer not to nap can come into the core to play quietly while others sleep. Siblings can be near one another, and a parent who comes to visit or share lunch can comfortably see all the family's enrolled children at one time.

In the course of using this common area, children of all ages, and the staff of the three rooms, come to know one another easily and informally. Children need only relocate three times from infancy through kindergarten. If not accompanied by their current teacher, children still have prior familiarity with the new teacher and room, and proximity to the former teacher and room. No child has to relate to more than 30–39 others. Most importantly, there is space for the occupants of each house—children, staff, and parents—to physically come together as a family and a community.

The descriptions and photographs that follow provide a detailed account of the design as it was rendered in one large building (Canada) and as separate structures (New Zealand).

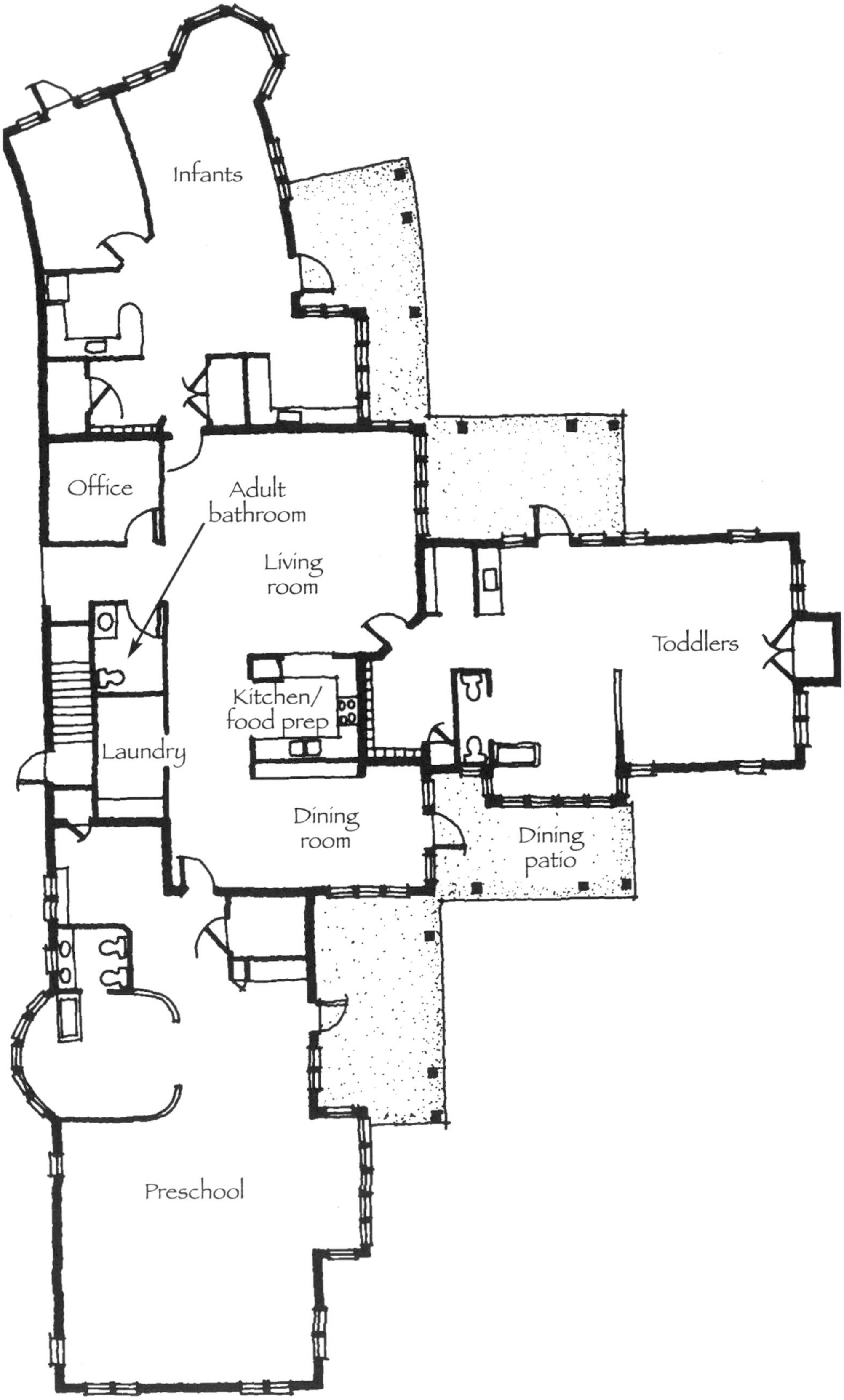

Figure 21.1
One "house" consists of a living room, dining room, kitchen/servery residential core, surrounded by an infant, a toddler, and a preschool room.

The Husky Child Development Center—The Copper House

The Canadian facility is located on the grounds of Husky Injection Molding Systems, Ltd., accommodating the children of 1,200 employees at the home facility in Bolton, Ontario, (approximately 45 minutes from downtown Toronto). Husky creates the machines and molds for many of the plastic objects in our lives: water/soda bottles, CD/audio tape cases, and containers of many kinds. The 50-acre Bolton site—formerly gently rolling pasture land—combines industrial manufacturing facilities, office headquarters, employee services, and an existing wetlands. In 1994, eight acres remained to be developed into a child care center, a wellness center, and ground-level parking.

Anita Olds and Associates initially conceived of the center as three separate houses sharing one administrative complex, plus an area for school-age children, as shown in Figure 21.2. However, as the design evolved, all the elements were placed under one roof incorporating only two houses, as in Figure 21.3, while allowing for future expansion to a third house, an atelier, and a gymnasium.

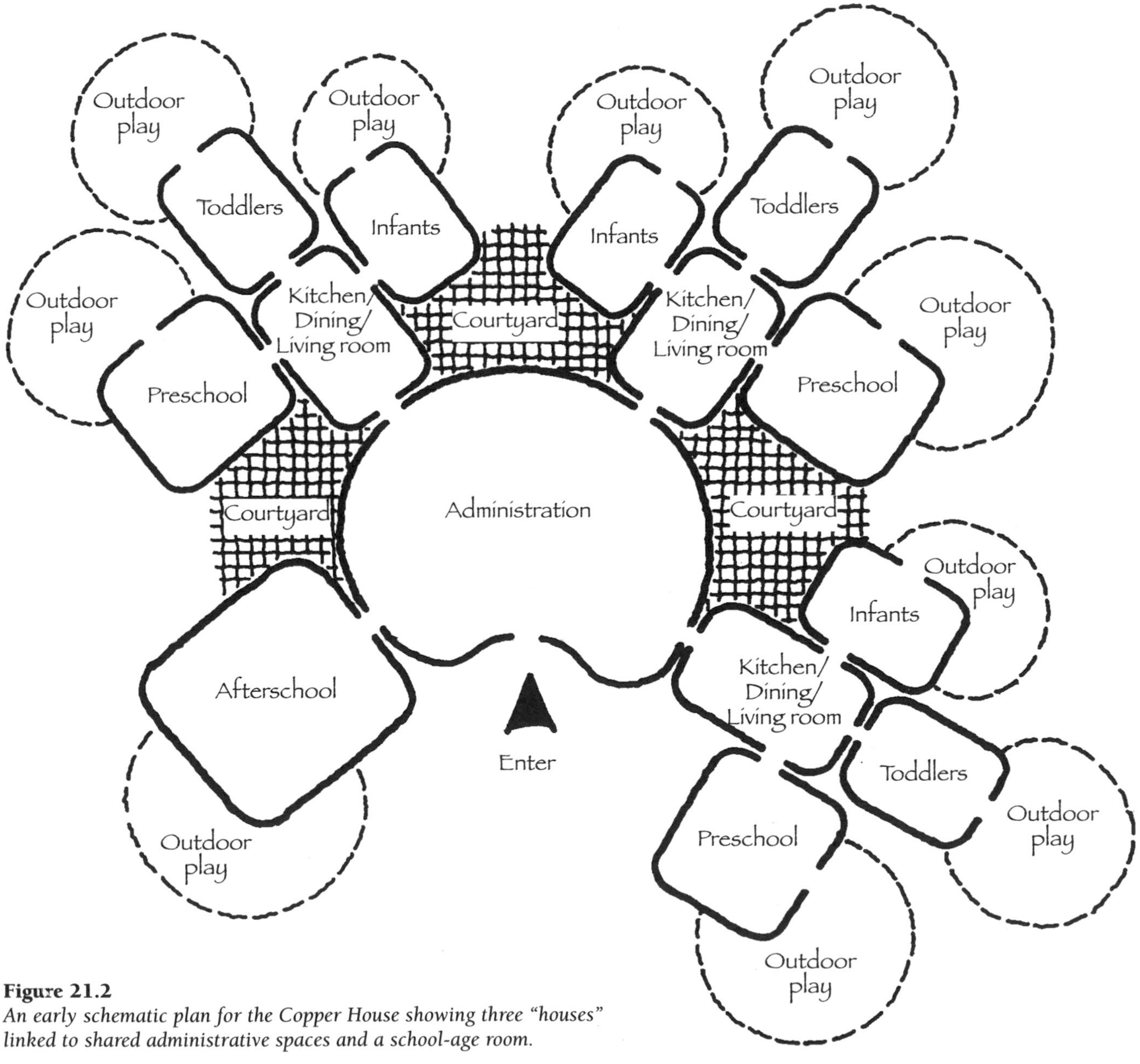

Figure 21.2
An early schematic plan for the Copper House showing three "houses" linked to shared administrative spaces and a school-age room.

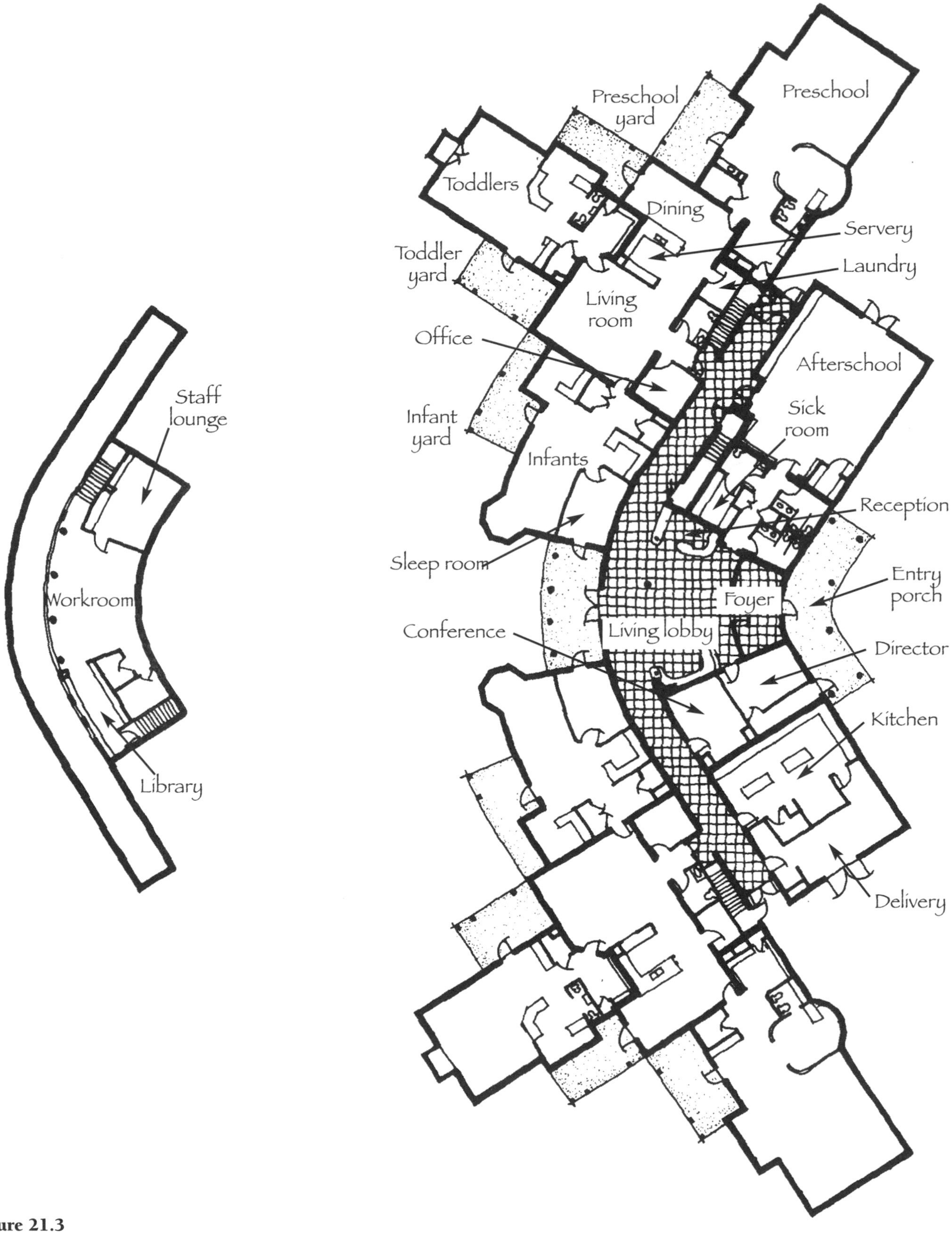

Figure 21.3
The plan of the Copper House as built.

BOX 21.1

Husky Child Development Center Specifics

Total Building Size: 15,800 sq ft — Each House Approximately 4,000 sq ft

Function	Interior	Porch	Play Yard
Infants (6/room)	900 sq ft/room	160 sq ft	1,800 sq ft
Toddlers (9/room)	810 sq ft/room	190 sq ft	4,400 sq ft
Preschoolers (16/room)	1,180 sq ft/room	195 sq ft	5,632 sq ft
Residential Core	1,000 sq ft/house	195 sq ft (Dining Patio)	
School-Age (20/room)	1,080 sq ft		2,200 sq ft
Staff Support Areas	1,000 sq ft		
Admin, Public, Circulation	3,300 sq ft		
Walls, mech/elec	1,700 sq ft		

We began by developing the concept and layout for one house and its residential core.[1] This primarily involved determining preliminary size and configuration of the core and group rooms so that the rooms could circle the core yet permit some natural light to enter it. Each group room was oriented to face south for maximum sunlight exposure, and to have its own exit to a south-facing covered porch and play yard.

Subsequently, Barbara Winslow, of Jacobson Silverstein Winslow/Degenhardt Architects (JSW/D), working with Anita Olds, was engaged to serve as Design Architect for the facility. The task included conceptual site and landscape planning to capitalize on views and screening offered by the wetlands area, the architectural design of a 16,000-square-foot facility with a phased development plan, and the selection/design of all interior finishes, fixtures, and furniture in collaboration with Carla Mathis, a color and interior style specialist.[2]

The Center uses passive solar design, a geothermal heat sink, and radiant heat floors for ecological soundness and maximum comfort. Large, low windows maintain a close indoor/outdoor relationship, filling the building with natural light. Natural materials were selected throughout. The copper roof (the choice of Husky's president and not specified by the design) gives the building its name. Wood is evident in the window frames and doors, the ceilings over the wet play bays, external and internal tree trunk columns, furnishings, and the reception desk, fireplace mantle, and benches.

The group rooms for infants, toddlers, preschoolers, and school-age children are depicted in photographs accompanying their floor plans in Chapters 16, 17, and 18, respectively. Other photos of the center used elsewhere in this guide are listed at the end of this chapter. As can be noted from studying these images and plans, the four zones in each group room (entry, messy, active, and quiet) were given architectural definition by varying ceiling heights, lighting, floor textures (ceramic tile, linoleum, carpet) and furnishings. Within the zones are numerous activity areas, many supported by the use of custom-designed equipment and furniture: risers, reading lofts, six-to-eight foot easels, built-in water-play tables, manipulative platforms, and dramatic-play climbers. Each room has a tiled, sun-filled "wet-play bay" to encourage the free exploration of messy materials, and a door leading directly to its own outdoor glass-covered porch and south-facing play yard (see Chapter 20).

Box 21.1 provides basic square footage information about the center, particularly its public spaces and residential core, which have not been discussed elsewhere.

The Presence of Curves

Because curves suggest nurturance and the feminine, a conscious attempt was made to incorporate curved

A view, from behind the fireplace (right), of the curved corridor linking the two houses. The south entrance is visible at left.

walls and forms into the architectural design. The curved central circulation spine linking the two houses with the lobby, administrative core, main kitchen, conference, and school-age rooms, creates a "visual hug." It gives the building a gracious "bend," resulting in an embracing concave entry with curved paths leading up to it on either side (see pages 87–88), and a houselike front porch supported by tree trunk columns (see pages 85 and 106). The spine also opens onto a fan-shaped courtyard on the opposite side, which is the pedestrian south entry, overlooking the wetlands and two ponds. Walking paths allow parents to easily access this entry from Husky's nearby corporate facility.

Curved walls also enclose the staff area upstairs, and an "eyebrow window" introduces a curve into the roof as well. Curved forms in the lobby banquette and reception desk; the infant room walls and octagon; many items of furniture; and the walls, windows, and ceiling of the preschool wet play bay (see pages 370–371) further expand the curvilinear effect.

The Experience of Entry

Either entrance—easily monitored by the receptionist—places families and visitors inside a welcoming, living room lobby complete with operative gas-fired fireplace, soft seating, and ethnic rugs and handcrafts. The lobby was designed to create a space inside the entries that would immediately put children and parents at ease, making the center understandable,

The light -filled south entrance at the end of the walking path, flanked by the octagon bays of the infant rooms.

A view of the Copper House from the factory side showing the two ponds. Parents can walk the path to reach the center from their offices.

A view of the front door and yard, showing the eyebrow window and curved roof of the partial second story.

The living room lobby of the Copper House.

intimate, and inviting. Because the Toronto area is a melting pot of many cultures, we wished to display the crafts, furnishings, and accessories of different ethnic groups without highlighting any single one. Important, as well, was the presence of handmade items and finishes as a contrast to the predominantly machine-made world in which most of today's children live. Thus, the banquette and fireplace, reminiscent of the American Southwest or the Middle East, are decorated with artifacts and pillows from Africa, Mexico, Turkey, Iran, India, Canada, and the United States, to name a few.

At the back of the banquette seating, and at the base of the reception desk, there is a decorative, highly

Low, lighted niches holding ethnic crafts children can touch.

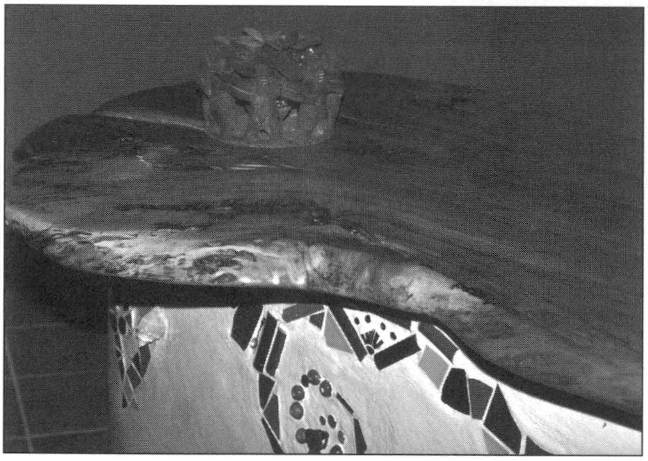

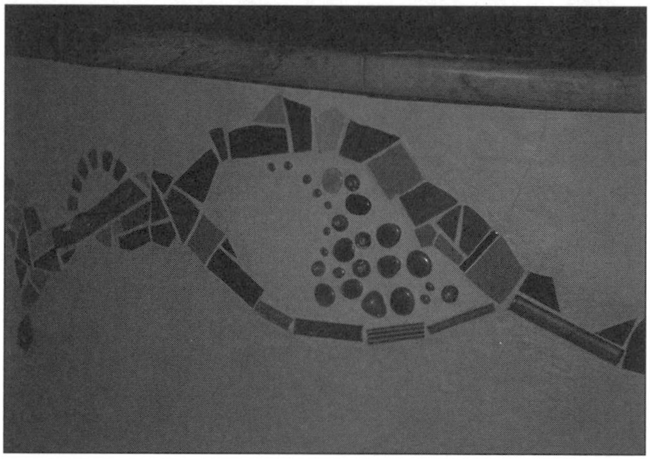

A polished tree burl forms the reception desk top; tactile elements embellish the surface below.

tactile border that we created with found objects and randomly broken bathroom tiles purchased on sale (see also page 98). Low, lighted niches behind the banquette, behind the fireplace, and down the corridor hold intriguing objects and ethnic crafts that children can touch and someday replace with creations of their own (see page 248). The tactile reception desk top, fireplace mantle, and benches in the vestibule, are made of polished tree burls.[3]

The director's office, immediately off the vestibule and lobby (see page 398) has older furniture, mixed with wicker seats for parents, and a small table and seat for a child. A sick bay rests in an alcove just beyond the receptionist's desk where an ill child can be easily monitored while waiting to be picked up. The area includes drawers for storing linens and blankets and a high-intensity gooseneck lamp to assist in close examination of a child (see page 399). The adjacent handicap-accessible bathroom for public use, softened by artwork, a wood cabinet, a throw rug, and soft colors and lighting, is available to an ill child as well. After greeting the receptionist, school-age children can reach their room and bathrooms via a corridor immediately off the lobby area.

Tree trunk columns extending through the second story mark the change in ceiling height from 10 feet in the lobby to 23 feet in the corridor. The sick bay is visible in the alcove beyond the reception desk.

A pleasant sitting area opposite wall niches displaying intriguing objects, marks the approach to the entrance of one house (left), the staircase to the second floor (right), and the school-age room (far right).

Corridors to Support Community

Passing through the lobby with its 10-foot-high ceiling, one enters the curved circulation spine whose height rises to 23 feet. The tree trunk columns found at the front porch are reiterated at the lobby/corridor boundary, rising through the ceiling to the staff area on the second floor. Advantage was taken of the space under the staircase to store large buggies used for transporting infants and toddlers (see page 310). As one traverses the corridor approaching House #1, it is possible to stop and rest on an old bench, surrounded by plants and an area rug, to look at the ethnic musical instruments, masks, and other objects in the niches on the staircase wall. Colorful, diaphanous banners decorated with jugglers, children, and animals,[4] help to lower the high ceiling and mark the entry to the house, the secondary school-age entrance, and the staircase to the partial second story.

Respite and Support for Staff

The upstairs floor houses the staff work and rest areas. It looks down onto the circulation spine and banners and out across the ponds to the Husky factory beyond. An enclosed staff lounge includes a couch and comfortable seating, a kitchenette, and an area for dining. (See page 400.) The large, open central work space can be variously configured for conferences, computers, and workstations of many sorts. It includes a separate bay housing curriculum resources and a library, as well

Some objects in the niches.

The restroom for adults in one "house."

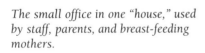

The small office in one "house," used by staff, parents, and breast-feeding mothers.

as a staff bathroom complete with a tiled sit-down shower. (See page 401.)

The Residential Core

Coming back downstairs, the entrance to House #1 is straight ahead. Once through its door, there is an adult toilet on the right, and a small office on the left. The office contains a love seat, side chairs, a desk, and a telephone. It is used by staff seeking a few moments of privacy, for parent-teacher conferences out of earshot of children, and by nursing mothers wishing some solitude.

Immediately ahead is the house living room. Similar to a living room at home, it is replete with soft couches, a large area rug, wood floors, bookcases, armoires, and even a window seat with storage underneath (see page 199)—in this case overlooking one of the play yards. Pillows in many different sizes make it possible to cozy up, to build forts, and even to have pillow fights. In addition to its use by children at all times of day, parents often linger to chat in the living room after dropping their children off, or before picking them up. Some use the area simply for a few moments of rest and retreat.

To the right of the living room is the servery and dining area. The servery is actually a complete residential-sized kitchen to which food is brought from the main kitchen to be reheated and served. It is also the place for preparing snacks and for doing cooking projects with the children. It includes a low counter at which they can work, or on which bowls of food can be placed for self-service. The dishwasher makes it possible to sterilize bottles, dishes, and infant/toddler toys. The dining area, which is used by the toddler and preschool groups in shifts, includes seating for 18–25, two window seats, and a door leading to a patio for eating outside in fine

The living room of one "house."

Views of the servery both inside. . . and outside.

weather. It also includes a low hutch where dishes, table linen, and flatware are accessible to the children helping to set the tables (see page 350).

The preschool room is located right off the dining area—the toddler and infant rooms right off the living room. This arrangement was intentional to enable the youngest children to access the living room most easily and the preschoolers to extend their projects into the dining room when desired. A laundry room, opposite the servery, allows staff to do the laundry and fold it with the children's help—informally, as one might at home—while sitting in the living room listening to stories or music.

Unique Features of the Center's Interior

A unique aspect of the center's design, contributing heavily to its residential feel, is the way in which all colors, furnishings, textiles, and accessories are employed to create an interior that nourishes the senses and the soul. Every item in the center—from crib bumpers and dishware, to planters, waste baskets, and artwork—was intentionally selected to create a harmonious, fully integrated interior, similar to the way one would furnish and decorate a home. Antique, second-hand, and new furniture; handwoven rugs; ethnic art; an abundance of pillows; natural fabrics on cushions, benches, waterbeds, and table linens; and soft color palettes were chosen to contribute to children's and adults' sense of well-being and safety. Posters, even those costing as little as one dollar, are matted and framed; artwork for children is mounted on boxes coated with a washable surface. (See page 381.)

After the center opened and all the furniture was in place, a number of days were spent "dressing the building." Each space was studied for decorative touches—artwork, vases, pillows, knick-knacks, accessories—that would help to make it balanced and complete. Items were purchased, hung, placed on shelves and surfaces, arranged and rearranged to make each room feel fully cared for and lived-in.

The Outdoor Play Yards

The outdoor play areas capitalize on views and screening offered by the wetlands. They include glass-covered porches at least ten feet deep; varied surfaces and changes in level; spray pools children can operate, with earth and sand to mix nearby; slides that extend down the hillside; an edible landscape of flowering trees and bushes attractive to birds, frogs, and butterflies; a castle on a mound; a steep hill for tobogganing in winter; and an organic garden complete with raised beds and its own tool shed. (See Chapter 20).

The Budget

Although the budget for this center was more generous than most, the center looks lavish less because of the money spent than because of the integrated nature of its interior design—and because of the extra care and effort of all parties involved. The total building cost, including raising the site by one meter (to clear the water table), the geothermal heat sink (an initially costly procedure involving multiple small rods dug deep into the ground to bring heat up from the earth's interior that is then available free), the building shell, the copper roof, roads, parking, grading, landscaping, four play yards, interior fixtures and finishes, commercial and custom furniture, and curriculum materials was approximately $3.5 million (U.S.).

New Generation Learning Centre

After studying the plans for *The Copper House*, Bruce and Shona Davison, owners/managers of *New Generation Children's Learning Centres,* in Papakura, New Zealand, hired Anita Olds and Associates and Murray Silverstein of JSW/D Architects to assist in the development of plans for a 1.5-acre site in South Auckland.[5] The flat site, formerly used for raising race horses, is bordered on one side by railroad tracks, on another by market gardens, and on a third by a minor city street. At the rear of the site, an existing house, which will eventually be torn down and replaced, currently serves as a child care center for 25 children.

The Davisons' design specifications were as follows:

- The site would consist of four buildings: three separate child care "houses," plus an additional facility for administration, resources, and staff training.
- Each child care house would consist of one room each for infants, toddlers, and preschool children. The children's rooms would be spaced around a residential core consisting of a living room, dining room, and kitchen to create a warm, friendly, family-centered environment.

One view of the New Generation Learning Centre.

Dining outdoors.

- Each of the children's rooms would have access to its own play yard.
- The design and construction would be on a cost-sustainable basis so the design could be replicated in any other location if/when required.
- The design, finishing, and landscaping would honor children's inherent affinity with the natural environment.[6]

The New Generation Centre is shown here, and a plan of the play yard is on the next page (Figure 21.4).

After investigating various alternatives, an "L"-shaped building configuration was chosen, with one wing shared by infants and toddlers, and the other wing used by preschoolers. The apex incorporates the entrance and the residential core. The compact floor plan optimizes ability to place multiple buildings onto a site with inherent space and shape limitations (see site plan on page 64 and building plan on page 128). The design also provides good connections between the three groups of children, and a superb courtyard for outdoor dining—well utilized in this temperate climate.

Box 21.2 provides basic information about the building's square footage.

Indoor versus Outdoor Space

The group rooms in this center are smaller than those of the Copper House, while the outdoor porches and play yards are considerably larger. This is because the temperate New Zealand climate enables children to be outdoors most of the year. In keeping with the visualizations described in Chapter 2, the Davisons chose to place a high priority on development of the natural terrain and on its use by children all year long and during most hours of the day. Bruce Davison has been designing the play yards himself, including a large aviary between the toddler and preschool yards. Eventually,

Figure 21.4
The building plan, courtyard, and play yards of the New Generation Learning Centre.

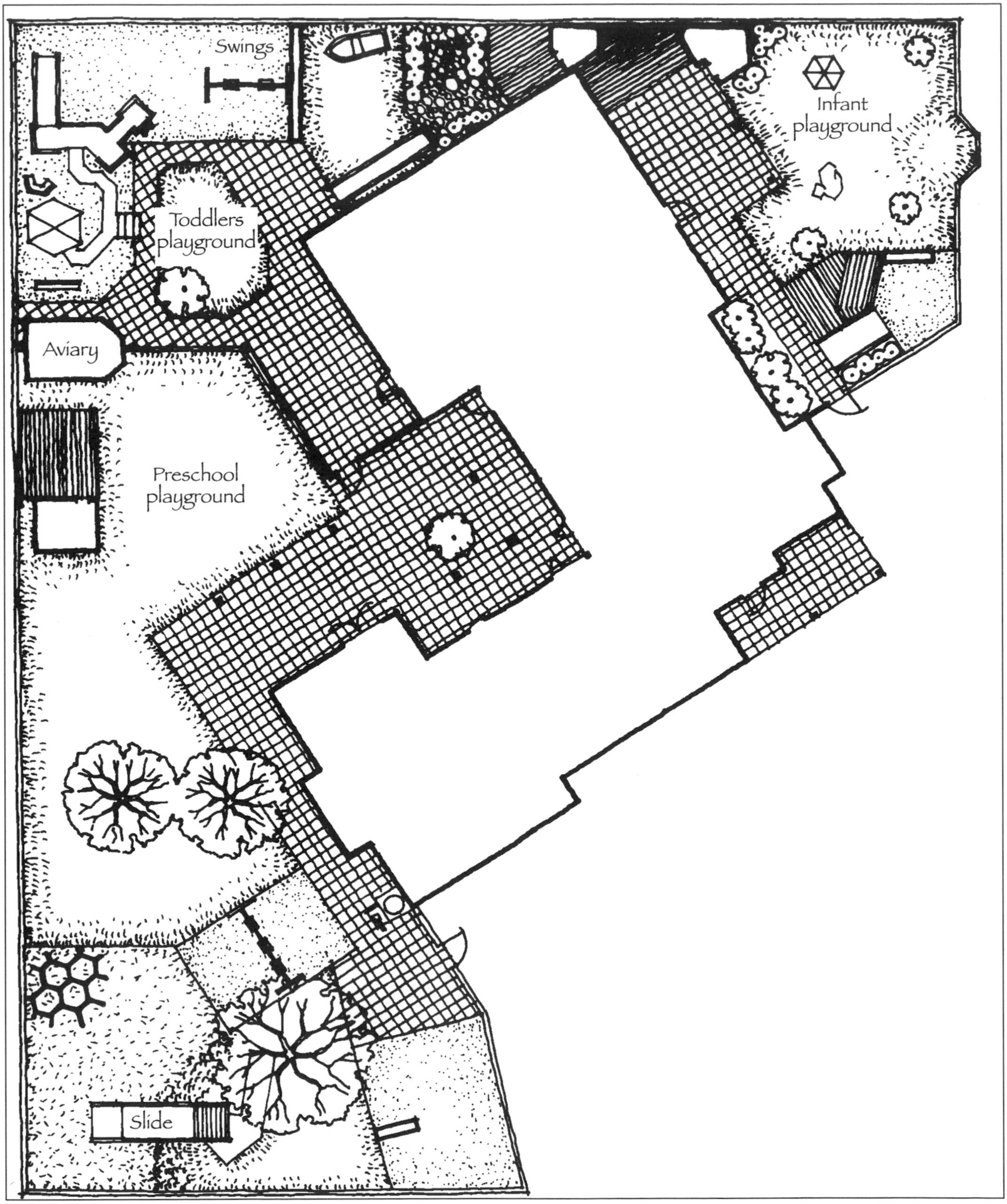

BOX 21.2

New Generation Learning Centre Specifics

Each House: 3,430 sq ft, housing 40 children

Function	**Interior**	**Porch**	**Play Yard**
Infants (8/room)	458 sq ft/room	364 sq ft	2,345 sq ft
Toddlers (12/room)	550 sq ft/room	364 sq ft	3,700 sq ft
Preschoolers (20/room)	950 sq ft/room	266 sq ft	11,200 sq ft
Residential Core	580 sq ft/house	287 sq ft (Dining Patio)	
Staff Support Areas	118 sq ft		
Admin, Public, Circulation	460 sq ft		
Walls, mech/elec	315 sq ft		

An aviary sits between the toddler and preschool play yards.

the entry will be flanked by a waterfall, stream, and small forest, along with exclusive use of native plants (to teach children local ecology). The entry porch, filled with potted plantings, includes a large alcove where strollers, car seats, and buggies can be stored.

Unique Interior Features

A unique feature of this center is a small fountain resting in the alcove just outside the infant and toddler rooms. The fountain is visible straight on from the building's front door and from the living room as well. This sonorous, interactive rock waterfall is a favorite attraction for the young ones! An additional feature is the preschool wet room. Similar to the one illustrated in Chapter 17, this 5-x-6-foot glass-enclosed space can be used for water play and extremely messy activities. Both the wet room and the preschool group's bathroom face their courtyard. The two rooms can be accessed from the play yard by a door to the exterior, which sits between them.

The entry to the center.

This fountain greets infants and toddlers as they approach their rooms.

The living room in this center includes a wood-burning fireplace, surrounded by a wooden gate. It is especially enjoyed on gray, rainy days—plentiful during New Zealand winters! The toddlers and preschoolers eat indoors or outside in two shifts, and a protected corner of the dining area is used by older infants as they get ready to graduate to the toddler room. The infant and toddler rooms share a diapering/toileting area which, by New Zealand licensing regulations, must be in a separate enclosed room with visibility panels. The infant sleep area is small because stacked cribs are permitted and preferred. In keeping with the residential feel of the center, the staff make a point of providing coffee, tea, and muffins in the kitchen at the start and end of each day, so parents will be nourished and encouraged to linger a while.

Anecdotal Responses to the Centers

The Copper House opened in October, 1996 and the first New Generations center in May, 1997. Two additional New Generations centers and an Administration/Training building will open in 2000. As of this writing, there has been ample opportunity to verify that the model is a huge success in both settings.

Children at the Husky center seem to show little separation anxiety when first enrolled. This may be attributable both to the homelike design and the fact that it is possible to view the factory from every child's

Eating indoors.

Making a later afternoon snack for parents.

room and indicate where "mommy or daddy is working." Groups of children come to sit around the fire and read stories in the lobby living room in winter. The Christmas tree and large center events take place here also. The residential core is used in all the ways anticipated and more. Barely a day goes by when each child has not spent some time curled up on the couch or playing on the living room rug. The school-age children also use this core as their residential base, thereby rubbing shoulders with the younger children at times. And the ease of moving from one room to another results in much cross-group and multiaged interaction, as evidenced in the photographs.

At the end of the day, all the children remaining at the New Generations Center are to be found hanging out in the living room, sprawled on a couch, playing a game, hugging a large stuffed teddy, or playing with an adult. It is not uncommon to find parents involved

Relaxing in the living room.

with children other than their own. One day, a mother coming to get her daughter sat down at a table in the living room to help another child with a puzzle before going to find her own offspring. Another day, a pregnant mom, due to deliver any moment, stretched out on a chair and fell asleep, while her husband relaxed on the couch in front of her. They had yet to get their son from his group room!

Getting From Here to There

To the author's knowledge, no U.S. child care center incorporates this residential core design or devotes so much space to communal activities.[7] The Husky and New Generation centers were designed to demonstrate that a child care center need not look or feel like an institution, even when it accommodates 100 children. It *is* possible to give children something functional and beautiful, commensurate with their spirits, and uplifting to adults as well. But to get from where child care center design is today to something more developmentally, socially, and emotionally appropriate, we as designers must be willing to change ourselves radically and to engage in a process of healing. In these concluding pages, I will draw upon concepts from three different sources to convey what I mean by these statements.

Mayer Spivak and Archetypal Place

Some years ago, in reflecting on the design of cities to support human endeavor, the environmental psychologist Mayer Spivak identified a minimal set of 13 archetypal place types used by both man and animals for the successful performance of daily life tasks.[8] These place types are behaviorally, psychologically, and culturally driven: They enable a species to live and thrive. The 13 behavioral tasks, for which specific types of places are created across cultures and species, include:

1. Shelter
2. Sleeping
3. Feeding
4. Excreting
5. Grooming
6. Meeting
7. Playing
8. Working
9. Competing
10. Storage
11. Territoriality

12. Routes linking places and leading in/out of the territory
13. Mating

It has occurred to me that aside from #13, Mating, all 12 of these functions need to be supported by places within a child care center in order to fulfill the developmental and social activities that occur there. If we look only at human societies, we may note that the *forms* the archetypal places have taken across the ages, and across cultures, as well as the physical elements within them, have varied dramatically. For example, sleeping can occur in beds, on pallets of straw, on tatami mats and futons, in hammocks, bunk beds, sleeping bags, etc. Places to eat range from fast food joints to fancy restaurants, kitchens, dining rooms, porches, campfires, and squatters' rights on a sidewalk. Appliances for cooking have included fireplaces; wood, gas, and electric-powered stoves; open fires; barbeque pits and charcoal-fired hibachis; clay ovens; and now microwave ovens. And the list goes on.

The first point is that for a child care center to truly support the activities of its occupants (both adult and child), it must provide in some way, shape, or form for the first twelve of these archetypal places. If it does not, it is seriously failing to support basic human needs.

Second, our culture has preferred designs for the types of places that will fulfill these functions. In the case of child care, many of these designs are borrowed from other contexts. For example, cribs are standard items of baby furniture in homes. If we were to be truly ingenious, and truly open to appropriate possibilities, it could well be that cribs might be better replaced by new designs specific to the child care setting—stacked bunks for example, or hammocks, or baskets, or swinging cradles or something as yet unknown. Much of the custom furniture I have designed for child care settings over the years has been in response to a felt need for which no supports were available commercially. A thorough rethinking of the design of spaces and furnishings in child care settings may be needed in order to create supports that are most appropriate to that unique context and set of behavioral activities.

My emphasis here is on opening up possibilities for creativity and change, for creating new models of this new building type. Why does this matter? Are we not doing a good enough job as it is? Not if we consider the unique time and place in history where we stand—a time when our children will spend their formative years growing up in centers.

Mimi Lobell and Spatial Archetypes

In her article entitled "Spatial Archetypes," the architect Mimi Lobell describes six archetypal ways of life, ways of knowing and of being in the world that are "inclusive of all of human civilization from the earliest evolution of our hominid ancestors to the present, including all the different historical periods and cultures that have existed in the world."[9] Each archetype is characterized by a unique social structure; economic base; world view, including attitudes toward time, religious beliefs, and cosmological concepts; and unique spatial organization related to the landscape, territoriality, and architectural forms and structures. The six archetypes are:

1. The sensitive chaos (world of the great spirit, represented by nomadic hunter-gatherers).
2. The great round (world of the goddess, represented by matrilineal clans utilizing predominantly round architectural structures such as kivas and yurts).
3. The four quarters (world of the hero, represented by the patriarchal revolution and by forts, walled cities, and quartered town plans).
4. The pyramid (world of the God-King, represented by pyramidal or octahedral structures resembling the world mountain).
5. The radiant axes (world of the emperor, represented by empires radiating outward from a central point).
6. The grid (world of the technocrat, represented by buildings and streets built according to an orthogonal grid, the dominance of the marketplace, statistics, and technology).

All six archetypes currently exist on earth, as the predominant social, psychological, and spatial organizing principle of one or another living culture. Lobell argues that, similar to stages of development, each archetype is a complete solution unto itself and no one archetype is better than another, although the six are sequential. Once a new archetype has taken hold in a given culture, it is impossible for a society to return to its previous archetype or mode of existence.

The dominant spatial archetype of twentieth century industrialized nations is the grid, as it was for the Roman Empire, the Aztec and Incan empires shortly before the Conquest, and Ptolemaic Egypt to the present. Grid cultures are marked by extreme specialization and fragmentation; an economy based on mass production, trade, and the marketplace; an international commercial and industrial network as the largest cohesive social unit; the movement of peasants to industrial urban centers; the prevalence of systems involving large groups of people organized into manageable, machinelike components; and extreme standardization of products, languages, currency, uniforms, education, housing, etc.

Architecture and town planning reflect the Grid in orthogonal street layouts, rectilinear rooms, modular building facades, uniform building units such as suburban tract houses, office modules, chain stores, and shopping malls. A primary characteristic of the Grid is that, unlike most of the other archetypes, it lacks a center. This may explain why it is currently so difficult for people to create community, to socialize spontaneously, and to come together in groups. The buildings we occupy support separatism, individuality, and isolation, not unity and collaboration.

In her analysis of each archetype, Lobell describes the concepts or forces representing the flowering of each archetype as well as those that lead to its death and decline. In her words: "The Grid represents the end of the sequence: the decline or death phase characterized by mechanization, commercialism, despiritualization, anonymity, and deflation." As in Rome, Egypt, and Cuzco during their respective Grid states, our Grid culture is in a process of dying. Lobell stops here. What will happen subsequently is unknown.

However, at this point my own speculation takes over. If we cannot go backwards, then perhaps a new archetype is actually in the process of formation. As with most evolutionary transformations, it is not possible to see the new manifestation from where we presently sit. One-celled organisms could not have imagined multicelled organisms or those with multiorgans!

Lobell alludes to this in saying that "the Grid represents the existential malaise of the deflated ego, with no centering Self to turn to and no sense of having any power in the world."[10] [However,] "Psychological liberation in the Grid can present great freedom of choice, releasing one from centralized authority and tradition. It can also contribute to the balanced perception that each individual is by turns the Great Spirit, Goddess, Hero, God-King, and Emperor—the archetypes are internalized in each of us; that we each embody the sum total of human experience and wisdom; and that we are individually capable of finding our own paths to illumination."[11]

What if a new, seventh archetype is forming as the Grid is dying? What if we are part of creating that seventh form? What if the children we are raising in child care centers will be the occupants of a new social, psychological, and spatial world view—an entirely different state of consciousness? In that case, how might we best support them for this evolutionary leap?

The Need for Healing

Creating a new building type that truly enables children to thrive, not simply survive, asks that we, as adults, heal our wounded egos and emotions and change our thoughts and beliefs about many things: the nature of childhood, the availability and deployment of resources, the worth of teachers, the needs of parents, the role of the environment, the purpose of design. The wounds and emotional traumas of separatism, uniformity, and marketplace-driven values characteristic of our culture divide us from ourselves and from one another. And, to the extent that these wounds are not healed, we perpetuate them on future generations. *Action follows thought.* We are called upon to change and heal outmoded thoughts, beliefs, and systems—before or at the same time as we strive to heal and improve the lives of our children. But what exactly is meant by "healing" and how might it occur?

Marco DeVries and Five Stages of Healing

A Dutch pathologist, Marco DeVries, defines healing as the body's attempt to reinstate wholeness when confronted with a breach in its integrity.[12] By analogy, one might say that, as a society, we need to heal from the breaches in integrity of our collective psyche.

DeVries describes the healing process as entailing the following five stages:

1. Pain
2. Temporary Repair
3. Destruction
4. Regeneration
5. Reorganization

DeVries explains that *pain* is actually the first stage of healing—the body's immediate response to any perceived breach in its integrity. Then there is usually an attempt on the part of the body or an outside agent to administer *temporary repair*, such as a blood clot or tourniquet to stop bleeding, or a cast to prevent movement. After temporary repair, the next stage of healing is not the repair itself but actually some form of *destruction*. Before the new can emerge, something must first be destroyed: damaged skin cells need to die and be sloughed off, diseased organs need to be removed, belief systems and lifestyles require radical alteration. Just as life's major passages of puberty, marriage, and parenthood are simultaneously the birth of the new and the death of a former way of being, healing demands that something be destroyed in order for something new to emerge. The destruction need not be violent, but it must occur.

Once destruction has taken place, *regeneration* of tissue, the growth of a scar, compensation for loss of an organ, a new way of looking at things, can follow. Normally, after some period of recuperation and regeneration we would say the person is "healed." However, DeVries differs with this viewpoint, arguing that unless there is also a *reorganization* of the person's life to incorporate the wounding, then true healing has not taken place. While hospitals and the medical profession can assist with the first four stages, there are few societally organized resources, aside from religious institutions, providing guidance for stage five. The number of personal growth and self-help books and programs increasingly available are perhaps a step in that direction.

DeVries goes on to say that there are three common ways of intepreting any healing:

1. The Status Quo Model: "I am as good as before."

2. The Deficient Model: "I will never be as good as before."

3. The Transformational Model: "I am bigger and better as a result of this wounding and healing experience."

The transformational model, in which the person emerges stronger and more whole than previously, can only occur where there is a willingness to complete stage five by reorganizing one's lifestyle, belief systems, and actions to embrace the wounding and give it meaning.

In my opinion, the process needed to heal our individual and collective wounds and to create personal and societal transformation may be the very same process required to take us beyond the grid to a new (seventh stage) form of social and spatial organization. In that process, we will find optimal ways to provide for the 13 basic place-related behavioral needs. One way to do this is to be open to new forms these places and supports might take. Most important of all is our willingness to let go of that which no longer serves us and to be open to finding new, more satisfying solutions which are as *heartfelt* as they may be technological.

A Vision for the Future

The concepts of archetypal place, evolutionary transformation, and stages of healing bring us full circle in the exploration of child care center design. *Action follows thought.* We cannot possibly create a new building type for child care unless we are willing to acknowledge the painful truth that all is not right with our present course of action. We cannot create a new building type unless we cease creating inferior designs as a form of temporary repair and are, instead, willing to give up outmoded beliefs and designs which do not optimally serve children and their caregivers. Our wounding has made us blind to new possibilities and to finding a way out. It has kept us from allowing the invisible carver's hands to bring the power of love to the forefront of our actions and thoughts.[13] Acknowledging all this, we can work together to regenerate our hearts and values, rejecting both the status quo and a concept based on deficits. Instead, we can embrace a belief in the transformative power of collective energy to create the spirited settings in which children, staff, and families *will* become all they possibly can be!

As Rudolf Steiner stated:[14]

> Until one is committed
> there is hesitancy, the chance to draw back,
> always ineffectiveness.
> Concerning all acts of initiative (and creation),

there is one elementary truth,
the ignorance of which kills countless ideas
and splendid plans:
that the moment one definitely commits oneself,
then providence moves too.

All sorts of things occur to help one that would never
otherwise have occurred.
A whole stream of events issues from the decision,
raising in one's favor all manner
of unforeseen incidents and meetings
and material assistance, which no man could have
dreamt
would have come their way.

I have learned a deep respect
for one of Goethe's couplets:

"Whatever you can do, or dream you can, begin it.
Boldness has genius, power and magic in it!"

Notes

[1]Ed Howe, Design Director of Anita Olds and Associates, was a significant contributor to this design.

[2]Owner: Husky Injection Molding Systems, Ltd., Bolton, Ontario, Canada; Conceptual Design: Anita Rui Olds, Anita Olds and Associates, Woodacre, CA; Architectural Design: Barbara Winslow, Jacobson, Silverstein, Winslow/Degenhardt Architects, Berkeley, CA; Interior Design: Carla Mathis Designs, Menlo Park, CA; Architect of Record: J.H. Rust, Architect, Toronto, Ontario; Landscape Design: Ruedi Hofer, PMA Landscape Architects, Etobicoke, Ontario.

[3]These burls and the plaster work for the fireplace and banquette were provided by New Hampshire master craftsman and woodworker Chance Anderson.

[4]Designed and fabricated by Robert Du Domaine.

[5]Owner: Bruce and Shona Davison, owners/managers, New Generation Children's Learning Centres, Papakura, New Zealand; Conceptual Design: Anita Rui Olds, Anita Olds and Associates, Woodacre, CA; Architectural Design: Murray Silverstein, Jacobson, Silverstein, Winslow/Degenhardt Architects, Berkeley, CA; Landscape Design: Bruce Davison, New Generation Child Care Centers, Papakura, New Zealand.

[6]Adapted from Bruce Davison, handout at NAEYC Conference, November, 1998.

[7]Although not as fully developed as the Canadian and New Zealand examples, the Magic Years Children's Center, Richmond, CA, depicted on page 129, to which Anita Rui Olds served as a consultant, was designed with the beginnings of a residential core: a living room at the entry and a kitchen/dining area at the rear of the main circulation corridor.

[8]Spivak, M., *Archetypal Place,* EDRA 4 Conference, Spring 1973.

[9]Lobell, M., *Spatial Archetypes, ReVISION*, Fall, 1983, Vol. 6, No. 2.

[10]Ibid pg. 74

[11]Ibid pg. 82

[12]Personal communication as part of a workshop at The Second International Psychosynthesis Conference, Toronto, Ontario, 1983.

[13]See quote at the beginning of Chapter 2.

[14]Rudolf Steiner

APPENDIXES

APPENDIX I

Questions to Ask Prospective Architects

Our child care center would like to get a sense of how your firm is structured, how you work with clients, and how closely your prior experience matches our needs. Please provide answers to the questions below.

Your Firm

1. How large is your firm? Please include the number of architects and the number of support personnel.
2. Which of the services we require (programming, architectural, interior, landscaping, etc.) is your firm prepared to provide?
3. What budget do you recommend for the required services we have identified? How do you propose to charge for your work on this project (hourly, percentage of construction costs, other)? If you propose an hourly fee, please indicate fees for each type of personnel whom you anticipate being involved in the project. If you propose to charge on a percentage basis, what percentage would you ask? Please describe your anticipated billing and payment schedule.
4. Are you proposing to collaborate with another architect, interior designer, consultant, or firm on this project. If so, why have you chosen this individual or firm? Please describe where and how you have worked together in the past. What are your respective strengths and weaknesses? Please provide details of the other firm, including number of architects and support personnel. In your collaboration, please describe who would do what tasks and how you propose setting fees for both firms.
5. Please indicate who from your firm would be assigned to this project and include résumés of key design personnel who would work with us.

How You Work With Clients

6. Please tell us what your process would be in working with us in the programming phase.
7. Please describe what your process would be in working with us through the design and construction phases.
8. Have you had experience working with design committees? Please provide details of each project, including client name, length of project, size of project (square feet and cost), and the type and size of the client group. Please describe your process in working with the client in each of these projects.

Your Prior Experience

9. Have you ever designed a child care center or educational facility for children? Please provide details of such projects, including client, location, acreage, number of buildings, square footage, and cost. Please highlight for us any creative solutions that you found for difficult projects, building sites, etc.
10. Have you worked on any other projects of a similar scale in terms of building size and cost? Please provide details of such projects completed, including client, location, square footage, and cost. You do not need to include projects designed but not executed.
11. Please describe your experience with residential construction, your design philosophy, and your approach to planning and designing small-scale buildings.
12. Please describe your experience with interior design and your approach to handling interior finishes and furniture.

13. Please describe your experience in planning, designing, and/or building for sites in ________________ county, city, municipality.
14. We are interested in your experience with the use of appropriate technology and renewable energy sources. Please provide details of (a) past designs that incorporated alternative energy sources, (b) projects that required the use of nontoxic materials for the environmentally sensitive, and (c) projects that required conformity to the latest Americans with Disabilities Act standards for handicapped accessibility. If these are not areas of your expertise, how would you propose to address these considerations? With whom might you consult?
15. Have you worked on any owner-builder projects or projects that incorporated volunteer labor? If so, please describe these.
16. Please provide a list of client references. Please indicate clients to whom we may talk by telephone and sites that we would be welcome to visit.

Your Thoughts on Our Center

17. What do you see as your greatest challenges in designing our center? Do you have any ideas at this stage of creative solutions you might offer to meet these challenges?
18. Our current budget calls for us to complete the building for ________ dollars, including (land, infrastructure, permits, architects' fees, construction costs, interior finishes, furnishings). Please comment on any implications that you are currently aware of that this budget would have on your design.
19. We recognize that this is a unique and challenging project. If may be that no single firm has all the expertise required to address all aspects of it. Do you foresee working with consultants on any aspects of the project. If so, towards what end? Whom might you consider (categories of experience and/or specific names)?
20. Do you have any other comments about this project that you would like to share with us at this time?

Thank you for your participation!

APPENDIX II

Comparison: Construction Manager (CM) versus General Contractor (GC) /Stipulated Sum

Issue	CM	GC/Stipulated Sum
Nature of Relationship with Owner	Trust and Confidence	Potential adversarial
Source of Responsibility	CM contracting directly with all subcontractors; architect contracts separately with owner	GC contracting directly with all subcontractors; architect contracts separately with the owner
Financial Risk of Owner	CM assumes financial responsibility by providing GMP—financial management is open book	GC assumes financial responsibility by providing stipulated sum—financial management is closed book
Loyalty to Whom or What	Loyalty to both owner and GMP—need owner reference for future local clients	Loyalty to bottom line
Design Phase Services	Value Engineering Quality Comparisons Review of Schedule and Phasing Design Document Review	None: If services similar to CM delivery are desired, they must be provided by independent consultants—(less continuity from design construction)
Competitiveness of Subbids	Local subs prequalified Bids competitive because sub wants to work with CM again Subbidding process is open book and is coordinated by CM in consultation with the owner CM already has the job and might be somewhat aggressive Subs not always marked up by CM	Local subs not prequalified with owner Subbidding is closed book GC wants the job and might be more aggressive Subs marked up by GC
Accounting Review	Owner has full access to CM's financial records for the project	None
Cost Savings	Split between owner and CM or entirely retained by owner	Entirely retained by GC
Cost Control	Opportunity for cost control and cost savings throughout the process through value engineering Open book process allows for constant financial monitoring	Cost control is maintained by GC alone with no outside input and motivation primarily by bottom line Closed book process does not allow monitoring by owner
Schedule Control	CM controls process in conjunction with owner Design of schedule allows for owner input	GC controls entire process Schedule designed solely by GC
Fast Tracking Possibility	Fully possible. CM retained before completion of design documents	None. GC retained only after general bid
Change Orders	Less severe because DM is part of team early and has fully reviewed design documents	Greater severity because GC less familiar with design documents. Unforeseen conditions and uncorrected errors in design documents are more probable
Flexibility of Process	CM is part of team from beginning and is amenable to change and flexibility of process within reason	GC relatively inflexible—wants to follow plan that produces maximum profit
Local Presence	Positive: If local CM is utilized, employs local personnel and supports state economy	Positive: If local GC is utilized Negative: If out of state GC controls process
Post Project Follow-Up: Punch List, Repairs, and Maintenance	Local: CM needs to stand behind his work in order to maintain his reputation CM likely to be involved in local support and maintenance contracts after the project	If local GC is utilized, impact would be similar to local CM. If out of state GC is utilized, they have less interest in follow-up, etc., because project is sole job in this area
Role of Architect	Agent of owner throughout design and construction Full owner input into design	Agent of owner throughout the design and construction Full owner input into design

APPENDIX III

A Summary of Low-Toxic Building Materials[1]

This outline is intended as an introduction to low-toxic building materials for the neophyte, a reminder and reference list for the experienced, and a point of departure for discussion for everyone. The information is offered as guidance, but nothing here is to be taken as a prescription, endorsement, or guarantee. Any material can be toxic if used without care, and individual responses to the same material can differ widely.

Key:
+ = generally low toxic
• = generally acceptable, with cautions
x = generally toxic

Foundation

+ Concrete *(avoid radon, curing compounds)*
• Concrete block *(avoid radon; admixtures and curing compounds may cause reactions, mostly when wet)*
• Treated wood

Structure

+ Stone
+ Brick
+ Earth *(adobe, rammed earth)*
+ Concrete *(avoid radon, curing compounds)*
• Wood *(treated wood affects some people)*
• Aluminum *(coatings affect some people)*
• Concrete block
x Laminated wood products with outgassing resins

Sheathing/Underlayment

+ Solid wood laid diagonally for wall or subfloor
+ Wood let-in lateral bracing for shear resistance
+ Diagonal metal straps for shear resistance
• Exterior-grade plywood, oriented strand board *(if outside an air barrier or sealed)*
• Hardboard
• Foil-faced laminated cardboard sheathing
x Particle board *(unless sealed or formaldehyde-free)*
x Medium-density fiberboard *(unless sealed)*

Damp-proofing

+ Cement-based sealants *(without petroleum products)*
x Asphalt-based sealants

Air and Vapor Barriers

+ Untreated building or kraft paper on exterior
+ Aluminum foil, paper-backed foil
x Polyethylene sheeting *(seal behind interior finish)*

Roofing

+ Metal *(copper, or steel with baked-enamel finish)*
+ Tile
+ Slate
• Wood *(treated wood contains toxic chemicals)*
• Concrete tiles require sealer
x Asphaltic roofing *(avoid where roof occurs near openings, dormer windows, etc., or for very sensitive people)*

Siding

+ Stucco *(if asphaltic building paper poses a problem, aluminum builders' foil my be substituted)*
+ Masonry *(may require sealing)*
• Wood *(require finishes or treatment that are often toxic; some people are sensitive to wood itself)*
• Synthetic additives in stucco should be avoided
• Hardwood siding *(emits some formaldehyde)*
• Metal *(possible electromagnetic influence, and lack of breathability can cause mold growth)*
x Vinyl
x Asbestos cement

Windows

+ Metal
+ Wood
• Manufactured wood windows *(usually treated with pesticides and fungicides)*
• Most window glass is held in place by synthetic materials, which may cause reactions in sensitive persons *(sealing is possible)*
x Vinyl

[1]Adapted from Carol Venolia, *Building with Nature: A Networking Newsletter* (November/December 1991).

Doors

+ Metal
+ Solid wood, panelized
• Sold-core doors usually have particleboard cores *(formaldehyde seal if used)*
• Some hollow-core doors have toxic glues
x Plastic *(note: may look like wood)*

Insulation

+ Air-krete
• Fiberglass *(usually tolerable after installed if sealed in: pink type has a dye that may irritate; loose fibers irritate; installers must be protected; avoid paper-faced type; some react to the formaldehyde resins)*
• Cellulose *(contains inks and added chemicals that can cause reactions)*
• Perlite *(possible nuisance dust)*
• Vermiculite *(settles in walls; best for horizontal applications; may contain small amounts of asbestos)*
• Rock wool; *(often contains some coal or mineral oil)*
• Foil-faced bubble pack *(includes plastic)*
• Cork *(may be chemically treated)*
• Expanded polystyrene, polyurethane, and polyisocyanurate *(may be tolerable outside the living space; all are toxic if burning)*
• Cotton batt insulation *(may be on the market soon)*
x Urea formaldehyde foam
x Asbestos

Weatherstripping

+ Metal
• Synthetic plastics *(may need to be sealed)*

Interior Wall and Ceiling Finish

+ Plaster *(unpainted)*
• Gypsum board *(use low-toxic joint compound and paint)*
x Laminated wood paneling
x Ceiling tiles or sprayed-on finish containing asbestos

Paint

+ Nontoxic paint
+ Natural paint *(not tolerated by some sensitive people)*
• Latex paint *(tolerated by many people after drying)*
x Oil-based paints
x Paint containing lead or mercury

Sealers

+ Low toxic formulations
+ Beeswax
• Natural shellac
• Lacquer *(after curing)*
• Urethane varnish *(after curing)*
x Epoxies
x Solvent-based furniture polish

Concrete Sealers

+ Sodium silicate
x Petrochemical-based sealers

Caulking, Sealants

• Clear silicone without additives *(keep well ventilated until cured)*
• Linseed-oil putty and caulking *(okay for most)*
• Acrylic sealant *(can be painted to reduce outgassing)*

Flooring

+ Ceramic tile *(mortar-set best, or use thinset without toxic additives; use low-toxic grout and seal grout lines with low-toxic sealer)*
+ Brick
+ Slate
+ Marble
+ Wood *(avoid toxic finishes and glues; some are allergic to wood itself; aluminum may be substituted for asphaltic paper under flooring)*
+ Untreated washable natural-fiber area rugs
• Natural linoleum *(some react to its natural ingredients; use a low-toxic adhesive)*
• Concrete *(avoid radon)*
• Some hard vinyls are tolerable *(use low-toxic adhesive; avoid asbestos)*
x Soft vinyl
x Wall-to-wall carpet *(most are loaded with toxic chemicals, most glues are highly toxic)*
x Vinyl asbestos tile

Adhesives

+ White and yellow glues *(in moderation)*
• Thinset mortar adhesives for ceramic tile *(avoid acrylic additives, use in well-ventilated area; use low-toxic type)*
x Standard carpet, panel, and construction adhesives

Cabinetry

+ Enameled metal
+ Solid wood
• Exterior-grade plywood *(outgasses some formaldehyde)*
x Interior-grade plywood *(unless sealed)*
x Particleboard *(unless formaldehyde is sealed in)*

Countertops

+ Granite
+ Marble
+ Ceramic tile (*see Flooring for notes)*
+ Metal
• Plastic *(high-pressure laminates, such as Formica, and molded plastic, such as Conan, are tolerated by most people)*
• Wood *(avoid in damp areas to minimize mold growth)*

Plumbing

+ Copper pipe *(mechanical joints or lead-free solder)*
x Cast-iron supply pipe
x Galvanized-steel supply pipe
x Polyvinyl chloride (PVC) supply pipe

APPENDIX IV

Carla Mathis' Living Colors

The following formulas for mixing one gallon of paint use both the Benjamin Moore Color system of 32 increments in an ounce (colors identified below by double letters), and the Universal Tint system of 48 increments in an ounce (identified by single letters). In each system, X = 1 ounce. For example, "2 X + 8 CR" = 2 ounces plus 8 increments of crimson. *(Note: Use lamp black only as a last resort, for it creates a shadow effect in the paint.)*

OY	=	oxide yellow
YE or A	=	bright yellow
GY	=	gray
BK or B	=	lamp black (last resort)
OG	=	orange
J	=	violet
CR	=	crimson
MG	=	magenta
RO	=	red oxide
BB or E	=	thalo blue
TG or D	=	green
L	=	raw umber
I	=	burnt umber
C	=	raw sienna
F	=	burnt sienna
WH	=	white

The Benjamin Moore system includes five tint bases that range from light-value colors to deep-toned bases. (Base 1 is light; base 5 is dark.) LB = light base. MB = medium base.

Whites

Cream (LB)

20 OY	(oxide yellow)
12 GY	(gray)
2 OG	(orange)
1 MG	(magenta)
1 I	(burnt umber)

Bisque (LB)

23 OY	(oxide yellow)
1 X +12 GY	(gray)
1 CR	(crimson)
1 TG	(green)
1 I	(burnt umber)

Creamy White(LB)

13 OY	(oxide yellow)
19 GY	(gray)
1 OG	(orange)
1 X + 28 WH	(white)
1 I	(burnt umber)
1 BB	(thalo blue)

Peach Blush (LB)

14 OY	(oxide yellow)
14 GY	(gray)
4 OG	(orange)
1 I	(burnt umber)
1 F	(burnt sienna)
1 BB	(thalo blue)

Dancing Colors

Toasted Plum Jam (MB)

Benjamin Moore # 215–3A	
24 YE	(yellow)
24 BB	(thalo blue)
1 X + 16 MG	(magenta)
2 X + 8 CR	(crimson)
2 X + 8 OG	(orange)
3 WH	(white)

Apricot Jam (MB)

Benjamin Moore # 215–3A	
23 OY	(oxide yellow)
26 OG	(orange)
16 RO	(red oxide)
4 L	(raw umber)
1 CR	(crimson)

Platinum (LB)

4 A	(bright yellow)
1 X + 28 OY	(oxide yellow)
1 X + 4 BK	(lamp black)
16 CR	(crimson)
8 WH	(white)

Silver Spruce Green (MB)

Benjamin Moore # 215–2A	
1 X OY	(oxide yellow)
1 X BK	(lamp black)
16 TG	(green)
1 X WH	(white)
1 YE	(bright yellow)

Apricot Pudding (MB)

Benjamin Moore # 215–3A	
4 YE	(bright yellow)
2 X + 4 OY	(oxide yellow)
14 RO	(red oxide)
1 X + 8 GY	(gray)

Rose Quartz(MB)

Benjamin Moore # 215–2A	
1 X OY	(oxide yellow)
2 X + 16 OG	(orange)
3 X + 16 GY	(gray)
1 J	(violet)
1 BB	(thalo blue)

Vanilla Milkshake(LB)

Benjamin Moore # 215–1A	
16 OY	(oxide yellow)
6 OG	(green)
20 GY	(gray)
1/2 BB	(thalo blue)

Silver Spruce Blue(MB)

2 YE	(bright yellow)
2 X OY	(oxide yellow)
4 BB	(thalo blue)
16 TG	(green)
8 OG	(orange)
4 X GY	(gray)
4 X WH	(white)

The following full-spectrum Donald Kaufman Colors, chosen and named by Carla Mathis, are appropriate for child care settings.[1]

Creamy Golden Browns

DKC–14 Barely Toast
DKC–32 Creme Caramel
DKC–35 Toasted Fawn

Peach Pink Soft Whites

DKC–22 Peach Pearl
DKC–27 Shell Peach

[1] Donald Kaufman Colors are available from the Color Factory, Englewood, NJ (201) 568-2226 and Santa Monica Painters Supply, Santa Monica, CA (310) 392-2339.

Sandy Neutrals

DKC–13 Adobe
DKC–16 Putty
DKC–21 Golden Sand
DKC–34 Chamois

Golden Creams, Creamy Yellows

DKC–2 Grapefruit
DKC–3 Straw
DKC–5 Milk
DKC–20 Yellow Dawn
DKC–24 Chalk White
DKC–28 Meringue
DKC–30 Misty Sun Beam

Misty Blues and Greens

DKC–8 Shale
DKC–11 Sea Foam Green
DKC–19 Lagoon Blue
DKC–29 Blue Mist
DKC–33 Robins' Egg Blue
DKC–37 Meadow Mist

CREDITS

Anita Rui Olds passed away on September 16, 1999. While she finished the writing of this book before her death, a large portion of the publication process had yet to be completed and some details were left unresolved. We have done our best to cite references and provide credits and acknowledgments to the many people (writers, editors, photographers, artists, architects, designers, consultants, and friends) whose contributions have made this endeavor possible. We apologize for any instance in which information may be confusing, incomplete, or unsatisfactory. We hope that Anita would be proud of this book and that many people will use and enjoy it.

Note: Photos not otherwise credited were taken by Anita Rui Olds. Text credits included here were not referenced in the footnotes or bibliography.

Foreword: xi, *Photographer:* Henry F. Olds, Jr.

Chapter 1: 3, Chance Anderson—builder and craftsman, Canterbury, New Hampshire; **4, Fig. 1.1,** *Source:* Adapted from *Young Children*; **8,** *Photographer:* Henry F. Olds, Jr.; **9** The Children's Hospital, St. Paul, MN; *Designer:* Anita Olds and Associates; **10 (top),** *Photographer:* Henry F. Olds, Jr.; **10 (bottom),** Infant/Toddler Family Creative Play Center, Shrewsbury, MA; *Designer:* Other Ways for Educational and Environmental Development, Cambridge, MA; **11,** Enchanted Forest, University of Maryland Hospital, Baltimore, MD; *Designer:* Anita Olds and Associates; *Photographer:* Gail Collins; **12,** Technology Child Care Center, M.I.T., Cambridge, MA; *Designer:* Other Ways for Educational and Environmental Development, Cambridge, MA

Chapter 2: 15, *Source:* David Whyte, excerpt from "The Faces At Braga," *Where Many Rivers Meet,* (Langley, Washington: Many Rivers Press, 1998), 26; **15,** The Nature Sanctuary, The Findhorn Foundation, Forres, Scotland; *Designer:* Ian Turnbull; **16,** *Photographer:* Henry F. Olds, Jr.; **21,** *Source:* Keith Critchlow, personal communication; **22,** Lindisfarne Chapel, Lindisfarne Foundation, Creston, Colorado; *Designer:* Keith Critchlow; **23, Fig. 2.1,** *Source/Architect:* Bruce Brook, Concord, NH; **24 (top),** Steiner School, Wales; *Designer:* Christopher Day, Dyfed, Wales; *Photographer:* Christopher Day; **24 (bottom),** Retreat Centre, Wales; *Designer:* Christopher Day; **25 (top),** Bandolier National Monument, Bandolier, NM; **25 (bottom),** Retreat Centre, Wales; *Designer:* Christopher Day, Dyfed, Wales; **27–31, Fig. 2.2-A, B, C, E, F, G, H,** *Source:* JSW, M. Jacobson, M. Silverstein, B. Winslow. *The Good House,* (Newtown, CT: The Taunton Press, 1990).

Chapter 3: 35, The Child Care Design Institute, Harvard University, Tufts University, 1996; *Photographer:* Gary Duart; **37, 42,** *Photographer:* Henry F. Olds, Jr.; **46,** *Photographer:* Gail Collins; *Designer:* Christopher Day; **49, Fig. 3.4,** Acton Infant/Toddler Center, Acton, MA; *Source/Designer/Architect:* Brook Design Associates, Concord, NH; **54,** *Designer:* Anita Olds and Associates; **55 (top),** Prototypes for box system for Child Development Assessment Program, Alfred I. Dupont Institute, Wilmington, DE; *Designer:* Anita Olds and Associates; **55 (bottom),** Alfred I. Dupont Institute, Wilmington, DE; *Designer:* Anita Olds and Associates

Chapter 4: 60, Fig. 4.3, The Child Care Design Institute, Harvard University, 1996; *Source/Architect:* Bruce Brook; **64, Fig. 4.7,** New Generation Children's Learning Centre, Papakura, New Zealand; *Designer/Architect:* Anita Olds and Associates, JSW, M. Jacobson, M. Silverstein, B. Winslow; **79, Fig. 4.10,** The Child Care Design Institute, Harvard University, 1996; *Source/ Architect:* Bruce Brook

Chapter 5: 83, *Source:* Christian Norberg-Schulz. *The Concept of Dwelling: On The Way To Figurative Architecture.* (New York: Rizzoli International Publications, Inc., 1985), 71; **84,** Nant-Y-Cum Steiner School Kindergarten, Wales; *Designer:* Christopher Day; *Photographer:* Christopher Day; **85 (top),** New Generation Children's Learning Centre, Papakura, New Zealand; *Designer/Architect:* Anita Olds and Associates, JSW, M. Jacobson, M. Silverstein, B. Winslow; *Photographer:* Bruce Davison; **85 (bottom),** The Copper House, Husky Child Development Center, Bolton, Ontario, Canada; *Designer/Architect:* Anita Olds and Associates, JSW, M. Jacobson, M. Silverstein, B. Winslow, Carla Mathis Designs; **86 (right),** Judge Baker Guidance Clinic, Children's Hospital, Boston, MA; *Mural artist:* Lilli Ann Killen Rosenberg; *Photographer:* Lilli Ann Killen Rosenberg; **87 (left),** The Copper House, Husky Child Development Center, Bolton, Ontario, Canada; *Designers:* Jacobson, Silverstein and Winslow, Anita Olds and Associates, Carla Mathis Designs; *Photographer:* Elaine Kilburn Photography; **87 (right),** Nant-Y-Cum Steiner Kindergarten, Wales; *Designer:* Christopher Day; *Photographer:* Christopher Day; **88,** The Copper House, Husky Child Development Center, Bolton, Ontario, Canada; *Designer/Architect:* Anita Olds and Associates, JSW, M. Jacobson, M. Silverstein, B. Winslow, Carla Mathis Designs; **89–90, Fig. 5.1, Fig. 5.2,** *Source/Architect:* Bruce Brook; *Project:* The Child Care Design Institute, Harvard University, 1996; **94, Fig. 5.4,** Eliot-Pearson Children's School, Tufts University, Medford, MA; *Designer/Architect:* Ed Howe Design and Construction, Janet Stork (Director of Eliot-Pearson), Kyna Healy, Kirk Abrams, AIA; **96 (top),** Eliot-Pearson Children's School, Tufts University, Medford, MA; *Designer:* Ed Howe Design and Construction, Janet Stork (Director of Eliot-Pearson, Kyna Healy, Kirk Abrams, AIA; *Photographer:* Ed Howe; **96 (bottom),** Eliot-Pearson Children's School, Tufts University, Medford, MA; *Designer:* Ed Howe Design and Construction, Janet Stork (Director of Eliot-Pearson), Kyna Healy, Kirk Abrams, AIA; *Photographer:* Kyna Healy; **97,** Developmental Child Care, St. Louis, MO; *Designer:* Anita Olds and Associates, Terry Bloomberg; **98 (left),** Eliot-Pearson Children's School, Tufts University, Medford, MA; *Designer:* Ed Howe Design and Construction, Janet Stork (Director of Eliot-Pearson), Kyna Healy, Kirk Abrams, AIA; *Photographer:* Janet Stork (Director of Eliot-Pearson); **98 (right),** Eliot-Pearson Children's School, Tufts University, Medford, MA; *Designer:* Ed Howe Design and Construction, Janet Stork, Kyna Healy, Kirk Abrams, AIA; *Photographer:* Kirk Abrams, AIA; **99 (top),** Community Child and Family Day Care Center, Peabody, MA; *Designer:* Anita Olds and Associates; **99 (bottom),** Child Care Design Institute, Harvard University, 1996; *Source/Designer/Architect:* Bruce Brook; **100 (bottom),** Community Child and Family Day Care Center, Peabody, MA; *Designer:* Anita Olds and Associates; **101,** Quincy Market, Faneuil Hall, Boston, MA; *Designer:* Benjamin Thompson and Associates, Cambridge, MA; **102,** Child Care Design Institute, Harvard University, 1996; *Source/Designer/Architect:* Bruce Brook; **103–104 (bottom),** Kindergarten, Auckland, New Zealand; **105, Fig. 5.8,** *Source:* C. Alexander et al., *A Pattern Language*, (Oxford University Press, 1977) Pattern 115, p. 564; **105, Fig. 5.9,** *Source:* C. Alexander et al., *A Pattern Language*, (Oxford University Press, 1977), Pattern 114, pp. 558–560; **106,**The Copper House, Husky Child Development Center, Bolton, Ontario, Canada; *Designer/Architect:* Anita Olds and Associates, JSW, M. Jacobson, M. Silverstein, B. Winslow, Carla Mathis Designs; *Photographer:* Elaine Kilburn Photography; **107,** *Source:* C. Alexander et al., *A Pattern Language*, (Oxford University Press, 1977) Pattern 116, pg. 565-568

Chapter 6: 109, *Source:* C. Alexander et al., *A Pattern Language*, (Oxford University Press, 1977), p. 628; **111, Fig. 6.1, 114, Fig. 6.3,** Child Care Design Institute, Harvard University, 1996; *Designer/Architect:* Bruce Brook; **116, Fig. 6.5,** *Source:* Illustration adapted/direct quote from C. Alexander et al., *A Pattern Language*, (Oxford University Press, 1977) p. 621; **117–118, Figs. 6.7, 6.8, 120, Fig. 6.10,** Child Care Design Institute, Harvard University, 1996; *Designer/Architect:* Bruce Brook; **124,** Cambridge Rindge and Latin High School, Infant/Toddler Center, Cambridge, MA; *Designer:* Anita Olds and Associates; **125,** Courtyard, The Child Development Center, Alfred I. Dupont Institute, Wilmington, DE; *Designer:* Anita Olds and Associates; **126, Fig. 6.14,** Developmental Child Care, St. Louis, MO; *Designer/Architect:* Anita Olds and Associates, Terry Bloomberg; **127, Fig. 6.15,** New Generation Children's Learning Centre, Papakura, New Zealand; *Designer/Architect:* Anita Olds and Associates, JSW, M. Jacobson, M. Silverstein, B. Winslow; **128, Fig. 6.16,** Richmond Magic Years Children's Center, Richmond, CA; *Designer/Architect:* Laura Shen, Tectonics, San Francisco, CA; **129, Fig. 6.17,** Cottage Kids Children's Center, Sacramento, CA; *Designer/Architect:* Janine Wilford, Tectonics, San Francisco, CA; **130–131, Fig. 6.18,** Irvine Child Care Center, Irvine, CA; *Designer/Architect:* Diane White (project architect); Cleg, Carter, and Vale Architects; **132, Fig. 6.19,** Cincinnati Children's Home, Cincinnati, OH; *Designer/Architect:* Steed, Hammond and Paul, Architects, Cincinnati, OH; **133, Fig 6.20,** GeoKids, Menlo Park, CA; *Designer/Architect:* Scotsman Buildings; **134, Fig. 6.21,** Omaha Toddler Room; Child Development Center of the Jewish Community Center of Omaha, NB; *Designer/Architect:* Mark Sanford Group;

Chapter 7: 137, *Source:* C. Alexander et al., *A Pattern Language*, (Oxford University Press, 1977), p. 941; **157–158,** Case Study I: Technology Child Care Center, M.I.T., Cambridge, MA; *Designer/Architect:* Other Ways for Educational and Environmental Development, Cambridge, MA; **158–159,** Case Study I: Technology Child Care Center, M.I.T., Cambridge, MA; *Designer:* Other Ways for Educational and Environmental Development, Cambridge, MA; Photos 1–16, Anita Rui Olds, Henry F. Olds, Jr., and Walter Drew; **160-162,** Case Study 2: Developmental Child Care, St. Louis, MO; *Designer/Architect:* Anita Olds and Associates, Terry Bloomberg; **161,** Case Study 2: Developmental Child Care, St. Louis, MO; *Designer:* Anita Rui Olds and Associates, Terry Bloomberg; **163–164,** Case Study 3: Community Child and Family Daycare Center, Peabody, MA; *Designer/Architect:* Anita Olds and Associates

Chapter 8: 167, 168, The Copper House, Husky Child Development Center, Bolton, Ontario, Canada; *Designer/ Architect:* Anita Olds and Associates, JSW, M. Jacobson, M. Silverstein, B. Winslow, Carla Mathis Designs; *Photographer:* Elaine Kilburn Photography

Chapter 9: 183, The Copper House, Husky Child Development Center, Bolton, Ontario, Canada; *Designer/Architect:* Anita Olds and Associates, JSW, M. Jacobson, M. Silverstein, B. Winslow, Carla Mathis Designs

Chapter 10: 188, New Generation Childcare Centre, Papakura, New Zealand; *Designer/Architect:* Anita Olds and Associates, JSW, M. Jacobson, M. Silverstein, B. Winslow; *Photographer:* Bruce Davison; **194,** Developmental Child Care, St. Louis, MO; *Designer:* Anita Olds and Associates, Terry Bloomberg; **195,** The Copper House, Husky Child Development Center, Bolton, Ontario, Canada; *Designer/Architect:* Anita Olds and Associates, JSW, M. Jacobson, M. Silverstein, B. Winslow, Carla Mathis Designs

Chapter 11: 197, *Source:* Christian Norberg-Schulz.*The Concept of Dwelling: On The Way To Figurative Architecture.* (New York: Rizzoli International Publications, Inc., 1985), p. 75; **197,** The Copper House, Husky Child Development Center, Bolton, Ontario, Canada; *Designer/ Architect:* Anita Olds and Associates, JSW, M. Jacobson, M. Silverstein, B. Winslow, Carla Mathis Designs; *Photographer:* Elaine Kilburn Photography; **198 (top),** The Copper House, Husky Child Development Center, Bolton, Ontario, Canada; *Designer/Architect:* Anita Olds and Associates, JSW, M. Jacobson, M. Silverstein, B. Winslow, Carla Mathis Designs; **198 (bottom),** Diona School, Reggio Emilia, Italy; *Photographer:* Angela Ferrario; **199 (top),** Nant-Y-Cum Steiner Kindergarten, Wales; *Designer:* Christopher Day, Dyfed, Wales; *Photographer:* Christopher Day; **199 (bottom), 200 (top and bottom),** The Copper House, Husky Child Development Center, Bolton, Ontario, Canada; *Designer/Architect:* Anita Olds and Associates, JSW, M. Jacobson, M. Silverstein, B. Winslow, Carla Mathis Designs; **201 (top),** Children's Hospital National Medical Center, Washington, DC; *Designer:* Anita Olds and Associates; **201 (bottom left),** The Copper House, Husky Child Development Center, Bolton, Ontario, Canada; *Designer/Architect:* Anita Olds and Associates, JSW, M. Jacobson, M. Silverstein, B. Winslow, Carla Mathis Designs; *Photographer:* Elaine Kilburn Photography; **201 (bottom right),** Developmental Child Care, St. Louis, MO; *Designer:* Anita Olds and Associates, Terry Bloomberg; **204,** Harvest Restaurant, Cambridge, MA; *Designer:* Benjamin Thompson and Associates, Cambridge, MA; **205, 208 (left),** The Copper House, Husky Child Development Center, Bolton, Ontario, Canada; *Designer/Architect:* Anita Olds and Associates, JSW, M. Jacobson, M. Silverstein, B. Winslow, Carla Mathis Designs; **210,** Fayerweather St. School; *Photographer:* Henry F. Olds, Jr.

Chapter 12: 213, *Source:* Wassily Kandinsky. *Concerning The Spiritual in Art* (New York: Dover Publications, Inc., 1977); **220,** The Copper House, Husky Child Development Center, Bolton, Ontario, Canada; *Designer/Architect:* Anita Olds and Associates, JSW, M. Jacobson, M. Silverstein, B. Winslow, Carla Mathis Designs; **221,** The Children's Barn, Acton, MA; *Designers:* Anita Olds and Associates, Gail Wheeler

Chapter 13: 231,Modular Boxes, Alfred I. Dupont Institute, Wilmington, DE; *Designer:* Anita Olds and Associates; Artist: Lilli Ann Killen Rosenberg; *Photographer:* Ken Wittenberg; **234,** The Copper House, Husky Child Development Center, Bolton, Ontario, Canada; *Designer/Architect:* Anita Olds and Associates, JSW, M. Jacobson, M. Silverstein, B. Winslow, Carla Mathis Designs; **235,** Children's Hospital National Medical Center, general medical playroom, Washington, DC; *Designer:* Anita Olds and Associates; **237 (top, bottom) 238, 239 (bottom),** The Copper House, Husky Child Development Center, Bolton, Ontario, Canada; *Designer/Architect:* Anita Olds and Associates, JSW, M. Jacobson, M. Silverstein, B. Winslow, Carla Mathis Designs; **240 (top),** Design Research, Cambridge, MA; *Designer:* Benjamin Thompson and Associates; **240 (bottom),** Community Child and Family Day Care Center, Peabody, MA; *Designer:* Anita Olds and Associates; **242,** Nant-Y-Cum, Steiner Kindergarten, Wales; *Designer:* Christopher Day, Dyfed, Wales; *Photographer:* Christopher Day; **243 (left),** Cambridge Rindge and Latin High School, Infant/Toddler Center, Cambridge, MA; *Designer:* Anita Olds and Associates; **243 (right),** The Copper House, Husky Child Development Center, Bolton, Ontario, Canada; *Designer/Architect:* Anita Olds and Associates, JSW, M. Jacobson, M. Silverstein, B. Winslow, Carla Mathis Designs; **244 (top left),** The Children's Barn, Acton, MA; *Designer:* Anita Olds and Associates, Gail Wheeler; **244 (top right),** Children's Hospital National Medical Center, general medical playroom, Washington, DC; *Designer:* Anita Olds and Associates; **244 (bottom right),** The University of Maryland Hospital, playroom, Baltimore, MD; *Designer:* Anita Olds and Associates; **245,** Harvest Restaurant, Cambridge, MA; *Designer:* Benjamin Thompson and Associates, Cambridge, MA; **246 (top),** The Children's Hospital, St. Paul, MN; *Designer:* Anita Olds and Associates; **246 (bottom),** Trudy's Community School, Taos, NM; **247, 248 (top),** The Copper House, Husky Child Development Center, Bolton, Ontario, Canada; *Designer/Architect:* Anita Olds and Associates, JSW, M. Jacobson, M. Silverstein, B. Winslow, Carla Mathis Designs; **249 (top),** Memorial Sloan-Kettering Cancer Center, Department of Pediatrics, New York, NY; *Mural artist:* Joan Drescher; *Photographer:* Joan Drescher; **249 (bottom),** Developmental Child Care, St. Louis, MO; *Designer:* Anita Olds and Associates, Terry Bloomberg

Chapter 14: 253, *Source:* Community PlayThings Catalog, Rifton, NY; **256,** The Copper House, Husky Child Development Center, Bolton, Ontario, Canada; *Designer/Architect:* Anita Olds and Associates, JSW, M. Jacobson, M. Silverstein, B. Winslow, Carla Mathis Designs; **257 (left),** Reggio Emilia Scuola di Ninos, Reggio Emilia, Italy; *Photographer:* Angela Ferrario; **257 (right),** *Source:* Wehrfritz Catalog, Rodach bei Coburg, Germany; **259 (top, bottom), 261 (left, right), 262,** The Copper House, Husky Child Development Center, Bolton, Ontario, Canada; *Designer/Architect:* Anita Olds and Associates, JSW, M. Jacobson, M. Silverstein, B. Winslow, Carla Mathis Designs

Chapter 15: 267, *Source:* C. Alexander et al., *A Pattern Language,* (Oxford University Press, 1977), p. 81; **269 (top),** Pre-K classroom, Wampatuck School, Scituate, MA; *Designer:* Other Ways for Educational and Environmental Development, Cambridge, MA; **270 (top), 271,** Developmental Childcare, St. Louis, MO; *Designers:* Anita Olds and Associates, Terry Bloomberg; **272 (left, right),** Pre-K, classroom, Wampatuck School, Scituate, MA; *Designer:* Other Ways for Educational and Environmental Development, Cambridge, MA; **273 (top left),** Infant/Toddler Creative Play Center, Shrewsbury, MA; *Designer:* Other Ways for Educational and Environmental Development, Cambridge, MA; **273 (top right, bottom left),** Wellesley College Child Care Center, Wellesley, MA; *Designer:* Other Ways for Educational and Environmental Development, Cambridge, MA; **273 (bottom right),** The Children's Barn, Acton, MA; *Designer:* Anita Olds and Associates, Gail Wheeler; **274,** Children's Hospital National Medical Center, Washington, DC; *Designer:* Anita Olds and Associates; **275 (top left and right),** Pre-K classroom, Wampatuck School, Scituate, MA; *Designer:* Other Ways for Educational and Environmental Development, Cambridge, MA; **275 (bottom left and right),** *Equipment/Designer:* Quadro/Horst Henke; *Photographer:* Horst Henke; **276 (top),** The Copper House, Husky Child Development Center, Bolton, Ontario, Canada; *Designer/Architect:* Anita Olds and Associates, JSW, M. Jacobson, M. Silverstein, B. Winslow, Carla Mathis Designs; **276 (bottom),** Developmental Child Care, St. Louis, MO; *Designer:* Anita Olds and Associates, Terry Bloomberg; **277 (top right),** Wellesley College Child Care Center, Wellesley, MA; *Designer:* Other Ways for Educational and Environmental Development, Cambridge, MA; **277 (bottom left and right),** The Children's Barn, Acton, MA; *Designer:* Anita Olds and Associates, Gail Wheeler; **278 (top),** Wellesley College Child Care Center, Wellesley, MA; *Designer:* Other Ways for Educational and Environmental Development, Cambridge, MA; **278 (bottom),** Lincoln Cooperative Nursery School, Lincoln, MA; *Designer:* Anita Olds and Associates; **280 (top),** Technology Child Care Center, M.I.T., Cambridge, MA; *Designer:* Other Ways for Educational and Environmental Development, Cambridge, MA; **280 (bottom),** Wellesley College Child Care Center; *Designer:* Other Ways for Educational and Environmental Development, Cambridge, MA; **281 (top and bottom),** Technology Child Care Center, M.I.T., Cambridge, MA; *Designer:* Other Ways for Educational and Environmental Development, Cambridge, MA; **284 (left and right), 285 (top left),** Creative Play Center, Shrewsbury, MA; *Designer:* Other Ways for Educational and Environmental Development, Cambridge, MA; **285 (top right),** Community Child and Family Day Care Center, Peabody, MA; *Designer:* Anita Olds and Associates; **285 (bottom left),** Creative Play Center, Shrewsbury, MA; *Designer:* Other Ways for Educational and Environmental Development, Cambridge, MA; **285 (middle right),** Developmental Child Care, Saint Louis, MO.; *Designer:* Anita Olds and Associates, Terry Bloomberg; **287, 288,** The Children's Barn, Acton, MA; *Designer:* Anita Olds and Associates, Gail Wheeler; **291, 292,** Creative Play Center, Shrewsbury, MA; *Designer:* Other Ways for Educational and Environmental Development, Cambridge, MA; **293, 294 (top left),** The Enchanted Forest, University of Maryland Hospital, Baltimore, MD; *Designer:* Anita Olds and Associates; *Photographer:* Gail Collins; **294 (top right, bottom left and right),** Creative Play Center, Shrewsbury, MA; *Designer:* Other Ways for Educational and Environmental Development, Cambridge, MA; **295 (top),** Children's Village, Ontario Place, Toronto; *Designer:* Erik MacMillan; **295 (bottom),** Creative Play Center, Shrewsbury, MA; *Designer:* Other Ways for Educational and Environmental Development, Cambridge, MA

Chapter 16: 300, *Photographer:* Henry F. Olds, Jr.; **302 (top),** The Enchanted Forest, University of Maryland Hospital, Baltimore, MD; *Designer:* Anita Olds and Associates; *Photographer:* Gail Collins; **302 (bottom),** *Mural artist:* Lilli Ann Killen Rosenberg; **305 (bottom left),** Children's Hospital National Medical Center, Washington, DC; *Designer:* Anita Olds and Associates; **305 (bottom right),** The Copper House, Husky Child Development Center, Bolton, Ontario, Canada; *Designer/Architect:* Anita Olds and Associates, JSW, M. Jacobson, M. Silverstein, B. Winslow, Carla Mathis Designs; **306 (top),** University of Maryland Hospital, Baltimore, MD; *Designer:* Anita Olds and Associates; **306 (bottom),** The Copper House, Husky Child Development Center, Bolton, Ontario, Canada; *Designer/Architect:* Anita Olds and Associates, JSW, M. Jacobson, M. Silverstein, B. Winslow, Carla Mathis Designs; *Photographer:* Elaine Kilburn Photography; **308, 310 (top right),** The Copper House, Husky Child Development Center, Bolton, Ontario, Canada; *Designer/Architect:* Anita Olds and Associates, JSW, M. Jacobson, M. Silverstein, B. Winslow, Carla Mathis Designs; **310 (bottom left),** *Source:* Community PlayThings Catalog, Rifton, NY; **313 (middle and bottom),** The Copper House, Husky Child Development Center, Bolton, Ontario, Canada; *Designers:* Jacobson, Silverstein and Winslow, Anita Olds and Associates, Carla Mathis Designs; **314 (bottom left),** *Source:* Nursery Maid Catalog, Dinuba, CA; **318,** Developmental Child Care, Saint Louis, MO; *Designer:* Anita Olds and Associates, Terry Bloomberg; **319 (top),** *Photographer:* Henry F. Olds, Jr.; **319 (bottom),** The Copper House, Husky Child Development Center, Bolton, Ontario, Canada; *Designer/Architect:* Anita Olds and Associates, JSW, M. Jacobson, M. Silverstein, B. Winslow, Carla Mathis Designs; **320 (bottom left),** Developmental Child Care Center, Saint Louis, MO; *Designer:* Anita Olds and Associates, Terry Bloomberg; **320 (bottom right),** The Copper House, Husky Child Development Center, Bolton, Ontario, Canada; *Designer/Architect:* Anita Olds and Associates, JSW, M. Jacobson, M. Silverstein, B. Winslow, Carla Mathis Designs; **320 (bottom left),** Developmental Child Care Center, Saint Louis, MO; *Designer:* Anita Olds and Associates, Terry Bloomberg; **323 (left),** The Copper House, Husky Child Development Center, Bolton, Ontario, Canada; *Designer/Architect:* Anita Olds and Associates, JSW, M. Jacobson, M. Silverstein, B. Winslow, Carla Mathis Designs; **323 (right),** The Copper House, Husky Child Development Center, Bolton, Ontario, Canada; *Designer/Architect:* Anita Olds and Associates, JSW, M. Jacobson, M. Silverstein, B. Winslow, Carla Mathis Designs; *Photographer:* Elaine Kilburn Photography; **324,** Newton Community Service Center, Newton, MA; *Designer:* Anita Olds and Associates; **325 (top left and right),** Developmental Child Care Center, Saint Louis, MO; *Designer:* Anita Olds and Associates, Terry Bloomberg; **325 (bottom right),** The Copper House, Husky Child Development Center, Bolton, Ontario, Canada; *Designer/Architect:* Anita Olds and Associates, JSW, M. Jacobson, M. Silverstein, B. Winslow, Carla Mathis Designs; **326 (bottom left), 327,** Developmental Child Care Center, Saint Louis, MO; *Designer:* Anita Olds and Associates, Terry Bloomberg; **328 (top left and right),** The Child Development Center, Alfred I. Dupont Institute, Wilmington, DE; *Designer:* Anita Olds and Associates, Lilli Ann Killen Rosenberg; *Mural artist:* Lilli Ann Killen Rosenberg; *Photographer:* Ken Wittenberg; **330, Fig. 16.8,** The Copper House, Husky Child Development Center, Bolton, Ontario, Canada; *Designer/Architect:* Anita Olds and Associates, JSW, M. Jacobson, M. Silverstein, B. Winslow, Carla Mathis Designs; **331, Fig. 16.8,** The Copper House, Husky Child Development Center, Bolton, Ontario, Canada; *Designer/Architect:* Anita Olds and Associates, JSW, M. Jacobson, M. Silverstein, B. Winslow, Carla Mathis Designs; **332, Fig. 16.9,** The Copper House, Husky Child Development Center, Bolton, Ontario, Canada; *Designer/Architect:* Anita Olds and Associates, JSW, M. Jacobson, M. Silverstein, B. Winslow, Carla Mathis Designs; **333, Fig. 16.9,** The Copper House, Husky Child Development Center, Bolton, Ontario, Canada; *Designer/Architect:* Anita Olds and Associates, JSW, M. Jacobson, M. Silverstein, B. Winslow, Carla Mathis Designs; Photos 1–3, 5–13: Anita Rui Olds; **333, Fig. 16.9,** Photo 4: *Photographer:* Elaine Kilburn Photography; **334, Fig. 16.10,** Developmental Child Care Center, St. Louis, MO; *Designer/Architect:* Anita Olds and Associates, Terry Bloomberg; **335, Fig. 16.10,** Developmental Child Care Center, St. Louis, MO; *Designer:* Anita Olds and Associates, Terry Bloomberg; **336, Fig. 16.11,** Developmental Child Care Center, St. Louis, MO; *Designer/Architect:* Anita Olds and Associates, Terry Bloomberg; **337, Fig. 16.12,** Rindge and Latin High School, Cambridge, MA; *Designer:* Anita Olds and Associates; **338, Fig. 16.13,** Child Development Center of The Children's Home of Cincinnati, OH; *Designer/Architect:* Anita Olds and Associates, Steed, Hammond & Paul, Cincinnati, OH; **339, Fig. 16.14,** Omaha Toddler Room; Child Development Center of the Jewish Community Center of Omaha, NB; *Designer/Architect:* Anita Olds and Associates, Mark Sanford Group

Chapter 17: 341, *Source:* Robert Fulghum. *All I Really Need To Know I Learned In Kindergarten* (New York: Villard Books, 1988), p. 7; **343,**

344, Wellesley College Child Care Center; *Designer:* Other Ways for Educational and Environmental Development, Cambridge, MA; *Photographer:* Henry F. Olds, Jr.; **346,** The Children's Barn, Acton, MA; *Designer:* Anita Olds and Associates, Gail Wheeler; **347, (top and bottom), 348 (left),** The Copper House, Husky Child Development Center, Bolton, Ontario, Canada; *Designer/Architect:* Anita Olds and Associates, JSW, M. Jacobson, M. Silverstein, B. Winslow, Carla Mathis Designs; **348 (right),** Pre-K classroom, Wampatuck School, Scituate, MA; *Designer:* Other Ways for Educational and Environmental Development, Cambridge, MA; **349, 350,** The Children's Barn, Acton, MA; *Designer:* Anita Olds and Associates, Gail Wheeler; **351,** Technology Child Care Center, M.I.T., Cambridge, MA; *Designer:* Other Ways for Educational and Environmental Development, Cambridge, MA; **352 (top),** Developmental Child Care, St. Louis, MO; *Designer:* Anita Olds and Associates, Terry Bloomberg; **352 (bottom left),** The Children's Barn, Acton, MA; *Designer:* Anita Olds and Associates, Gail Wheeler; *Photographer:* Henry F. Olds, Jr.; **352 (bottom right), 353 (left and right),** Developmental Child Care, St. Louis, MO; *Designer:* Anita Olds and Associates, Terry Bloomberg; **355 (left),** Pre-K classroom, Wampatuck School, Scituate, MA; *Designer:* Other Ways for Educational and Environmental Development, Cambridge, MA; **355 (right),** Developmental Child Care, St. Louis, MO; *Designer:* Anita Olds and Associates, Terry Bloomberg; **356,** The Children's Barn, Acton, MA; *Designer:* Anita Olds and Associates, Gail Wheeler; **357 (top),** Trudy's Community School, Taos, NM; **357 (bottom),** The Phillips School, Watertown, MA; *Designer:* Other Ways for Educational and Environmental Development, Cambridge, MA; *Photographer:* Henry F. Olds, Jr.; **358 (top),** Technology Child Care Center, M.I.T., Cambridge, MA; *Designer:* Other Ways for Educational and Environmental Development, Cambridge, MA; **358 (bottom),** Pre-K classroom, Wampatuck School, Scituate, MA; *Designer:* Other Ways for Educational and Environmental Development, Cambridge, MA; **359,** Trudy's Community School, Taos, NM; **360, 361,** The Children's Barn, Acton, MA; *Designer:* Anita Olds and Associates, Gail Wheeler; **362 (left and right), 363,** Technology Child Care Center, M.I.T., Cambridge, MA; *Designer:* Other Ways for Educational and Environmental Development, Cambridge, MA; **365 (top),** The Children's Barn, Acton, MA; *Designer:* Anita Olds and Associates, Gail Wheeler; **365 (bottom), 366 (top),** Pre-K classroom, Wampatuck School, Scituate, MA; *Designer:* Other Ways for Educational and Environmental Development, Cambridge, MA; **366 (bottom),** The Children's Barn, Acton, MA; *Designer:* Anita Olds and Associates, Gail Wheeler; **367 (top),** Wellesley College Child Care Center, Wellesley, MA; *Designer:* Other Ways for Educational and Environmental Development, Cambridge, MA; **367 (bottom),** Pre-K classroom, Wampatuck School, Scituate, MA; *Designer:* Other Ways for Educational and Environmental Development, Cambridge, MA; **369,** The Copper House, Husky Child Development Center, Bolton, Ontario, Canada; *Designer/Architect:* Anita Olds and Associates, JSW, M. Jacobson, M. Silverstein, B. Winslow, Carla Mathis Designs; **370, Fig. 17.2,** The Copper House, Husky Child Development Center, Bolton, Ontario, Canada; *Designer/Architect:* Anita Olds and Associates, JSW, M. Jacobson, M. Silverstein, B. Winslow, Carla Mathis Designs; **371, Fig. 17.2,** The Copper House, Husky Child Development Center, Bolton, Ontario, Canada; *Designer/Architect:* Anita Olds and Associates, JSW, M. Jacobson, M. Silverstein, B. Winslow, Carla Mathis Designs; photos 1, 8, 11, 12: *Photographer:* Anita Rui Olds; Photos 2–7, 9, 10: *Photographer:* Elaine Kilburn Photography; **372, Fig. 17.3,** Developmental Child Care, St. Louis, MO; *Designer:* Anita Olds and Associates, Terry Bloomberg; **373, Fig. 17.3,** Developmental Child Care, St. Louis, MO; *Designer:* Anita Olds and Associates, Terry Bloomberg; **374, Fig. 17.4,** Eliot-Pearson Children's School, Tufts University, Medford, MA; *Designer/Architect:* Anita Olds and Associates, Ed Howe Design & Construction, Janet Stork (Director of Eliot-Pearson School); **375, Fig. 17.5,** The Child Development Center of The Children's Home of Cincinnati, OH; *Designer/Architect:* Anita Olds and Associates, Steed, Hammond & Paul, Cincinnati, OH

Chapter 18: 377, *Source:* Walt Whitman, excerpt from "Leaves of Grass," *American Poetry: The Nineteenth Century*, Vol. I (NY: Penguin Books, 1993), p. 826; **381,** The Copper House, Husky Child Development Center, Bolton, Ontario, Canada; *Designer/Architect:* Anita Olds and Associates, JSW, M. Jacobson, M. Silverstein, B. Winslow, Carla Mathis Designs; **382,** Fayerweather St. School, Cambridge, MA; *Photographer:* Henry F. Olds, Jr.; **385,** Fayerweather St. School, Cambridge, MA; *Designer:* Kenneth Redmond; **386 (top),** *Photographer:* Henry F. Olds, Jr.; **388 (left),** The Leahy School, Lawrence, MA; *Photographer:* Henry F. Olds, Jr.; *Designer:* Other Ways for Educational and Environmental Development; **388 (right),** The Children's Barn, Acton, MA; *Designer:* Anita Olds and Associates, Gail Wheeler; *Photographer:* Henry F. Olds, Jr.; **389,** Fayerweather St. School, Cambridge, MA; *Photographer:* Henry F. Olds, Jr.; **391,** *Photographer:* Henry F. Olds, Jr.; **392, Fig. 18.1,** The Copper House, Husky Child Development Center, Bolton, Ontario, Canada; *Designer/Architect:* Anita Olds and Associates, JSW, M. Jacobson, M. Silverstein, B. Winslow, Carla Mathis Designs; **393, Fig. 18.1,** The Copper House, Husky Child Development Center, Bolton, Ontario, Canada; *Designer/Architect:* Anita Olds and Associates, JSW, M. Jacobson, M. Silverstein, B. Winslow, Carla Mathis Designs; Photos 1, 4: *Photographer:* Elaine Kilburn Photography; Photos 2, 3, 5: *Photographer:* Anita Rui Olds

Chapter 19: 395, *Source:* Johann Christoph Arnold. *A Little Child Shall Lead Them: Hopeful Parenting in a Confused World* (Farmington, Pennsylvania: Plough Publishing House,1997), p. 137; **396, Fig. 19.1,** The Copper House, Husky Child Development Center, Bolton, Ontario, Canada; *Designer/Architect:* Anita Olds and Associates, JSW, M. Jacobson, M. Silverstein, B. Winslow, Carla Mathis Designs; Photos 1–4: *Photographer:* Elaine Kilburn Photography; **398 (top),** The Copper House, Husky Child Development Center, Bolton, Ontario, Canada; *Designer/Architect:* Anita Olds and Associates, JSW, M. Jacobson, M. Silverstein, B. Winslow, Carla Mathis Designs; **398 (bottom),** *Photographer:* Elaine Kilburn Photography; **399,** The Copper House, Husky Child Development Center, Bolton, Ontario, Canada; *Designer/Architect:* Anita Olds and Associates, JSW, M. Jacobson, M. Silverstein, B. Winslow, Carla Mathis Designs; **400 (left), 401 (top and middle right),** The Copper House, Husky Child Development Center, Bolton, Ontario, Canada; *Designer/Architect:* Anita Olds and Associates, JSW, M. Jacobson, M. Silverstein, B. Winslow, Carla Mathis Designs; *Photographer:* Elaine Kilburn Photography; **401 (bottom), 407 (left),** Creative Play Center, Shrewsbury, MA; *Designer:* Other Ways for Educational and Environmental Development; **407 (right),** Wellesley College Child Care Center, Wellesley, MA; *Designer:* Other Ways for Educational and Environmental Development; **409,** *Photographer:* Henry F. Olds, Jr.

Chapter 20: 411, *Source:* Gary Paul Nabhan and Stephen Trimble, *The Geography of Childhood: Why Children Need Wild Places* (Boston: Beacon Press, 1994), p. 75; **419, Fig. 20.1,** The Copper House, Husky Child Development Center, Bolton, Ontario, Canada; *Designer/Architect:* Anita Olds and Associates, JSW, M. Jacobson, M. Silverstein, B. Winslow, Carla Mathis Designs; **423, 424,** Arlington, MA; *Photographer:* Horst Henke; *Designer:* Anita Olds and Associates, Horst Henke; Designer of Equipment: Horst Henke

Chapter 21: 432, Fig. 21.1, 433, Fig. 21.2, 434, Fig. 21.3, The Copper House, Husky Child Development Center, Bolton, Ontario, Canada; *Designer/Architect:* Anita Olds and Associates, JSW, M. Jacobson, M. Silverstein, B. Winslow, Carla Mathis Designs; **436 (top and bottom), 437 (top and bottom), 439 (left and right),** *Photographer:* Elaine Kilburn Photography; **437 (middle), 438** *Photographer:* Anita Rui Olds; **440,** The Copper House, Husky Child Development Center, Bolton, Ontario, Canada; *Designer/Architect:* Anita Olds and Associates, JSW, M. Jacobson, M. Silverstein, B. Winslow, Carla Mathis Designs; **441,** *Photographer:* Elaine Kilburn Photography; **443 (top and bottom),** New Generation Children's Learning Centre, Papakura, New Zealand; *Designer/Architect:* Anita Olds and Associates, JSW, M. Jacobson, M. Silverstein, B. Winslow; *Photographer:* Bruce Davison; **444, Fig. 21.4,** New Generation Children's Learning Centre, Papakura, New Zealand; *Designer/Architect:* Bruce Davison; **445, 446, 447, 448,** New Generation Children's Learning Centre, Papakura, New Zealand; *Designer/Architect:* Anita Olds and Associates, JSW, M. Jacobson, M. Silverstein, B. Winslow; *Photographer:* Bruce Davison; **451,** *Source:* Adapted from: Marco Devries, personal communication

BIBLIOGRAPHY

ADA Accessibility Guidelines for Buildings and Facilities: Rules and Regulations, Vol. 63, No. 8 (Federal Register 1998)

Alexander, C. *The Timeless Way of Building* (New York: Oxford University Press, 1979)

Alexander, C., et al., *A Pattern Language* (New York: Oxford University Press, 1977)

Anderson, Gretchen Lee. *Removing Barriers to Childcare Facilities Development* (California State University, Northridge, CA, 1993)

Ayres, A. J. *Sensory Integration and Learning Disorders* (Los Angeles: Western Psychological Services, 1973)

Bachelard, G. *The Poetics of Space* (Boston: Beacon Press, 1969)

Birren, F. *Light, Color and Environment* (New York: Van Nostrand Reinhold, 1982)

Bower, T. G. R. *The Perceptual World of the Child* (Cambridge, MA: Harvard University Press, 1977)

Carnegie Corporation of New York, *Starting Points: Meeting the Needs of Our Youngest Children* (Carnegie Task Force on Meeting the Needs of Young Children, August, 1994)

Carnegie Corporation of New York, (CarnegieTask Force on Learning in the Primary Grades, September 15, 1996)

Cost, Quality, and Child Outcomes in Child Care Centers (Denver: University of Colorado at Denver, 1995)

Dadd, Debra Lynn. *Home Safe Home: Protecting Yourself and Your Family from Everyday Toxics and Harmful Household Products* (New York: Tarcher/Putnam, 1997).

Day, Christopher. *Places of the Soul: Architecture and Environmental Design as a Healing Art* (San Francisco: Harper, 1994)

Erikson, E. *Childhood and Society,* 2d ed. (New York: W.W. Norton & Co. Inc., 1963)

Fiske, D. W. and Maddi, S. R. *Functions of Varied Experience* (Homewood, IL: Dorsey, 1961)

Girdlestone, Rodney. "Electromagnetic Fields," *Mind Body Soul: The Alternative Lifestyle Magazine* (Sept/Oct. 1994)

Girdlestone, Rodney and Cowan, David. *Safe as Houses? Ill-health and Electro-stress in the Home* (Gateway Books, 1994).

Halpern, Steven. *Sound Health: The Music and Sounds that Make Us Whole* (New York: Harper & Row, 1985)

Hillman, James. "One Man's Ceiling is Another Man's Horror," in *Utne Reader* (Feb/March, 1985)

Hiss, Tony. *The Experience of Place: A New Way of Looking at and Dealing with Our Radically Changing Cities and Countryside* (New York: Vintage Books, 1990)

Hollowich, Fritz. *The Influence of Ocular Light Perception on Metabolism in Man and in Animals* (New York: Springer Verlag, 1980)

Hughes, P. C. "The Use of Light and Color in Health" in A. C. Hasings, J. Fadiman, J. S. Gordon (eds.) *Health for the Whole Person; The Complete Guide to Holistic Medicine* (Boulder, CO; Westview Press, 1980)

Itten, Johannes. *The Elements of Color* (New York: Van Nostrand Reinhold, 1970)

Ittleson, W. H., Rivlin, L. G., and Proshansky, H. M. "The Use of Behavioral Maps in Environmental Psychology," in *Environmental Psychology: Man and His Physical Setting* (New York: Holt, Rinehart, and Winston, Inc., 1970)

Jacobson, Silverstein, and Winslow, *The Good House* (The Taunton Press (1990)

Kaplan, Stephen and Kaplan, Rachel. *Cognition and Environment: Functioning in an Uncertain World* (New York: Praeger Publishers, 1982)

Katz, L., Evangelou, D., and Hartman, J. A. *The Case for Mixed-Age Grouping in Early Education* (Washington, D. C.: NAEYC), 1990

Kaufman, Donald and Dahl, Taffy. *Color: Natural Palettes for Painted Rooms* (New York: Clarkson Potter/Publishers, 1992)

Kritchevsky, S., Prescott, E., and Walling, L. "Planning Environments for Young Children." *Physical Space.* (Washington D.C.: National Association for the Education of Young Children 1977)

Lawlor, Anthony. *The Temple In The House* (New York: Tarcher/Putnam, 1994)

Lawlor, R. *Parabola: Myth and the Quest for Meaning,* Vol III, Number 1, (Brookline, NY, 1978)

Liedloff, J. *The Continuum Concept.* (New York: Addison-Wesley, 1977)

Lillard, Paula Polk. *Montessori—A Modern Approach* (New York: Schocken Books, 1972)

Lobell, M. Spatial Archetypes, *ReVISION*, Fall, 1983, Vol. 6, No. 2

Lynch, Kevin. *The Image of the City* (Cambridge: The M.I.T.Press, 1977)

"Making a Difference: An Introduction to the Environmental Resource Guide," *Architecture* (May 1991)

Mahnke, Frank H. and Mahnke, Rudolf H. *Color and Light in Man-Made Environments.* (New York: Van Nostrand Publishing Company, 1987)

Marcus, Clare Cooper. *House As a Mirror of Self: Exploring the Deeper Meaning of Home* (Berkeley, CA: Conari Press, 1995)

Marino, A. A. "Electromagnetic Fields, Cancer, and the Theory of Neuroendocrine-Related Promotion," *Bioelectrochemistry & Bioenergetics* 29 (1993)

Mathis, Carla Mason and Conner, Helen Villa. *The Triumph of Individual Style* (Menlo Park, CA: Timeless Editions, 1993)

McDonough, W. *Design, Ecology, Ethics and the Making of Things,* (the Centennial Sermon presented at the Cathedral of St. John The Divine, New York, N.Y., February 1993)

Miller, Norma L. ed., *The Healthy School Handbook* (Washington, D.C.: NEA Professional Library, 1995)

Montessori, M. *The Montessori Method* (New York: Schocken Books, 1964)

Moore, Gary T. "Determining Overall Space Needs in Campus Child Care Centers," *Campus Child Care News*, (January 1996)

Pearce, J. C. *Evolution's End: Claiming the Potential of Our Intelligence* (San Francisco: Harper, 1992)

Pearson, David. *The Natural House Catalog,*(Simon & Schuster, 1996).

Powell, W. F. *Color and How to Use It* (Walter Foster Publishing, Inc., 1984)

Prescott, E. "The Environment as Organizer of Intent in Child-Care Settings," in C. Weinstein and T. G. David, *Spaces for Children: The Built Environment and Child Development* (New York: Plenum Press, 1987)

Prescott, Elizabeth and David, Thomas G. "Concept Paper on the Effects of the Physical Environment on Day Care" (Pasadena, CA: Pacific Oaks College, 1976)

Prescott, J. W. "Transforming the American Family," *Touch the Future* (Winter 1997/1998)

Rosenthal, N. E., et al. "Antidepressant Effects of Light in Seasonal Affective Disorder,"*American Journal of Psychiatry* 142, no.2 (1985), Ott, J. N. *Health and Light* (New York: Simon & Schuster, 1973).

Ruopp et al., *Children at the Center: Final Report of the National Day Care Study*. (Cambridge, MA: Abt Associates, 1979)

Satterfield, J. H., et al. "Response to Stimulant Drug Treatment in Hyperactive Children: Prediction from EEG and Neurological Findings," *J. Autism Child Schizo*. 3 (1973)

Spivak, M. and Tamer, J. *Light and Color: A Designer's Guide* (Washington, D.C.: AIA Press, 1983)

Spivak, M. *Archetypal Place,* EDRA 4 Conference, Spring 1973

Stephens, Karen. "Small is Beautiful—Advantages of a Small Center," *Exchange* (January 1995)

Tame, David. *The Secret Power of Music* (Rochester, NY: Destiny Books, 1984)

Theilheimer, R. "Something for Everyone: Benefits of Mixed-Age Grouping for Children, Parents, and Teachers," *Young Children* (July 1993)

Tomatis, A. "Chant, the Healing Power of Voice and Ear," in *Music, Physician for Times to Come,* ed. Don Campbell (Wheaton, Ill: Quest, 1991)

Venolia, Carol. *Healing Environments: Your Guide to Indoor Well-Being* (Berkeley, CA: Celestial Arts, 1988)

von Goethe, Johann Wolfgang. *Theory of Colours* (Farberwehre), trans. Charles Lock Eastlane (London: John Murray, 1980)

Wolfe, M. and Laufer, R. "The Concept of Privacy in Childhood and Adolescence," in *Man-Environment Interaction*. ed. D.H. Carson (Milwaukee, WI:EDRA, 1974)

Wolfe, Maxine, and Rivlin, Leanne G. "The Institutions in Children's Lives," in *Spaces for Children*

Wurtman, Richard J. "The Effects of Light on the Human Body," *Scientific American,* Vol. 1, 233, (1982)

INDEX

About the Author

Anita Rui Olds held a doctorate in Human Development and Social Psychology from Harvard University and was on the faculty of the Elliot-Pearson Department of Child Study from 1969 to 1999. She was the founder and director of The Child Care Institute, an annual training program for designers and child-care professionals, co-sponsored by Tufts University and The Harvard Graduate School of Design. Her firm, Anita Olds & Associates, in Woodacre, California, amassed more than 30 years of experience in the design of children's environments, including hospitals, playgrounds, and schools. As both a social scientist and designer, she often served as a consultant to architectural and design firms, helping to determine user response to built space and its interior details. Her work was devoted to exploring ways in which the built environment contributes to healing, communication, and the realization of personal and societal transformation.